Housing for All
Under Law

Housing for All Under Law

New Directions in Housing, Land Use and Planning Law

*A Report of
the American Bar Association
Advisory Commission on
Housing and Urban Growth*

Edited by Richard P. Fishman

Ballinger Publishing Company • Cambridge, Massachusetts
A Subsidiary of J.B. Lippincott Company

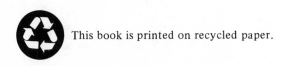
This work was prepared in part under Contract No. HUD Ill., PD 12, Department of Housing and Urban Development. The United States Government reserves a royalty free, nonexclusive and irrevocable license to reproduce, publish or otherwise use, and to authorize others to use, for United States Government purposes, all copyrighted material resulting from the work performed under the HUD Ill., PD 12 contract.

International Standard Book Number: 0-88410-751-5

Library of Congress Catalog Card Number: 77-810

Printed in the United States of America

Library of Congress Cataloging in Publication Data

American Bar Association. Advisory Commission on
   Housing and Urban Growth.
   Housing for All Under Law.

   Includes bibliographical references.
   1. Housing—United States—Law and legislation. 2. City planning and redevelopment law—United States. 3. Zoning law—United States. 4. Land use, Urban—United States. I. Fishman, Richard P. II. Title.
KF5729.A8   346'.73'045   77-810
ISBN 0-88410-751-5

MEMBERS OF THE ABA ADVISORY COMMISSION ON HOUSING AND URBAN GROWTH

Chairman
W. Carloss Morris, Jr.
Morris, Harris, McCanne, Tinsley
& Snowden, P.C.

Vice Chairman
Richard H. Keatinge
Keatinge, Bates & Pastor
Los Angeles, California

Richard F. Babcock
Ross, Hardies, O'Keefe, Babcock
& Parsons
Chicago, Illinois

Derrick A. Bell, Jr.
Professor
Harvard Law School
Cambridge, Massachusetts

Panke Bradley
Atlanta City Council Member
Atlanta, Georgia

John G. Burnett
Vice President
Rockefeller Center Management
Corporation
New York, New York
(Former President, New York State
Urban Development Corporation)

Lewis Cenker (1916–1975)
Smith, Cohen, Ringel, Kohler,
Martin & Lowe
Atlanta, Georgia
(Former President, National
Association of Home Builders)

Marion Clawson
Economic and Planning Consultant
(Former Acting President, Resources
for the Future, Inc.)
Washington, D.C.

John J. Costonis
Professor
University of Illinois School of Law
Champaign, Illinois

Robert S. DeVoy
Real Estate Economist and Planner
Robert S. DeVoy Associates
Washington, D.C.

Herbert M. Franklin
Lane & Edson, P.C.
Washington, D.C.

Robert H. Freilich
Hulen Professor of Law in
Urban Affairs
University of Missouri-Kansas City
School of Law
Kansas City, Missouri

Robert Graham
Senator
State of Florida
Tallahassee, Florida

Frederick W. Hall
Associate Justice (Retired)
New Jersey Supreme Court
Somerville, New Jersey

George Lefcoe
Professor
University of Southern California
Law Center
Los Angeles, California

Daniel R. Mandelker
Howard A. Stamper Professor of Law
Washington University School of Law
St. Louis, Missouri

William K. Reilly
President
The Conservation Foundation
Washington, D.C.

Florence W. Roisman
Attorney at Law
Washington, D.C.

William L. Slayton
Executive Vice President
The American Institute of Architects
Washington, D.C.

R. Joyce Whitley
Whitley & Whitley, Inc.
Architects & Planners
Shaker Heights, Ohio

Pete Wilson
Mayor of San Diego
San Diego, California

Donald G. Glascoff, Jr.
Cadwalader, Wickersham and Taft
New York, N.Y.
(Associate Member Appointed 1975)

ABA SPECIAL COMMITTEE ON HOUSING AND URBAN DEVELOPMENT LAW

Chairmen
John Edward Smith
(August 1973–August 1976)
Steel, Hector & Davis
Miami, Florida

Laughlin E. Waters
(August 1976–Present)
Judge, United States District Court
Central District of California
Los Angeles, California

ADVISORY COMMISSION STAFF

Director
Richard P. Fishman

Assistant Directors
Katherine McG. Sullivan
Timothy J. Hartzer
Randall W. Scott
Scott M. Reznick

Research Assistants
Jane S. Hardin
Ira J. Botvinick
Michael B. Phillips

Support Staff
Mavis W. Walker
Sophia C. Hantzes
Barbara J. Merryman
Barbara B. Egan

PRINCIPAL CONTRIBUTING CONSULTANTS

I. Michael Heyman
Vice-Chancellor and Professor of Law
University of California-Berkeley
Berkeley, California

Roselyn B. Rosenfeld
Attorney at Law
Berkeley, California

David Falk
Lane & Edson, P.C.
Washington, D.C.

Lawrence E. Susskind
Associate Professor
Department of Urban Studies
and Planning
Massachusetts Institute of Technology
Cambridge, Massachusetts

Anne D. Aylward
Research Associate
Massachusetts Institute of Technology
Cambridge, Massachusetts

Mary E. Brooks
Director of Research
Suburban Action Institute
New York, New York

Connie Lieder
Housing and Planning Consultant
Baltimore, Maryland

Edward J. Sullivan
Legal Counsel to the Governor
Salem, Oregon

Michael J. Meshenberg
Daniel Lauber
American Society of Planning Officials
Chicago, Illinois

Contents

POLICY STATEMENTS

The Advisory Commission has adopted specific Policy Statements which
summarize the major themes and findings of its Report. Policy Statements
follow Chapters Two, Three, Four, Five and Six.

Preface

The American Bar Association Advisory Commission on Housing and Urban Growth was created in 1974, on the recommendation of the ABA's Special Committee on Housing and Urban Development Law. The Advisory Commission was charged with examining some of the major legal interrelationships among land-use controls, planning, and housing, with the aim of formulating legislative, administrative, and judicial alternatives and reforms that will increase housing opportunity and choice and promote a more rational urban growth process. This Report is the product of the Advisory Commission's efforts.

Since World War II, urbanization in America has been characterized by unplanned and haphazard growth that has spawned complex problems at every level of government, imposing huge social, environmental, and economic costs on the public and private sectors. This growth has been typified by sprawl and low-density development on the urban-rural fringe and decline in the central city. It has been accompanied by serious racial and economic polarization, with the poorer, minority population left in the central city while the more affluent white population spreads to the suburbs. As a result, housing choice and the opportunity for social mobility have been thwarted for millions of Americans.

The residential segregation of our metropolitan areas, the sprawl on the edge, and the decay within the cities are the outgrowth of many complex forces too numerous to be completely analyzed in this book. It is clear that zoning and other traditional land-use controls, in attempting to guide growth, have too often prevented access to decent housing and instead have reinforced and aggravated patterns of racial and economic segregation. Moreover, our courts and legislatures have done far too little to prevent this abuse of government power.

While land-use controls—absent supporting market forces and other government actions—are not necessarily the most significant factor affecting patterns of growth, they are exceedingly important. It is through such controls that local governments substantially influence where, for what, and when growth will occur.

The nature of zoning—the workhorse of American land-use regulations—is such that it is difficult to distinguish its control over physical development and land use per se from its influence over the economic status of prospective residents and its intentional or effective use in discriminating against ethnic or racial groups. However, large-lot zoning, prohibitions on multiple dwellings, minimum building sizes, bedroom limitations, and other such devices have helped make the cost of new housing prohibitive for over half the population. Whether the aim is to exclude persons unable to afford such housing or to achieve some other legitimate regulatory purpose, the effect is the same. Those with the lowest incomes have a limited choice of where to live and work, and where to send their children to school.

Even in the absence of excessive or discriminatory government control over land use, most lower income families would nevertheless find new housing beyond their reach. The only way these people could afford new housing would be through some form of subsidy or assistance. This situation has always existed, although it may have become more critical in recent years. However, land-use controls have frequently aggravated a situation that would have been difficult enough at best, and have frequently operated to make various proposed solutions to the problems of housing for the lower income population more difficult or even impossible.

Breaking down restrictive land-use practices would thus not only help increase housing choice and freedom of movement—justifiable ends in themselves—but might also create a more equitable geographic distribution of the fiscal and social costs of dealing with other metropolitan-area problems such as transportation, education, and environmental degradation. It would, moreover, help to improve declining central-city areas without displacing urban decay to adjacent neighborhoods. Eliminating the abuses in the administration of land-use controls and providing an adequate planning base where none currently exists would promote more rational land-use decision-making.

If, however, current patterns of growth continue, greater numbers of Americans will be denied housing choice, our cities will continue to decline, and racial and economic segregation will be perpetuated. The Advisory Commission on Housing and Urban Growth views this prospect with great dismay. It believes that the available legal and institutional devices must be reformed to shape and direct in a more sensitive way our metropolitan regions, and to promote the "living welfare of the people."

It is particularly appropriate that the organized bar be in the forefront of this important undertaking. Having fashioned the planning and zoning concepts under which the comprehensive allocation of land uses in our communities was first secured, and having drafted the initial enabling statutes, lawyers took zoning to the Supreme Court of the United States and won its legal acceptance over 50 years ago in the landmark case of *Village of Euclid v. Ambler Realty Co.*, 272 U.S. 365 (1926).

The planning and zoning process that confronted the Supreme Court in the *Euclid* case, premised on assumptions of rather rigid patterns of land use and urban development, has been substantially strained over the years in order to accommodate rapidly changing social, economic, and environmental concerns. As early as 1946, before the postwar building boom had gained much momentum, many of the shortcomings of the system were noted in a truly prescient report by the ABA's Committee on Planning, Rebuilding, and Developing Metropolitan Communities. Questioning how Americans can best use their land to make urban life more humane and worthwhile and to secure basic community and national values, the Committee expressed particular concern over the fragmentation of planning and land-use controls at the local level, and the need for a broader metropolitan or regional perspective. "The first big trouble in most metropolitan communities in the United States today," the Committee Report observed, "is that the community as a whole does not have control of its problem as a whole. . . ."

In the late 1960s following the racial conflagrations that tore apart many of America's cities, two prominent presidential commissions—the National Commission on Urban Problems (the Douglas Commission) and the President's Committee on Urban Housing (the Kaiser Committee)—issued major reports that shared many of the conclusions reached earlier by the ABA's Committee on Planning, Rebuilding, and Developing Metropolitan Communities. The presidential commissions also made comprehensive recommendations for institutional reform, all too few of which were ultimately implemented. Nonetheless, the reports were profoundly significant in raising the national consciousness about urban problems.

In 1967 the American Bar Association created the Special Com-

mittee on Housing and Urban Development Law to assist the organized bar in modernizing housing and urban development law and in
increasing lawyer involvement in the housing development process.
With funding from the Ford Foundation, the American Bar Endow-
ment, and the U.S. Department of Housing and Urban Development,
the Special Committee established Lawyers for Housing programs in
seven cities, and spurred the creation of state and local bar committees to assist in the local implementation of national housing programs and strategies. Unfortunately, the 1973 moratorium on federal
funds for housing and community development programs obviated
plans for new Lawyers for Housing programs, and pulled the underpinnings from many national efforts aimed at promoting housing
opportunity and solving urban problems.

In light of this development and the seeming intractability of our
urban problems, the Special Committee concluded that a new orientation was in order; the time was ripe for a concerted effort by the
organized bar to examine the major legal constraints to housing and
urban growth with the aim of formulating new strategies and alternatives. Other prominent groups and professional organizations, such as
the Task Force on Land Use and Urban Growth of the President's
Citizens' Advisory Committee on Environmental Quality, the American Institute of Architects' National Policy Task Force on Urban
Growth, and the National Academy of Sciences–National Academy
of Engineering, had recently documented the way in which land-use
policies of local governments have degraded our physical environment and exacerbated patterns of racial and economic concentration
by denying housing opportunity and limiting mobility. Their reports
all called upon the courts and the legal profession to reform and formulate the legal doctrines necessary to solve the problems of urban
growth.

The ABA's Special Committee on Housing and Urban Development Law also hoped to build upon the prodigious work of the
American Law Institute, whose comprehensive revision of the statutory law of zoning, planning, and the physical development of land—
embodied in *A Model Land Development Code*—was nearing completion after over a decade of scholarly effort. The Special Committee,
however, contemplated a different focus from that employed by the
American Law Institute. Its efforts would concentrate more narrowly
on the special needs and character of desirable community development; deal more broadly with the socioeconomic considerations that
increasingly affect and are affected by local urban growth and land-
use policies; and address courts as well as legislatures with recommended approaches to urban growth.

Recognizing the complexities, legal and otherwise, that such a task would engender, the Special Committee realized that a multiplicity of skills would be essential for its undertaking to be meaningful. Consequently it recommended the creation of an interdisciplinary Advisory Commission on Housing and Urban Growth comprised of leading practicing attorneys, legal scholars, planners, economists, urbanologists, and public officials that would undertake the in-depth study and analysis contemplated, and report its findings to the Special Committee. Former ABA President Chesterfield Smith and then President-Elect James D. Fellers responded to the Special Committee's request by appointing as members of the Advisory Commission a highly distinguished panel of experts with diverse backgrounds, interests, and points of view.

Aided by a substantial grant from the Office of Policy Development and Research of the U.S. Department of Housing and Urban Development, the Advisory Commission assembled a staff of attorneys and planners in the ABA's Washington, D.C. office under the direction of Richard P. Fishman. In November 1974 the Advisory Commission held its first meeting at the Smithsonian Institute's Belmont Conference Center at Elkridge, Maryland. Subsequent meetings of the full Commission were held over the next year and a half in Chicago, New Orleans, Columbia, Maryland (graciously hosted by Columbia's visionary creator and developer, James W. Rouse), and Washington, D.C.

The Commission's meetings focused on the discussion and adoption of Policy Statements—summary "black-letter" statements, distilling positions that had been advanced by Commission members and developed in detailed background research papers prepared by the staff and consultants. At several meetings, outside experts were called upon to make presentations in conjunction with the Policy Statements that were on the agenda. At each meeting the Commission was asked to vote on the various Policy Statements presented. Debate among the Commission was frequently lengthy and always stimulating; but consensus was ultimately achieved.

As this Report grew in volume and the Policy Statements were refined, an additional procedure was established to assure thorough review. The Commission established an Executive Committee, composed of Chairman Morris and members Keatinge, Babcock, Franklin, Freilich, Burnett, and DeVoy, to oversee the details of preparing the final Report. In turn the Executive Committee divided the Commission into seven subcommittees and assigned each the responsibility of reviewing and approving a draft chapter and its accompanying Policy Statements before the chapter was submitted to the full Commission for final endorsement. All Commission members were then given additional time to express disagreements and file dissenting statements.

No such dissenting opinions were filed. In a true spirit of consensus-building, any disagreements expressed were resolved or accommodated through modifications in the text or Policy Statements. While it cannot reasonably be expected that there could be complete accord on every point or issue raised in a work of this size, it can, however, fairly be said that the entire Advisory Commission shares the strong conviction that the principal themes of the Report, as expressed in the Policy Statements at the ends of the various chapters, are sound.

In receiving this Report, the Special Committee is truly gratified with the unanimity of the Advisory Commission. In light of the diversity of interests represented by the Commission's members and the strong positions taken by the Commission as a body—often diverging from established doctrinal trends—the Special Committee regards *Housing For All Under Law* as a very significant contribution, meriting the most serious consideration. We are pleased to fully endorse the Report, and enthusiastically commend it as a vital resource and working document for private attorneys and planners as well as for courts and public policy-makers.

> John Edward Smith, Esq.
> Chairman, ABA Special Committee on Housing and Urban Development Law (August 1973–August 1976).
>
> Judge Laughlin E. Waters
> Chairman (August 1976–Present)

Acknowledgments

Many individuals and numerous organizations provided invaluable assistance to the Advisory Commission. We would first like to express our appreciation to those who made major contributions to the text of the Report: David Falk of the Washington, D.C. law firm of Lane & Edson, P.C., for his work on Chapter 2; and Ira Michael Heyman, Vice-Chancellor and Professor of Law at the University of California-Berkeley, and Roselyn B. Rosenfeld, Attorney at Law, Berkeley, for their work on Chapter 3. Edward J. Sullivan, Legal Counsel to the Governor of Oregon, and Daniel Lauber and Michael J. Meshenberg of the American Society of Planning Officials, Chicago, all prepared papers that were incorporated into Chapter 4. Daniel R. Mandelker, Howard A. Stamper Professor of Law at Washington University School of Law, St. Louis, prior to being appointed to the Advisory Commission, wrote the legal analysis for Chapter 5, and Professor Lawrence E. Susskind and Research Associate Anne D. Aylward of the Department of Urban Studies and Planning at Massachusetts Institute of Technology prepared the survey and evaluation of the state of the art in comprehensive planning that is included in Chapter 5. Mary E. Brooks, Research Director of the Suburban Action Institute, New York City, and Constance Lieder, Housing and Planning Consultant, Baltimore, contributed portions of Chapter 6, as did Advisory Commission member Robert S. DeVoy. Richard E. Blumberg and Brian Quinn Robbins, staff attorneys for the National Housing and Economic Development Law Project, Berkeley, wrote on developments in landlord and tenant law for Chapter 7. Finally, Advisory Commission members Marion Clawson and Robert Freilich prepared background papers in areas of their special expertise to assist the staff.

The following individuals made valuable oral presentations at Commission meetings and submitted helpful briefing papers: Professor Michael Heyman and Edward Sullivan; Professor Norman Williams, Jr., of Vermont Law School; Professor James A. Kushner of Southwestern Law School; and J. Fred Silva, Chief of Research and Policy Development, Office of the Governor of California. In addition, the following were guests of the Advisory Commission at various Commission meetings or subcommittee meetings, at which they contributed their expertise to the discussions at hand: Robert Elliot, former General Counsel of the U.S. Department of Housing and Urban Development; Donald Glascoff, former Deputy General Counsel of HUD and now with the New York law firm of Cadwalader, Wickersham & Taft; Robert Einsweiler, former President of the American Institute of Planners and a private planning consultant in Minneapolis; Marlin Smith of the Chicago law firm of Ross, Hardies, O'Keefe, Babcock & Parsons; Malcolm A. Misuraca of the Santa Rosa, California law firm of Misuraca & Beyers; Paul Davidoff, Executive Director of the Suburban Action Institute, New York City; and Professor John Ragsdale of the University of Missouri–Kansas City School of Law.

We are also grateful for the papers prepared by Jane Silverman of the Urban Land Institute, Washington, D.C.; Joel Brenner of the Washington, D.C. law firm of Lane & Edson, P.C.; Michael A. Agelasto, Congressional Research Service; David L. Colgan of the Santa Ana, California law firm of Rutan & Tucker; Scott Peters, an attorney and political science graduate student at Washington University; and William C. Cramer, Jr., a third-year student at Harvard Law School.

Helpful advice, information, verification, and critiques of drafts were provided by many persons. We would like to acknowledge particularly the comments and advice of Dina Lassow, Attorney at Law, Washington, D.C.; Judge Edward Howell of the Oregon Supreme Court; Judge Paul Garrity, Superior Court, Commonwealth of Massachusetts; Conrad Bagne, University of Washington Graduate School of Planning; Duane Searles, National Association of Home Builders; David Solomon, City Attorney, Lakewood, Colorado; Craig Peterson, John Marshall Law School, Chicago.

Without the sponsorship of the ABA Special Committee on Housing and Urban Development Law, this Report would not have been possible. Our appreciation goes to each member of the Special Committee: Judge Richard L. Banks, Boston; Conrad Robert Belt, New York City; William D. Browning, Tucson; Daniel N. Epstein, Chicago;

James A. Heeter, Kansas City, Missouri; Bruce B. Johnson, Denver; Andrew H. Mott, Washington, D.C.; Roy H. Semtner, Oklahoma City; George M. Shapiro, New York City; Fred J. Livingston, Cleveland; and its chairmen, John Edward Smith of Miami and Judge Laughlin E. Waters of Los Angeles.

Finally special words of thanks go to David James, Director of the American Bar Association's Division of Public Services, who provided invaluable assistance in securing the necessary approvals from the Association at each step along our lengthy course to publication, and to James Hoben, Edward N. Reiner, and Paul McAuliffe of the Department of Housing and Urban Development, who provided us with support throughout the project.

W. Carloss Morris, Jr.
Chairman, ABA Advisory Commission on
Housing and Urban Growth

The Report in Brief

Chapter 1, "Current Dilemmas and Legal Issues in Housing and Urban Growth: An Overview," sets forth many of the problems that will be addressed in subsequent chapters. It discusses some of the complex forces that have affected growth and housing opportunity in metropolitan America, with particular emphasis on the inadequacies of our land-use control system.

Chapter 2, "Judicial Doctrine for Inclusionary Land-Use Programs," explores the evolution and status of federal and state judicial doctrine relating to the validity of local land-use regulations and the application of various federal programs that may inhibit housing choice among persons and families of low income. The analysis traces two diverging trends in the state and federal courts. The first is a growing retreat of the federal courts as a sympathetic forum for constitutional challenges to exclusionary housing and land-use constraints. The other is a more enlightened anti-exclusionary attitude being exhibited by a number of important state courts that are closely scrutinizing local actions to evaluate their real impact on the public, both within and beyond a locality's boundaries. The Advisory Commission notes that under our system of federalism, and in constitutional jurisprudence, state courts may properly construe state constitutional counterparts of provisions of the Bill of Rights as guaranteeing citizens of their states even more protection than identically phrased federal provisions.

The doctrine of "regional general welfare" developed in Chapter 2 asserts that the "general welfare," as a basic state constitutional principle and the predicate for local police power regulations, should be regional and include the fundamentally important state interest that the housing needs of all income groups of the state be promoted and enhanced. Moreover, in exercising their police power authority, local governments have an affirmative legal duty to promote the "general welfare," which includes the welfare of the housing market area of which the jurisdiction is a part. This includes the affirmative duty to: (1) plan for present and prospective housing in a regional context; (2) eliminate those local regulatory barriers that make it difficult to provide housing for persons of low-and moderate-income; and (3) offer regulatory concessions and incentives to the private sector in this regard.

The central issue addressed in Chapter 3, "The Role of the Courts," is the appropriateness of judicial intervention in reviewing and remedying legislative and administrative land-use decisions alleged to frustrate housing choice. The Advisory Commission advocates a strong judicial role in entertaining challenges to exclusionary land-use regulations on the basis of its conclusions that: (1) opportunities for decent living accommodations in decent environments, freedom from law imposed discrimination based on income (and income as a surrogate for race), and access to employment opportunities are fundamental values; (2) these values will not be satisfactorily achieved in the absence of judicial intervention since those adversely affected by parochial exclusionary decisions have little, if any, voice in their formulation and few effective political means to overturn them; and (3) the courts are competent to handle this type of litigation and to fashion effective remedies to help bring about fundamental changes in metropolitan housing patterns. An active judicial role, moreover, invites an appropriate political response, namely, the creation of a regional planning structure.

Chapter 3 examines procedural matters likely to arise in exclusionary cases, including standing, joinder of parties, and burden of proof. It also deals with remedies available to a court, in the face of legislative intransigence, for restructuring all or portions of a zoning ordinance that has been invalidated because it precludes access to housing by any or a "fair share" of lower income households. Also explored is the use of a special master or a consultant to assist the court in assembling data and designing a regional housing allocation plan, in examining the adequacy of plans produced by the parties, or in monitoring local compliance. Finally, the chapter discusses the various options available to the court in enforcing its order when dealing with a recalcitrant municipality, such as suspension of state or federal grants or local laws that obstruct compliance, invalidation of all zoning, and contempt. It explains how a municipality can affirmatively foster the construction of low- and moderate-income housing by such means as establishing a local housing authority, granting incentives to private developers, and ordering required municipal services.

Chapter 4, "Improving the Administration of Land-Use Controls," traces the evolution of land-use controls from a self-executing and relatively rigid system that preregulated land uses, to a highly discretionary system of administrative control in which applications for development are considered on an ad hoc case-by-case basis. Fairness and rationality have often been severely strained. To inject greater procedural fairness and predictability into the system, the Advisory Commission endorses a recent judicial trend which treats zoning amendments that affect only individual parcels of property, as opposed to the community at large, as "adjudicatory" acts. These decisions have traditionally been considered "legislative" because they are made by the local legislature. If zoning changes are treated as adjudicatory, they will be subject to the essentials of procedural due process that are traditionally expected of administrative bodies—adequate notice, an opportunity to present and rebut evidence, a record, a statement of findings—and will not be subject to voter referendum.

Chapter 4 also examines such land-use controls as planned unit developments, special permits, incentive zoning, and transferable development rights, which allow more flexible control over development but are subject to a high degree of administrative discretion and thus uneven application. It suggests that these techniques be applied so that they are consistent with comprehensive planning, encourage housing opportunity for all income groups, and accommodate the procedural safeguards essential to fair administration. Numerous other procedural and substantive changes are discussed, including limitations on ex parte contacts between the parties to an action and the public officials involved, citizen participation in the decision-making process, and consolidation of administrative reviews and development permits.

The implementation of many of the changes suggested in Chapter 4 may impose additional administrative burdens on local government. To lessen these burdens, while at the same time assuring a more efficient and professional process, the utilization of a hearing examiner system should be considered. The experiences of hearing examiners in numerous locations throughout the country are evaluated.

As the substantive and procedural elements of land-use decisions increase in complexity (often reinforced by federal and state legislation) to include new objectives—such as lower income housing, environmental protection, and regional growth management—comprehensive planning is essential as a policy base to insure internal consistency, to provide predictability, and to reduce the tendency toward arbitrary local decisionmaking. Chapter 5, "The Role of the Local Comprehensive Plan in Land-Use Regulation," explores the changing nature of planning practice, the evolving judicial attitude toward the role of the plan in land-use administration, and new legislation that mandates comprehensive planning. In Chapter 5 the Commission concludes that state enabling legislation, traditionally permissive in its approach to local planning, should be amended to require local comprehensive planning and to require that local land-use controls be consistent with local comprehensive plans. The essential elements of the mandatory planning process are therefore discussed, as well as the implications of the consistency requirement for judicial and state review of local land-use decisions. Finally, using a national survey of current planning practice, the chapter examines the capability of local governments to undertake mandatory planning.

The Advisory Commission considers housing planning to be an essential element of the local comprehensive plan. As discussed in Chapter 6, "Housing Planning," the plan should consider housing for all economic segments of a community, particularly low- and moderate-income households, as well as regional housing circumstances and needs. Comprehensive plans should include specific implementation proposals that are clearly related to the assessment of needs, resources, likely achievements, and other human and community development objectives. They should also be formulated as comprehensive housing strategies that involve citizen groups and representatives of the public and private sectors interacting in an ongoing process of education, consensus, monitoring, goal-setting, action, and evaluation. Chapter 6 attempts to provide the basic information necessary for formulating housing plans and strategies and for facilitating judicial review of alleged exclusionary land-use actions.

Chapter 7, "State and Local Roles in Housing and Community Development," examines the legal underpinnings of strategies that state and local governments can undertake to increase housing choice and opportunity. Some of the activities, such as financing low- and moderate-income housing by state housing finance agencies, reforming landlord and tenant law to equalize the bargaining power between the parties, and instituting property tax relief, have generally produced positive results. Others, such as land banking and "inclusionary" zoning ordinances, are somewhat speculative, as there has not been sufficient experience to evaluate their potential efficacy. Still others, such as state review or override of local regulatory actions

, that adversely affect low- and moderate-income housing, have had mixed results, but these can be improved.

While the Advisory Commission believes that the federal government has the primary resources and responsibility for meeting the national housing goal of "a decent home and suitable living environment for every American family," there is little doubt that more effort and cooperation from all levels of government and the private sector is essential for achieving this goal.

Housing for All
Under Law

Current Dilemmas and Legal Issues in Housing and Urban Growth: An Overview

THE NEXUS BETWEEN HOUSING AND URBAN GROWTH: THE CONCERNS OF THE ADVISORY COMMISSION

Housing, land use, and urban growth—the principal issues addressed in this Report—must be viewed in the context of the economic, social, political, and legal structure of the United States. The term growth, as used herein, refers to population growth and urban expansion in general, and necessarily to economic growth and development as well. Some growth is both inevitable and essential, and more would be desirable, up to some limit or rate.[1]

The people now living and those to be born must live somewhere; the only real questions are where and how. The children of the postwar baby boom are now forming households, ensuring continued growth pressures. Notwithstanding a 1975 fertility rate of only 0.8 percent, population is predicted to grow by more than a million annually through at least the 1990s.[2] The relatively young age structure of our population ensures that births will exceed deaths by such a margin that zero population growth is unlikely to be reached in this

---

1. *See* D. Meadows *et al.*, Limits to Growth (1974). *But see* W. Leontief, The Future of the World Economy (Report Prepared for the United Nations Department of Economic and Social Affairs 1976), *as reported in* N.Y. Times, Oct. 14, 1976, at 14.
2. The Domestic Council, The 1976 Report on National Growth and Development 18-20 (1976) [hereinafter cited as 1976 Growth Report].

century. Consequently, this nation of over 213 million will have to shelter and feed an additional 50 million by the year 2000.[3]

The magnitude of these figures take on a greater poignancy in light of our current housing situation. Today it is not merely the poor or lower-income people who cannot afford new housing or otherwise participate in the housing market. Nearly 43 percent of all American working households earned less than $10,000 in 1975, and nearly two-thirds of the households earned less than $15,000. The cost of new housing is thus already beyond the capability of between one-half and two-thirds of all American families.[4] And while 30.8 percent of American renters paid one-fourth or more of their incomes to their landlords in 1950, approximately 42 percent did so by 1976.[5]

With inflation pushing labor and construction costs to new heights, the median sales price of a new house almost doubled between 1970 and 1976, increasing from $23,400 to $44,200.[6] In the existing housing market the median sales price in 1976 was $38,100, with fewer than 10 percent of existing houses being sold for less than $20,000. Since 1970, increases in the sales price of both new and existing housing and the costs of homeownership—including fuel, repairs and maintenance, mortgage payments, taxes, and insurance—outpaced increases in personal income.

While the number of low-income families living in physically inadequate housing has declined since 1960, the number paying an unreasonably high percentage of their incomes for rent increased dramatically. And still it is estimated that as of 1973, 16.8 million families—one of every four in the nation—lived with at least one form of housing deprivation.

The 1976 *Report on National Growth and Development* summed up the nation's current housing situation as follows:

> For the middle class, rapidly rising costs of living and a drop in real disposable income since 1973 have meant revision in home-ownership expectations. There is some home ownership among families with income below $5,000, but for the most part poor and moderate income families are

3. *Id.*

4. U.S. League of Savings and Loan Associations, 1976 Sav. & Loan News 36–37 (March).

5. These figures are from a speech by former HUD Deputy Assistant Secretary for Economic Affairs John C. Weicher, to the American Real Estate and Urban Economics Association, May 21, 1976, as reported in 3 Hous. & Dev. Rep. 1230 (May 31, 1976).

6. These figures and those in the following paragraph are drawn from Joint Center for Urban Studies of M.I.T. & Harvard University, The Nation's Housing, 1975 to 1985 (Press Release, March 3, 1977) [hereinafter cited as Nation's Housing].

limited in their choice of existing housing units to those available for low rents and thus to those of lower quality neighborhood environments.[7]

The future appears to be even more bleak. In a report issued in March 1977, the joint center for Urban Studies of the Massachusetts Institute of Technology and Harvard University estimated that in the face of the extraordinary population and economic pressures that the country is facing, and given the neglect of housing needs on the part of the United States government, the average price for a typical home could reach $78,000 by the early 1980s, if trends from 1971 to 1976 continue for another five years. Moreover, according to the Joint Center report, even after the upturn of 1976, housing starts are 20 percent below the number necessary to meet household growth and to replace physically obsolete units; with some 20.2 to 22.6 million new housing units needed between 1975 and 1985.[8]

This Advisory Commission, as does the American public generally, regards some growth as more desirable than no growth; the latter would require both a continuation of poverty for large numbers of people and an exacerbation of our housing problem, neither of which is acceptable. The precise form of growth and its environmental consequences present policy issues beyond the scope of this book. But the Advisory Commission does consider increases in housing stock for all income groups in the United States as highly desirable.

In the Advisory Commission's view it will take more than the construction of new housing to solve the nation's housing problem.[9]

7. 1976 Growth Report, *supra* note 2, at 40.

8. Nation's Housing, *supra* note 6. The report estimated that 11.9 to 13.6 million of the 20.2 to 22.6 million new units would be required because of expected growth in the number of households; most of the remainder would be needed to replace physically obsolete units and to allow families to upgrade existing housing.

9. Moreover, in the Advisory Commission's view the "filtering" or "trickle-down" principle that has been at the heart of U.S. housing efforts for years is not sufficient, in itself, to constitute a national housing policy. In strictly economic terms, filtering is essentially a neutral system characteristic of the U.S. housing market; it has been defined as the "changing of occupancy as the housing that is occupied by one income group becomes available to the next lower income group as a result of decline in market price." R. Ratcliff, Urban Land Economics 17 (1949). However, when relied upon as a housing policy or strategy, the filtering principle in effect holds that by assisting the middle class rather than the neediest, the entire society, including the poor, will benefit; *i.e.*, when new middle-class housing is constructed, the units thereby vacated trickle down to the poor. This principle can only work if the people whom trickle-down is intended ultimately to benefit—the poor—are fairly well economically integrated into the rest of society. The fact is, however, that the poor are not usually noticeably less poor after abandoning one dwelling unit in favor of another, and concentrations of urban poverty are not affected by the trickle-down process. When the urban poor do move, they nearly always move to ad-

Housing is far more than mere shelter, although that is important in itself. Housing involves access to good jobs, to good schools, to attractive shopping districts and stores, to parks and recreation areas, and to other positive aspects of urban life. Housing is not merely an individual matter; it concerns the community and its total environment, including the whole complex of land uses and activities within which the householder moves. More rational patterns of growth, which will alter current concentrations of poverty and race, are therefore essential.

PATTERNS OF URBAN GROWTH IN METROPOLITAN AMERICA

The dynamics of urban growth in America—the decline of our central cities, the wasteful and inefficient use of land on the urban fringes, the marked separation of our people by racial and economic class—are only imperfectly understood. Part of the reason, as noted in a recent study commissioned by the Urban Institute, is that "much of the information available about the city over time is not in an idiom suitable for technological analyses. . . . [R]esearch is confounded by the infinitely various fragmentation of the city, by the intense complexity of its behavior patterns, and by the urgency of its highly apparent problems with housing, poverty, education, transportation, racial hostility, governance, pollution and crime."[10] Stated somewhat differently, the problem is that "the city has not just grown bigger than its boundaries—it has outgrown the concept and the vocabulary of the city itself."[11]

Recognizing these analytical shortcomings, we shall highlight some of the major forces that have collectively shaped metropolitan America,[12] and direct the readers' attention to some of the major themes that will be addressed in this book.

---

jacent neighborhoods. No policy will break this cycle if it fails to destroy the concentrations of poverty in the central city. *See* A. Downs, Opening Up the Suburbs (1973). For economic models of filtering, *see* W. Smith, *A Theory of Filtering*, in Filtering and Neighborhood Change (1964); W. Grigsby, Housing Markets and Public Policy (1963).

10. B. Harrison, Urban Economic Development: Suburbanization, Minority Opportunity, and the Condition of the Central City xiii (Urban Institute, 1974).

11. Ylvisaker, *The Shape of the Future*, in Metropolis: Values in Conflict 63, 68 (Elias, Gillies, & Reimer, eds. 1964).

12. A more comprehensive treatment of the subject is in M. Clawson, Suburban Land Conversion in the United States: An Economic and Governmental Process (1971).

The Racial and Economic Polarization
of Metropolitan Areas

The United States is a preponderantly urban nation. Approximately 70 percent of all Americans live in metropolitan areas, and over half of those in the surburbs.[13] The great proportion of our national growth since World War II has taken place in the suburbs and on the urban-rural fringe of major metropolitan centers.[14] During the 1960s the population of the suburbs increased by nearly six times that of the population of the central cities. This population shift resulted in a 31 percent increase in the number of dwelling units in suburban areas.[15]

Between 1951 and 1970, manufacturing employment significantly declined within 12 of the 30 largest cities in the nation, primarily in the older and more industrialized centers of the Northeast and North Central regions. In Boston and Philadelphia, the declines exceeded 10 percent of the industrialized labor force.[16] At the same time, suburban employment increased around the 30 largest cities (with the exception of San Antonio). In 9 of the metropolitan areas involved, suburban jobs at least doubled. Nationally, between 1973 and 1975, suburban employment grew by 3.2 percent, while employment in central cities declined by 3.7 percent.[17]

This significant relocation of manufacturing and office employment and residential development from central cities to suburbs has resulted in rather profound social and economic disparities, with the central city taking in and retaining the lower income minority population and the suburbs generally absorbing the more affluent

13. Environmental Quality: Fifth Annual Report of the Council on Environmental Quality (G.P.O. 1974) [hereinafter cited as Environmental Quality].

14. The 1976 Growth Report, *supra* note 2, at 23, describes a continuing loss of population by the older eastern cities to the Gulf, Great Lakes, and Rocky Mountain regions; with more than 80 percent of the nation's population growth since 1970 having occurred in the South and West together. The report also notes that Census Bureau estimates indicate that nonmetropolitan areas are for the first time growing more rapidly than metropolitan areas. The report acknowledges, however, that more needs to be known about the durability of this trend and its precise dimensions before its implications for national growth can be fully drawn. *Id.* at xi.

Even assuming that nonmetropolitan growth continues, there is no indication that there will not also be further growth and further rebuilding in suburban areas and in urban centers. The Advisory Commission's discussion of the land-use regulatory situation should continue to be fully relevant in the future.

15. Environmental Quality, *supra* note 13, at 3–4.

16. 1976 Growth Report, *supra* note 2, at 33.

17. *Id.*

white population.[18] This loss of industry and jobs to suburbia has left central urban areas without enough jobs for the relatively poor, unskilled labor force remaining, and with an insufficient tax base to provide municipal services for those still living there, much less to stem the tide of further urban deterioration.[19] Housing left behind by white flight, furthermore, tends to be older, in worse condition, and in less desirable neighborhoods than its counterpart in suburbia. As a result, financial institutions and even residents have "disinvested" in urban housing stock until vast areas of our central cities have become abandoned wastelands where crime, pollution, poverty, and psychological deterioration are everyday occurrences.[20]

In 1968 both the National Commission on Urban Problems[21] and the National Advisory Commission on Civil Disorders[22] documented the pervasive racial and economic polarization existing between central cities and their suburbs, and warned in the strongest terms of the

---

18. The Central City Problem and Urban Renewal Policy: A study prepared by Congressional Research Service, Library of Congress, for the Subcommittee on Housing and Urban Affairs Committee on Banking, Housing, and Urban Affairs, U.S. Senate 3 (G.P.O. 1973) [hereinafter cited as Central City Problem]. *See also* text at note 24 *infra.*

19. *See generally* T. Muller, Growing and Declining Urban Areas: A Fiscal Comparison (Urban Institute 1975).

20. *See, e.g.,* Center for Community Change, National Urban League, The National Survey of Housing Abandonment (1971); G. Sternlieb & R. Burchell, Residential Abandonment—The Tenement Landlord Revisited (1973); Note, *Project Abandonment of Residential Property in an Urban Context,* 23 DePaul L. Rev. 1186 (1974); Comment, *Property Abandonment in Detroit,* 20 Wayne L. Rev. 845 (1974); Note, *Building Abandonment in New York City,* 16 N.Y.L.F. 798 (1970).

21. The National Commission on Urban Problems observed that "the increases of nonwhites in central cities is accompanied by just as big a movement of whites from the central cities to the suburbs. The result is an almost unyielding pattern of segregation." Building the American City 4 (1968) [hereinafter cited as Building the American City].

22. The National Advisory Commission on Civil Disorders commented on the pervasiveness of metropolitan racial segregation:

> The nation is rapidly moving toward two increasingly separate Americas. Within two decades, this division could be so deep that it would be almost impossible to unite: a white society principally located in suburbs, in smaller central cities, and in the peripheral parts of large central cities, and a Negro society largely concentrated within large central cities. The Negro society will be permanently relegated to its current status, possibly even if we expend great amounts of money and effort in trying to "gild" the ghetto. In the long run, continuation and expansion of such a permanent division threatens us with two perils. The first is the danger of sustained violence in our cities. . . . The second is the danger of a conclusive repudiation of the traditional American ideals of individual dignity, freedom, and equality of opportunity.

Report of the National Advisory Commission on Civil Disorders xii (Bantam Books ed. 1968).

critical problems this posed, both for the groups involved and for society at large. While the Civil Rights Acts of 1964 and 1968 provided an unequivocal bar against racial discrimination in the rental and sale of housing,[23] the commitment to integrated housing has not been widespread. Several years later, in 1973, a report of the Advisory Commission on Intergovernmental Relations observed little change:

> Taxable wealth and personal income are growing faster in suburban areas than in their central cities and the disparity continues to widen. As suburbs grow, central cities, for the most part, face the problems of population loss; increasing concentrations of poor, nonwhite, and elderly; ever-increasing obsolescence in housing; and above average crime rates.[24]

There is no indication that this pattern is changing. In 1960, 16.4 percent of the total population in central cities was black; in 1974 the figure had grown to 22 percent.[25] Income differences between central-city and suburban families are also continuing to increase.[26] The percentage of central-city poor who are black has increased dramatically, from 37 percent in 1959 to 47 percent in 1974.[27] The implications of these trends in residential segregation is that we have and will continue to have large urban ghettos, substantial sections of which are in sharp decline.

By most standards of urban well-being, these declining areas offer unsatisfactory living environments and markedly inferior opportunities for improved income and greater social mobility. The opportunity for obtaining an adequate education in inner-city ghetto schools is far from optimal. Security of person and property is also vastly lower—a ghetto-dweller is about four times more likely to be robbed and about seven times more likely to be murdered than is a nonghetto-dweller.[28]

Beyond education and security, there is insufficient opportunity in urban ghettos to earn an adequate living or to accumulate personal wealth. *The Urban Predicament*, a 1976 report by the Urban Institute, explained this opportunity gap:

23. *See* discussion in text accompanying notes 111–17 *infra.*

24. Sacks & Callahan, *Central City Suburban Fiscal Disparity*, in City Financial Emergencies: The Intergovernmental Dimension 151 (Advisory Commission on Intergovernmental Relations 1973).

25. 1976 Growth Report, *supra* note 2, at 33.

26. *Id.* at 37–38.

27. W. Gorham & N. Glazer, The Urban Predicament 21 (1976) [hereinafter cited as Urban Predicament].

28. *Id.* at 30.

[M]ost ghettos are increasingly poorly located with respect to new job opportunities. The large black ghettos of Chicago, Philadelphia, and Cleveland are not where the incremental jobs are being created. The locational handicap is exacerbated by the weakness of the information resources of ghetto communities. . . .

When the national economy was doing very well in 1959, the overall black unemployment rate in urban areas was 7.2 percent, twice the national average; the rate for black teen-age youth was 27.9 percent, 8 times the national average. In the third quarter of 1975, with overall average unemployment at 8.3 percent, black unemployment was 41.4 percent. While many different reasons can be offered to explain these extraordinarily high unemployment rates, almost all of them stem from the dual handicaps of race and place.[29]

While employment provides income, it is not in itself the road to financial security and, ultimately, upward mobility. The Urban Institute report notes the fundamental importance of homeownership in this regard:

Most Americans . . . who have managed to develop net worth in the past 30 years have done so through homeownership. The owned home has been the means by which persons of low income, through "sweat" equity (i.e., enhancing the value of the property by working on its maintenance and improvement) and market appreciation, put something aside for a rainy day. The opportunity to do that in most parts of our urban ghettos is extremely limited. . . . [S]ince ghetto property values are not increasing as much as they are in other neighborhoods, the incentive for individual homeowners to make improvements is relatively low. High crime, poor schools, poorer than average amenities, all undermine the promise of property appreciation in exchange for the struggle of investing in homes and maintaining them.[30]

Policies initiated in suburbia have had a tremendous impact on reinforcing these conditions in the central city. Exclusionary techniques designed to keep "undesirables" from moving into predominantly middle-class suburban areas have the effect of placing a heavy burden on other areas of the region, including the central city. Through restrictive zoning ordinances—minimum lot-size or floor-area requirements, exclusive single-family limitations, noncumulative industrial zones, and other practices[31] —the cost of suburban housing is raised to a level too high for low- and moderate-income buyers to afford. Through zoning and other local devices, public housing has also been

29. *Id.*
30. *Id.* at 30–31.
31. *See* discussion in text accompanying notes 249–69 *infra.*

effectively excluded from many suburban communities,[32] with the burden for such housing falling on the central city. Discriminatory lending and selling practices have meanwhile assured that suburban residential areas can maintain their status as havens for the white middle class.[33]

Growth in Suburbia

The other major characteristic so prevalent in our metropolitan areas is the sporadic pattern of growth by which close-in, more expensive land surrounding the urban core is withheld from development,[34] while less expensive land—often scattered in isolated locations on the urban fringe—is developed. This pattern of growth has been aptly termed urban sprawl.[35]

Sprawl is characterized by low population density, which produces inefficient resource allocations and impairs the esthetic aspects of the metropolis. As land is divided and subdivided for scattered, small-scale development, irreplaceable natural and recreational resources are unnecessarily consumed. Basic services such as water supply and sewage removel must be extended over great distances, resulting in higher per capita costs.[36] Existing roads prove inadequate to accommodate newly scattered populations commuting into the increasingly distant city.[37] Schools also prove inadequate to handle the increased suburban population; consequently, new schools and new roads must be constructed, and local residents must bear additional taxes.

The Advisory Commission on Intergovernmental Relations has described the fiscal side of the mounting urban growth problems being felt in the suburbs:

32. *See* discussion in text accompanying notes 102–22 *infra.*
33. *See, e.g.,* Building the American City, *supra* note 21, at 100; Searing, *Discrimination in Home Finance,* 48 N.D.L. 1113 (1973); Silverman, *Home-ownership for the Poor: Subsidies and Racial Segregation,* 48 N.Y.U.L. Rev. 72 (1973); Stegman, *Low-Income Ownership: Exploitation and Opportunity,* 50 J. Urb. L. 371 (1973); Comment, *Exploiting the Home-Buying Poor: A Case Study of Abuse of the National Housing Act,* 17 St. Louis U.L.J. 525 (1972).
34. *See* Clawson, *supra* note 12, at 134–35.
35. For excellent accounts of sprawl in action, see Clawson, *id.,* and W. Whyte, The Last Landscape (1970). While in recent years the problems of sprawl have received considerable attention from urban commentators and have stimulated more public concern than ever before, the phenomenon of sprawl is by no means of recent vintage. *See* R. Fogelson, The Fragmented Metropolis: Los Angeles, 1850–1930, at ch. 12 (1967).
36. Alternatively, if separate new public services are provided by installing new plants and utility facilities, high costs will be encountered because of the diseconomies of small-scale operations.
37. *See* F. Bosselman, Alternatives to Urban Sprawl: Legal Guidelines for Governmental Action 6 (Prepared for the consideration of the National Commission on Urban Problems, Research Report No. 15, 1968).

While not experiencing drastic changes in the socioeconomic character of their population, they are faced with the prospect of developing an urban infrastructure which carries with it substantial expenditure demands. Thus while tax levels and tax rates remain higher in central cities, suburbs have experienced percentage increases in taxes and expenditures that are remarkably similar to those of central cities. It is beginning to appear that many suburbs can no longer devote ever increasing proportions of their budget to educational programs and defer non-educational expenditure requirements.[38]

The high economic and environmental costs associated with sprawl have stimulated hundreds of suburban communities throughout America to analyze their long-term growth options and take actions to slow or control their growth.[39] These growth-control measures take many forms, including moratoria on sewer hookups, building permits, subdivision approvals, and rezonings; "down-zoning" for lower densities (e.g., from two units per acre to one unit per six acres); temporary holding zones; tax relief to forestall conversion of agricultural land to urban use; and timing and sequential controls.[40] Such measures taken in one community may, however, merely re-direct development further out into the rural fringe and encourage even greater metropolitan sprawl.[41] Growth-control measures that restrict the amount of land available for housing, thereby increasing its cost, effectively preclude all but upper income groups from living in the community.[42]

The findings of a recent government-commissioned study, *The Costs of Sprawl*,[43] offer important insights on the issue of growth control. The study analyzed a wide range of economic, environmental, and social effects associated with three prototypical community developments located on the urban fringe: low-density sprawl, a combination mix, and high-density planned.[44] The study

38. Sacks & Callahan, *supra* note 24, at 151.

39. *See* W. Reilly, ed., The Use of Land: A Citizens' Policy Guide to Urban Growth (1973).

40. *See* discussion in text accompanying notes 280–306 *infra*.

41. F. Bosselman, *Can the Town of Ramapo Pass a Law to Bind the Rights of the Whole World?* 1 Fla. St. U.L. Rev. 234, 248 (1973).

42. *Id.* at 248. *See also* H. Franklin, Controlling Growth: But for Whom? (Potomac Institute, 1973).

43. Real Estate Research Corporation, The Costs of Sprawl: Environmental and Economic Costs of Alternative Residential Development Patterns at the Urban Fringe (G.P.O. 1974) [hereinafter cited as Costs of Sprawl].

44. Low-density sprawl was defined as a community composed of detached single-family homes, 75 percent sited in a traditional grid pattern and the rest clustered, with neighborhoods sited in a noncontiguous, leapfrog pattern; high-density planned is a community composed of 40 percent six-story high-rise apartments, 30 percent walkup apartments, 20 percent townhouses, and

disclosed that the high-density planned community costs 21 percent less in terms of total public and private investment to occupants, taxpayers, and local governments than the combination mix community, and 44 percent less than the low-density sprawl.[45] Because of reduced automobile usage, the high-density planned community was found to generate about 45 percent less air pollution than the low-denisty sprawl community, which housed the same number of people,[46] and also to significantly reduce energy consumption.[47] Other studies indicate that the conclusions reached in the community-level analysis of *The Costs of Sprawl* are applicable to an entire metropolitan area.[48] Collectively these studies demonstrate that the adverse effects of growth can be minimized by increased densities and better planning. America's communities must learn to think not in terms of "growth or no growth," but rather in terms of how, where, and under what conditions growth should occur.

The Metropolitan Problem and The Search for a Metropolitan Solution

Many of the major problems confronting our urban society today —racial and economic segregation, the rising cost of land and housing, central-city deterioration, the alleged mismatch between housing and employment opportunities,[49] urban-suburban fiscal disparities in the

---

10 percent clustered single-family homes, and all clustered in contiguous neighborhoods, much in the pattern of a high-density "new community." For comparative purposes, an intermediate pattern, called combination mix, included both traditional subdivisions and more clustered developments. *Id.*

45. *See Executive Summary*, Costs of Sprawl, *id.* at 3.

46. *Id.* at 4.

47. *Id.* at 5.

48. *See, e.g.*, Development Research Associates, The Case for Open Space (Prepared for People for Open Space in the San Francisco Bay Area, Los Angeles 1969); J. Recht & R. Harmon, Open Space and the Urban Growth Process: An Economic Evaluation Using a Growth Allocation Model, (Berkeley, Institute of Urban and Regional Development, Research Report 31, 1969).

49. Numerous urban commentators have asserted the existence of a mismatch between centrally located workers and increasing employment opportunities in the suburbs. Daniel Moynihan, for example, explains that "it is the low-skilled jobs [which] seem increasingly to be located in the suburban fringe, far from the homes of the central city poor." *Poverty in the Cities*, in The Metropolitan Enigma 348 (J. Wilson ed. 1968). Schreiber *et al.* likewise conclude that "the unskilled and semi-skilled jobs in the manufacturing and service sectors of the economy have become increasingly decentralized and therefore inaccessible [to] low-income people in the central cities." Economics of Urban Problems 13 (1971). Similar assertions are made in L. Rubinowitz, Low Income Housing 11–18 (1974); Advisory Commission on Intergovernmental Relations, Urban and Rural America: Policies for Future Growth 58 (G.P.O. 1968); A. Downs, Opening Up the Suburbs (1970). An argument for the mismatch contention based on statistical data from Chicago and Detroit is presented in J. Kain, *Housing Segregation, Negro Employment and Metropolitan Decentralization*, Q.J. Econ. (May 1968).

provision of education and other services,[50] suburban sprawl and a lack of accessible open space, and increasing crime and pollution—are metropolitan or regional in scope; they do not respect municipal boundaries.[51] The "metropolitan problem," as these enumerated urban ills have been collectively called, has been studied, analyzed, dissected, and decried by a generation of urban scholars.[52] The fundamental problem they identify is "the noncongruence of problem units with policy-making units."[53] Metropolitan areas are interdependent social and economic units, but they are generally comprised of a multiplicity of local governments that, by and large, act in their own self-interests. Because of the interdependent nature of the metropolis, the policies undertaken by independent municipal cor-

---

The mismatch hypothesis, however, is by no means universally accepted. Charlotte Fremon, for example, finds that "there is no conclusive evidence at all to support the mismatch hypothesis—or to refute it. There exist no time series data for employment, by occupation, in cities and suburbs. The central hypothesis of the argument—that the jobs growing in the central cities are high-skilled ones compared to those growing in the suburbs—had only been assumed." Central City and Suburban Employment Growth, 1965-1967 at 8 (Urban Institute, 1970). Other commentators who question or take exception to the mismatch hypothesis can be found in the sources collected in Harrison, *supra* note 10, at 42-59.

50. Suburban communities spend approximately 50-60 percent of their total budget for education, while core cities spend for education at a rate of about 35 percent. The most widely cited reasons for this pattern of fiscal disparity are the uneven distribution of wealth between city and suburban residents and the overburden of noneducational services on central-city budgets. Bahl & Puryear, *Regional Tax Base Sharing: Possibilities and Implications*, 29 Nat'l Tax J. 328, 332 (1976). For other views on the subject of fiscal disparities, *see* articles collected in 29 Nat'l Tax J. 223. *See also* Sacks & Callahan, *supra* note 24, at 91; Rubinowitz, *supra* note 49, at 11-18. *See generally*, W. Oates, Fiscal Federalism (1972).

51. Former Secretary of HUD George Romney spoke of the need for thinking in terms of the "real city":

[I]t is time to recognize that the effort to meet central city needs separately from suburban needs is as futile as it would have been for the United States to try to continue as a Nation under the Articles of Confederation. . . . Today the Nation's future is jeopardized by the mounting problems in our cities as a result of the refusal to recognize the common needs of the central cities and the suburbs. Surely, it is clear that the Real City consists of both the central city and its surrounding suburbs.

George Romney, Remarks Prepared for Delivery at the 41st Annual Convention of the National Housing Conference, Washington, D.C., March 6, 1972.

52. *See, e.g.*, E. Banfield & M. Grodzins, Government and Housing in Metropolitan Areas (1958); R. Wood, Metropolis Against Itself (1959); Council of State Governments, The State and the Metropolitan Problem (1956); L. Gulick, The Metropolitan Problem and American Ideas (1962); J. Wilson, ed., The Metropolitan Enigma (1968); M. Danielson, ed., Metropolitan Politics (1971); W. Gorham & N. Glazer, The Urban Predicament (1976).

53. R. Lineberry & I. Sharkansky, Urban Politics and Public Policy 132 (1974).

porations, townships, and special districts may have effects, often unintended, upon other parts of the region. Economists call such consequences "externalities" or, more descriptively, "spillover effects."

Land-use and zoning regulations are particularly illustrative of the spillover effect of municipal policies. Through zoning and planning enabling acts, a large number of jurisdictions within metropolitan areas exercise land-use controls. In 1968, of over 7,600 local governments within standard metropolitan statistical areas, nearly 5,200 (68 percent) had a zoning ordinance in force.[54] In the Philadelphia metropolitan area alone, where there are 238 cities, boroughs, and townships, nearly 200 have zoning ordinances.[55] More than 112 of the 129 localities in Chicago's Cook County have zoning; and within the New York area, as defined by the Regional Plan Association, more than 500 jurisdictions exercise zoning power.[56] Thus has metropolitan governmental structure been variously characterized by such terms as "balkanization," "fragmentation," or "fractionalization." The National Commission on Urban Problems has described the nature of local land-use controls:

> Today, a basic problem results because of the delegation of the zoning power from states to local governments of any size. This often results in a type of Balkanization, which is intolerable in large urban areas where local government boundaries rarely reflect the true economic and social watersheds. The present indiscriminate distribution of zoning authority leads to incompatible uses along municipal borders, duplication of public facilities, [and] attempted exclusion of regional facilities.[57]

By careful manipulation of zoning regulations, local governments can determine, to a large extent, the type of families and persons, businesses, and industries that will locate within their borders. Affluent suburban communities, through their zoning policies, have in this way been able to minimize their own tax burdens while increasing those of the central cities by excluding "bad" tax ratables (such as low-income housing), and attracting "good" tax ratables (such as commercial uses and expensive single-family housing).[58] This "fiscal zoning game" can thus be a method for maximizing benefits for

54. Building the American City, *supra* note 21, at 209.
55. *Id.*
56. *Id.*
57. *Id.* at 18–19.
58. *See generally* N. Williams, American Land Planning Law: Land Use and the Police Power ch. 14 (1974) [hereinafter cited as Williams]; *and see* discussion of fiscal zoning in text at notes 253–62 *infra*.

one's own community while shifting the costs to others.[59] Decisions made in numerous functional areas other than land use—such as pollution control, crime prevention, transportation, education, and attraction of industry—also may engender externalities to other communities.

A common suggestion of economists and political scientists is to "internalize the externalities" by enlarging and reorganizing the structure of metropolitan government.[60] But surburban domination of state legislatures has impeded such efforts and has further strengthened the division of metropolitan areas into a relatively impoverished core and a relatively affluent outer ring. With the exception of some newer urban areas in the South and West, attempts to expand government jurisdiction through annexation to a base large enough to deal effectively with regional problems have been consistently circumscribed.[61] Similarly, efforts at the reorganization of metropolitan government while long advocated by political scientists and urban reformers, have not met with substantially greater success.[62] As one commentator has observed:

> [T]hrough the second quarter of this century many political scientists were writing on why metropolitan areas needed to be politically integrated through local government consolidation. Thus far, in the third

---

59. *See* Campbell & Sacks, *The Fiscal Zoning Game*, 30 Municipal Finance 40 (1964); D. Netzer, Economics of the Property Tax 131-36 (1966); Hamilton, *Property Taxation's Incentive to Fiscal Zoning*, in Property Tax Reform 125 (G. Peterson ed. 1973); Clawson, *supra* note 12, at 166-87.

60. *See generally* Lineberry, *Reforming Metropolitan Governance: Requiem or Reality*, 58 Geo. L.J. 675 (1970); Clawson, *supra* note 12, at 166-87. Most economists, however, readily point out that one of the major problems with this suggestion is that in the case of most public services the efficiency losses resulting from externalities, and indeed the externalities themselves, are extremely difficult to measure. *Id.* at 180-82. Consequently, it is difficult to use the concept of externalities to justify regional or metropolitan taxation or government reorganization in the face of generally strong opposition.

61. For example, suburban pressures caused the Florida legislature in 1974 to curb the power of annexation enjoyed by central cities. Urban Predicament, *supra* note 27, at 79. *See also* Muller and Dawson, An Evaluation of the Fiscal Impact of Annexation in Richmond, Virginia (Urban Institute, 1975); Holliman, *Invisible Boundaries and Political Responsibility: A Proposal for Revision of California Annexation Law* 13 Pac. L.J. 533 (1972); Comment, *Annexation Elections and the Right to Vote*, 20 U.C.L.A. L. Rev. 1093 (1973).

62. *See generally* sources collected in note 52 *supra;* M. Mogulof, Governing Metropolitan Areas (1971); R. Hanson, *Land Development and Metropolitan Reform*, in Reform as Reorganization (L. Wingo ed. 1974); L. Wingo, ed., Reform of Metropolitan Governments (1972); W. Harvey, ed., Where Governments Meet: Emerging Patterns of Intergovernmental Relations (1967). *Cf.* R. Bish & V. Ostrom, Understanding Urban Government: Metropolitan Reform Reconsidered (1973).

quarter, a major theme has been documentation of how thoroughly this advice has been rejected by the American people.[63]

It is unlikely that metropolitan general-purpose governance, regardless of its inherent advantages or disadvantages, will be a major component of urban reform, at least in the near future. A more realistic possibility is for increased federal and state aid and for federal or state assumption of greater responsibility in functional areas. The recent trend toward an increased state role (through a reassertion of the state's sovereign authority) in land-use control and planning[64] must be viewed as a salutory development. It holds a strong potential for minimizing the adverse effects of parochial land-use decisions while maximizing the favorable ones. Similarly, the states have recently emerged as a force in housing finance, with some 40 state housing finance agencies having been established since 1970.[65] Education, health care, transportation, tax relief, and other areas in which the states have been dormant or ignored for decades, are now receiving increased state attention and assistance. Thus the states must now be viewed as relatively stable and powerful instruments of government, better financed (in general) by income and sales tax than local governments and capable of assuming a much more vigorous role in the federal system, and more specifically in the solution of urban problems.[66]

63. Williams, "Life Style Values and Political Decentralization in Metropolitan Areas," 48 Sw. Soc. Sci. Q. 299 (1967). Other explanations of why the metropolitan reform drive never got far can be found in R. Lineberry & L. Masotti, The New Urban Politics 9-11 (1976); Marando, *The Politics of Metropolitan Reform*, in State and Local Government: The Political Economy of Reform (Campbell & Bahl eds. 1975).
There is some evidence, however, that a few of the more sophisticated metropolitan governments or councils now in existence, such as that in the Minneapolis–St. Paul area, are beginning to make inroads into the problems of externalities through efforts to eliminate fiscal and service disparities and promote greater coordination and political accountability. *See* discussion of the Minnesota Metropolitan Revenue Distribution Act, Minn. Stat. Ann. ch. 472F (1974), in Chapter 7 *infra.*
64. *See* text accompanying note 306 *infra*, and discussion of state land-use initiatives in Chapters 4 & 5 *infra. See generally*, N. Rosenbaum, Land Use and the Legislatures: The Politics of State Innovation (1976).
65. *See* discussion of state housing finance agencies in Chapter 7 *infra.*
66. On the states' resurgence in a variety of functional areas, *see generally* A Campbell, ed., The States and the Urban Crisis (1970); I. Sharkansky, The Maligned States (1972); Center for Policy Research and Analysis of the National Governors' Conference, States' Responsibilities to Local Governments: An Action Agenda (1975). Much of the impetus for an increased state role has come from the federal government, e.g., through grants-in-aid for state housing and land-use planning (see text at notes 182-95 *infra*); through matching capital grants for highway and mass-transit construction (see notes 144-46 and accompanying text *infra*); or special set-asides of scarce housing subsidy

THE FEDERAL ROLE IN INFLUENCING PATTERNS OF URBAN GROWTH AND METROPOLITAN DEVELOPMENT

The federal government has never had an explicit national growth or land-use policy;[67] yet federal actions have significantly influenced the spatial configuration of our metropolitan areas.[68] Indeed, without federal housing, urban renewal, and highway programs, it is unlikely that growth (and sprawl) on the fringe would have been as dominant and decline in the cities as rapid. Nor is it likely that patterns of residential segregation would be so pronounced. This section examines some of the federal programs that have markedly affected patterns of metropolitan growth, and particularly impacted on housing and economic opportunities. It also touches upon recent federal environmental laws, which hold the prospect of significantly influencing local land-use decisionmaking, and also indirectly affecting housing construction and costs.

There are many other significant federal growth determinants that are well beyond the scope of this book and can only be mentioned in passing. For example, federal expenditures for defense and space programs, and for other government facilities, have substantially contributed to the development of specific regions of the country,[69] as have federal programs for mass transit and public facility infra-

---

funds to states possessing a housing finance capability (see discussion of state housing finance agencies in Chapter 7 *infra*). Sometimes, as in education finance, it has taken prodding by the judiciary to force the states to act. *See, e.g.,* Robinson v. Cahill, 69 N.J. 449, 355 A.2d 159; 69 N.J. 155, 358 A.2d 457 (1976); Serrano v. Priest, 5 Cal. 3d 584, 487 P.2d 1241 (1971); —— Cal. 3d——, 557 P.2d 929 (1976), and other school finance cases discussed in Chapter 7 *infra*.

67. The requirement of Title VII of the Housing and Urban Development Act of 1970, P.L. 910609, 84 Stat. 1770, for the furnishing of a biennial report on urban growth by the President, can hardly be considered a "national growth policy." And proposals for a National Land Use Policy Act have been consistently defeated over the past several years. *See* N. Lyday, The Law of the Land: Debating National Land Use Legislation, 1970–1975 (Urban Institute, 1976); Reilly, *New Directions in Federal Land Use Legislation,* in Land Use Controls: Present Problems and Future Reforms 331 (Center for Urban Policy Research, Listokin ed. 1975).

68. *See generally* J. Stevens, Impact of Federal Legislation and Programs on Private Land in Urban and Metropolitan Development (1973).

69. For example, the development of Cape Canaveral stimulated tremendous growth over a short period of time in Brevard County, Florida, during the 1960s. The growth of the city of Seattle has been substantially affected by defense spending. And development along a 60-mile corridor of interstate highway leading to Frederick, Maryland from Washington, D.C. was stimulated by the location of the Atomic Energy Commission and the National Bureau of Standards. *See* Environmental Quality, *supra* note 13, at 27.

structure (such as sewers and sewage treatment plants).[70] More recently, as the 1976 *Report on National Growth and Development* documents, capital shortages, inflation, higher interest rates, and relative scarcities of energy and other natural resources—all of which are affected by federal policies—are altering in new but not yet precisely definable ways, the context of land conversion, and growth in America.

Federal Housing Programs: A Major Spur for Suburbanization and Residential Segregation

Single-Family Homes. Among the programs that have greatly influenced metropolitan growth and social and economic opportunity in America were those enacted during the New Deal to stimulate the private sector to build housing and to help individuals retain their homes or acquire new housing.[71] Many of the institutions that were created in the 1930s, such as the Federal Housing Administration (FHA), the Federal Savings and Loan Insurance Corporation, and the Federal National Mortgage Association (FNMA), provided enormous impetus to the large-scale provision of single-family homes over the next several decades, and continue to this day to exercise vast influence over the housing credit markets and the housing industry.[72] The FHA, for example, through the provision of mortgage insurance, made low down payments and long-term fully amortized mortgage loans feasible.[73] FHA also standardized the provisions of the mortgage instrument, thereby converting mortgages into national credit market instruments and attracting new types of lenders into the mortgage market.

After World War II an enormous program of guaranteed home loans for veterans was extended through the Veterans Administration (VA). Interestingly, the VA housing program, established by the

70. Urban Systems Research and Engineering, Inc., The Growth Shapers: The Land Use Impacts of Infrastructure Investments (Prepared for the Council on Environmental Quality, G.P.O. 1976).

71. During the Great Depression, some 50 percent of all home mortgages in the nation were in default; foreclosures approached the rate of 1,000 per working day in late 1931 and 1932; and new mortgage lending and new homebuilding were sharply reduced. HUD, Housing in the Seventies: A Report of the National Housing Policy Review 7 (G.P.O. 1974) [hereinafter cited as Housing in the Seventies].

72. For example, to this day most FHA mortgage insurance has been written on one- to four-family houses under the basic mortgage insurance program, Section 203 of the National Housing Act of 1934, as amended.

73. Prior to the Depression, typical mortgage loans were unamortized, with all principal being paid to maturity. The term to maturity was usually between five and ten years, and borrowers were required to make 50 percent down payments. Housing in the Seventies, *supra* note 71, at 8.

Servicemen's Readjustment Act of 1944 (the G.I. Bill), constitutes the largest program ever enacted for a single target group, dwarfing all other programs for the poor, the elderly, handicapped, or minority groups.[74] The VA and FHA programs enabled the production of enough housing to satisfy the enormous demand for new residences resulting from the Depression and World War II. Production jumped from 140,000 units in 1944 to a million in 1946, and was close to 2 million in 1950.

Perhaps the most important housing program administered by the federal government, however, has not been created under the rubric of national housing legislation. The federal income tax law, by allowing the homeowner to deduct interest payments and property taxes from his or her income,[75] provides an incentive favoring the construction of low-density, single-family homes.[76] The incentive is stronger for more expensive housing because high-income families obtain more tax relief from deductions than do low-income families. This preference in the income tax provisions for homeowners over renters costs the Treasury at least $7 billion per year in foregone tax revenues[77]—substantially exceeding the costs of all programs designed for lower income persons and families. Another feature of the federal tax laws that affects patterns of housing and development is the treatment of profits from buying and selling land as capital gains, which are taxed at a lower rate than other types of income. This serves as a stimulus for land speculation. Some observers identify the capital gains treatment as perhaps the most important federal tax provision in stimulating the development of open rural land.[78]

In sum, these federal programs, by facilitating low down payment, long-term loans, with lower monthly payments, and by providing beneficial income tax treatment, have stimulated the construction of single-family homes. Since the single-family home, on its separate lot, is a voracious consumer of land, and since reasonably priced land is not available in the central city, the effect of federal policy has been to encourage suburbanization.[79]

The early administration of mortgage insurance and loan programs has had a more insidious impact on metropolitan growth patterns. As

74. *Id.* at 10.

75. I.R.C. §§ 163, 164.

76. *See* Gurko, *Federal Income Taxes and Urban Sprawl,* 48 Denver L.J. 329 (1972); R. Slitor, The Federal Income Tax in Relation to Housing (Prepared for the National Commission on Urban Problems, G.P.O. 1968).

77. H. Aaron, Shelter and Subsidies: Who Benefits from Federal Housing Policies? 53 (1972).

78. Gurko, *supra* note 76, at 346.

79. Clawson, *supra* note 12, at 43.

the United States Commission on Civil Rights has concluded, "for nearly 30 years after the first federal housing programs were initiated, the Federal Government either actively or passively promoted racial and ethnic discrimination in housing."[80] From 1935 to 1950, the *FHA Underwriting Manual* warned of "the infiltration of inharmonious racial and national groups," "a lower class of inhabitants," or the "presence of incompatible racial elements" in new neighborhoods.[81] Zoning was advocated as a device for exclusion, as was the use of racial covenants. A model restrictive covenant was prepared by FHA itself, with a space left blank for the prohibited races and religions, to be filled in by the builder.[82] The Home Loan Bank System, the federal agency that regulates savings and loan institutions, as well as the VA, urged similar practices. This policy was in full effect during the first five years of the building boom after World War II, when over 900,000 units of FHA housing were produced.[83] Even by 1948, federally approved racial covenants covered large portions of suburbia and had established a pattern of suburban bias against blacks.[84]

In December 1949, FHA and VA reversed the policy of promoting racial segregation in housing, following the 1948 decision in *Shelley v. Kraemer*,[85] which prohibited judicial enforcement of restrictive covenants.

---

80. Twenty Years After Brown: Equal Opportunity in Housing—A Report of the U.S. Commission on Civil Rights 39 (G.P.O. 1975) [hereinafter cited as Equal Opportunity in Housing].

81. *Id.* at 39–40. *See also* C. Abrams, The City is the Frontier 62 (1965).

82. The sections of the official *FHA Manual* in which these provisions appeared are cited in Abrams, *id.* at 78 n.8. *See also* Equal Opportunity in Housing, *supra* note 80, at 40.

83. Shelley v. Kraemer, 334 U.S. 1 (1948).

84. Abrams estimated that in the New York City suburbs, five-sixths of the subdivisions were racially restricted. And in a sample survey of 315 developments in the area, 56 percent of all homes were forbidden to blacks. Abrams, *supra* note 81, at 62. *And see* Equal Opportunity in Housing, *supra* note 80, at 40.

The U.S. Civil Rights Commission has observed that changes in FHA policy toward segregation "had little real effect in increasing minority participation in FHA and VA programs on an integrated basis." The report continues:

> "As late as 1959, it was estimated that less than two percent of the FHA-insured housing built in the post-war housing boom, had been made available to minorities." The intent to promote minority housing opportunity was not matched by action to prevent builders and owners who participated in federally sponsored programs from behaving much as they had in the past.

Equal Opportunities in Housing, *supra* note 80, at 41.

85. Equal Opportunity in Housing, *supra* note 80, at 40.

A Decent House for Every American. During the New Deal era the first federal program designed to finance housing construction for low-income families was created. The Housing Act of 1937[86] established the U.S. Housing Authority to provide financial assistance to local government bodies, usually semiautonomous local housing authorities (LHAs), which would construct and manage the housing. Although the public housing program was intended primarily as a means of stimulating employment and clearing slums,[87] it remained the principal form of federal housing assistance to low-income families until the 1970s.

In the Housing Act of 1949, Congress for the first time recognized decent housing as a national goal:

> The Congress hereby declares that the general welfare and security of the Nation and the health and living standards of its people require housing production and related community development sufficient to remedy the serious housing shortage, through the clearance of slums and blighted areas, and the realization as soon as feasible of *the goal of a decent home and a suitable living environment for every American family*, thus contributing to the development and redevelopment of communities and to the advancement of the growth, wealth and security of the Nation [emphasis added].[88]

The act provided for the creation of the Urban Redevelopment Program,[89] later to become the Urban Renewal Program,[90] and a greatly expanded public housing program.[91]

During the 1960s, new programs established a system of interest subsidies for low- and moderate-income housing outside the traditional public housing program.[92] In 1961 Congress authorized the Section 221(d)(3) program[93] —a new, subsidized, below-market-interest-rate mortgage insurance program to provide rental housing for moderate-income families. In 1965 Congress authorized the establishment of the rent supplement program,[94] to provide a federal pay-

86. 50 Stat. 888 (codified in scattered sections of 42 U.S.C. (1970)).
87. Housing in the Seventies, *supra* note 71, at 1.
88. 42 U.S.C. § 1441.
89. 42 U.S.C. §§ 1450 *et seq.* (1970), *as amended by* 42 U.S.C. § 1452(b) *et seq.* (Supp. III 1973).
90. Housing Act of 1954, 68 Stat. 590 (codified in scattered sections of 12, 18, 20, 31, 38, 40 U.S.C. (1970)).
91. 63 Stat. 413, 42 U.S.C. §§ 1401 *et seq.* (1970), *as amended by* 42 U.S.C. § 1042 *et seq.* (Supp. III 1973).
92. For a history of the housing subsidy programs, *see* Housing in the Seventies, *supra* note 71, at 14–19.
93. Section 221(d)(3) of the 1961 Housing Act, 12 U.S.C. §§ 1715 *l*(d)(3) (1970), 1715*l*(d)(3) (Supp. IV, 1974).
94. 12 U.S.C. § 1701s (1970).

ment to meet a portion of the rent of low-income families in privately owned housing built with FHA mortgage insurance assistance.

In the Housing and Urban Development Act of 1968,[95] Congress for the first time specified a housing goal in terms of housing units to be produced (26 million units, including 6 million for low- and moderate-income families) and established a ten year time frame for production.[96] To meet the new lower income housing goals, Congress created several new housing programs for low- and moderate-families, and authorized additional funding for the public housing program. Section 235 of the Housing and Urban Development Act of 1968[97] created a homeownership program providing special mortgage insurance and interest subsidy payments, which reduced the effective interest rate to 1 percent, to help lower income home purchasers meet mortgage payments. Section 236[98] established a multifamily, rental housing program for moderate-income families, again with interest subsidy payments to reduce the effective interest rate to 1 percent. These were to be produced and managed by private interests. Prior to their suspension in January 1973,[99] the section 235 and 236 programs alone had produced 655,923 units, a figure that almost exceeds the amount of federally assisted housing produced for low- and moderate-income families during the 30 years from 1942 to 1972.[100] However, the Nixon Administration's moratorium on these programs and HUD's subsequent inertia in implementing replacement programs effectively obviated any possibility of meeting the housing goals set in 1968.

Like FHA- and VA-insured private housing, federally assisted low-income housing has had a marked effect on metropolitan residential patterns. When public housing legislation was first enacted in 1937, the separate-but-equal doctrine of *Plessy v. Ferguson*[101] still enjoyed judicial sanction. There was no compelling reason for the Public Housing Administration either to object to the construction of segre-

95. 82 Stat. 476 (codified in scattered sections of 5, 12, 15, 18, 20, 31, 38, 40, 42, 49 U.S.C. (1970)).

96. 42 U.S.C. § 1441(a) (1970).

97. 12 U.S.C. § 1715 z-2 (1970).

98. 12 U.S.C. §§ 1715 z-1(a)-(m), (o) (1970), 1715 2-1(f), (g), (i), (n), (p) (Supp. IV 1974).

99. The Nixon Administration's justification for the suspension of these programs can be found in Housing in the Seventies, *supra* note 71, at 83–136. *But cf.* A. Downs, Federal Housing Subsidies: Their Nature and Effectiveness and What We Should Do About Them (Prepared for National Association of Home Builders, National Association of Mutual Savings Banks, & U.S. Savings and Loan League Oct. 19, 1972).

100. Mageda, *Housing Report/Major Programs Revised to Stress Community Control*, 1974 Nat'l J. Reps. 1376 (Sept. 14).

101. 163 U.S. 537 (1896).

gated public housing or to encourage racial integration. Local housing authorities regularly selected—and the Public Housing Administration approved—separate locations for the units to be occupied by white and minority families.[102] In virtually all metropolitan areas the location of public housing accentuated the concentration of both minority groups and the poor in central cities.[103] If the tenants were to be poor blacks, the project was located where poor blacks already lived; if the tenants were to be poor whites, the projects were located where poor whites already lived. Local opposition to the construction of public housing in more desirable locations assured this result.

In some localities, as the United States Commission on Civil Rights has observed, the federally approved policies pursued by the local housing authorities actually created segregated residential patterns and concentrations of minority poor where they had not previously existed.[104] Even after the United States Supreme Court struck down the separate-but-equal doctrine in *Brown v. Board of Education* in 1954,[105] public housing authorities continued to acquiesce in the perpetuation of segregated facilities.[106] In 1962 a Presidential Executive Order on Equal Opportunity in Housing declared that tenants in federally supported housing projects could not be selected on the basis of race.[107] The federal Public Housing Administration, however, interpreted this order narrowly, limiting its effect to public housing completed after the date of the order,[108] and applied it solely to tenant selection. This left site selection unregulated.[109] In addition, FHA exempted federally assisted one- and two-family owner-occupied dwellings from the scope of the order.[110]

The Civil Rights Act of 1964[111] required more positive measures to correct discrimination. Title VI prohibited discrimination against persons who were eligible to participate in and receive the benefits of any program receiving federal financial assistance. Any such public facility, regardless of the date of completion, was to be integrated.

102. In addition, with Federal approval, local housing authorities established separate management offices for projects occupied by whites and blacks, and separate waiting lists based on race. Equal Opportunity in Housing, *supra* note 80, at 47.

103. *Id.*

105. 347 U.S. 483, 495 (1954).

106. *See* Comment, *The Public Housing Administration and Discrimination in Federally Assisted Low-Rent Housing*, 64 Mich. L. Rev. 871 (1966).

107. Exec. Order No. 11,083, 3 C.F.R. 6562 (1964). *See* 42 U.S.C. § 1982 (1964).

108. *See* Comment, *supra* note 106, at 879.

109. *Id.*

110. U.S. Commission on Civil Rights, Federal Civil Rights Enforcement Effort 155 (1971). This exemption was removed in June 1969.

111. 42 U.S.C. § 2000(d) (1964).

In 1966 the Department of Housing and Urban Development (HUD) issued detailed regulations for the implementation of Title VI, which applied to both site selection and tenant selection. These regulations created the first explicit federal policy against discriminatory site selection, which made "any proposal to locate housing only in areas of racial concentration . . . prima facie unacceptable."[112]

Under the affirmative mandate and expanded coverage of Title VIII of the Civil Rights Act of 1968[113] (commonly called the Fair Housing Act), federal activity to assure equal opportunity in housing for minorities increased. The Fair Housing Act bars discrimination in the sale or rental of private as well as publicly assisted housing, when such discrimination is based upon race, color, religion, or national origin. Exempted from coverage under this act are single-family homes sold or rented without a broker or advertisement[114] and owner-occupied dwellings in which no more than three rooms or units are to be rented.[115] The racial discrimination gap was filled by the U.S. Supreme Court in *Jones v. Alfred H. Mayer, Co.,*[116] which held that the Civil Rights Act of 1866[117] "bars *all* discrimination, private as well as public, in the sale or rental of property" (emphasis added).

Notwithstanding these important administrative, legislative, and judicial developments, the United States Commission on Civil Rights found that in 1971 the traditional pattern of racial residential segregation was being perpetuated in the Section 235 homeownership program. It pointed out the urgent need for improved site-selection standards that would prevent the continuing concentration of low-income and minority families resulting from federally assisted housing programs.[118]

---

112. HUD, Low Rent Housing Manual § 205.1(g) (1967). These regulations were not without shortcomings. They permitted waiver of the nondiscrimination requirement if the local housing authority could show: (1) that no sites with costs under the cost-acquisition limits for public housing were available outside racially concentrated areas; (2) that proper rezoning could not be obtained from the city for any acceptable site outside these areas; or (3) that local officials had denied all acceptable sites in white areas. Note, *Racial Discrimination in Public Housing Site Selection,* 23 Stan. L. Rev. 63, 73 (1970).

113. 42 U.S.C. §§ 3601–3619, 3631 (1970).

114. 42 U.S.C. § 3603(b) (1970).

115. 42 U.S.C. § 3603(c) (1970).

116. 392 U.S. 409, 421 (1968).

117. The Civil Rights Act of April 9, 1866, ch. 31, § 1, codified as 42 U.S.C. § 1982, provides: "All citizens of the United States shall have the same right, in every State and Territory, as is enjoyed by white citizens thereof to inherit, purchase, lease, sell, hold, and convey real and personal property."

118. U.S. Commission on Civil Rights, Homeownership for Lower Income Families 89 (G.P.O. 1971).

In 1972, in response to federal court decisions in cases concerning the siting of federally assisted housing[119] and in order to implement more fully the mandates of Title VI and Title VIII, HUD issued new project selection criteria[120] to provide a uniform standard governing the selection of locations for most subsidized housing for low- and moderate-income families. Affirmative marketing requirements were also developed to govern the marketing of all FHA-subsidized and -insured housing.[121] Whether these new administrative criteria would have effectively prevented further discriminatory site selection is unclear, for the federally assisted housing programs they were intended to regulate were suspended in January 1973, less than a year after the criteria were released in final form.

The federal subsidy programs existing then along with traditional public housing, were largely replaced by the Housing and Community Development Act of 1974, which established the Section 8 leased housing program as the principal vehicle for federally assisted lower income housing. Under Section 8, HUD provides for existing, newly constructed, and substantially rehabilitated housing assistance payments to cover the difference between the rent charged by the landlord and 15 to 25 percent of the eligible "lower income" families adjusted income.[122]

The 1974 Act also contains strong congressional objectives for achieving social and economic integration. Departing significantly from past housing legislation, it conditions the payment of federal community development funds on the willingness of a community to assess and provide for low- and moderate-income housing needs. The recipient of community development funds must prepare a housing assistance plan (HAP) that must, *inter alia*, accurately survey the condition of the community's housing stock and assess the housing assistance needs of "lower-income persons residing in or expecting to reside in the community," and indicate the general locations of proposed

119. Shannon v. HUD, 436 F.2d 809 (3d. Cir. 1970); Gautreaux v. Chicago Housing Authority, 362 F. Supp. 582 (N.D. Ill. 1967), 296 F. Supp. 907 (N.D. Ill. 1969), 304 F. Supp. 736 (N.D. Ill. 1969), (judgment order reported), 503 F.2d 930 (7th Cir. 1974), *aff'd* 425 U.S. 284 (1976). (There is a discussion of *Gautreaux* in Chapter 3 *infra.*)
120. 24 C.F.R. § 200.700 (1973). *See* Lefcoe, *From Capitol Hill: The Impact of Civil Rights Litigation on HUD Policy*, 4 Urb. Law. 112 (1972).
121. 24 C.F.R. § 200.600 (1973). These regulations were issued pursuant to Executive Order 11063 as well as Title VIII. They state that "it is the policy of [HUD] to administer its FHA housing programs affirmatively so as to achieve a condition in which individuals of similar income levels in the same housing market area have a like range of choices available to them regardless of their race, color, religion or national origin." *Id.* at § 200.610 (1975).
122. 42 U.S.C. § 1437(f)(c)(3). The Section 8 program is discussed in detail in Chapters 6 & 7 *infra.*

housing for lower income persons, with the objectives: (1) to further the revitalization of the community; (2) to promote greater choice of housing opportunities and avoid concentrations of assisted persons in areas containing a high proportion of low-income persons; and (3) assure the availability of public services for such housing.[123] Every application for housing assistance under HUD programs must be submitted to the local government for certification that it is consistent with the HAP.[124] The allocation of housing assistance funds to communities is to be based, furthermore, in part on the housing needs specified in these plans.[125]

HUD had formerly permitted a locality to receive funds under categorical grant programs for community development, while disregarding the need for lower income housing in the locality. Now a suburban community that has excluded lower income housing must prepare such a plan for meeting lower income housing needs if it wants community development funds.

It is still too early to tell whether the new approaches embodied in the 1974 Act can successfully achieve Congress's strongly stated objectives for promoting social and economic integration. The answer will depend largely on the manner in which local governments respond to the greater discretion and more sophisticated planning responsibilities presented to them, the extent to which local actions and HAPs are scrutinized by HUD for compliance with the act's objectives,[126] and HUD's ability to make the new Section 8 program truly operational.[127]

123. *Id.* § 5304(a)(4) (1974).

124. *Id.* § 1439(a) (1974). This requirement does not apply, inter alia, to applications for federal housing assistance involving twelve or fewer housing units. *Id.* § 1439(b).

125. *Id.* § 1439(d)(1).

126. *See* Fishman, *Title I of the Housing and Community Development Act of 1974: New Federal and Local Dynamics in Community Development,* 7 Urb. Law. 189 (1975). HUD's administrative review of local housing assistance plans has been criticized in a number of studies evaluating first-year performance under the act. *See* H. Franklin, The Housing Assistance Plan: A Non-Working Program for Community Improvement (Potomac Institute 1975); U.S. Gen'l Accounting Office, Meeting Application and Review Requirements for Block Grants under Title I of the Housing and Community Development Act of 1974 (Report No. RED-76-106, June 1976); Joint Center for Political Studies, New Federalism and Community Development (1976).

127. From the time the 1974 act was signed into law (August 1974) until August 1976, HUD managed to place only 33,000 families in Section 8 housing. Holsendolph, *Rent Subsidy Plan Lagging, But Backers Are Hopeful,* N.Y. Times, August 8, 1976, at 16. By the end of calendar 1976, however, HUD's record had substantially improved, with a total of nearly 154,000 units leased under the Section 8 program. 4 Hous. & Dev. Rep. 874 (Feb. 21, 1977). Yet a preliminary

Urban Renewal and the Central City

Urban renewal—one of the programs consolidated by the Housing and Community Development Act of 1974—has had a profound impact on metropolitan development, particularly on central-city residential patterns.[128] Established by Title 1 of the Housing Act of 1949, and subsequently revised and amended many times, the original urban renewal process and funding formula and the program's primary objectives—the physical renewal of inner-city slums and blighted areas —remained basically the same throughout the life of the program.[129]

---

report issued by HUD indicates that the Section 8 existing housing program is not achieving significant dispersal of low-income families into new neighborhoods. The HUD survey showed that 48 percent of those receiving subsidies continue to occupy their current dwellings. 4 Hous. & Dev. Rep. 59 (June 28, 1976).

128. An extensive bibliography on the urban renewal program is contained in Central City Problem, note 18 *supra*. Some of the more comprehensive works include J. Wilson, ed., Urban Renewal: The Record and the Controversy (1966); J. Lowe, Cities in a Race with Time (1968); C. Abrams, The City is the Frontier (1965); J. Bellush & M. Hausknecht, Urban Renewal: People, Politics, and Planning (1967). For a more journalistic account of urban renewal, *see* R. Caro, The Power Broker: Robert Moses and the Fall of New York chs. 33, 41, 43, 45 (1974).

129. The major legislative changes were in the scope of the program. The first substantial revision was made by the Housing Act of 1954, 68 Stat. 590, 622, which changed the name of the program from urban redevelopment to urban renewal, a term then not in common use. This shift was purported to represent a broader, more comprehensive approach to the problems of slums and blight, with a new emphasis on conservation and rehabilitation as well as slum clearance as a means to prevent and eliminate blight. Prior to 1954, under Title I of the 1949 act, urban redevelopment project areas were limited to those which were primarily residential in character before redevelopment, or which were to be developed for predominantly residential uses. The 1954 Act amended this requirement, permitting 10 percent of the authorized federal capital grant funds to be used for nonresidential projects. This exception was increased to 20 percent in 1959, 30 percent in 1961, and 35 percent in 1965. *See generally,* Foard & Fefferman, *Federal Urban Renewal Legislation,* 25 Law & Contemp. Probs. 635 (1960); Stein, *The Housing Act of 1964: Urban Renewal,* 11 N.Y.L.F. 1 (1965). Other programmatic changes included increased citizen participation and greater concern for the provision of adequate housing for displaced families and individuals (and particularly with the availability of low- and moderate-income housing within urban renewal areas).

The first alternative method of executing the urban renewal program since 1949 was authorized by the Housing and Urban Development Act of 1968, which established the Neighborhood Development Program (NDP) to "facilitate more rapid renewal and development of urban areas on an effective scale, and to encourage more efficient and flexible utilization of public and private opportunities in such areas. . . ." Pt. B § 131(a), Title I of the Housing Act of 1949, as amended. While the urban renewal program remained essentially the same in terms of application, planning, and execution of the NDP, a principal difference was that federal assistance for an NDP could cover activities in several contiguous or noncontiguous urban renewal areas, and that funding proceeded on an annual incremental basis. The NDP process was designed to emphasize shorter range, more comprehensive action than the standard urban renewal

The federal government provided grants to local authorities for the acquisition, assembly, clearance, and site preparation of slum property. The cleared land was subsequently sold at a write-down to private developers for redevelopment in accordance with a locally prepared, federally approved plan.[130] By 1968 well over $7 billion in public funds had been spent or committed for urban renewal in well over a thousand cities. In addition, billions of dollars have been spent by the private sector in rebuilding the cleared areas.[131]

Since its inception the urban renewal program has come under vehement attack for its role in divesting minorities of housing and causing massive shifts of minority populations to nearby neighborhoods, which frequently became the new ghettos. One commentator found that during the first decade of urban renewal

> more than 60 percent of the families displaced were blacks, although blacks numbered less than a third of the total city populations involved. Through June 1965, reconstruction of urban renewal land was mainly for institutional and public purposes (27 percent), and housing (36 percent), and prior to 1963, most of the new housing was for upper middle-income occupancy.[132]

At the end of 1971, approximately 600,000 housing units had been demolished on urban renewal sites, but only 201,000 new units had been completed, with an additional 43,000 units under construction, the majority of which were unsubsidized.[133] While construction of replacement units accelerated for several years under the Section 236 program,[134] the suspension of this program effectively killed any possibility of replacing even one-half the total number of demolished units.

Notwithstanding the program's serious weaknesses, urban renewal has achieved a number of successes. It has improved the physical appearance of hundreds of American cities; and the offices and commercial facilities built within central-city urban renewal areas have increased land values and raised the tax base, arresting at least to some degree the economic decline that would otherwise have occurred.[135]

---

process. Again, the major physical objectives of urban renewal did not fundamentally change. Real Estate Research Corporation, Legislative History of Urban Renewal (Prepared for HUD, 1974).

130. Central City Problem, *supra* note 18, at 53.

131. Building the American City, *supra* note 21, at 165.

132. Shussheim, *Housing in Perspective*, 19 Pub. Interest 27 (1970).

133. Central City Problem, *supra* note 18, at 56.

134. *Id.*

135. Building the American City, *supra* note 21, at 165. For an enumeration of many of the costs and benefits commonly associated with urban re-

Yet on balance—and certainly when measured in human terms—urban renewal has failed to help the poor and near-poor who make up most of those who have been displaced, and has created severe dislocations in central-city residential patterns, as well.

One of the major aims of the Housing and Community Development Act of 1974, in linking the provision of community development block grants to the submission of a HAP, was to avoid the social and economic dislocations associated with urban renewal, and to permit the planning of unified community development and housing programs that would achieve the primary objective of Title VI—"the development of viable urban communities by providing decent housing and a suitable living environment and expanding economic opportunity, primarily for persons of low and moderate income."[136] The House Report, in explaining the provisions of the Act that attempt to coordinate housing and community development, expressly recognized the failure of past programs:

> For the first time, after nearly three decades of Federal aid for housing and community development, communities will be able to coordinate the location of new housing units with existing or planned public facilities and services, such as schools, transportation, police and fire protection, recreational facilities, and job opportunities. The . . . bill will put an end to a system of support for community development and housing activities which recognized their close relationship but fails to provide the mechanisms necessary to permit them to be undertaken on a unified basis.[137]

To date the results of this approach have not been altogether satisfying. For one thing there is general acknowledgement that the systems for allocating block grant funds and housing assistance subsidies have not been coordinated.[138] It appears, furthermore, that during the program's second full year of operations the share of block grant funds going to low- and moderate-income areas is declining.[139] Con-

---

newal, *see* Real Estate Research Corp., The Future of Local Urban Redevelopment (Prepared for HUD, 1975).

136. 42 U.S.C. § 5301(c).

137. H.R. Rep. No. 93-1114, 93d Cong., 2d Sess. 3 (1974).

138. Jacobs, *Annual Report May Provide Fuel for Block Grant Debate*, 4 Hous. & Dev. Rep. 888–89 (Feb. 21, 1977). The second annual HUD report does indicate that there is a fairly high level of co–location of housing and block grant activities, *i.e.*, census tracts receiving both housing and community development funds. The report also notes, however, that high percentage of co–location within census tracts does not necessarily mean *coordinated* housing and community development programs. *Id.* at 889.

139. According to HUD's second annual report on program operations, entitlement communities plan to spend 57.3 percent of their second-year funds on activities benefitting low- and moderate-income families; in the first year of

gressional action may thus be necessary to ensure that the act's objectives and conceptually sound method of addressing them—by linking housing and community development activities—are realized.

The Federal Highway Program

The federal-aid highway program, which has been in existence since 1916,[140] has had a massive influence on land development and residential patterns in the United States.[141] Designed initially to promote the national defense, to improve highway safety, and to facilitate commerce and mail delivery, and constrained by scarce funds and the high cost of improvements in developed areas, the program in its earlier years tended to support highway work predominantly on the rural-urban fringe or in small municipalities.[142] It was not until 1944 that urban roads even became eligible for assistance. By 1956, with the enactment of the federal interstate highway program[143] large-scale intervention and expenditures on the nation's urban network began. In 1955, combined federal and state expenditures for urban highway construction had been $718 million (only 22 percent of total federal and state highway expenditures); by 1962, federal and state expenditures for urban highways had more than tripled, to $2.07 billion, and the urban share had increased to 35 percent of total expenditures.[144] The magnitude of these figures become clear when one notes that in 1960, highway aid represented nearly half of all federal grants to state and local governments, and that between 1950 and 1966, of the 385,000 miles of new highway built, 271,000 miles were federally aided.[145] And much of this investment and con-

---

the program the figure was 64 percent. Not only is the expenditure of funds shifting away from lower income families, but it has also become more diffuse, with lower income census tracts receiving less funds than in the prior year. *Id.* at 888.

140. Federal-Aid Highway Act of 1916, 39 Stat. 355.

141. *See* Building the American City, *supra* note 21, at 231; Reiter, *Impact of the Federal Highway Program on Urban Areas*, 1 Urb. L. Ann. 76 (1969). *See generally Symposium: Urban Transportation Systems: Problems, Policies, and Planning*, 2 Urb. L. Ann. 1 (1970).

142. For a history of highway policy developments through 1960, *see* P. Burch, Highway Revenue and Expenditure Policy in the United States (1962).

143. Federal-Aid Highway Act of 1956 ch. 462, 70 Stat. 374.

144. Federal Highway Administration, Highway Statistics, Summary to 1965, at 75-76 (1966). Under the federal highway program, the basic scheme for assistance, which dates back to the Federal-Aid Highway Act of 1916, *supra* note 140, is for grants-in-aid to the states for the construction, rather than maintenance or ownership, of federal-aid highways. D. Hagman, Urban Planning and Land Development Control Law 29 (1975).

145. Hagman, *supra* note 144, at 28.

struction took place for the first time in inner-city, high-density sections of large urban areas.[146]

Like urban renewal, the federally assisted highway construction program caused massive displacements of minorities and the poor in central cities, and in some suburban areas as well. By the mid-sixties the highway program was displacing 35,000 people a year from their homes.[147] In fact, the claim has been made in various cities that highways have been intentionally used to separate black and white neighborhoods, or to isolate minority neighborhoods from the mainstream of community life.[148] Until the enactment of the Uniform Relocation Act of 1970,[149] the federal highway program imposed no meaningful requirement on either the federal government or states to consider the impact of highway location plans on minority communities, or on neighborhood character in general. Most important, no relocation housing or monetary assistance to displacees was required.

The impact of highway construction, however, has extended far beyond central-city displacement. The expenditure of billions of dollars for new highways has affected the entire pattern of metropolitan development, and particularly the sprawling growth of the suburbs. As the National Commission on Urban Problems observed in 1968:

> Probably there is no more important single determinant of the timing and location of urban development than highways. Highways in effect "create" urban land where none existed before by extending the commuting distance from existing cities. The low-density pattern found in most of the Nation's suburban area would never have been possible without the effect of high-speed highways in reducing the importance of compact urban development. As highways stretch out from existing urban areas, development quickly follows, with even the most carefully considered plans and zoning ordinances rarely proving a match for the development pressures

146. Altshuler & Curry, *The Changing Environment of Urban Development Policy—Shared Power or Shared Impotence?* 10 Urb. L. Ann. 3, 7 (1975). Federal expenditures on mass transit did not achieve substantial scale until after the enactment of the Urban Mass Transportation Assistance Act of 1970, 49 U.S.C. § 1602, as amended. Between 1970 and 1976, expenditure obligations for the federal transit program have risen by more than 1,300 percent, from $133 million to $1.924 billion. Altshuler & Curry, *supra*, at 7.

147. For statistics on human displacement and relocation caused by government projects, including highways, urban renewal, and public housing, *see* Leary & Turner, *The Injustice of "Just Compensation" to Fixed Income Recipients—Does Recent Legislation Fill the Void?* 48 Temple L.Q. 1 (1974).

148. Building the American City, *supra* note 21, at 231. *See also* Caro, *supra* note 128.

149. Uniform Relocation Assistance and Real Property Acquisition Policies Act of 1970, 42 U.S.C. §§ 4601–4602, 4621–4638, 4651–4655 (1970).

generated. The phenomenon of strip commercial development along non-limited access roads is one example of the irresistability of such pressures.[150]

Highways of the past were routed with little concern for their environmental, social, or economic effects. These matters are now taken into consideration through complex requirements for environmental impact statements,[151] citizen participation and public hearings,[152] and a comprehensive planning process.[153] It has been forcefuly argued that while these new requirements are good for environmental amenity, participatory democracy, and respect for minority interests, they also are increasing the opportunities and risks for paralysis and stalemate in urban development activity.[154] In many respects this is a healthy dilemma, particularly in light of the deleterious external effects that ill-conceived public actions have had in the past. The unresolved problem is in achieving the right balance—stopping undesirable development while allowing desirable development to go forward with reasonable dispatch.

Federal Environmental Protection Legislation and Land-Use Controls

Since the passage of the National Environmental Policy Act of 1969 (NEPA),[155] a series of federal environmental protection programs have been enacted that have combined to form a quasi–national land-use control structure. Other significant environmental laws include the Clean Air Act Amendments of 1970,[156] the Federal Water

150. Building the American City, *supra* note 21, at 231.

151. *E.g.*, the National Environmental Policy Act of 1969 (NEPA), 42 U.S.C. §§ 4321–4347 (1970), *as amended by* 42 U.S.C.A. 4332(2)(d) (Pamphlet No. 5, 1975) requires, inter alia, a comprehensive analysis of alternatives (including no-build alternatives) before definitive public actions are taken. *See, e.g.*, Morningside-Lenox Park Ass'n v. Volpe, 334 F. Supp. 132 (N.D. Ga. 1971); Arlington Coalition v. Volpe, 332 F. Supp. 1218, *rev'd*, 458 F.2d 1323 (4th Cir. 1972), *cert. denied sub nom.*, Fugate v. Arlington Coalition, 401 U.S. 1000 (1972); and discussion of NEPA in text *infra*.

152. *E.g.*, 23 U.S.C. § 128 (1970) (hearing process for federally aided highways); 42 U.S.C. § 1602(d) (1970) (public hearings for federally aided transit projects).

153. *E.g.*, 23 U.S.C. § 109(h) (1970) (highway planning process guidelines to insure consideration of social, economic, and environmental factors); 23 U.S.C. § 134 (1970) (urban transportation planning process). The plethora of current transportation planning requirements are discussed in Altshuler & Curry, *supra* note 146, at 11–21.

154. *See* Altshuler & Curry, *supra* note 146, at 10–11, 38–41.

155. 42 U.S.C. §§ 4321–4347 (1970), *as amended by* 42 U.S.C.A. § 4332(2)(d) (Pamphlet No. 5, 1975).

156. 42 U.S.C. § 1857 (1970).

Pollution Control Act Amendments of 1972,[157] the Coastal Zone Management Act of 1972,[158] and to a lesser extent the Noise Control Act of 1972.[159]

NEPA requires that all federal agencies prepare environmental impact statements for "major Federal actions significantly affecting the quality of the human environment."[160] Another statutory mandate of NEPA requires that all federal agencies plan and develop alternative management strategies for the optimal use of natural resources.[161] Through these action-forcing procedures and public-interest litigation, substantial progress has been made in effecting an integrated decision-making process, balancing economic, engineering, and community interests with environmental protection.

Yet NEPA has been criticized as forcing public administrators to recognize environmental concerns as dominant over such socioeconomic factors as community economic development, maintaining neighborhood integrity, the efficient construction of metropolitan transportation networks, and public capital infrastructure construction.[162] A recent appraisal of the impact of NEPA and other federally imposed requirements on urban development policy led to the following conclusion:

> We have, in short, decisively entered a new era with respect to urban physical development, one in which the private sector is regulated as never before, in which public agencies with developmental mandates are hemmed in by a dense forest of qualifiers and restrictions, and in which federal aid policy is being revised to offer state and local officials attractive alternatives to disruptive public works programs in urban areas.[163]

NEPA requirements have recently been involved in federal legislative developments and court decisions affecting urban housing de-

157. 33 U.S.C. §§ 1251–1376 (Supp. II 1972).

158. 16 U.S.C. § 1451 *et seq.*

159. 42 U.S.C.A. § 4901. *See* Comment, *Toward the Comprehensive Abatement of Noise Pollution: Recent Federal and New City Noise Control Legislation,* 4 Ecology L.Q. 109 (1974).

160. 42 U.S.C. § 4332(2)(c) (1970), *as amended by* 42 U.S.C.A. § 4332(2)(c) (Pamphlet No. 5, 1975).

161. *Id.* at § 4332(2)(d).

162. *See* Hagman, *supra* note 144, at 558–60. For an analysis of SEPAs or "little NEPAs" at the state level as enacted by 30-odd states, *see* Hagman, NEPA's *Progeny Inhabit the States—Were the Genes Defective?* 7 Urb. L. Ann. 3 (1974); Yost, *NEPA's Progeny: State Environmental Policy Acts,* 3 Environ. L. Rep. 50090 (1973). The state environmental impact process has also been criticized for providing insufficient data to give adequate guidance in environmental vs. socioeconomic tradeoffs. *See* Muller, State-Mandated Impact Evaluation: A Preliminary Assessment (Urban Institute, April 1976).

163. Altshuler & Curry, *supra* note 146, at 39.

velopment. Under the Housing and Community Development Act of 1974, NEPA review of proposed activities has been delegated from HUD to the local recipient.[164] In *Flint Ridge Development Co. v. Scenic Rivers Association of Oklahoma*,[165] the U.S. Supreme Court held that HUD's responsibility under the Interstate Land Sales Full Disclosure Act were not covered by NEPA.[166] In *Nucleus of Chicago Homeowners Association v. Lynn*,[167] the Court of Appeals for the Seventh Circuit held that NEPA did not apply in a homeowner's suit to keep public housing from a white neighborhood. The suit was based on the allegation that "the social characteristics of the prospective tenants of the housing units will have an adverse impact on the quality of the environment."[168]

The Clean Air Amendments of 1970 and the Federal Water Pollution Control Act Amendments of 1972, as well as the Coastal Zone Management Act of 1972, are likely to have a direct impact on the location and timing of development and other decisions that shape land-use patterns.[169] These laws and other environmental legislation explicitly or implicitly authorize—and in some cases require—the Environmental Protection Agency (and state and regional planning agencies implementing programs under such legislation) to consider land-use measures as alternative or supplemental means for achieving environmental quality standards and objectives.

Planning and implementation requirements for pollution control under federal legislation include: (1) basin, areawide, and facilities plans to meet water-quality objectives; (2) state implementation plans and related transportation and stationary source controls to achieve air-quality objectives; and (3) the development of state and local controls for land development in coastal zones. These requirements may affect land uses by restricting the nature and location of pollution sources or by determining the need for state and local governments to employ land-use measures to control the location of pollution sources. The Clean Air Act provides, for instance, that plans prepared by air-pollution control agencies receiving EPA grants must include "emission limitations . . . and such other measures as may be necessary to insure attainment and maintenance of . . . primary or

---

164. *See* Thomas, *Hud's NEPA Responsibilities Under the Housing and Community Development Act of 1974: Delegation or Designation?* 10 Urb. L. Ann. 179 (1975).
165. 423 U.S. 1013 (1976).
166. 15 U.S.C. § 1701 *et seq.* (1975).
167. 524 F.2d 225 (7th Cir. 1976).
168. *Id.* at 228.
169. *See generally* Hagman, *supra* note 144, at 565–89.

secondary standard[s] including . . . land use and transportation controls."[170]

Regulatory measures designed to achieve and maintain environmental quality standards, such as transportation-control plans, review of new sources of air pollution, limitations on the degradation of existing clean air, and the issuance of waste water discharge permits to industries and municipalities, may affect land-use decisions by restricting or altering the nature and location of pollution sources. The award of grants for the planning and construction of needed additional municipal sewage treatment capacity may affect land-use decisions by encouraging and accommodating new development or expansion.

In its 1974 *Annual Report*, the Council on Environmental Quality (CEQ) identified a number of ways in which the federal environmental control laws and regulations—which were adopted to attain positive goals—may have negative effects on land use and, ironically, even on the environment they are designed to protect.[171] For example, the Clean Air Act of 1970 mandates regulations for formulating transportation control plans for selected metropolitan areas to meet ambient air-quality standards.[172] These controls have included strategies such as the elimination of on-street parking and a parking tax on off-street parking in the central business district in order to make automobile commuting more expensive and to encourage more commuters to use public transit. But if these regulations are not vigorously enforced throughout the metropolitan areas, they might, according to CEQ, have the effect of

encouraging the dispersal of employment centers out of the central city. Such dispersal could in turn affect the economic viability of the central city, as well as make it more difficult for lower-income central city residents to get to their jobs. It would also adversely affect the viability of the public transit systems that are supposed to be encouraged by other measures and would tend to encourage more development at the urban fringe. . . . In some instances—for example, if parking controls cause residential and industrial location patterns that discourage mass transit use—

170. 42 U.S.C.A. § 1857 (C-5(a)(z)(B).

171. *See* Environmental Quality, *supra* note 13, at 31–36. *See also* F. Bosselman *et al.*, EPA Authority Affecting Land Use (Report Submitted to the Environmental Protection Agency under Contract No. 68-01-1560, March 12, 1974).

172. *See generally* Mandelker & Rothschild, *The Role of Land-Use Controls in Combatting Air Pollution Under the Clean Air Act of 1970*, 3 Ecology L.Q. 235 (1973); Note, *EPA Regulation of "Indirect Sources": A Skeptical View*, 12 Harv. J. Legis. 111 (1974).

the incentives may work against each other and result in land use patterns that actually increase the amount of air pollution generated.[173]

Similarly, the 1972 amendments to the Federal Water Pollution Control Act have the potential to stimulate dispersed development and encourage sprawl on the fringe:

> Because it is generally less expensive to build pollution abatement technology into a new plant than to add it to an old one, and because abatement devices require space which may not be available at older congested industrial sites, the effluent standards may induce firms to abandon old plants, particularly those located in high density urban areas, sooner than they otherwise might have. Usually a new plant will be located outside the central city where more land is available at a lower price.[174]

Controls to be developed and implemented by the Section 208 regional waste-water management program of the 1972 Act will have a significant effect on future industrial decisions about both the scope and location of future expansion.[175]

In the Coastal Zone Management Act of 1972 (CZMA), as amended in 1976,[176] federal funds have been made available for state planning and control for the protection of environmentally critical areas bordering coastal waters.[177] Under the Act, however, the details of the state and local management programs are left to the states. Included in the act's requirements are: "(1) an identification of coastal zone boundaries; (2) a definition of permissible land and water uses; (3) 'an inventory and designation of areas of particular concern'; (4) an identification of the means by which the state proposes to exert control over land and water uses; (5) 'broad guidelines on priority of uses'; and (6) a description of a proposed organizational structure."[178] A recent analysis of future implementation problems under the act has stated:

> The federal guidelines under the CZMA give the states a choice of several possible methods: state standards for local implementation subject to state review and approval, direct state regulation and implementation, state ad-

173. Environmental Quality, *supra* note 13, at 33–34.
174. *Id.* at 35.
175. *See* Phillips, *Developments in Water Quality and Land Use Planning: Problems in the Application of the Federal Water Pollution Control Act Amendments of 1972*, 10 Urb. L. Ann. 119 (1974).
176. *See* U.S. Code Cong. & Ad. News 1013 (1976).
177. *See generally*, Mandelker and Sherry *The National Coastal Zone Management Act of 1972*, 7 Urb. L. Ann. 119 (1974).
178. *Id.* at 130.

ministrative review of all land and water use decisions, or a combination of these techniques. This is not much help since total control by the state is seldom politically feasible, and zoning, which is the only local mechanism specifically mentioned in the federal guidelines, is subject to well-known deficiencies.[179]

In sum, analyzing all the potential land-use implications of recent environmental legislation, developing the requisite complementary guidelines, and overseeing the responsibility for preparing integrated plans which balance all the various environmental, economic, and social objectives is an extremely complex undertaking. In the Advisory Commission's view the planning required by the federal environmental protection legislation and by EPA as well as that required by legislation not specifically environmental, such as the Federal Aid Highway Act[180] and the Housing and Community Development Act of 1974,[181] can be better coordinated with local land-use policies through a mandatory comprehensive planning process such as that called for in this book.

Federal Encouragement of Regional Planning

We have seen in this chapter how federal programs have often had a deleterious impact on growth in urban America. In rather schizophrenic fashion, other federal policies have also provided the major impetus for regional comprehensive planning and metropolitan coordination. Federal encouragement of regional planning can be traced directly to the 701 assistance program of the Housing Act of 1954.[182] The Comprehensive Planning Assistance Program created by this Act provided funds for comprehensive regional planning, thereby stimulating the formation of regional planning bodies.

Regional planning received a further boost through the A-95 review process, established pursuant to the Intergovernmental Cooperation Act of 1968[183] and administered under rules promulgated by the Office of Management and Budget (OMB). OMB Circular A-95[184] requires that all applications for federal grants be reviewed by a state,

---

179. *See* Schoenbaum & Rosenberg, *The Legal Implementation of Coastal Zone Management: The North Carolina Model*, 1976 Duke L.J. 2.

180. *See* Mashaw, *The Legal Structure of Frustration: Alternative Strategies for Public Choice Concerning Federally Aided Highway Construction*, 122 U. Pa. L. Rev. 1 (1973).

181. *See* text following notes 122 *supra*.

182. 40 U.S.C. § 461(a).

183. 42 U.S.C. § 4201 *et seq.* (1968).

184. U.S. Office of Management and Budget Circular A-95 (Revised 1973/74/75/76. *And see* Brussat, *Knowing Your A-95*, 32 Urb. Land 13 (March 1973); Myhra, *A-95 Review and the Urban Planning Process*, 50 J. Urb. L. 449 (1973).

regional, or metropolitan clearinghouse. The purpose of the review is to identify the relationship of the proposed project to area-wide comprehensive plans, and to identify any possible interjurisdictional problems or opportunities associated with the proposal.[185] Any comments or recommendations made after review are submitted with the grant application to the federal agency to assist the federal official in the evaluation process. The stated purpose of A-95 review is

> To encourage the establishment of a network of state, regional, and metropolitan planning and development clearinghouses which will aid in the coordination of federal or federally assisted projects and programs with state, regional and local planning for orderly growth and development.[186]

The regional agencies that usually perform the review task are Councils of Government (COGs)—voluntary associations of elected officials from jurisdictions in the region, established either by local initiative or state enabling legislation. Examples include the Association of Bay Area Governments (ABAG) in the San Francisco–Oakland area, and the Association of Central Oklahoma Governments (ACOG).[187] Their most important function is to comment on applications for federal grants based on the consistency of the submitted proposals with metropolitan area objectives.

Most of the powers of the metropolitan COGs are negative rather than positive and advisory rather than mandatory. They can recommend disapproval of local grant applications that are inconsistent with often vaguely drawn metropolitan criteria, but they cannot compel a local government to do anything against its will. (Indeed, as a practical matter, the constituent local governments usually have a strong interest in seeing additional federal money spent in their jurisdiction.) Generally, their limited powers extend only to matters involving federal money and not to local decisions on zoning, taxation, spending, and so forth. While it is generally acknowledged that COGs have done little in solving metropolitan problems, many have made at least embryonic strides in regional planning and coordination in a number of functional areas such as fair-share housing, and have opened up a much-needed dialog between constituent governments.

185. Myhra, *supra* note 184, at 450–51. *See also* discussion of the A-95 review process in Chapter 6 *infra*.
186. Office of Management and Budget, Circular A-95: What It is and How It Works (1974).
187. For an analysis of a wide variety of COGs, see Advisory Commission on Intergovernmental Relations, Substate Regionalism and the Federal System (1973); M. Mogulof, Governing Metropolitan Areas (1971).

In 1968 the 701 program was amended to require the preparation of a housing element as part of the overall work program of any agency receiving federal urban planning assistance funds.[188] The housing element, according to HUD regulations, was to coordinate housing plans with other regional plans, to identify housing needs, and to define strategies for meeting them.[189] The housing element of the 701 program, the A-95 review process, and judicial pressure to disperse federally assisted housing (subsequently codified in HUD's project-selection criteria), combined to catalyze efforts at implementing regional housing allocation plans. The Miami Valley Regional Planning Commission (MVRPC) in Dayton, Ohio was the prototype. In 1970 it adopted a regional housing allocation plan calling for the construction of 14,000 units of low- and moderate-income housing. Initially HUD gave special consideration to MVRPC's housing allocation plan, and encouraged the preparation of similar plans elsewhere.[190] The termination of federally subsidized housing in January 1973, however, marked a severe setback for all fair-share housing efforts.[191]

The Housing and Community Development Act of 1974 contains several provisions which, if properly implemented, have the potential for revitalizing the fair-share plans and for stimulating a greater degree of coordination among neighboring jurisdictions within metropolitan areas. As noted earlier the Act requires recipients of community development block grants to prepare a HAP that assesses, *inter alia*, the housing needs of lower income persons "residing in or *expected to reside in* the community" (emphasis added).[192] To comply with the letter of this requirement, a community would necessarily have to look beyond its own boundaries, and an interjurisdictional dialog and response should logically fol-

---

188. Housing and Urban Development Act of 1968, P.L. 90-448, 82 Stat. 476, 528 *amending* 40 U.S.C. § 461(a).

189. For the program requirements prior to the Housing and Community Development Act of 1974, *see* HUD, Comprehensive Planning Assistance Requirements and Guidelines for a Grant—Handbook I (CPM Circular No. 6041.1A, March 1972). The "701" planning program is also discussed in greater detail in Chapter 6 *infra*.

190. *See* Listokin, *Fair Share Housing Distribution: Will It Open the Suburbs to Apartment Development?* 2 Real Estate L.J. 740 (1974); and discussion of housing allocation plans in Chapter 6 *infra*.

191. *Id. See also* H. Franklin, D. Falk, & A. Levin, In-Zoning: A Guide for Policy Makers on Inclusionary Land Use Programs 169 (1974) [hereinafter cited as In-Zoning] for an evaluation of the early housing allocation plans.

192. 42 U.S.C. § 5304(a)(4)(A) (1974), and text accompanying note 122 *supra*. The "expected to reside" requirement is discussed in greater detail in Chapters 2, 3 & 6 *infra*.

low. The 1974 act also amended the 701 Comprehensive Assistance Planning Program, by mandating a land-use element in addition
to a housing element.[193] Each of the elements, which are to be consistent with one another and with national growth policy, are required
to specify annual goals and objectives, programs designed to achieve
these objectives, and procedures for evaluating whether the programs
are meeting the objectives. Recipients of funds who are not engaged
in comprehensive planning and have not completed both housing and
land-use elements by August 1977 become ineligible for additional
planning funds.[194]

HUD programs, in large part, gave birth to regional planning and
to regional housing allocation strategies. Whether such plans mature
to influence metropolitan housing and land-use policy will depend
largely on continued administrative and financial support by HUD,
and to a lesser extent on judicial willingness to assure compliance
with federal laws.[195]

INADEQUACIES OF THE PRESENT
LAND-USE CONTROL SYSTEM IN
PROMOTING HOUSING OPPORTUNITIES
AND RATIONAL GROWTH: THE
MOVEMENT TOWARD REFORM

Zoning—the basic governmental mechanism for land-use regulation in
this country—has not worked well in coping with the complexities
and problems of growth in urban America.[196] Land use-regulations,

193. 40 U.S.C. § 461(c) (1974). *See* discussion of the 701 program in Chapter 6 *infra*.
194. *Id.*
195. *See* Kushner, Litigation Strategies and Judicial Review Under Title I
of the Housing and Community Development Act of 1974, 11 Urb. L. Ann.
37 (1976); Fishman *supra* note 126.
196. In 1963, a study group established by the prestigious American Law
Institute (ALI) to examine the law relating to public control of land use and
development concluded, inter alia:

> The present legal framework for decision-making in the field of land use
> planning and regulation remains a product of the twenties, notwithstand-
> ing a mass of encrustations. When measured against the needs and aspira-
> tions of an increasingly urban and mobile society, this framework fails to
> provide the necessary guidance to local legislative and administrative
> bodies, to reviewing courts and practicing lawyers, to land developers
> and, indeed, to the planning profession. This framework not only fails to
> further the accomplishment of reasonable planning goals but its use is
> often incompatible with the functioning of the democratic process.

ALI, A Model Land Development Code ix–x (adopted May 21, 1975) (1976)

of course, in and of themselves, cannot build housing, create jobs, or assure suitable environments. When governments at all levels build and spend and tax, they shape cities directly, and they set in motion market forces that regulations cannot fundamentally alter. Yet, although regulations are not the most important of public actions that guide development, they do significantly influence the complex process of urban growth. And that influence extends beyond physical relationships and affects such diverse matters as housing opportunity, employment opportunity, racial and economic patterns, and local tax rates. (Federal housing programs, for example, have always deferred to local land-use controls.) In the remainder of this chapter we will examine how traditional land-use controls have adversely affected housing opportunities and patterns of urban growth, and note some of the important incipient reforms explored in much greater depth in subsequent chapters.

The Advent of Zoning as The Basic Land-Use Control

Urban reformers, influenced primarily by the successful use of zoning by German municipalities, first introduced the concept to America in the early 1900s.[197] Historical inquiry has made clear that zoning was never conceived as a means to guide the urban development process.[198] In Germany, where municipalities did not experience the rapid growth and transformation of neighborhoods characteristic of American cities, zoning was used simply to register "conditions that were more or less permanent."[199] From the outset, then, zoning in the United States was viewed as a means to protect property values[200] —a tool for segregating undesirable land uses and designating compatible use districts.[201] It was premised on assump-

---

[hereinafter cited as ALI Code]. In the late 1960s several prominent commissions called for a major restructuring of the entire U.S. land-use regulatory system. While their proposals for reform were in no way as comprehensive or detailed as those proposed by the American Law Institute (a task that took the ALI reporters over 10 years to complete), their findings and recommendations are in striking agreement. *See* Building the American City *supra* note 21; Advisory Commission on Intergovernmental Relations, Urban and Rural America: Policies for Future Growth (1968); President's Committee on Urban Housing, A Decent Home (1968).

197. For an excellent treatment of the historical antecedents of zoning and its evolution in the United States, *see* S. Toll, Zoned American (1969).

198. Mandelker, Role of Zoning in Housing and Metropolitan Development 785 (Papers Submitted to Subcommittee on Housing Panels, Committee on Banking and Currency, 92d Cong., 1st Sess. 1971).

199. Toll, *supra* note 197, at 138.

200. *See* J. Delafons, Land Use Controls in the United States 23 (1969).

201. The concept that all urban uses could be isolated into appropriate land areas seems to have been derived from the law of nuisance. While the U.S. Su-

tions of a rigid and ordered pattern of land and urban development in which a community could be easily divided or preregulated into well-defined districts with fixed boundaries.

Also from the beginning, zoning in the United States was commonly used as a device to exclude undesirable persons or groups.[202] What is generally regarded as the first modern comprehensive zoning ordinance in the United States was enacted by New York City in 1916, and was an outgrowth of the desire of Fifth Avenue merchants to keep the women's garment industry from encroaching into their fashionable shopping district. The merchants feared that the presence on the streets of the large numbers of immigrants employed in the garment factories would repel their carriage-trade customers.[203]

The New York City ordinance was a huge success, and the concept began to be widely replicated.[204] Zoning was particularly popular in the suburbs, where it provided an excellent device for the insulation of the single-family detached dwelling.[205] In 1926 the constitution-

---

preme Court, in Euclid v. Ambler Realty Co., 272 U.S. 365 (1926), disclaimed nuisance as the predicate of zoning's constitutionality, Justice Sutherland's aphorism shows the close connection: "A nuisance may be merely a right thing in the wrong place—like a pig in the parlor instead of the barnyard." *Id.* at 388.

202. Zoning's potential for class stratification was prophetically identified in the 1927 district court opinion in Village of Euclid v. Ambler Realty Co., 297 F. Supp. 307, 316 (N.D. Ohio), *rev'd,* 272 U.S. 365 (1926). The district court said that the ordinance amounted to a taking of property without just compensation, and declared:

> The plain truth is that the true object of the ordinance in question is to place all the property in an undeveloped area of 16 square miles in a strait-jacket. The purpose to be accomplished is really to regulate the mode of living of persons who may hereafter inhabit it. In the last analysis, the result to be accomplished is to classify the population and segregate them according to their income or situation in life. The true reason why some persons live in a mansion and others in a shack, why some live in a single-family dwelling and others in a double-family dwelling and others in an apartment, or why some live in a well-kept apartment and others in a tenement, is primarily economic.

Id. at 316.

203. Toll, *supra* note 197, at 138. For an interesting account of the unholy alliance between the Fifth Avenue Association, city planning advocates, and urban reformers, which resulted in the first comprehensive zoning ordinance, *see generally* Toll, *supra.*

204. The New York City ordinance was upheld in Lincoln Trust Co. v. Williams Building Corp., 229 N.Y. 313, 128 N.E. 209 (1920). By 1925, 368 municipalities had enacted zoning ordinances. Building the American City, *supra* note 21, at 200.

205. *See* R. Babcock, The Zoning Game 3, 6 (1966). A manual prepared in 1926 by Secretary of Commerce Herbert Hoover's Advisory Committee on Zoning, and widely disseminated throughout the country by the U.S. Department of Commerce, extolled the virtues of zoning in the following terms:

> Suppose you have just bought some land in a neighborhood of houses and built a cozy little house. There are two vacant lots south of you. If your

ality of local comprehensive zoning was sustained by the United States Supreme Court in *Village of Euclid v. Ambler Realty Co.*,[206] in which the Court held that the exclusion of industrial and commercial uses from a single-family residential district was a valid exercise of the state's police power.

In upholding the *Euclid* ordinance, the Supreme Court accorded to local zoning enactments a presumption of validity that is still very much the rule today. Under this presumption—predicated on the doctrine of separation of powers—before an ordinance, or portions of an ordinance, can be declared unconstitutional, it must be shown "that such provisions are clearly arbitrary and unreasonable, having no substantial relation to the public health, safety, morals, or general welfare."[207] When a plaintiff fails to carry this heavy burden of proof, the challenge fails. "If the validity of the legislative classification for zoning purposes be fairly debatable, the legislative judgment must be allowed to control."[208] These standards, articulated by the *Euclid* Court, have, as we shall see, tipped the scales in zoning litigation in favor of the local government and resulted in an almost unyielding—and often myopic—judicial deference to local actions.

With the legal hurdles cleared, zoning raced across the country. Much of the impetus for the widespread adoption of local zoning came, curiously enough, from the federal government. In 1922 the U.S. Department of Commerce issued model zoning legislation—the Standard State Zoning Enabling Act (SZEA)[209]—and furnished copies of the model law, at the government's expense, to all legislatures and municipalities.[210] The Commerce Department also prepared and disseminated supplementary literature extolling in the most glowing terms the virtues of zoning, supporting its legality (even before the *Euclid* decision was rendered), and explaining how public

---

town is zoned, no one could put up a large apartment house on those lots, overshadowing your home, stealing your sunshine and spoiling the investment of 20 years' saving. Nor is anyone at liberty to erect a noisy, malodorous public garage to keep you awake at night or to drive you to sell out for half of what you put into your house.

If a town is zoned, property values become more stable, mortgage companies are more ready to lend money. . . .

A zoning law, if enacted in time, prevents an apartment house from becoming a giant airless hive, housing human beings like crowded bees.

U.S. Dept. Commerce, Advisory Committee on Zoning, A Zoning Primer 3 (1926).
    206. 272 U.S. 365 (1926).
    207. *Id.* at 395.
    208. *Id.*
    209. The Standard State Zoning Enabling Act (SZEA), as revised by the U.S. Dept. of Commerce in 1926, is reprinted in A. Rathkopf, 3 The Law of Zoning and Planning 100 (1967).
    210. *See* E. Bassett, Zoning: Laws, Administration and Court Decisions During the First Twenty Years 29 (1936).

support could be gathered and a zoning program implemented.[211] By the end of 1927, some 45 states had enacted zoning laws (although the laws in some states only applied to certain classes of cities).[212] At the close of 1930, zoning ordinances were in effect in 981 municipalities, representing a population of more than 46 million or some 67 percent of the country's urban population.[213] Today, municipalities in over 40 states still operate under the basic provisions of the Standard State Zoning Enabling Act (SZEA).[214]

In addition to prescribing bulk, use, height, and area requirements, the SZEA established the framework for the now familiar triumvirate of legislative body, zoning commission, and board of appeals (or board of adjustment). The local legislative body was empowered to create a zoning commission that would draw up the zoning ordinance and recommend the boundaries of the districts. The SZEA suggested that if a city planning commission already existed, it be appointed as the zoning commission. The early zoning proponents expected that zoning would operate as a simple system of preregulating land use in accordance with the goals of a master or comprehensive plan.[215] The master plan would have a long-range perspective and would indicate broad categories of land use for general areas of the city. The zoning ordinance would delineate the exact boundaries of districts and specify the detailed regulations that would apply to them.

The SZEA also provided for the creation of a board of adjustment or board of appeals to consider appeals from rulings under the ordinance, to hear and decide special exceptions, and to grant variances from the ordinance under "special conditions" where strict application of the ordinance would result in "unnecessary hardship" (the latter term was left undefined). The variance was also intended to safeguard the constitutionality of the ordinance where a strict application of its provisions might amount to a taking. The occasional requests for rezonings (amendments to the zoning ordinance) were to be heard by the local legislative body. The decisions were to be made "in accordance with a comprehensive plan"[216] and to further

211. *See* note 205 *supra.*
212. U.S. Dept. Commerce, Survey of Zoning Laws and Ordinances 2 (1928), *cited in* C. Haar, Land Use Planning 1973 (1971).
213. *Id.*
214. *See* 1 Williams, *supra* note 58, at 357.
215. *See generally* Bassett, *supra* note 210.
216. Section 3 of the Standard State Zoning Enabling Act spells out the purposes of zoning in the following language: "Such regulation shall be made in accordance with a comprehensive plan. . . ." A large body of case law, discussed at length in Chapter 5 *infra,* has interpreted this requirement in a confusing variety of ways. *See* text accompanying notes 238–43 *infra.*

such purposes as promoting the "health and the general welfare" and avoiding "undue concentration of population."

In sum, the zoning ordinance was to be a neutral tool for implementing the master plan. It was to be largely self-executing and therefore would need little administrative machinery. A building inspector, functioning as a zoning officer, would review all applications for (zoning) use permits. Individual applications would be compared with the regulations of the zoning ordinance. If the application did not fit the specifications of the ordinance, a permit would not be issued. In the unusual instances in which this system of nondiscretionary review might be inadequate, the SZEA provided safeguards through the use of special exceptions, variances, and rezonings.

Failure of the Fundamental Assumptions of Euclidean Zoning: The Ability to Predesignate and Separate Incompatible Uses

Almost from the beginning zoning did not operate as was originally envisioned.[217] The basic policy assumptions behind Euclidean zoning[218]—that homogeneity of uses is desirable and that a community could be divided in advance into broad compatible-use districts—have been substantially strained by an increasingly complex and changing urban environment that requires delicate adjustments among competing land uses.

When zoning was originally conceived, urban land uses seemed to be compartmentalized. The typical ordinance of the 1920s divided the municipality into three zones: residential (single family), commercial, and unrestricted—expressed in separate sets of maps dealing with use, height, and land coverage. No attempt was made to cure past or existing evils by demolition or removal to other areas. Instead, zoning was used only to impose some sort of rational plan for future building. Its proponents expected that once zones were established and guidelines promulgated, every use would be segregated into its appropriate land area and nonconforming uses would disappear.[219]

217. As early as 1937 a presidential committee criticized the zoning and planning process. The National Resources Committee observed that "[n]ew methods of transportation have made unprecedented urban decentralization possible. The planning of our cities, however, has not changed to conform with the new mobility." Report on Our Cities—Their Role in the National Economy 47 (1937).

218. Zoning was "Euclidean" in two senses: (1) the kind of zoning that was widely adopted was similar to that used in the Village of Euclid v. Ambler Realty Co., 272 U.S. 365 (1926); (2) the community was divided into a geometric pattern of use districts. See Hagman, *supra* note 144, at 71.

219. In the early days of zoning, Edward Bassett, one of the fathers of modern planning law, exhorted: "Zoning has sought to safeguard the future, in the expectation that time will repair the mistakes of the past." Bassett, *supra* note 210, at 105.

Nonconforming uses, however, have persisted for almost a half-century since zoning has become common,[220] and the problem has been intensified by the development of new methods of building production and by greater mobility, which in turn have created uses that could not have been predicted in the 1920s and 30s when many existing zoning ordinances were adopted.[221]

Another problem with zoning's underlying assumption that different uses could be segregated is that it prohibited certain types of intermingling of uses now viewed as desirable. In terms of convenience, efficiency, environmental amenity, and energy consumption, for example, there are often significant advantages to locating non-residential neighborhood facilities such as a grocery store or pharmacy within a residential area.[222] Still another result of the traditional system of separating residence from industrial and commercial areas has been to stimulate sprawl and increased automobile usage.[223] With such development patterns people must travel farther to get from one type of area to another.

The Growth of Discretion and Flexibility and the Lack of Procedural Safeguards

Unable to foresee and provide for long-range trends affecting land use, and unable to make the subtle differentiations in land uses de-

220. Provisions requiring the "amortization" of nonconforming uses over a specified period of time have come into more common use only since the 1950s. Present-day zoning ordinances, however, generally limit amortization to open uses involving no substantial structures, to uses deemed especially objectionable, like auto wrecking, junk yards, coal storage dumps, and to heavy service establishments not designed for such use. Such amortization provisions raise perplexing constitutional issues. *See, e.g.*, the leading amortization case, Los Angeles v. Gage, 127 Cal. App. 2d 442, 274 P.2d 34 (1954). *See generally*, Hagman, *supra* note 144, at 154-62; ALI Code, *supra* note 196, at art. IV.

221. Professor Daniel Mandelker has observed (*supra* note 198, at 787):

> While development in the early decades of the century took place piece-meal, on small lots, changes in building methods stimulated by the greater accessibility induced by the automobile led to newer development techniques in which urban development came to occur on large aggregates of land especially assembled for development purposes. The large subdivision or apartment complex replaced the single home on the individual lot. Extensive regional shopping centers replaced the corner store. Where these massive developments would go would have important effects on the shape and character of urban areas. Moreover, the coming of the automobile and the high-speed expressway significantly widened the area in which new development could occur. Control over the location of major developments in largely open territory came to be an important zoning problem. No longer could the exercise of zoning controls be justified in the name of preventing narrow land use incompatibilities.

222. Subsequently developed techniques, such as planned unit developments (discussed in Chapter 4 *infra*), seek to remedy this deficiency by permitting a more beneficial integration of land uses at a proper scale.

223. *See* discussion of the findings of the study, Costs of Sprawl, note 43 *supra*, in the text accompanying notes 43–48 *supra*.

manded by new modes of urban development, zoning was gradually converted from what was intended to be a comparatively simple, self-executing system for preregulating land use into a system of administrative control in which applications for development were frequently considered on an ad hoc basis. Amendments, variances, and special exceptions, originally intended as rarely used safety valves, often became the rule. The reporters for the American Law Institute's *Model Land Development Code* made the following observation in this regard:

> A person who looks at the text of a zoning ordinance or the zoning map in order to ascertain the community's policies toward land use may be accumulating only meaningless information. . . . "The community's real land use policy comes to be expressed in the zoning amendment."[224]

A number of other administrative techniques have evolved to assure that any future development receives discretionary review by the local zoning body—a system referred to by the National Commission on Urban Problems (the Douglas Commission) as the "wait-and-see" approach to regulation.[225] Large-lot zoning is typical of this approach. By zoning undeveloped areas for very low densities and then waiting for landowners to seek a map change or a rezoning, a community obtains de facto control over land development. When the owner applies for that rezoning, the municipality has an option to give it the broadest discretionary review.

Special exceptions or permits (for uses tentatively approved by the regulation, but only if each applicant satisfies stated—but often intentionally vague—standards) have always been available and employed as wait-and-see devices.

Other commonly used techniques now include "floating zones" (uses described in the text of the regulations but not placed on the map until an application is made for rezoning), "conditional rezonings" (imposition of specific conditions on the future use of the rezoned land), and, of more recent vintage, "planned unit developments" (PUDs) (which apply requirements to entire projects rather than to individual lots as in traditional zoning, and which require discretionary public review of proposed site plans or designs).

While wait-and-see devices have provided municipalities with much-needed flexibility in responding to rapidly changing urban

224. ALI Code, *supra* note 196, at 152, *citing* Krasnowiecki, *The Basic System of Land Use Control: Legislative Preregulation v. Administrative Discretion,* in The New Zoning: Legal, Administrative and Economic Concepts and Techniques 3, 6 (Marcus & Groves eds. 1970).

225. Building the American City, *supra* note 21, at 206.

conditions, they have also afforded municipalities an opportunity to abuse their discretion. The often arbitrary and capricious decision-making that has resulted has strained the fairness and rationality of the entire land-use regulatory process.[226] Where development proposals are evaluated under a process that lacks meaningful guidelines or standards, local decisionmakers can attempt to obtain concessions that cannot be demanded legally. Also, the ad hoc utilization of flexible techniques without a sound planning basis will further lower standards and likely result in an unsatisfactory, haphazard pattern of development.[227] One of the most objectionable results of the wait-and-see approach, in the view of the Douglas Commission, is its potential for exclusion: "The developer who seeks to build a racially integrated project or moderate-income housing may find that his plans do not receive approval or that minor objections to various aspects of his plan drag on interminably."[228]

The likelihood of unfairness in the land-use decisionmaking process is enhanced by a pervasive lack of procedural safeguards. Most enabling acts do not establish clear guidelines for the conduct of hearings or require local governments to adhere to other significant procedural or substantive standards.[229] In part this situation is a manifestation of the traditional view that local land-use actions—even those affecting only individual parcels of property, as opposed to the community at large—are legislative in character and are thus not entitled to the due process requirements that apply to adjudicatory proceedings. Hearings before local zoning boards consequently tend to be extraordinarily informal. Witnesses often are not required to testify under oath, the presentation and rebuttal of evidence is limited, records of the proceedings are not kept, and written opinions are not provided. *Ex parte* contacts between interested parties and the decision-maker are common. Uner these situations the citizen is often no match for the well-placed and sophisticated private developer, and adequate judicial review is severely circumscribed. Richard Babcock has described the chaos in the local zoning process in these graphic terms:

> The running, ugly sore of zoning is the total failure of this system of law to develop a code of administrative ethics. Stripped of all planning jargon, zoning administration is exposed as a process under which isolated social and political units engage in highly emotional altercations over the use of

226. *See* Babcock, *supra* note 205, at 135.
227. Building the American City, *supra* note 21, at 222.
228. *Id.* at 227.
229. *See* Delafons, *supra* note 200, at 41–97; Babcock, *supra* note 205; D. Mandelker, The Zoning Dilemma (1971).

land, most of which are settled by crude tribal adaptations of medieval trial by fire, and a few of which are concluded by confused ad hoc injunctions of bewildered courts.[230]

A number of courts, recognizing the abuses common in zoning administration, have devised often rather crude methods to correct them. Some courts have employed the little understood "spot zoning" technique as a means to invalidate a rezoning that unfairly favors one landowner at the expense of neighboring landowners.[231] Other courts employ the rule of "change or mistake," whereby amendments to the original regulations are not accorded the full presumption unless there is shown to be a change in neighborhood circumstances or a mistake in the original regulations;[232] still others use the "appearance of fairness" rule, which requires that not only must land-use hearings *be* fair but *appear* so to the parties and disinterested persons.[233] Finally, there has been increasing utilization of the comprehensive plan as a standard for such decisions.[234]

An important judicial reform in this area is the recharacterization of the rezoning of a single parcel of property as an adjudicatory process rather than a legislative one. Rezonings have traditionally been considered legislative because they are granted by the local legislature. In *Fasano v. Board of County Commissioners*[235] the Supreme Court of Oregon rejected the traditional view and explained the distinction:

> Ordinances laying down general policies without regard to a specific piece of property are usually an exercise of legislative authority, are subject to limited review, and may only be attacked upon constitutional grounds for an arbitrary abuse of authority. On the other hand, a determination whether the permissible use of a specific piece of property should be changed is

230. Babcock, *The Chaos of Zoning Administration*, 12 Zoning Dig. 1 (1960).
231. Professor Daniel Mandelker explains spot zoning as follows:

> If one developer receives a zoning amendment for apartment development in one quadrant [of an intersection], why can't another developer likewise receive a zoning amendment for apartment development in another quadrant? The situation suggests favoritism and discrimination and the courts are skeptical. They exhibit their skepticism by characterizing a rezoning of this kind as a "spot" zoning, with overtones that it is presumptively invalid.

Mandelker, *supra* note 229, at 72.
232. *See, e.g.*, McDonnald v. Board of County Comm'rs, 238 Md. 549, 210 A.2d 325 (1965).
233. *See, e.g.*, Fleming v. City of Tacoma, 81 Wash. 2d 292, 502 P.2d 327 (1972).
234. *See* discussion in text accompanying notes 238–46 *infra*.
235. 264 Or. 574, 507 P.2d 23 (1973).

usually an exercise of judicial authority and its property is subject to an altogether different test.[236]

Viewing these rezonings as quasijudicial both lessens the otherwise heavy burden of overcoming the presumption of legislative validity (by utilizing the comprehensive plan as the standard for such decisions), and affords the due process guarantees traditionally expected of administrative bodies. Several state supreme courts, as well as the ALI *Model Land Development Code*, have followed *Fasano* and adopted this approach.[237] When tied to a mandatory comprehensive plan with a housing element (as recommended in this Report) this reform can have particular importance for low-cost housing projects, which often necessitate single-parcel rezonings. Under the traditional legislative characterization, local adverse decisions about such projects are subjected to very limited judicial review.

Absence of an Adequate Planning Base—
The Trend Toward Mandatory
Comprehensive Planning

Contributing to the likelihood of arbitrary decisionmaking, and reducing the opportunities for recognizing it as such, has been the failure of local governments to make plans or policies to serve as a basis for local zoning actions. Even when such plans existed, they often have not been accorded any legal effect by the courts. While the SZEA provides that zoning shall be "in accordance with a comprehensive plan," the proper relationship between planning and zoning has been clouded by the untidy historical fact that the Standard Zoning Act of 1922 preceded by over six years the Standard Planning Enabling Act (SPEA), which was also promulgated by the U.S. Department of Commerce. Consequently, zoning preceded planning in most parts of the country.[238]

Complicating the problem is the fact that the Standard Planning Act only made planning advisory. Accordingly, the courts traditionally avoided inquiry into the specific relationship between plan-

236. *Id.* at 580, 581, 507 P.2d at 26.
237. For a detailed discussion of *Fasano*, the cases that have followed it, and the implications of this new doctrine on the land-use regulatory process, *see* Chapter 4 *infra*.
238. Planning enabling legislation did not spread nearly as quickly as did zoning enabling legislation; it took over twenty years for planning enabling legislation to be enacted by twenty states. The difference has been attributed, at least in part, to the fact that the federal government (*i.e.*, the Commerce Department) pushed its model zoning legislation—the SZEA—much harder than its model planning act (SPEA). *See* N. Rosenbaum, Land Use and the Legislatures: The Politics of State Intervention 6 (1976).

ning and zoning. When discussing the "in accordance" requirement of the Zoning Act, they often looked to the comprehensiveness of the zoning ordinance itself, rather than to an external standard embodied in a master plan. Utilizing this "unitary view"—equating comprehensive plans, where they were required, with the zoning regulations themselves[239]—the courts have traditionally tested zoning decisions under constitutional due process and equal protection standards. Generally, given the presumption of validity attaching to legislative acts,[240] these standards were easily satisfied.

A more recent trend in court decisions reflects an increasing judicial disposition to grant legal status, if not controlling weight, to officially adopted comprehensive plans. Under one view in this trend, while a plan is not a sine qua non of valid zoning, if a plan has been adopted, land-use decisions are at least examined in light of its standards and policies.[241] Other courts have held that the absence of a formally adopted plan severely weakens the presumption of validity accorded zoning decisions.[242] Both these approaches represent a general view that local land-use decisions can confer both benefits and detriments, and that a local decision is entitled to more respect if the alternatives and their implications were considered prior to the adoption of the land-use regulation. Courts are becoming far less willing to uphold a regulation whose purpose or reasonableness cannot be so established.

In addition, a growing number of states, under recently enacted legislative authority, are specifically requiring consistency between local land-use actions and a separately adopted, statutorily defined master or comprehensive plan.[243] Several of these states require housing planning as a component of the local comprehensive plan.[244]

239. *See, e.g.*, Kozesnik v. Township of Montgomery, 24 N.J. 154, 131 A.2d 1 (1957), which is often cited as an illustration of the unitary view. *See generally* Sullivan & Kressel, *Twenty Years After: Renewed Significance of the Comprehensive Plan Requirement*, 9 Urb. L. Ann. 33 (1975).

240. *See* text accompanying notes 207–08 *supra*.

241. The case that best illustrates this approach is Udell v. Haas, 21 N.Y.2d 463, 288 N.Y.S.2d 88, 235 N.E.2d 877 (1968). *See* discussion of this case in Sullivan & Kressel, *supra* note 239, at 45–47; and in Chapter 5 *infra*.

242. *See, e.g.*, Forestview Homeowners Ass'n v. County of Cook, 18 Ill. App. 3d 230, 242–43, 309 N.E.2d 763, 772–73 (1974); Raabe v. City of Walker, 383 Mich. 165, 178–70, 174 N.W.2d 789, 796 (1970).

243. These jurisdictions are cited in Chapter 5 *infra. See also* Rosenbaum, *supra* note 238, at 18–21.

244. Florida, for example, in its Local Government Comprehensive Planning Act of 1975, 1975 Fla. Laws ch. 75-257, requires localities to:

[prepare a] housing element consisting of standards, plans and principles to be followed in the provision of housing for existing residents and the anticipated population growth of the area; the elimination of substandard dwelling conditions; the improvement of existing housing; the provision

This approach to planning, which is generally endorsed by this Advisory Commission (see Chapter 5 *infra*), has the advantage of allowing localities to participate in developing their own strategies for resolving their housing needs while assuring that consideration is given to promoting housing opportunity as part of local growth-management programs.

As is discussed in this chapter and throughout this book, the case for according legal effect to comprehensive planning is even stronger when dealing with more complex environmental and growth-control programs. Growth controls that limit the availability of land development due to local service inadequacies may unduly restrict the amount of land available for development, and resulting land shortages may in turn inflate land prices so that housing opportunities for lower- and even middle-income groups are diminished. Moreover, comprehensive planning is needed more than ever to rationalize public decisions to restrict or intensify development, so that land-owners affected by these decisions will be fairly treated.[245]

Fairness in treatment becomes imperative whenever a managed growth program includes a timing element and defers growth in some parts of a community until public facilities become available. Mandatory planning may help forestall due process taking objections to land use restrictions. Finally, as indicated earlier, regional planning mandated by such diverse federal legislation as the Federal Aid Highway Act, the Federal Water Pollution Control Act of 1972, the Clean Air Act of 1970, the National Coastal Zone Management Act of 1972, and, to an extent, by the Housing and Community Development Act of 1974, can be better oriented to local land-use policies through a comprehensive planning process.[246]

Exclusionary Land-Use and Growth-Control Policies: Expanding the Role of the Courts and State Legislatures in Overcoming Municipal Parochialism

Since the earliest days of zoning, localities have enjoyed nearly complete autonomy in the exercise of their land-use regulatory powers. Zoning and planning enabling acts have delegated the state's sovereign authority over land use to literally thousands of local

---

of adequate sites for future housing including housing for low and moderate income families and mobile homes, with supporting infrastructure and community facilities . . . ; provision for relocation housing, identification of housing for purposes of conservation, rehabilitation or replacement; and formulation of housing implementation programs.

245. *See* Chapter 5 *infra*.
246. *See* text accompanying notes 155–181 *supra;* and Chapter 5 *infra*.

governments throughout the nation—and often to hundreds of jurisdictions within a single metropolitan area[247]—while they provided no mechanism for coordination among jurisdictions. The fragmentation or balkanization of authority that has thereby resulted—with each community acting independently of its neighbors and attempting to solve its own parochial needs without regard to potential impacts of its decisions on surrounding areas—has proved to be a major obstacle to dealing with urban problems that are areawide in scope (such as housing, transportation, pollution, education). As the National Commission on Urban Problems observed: "Although the basic justification for zoning is to protect the overall public good, this often appears to be the last consideration as zoning is now practiced.[248]

To illustrate, the interests of the constituency served by local officials making land-use decisions in an affluent suburban bedroom community are often substantially different from those of its central city, or of the metropolitan area as a whole, whose concerns are affected by those decisions. While the need for and inevitability of regional developments—such as solid-waste disposal plants or electrical energy generators—may be clear to suburban officials and their constituents, it may be equally clear that they should be located somewhere else. Likewise, it may be recognized that low- and moderate-income families need to be housed somewhere within the metropolitan area, but that they need be housed within any given jurisdiction in that area is another matter. If every municipality in a region can exercise its land-use controls to exclude low- and moderate-cost housing, there will be no suitable place for low- and moderate-income families to reside. The use of the zoning power by municipalities to take advantage of the benefits of regional development without having to bear the burdens of such development, and to maintain themselves as enclaves of social or economic homogeneity, is generically described as exclusionary zoning.[249]

The reliance of local governments on the property tax as their major source of local revenues[250] contributes substantially to the exclusionary tendencies of local land-use controls. Pressures are imposed on local communities to compete within metropolitan areas

247. *See* text accompanying notes 54–56 *supra.*
248. Building the America City, *supra* note 21, at 18–19.
249. M. Brooks, Exclusionary Zoning 3 (American Society of Planning Officials, 1970). *See also* Sager, *Tight Little Islands: Exclusionary Zoning, Equal Protection and the Indigent,* 21 Stan. L. Rev. 767 (1969).
250. The property tax accounts for almost 66 percent of all locally collected general revenues and 80 percent of local taxes. Urban Predicament, *supra* note 27, at 52.

for those land uses that generate the highest tax returns, or at least pay their way in taxes for the services they require, and to restrict or at least discourage those uses that impose tax burdens.

A recent report of the Regional Plan Association to the New Jersey Tax Policy Committee states:

> Local leaders justify "home rule" in planning and zoning on the basis that local people should have the right to determine the kind of community they want. But debate on most plans or zoning ordinances in New Jersey focuses almost entirely on taxes, not the pattern of community that will result. . . . [A]lmost all communities on the fringe [of] urbanization are zoned with the intention of keeping school taxes in check.[251]

Similarly, economist Dick Netzer, explaining the process by which large numbers of communities zone to attract or import tax base and

---

251. Report of the New Jersey Tax Policy Committee, The Property Tax 19 (1972). The Supreme Court of New Jersey, in the leading case of *Southern Burlington County NAACP v. Township of Mount Laurel*, vividly described the process of fiscal zoning as practiced by suburban municipalities, and further related this practice to the loss of tax base and decline of the central cities:

> There cannot be the slightest doubt that the reason for this course of conduct [exclusionary zoning] has been to keep down local taxes on *property*. . . . This policy of land use regulation for a fiscal end derives from New Jersey's tax structure, which has imposed on local real estate most of the cost of municipal and county government. . . . Sizable industrial and commercial ratables are eagerly sought and homes and the lots on which they are situated are required to be large enough, through minimum lot sizes and minimum floor areas, to have substantial value in order to produce greater tax revenues to meet school costs. . . . Almost every [municipality] acts solely in its own selfish and parochial interest and in effect builds a wall around itself to keep out those people or entities not adding favorably to the tax base. . . .
> The other end of the spectrum should also be mentioned. . . . Core cities were originally the location of most commerce and industry. Many of these facilities furnished employment for the unskilled and semi-skilled. These employees lived relatively near their work, so sections of cities always have housed the majority of people of low and moderate income, generally in old and deteriorating housing. Despite the municipally confined tax structure, commercial and industrial ratables generally used to supply enough revenue to provide and maintain municipal services equal or superior to those furnished in most suburban and rural cases.
> The situation has become exactly the opposite since the end of World War II. Much industry and retail business, and even the professions, have left the cities. . . . The economically better situated city residents helped to fill up the miles of sprawling new housing developments. . . . There has been a consequent critical erosion of the city tax base and inability to provide the amount and quality of those governmental services—health, education, police, fire, housing and the like—so necessary to the very existence of safe and decent city life.

67 N.J. 151, 336 A.2d 713, 723-24; *appeal dismissed*, 96 S. Ct. 18 (1975).

repel consumers of public services (termed by Netzer, "fiscal mercan-
tilism"), states:

> From a fiscal standpoint, the best of all possible worlds appears, to many
> suburban decision-makers, to be development of the community's vacant
> land by campus-type offices and laboratories and by housing expensive
> enough to assure that there will be few schoolchildren (because of the
> anticipated age levels of the owners).[252]

Low- and moderate-income housing and housing for large families
is generally regarded as involving increased municipal expenditures
without generating compensatory property tax revenues.[253] A locality may thus attempt to divert such housing by a variety of "fiscal
zoning" techniques that can significantly affect two of the major
components of the cost of housing—the cost of land, including servicing, and the cost of the structure itself—thereby effectively
pricing housing beyond the means of particular segments of the
populace.[254] In its national survey of fiscal zoning techniques, the
National Commission on Urban Problems listed the following practices as having potential exclusionary effects:[255]

1. *Large-lot zoning.*—By restricting development in a jurisdiction
substantially to single-family dwellings on large lots (one-half acre
and more),[256] a community can limit the supply of housing sites and

252. Netzer, *supra* note 59, at 131.
253. For a view asserting that local finances may not be as significant a
determinant for exclusionary policies as the number of zoning authorities per
million population, and the desire to maintain a community's life-style by
keeping out those who are racially, ethnically, or economically different, *see*
Branfman, Cohen & Trubek, *Measuring the Invisible Wall: Land Use Controls
and Residential Patterns of the Poor*, 82 Yale L.J. 483 (1973); Branfman et al. do
not regard the number of zoning authorities as a fiscal variable, and hence find
little evidence that fiscal considerations lead to income stratification. *But see*
Hamilton, *supra* note 59, at 129. He disagrees with the Branfman approach,
interprets the number of school districts as a fiscal variable, and finds that it
contributes significantly to segregation by income.
254. While there is general concensus that restrictive land-use controls have
an inflationary impact on the cost of housing and land, it must be noted that
it is extremely difficult to isolate or measure the precise effects. *See* E. Bergman,
Development Controls and Housing Costs: A Policy Guide to Research (National Science Foundation, 1975); L. Sagalyn & G. Sternlieb, Zoning and Housing Costs: The Impact of Land Use Controls on Housing Prices (1973). *See
also* note 264 *infra.*
255. Building the American City, *supra* note 21, at 213–17. A large number
of articles on exclusionary zoning have been written in recent years. An exhaustive research bibliography can be found in National Committee Against Discrimination in Housing & The Urban Land Institute, Fair Housing and Exclusionary Land Use 53 (1975).
256. Building the American City, *supra* note 21, at 214. *See, e.g.,* National
Land Investment Co. v. Kohn, 419 Pa. 504, 215 A.2d 597 (1966) (invaludating

thereby increase residential land costs generally, particularly where the demand for new housing is strong; moreover, large lot sizes can also add costs to land improvements by increasing the required linear feet of streets, sidewalks, gutters, sewers, and water lines.

2. *Minimum house size requirements.*—By raising the lower limit of construction costs, such requirements can be the most direct and effective exclusionary tool.[257]

3. *Prohibition of multifamily housing.*—By limiting development to single-family dwellings,[258] a community can effectively eliminate the most realistic opportunity for housing persons of low- and moderate-incomes; multifamily housing generally represents such an opportunity because their higher densities usually mean lower land costs per unit, and federal subsidies are most frequently geared to this type of housing.

4. *Prohibition of mobile homes.*—As the average price for a single-family conventional home continues to climb beyond the reach of a large proportion of the population, the only available nonsubsidized form of housing for those persons who wish to own rather than rent is the mobile home.[259]

5. *Unnecessarily high subdivision requirements.*—When a community requires a developer to provide land improvements, far above the necessary minimum or to dedicate substantial amounts of land (or pay fees in lieu of such dedication) for open space, schools, recreation facilities, and so forth,[260] these costs are passed on to the consumer and the cost of housing is effectively increased.

6. *Administrative practices.*—Improper notice, *ex parte* contacts, administrative delays, the imposition of arbitrary development demands in exchange for local permits, and other local practices can also be used for exclusionary ends.[261]

---

four-acre minimum lot sizes). *Cf.* Ybarra v. Town of Los Altos Hills, 503 F.2d 250 (9th Cir. 1974) (upholding one- and two-acre minimum lots to preserve the rural environment).

257. *See, e.g.,* Lionshead Lake, Inc. v. Township of Wayne, 10 N.J. 165, 89 A.2d 693 (1952). *Cf.* Molino v. Mayor and Council 116 N.J. Super. 195, 281 A.2d 401 (1972).

258. *See, e.g., In re* Appeal of Girsh, 437 Pa. 237, 263 A.2d 395 (1970); Southern Burlington NAACP v. Township of Mount Laurel, 67 N.J. 151, 336 A.2d 713 (1975); *appeal dismissed* 96 S. Ct. 18 (1975).

259. *See, e.g.,* Bristow v. City of Woodhaven, 35 Mich. App. 205, 192 N.W.2d 322 (1971). *But see* Kropf v. City of Sterling Heights, 391 Mich. 139, 215 N.W.2d 179 (1974). A discussion of mobile homes is contained in Chapter 7 *infra.*

260. *See, e.g.,* Associated Home Builders v. City of Walnut Creek, 4 Cal. 3d 633, 484 P.2d 606 (1971). *Cf.* Pioneer Trust and Savings v. Village of Mount Prospect, 196 N.E.2d 79 (Ill. 1961).

261. *See* text accompanying note 228 *supra.*

These techniques and others, such as minimum frontage requirements, bedroom restrictions, and overzoning for nonresidential uses,[262] bar more than lower income persons from living within a municipality. A much broader category of excluded persons has been defined to encompass "young and elderly couples, single persons, and large, growing families not in the poverty class . . . [who] cannot afford the only kinds of housing permitted in most places—relatively high-priced, single-family detached dwellings on sizable lots and, in some municipalities, expensive apartments."[263]

All these exclusionary practices, moreover, are fairly widespread. In the New York metropolitan area, for example, 99.2 percent of the undeveloped land zoned for residential purposes is restricted to single-family dwellings.[264] In Connecticut, more than half of all vacant land zoned for residential use is for minimum lots of one to two acres. Nationally, 25 percent of metropolitan-area municipalities of over 5,000 population permit *no* single-family houses on lots of less than one-half acre.[265]

Municipalities have in this way used their zoning powers to advance their parochial interests at the expense of the surrounding region. They have furthermore established and perpetuated social and economic segregation. As the exclusionary practices of localities are permitted to continue, presently developing municipalities acquire permanent exclusionary characteristics.[266] As the cost of housing continues to climb through inflationary forces, the effect of restrictive land-use practices is compounded and the value of zoning reform is diminished.[267]

262. These techniques are discussed in the concurring opinion in Southern Burlington County NAACP v. Township of Mount Laurel, 67 N.J. 151, 336 A.2d 713, *appeal dismissed*, 96 S. Ct. 18 (1975).

263. *Id.* at 717.

264. Building the American City, *supra* note 21, at 215. One calculation of the inflationary effect of land-use restrictions on housing costs estimated that the percentage of New York region families that could afford to own houses would have increased from 20 percent in 1973 to 47.5 percent if suburban zoning were more permissive. *See* Caldwell, How to Save Urban America: Regional Plan Association Choices for 1976, at 18–22 (1973).

265. Building the American City, *supra* note 21, at 214.

266. Southern Burlington NAACP v. Township of Mount Laurel, 336 A.2d 713, at 742 (Pashman, J, concurring).

267. It must be noted at this point that true zoning reform, or at least bringing about an end to the fiscal-exclusionary zoning dilemma, inevitably involves matters beyond land-use controls alone. Under our current property tax system the incentive to zone for fiscal purposes is so strong that meaningful long-term reform of the land-use control process will necessarily entail some altering of the structure and administration of the property tax—more specifically, a shifting of a greater portion of the burden of financing educational and other services from localities to the states. Municipalities would thus be deprived of their principal raison d'être for exclusionary zoning. The school finance cases

Yet, until recently, restrictive land-use practices have been almost universally condoned by the courts. When local practices have been contested, the courts have tended to view such cases largely as matters of police power versus private property rights, with little consideration of the broader social implications or the rights of those who are excluded.[268] Courts have often lost sight of the fact that a local jurisdiction, in exercising its zoning powers, is acting only as a delegate of the state—and that the "general welfare" that must be served extends beyond the borders of the particular municipality.

Disregarding the warning of the U.S. Supreme Court in the *Euclid* case about "the possibility of cases where the general public interest would so far outweigh the interest of the municipality that the municipality would not be allowed to stand in the way,"[269] most judicial decisions have treated general welfare only as the interest of the enacting municipality, even when the regulation has a substantial external impact.[270] Moreover, using the presumption of validity and the "fairly debatable"[271] test of *Euclid* as a crutch, courts have been reluctant to consider the motivation of public officials in arriving at particular decisions.

Justice Frederick W. Hall, in his classic dissent in the 1962 case of *Vickers v. Gloucester Township*[272] (involving the exlusion of mobile

---

and the remedial legislation generated thereby may, in time, achieve such results. *See* 5 Williams, *supra* note 58, at 481–483; Heyman, *Legal Assault on Municipal Land Use Regulations*, 5 Urb. Law. 14 (1973). *See also* discussion of property taxation and school finance cases in Chapter 7 *infra*.

268. *See* the discussion of cases in Chapter 2 *infra*. For two interesting critiques of the role of the judiciary on the zoning process, *see* 1 Williams, *supra* note 58, at 85–111; Babcock, *supra* note 205, at ch. 6.

269. Village of Euclid v. Ambler Realty Co., 272 U.S. 365, 390 (1926).

270. In an early decision *contra*, recognizing that the "general welfare" for zoning purposes transcends the purely parochial interests of one municipality, Justice Frederick W. Hall of the New Jersey Supreme Court stated:

> Regional or for that matter, local institutions generally recognized as serving the public welfare are too important to be prevented from locating on available, appropriate sites, subject to reasonable qualifications and safeguards, by the imposition of exclusionary or unnecessarily onerous municipal legislation enacted for the sake of preserving the established or proposed character of a community or some portion of it . . . or to further some equally indefensible parochial interest. And, of course, if one municipality can so act, all can, with the result that needed and desirable institutions end up with no suitable place to locate. In my view, such action is not legitimately encompassed by the zoning power and the courts have the power to and should say so. The substantive question seems to me to fall clearly within the . . . language from Village of Euclid v. Ambler Realty Co.

See the concurring opinion in Roman Catholic Diocese v. Borough of Ho-Ho-kus. 47 N.J. 211, 223, 220 A.2d 97, 103 (1966).

271. *See* discussion in text accompanying notes 207–08 *supra*.

272. 37 N.J. 232, 181 A.2d 129, *appeal dismissed*, 371 U.S. 233 (1963).

homes), which is widely regarded as one of the best modern zoning opinions,[273] took issue with the then-prevalent nature of judicial review and eloquently described his view of the proper function of a court:

> [O]ur courts have in recent years, made it virtually impossible for municipal zoning regulations to be successfully attacked. Judicial scrutiny has become too superficial and one-sided. . . .
>
> While it has long been conventional for courts to test the validity of local legislation by the criterion of whether a fairly debatable issue is presented, and if so to sustain it, it makes all the difference in the world how a court deals with that criterion. Proper judicial review to me can be nothing less than an objective, realistic consideration of the setting—the evils or conditions sought to be remedied, a full and comparative appraisal of the public interest involved and the private rights affected, both from the local and broader aspects, and a thorough weighing of all factors, with government entitled to win if the scales are at least balanced or even a little less so. Of course, such a process involves judgment and the measurement can never be mathematically exact. But that is what judges are for—to evaluate and protect all interests, including those of individuals and minorities, regardless of personal likes or views of wisdom, and not merely to rubber-stamp governmental action in a kind of judicial laissez-faire. The majority approach attaches exclusive significance to the view of the governing body that, in its summary opinion the "welfare" of the municipality would be advanced. On this criterion it is hard to conceive of any local action which would not come within the "debatable" class.
>
> . . . In my opinion legitimate use of the zoning power by such municipalities does not encompass the right to erect barricades on their boundaries through exclusion or too tight restriction of uses where the real purpose is to prevent feared disruption with a so-called chosen way of life. Nor does it encompass provisions designed to let in as new residents only certain kinds of people, or those who can afford to live in favored kinds of housing, or to keep down tax bills of present property owners. When one of the above is the true situation deeper considerations intrinsic in a free society gain the ascendency and courts must not be hesitant to strike down purely selfish and undemocratic enactments.[274]

Thirteen years later Justice Hall was able to express his views for a unanimous New Jersey Supreme Court in the landmark case of *Southern Burlington County NAACP v. Township of Mount Laurel.*[275] The court held that Mount Laurel's general zoning ordinance, which

273. *See* 3 Williams, *supra* note 58, at 6.
274. Vickers v. Gloucester Tp., 37 N.J. 232, 260, 181 A.2d 129, 144 (1962).
275. 67 N.J. 151, 336 A.2d 713 (1975), *appeal dismissed*, 96 S. Ct. 18 (1975). *See* discussion of *Mount Laurel* in Chapters 2 & 3 *infra*.

permitted only single-family detached dwellings, was invalid to the extent that it failed to provide a realistic opportunity for the development of low- and moderate-income housing. Relying on the substantive due process and equal protection provisions of the state constitution, the court placed a presumptive obligation on each developing municipality to regulate its land in a manner permitting residential development for a "fair share" of its region's housing needs.[276] Already the *Mount Laurel* decision has had a favorable influence on important judicial developments in other states.[277]

The importance of *Mount Laurel* also lies in the court's recognition of the difficulty of attempting a regional solution to regional housing problems through the judicial process. While mandating that a developing municipality must zone for its fair share of the region's housing needs, the court realized that "[f]requently it might be sounder to have more of such housing . . . in one municipality in a region than in another, because of greater availability of suitable land, location of employment, accessibility of public transportation or some other significant reason."[278] A more flexible remedy, however, was limited by New Jersey legislation that restricts zoning to individual municipalities. In the court's view, "Authorization for regional *zoning*—the implementation of planning—, or at least regulation of land uses have a substantial external impact by some agency beyond the local municipality, would seem to be logical and desirable as the next legislative step."[279]

Recently, the realization that uncontrolled development may be harmful to both the urban environment and the local tax base has led many communities to adopt newer types of restrictive methods

---

276. The *Mount Laurel* court's highly advanced articulation of an anti-exclusionary doctrine takes on added significance in view of the historical fact that it was in New Jersey where the judicial rationale to uphold exclusionary zoning was originated. *See* Pierro v. Baxendale, 20 N.J. 17, 118 A.2d 401 (1955); Fisher v. Bedminster, 11 N.J. 194, 93 A.2d 378 (1952); Lionshead Lake, Inc. v. Wayne, 10 N.J. 165, 89 A.2d 693 (1952). These early decisions attracted a good deal of scholarly attention. *See, e.g.,* Haar, *Zoning for Minimum Standards: The Wayne Township Case,* 66 Harv. L. Rev. 1051 (1953); Nolan & Horack, *How Small a House? Zoning for Minimum Space Requirements,* 67 Harv. L. Rev. 967 (1954); Williams, *Planning Law and Democratic Living,* 20 Law & Contemp. Probs. 317 (1955).

277. *See, e.g.,* Township of Willistown v. Chesterdale Farms, Inc., 341 A.2d 466 (Pa. 1975); Berenson v. Town of New Castle, 38 N.Y.2d 102, 341 N.E.2d 236 (1975). These cases are discussed in Chapter 2 *infra.*

278. 336 A.2d at 732.

279. *Id.* n.22. The New York Court of Appeals, in 285 N.E.2d 296, (see text accompanying note 304 *infra*), and the Pennsylvania Supreme Court, in *In re* Appeal of Girsh, 437 Pa. 237, 263 A.2d 395 n.4 (1970), are in accord on the desirability of a regional land-use mechanism.

aimed at controlling, slowing, or even halting growth.[280] While such efforts may represent an enlightened attitude about the deleterious effects of uncontrolled growth, they may also have serious exclusionary implications.[281] In the most extreme form, communities have decided that at some point in the future they want no more growth and will permit no more development. The citizens of Boca Raton, Florida, for example, amended their city charter through a voter referendum in November 1972 to impose an absolute limit of 40,000 on the number of dwelling units that can ever be built in the city. To implement the charter amendment, the city reduced densities for all multiple dwellings by 50 percent. A Florida circuit court has recently ruled that the dwelling-unit cap as well as the implementing ordinance violates constitutional due process requirements and is confiscatory.[282] The court found that the building cap was "developed through emotional guess-work," noting that the data generated to rationalize the amendment were developed *after* the building cap was adopted rather than before. With regard to the 50 percent density reduction in multi-family zoning classifications, the court concluded that "if . . . [the reduction] bears any reasonable relationship to characteristics of the properties or areas involved, it is by pure accident."[283] Finally, in strongly worded dicta, the court recognized the serious exclusionary effect of the building cap by pointing out that "its effect on housing supply has been to eliminate the possibility of private construction of low- and moderate-income housing."[284]

Growth-control measures commonly take the form of moratoria on various phases of development. These moratoria are generally temporary, permitting localities to reassess their comprehensive plans and to create new development policies.[285] A recent study found that nearly one-fifth of all local governments surveyed had imposed

280. *See generally* Reilly, *supra* note 39.

281. *See generally* H. Franklin, Controlling Urban Growth—But for Whom? (Potomac Institute, 1973); Bosselman, *Can the Town of Ramapo Pass a Law to Bind the Rights of the Whole World?* 1 Fla. St. U.L. Rev. 234 (1973).

282. Boca Villas Corp. v. Pence; Keating-Merideth Properties, Inc. v. City of Boca Raton (consolidated C.A. No. 73-1061540, Palm Beach Circuit Court, Sept. 30, 1976).

283. *Id.*, slip op. at 11. The court rejected the environmental and fiscal justifications offered by the city as not substantially or factually related to any possible public benefit that could outweigh the property loss to the plaintiffs. *Id.* at 15-17.

284. *Id.* at 17-18. The case is being appealed. 4 Hous. Dev. Rep. 499 (Nov. 1, 1976).

285. Being temporary and presumably directed toward promoting more rational growth, these moratoria are generally invulnerable to legal attack. *See, e.g.,* Meadowland Reg. Dev. Agency v. Hackensack Dev. Comm'n, 119 N.J. Super. 572, 293 A.2d 192 (1972).

some type of moratorium, most frequently on building permits.[286] Another type of moratorium in frequent use is on new sewer hookups or sewer construction. During 1973 over 200 such moratoria were in force.[287] These moratoria are usually justified on environmental grounds—to prevent overloading of treatment-plant capacity, for instance—and are generally instituted to comply with state and federal water quality laws. There is usually a schedule for the construction of new treatment facilities which provides assurance that the moratorium will be lifted in the foreseeable future.[288]

Some communities, however, have adopted such moratoria in a more open attempt to control rates or patterns of population growth.[289] While such actions may well limit the amount of growth taking place in one community, it is likely that growth will occur somewhere else, perhaps with more adverse economic environmental and social effects.[290] Since package plants and septic systems are costly and generally require large lots, sewer moratoria can seriously effect low- and moderate-income housing opportunities by tightening the housing market and increasing housing costs. A report of the County Executive's Office in Montgomery County, Maryland, stated some of the difficulties of sewer moratoria:

> The results [of the moratorium] have been disappointing. The increase in sewage flows has not tapered off. The residential construction rate has actually increased. . . . The price of housing, both rental and sale, has risen extraordinarily in recent years, making it increasingly difficult for people in lower and moderate income ranges to obtain housing in the county. The end result is that both water quality and socioeconomic problems have gotten worse.[291]

Even more sophisticated growth-management schemes can have exclusionary effects when applied in a strictly local context. In 1972, the City of Petaluma, California adopted a growth-control ordinance (actually the aggregation of a number of resolutions, ordinances, and plans) that employed a staging formula to regulate development. The preamble to Petaluma's plan explained that "[i]n order to pro-

<hr>

286. S. Carter *et al.*, Environmental Management and Local Government (Prepared by International City Management Association for Environmental Protection Agency, G.P.O. 1974).

287. Rivkin/Carson, Inc., The Sewer Moratorium as a Technique of Growth Control and Environmental Protection 14, 15 (Prepared for HUD, 1973).

288. *Id.*

289. *Id.* at 1–4.

290. For a discussion of how sewer moratoria can accelerate sprawl see Rivkin/Carson, id.

291. *Quoted in id.* at 25–27.

tect its small-town character and surrounding open spaces, it shall be the policy of the city to control its future rate and distribution of growth. . . ."[292] To this end the city fixed its annual housing growth rate at not more than 500 dwelling units—the average annual growth experienced during the 1960s—and established, inter alia, a rating system for allocating the units.[293]

In *Construction Industry Association of Sonoma County v. City of Petaluma*,[294] the federal district court invalidated the Petaluma growth-control ordinance as a violation of the constitutional right to travel. The Ninth Circuit Court of Appeals reversed, holding that the landowners and builders association did not have standing to assert the right-to-travel claim of those persons who were excluded from residence.[295] In so holding, the court of appeals accepted the undisputed evidence that were the plan adopted by municipalities throughout the San Francisco region, "the impact on the housing market would be substantial. . . ."[296] The court, however, taking note of the fact that the Petaluma ordinance provides that 8 to 12 percent of the 500 units authorized each year must be for low- and moderate-income housing, concluded that the Petaluma scheme was not exclusionary.[297] Moreover, in the court's view, to the extent that local zoning thwarts the general welfare of the region or the state, it is the responsibility of the state legislature, not the federal courts, to adjust the system.[298]

292. *Cited in* Construction Industry Ass'n v. City of Petaluma, 522 F.2d 897, 902 (9th Cir. 1975), *cert. denied*, 424 U.S. 934 (1976).

293. The city adopted a residential development evaluation system to implement the official development policy and an environmental design plan. Under the system, residential units are to be allocated by what is in effect an annual competition, in which units are awarded to the applicants obtaining the highest number of points on a rating system established by the plan. Resolution No. 6113, §V, City of Petaluma, Aug. 21, 1972. Other aspects of the Petaluma ordinance are explained in some detail in the decisions in Construction Industry Ass'n v. City of Petaluma, 522 F.2d 897 (9th Cir. 1975), *cert. denied* 424 U.S. 934 (1976), *reversing* 375 F. Supp. 574 (N.D. Cal. 1974).

294. 375 F. Supp. 574 (N.D. Cal. 1974).

295. 522 F.2d 897. The doctrinal issues raised in the *Petaluma* litigation are discussed in depth in Chapters 2 & 3 *infra*.

296. According to the court, "the aggregate effect . . . would be a decline in regional housing stock quality, a loss of the mobility of current and prospective residences and a deterioration in the quality and choice of housing available to income earners with real incomes of $14,000 per year or less."

297. *Id.* at 908. The court was obviously impressed with the fact that the Petaluma plan specifically made provision for low- and moderate-income housing, which had previously been unavailable in the community. In fact, the court termed the plan "inclusionary" and distinguished it from "exclusionary" zoning regulations that have been invalidated in recent years. *Id.* at n.16.

298. The court stated:

If the present system of delegated zoning power does not serve the state interest in furthering the general welfare of the region or entire state,

One of the most innovative, comprehensive and certainly controversial[299] techniques for controlling growth (and the prototype for many of the growth-control measures subsequently enacted throughout the nation) is that adopted by the town of Ramapo, New York in 1969, and upheld by the state's highest court in 1972 in the case of *Golden v. Planning Board of Ramapo.*[300] The Ramapo plan is based upon the concept of timing and sequential controls—that is, all residential development other than single-lot development must proceed in accordance with the provision of adequate municipal facilities.[301] To obtain a special-use permit for residential development, a developer must demonstrate that the development is adequately served by utilities and other municipal services. Specifically, the standard for granting a residential use permit is based on the availability to the proposed development of five essential public improvements and services: (1) sewers or an improved substitute; (2) drainage facilities; (3) parks or recreational facilities, including public school sites; (4) state, county, or town roads improved with curbs and sidewalks; and (5) firehouses. The city has an eighteen-year capital improvement program that schedules the construction of facilities for the entire area.

In upholding the Ramapo ordinance, the New York Court of Appeals was favorably impressed with the town's extensive use of professionals in formulating the plan, the town's positive commitments to assimilate growth and to accommodate at least some lower income housing to assure balanced growth,[302] and the town's efforts

---

it is the state legislature's and not the federal court's role to intervene and adjust the system. . . . The federal court is not a super zoning board and should not be called on to mark the point at which legitimate local interests in promoting the welfare of the community are outweighed by legitimate regional interests.

Id. at 98.

299. The Ramapo plan has generated literally scores of articles in the legal and planning literature. Among the more provocative writings are those by Franklin and Bosselman, *supra* note 281; and the articles which appear in R. Burchell & D. Listokin, eds., Future Land Use; Energy, Environmental and Legal Constraints (1975). *See also* Note, *A Zoning Program for Phased Growth: Ramapo Township's Time Controls on Residential Development*, 47 N.Y.U.L. Rev. 723 (1973); Note, *Phased Zoning: Regulation of the Tempo and Sequence of Land Development*, 126 Stan. L. Rev. 585 (1974).

300. Golden v. Planning Bd. of Ramapo, 30 N.Y.2d 359, 285 N.E.2d 291, *appeal dismissed*, 409 U.S. 1003 (1972).

301. For a thorough description of the Ramapo plan, *see* Freilich & Greis, *Timing and Sequential Development: Controlling Growth*, in Burchell & Listokin, *supra* note 299, at 59.

302. Subsequent reports, however, indicate that housing prices in Ramapo are already experiencing an inflation that is apparently attributable to the development timing ordinance. *See* New Jersey Division of Legislative Infor-

at economic adjustments to reduce the burden on property owners caused by the temporary deferral of development.[303] The court, however, was not altogether satisfied with the ordinance's failure to accommodate regional concerns. Yet in the absence of state or regional planning and land-use controls, the court held that the Ramapo plan was a good-faith effort that constitutionally could be tolerated until a better method was found:

> Of course, these problems cannot be solved by Ramapo or any single municipality, but depend upon the accommodation of widely disparate interests for their ultimate resolution. To that end, statewide or regional control of planning would insure that interests broader than that of the municipality underlie various land use policies.
>   . . . The answer which Ramapo has posed can by no means be termed definitive; it is, however, a first practical step toward controlled growth achieved without foresaking broader social purposes.[304]

The Ramapo holding, while bolstering the power of local government to plan and zone, also foreshadowed heightened judicial scrutiny of such actions. The court made it clear that any zoning scheme that could be demonstrated to impede growth, or to be exclusionary, would not be countenanced.[305]

---

mation and Research, Legislative Services Agency, Planned Growth Seminar 143 (Jan. 16, 1975), *cited in* Ackerman, *The Mount Laurel Decision: Expanding the Boundaries of Zoning Reform,* 1976 Ill. L.F. 1, 69.

303. *See* Falk & Franklin, Local Growth Management Policy: A Legal Primer 15 (Potomac Institute, 1975).

304. 285 N.E.2d 291, 301.

305. *Id.* Professor Robert H. Freilich, the draftsman of the Ramapo ordinance, has advocated timing and sequential controls on the regional level. Such controls must be tied to other programs that provide:

1. A review of federal subsidy applications to insure that projects are located in areas of new development.
2. The development and implementation of regional "fair share" plans for housing of low- and moderate-income families in suburban and new development locations.
3. The development of a regional housing authority with capacity to develop public and turnkey housing throughout the region.
4. The development, through legislation, of powers to finance and construct low-moderate income housing through sale of tax exempt bonds, and with exemption from local zoning and planning restrictions.
5. A request to regional planning authorities to review local zoning and planning to ensure that they conform to regional plans, are nonexclusionary, and make provision for low-moderate income housing.

Freilich & Ragsdale, *Timing and Sequential Controls—The Essential Bases for Effective Regional Planning: An Analysis of New Directions for Land Use Control in the Minneapolis–St. Paul Metropolitan Region,* 58 Minn. L. Rev. 1009, 1085–86 (1974).

In recent years the state legislatures, in addition to the more progressive courts, have begun to take an increasing role in land-use and growth-management matters that were once viewed as being totally within the local domain.[306] A diverse body of legislation has been enacted under which state or regional bodies are authorized, in varying degrees, to plan, review local plans, or mandate local planning and the components of local plans (such as housing, open space, and circulation elements); to directly regulate land use (through zoning or subdivision controls) in environmentally sensitive or in unincorporated areas; to regulate or review the siting of power plants, large-scale industrial and commercial facilities, surface mines, and low-income housing; or to provide preferential tax treatment for withholding, preserving, or delaying development of prime agricultural land or committing it to permanent open-space usage.[307]

306. The recent realignment of land-use regulatory powers by the states vis à vis local government has been termed by Bosselman & Callies at "the quiet revolution in land use control." In their highly influential monograph, published by the Council on Environmental Quality, the authors explain "the quiet revolution" in this way:

> This country is in the midst of a revolution in the way we regulate the use of our land. It is a peaceful revolution, conducted entirely within the law. It is a quiet revolution, and its supporters include both conservatives and liberals. It is a disorganized revolution, with no central cadre of leaders, but it is a revolution nonetheless.
>
> The *ancien régime* being overthrown is the feudal system under which the entire pattern of land development has been controlled by thousands of individual local governments, each seeking to maximize its tax base and minimize its social problems, and caring less what happens to all the others.
>
> The tools of the revolution are new laws taking a wide variety of forms but each sharing a common theme—the need to provide some degree of state or regional participation in the major decisions that affect the use of our increasingly limited supply of land.

F. Bosselman & D. Callies, The Quiet Revolution in Land Use Control: A Report to the Council on Environmental Quality 1 (1971). The first major state initiative in "the quiet revolution" was the adoption by Hawaii in 1961 of a land-use law that directed the classification of all the state's land into urban, rural, agricultural, and conservation districts, and gave the state's government unprecedented control over the state's land resources. Innovative laws dealing with various facets of land-use policy were enacted over the next ten years in Massachusetts, Maine, Vermont, California, Oregon, Wisconsin, and Minnesota. These laws are discussed and analyzed in The Quiet Revolution.

307. Virtually every state has enacted some kind of land-use legislation since the publication of *The Quiet Revolution*. For a summary of recent state land-use initiatives, *see generally* 1976 Growth Report, *supra* note 2, at 130–34; Environmental Quality: Seventh Annual Report of the Council on Environmental Quality 66–76 (1976); Rosenbaum, *supra* note 64. For more analytical treatments of selected land-use laws, *see* R. Healy, Land Use and the States (1976); D. Mandelker, Environmental and Land Controls Legislation (1977). *See also* discussion of mandatory planning legislation in Chapter 5 *infra*; and the Massachusetts "Anti-Snob" Zoning Law, in Chapter 7 *infra*.

This reassertion by the states of their sovereign power to regulate certain land-use and development matters, rather than delegating plenary control to local governments, is predicated on the realization that a municipality cannot provide rational treatment for complex growth management problems that transcend local boundaries,[308] and on an awareness that a local jurisdiction, because of perceived self-interest, may take actions that are harmful to the combined interest of a larger constituency.[309] While state land-use initiatives to date have focused primarily on environmental concerns,[310] the rationale underlying such actions is applicable to housing and a broad range of urban problems that similarly transcend local political boundaries.[311]

In the chapters that follow, the Advisory Commission will examine the vital and interdependent roles that legislatures, courts, lawyers, planners, and public officials—at all levels of government—must play in improving the administration of land use controls in order to increase housing choice and opportunity and to promote more rational urban growth.

308. The reporters for the American Law Institute's Model Land Development Code stated the matter succinctly: "The judgement is that total localism in the regulation of land development has now become anachronistic. . . ." ALI Code, *supra* note 196, at xii.

309. *See* Heyman, *supra* note 267, at 4.

310. *Id.*

311. For example, a state-mandated local comprehensive planning process (with a housing element geared to regional needs) might be useful in relieving or accommodating the restrictive pressures on housing opportunity imposed by growth-control programs, and also in helping to coordinate the multiple planning requirements mandated by diverse federal laws. *See* text accompanying notes 244–46 *supra*, and more extended discussions in Chapters 5 & 6 *infra*.

Chapter 2

Judicial Doctrine for Inclusionary Land-Use Programs

INTRODUCTION

Competing Values and the Language of Land-Use Decisions

In deciding land-use cases, as in deciding other types of cases, judges weigh competing values to resolve the conflicts that arise out of the specific facts of the dispute. That is the essence of judging. Meaningful analysis and evaluation of the decisions of courts cannot be limited to the rationales set forth in the written opinions, but should also discern the underlying determinative values. These values, however, and the judicial discussion of them, are often embodied in legal terms that carry more social significance than their legal dictionary definitions would suggest. In land-use decisions, the critical concepts in this respect are: (1) standing; (2) justiciability; (3) burden of proof; and (4) remedies—all legal terms that may actually veil deeper political, social, and economic beliefs.

Standing. Standing answers the question: Who is permitted to bring a dispute to a court for resolution?[1] People with standing are

1. Baker v. Carr, 369 U.S. 186, 204–08 (1962). A leading treatise phrases the issue of standing in this way:

> More precisely stated, the question of standing in this sense is the question whether the litigant has a sufficient personal interest in getting the relief he seeks, or is a sufficiently appropriate representative of other interested persons, to warrant giving him the relief, if he establishes the illegality alleged—and, by the same token, to warrant recognizing him as entitled to invoke the court's decision on the issue of illegality.

thus recognized as being involved in the set of facts giving rise to a dispute and as having a stake in a court's judgment. People with standing also bring their own perspectives to a case; a court that gives them a hearing is recognizing that the values they represent are values that must compete with others in the ultimate judgmental process. Traditional land-use litigation has involved the resolution of conflicts between the values represented by property rights—the right to use one's property for economic gain or for private enjoyment—and the values of local self-determination as expressed by the municipal legislature—the right of the community to place restrictions on the use of private property to promote the community's vision of the common good.[2]

The undecided question is whether standing should also be given to others who have an interest in the outcome of the dispute, even though that interest is not based on a threat to their legal property rights.[3] At issue is the standing of individual members of minority or low-income groups, and of associations that represent them, to challenge municipal land-use regulations that limit their options to find housing they can afford in locations they consider desirable. They bring a different set of values to bear on the dispute—a right to be free from unreasonable governmental interference in obtaining decent housing in a suitable environment and nearer improved employment and educational possibilities. A court that gives them standing will be saying that these values, too, deserve consideration in the resolution of a specific controversy. To deny standing to such parties may be tantamount to saying that these values have no place in the evaluation of municipal land-use regulations.

Justiciability. Closely related to standing is the concept of justiciability, the question of whether a dispute is appropriate for resolution by a court.[4] Nonjusticiability might be found for a number of reasons.[5] Sometimes courts refuse to hear a dispute because the gov-

---

H. Hart & H. Wechsler, The Federal Courts and the Federal System 174 (1953).

2. *See* N. Williams, 1 American Land Planning Law ch. 2 (1974) [hereinafter cited as Williams].

3. *See id.* at 74-75; American Law Institute, A Model Land Development Code (adopted May 21, 1975) (1976), *Commentary* at 416–17 [hereinafter cited as ALI Code]. *See also* discussion in text following note 139 *infra.*

4. Hart & Wechsler, *supra* note 1, at 174:

Would clarity be gained by viewing standing as involving problems of the nature and sufficiency of the litigant's concern with the subject matter of the litigation, as distinguished from problems of justiciability—that is, the fitness for adjudication—of the legal questions which he tenders for decision?

5. Baker v. Carr, 369 U.S. at 217.

erning facts are not yet sufficiently in focus to enable the court to obtain an accurate picture of the dispute; these types of cases are called "premature" or not yet "ripe" for judicial resolution.[6] At other times courts will not entertain suits because they lack any clear legal standards for making a decision or for devising a remedy.[7] In cases where a court finds nonjusticiability, the status quo is preserved. The aggrieved party's only recourse is from the political branches of government or self-help.

Burden of Proof. Parties with standing to bring their dispute to the courts for resolution have some prior knowledge as to how the court is likely to decide their case on the basis of how the judges have treated similar cases. Particularly important is what a court has said about each party's burden of proof. Under the adversary system of Anglo-American justice, the party that brings the action bears the initial burden of proof. Preserving the status quo is a fundamental value of the system, and judicial intervention is not to be lightly granted. Specifying the quantity of evidence necessary to sustain the plaintiff's burden of proof and shifting the responsibility onto the other party to rebut it is the court's way of adjusting the relative weights of the values asserted by the plaintiffs to the values asserted by the defendants.

In the land-use area there has been for the last 50 years a strong judicial bias against those attacking governmental land-use regulations. It is more than a plaintiff's initial burden of proof. Most courts, following the United States Supreme Court in the *Village of Euclid v. Ambler Realty Co.*,[8] have attached a presumption of validity to the municipal regulation, thus elevating to the highest value those community judgments that are expressed through the locally elected legislative body.[9] Only when property values are threatened with

6. *See* K. Davis, Administrative Law Treatise, at §§ 21.01, 21.09 (1958).
7. Baker v. Carr, 369 U.S. at 217.
8. 272 U.S. 365 (1926).
9. Under the rule announced in *Euclid*, in order to declare invalid the provisions of a local zoning enactment, it must be shown "that such provisions are clearly arbitrary and unreasonable, having no substantial relation to the public health, safety, morals or general welfare." Moreover, "[i]f the validity of the legislative classification for zoning purposes be fairly debatable, the legislative judgment must be allowed to control." *Id.* at 395. For typical expressions of the presumption-of-validity rule, *see* Nickola v. Township of Grand Blanc, 394 Mich. 589, 232 N.W.2d 604 (1975); South Gwinnett Venture v. Pruitt, 491 F.2d 5 (5th Cir. 1974). And for a classic critique of the near total, one-sided judicial deference often accorded to local regulations under the presumption, *see* Vickers v. Gloucester Tp., 37 N.J. 232, 181 A.2d 129, *appeal dismissed,* 371 U.S. 233 (1963) (Hall, J., dissenting), cited in text of Chapter 1 *supra*, at note 274.

virtually complete destruction will this presumption be overcome by virtue of the constitutional protection against the taking of private property without just compensation or due process of law.[10] A leading example of such a case is *Nectow v. City of Cambridge*,[11] where the Supreme Court, two years after *Euclid*, invalidated a municipal land-use regulation as applied to the plaintiff's land. The Court held that by zoning the plaintiff's land for residential use, the municipality was in effect denying the landowner any revenue-producing use of his property, because it was completely surrounded by industrial property and was suitable only for industrial uses.

Remedy. A court believing it is faced with a situation that exceeds its power to remedy will tend to refrain from making the decision that requires the remedy, even though the judge might share the values of the plaintiff.[12] In land-use litigation, site-specific remedies present no unusual difficulties. While a judicial order to a municipality to rezone a specific site for multifamily development or to issue building permits for a development is readily manageable,[13] extensive revisions of a municipality's zoning ordinance raise problems of an entirely different nature that caution courts from becoming involved.[14] This may be called judicial prudence or statesmanship, but may more appropriately be viewed as a reflection of the limitations of the judicial system for effecting broad social reforms. (These problems are dealt with in Chapter 3.

A Reassessment of the Role of Courts in Land-Use Controversies

Land-use law, as it has developed over the past half-century, recognizes two fundamental values: (1) the rights of property owners to use their property; and (2) the rights of municipalities to regulate private property. Excluded from view, largely through application of concepts of standing and justiciability, have been the interests of people—principally from low-income and minority groups—who have

10. *See* 1 Williams, *supra* note 2, at ch. 7. Another ground for invalidating a zoning ordinance is presented when the ordinance does not aim to achieve a legitimate subject for public regulation. *Id.*

11. 277 U.S. 183 (1928).

12. *See* Baker v. Carr, 369 U.S. at 217.

13. *See* discussion in Chapter 3 *infra*.

14. *See, e.g.*, Pennsylvania v. County of Bucks, 22 Bucks County Rep. 179 (1972), *appeal dismissed*, 8 Pa. Commw. Ct. 294, 302 A.2d 897 (1973), *cert. denied*, 414 U.S. 1130 (1974). *See generally* Hartman, *Beyond Invalidation: The Judicial Power to Zone*, 9 Urb. L. Ann. 159 (1975); and Chapter 3 *infra*.

housing needs that must be met and that private enterprise may be capable of meeting if local government constraints are eliminated.[15]

The Advisory Commission believes that their interests should now be given due regard. Specifically, opportunities for decent living accommodations in decent environments, freedom from legally imposed discrimination based on income, and access to employment and educational opportunities are fundamental values that must be given equal consideration with values relating to private property rights and to municipal self-determination in making land-use decisions. The Advisory Commission adopts this position because it views with alarm the growing racial and economic polarization in our society—as has been described in Chapter 1—which denies to substantial numbers of American citizens those values the nation deems fundamental.

There will be some who argue that to expand the scope of judicial concern beyond the protection of private property rights and municipal self-determination is to embark on a course of unprecedented and unwarranted judicial activism that would be better left to state and national legislative bodies.[16] A short reply would be that state and national legislatures have displayed a reluctance to take strong affirmative actions (except in some notable instances described in Chapters 6 and 7. But the case for greater judicial involvement rests on firmer ground than this.

Courts have for decades actively engaged in the land-use regulatory process by hearing and judging land-use disputes brought before them. Their influence extends beyond the cases they decide, for the knowledge of how a court would decide a dispute influences the business decisions and legislative actions of landowners, developers, and municipal officials. Yet court cases are decided, and their influence radiates, without taking into account the needs and interests of the many Americans who live in inadequate shelter, or in unhealthy neighborhoods with inadequate access to employment and education opportunities.[17]

Too few courts recognize the demonstrable facts about urban America and see that other people and other interests and the values they represent have a claim to consideration in land-use litigation. Thus, to extend the scope of judicial concern in land-use cases merely opens judicial eyes to the real context for proper decision of the

15. *See* Report of the President's Committee on Urban Housing, A Decent Home 25 (G.P.O. 1968) [hereinafter cited as Decent Home].
16. *See* Pennsylvania v. County of Bucks, 302 A.2d at 902.
17. *See* R. Babcock, The Zoning Game 101–11 (1969).

same types of cases that presently engage the courts. The courts will continue to be active in land-use litigation, and they should have under review a broader and more representative set of values. In this sense they will be discharging their judicial duties more responsibly than before.

Bringing the process whereby courts now resolve land-use regulatory disputes back in touch with the real facts is not the only reason for greater judicial activism. Government at local, state, and national levels has been an important contributor to the racial and economic polarization that now marks our society. The responsibility of government for this situation has resulted primarily from the following four factors:

1. Overt and covert government discrimination on the basis of race or income disparities.[18] While racial discrimination in government programs is now universally prohibited,[19] economic discrimination is not. And economic discrimination often has the same effect —and at times the same motivation—as racial discrimination.

2. The unequal distribution of the benefits of government programs, particularly of the federal government, between the economically advantaged and the economically disadvantaged, with the former receiving a far greater share. As illustrated in Chapter 1, the monetary value of the tax benefits to middle- and upper-income families available through deductions for federal income taxes of mortgage loan interest and real estate taxes is many times the value of the annual subsidies for housing low- and moderate-income families. Other federal government programs, such as the massive federal highway program, have benefited high-income families by expanding their housing opportunities, while it has created dislocations and added burdens to the poor left behind in the central cities.

3. Purposefully exclusionary land-use policies of municipalities, through many of the devices identified in Chapter 1.[20] These have restricted housing and employment opportunities in the suburbs for low-income and minority persons, and reinforced the polarizing tendencies of other government programs.

4. The balkanization of municipal government, created by state law.[21] Fractionalized local government has prevented the development

18. *See* U.S. Commission on Civil Rights, Twenty Years After Brown: Equal Opportunity in Housing (G.P.O. 1975). *See also* discussion in Chapter 1 *supra*, in text accompanying notes 80–119.

19. *See* D. Falk & H. Franklin, Equal Housing Opportunity: The Unfinished Federal Agenda 53–63 (Potomac Institute 1976). *See also* discussion in Chapter 1 *supra*, at text accompanying notes 113–17.

20. *See* Chapter 1 *supra*, at text accompanying notes 255–62.

21. *See id.*, at notes 49–62.

of regional solutions to what are regional problems. State governments have rarely stepped in, and, where metropolitan areas cross state boundaries, would not be effective without further interstate cooperation. The courts, too, are an organ of government; yet by their noninvolvement they have actively permitted these conditions to persist. The Advisory Commission believes that the courts must accept the burden of responsibility to do their part in reversing the effect of these past and often continuing government policies.

Federal and State Courts in Land-Use Litigation

American land law has been the almost exclusive province of state courts.[22] After *Nectow v. City of Cambridge*,[23] decided in 1928, the United States Supreme Court heard only one case involving municipal land-use controls in the next 45 years.[24] Yet when the legal assault on municipal exclusionary land-use practices began in earnest in the latter part of the 1960s, the cases were brought more often in federal court than in state courts.[25] Many of these challenges to municipal autonomy involved federally subsidized housing developments,[26] and the litigating attorneys believed that federal courts were more likely than state courts to be receptive to assertions that local regulations were frustrating achievement of national housing policy.[27]

The United States Supreme Court had led the lower federal courts to major breakthroughs in other areas of civil and political rights, most dramatically in reversing the separate-but-equal doctrine as applied to public education and other public facilities,[28] and in equalizing representation in national and state legislative bodies.[29] There was every reason to hope that these constitutional doctrines would be extended to recognize the claims of minority and low-income families seeking better housing opportunities. Enactment of

22. 1 Williams, *supra* note 2, at ch. 3.
23. 277 U.S. 183 (1928).
24. Goldblatt v. Town of Hempstead, 369 U.S. 590 (1962).
25. Sloane, *Changing Shape of Land Use Litigation: Federal Court Challenges to Exclusionary Land Use Practices,* 51 Notre Dame Law. 48 (1975).
26. *Id. See also* Sager, *Troubled Waters: Litigation in the Federal Courts Against Exclusionary Land Use Restraints,* in Exclusionary Land Use Litigation: Policy and Strategy for the Future (National Committee Against Discrimination in Housing 1975).
27. *Id.*
28. *E.g.,* Brown v. Board of Education, 347 U.S. 483 (1954); New Orleans City Park Imp. Ass'n v. Detiege, 358 U.S. 54 (1958).
29. *E.g.,* Baker v. Carr, 369 U.S. 186 (1962); Reynolds v. Sims, 377 U.S. 533 (1964).

the federal civil rights laws in 1964[30] and 1968,[31] and the expectation that a favorable federal court decision would make a more widespread impact than a state court decision, gave added impetus to seek relief in the federal courts. Thus there developed an involvement by the federal courts in land-use regulation controversies that, for a short period, almost eclipsed that of the states.

But the federal courts are also subject to limitations not applicable to state courts in dealing with land-use regulatory issues. The federal courts are limited to interpreting and applying the provisions of the U.S. Constitution and of relevant federal statutes.[32] Until 1974 the only directly applicable federal statutes were the civil rights acts, which prohibit discrimination on the basis of race, color, national origin, religion, and (since 1974) sex,[33] but do not by their direct terms deal with the interests of low-income persons. Since 1974, the federal laws have also imposed requirements relating to some substantive aspects of municipal planning in the limited context of the federal community development block grant and planning assistance programs.[34] By contrast, federal housing subsidy and insurance programs have always deferred to locally imposed land-use controls.

The applicable federal constitutional principles are general in concept. While they can be effectively applied to prescribe unlawful municipal conduct, they provide less guidance to courts for framing broad affirmative relief on complex land-use regulatory issues. Further, affirmative relief by an activist federal court begins to stretch the principles of federalism underlying our constitutional system. Congress has not indicated that land-use planning should be a federal function,[35] and federal courts will therefore be hesitant to interfere with state and municipal land-use regulatory processes be-

30. Title VI of the Civil Rights Act of 1964, P.L. 88–352, 42 U.S.C. § 2000(d) (1964).

31. Title VIII of the Civil Rights Act of 1968, P.L. 90–284, 42 U.S.C. §§ 3601–3619, 3631 (1970). *See* discussion of the civil rights laws in Chapter 1 *supra*, at text accompanying notes 111–21.

32. Federal courts, of course, also assume jurisdiction when the diversity of citizenship requirements are met, 28 U.S.C. § 1332, but they apply the law of the state where they sit except to the extent that federal constitutional or statutory matters may be involved. Erie R.R. v. Tompkins, 304 U.S. 64 (1938).

33. 42 U.S.C. § 5309 (a) extending coverage of title VIII of the Civil Rights Act of 1968 to discrimination based on sex.

34. Housing and Community Development Act of 1974, *as amended*, § 701, 42 U.S.C. § 5304(a)(4); Housing Act of 1954, *as amended*, § 701, 40 U.S.C. § 461.

35. Several attempts have failed in Congress during the past five years to enact a mild national land-use planning law. *See* President's 1976 Report on National Growth and Development: The Changing Issues for National Growth 134 (G.P.O. 1976) [hereinafter cited as 1976 Growth Report].

yond what is minimally necessary to correct past constitutional violations.[36]

State courts do not labor under these limitations. The inherent police power of the state underlies land-use regulations, and statutes enacted by state legislatures delegate these powers to municipalities. Thus a state court can develop its jurisprudence through interpretations of its own state laws and constitution and can develop doctrines about what is the proper exercise of the state's police powers. Further, most state constitutions contain provisions closely resembling the substantive provisions of the Fifth and Fourteenth Amendments to the Constitution, and these provide an independent basis for the protection of fundamental individual rights. This is particularly important because the United States Supreme Court appears to be receding from its former leadership in this area.[37]

Mr. Justice Brennan recently noted with approval that state courts were again looking to the provisions of their own constitutions for protecting individual rights:

> I suppose it was only natural that when during the 1960s our rights and liberties were in the process of becoming increasingly federalized, state courts saw no reason to consider what protections, if any, were secured by state constitutions. It is not easy to pinpoint why state courts are now beginning to emphasize the protections of their states' own bills of rights. It may not be wide of the mark, however, to suppose that these state courts discern, and disagree with, a trend in recent opinions of the United States Supreme Court to pull back from, or at least suspend for the time being, the enforcement of the *Boyd* principle [that "constitutional provisions for the security of person and property should be liberally construed"] with respect to application of the federal Bill of Rights and the restraints of the due process and equal protection clauses of the Fourteenth Amendment.[38]

After approvingly referring to numerous state court decisions where state constitutional provisions have been interpreted to protect individual rights not given protection in similar factual situations by

---

36. *See* Hills v. Gautreaux, 425 U.S. 284 (1976).

37. *See generally* Comment, *Protecting Fundamental Rights in State Courts: Fitting a State Peg to a Federal Hole,* 12 Harv. Civ. Rts.–Civ. Lib. L. Rev. 63 (1977); Note, *Of Laboratories and Liberties: State Court Protection of Political and Civil Rights,* 10 Ga. L. Rev. 533 (1976); Wilkes, *The New Federalism in Criminal Procedure: State Court Evasion of the Burger Court,* 62 Ky. L.J. 421 (1974).

38. Brennan, *State Constitutions and the Protection of Individual Rights,* 90 Harv. L. Rev. 489, 495 (1977).

the United States Supreme Court under similar or identical language in the U.S. Constitution,[39] he concluded:

> . . . [T]he decisions of the [Supreme] Court are not, and should not be, dispositive of questions regarding rights guaranteed by counterpart provisions of state law. Accordingly, such decisions are not mechanically applicable to state law issues, and state court judges and the members of the bar seriously err if they so treat them. Rather, state court judges, and also practitioners, do well to scrutinize constitutional decisions by federal courts, for only if they are found to be logically persuasive and well-reasoned, paying due regard to precedent and the policies underlying specific constitutional guarantees, may they properly claim persuasive weight as guideposts when interpreting counterpart state guarantees.[40]

The Advisory Commission agrees. While recent federal court decisions have, in our view, unduly limited access to federal courts to contest municipal land-use regulations and have improperly failed to extend the protections of the equal protection clause of the Fourteenth Amendment to the claims of lower-income families disadvantaged by municipal land-use regulations, the Advisory Commission firmly believes that these judgments should not be reflected in the decisions of state courts interpreting their own state constitutions and statutes.

DOCTRINE IN THE FEDERAL COURTS

Standing and Related Procedural Problems

The doctrine of standing, as applied by the federal courts, rests on two legal foundations. First, Article III of the Constitution authorizes the federal judiciary to decide only "cases" or "controversies." This means, at its irreducible minimum, that there must be an actual dispute between two parties and that the interests of the party bringing the action will be affected by the judgment of the court. As stated recently by Mr. Justice Powell:

39. *E.g.*, People v. Brisendine, 13 Cal. 3d 528, 531 P.2d 1099, 119 Cal. Rptr. 315 (1975) (California citizens entitled to greater protection against unreasonable searches and seizures under state constitution than offered by federal Constitution); State v. Johnson, 68 N.J. 349, 346 A.2d 66 (1975) (state constitution imposes higher standards for voluntariness of consent to search than those of Schneckloth v. Bustamonte, 412 U.S. 218 (1973)). Many other cases supporting this proposition are cited by Justice Brennan; more are collected in articles at note 37 *supra* and in the following articles: Howard, *State Courts and Constitutional Rights in the Day of the Burger Court*, 62 Va. L. Rev. 873 (1976); Project, *Toward an Activist Role for State Bills of Rights*, 8 Harv. Civ. Rts.-Civ. Lib. L. Rev. 271 (1973).

40. Brennan, *supra* note 38, at 502.

> In sum, when a plaintiff's standing is brought into issue the relevant inquiry is whether, assuming justiciability of the claim, the plaintiff has shown an injury to himself that is likely to be redressed by a favorable decision. Absent such a showing, exercise of its power by a federal court would be gratuitous and thus inconsistent with the Art. III limitation.[41]

The injury to a plaintiff is not limited to economic injury, and this represents a major advance. Prior to 1968 a plaintiff had to establish that a suit was based on an infringement of legal rights, generally described as "one of property, one arising out of contract, or one founded on a statute which confers a privilege."[42]

Beginning with *Flast v. Cohen*[43] in 1968, and *Association of Data Processing Service Organizations, Inc. v. Camp*[44] in 1970, the Supreme Court said that any type of real injury, "economic or otherwise," would be sufficient. In *Flast*, the plaintiff was a taxpayer, challenging a congressional spending program alleged to be unlawful under the First Amendment. In the *Data Processing* case, the plaintiff complained that his business rivals would be substantially aided by the alleged unlawful federal regulation. In another case, *Sierra Club v. Morton*,[45] the injury was to the enjoyment of the environment. But while not necessarily economic, the injury must be real: there must be "injury in fact."[46] This serves to assure that the dispute is genuine so that the court is not giving a purely advisory opinion. It also brings the relevant facts into focus and sharpens the issues. This assists the court to evaluate the factual situation, weigh the competing interests and the underlying values they represent, make a decision, and frame appropriate relief.

The second basis for standing rests on the Supreme Court's own conception of its proper role in American constitutional government, a role that the Court has been narrowing over the past few years. Thus, standing may be denied to a party asserting "a 'generalized grievance' shared in substantially equal measure by all or a large class of citizens."[47] A party may assert rights under a statutory or constitutional provision only if that party lies within the "zone of interests" intended to be protected by that provision.[48] And a

---

41. Simon v. Eastern Ky. Welfare Rts. Org., 426 U.S. 26, 38 (1976).
42. Tennessee Elec. Power Co. v. T.V.A., 306 U.S. 118, 137–38 (1939).
43. 392 U.S. 83 (1968).
44. 397 U.S. 150 (1970).
45. 405 U.S. 727 (1972). *See also* United States v. SCRAP, 412 U.S. 669 (1973).
46. Ass'n of Data Processing Serv. Org. v. Camp, 397 U.S. at 152.
47. Warth v. Seldin, 422 U.S. 490, 499 (1975).
48. Ass'n of Data Processing Serv. Org. v. Camp, 397 U.S. at 153.

party is usually not allowed to assert the rights of other parties not before the Court.[49] These discretionary limitations have been imposed because, according to Mr. Justice Powell:

> Without such limitations—closely related to Art. III concerns but essentially matters of judicial self-governance—the courts would be called upon to decide questions of wide public significance even though other governmental institutions may be more competent to address the questions and even though judicial intervention may be unnecessary to protect individual rights.[50]

Paradoxically, in land-use litigation the lower federal courts initially widened access to federal courts when they permitted minority and low-income individuals to join as plaintiffs with landowners and developers suing to set aside municipal land-use restrictions impeding proposed federally subsidized housing developments.[51] This was a break with tradition, even though often not specifically dealt with in the reported decisions. On occasions when the participation of low-income and minority plaintiffs was challenged, it was not in terms of their standing, but on the question of whether the issues relating to their interests were yet ripe for judicial determination, given the fact that they might not actually want the housing or be selected as tenants if the housing were built.

One court of appeals[52] dealing with this issue concluded, first, that the facts framing the legal issues about the validity of the municipal regulations were as well defined as they could ever be, since the housing development was ready to be built but for the adverse zoning; and second, that withholding a judicial determination would result in considerable hardship to the plaintiffs:

> The individual plaintiffs have presented a strong case for consideration at this time. They allege that they are subject to the serious consequences of segregation in housing and education, as well as the economic consequences of decreasing access to jobs due to their inability to escape from the inner city.
>
> The statistics cited by the plaintiffs indicate a great need to provide low and moderate income housing in the suburban areas, a need which Park

49. Warth v. Seldin, 422 U.S. at 499. *But see* Craig v. Boren, 50 L. Ed. 397 (1976).

50. Warth v. Seldin, 422 U.S. at 500.

51. *E.g.*, Park View Heights Corp. v. City of Black Jack, 467 F.2d 1208 (8th Cir. 1972); Kennedy Park Homes Ass'n v. City of Lackawanna, 436 F.2d 108 (2d Cir. 1970), *cert. denied*, 401 U.S. 1010 (1971); Daily v. City of Lawton, 425 F.2d 1037 (10th Cir. 1970).

52. Park View Heights Corp. v. City of Black Jack, 467 F.2d 1208 (8th Cir. 1972).

View and ICUA [the housing sponsors] are trying to fill. Any attempt to interfere with this program may work a visible and immediate hardship on the class of low and moderate income citizens of the City of St. Louis.[53]

By thus allowing low-income and minority persons as plaintiffs, the court was explicitly recognizing that their needs deserved consideration and would likely be a significant factor influencing its judgment. The court also implicitly recognized that persons not residing in the municipality had a legally sufficient interest in that municipality's land-use regulations to have standing to challenge those aspects that were harmful to them.

While the United States Supreme Court has approved these lower court cases where specific projects have been involved,[54] the Court has declined to adjudicate challenges to municipal land-use regulations where specific housing developments are not being proposed. In *Warth v. Seldin*,[55] decided in 1975, a divided Court was faced with a broad challenge to the exclusionary zoning ordinances of a suburban community near Rochester, New York, and denied standing for all the plaintiffs, including: (1) nonresident low-income individuals, some of whom were minorities and all of whom claimed to have been unsuccessful in locating adequate housing in the community that they could afford; (2) nonresident taxpayers of Rochester, who claimed that the municipality's policies required Rochester to build more low-income housing and thereby increase the city's tax burden; (3) a housing advocacy association representing both residents and nonresidents; (4) an association representing developers doing business in the metropolitan area who claimed to be losing business because of the municipality's practices; and (5) another association representing nonprofit housing sponsors.

The opinion by Mr. Justice Powell left unclear whether this denial of standing was mandated by the "case or controversy" requirement of Article III of the Constitution or by "prudential considerations defining and limiting the role of the courts."[56] The message delivered quite clearly, however, was that broad reform of municipal land-use regulations was not a task to be assumed by the federal courts. The proper institutions for change were elsewhere, as Mr. Justice Powell stated in a footnote:

53. *Id.* at 1216.
54. Village of Arlington Heights v. Metropolitan Housing Dev. Corp., 97 S. Ct. 555 (1977); Warth v. Seldin, 422 U.S. at 507–08 nn. 17&18.
55. 422 U.S. 490 (1975).
56. *Id.* at 517–18.

We also note that zoning laws and their provisions, long considered essential to effective urban planning, are peculiarly within the province of state and local legislative authorities. They are, of course, subject to judicial review in a proper case. But citizens dissatisfied with provisions of such laws need not overlook the availability of the normal democratic process.[57]

The *Warth* decision is but one of a number of recent Supreme Court decisions where technical procedural barriers have been raised to avoid the resolution of controversies on their merits, even though the vindication of substantial constitutional rights has been at stake. The Advisory Commission notes with approval the recent critical findings of the Council for Public Interest law that:

A substantial number of important cases involving aggrieved parties prepared to litigate issues on the merits have been dismissed by the federal courts on technical grounds under new, shifting, and progressively more stringent procedural rulings. In consequence, many citizens, including minorities, the poor, and victims of official abuses, have been left without judicial remedies. As the courts have turned from the substance of justice to the niceties of pleading, citizens have found greater cause for dissatisfaction with the administration of justice.[58]

In the Advisory Commission's view, the Supreme Court in *Warth* conceived too narrowly its role in land-use litigation. Even though state courts may be preferable forums for dealing with broad challenges to municipal land-use regulations, it does not follow that the door to the federal courts should be closed when federal constitutional or statutory rights are asserted. The federal courts may, in fact, be the only available tribunal where the claims of minority and low-income persons can be heard, since courts in most states are still unreceptive to consideration of their interests. The framers of the Constitution established the federal judiciary precisely to provide a practical alternative to the often-parochial state courts for the adjudication of issues of national importance.[59] The considerations that led the lower federal courts, with subsequent Supreme Court approval, to recognize the interests of minority and lower income persons when specific developments are proposed, do not change when a municipality's land-use regulations are challenged apart from an identifiable project. The principal difference is that, in the latter case,

57. *Id.* at 508 n.18.
58. Council for Public Interest Law, Balancing the Scales of Justice: Financing Public Interest Law in America 357 (1976).
59. The Federalist No. 81, *reprinted in* H. Hart & H. Wechsler, The Federal Courts and the Federal System 27–29 (2d ed. 1973).

the municipality's exclusionary practices have been more effective. As Mr. Justice Brennan noted in his dissent in *Warth*:

> Because of this scheme, those interested in building homes for the excluded groups were faced with insurmountable difficulties, and those of the excluded groups seeking homes in the locality quickly learned that their attempts were futile. Yet, the Court turns the very success of the allegedly unconstitutional scheme into a barrier to a lawsuit seeking its invalidation. In effect, the Court tells the low-income-minority and building company plaintiffs they will not be permitted to prove what they have alleged—that they could and would build and live in the town if changes were made in the zoning ordinance and its application—because they have not succeeded in breaching, before the suit was filed, the very barriers which are the subject of the suit.[60]

Concern for the interests of minority and low-income families in securing better housing opportunities does not permit the distinction that governs who has standing to depend upon whether a specific proposed development is an element of the controversy. Of course, it is necessary to observe the outer limits defining who may sue contained in the requirements of Article III that the plaintiff must have suffered injury capable of redress by a federal court. Quite clearly, not every resident of the United States would have standing to challenge a suburban municipality's restrictive zoning. Yet it must be recognized as a fact that the metropolitan area is the true geographic unit for assessing economic and social opportunities and the quality of life.

As the Supreme Court recognized in *Hills v. Gautreux*,[61] the metropolitan area encompasses the operative housing market area. It necessarily follows that any action a municipality takes that will have the effect of restricting the availability of housing for an identifiable income or racial segment of the population of the metropolitan area will necessarily have an adverse impact on members of that group. Accordingly, it should be considered to have directly injured them a constitutional sense. And the relief requested—lifting the restrictive municipal regulations to free private enterprise to build low-income housing in that community—will directly benefit the low-income plaintiffs, and the group they represent, by increasing their housing opportunities in the metropolitan area in which they live.

Thus, Article III of the Constitution should not be asserted as the basis for denying standing to any minority or lower income person

60. Warth v. Seldin, 422 U.S. at 523.
61. 425 U.S. at 299–300.

living in a metropolitan area who alleges that the restrictive land-use regulations of any municipality in that same area have the effect of reducing the availability of suitable housing. To the extent that the result in *Warth* depends upon consitutional limitations on the federal courts, it is a too-restrictive interpretation of a "case" or "controversy." Even if the Supreme Court adheres to its decision in *Warth*, where unconstitutional economic discrimination is alleged, the result in the case should not be extended to cases involving charges of racial discrimination or violations of other specific federally created rights. Racial discrimination has no place in our society, and racial discrimination by public bodies cannot be tolerated. Since the *Brown v. Board of Education* decision in 1954,[62] the Supreme Court has been particularly receptive to charges of officially sponsored or sanctioned racial discrimination, and, in Title VIII of the Civil Rights Act of 1968,[63] Congress has provided that discrimination in housing on the basis of race, color, national origin, religion, or sex is unlawful. This prohibition applies equally to private persons, federal agencies, and municipalities.[64]

Similarly, the Civil Rights Acts of 1964 and 1968 create additional duties on the Department of Housing and Urban Development and other federal agencies to administer their housing and urban development programs in a nondiscriminatory manner and to affirmatively promote equal housing opportunities.[65] With its tradition of protecting minority rights and in the face of these unequivocal congressional expressions of overriding national policy, the doors to the federal courts must remain open to a party alleging the minimal injury required by Article III, when racial discrimination in municipal land-use regulations or in any aspect of federal housing programs is the basis of the claim.

The case for federal court adjudication of nonracial claims arising under federal statutes is as compelling. For example, the Housing and Community Development Act of 1974 creates housing and planning duties on the part of municipalities participating in the community development block grant program and on the part of the Department of Housing and Urban Development in monitoring and

62. 347 U.S. 483.

63. 42 U.S.C. §§ 3601-19, 3631.

64. United States v. City of Black Jack, 508 F.2d 1179 (8th Cir. 1974), *cert. denied*, 422 U.S. 1042 (1975) (Title VIII applies to municipalities).

65. *See* notes 29 and 30 *supra; see also* Falk & Franklin, *supra* note 19, at 53-55.

66. Housing and Community Development Act of 1974, §§ 104(a)(3) and (4), 104(d), 42 U.S.C. §§ 5304(a)(3) and (4), 5304(d). The responsibilities of block grant recipients and HUD are discussed in Chapter 6 *infra*.

enforcing them.[66] The beneficiaries of these legal duties are the minority and low-income segments of the American population that have been continually promised better housing and improved living environments by successive Congresses.[67] The primary purpose of the 1974 Act is stated to be "providing decent housing and a suitable living environment and expanding economic opportunities, principally for persons of low and moderate income."[68] When municipal governments or agencies of the federal government fail to meet their statutory obligations, the intended beneficiaries need to be able to seek redress in federal court, for they are the persons who suffer when government fails. And since these are duties created solely under federal law, state courts do not provide a suitable alternative forum for relief.

Warth v. Seldin is, unfortunately, adversely influencing the lower federal courts considering standing in these kinds of cases.[69] For example, the Court of Appeals for the Second Circuit,[70] sitting en banc, recently denied standing to a minority nonresident individual challenging the right of HUD to make certain urban grants to two suburban communities in Westchester County, New York, that allegedly maintained restrictive land-use regulations. The complaint charged HUD with violating the Civil Rights Acts of 1964 and 1968 in making these grants. The court denied standing to the plaintiff for the reason that he had not suffered any injury from either the making of the grants or from the alleged discriminatory municipal land-use regulations.

More recently, the Second Circuit, sitting *en banc*, reversed the decision of a federal district court and a three-judge court of appeals panel barring the release of community development block grant funds to suburbs of Hartford, Connecticut.[71] The Second Circuit (in a sharply divided 6-4 decision), relying on *Warth*, found that the City of Hartford lacked standing to challenge HUD's waiver of the "expected to reside" requirement of the housing assistance plans in the first year block grant applications of seven Hartford suburbs.

67. Housing Act of 1949, § 2, 42 U.S.C. § 1441; Housing and Urban Development Act of 1968 § 1601, 42 U.S.C. § 144(a); Housing and Community Development Act of 1974 § 101(c), 42 U.S.C. § 5301(c).

68. Housing and Community Development Act of 1974 § 101(c), 42 U.S.C. § 5301(c).

69. *See* Sager, *Burnt Bridges: Retreat of the Federal Judiciary from Land Use Litigation,"* 1976 Land Use L. & Zoning Dig. 7.

70. Evans v. Lynn, 537 F.2d 571 (2d Cir. 1976) (en banc), *cert. denied*, 45 U.S.L.W. 3489 (1977).

71. City of Hartford v Hills, 408 F. Supp. 889 (D. Conn. 1976), *rev'd. sub nom.* City of Hartford v Town of Glastonbury, ——F.2d—— (2d. Cir., Aug. 15, 1977) *(en banc)*.

The Court of Appeals found, that the City of Hartford had not shown a "specific and perceptible harm" in HUD's action nor had it shown that the requested relief would redress Hartford's alleged injury.

It is demeaning to the judicial process, and demonstrates the artificiality of the Supreme Court's doctrine on standing, to require that a federal court fabricate an artificial "interest" to satisfy technical procedural requirements. There should be a straightforward recognition that a central city has an interest, cognizable in federal court, in seeing that its suburban communities meet their federally imposed housing and community development obligations. Likewise, minority and lower income persons have a similar interest in assuring that the municipalities in the metropolitan area in which they live, and the supervising federal agencies, comply with their statutory duty to provide subsidized housing outside areas of low-income and minority concentration in better living environments. With their stake in the outcome of the litigation so clear, justice requires that they be given the opportunity for a judicial determination in a federal court.

The Supreme Court has acknowledged that its discretionary denial of standing to plaintiffs may in certain circumstances be reversed by congressional action.[72] There are statutes where Congress has specifically authorized citizen suits, giving a right of appeal to a class broadly defined as "any person." For example, under the Clean Air Act, Congress has authorized any person to bring suit "in his own behalf" against the Environmental Protection Agency where there is "alleged a failure of the Administrator to perform any act or duty . . . which is not discretionary. ∴ ."[73] Such explicit congressional direction should not be necessary in the case of the primary beneficiary of a federal program who claims that the program is not being administered in the interest of the group he or she represents. But if the Supreme Court is going to insist on specific congressional direction, then the Advisory Commission urges that Congress amend its statutes dealing with housing, community development, and civil rights to accomplish this.

The federal courts must once again resume their role as the forum in which individuals seek redress for rights and benefits denied them by the unlawful conduct of government. Where federal courts decide to shirk their responsibility, Congress should clearly reimpose it. In this connection the Advisory Commission endorses the recommendation of the Council for Public Interest Law:

72. *E.g.*, Warth v. Seldin, 422 U.S. at 501.
73. 42 U.S.C. § 1857h-2(a).

Congress should adopt legislation designed to reduce procedural barriers in the federal courts, and to reverse the current trend toward an elaboration of the technical rules of standing, ripeness, sovereign immunity, and exhaustion of administrative remedies.[74]

Racial Discrimination: Equal Protection and the Civil Rights Acts

The central purpose of the equal protection clause of the Fourteenth Amendment is the prevention of official conduct discriminating on the basis of race.[75] Under the Supreme Court's equal protection doctrine, government actions based on considerations of race are inherently suspect, and can be upheld only if justified by a compelling state interest.[76] Only once in this century—in the case of the detention of Americans of Japanese descent during World War II—has the Court found a governmental interest compellingly justified by the race or national origin of those purposefully disadvantaged.[77] And this exception was not a shining hour for American jurisprudence.

Municipal land-use regulations utilizing racial classifications are of course subject to challenge on equal protection grounds. As long as 60 years ago the Supreme Court invalidated a local ordinance prohibiting "non-Caucasians" from occupying residences in city blocks in which a majority of homes were occupied by Caucasians.[78] But municipal ordinances today do not draw explicitly racial distinctions, so the possibility that there has been "official conduct discriminating on the basis of race" must be inferred from other facts.[79] What constitutes proof of unconstitutional racial discrimination thus became the central problem facing courts in the late 1960s applying the equal protection clause to municipal land-use regulations.[80]

The courts had first to decide a fundamental issue that was posed as a question of proof, but in reality defined the nature of the racial discrimination that would be found to violate the commands of the Constitution. The question was: Would a "suspect classification" be found whenever the municipal action or regulation is shown to have an unequal adverse effect on a racial minority by imposing extra burdens or by unequally denying benefits, or must such an unequal

74. Council for Public Interest Law, *supra* note 58, at 357.
75. *See* Washington v. Davis, 426 U.S. 229, 239 (1976).
76. *E.g.*, Loving v. Virginia, 388 U.S. 1 (1967).
77. Korematsu v. United States, 323 U.S. 214 (1944).
78. Buchanan v. Warley, 245 U.S. 60 (1917).
79. *See generally* Bogen & Falcon, The Use of Racial Statistics in Fair Housing Cases, 34 Md. L. Rev. 59 (1974); Note, *Beyond the Prima Facie Case in Employment Discrimination Law: Statistical Proof and Rebuttal*, 89 Harv. L. Rev. 387 (1975).
80. *See* Sloane, *supra* note 25; Sager, *supra* note 26, at 20.

effect also be proved to have been the purpose of the official action? Some of the initial decisions in 1969 and 1970 in suits brought to invalidate municipal actions blocking the construction of federally assisted housing projects read as if a racially discriminatory effect might be sufficient.[81]

Since effects can be proved by objectively verifiable facts, this promised to be a manageable standard. That this approach would ultimately be adopted seemed nearly certain from the Supreme Court's 1971 decision in *Palmer v. Thompson*,[82] which warned against the difficulty of an inquiry into "the motivation, or collection of different motivations, that lie behind a legislative enactment."[83] The Supreme Court in *Palmer* upheld the decision of the city council of Jackson, Mississippi to close its municipal swimming pools in response to a court order to integrate all of its public facilities. In doing so the Court accepted the municipality's assertion that it could not safely or economically operate integrated pools, and did not permit an examination into what the municipality's councilmen had intended by closing the pools.[84] In his opinion for a closely divided Court, Mr. Justice Black conceded that some of the Court's precedent "may suggest that the motive or purpose behind a law is relevant to its constitutionality";[85] however, upon reanalyzing that precedent,[86] he concluded that it turned "on the actual effect of the enactments, not upon the motivation which led the states to behave as they did."[87]

But in 1976, the Supreme Court, in *Washington v. Davis*,[88] distinguished *Palmer v. Thompson*[89] and held that a racially discrimina-

81. *See* Dailey v. City of Lawton, 425 F.2d 1037 (10th Cir. 1970); Kennedy Park Homes Ass'n v. City of Lackawanna, 436 F.2d 108 (2d Cir. 1970), *cert. denied*, 401 U.S. 1010 (1971); SASSO v. Union City, 424 F.2d 291 (9th Cir. 1970). None of these cases rested its holding entirely on proof of a racially discriminatory effect. *See* United States v. City of Black Jack, 508 F.2d 1179 (8th Cir. 1974), *cert. denied*, 422 U.S. 1042 (1975) (racially discriminatory effect is sufficient to establish official action by municipality in violation of Title VIII of Civil Rights Act of 1968).

82. 403 U.S. 217 (1971). *See generally* Brest, *Palmer v. Thompson: An Approach to the Problem of Unconstitutional Legislative Motivation*, 1971 Sup. Ct. Rev. 95; Ely, *Legislative and Administrative Motivation in Constitutional Law*, 79 Yale L.J. 1205 (1970).

83. 403 U.S. at 224.

84. Overwhelming evidence was presented, and is summarized in Mr. Justice White's dissenting opinion, demonstrating that the pools were closed solely to avoid desegregating them. 403 U.S. at 246-54.

85. 403 U.S. at 225.

86. Specifically, the Court reanalyzed its decision in Griffin v. County School Bd., 377 U.S. 218 (1964); and Gomillion v. Lightfoot, 364 U.S. 339 (1960).

87. 403 U.S. at 225.

88. 426 U.S. 229 (1976).

89. The opinion [in *Palmer v. Thompson*] warned against grounding de-

tory effect or a racially disproportionate impact, standing alone, would not suffice to establish a violation of the equal protection clause. There had also to be proof of a discriminatory purpose.[90] Because no discriminatory purpose had been proved, the Court upheld the use of written tests required of all applicants to the District of Columbia police force even though this resulted in the disqualification of more minority than white applicants. The Supreme Court seemed impelled not to cast a cloud of constitutional doubt over the many hundreds of government programs and actions, arising under "a whole range of tax, welfare, public service, regulatory, and licensing statutes that may be more burdensome to the poor and to the average black than to the more affluent white."[91] After *Washington v. Davis*, unintended racial consequences from official actions would not constitute a violation of the equal protection clause.

Proving a purpose to discriminate remains a problem, and no clear standards have been provided. The Supreme Court in *Washington v. Davis* said that a purpose to discriminate could be discerned only by looking at all the facts.[92] For example, a consistent practice of treat-

---

cision on legislative purpose or motivation, thereby lending support for the proposition that the operative effect of the law rather than its purpose is the paramount factor. But the holding of the case was that the legitimate purposes of the ordinance—to preserve peace and avoid deficits—were not open to impeachment by evidence that the councilmen were actually motivated by racial considerations. Whatever dicta the opinion may contain, the decision did not involve, much less invalidate, a statute or ordinance having neutral purposes but disproportionate racial consequences. *Id.* at 243.

90. "But our cases have not embraced the proposition that a law or other official act, without regard to whether it reflects a racially discriminatory purpose, is unconstitutional solely because it has a racially disproportionate impact." *Id.* at 239. For a thorough analysis of the racial discrimination cases, concluding, inter alia, that notwithstanding Washington v. Davis, the "disproportionate impact" doctrine will continue to play a useful role in antidiscrimination litigation, *see* Brest, *The Supreme Court, 1975 Term, Foreward: In Defense of the Antidiscrimination Principle*, 90 Harv. L. Rev. 1 (1976). *See also* note 99 *infra.*

91. 426 U.S. at 248.

92. "Necessarily, an invidious discriminatory purpose may often be inferred from the totality of the relevant facts, including the fact, if it be true, that the law bears more heavily on one race than another." *Id.* at 242.

In a concurring opinion, Mr. Justice Stevens cautioned that "the line between discriminatory purpose and discriminatory impact is not nearly as bright, and perhaps not as critical, as the reader of the Court's opinion might assume." *Id.* at 254. In choosing to sustain the challenged verbal ability test "on a ground narrower than the Court describes," *id.*, Mr. Justice Stevens stressed that there was not enough evidence of disproportionate impact "to overcome the presumption that a test which is this widely used by the Federal Government is in fact neutral in its effect as well as its 'purpose' as that term is used in constitutional adjudication." *Id.* at 255.

ing racial groups differently under a statute that is racially neutral on its face would establish purposeful discrimination.[93] Even a discriminatory effect from a government action could evidence a purpose to discriminate, particularly if "the discrimination is very difficult to explain on non-racial grounds."[94] Nevertheless, this is all circumstantial evidence that in the last analysis requires the court to make what Professor Lawrence Sager has described as a "considerable leap of faith"[95] in concluding that the discrimination was purposeful. The outcome from case to case becomes difficult to predict.[96]

Fortunately, in Title VIII of the Civil Rights Act of 1968, Congress has provided an independent statutory basis for invalidating municipal actions that "make unavailable or deny, a dwelling to any person because of race, color, religion, or national origin."[97] As the Supreme Court made clear in *Washington v. Davis*, Congress can provide a less stringent standard of proof of racial discrimination made unlawful by statute than the standard of proof required to show an unconstitutional discrimination. The federal courts have held that

93. *See, e.g.*, Yick Wo v. Hopkins, 118 U.S. 356 (1886); United Farmworkers v. City of Delray Beach, 493 F.2d 799 (5th Cir. 1974); Village of Arlington Heights v. Metropolitan Housing Dev. Corp. 97 S. Ct. 555, 564 (1977).

94. Washington v. Davis, 426 U.S. at 242. The kind of evidence that might prove an invidious discriminatory purpose was further explicated by the Supreme Court in Village of Arlington Heights v. Metropolitan Housing Dev. Corp., 97 S. Ct. 555, discussed in note 96 *infra* and more fully in Chapter 3 *infra*. Among the kinds of probative evidence mentioned by Mr. Justice Powell in *Arlington Heights* include "the impact of the official action—whether it 'bears more heavily on one race than another'"; the emergence from the effect of state action of "a clear pattern, unexplainable on grounds other than race"; "the historical background . . . particularly if it reveals a series of official actions taken for invidious purposes"; and "the specific sequence of events leading up to the challenged decision," especially "departures from the normal procedural sequence" and "contemporary statements by members of the decision-making body, minutes of its meetings, or reports." *Id.* at 564–65.

95. Sager, *supra* note 26, at 22.

96. In Village of Arlington Heights v. Metropolitan Housing Dev. Corp., 97 S. Ct. 555, the Supreme Court applied the *Washington v. Davis* rule and held that, on the evidence presented, the plaintiffs had failed to meet their burden of proving that the village's refusal to rezone the plaintiff's site for multifamily uses, so that a federally subsidized housing development could be built, was motivated by a racially discriminatory purpose. Thus the Court refused to find any violation of the equal protection clause of the Fourteenth Amendment. The Court remanded the case for consideration of the same claims under Title VIII of the Civil Rights Act of 1968.

The Supreme Court has since (without opinions) remanded to the lower courts for reconsideration, in light of the principles of *Washington v. Davis* and *Arlington Heights*, several other cases involving claims of racial discrimination in local housing policies. *See* Joseph Skilken and Co. v. City of Toledo, 528 F.2d 867 (6th Cir. 1975), *judgment vacated*, 45 U.S.L.W. 3508 (1977); Board of School Comm'rs v. Buckley, 541 F.2d 1121 (7th Cir. 1976), *judgment vacated*, 45 U.S.L.W. 3508 (1977).

97. Civil Rights Act of 1968 § 804(a), 42 U.S.C. § 3604(a).

discrimination in employment in violation of Title VII of the Civil
Rights Act of 1964 can be proved by evidence of discriminatory
effects alone.[98] Title VIII, prohibiting discrimination in housing, and
in municipal land-use regulations affecting housing, should be given
the same construction.[99] In this way the congressional purpose in
Title VIII of rooting out racial discrimination in housing in all its
facets can be served, without at the same time raising constitutional
questions about the host of other government programs outside of
housing, employment, voting, and the other areas specifically covered
by the civil rights acts.

Economic Discrimination and Equal Protection

Municipal land-use regulations that make no provision for the development of low- and moderate-income housing have the effect—
and often the purpose—of keeping low-income persons out of the
community.[100] The federal district judge whose decision was reversed
by the Supreme Court in *Village of Euclid v. Ambler Realty Co.* had
warned of this: "In the last analysis, the result to be accomplished is
to classify the population and segregate them according to their in-

98. *See* Griggs v. Duke Power Co., 401 U.S. 424 (1971); Gregory v. Litton
Systems, Inc., 472 F.2d 631 (9th Cir. 1972); Wallace v. Debron Corp., 494 F.2d
674 (8th cir. 1974); General Electric Co. v. Gilbert, 50 L. Ed. 2d 343 (1976).
And see Note, *supra* note 79.

99. *See, e.g,* Williams v. Matthews Co., 499 F.2d 819 (8th Cir. 1974); United
States v. City of Black Jack, 508 F.2d 1179 (8th Cir. 1974), *cert. denied,* 422
U.S. 1042 (1975). In *Black Jack* the court of appeals invalidated an ordinance
that prohibited the construction of any new multiple-family dwellings on the
ground that it effectively excluded black families from a white suburb of St.
Louis, Missouri and thereby violated the Fair Housing Act of 1968:

> To establish a prima facie case of racial discrimination, the plaintiff need
> prove no more than that the conduct of the defendant actually or pre-
> dictably results in racial discrimination; in other words that it has a dis-
> criminatory effect. . . . [T]he plaintiff need make no showing whatsoever
> that the action resulting in racial discrimination in housing was racially
> motivated. . . . Effect, and not motivation, is the touchstone, in part be-
> cause clever men may easily conceal their motivations, but more im-
> portantly, because . . . "we now firmly recognize that the arbitrary quality
> of thoughtlessness can be as disastrous and unfair to private rights and the
> public interest as the perversity of a willful scheme. . . ." Hobson v. Han-
> son, 269 F. Supp. 401, 497 (D.D.C. 1967) (Wright, J.), *aff'd sub nom.,*
> Smuck v. Hobson, 408 F.2d 175 (D.C. Cir. 1969) (en banc).
> Once the plaintiff has established a prima facie case by demonstrating
> racially discriminatory effect, the burden shifts to the governmental
> defendant to demonstrate that its conduct was necessary to promote a
> compelling governmental interest.

Id. at 1184–85. *See* Comment, *Applying the Title VII Prima Facie Case to Title
VIII Litigation,* 11 Harv. Civ. Rts.–Civ. Lib. L. Rev. 128 (1976); Brest, *supra*
note 90.

100. *See* discussion of "exclusionary" land-use controls in Chapters 1 & 4.

come or situation in life."[101] This may be official discriminatory action directed at an identifiable segment of the population, but unless there is also proof that the discrimination is purposefully directed against a racial minority, Supreme Court decisions make it clear that the municipal regulations do not violate the equal protection clause of the fourteenth amendment.

Thus, the Supreme Court has held that government classifications on the basis of income are not inherently "suspect,"[102] and that housing is not a "fundamental interest" protected by the Fourteenth Amendment.[103] Municipal land-use regulations that have the intent or effect of barring low- and moderate-income housing are treated under the federal Constitution like other governmental legislation: they are entitled to a presumption of validity and will be upheld unless the regulation can be shown to bear no rational relationship to any legitimate government interest.[104]

Few municipal land-use regulations have failed to pass this test. Large-lot zoning in a San Francisco suburb was upheld as being "rationally related to preserving the town's rural environment."[105] Another San Francisco suburb's comprehensive growth limitation program was similarly approved on the basis that the regulation of growth is a legitimate municipal concern.[106] Similarly, a California constitutional provision requiring special voter approval for all public housing projects that serve lower income persons, but not for any other type of new housing proposed for the municipality, was ap-

101. 297 F.307, 316 (N.D. Ohio, 1924).

102. *See, e.g.*, James v. Valtierra, 402 U.S. 137 (1971); San Antonio Ind. School Dist. v. Rodriguez, 411 U.S. 1 (1973). *See also* discussion in Chapter 3 *infra*. Wealth discrimination as a basis for finding a violation of the equal protection clause of the Fourteenth Amendment retains vitality in questions involving both the administration of justice [Griffin v. Illinois, 351 U.S. 12 (1956); Williams v. Illinois, 399 U.S. 235 (1970)], and the right to vote [Harper v. Virginia State Bd., 383 U.S. 663 (1966)].

103. *See* Lindsey v. Normet, 405 U.S. 56 (1972). *Cf.* note 109 *infra*.

104. *See, e.g.*, Ybarra v. Town of Los Altos Hills, 503 F.2d 250 (9th Cir. 1974). The Supreme Court in recent years has, on occasion—but with little apparent consistency—utilized a more flexible variation of the "rational relationship" test in equal protection adjudication. *See, e.g.*, Eisenstadt v. Baird, 405 U.S. 438 (1972); James v. Strange, 407 U.S. 128 (1972). *See generally* Gunther, *Supreme Court, 1971 term, Foreward: In Search of Evolving Doctrine on a Changing Court: A Model for a New Equal Protection*, 86 Harv. L. Rev. 1 (1972); Note, *Legislative Purpose, Rationality and Equal Protection*, 82 Yale L.J. 123 (1972). The Court, however, showed no inclination to apply its more flexible form of equal protection review to the challenged zoning ordinance in Village of Belle Terre v. Boraas, 416 U.S. 1, 7–8 (1974). *See* Note, *Boraas v. Village of Belle Terre: The New, New Equal Protection*, 72 Mich. L. Rev. 508 (1974).

105. Ybarra v. Town of Los Altos Hills, 503 F.2d at 254.

106. Construction Industry Ass'n v. City of Petaluma, 522 F.2d 897 (9th Cir. 1975), *cert. denied*, 424 U.S. 934 (1976).

proved by the Supreme Court because it "ensured that all the people of a community will have a voice in a decision which may lead to large expenditures of local governmental funds for increased public services or to lower tax revenues."[107] Possibly the only instance where a state or municipal land-use regulation—not involving a claim of racial discrimination—has been invalidated on equal protection grounds was an ordinance prohibiting the issuance of building permits for single-family housing built under the federal Section 235 housing subsidy program.[108] The court could not find that the federal program provided any reason to distinguish between otherwise similar types of single-family homes.

The Advisory Commission believes that the Supreme Court has adopted too narrow a view of the equal protection clause of the Fourteenth Amendment. Lower income groups are not generally able to make their influence felt in the political processes of the nation, and thus need judicial protection from laws and other official acts that are targeted directly against their interests. There can be no greater justification for upholding a law that purposefully disadvantages lower income groups than for upholding a law intentionally harmful to racial minorities. Government actions that intentionally impose unequal burdens on lower income persons, or deny them significant opportunities made available to wealthier people, should require some greater justification in the public interest than simply that they bear a rational relationship to a legitimate government interest.

Only a truly compelling state interest should warrant the continuation of purposeful official discrimination against lower income people. Moreover, the Advisory Commission believes that the right to decent living accommodations in decent environments and access to employment and educational opportunities should be treated as fundamental values (as state courts may decide under their state constitutions).[109] Municipal actions that inhibit the enjoyment of these

107. *See* James v. Valtierra, 402 U.S. at 143. *See generally* Lefcoe, *The Public Housing Referendum Case: Zoning and the Supreme Court,* 59 Cal. L. Rev. 1384 (1971).

108. *See* Morales v. Haines, 349 F. Supp. 684 (N.D. Ill. 1972), *reversed in part on other grounds,* 486 F.2d 880 (7th Cir. 1973). The case was brought by a minority citizen who had contracted with the builder for a house to be built with Section 235 interest-reduction payments. The court of appeals remanded the case to the district court to determine whether there was racial discrimination in the denial of the building permits on the basis of which the district court would reconsider its denial of actual and punitive damages and attorneys' fees.

109. For example, in Southern Burlington County NAACP v. Township of Mount Laurel, 67 N.J. 151, 336 A.2d 713 (1975), *appeal dismissed and cert. denied,* 423 U.S. 808 (1975), the New Jersey Supreme Court stated that access

fundamental values should likewise be held to a stricter standard of justification than under present federal court decisions.

The Unequal Burden of Voter Referendums

Several recent Supreme Court decisions have failed to find a violation of the equal protection clause of the Constitution in state or municipal laws that require the affirmative approval by the municipality's voters to authorize any zoning change or development proposal. In *James v. Valtiera*,[110] noted earlier, the Supreme Court upheld a California constitutional provision requiring that a voter referendum approve each proposed public housing project. It was argued that this would violate the equal protection clause because no other type of housing than public housing required approval by popular vote. Mr. Justice Black's opinion suggested that the value of direct popular involvement in municipal decisions directly affecting the lives of municipal residents was generally more important than the resulting unequal treatment to the lower income households needing the housing:

> A lawmaking procedure that "disadvantages" a particular group does not always deny equal protection. Under any such holding, presumably a State would not be able to require referendums on any subject unless referendums were required on all, because they would always dissatisfy some group.[111]

In Mr. Justice Black's view, the "[p]rovisions for referendums demonstrate devotion to democracy, not to bias, discrimination, or prejudice."[112] He distinguished the earlier case of *Hunter v. Erick-*

---

to housing, as one of the major elements of the "regional general welfare," was, in fact, a constitutional question "of fundamental import." *Id.* at 725. Reviewing a substantial body of legislative findings and cases, the court concluded: "There cannot be the slightest doubt that shelter, along with food, are the most basic human needs. . . . It is plain beyond dispute that proper provision for adequate housing of all categories of people is certainly an absolute essential in promotion of the general welfare. . . ." *Id.* at 727. The Michigan Supreme Court has characterized housing as "essential to the human condition," although not among the enumerated rights specifically mentioned in the state constitution. Nickola v. Township of Grand Blanc, 394 Mich. 589, 232 N.W.2d 604, 610 (1975). In more measured words the California Supreme Court identified the conflicting interests concerned with the impact of a local ordinance limiting growth to include the interest of "outsiders searching for a place to live in the face of a growing shortage of adequate housing." Associated Homebuilders v. City of Livermore, 135 Cal. Rptr. 41, 56 (1976).

110. 402 U.S. 137 (1971).

111. *Id.* at 142.

112. *Id.* at 141. For an analysis of *Valtierra*, concluding that its potential implications for zoning and housing discrimination may not be as serious as the above-quoted passage from the majority opinion might suggest, *see* Lefcoe, *supra* note 107.

son,[113] where the Supreme Court had invalidated—as constituting racial discrimination—a municipal charter provision requiring voter approval before any fair housing ordinance the city council might enact could become effective. By contrast, in *Valtierra* the Court did not find that the public housing referendum requirement was aimed at a racial minority.

The principles in *Valtierra* were reaffirmed and expanded in 1976 in *City of Eastlake v. Forest City Enterprises, Inc.,*[114] where the Supreme Court upheld a municipal charter provision requiring the approval of 55 percent of the municipal electorate for any change in the zoning ordinance, a provision of the charter added by voter initiative just after the city council had rezoned a site for a proposed multifamily housing development. Adopting the Ohio Supreme Court's characterization of the rezoning as "legislative in nature,"[115] the Court held that legislative actions can constitutionally be reserved by the people for decision by popular vote instead of by the legislature. Yet the results of the popular action could still be reviewed under the same standards of judicial review as are applicable to any other government action.[116] For example, public taking of private property by direct popular vote is no less a taking than when voted by the municipal legislative body.

Although official action is not immunized from judicial review by having been approved by direct popular vote, there are circumstances where the procedures by which that action is taken must also be evaluated against constitutional principles. Voter referendum requirements for certain types of land-use and housing decisions present one such situation. The voter referendum requirements in *Valtierra* and *Eastlake*, like the requirement in *Hunter v. Erickson*, were not imposed out of devotion to abstract principles of direct democracy. They were imposed to raise difficult, and frequently insuperable, barriers to the provision of needed lower income housing or to any change in the municipality's existing land-use regulations. As Mr. Justice Stevens's dissenting opinion in *Eastlake* pointed out:

> There can be little doubt of the true purpose of Eastlake's charter provision—it is to obstruct change in land use, by rendering such change so burdensome as to be prohibitive. The Charter provision was apparently adopted specifically to prevent multifamily housing . . . .

113. 393 U.S. 385 (1969).
114. 426 U.S. 668 (1976).
115. *Id.* at 673-74, relying on statements in City of Eastlake v. Forest City Enterprises, 41 Ohio 2d 187, 324 N.E.2d 740 (1975).
116. 426 U.S. at 676-77. *See* SASSO v. Union City, 424 F.2d 291, 295 (9th Cir. 1970).

There is no subtlety to this; it is simply an attempt to render change difficult and expensive under the guise of popular democracy.[117]

Certainly both the purpose and the practical effect of a direct-vote requirement is a proper matter for a court to consider in passing on the validity of the requirement itself.

Municipalities seeking to perpetuate their restrictive land-use regulations may be tempted to enact similar voter referendum requirements on the basis of the *Eastlake* decision.[118] State courts, however, are not bound by the Supreme Court's decisions that are based solely on the U.S. Constitution, but are free to apply their own notions of equal protection under the provisions of their state constitutions. A state court may therefore weigh the unequal burden of the referendum against the value of democracy, and reach its own judgment.

State courts should also question the characterization of the rezoning action in *Eastlake* as "legislative." Consistent with the positions adopted by a number of state courts,[119] the Advisory Commission believes that the granting or denial of development permission that is specific to a parcel of land is an adjudicatory (rather than a legislative) process to which the essentials of procedural due process must apply.[120] These would include adequate notice, an opportunity to be heard, a fair and impartial tribunal, and a decision based on an adequate record—almost none of which can be achieved if the de-

117. 426 U.S. at 689, *quoting* 41 Ohio 2d 187, 200, 324 N.E.2d 740, 748-49 (1975) (Blank, J., concurring). For similar sentiments, *see* Report of the National Commission on Urban Problems, Building the American City 190-91 (G.P.O. 1968) [hereinafter cited as Building the American City].

118. *See* Cornelius v. City of Parma, 374 F. Supp. 730 (N.D. Ohio), *vacated and remanded,* 506 F.2d 1400 (6th Cir. 1974) (referendum requirement of Ohio town for federally subsidized housing remains in force after inconclusive federal court litigation).

119. *See, e.g.,* Fasano v. Board of County Comm'rs, 264 Or. 574, 507 P.2d 23 (1973); Fleming v. City of Tacoma, 81 Wash. 2d 292, 502 P.2d 327 (1972); Snyder v. City of Lakewood, 542 P.2d 371 (1975); West v. City of Portage, 392 Mich. 458, 221 N.W.2d 303 (1974); Forman v. Eagle Thrifty Drugs and Markets, 89 Nev. 533, 516 P.2d 1234 (1973); and other cases cited in Chapter 4 *infra,* where this issue is discussed in substantial detail.

120. *See* Chapter 4 *infra,* and Mr. Justice Stevens's dissenting opinion in City of Eastlake v. Forest City Enterprises, 426 U.S. at 693-95. The Supreme Court of Oregon, in *Fasano,* explained the distinction in these words:

Ordinances laying down general policies without regard to a specific piece of property are usually an exercise of legislative authority, are subject to limited review, and may only be attacked upon constitutional grounds for an arbitrary abuse of authority. On the other hand, a determination whether the permissible use of a specific piece of property should be changed is usually an exercise of judicial authority and its property is subject to an altogether different test.

264 Or. at 580, 581, 507 P.2d at 26.

cision is made by popular vote. Thus, while the Supreme Court was correct in holding that the Constitution does not prevent voters from acting directly on all *legislative* matters, site-specific rezonings should not be among those matters. If state courts adopted sound principles for distinguishing between legislative and adjudicatory processes in land-use law, voter referendum requirements could be limited to their proper sphere.[121]

The Right to Travel

Although the right to shelter is not in the Supreme Court's view a fundamental interest deserving of special protection under the Constitution, the right of residential mobility is. The doctrine arises out of a fundamental objective of the Constitution—the creation of a single nation from the union of the states throughout which people may freely move without unwarranted governmental interference.[122] Implied in the right of free movement is the right to "migrate, resettle, find a new job, and start a new life."[123] This doctrine, long dormant in constitutional jurisprudence,[124] has assumed renewed

121. In circumstances very similar to those in *Eastlake*, the Michigan Supreme Court ruled in West v. City of Portage, 342 Mich. 458, 221 N.W.2d 303 (1974), that an amendment to a city zoning ordinance changing the zoning for a particular piece of property was not subject to a referendum. The court, relying on similar decisions from other jurisdictions, held:

> The issue is whether an amendment to a city zoning ordinance changing the zoning of particular property is subject to a referendary vote of the electors of the city.
> We hold that such a change in zoning is not subject to a referendum. The right of referendum extends only to legislative acts. A change in the zoning of particular property, although in form (amendment of a zoning ordinance) and in traditional analysis thought to be legislative action, is in substance an administrative not legislative, act.

Id. at 460–61, 221 N.W.2d at 304. The Washington State Supreme Court recently held that a site-specific rezoning action by the municipal council was an administrative, not legislative, action, and therefore could not be subsequently challenged by a voter referendum. Leonard v. City of Bothell, —— P.2d —— (Dec. 16, 1976). By contrast the California Supreme Court upheld a voter initiative establishing criteria governing the issuance of residential building permits, without distinguishing between legislative and administrative actions. Associated Homebuilders v. City of Livermore, 135 Cal. Rptr. 41 (1976).

122. United States v. Guest, 383 U.S. 745, 758 (1966). Although the Articles of Confederation provided that "the people of each State shall have free ingress and egress to and from any other State," that right finds no explicit mention in the Constitution. The reason, it has been suggested, is that a right so elementary was conceived from the beginning to be a necessary concomitant of the stronger Union the Constitution created. In any event, freedom to travel throughout the United States has long been recognized as a basic right under the Constitution.

123. Shapiro v. Thompson, 394 U.S. 618, 629 (1969).

124. *See* Crandall v. Nevada, 73 U.S. 35 (1868); Edwards v. California, 314 U.S. 160 (1941); United States v. Guest, 383 U.S. 745 (1966).

importance in the last decade as the Supreme Court has been called upon to evaluate the right of governments to withhold government benefits on the basis of the residency of the beneficiaries.

Under the Court's two-stage analysis,[125] the regulation in issue is first evaluated to determine whether it constitutes a burden on the right of mobility. A burden will be found if either the regulation would have the effect of actually deterring migration or if it would impose a penalty relating to a "basic necessity of life"[126] on persons who had already moved to the community that imposes the regulation. Once a burden on mobility is established, the evidentiary burden of proof shifts to the state or municipality imposing the regulation to show both that there is a compelling state interest that justifies the imposition of the regulation and that the compelling state interest cannot be served in a way that would impose a less onerous burden on personal mobility. If these showings cannot be made, the regulation will be invalidated.

The right-to-travel principle is, in effect, a means for subjecting state and local regulations that have some inhibiting effect on residential mobility to closer judicial scrutiny than is generally accorded legislative actions. But not every regulation found to burden the right to travel has been invalidated. While residency of periods of from one to five years have been declared unlawful when made a requirement for receiving welfare assistance payments,[127] voting,[128] free nonemergency medical care,[129] and admission to public housing projects,[130] similar durational residency requirements have been upheld when imposed for obtaining lower tuitions at state universities[131] and access to state courts for adjudications of divorce.[132]

The right-to-travel doctrine can serve as a measure for evaluating municipal land-use regulations[133] since the doctrine provides criteria

125. *See* Memorial Hospital v. Maricopa County, 415 U.S. 250 (1974).

126. *Id.* at 259.

127. Shapiro v. Thompson, 394 U.S. 618 (1969).

128. Dunn v. Blumstein, 405 U.S. 330 (1972) (three-month county residency requirement invalidated along with one-year state residency requirement).

129. Memorial Hospital v. Maricopa County, 415 U.S. 250 (1974).

130. Cole v. Housing Authority, 435 F.2d 807 (1st Cir. 1970); King v. New Rochelle Municipal Housing Authority, 442 F.2d 646 (2d Cir. 1971). Both cases applied the right-to-travel principle to intrastate travel, a question not yet directly faced by the Supreme Court. *See* Memorial Hospital v. Maricopa County, 415 U.S. at 255–56.

131. Vlandis v. Kline, 412 U.S. 441 (1973).

132. Sosna v. Iowa, 419 U.S. 393 (1975).

133. *See generally* Note, *Freedom of Travel and Exclusionary Land Use Regulations,* 84 Yale L.J. 1564 (1975); Note, *The Right to Travel: Another Constitutional Standard for Local Land Use Regulations,* 39 U. Chi. L. Rev. 612 (1972) (providing right-to-travel analyses for assessing restrictive land-use controls).

to weigh the public purposes served by the regulations against the extent to which they restrict families seeking improved housing, more satisfactory environments, and access to better jobs and educational opportunities. With this doctrine it becomes possible to balance the right of municipal self-determination with the housing needs of people, particularly of low- and moderate-income people whose needs for adequate housing are most pressing.

All municipal land-use regulations are to some extent restrictive; that is their very purpose. Application of the right-to-travel principle can serve to identify which municipal land-use regulations impose restrictions with significant extramunicipal impacts so that further evaluation is warranted. To make this threshold determination, the court would have to review the municipality's entire land-use regulatory program, its zoning ordinances, its land-use and housing plans, its building regulations, and the history of their administration. It would be appropriate to determine the extent to which the municipality was taking care of a reasonable share of the region's housing needs at all income levels. If, on the basis of this examination, the court concluded that the opportunity for mobility was indeed restricted to a significant extent, then the burden of proof would shift to the municipality to establish the compelling need for its restrictive land-use regulations.

Exclusionary land-use regulations would not fare well under this analysis. A sizable suburban community that permitted only expensive housing to be built through large-lot zoning and other exclusionary devices could be found to be hindering the movement of lower income families to that municipality. And its assertions of compelling government interests would most likely be rationalizations for the municipality's desire to retain its exclusive character, which would not be an acceptable justification. At the same time, the right-to-travel principle can enable a court to avoid excessive involvement in local land-use regulatory issues, for the initial burden on residential mobility will not be proved if the municipality makes a reasonable provision for all types of housing in relation to reasonable estimates of regional need and demand, no matter how exclusionary the rest of its regulations might be.

The right-to-travel principle as applied to municipal land-use regulations is at its initial stage of judicial development in federal courts. It has been applied only once by a federal district court, in *Construction Industry Ass'n of Sonoma County v. City of Petaluma*,[134] to invalidate a suburban community's development timing growth-

134. 375 F. Supp. 574 (N.D. Cal. 1974).

control plan.[135] The Court of Appeals for the Ninth Circuit reversed the judgment,[136] entirely avoiding consideration of the merits of the right-to-travel principle by holding that the developers who brought the lawsuit lacked standing to assert the right-to-travel rights of non-residents not parties to the litigation.

It is the hope of the Advisory Commission that the federal courts will in the future recognize that restrictive municipal land-use regulations can limit the exercise of the basic constitutional right of Americans to move "throughout the length and breadth of our land uninhibited by statutes, rules, or regulations which unreasonably burden or restrict this movement,"[137] and will subject such government controls to the same degree of judicial scrutiny as accorded to other official actions that exceed their constitutional boundaries.[138]

DOCTRINE IN STATE COURTS

The Restrictive Doctrine of Standing

The ability of persons to challenge municipal land-use regulations in state court is traditionally more limited than in federal court,[139] even after *Warth v. Seldin.*[140] The expansion of the kind of interests which, when invaded, will give rise to standing—as represented by the U.S. Supreme Court *Data Processing* and *Sierra Club* cases[141] —has not been matched in state court decisions. Yet, ironically, some state courts allow a party with standing to raise issues questioning the constitutionality of the municipal regulation because of adverse effects

135. The Petaluma plan is discussed in the lower court opinion and in Mc-Givern, *Putting a Speed Limit on Growth,* 1972 Planning 264–65.

136. 522 F.2d 897 (9th Cir. 1975), *cert. denied,* 424 U.S. 934 (1976).

137. Shapiro v. Thompson, 394 U.S. at 629.

138. The California Supreme Court has recently rejected this approach to the right-to-travel principle in Associated Homebuilders v. City of Livermore, 135 Cal. Rptr. 41 (1976). The California court characterized the United States Supreme Court precedents as involving laws that "penalize travel and resettlement," whereas the local growth-limitation measure before the California court "merely makes it more difficult for the outsider to establish his residence in the place of his choosing." *Id.* at 52. The California court appeared concerned that application of the federal right-to-travel principle would severely limit all local efforts to engage in rational planning and zoning. *See id.* at 53. While eschewing the right-to-travel principle, the California Supreme Court did impose new limits on local autonomy in land-use control matters under the "regional general welfare" doctrine, discussed in text following note 170 *infra.*

139. *See generally* Walsh, *Alternatives to Warth v. Seldin: The Potential Resident Challenges of an Exclusionary Zoning Scheme,* 11 Urb. L. Ann. 223 (1976); Ayer, *The Primitive Law of Standing in Land Use Disputes: Some Notes from a Dark Continent,* 55 Iowa L. Rev. 344 (1969).

140. 422 U.S. 490 (1975); discussed in text accompanying notes 55–60 *supra.*

141. *See* text at notes 44–46 *supra.*

on parties not before the court and to whom the court would not have conferred standing.[142]

The general rule in state courts (except New Jersey) is that to have standing a party must demonstrate that the municipal land-use regulation has invaded a legal interest that is personal to him.[143] The clearest case, of course, is made by an owner of the land that is subject to the municipal regulation. While the procedural processes vary significantly from state to state, in general a landowner may challenge the regulation either under a right of judicial review specifically conferred by the state zoning enabling act on "aggrieved persons"[144] or under the state's general jurisdictional grant of authority to courts to hear constitutional claims. However, state courts have equated the criteria for standing under both procedures.[145]

Injury to an interest in land is also the touchstone for standing of owners of land affected by a municipal regulation applied to another person's real property. The state courts will confer standing on any landowner in the municipality who can show that the municipal regulation has or will cause special damage either to the economic interest in the property or to the quiet enjoyment of the property.[146] A generalized claim that the municipal regulation will be harmful to the landowner as a member of the community will not be sufficient.[147] Since the impact of land-use regulations is felt most directly by adjacent properties, a sufficient injury for standing purposes is presumed in many states (either by statute or by judicial decision) to any landowner of adjacent property or of property within reasonably close proximity to the property that is subject to the municipal regulation.[148] Landowners outside this circle must still prove special damage to their property interests before being given standing.[149]

State courts have found more troublesome the question of whether the ownership of property outside the municipality imposing the

142. *See* cases cited at notes 189-92 *infra.*
143. *See* Walsh, *supra* note 139, at 226-27; Comment, *Standing to Appeal Zoning Determinations: The "Aggrieved Person" Requirement,* 64 Mich. L. Rev. 1070 (1966); ALI Code, *supra* note 3, at 409-19.
144. Standard State Zoning Enabling Act § 7 (Department of Commerce rev. 1926), *reprinted in* A. Rathkopf, 3 Law of Zoning and Planning 100 (1967).

Any person or persons, jointly or severally, aggrieved by any decision of the board of adjustment, or any taxpayer, or any officer, department, board, or bureau of the municipality, may present to a court of record a petition, duly verified, setting forth that such decision is illegal, in whole or in part, specifying the gounds of the illegality.

145. *See* ALI Code, *supra* note 3, at 416.
146. *Id.* at 411-12.
147. Comment, *supra* note 143, at 1084.
148. ALI Code, *supra* note 3, at 466.
149. Comment, *supra* note 143, at 1079-80.

regulations but adjacent or near to the affected land confers standing to challenge the municipal regulation. Most state courts have denied standing in this circumstance on the ground that the municipality administering its land-use controls need be concerned only with the impact of its regulations within its own boundaries;[150] thus a land-owner outside the municipality, whose interests are not entitled to consideration, has no claim to assert and thus need not be accorded standing.

But state courts are gradually abandoning this narrow view and have conferred standing on property owners showing special injury to their land outside the municipality resulting from the municipal regulation.[151] A few courts have likewise conferred standing on neighboring municipalities themselves.[152] In expanding this circle of parties with standing, these state courts have recognized, usually explicitly, that municipal regulation can have an extraterritorial impact on neighboring land that may be just as important for evaluating the validity of the regulation as its intramunicipal impact.[153]

Persons not owning property generally cannot challenge municipal land-use regulations in state courts. Neighborhood and civic improvement associations are not given standing.[154] Neither are businesses, when the creation of competition is the basis of their claim rather than an injury to their real property.[155] Taxpayers' suits are also not permitted—a curious result, since the Department of Commerce's Standard State Zoning Enabling Act specifically conferred a right of judicial review on "any taxpayer."[156] Although over half the states

150. *Id.* at 1080.

151. *See, e.g.,* Scott v. City of Indian Wells, 6 Cal. 3d 541, 99 Cal. Rptr. 745, 492 P.2d 1137 (1972); Allen v. Coffel, 488 S.W.2d 671 (Mo. Ct. App. 1972).

152. *See* Township of River Vale v. Township of Orange, 403 F.2d 684 (2d Cir. 1968); *see, e.g.,* Borough of Cresshill v. Borough of Dumont, 28 N.J. Super. 26, 100 A.2d 182 (Super Ct. 1953), *aff'd,* 15 N.J. 238, 104 A.2d 441 (1954).

153. Allen v. Coffel, 488 S.W.2d at 679.

The Enabling Act is reasonably to be understood to extend the benefit of its sanction, that a zoning shall be for the public welfare, not only to the residents of the enacting municipal community, but also to affected non-resident owners of property contiguous to the municipal zoning.

154. *See* Comment, *supra* note 143, at 1084; Ayer, *supra* note 139, at 3?9. An intermediate Florida appellate court recently gave standing to a citizens' association to challenge a PUD rezoning on the grounds that the rezoning ordinance was enacted contrary to the state's "sunshine law." Upper Keys Citizens Ass'n. v. Wedel, No. 76-680 (Fla. Dist. Ct. App., 3d Dist., Feb. 1, 1977).

155. Comment, *supra* note 143, at 1082-83; Ayer, *supra* note 139, at 353-56. *But see* Walker v. Stanhope, 23 N.J. 657, 130 A.2d 372 (1957) (nonresident seller of mobile homes held to have standing to challenge municipal ordinance excluding mobile home parks).

156. *See* note 144 supra.

enacting zoning enabling acts following the Department of Commerce model eliminated this provision, courts in states retaining it have nonetheless required a showing of special damage to real property interests as a condition to suit by a taxpayer.[157]

With standing to sue so narrowly limited in state courts to persons demonstrating an invasion of their real property interests, the decision of the Supreme Court of New Jersey, in *Southern Burlington County NAACP v. Township of Mount Laurel*,[158] takes on enormous significance for its conclusion that both resident and nonresident persons occupying substandard housing and presumably earning low incomes had standing to challenge Mount Laurel's zoning ordinance.[159] There was support in prior New Jersey Supreme Court decisions for conferring standing on nonresidents, since New Jersey was one of those states recognizing the rights of landowners in neighboring municipalities to sue.[160] And in 1975 the New Jersey legislature amended its zoning enabling act to confer a right of judicial review specifically on nonresidents as well as residents.[161] Yet there was no direct precedent for the New Jersey Supreme Court's holding that persons not owning property, but living in substandard housing, had a sufficient interest to have standing—a result not required by the 1975 amendment to the zoning enabling act.

With this decision the New Jersey Supreme Court has recognized that courts properly function to protect all individuals harmed by unlawful government action. Exclusionary municipal land-use regulations, by limiting housing opportunities for lower income households, certainly cause them injury. As persons injured by allegedly unlawful government action, they have as much justification to seek

---

157. *See* Comment, *supra* note 143, at 1083; ALI Code, *supra* note 3, at 409-10.

158. 67 N.J. 151, 336 A.2d 713 (1975), *appeal dismissed and cert. denied*, 423 U.S. 808 (1975).

159. 336 A.2d at 717 n.3.

160. *See* Borough of Cresshill v. Borough of Dumont, 15 N.J. 238, 104 A.2d 441 (1954); Walker v. Stanhope, 23 N.J. 657, 130 A.2d 372 (1957).

161. N.J. Stat. Ann. § 40:55-57.1 (Supp. 1975) provides:

For purposes of this article . . . the term "other interested party" . . . shall include . . . (b) in the case of a civil proceeding in any court or in an administrative proceeding before a municipal agency, any person, whether residing within or without the municipality, whose right to use, acquire, or enjoy property is or may be affected by any action taken under the act to which this act is a supplement, or whose rights to use, acquire, or enjoy property under the act to which this act is a supplement or under any other law of this State or of the United States have been denied, violated or infringed by an action or a failure to act under the act to which this act is a supplement.

redress in the courts of their state, and as much need, as owners of land who may also have suffered injury in their property rights.

There is no rational justification for enabling injured property owners to challenge unlawful municipal regulations, but not injured non-property owners. This is a remnant of a bygone day when the vision of courts was limited to the protection of private property.[162] In today's climate, human rights have an equal, if not greater, claim to consideration. As the court in *Mount Laurel* so clearly stated, "municipalities must zone primarily for the living welfare of people."[163]

How many state courts are likely to follow the example of the New Jersey Supreme Court? Some, by virtue of rigid conservatism and strict adherence to principles of *stare decisis*, will continue to confer standing only on persons having a legal interest in land. Other courts, for more practical reasons similar to those persuasive to the United States Supreme Court in *Warth v. Seldin*, will not permit litigation that challenges a municipal land-use ordinance unless a specific proposed housing development or parcel of land is directly involved to give the controversy concreteness.

The courts in Pennsylvania provide an illustration. They have recognized the adverse extraterritorial impact of municipal land-use regulations that totally exclude higher density residential uses.[164] But the Pennsylvania courts refused to hear a case brought by lower income persons and several associations challenging the allegedly exclusionary zoning ordinances in Bucks County in suburban Philadelphia, and its 54 constituent municipalities, because the case did not present a sufficiently concrete set of facts:

> In reality, plaintiffs seek a premature and merely advisory opinion or adjudication of the theoretical or abstract invalidity of the various zoning ordinances, as they might relate to persons of the classes they purport to represent, if and when such persons should take actual steps to procure low or moderate cost housing in Bucks County. The rendering of advisory opinions on hypothetical facts is no part of the judicial function.[165]

162. For example, this statement was made by a New Jersey Superior Court Judge in 1953:

> The real object, however, of promoting the general welfare by zoning ordinances is to protect the private use and enjoyment of property, and to promote the welfare of the individual property owner. In other words, promoting the general welfare is a means of protecting private property.

Borough of Cresshill v. Borough of Dumont, 100 A.2d at 190.
163. 336 A.2d at 732.
164. *See* cases cited in notes 189–92 *infra*.
165. Pennsylvania v. County of Bucks, 302 A.2d 897 at 900 (1973), *cert. denied*, 414 U.S. 1130 (1974).

Equally important to the Pennsylvania court was the requested relief that would require restructuring the land-use regulatory system in that heavily populated county. The court feared it would be required to assume the awesome task of becoming a super planning agency, with no expertise in the field."[166] By contrast, when a specific parcel of land is involved on which a housing development is being proposed, the court can find the entire ordinance invalid, but its remedial decree can be limited to ordering that the development proposed for the site be permitted to proceed.[167]

The Pennsylvania courts, and those in other states that follow their reasoning, are too cautious. The judicial remedies that the court would have to grant for effective relief are manageable, as discussed in considerable detail in Chapter 3. And the element of concreteness in the case necessary to enable the court to make an informed judgment on the facts is not lacking. The adverse impact of a system of municipal land-use controls on meeting regional housing needs and expanding housing opportunities for lower income persons throughout a metropolitan area is demonstrated by a careful analytical and historical study of the land-use controls and physical characteristics of the municipality, and local and regional data on housing, employment, education, and growth trends. Additional data relating to a single proposed development barred by the municipal regulation adds little meaningful information to the analysis of the macro effect of the municipality's total regulatory program. The relevant facts required to be known by a court can be presented just as well by an attorney representing lower income families claiming to have been denied housing opportunities by an alleged exclusionary municipality as by an attorney representing a landowner seeking to develop multifamily housing.

The American Law Institute, in its *Model Land Development Code*, has taken this newer and broader view of standing. According to the Code, standing to sue should be conferred by state courts on any "person who has, or represents persons who have, a significant interest that has been affected by the ordinance or rule,"[168] with the

166. *Id.* at 905, *cert. denied*, 414 U.S. 1130.
167. *See, e.g.,* Township of Williston v. Chesterdale Farms, Inc., 462 Pa. 445, 341 A.2d 466 (1975).
168. ALI Code, *supra* note 3, at 416. The quoted provision of the *Model Land Development Code* resulted from merging two provisions in the immediately preceding draft that read as follows:

(4) a person claiming that the order or rule deprives him or persons he represents of rights given to him by the Constitution or laws of the United States or his state;
(5) any person satisfying the court that he has a significant interest that has been affected by the order or rule;

express purpose of permitting "a person who does not reside on land in an area a right to challenge the restriction, even though the landowners do not wish to challenge."[169]

The Regional General Welfare as the Measure of Municipal Land-Use Regulations

Two decisions have marked major watersheds in the law of municipal land-use regulations. The first was the U.S. Supreme Court's decision in *Village of Euclid v. Ambler Realty Co.*,[170] handed down in 1926, in a decade when over 54 million people (constituting for the first time over half of America's population) lived in metropolitan areas marked by urban centers beginning to spill out beyond their borders into the surrounding countryside.[171] That decision resolved conflicting state and federal court decisions in holding that municipal zoning was a valid exercise of the state police power and establishing the legal principles—including the presumptive validity of municipal zoning decisions—that were to provide the foundation for court decisions for the next half century and beyond. With this decision, municipalities were provided with the legal tools with which to influence the character of their communities in the face of anticipated pressures for growth from the burgeoning urban population.

By 1975, the year in which the New Jersey Supreme Court decided its landmark *Southern Burlington County NAACP v. Township of Mount Laurel*,[172] 154 million people—over 70 percent of America's population—lived in metropolitan areas characterized by the spatial separation of racial and economic groups.[173] In that case, the Supreme Court of New Jersey broke with precedent on questions of standing by opening its state courts to persons not owning land who could claim a deprivation of housing opportunities resulting from restrictive municipal land-use regulations. The court also forced a re-

---

American Law Institute, A Model Land Development Code (Prop. Off. Draft, 1975), at 475. No more restrictive rules of standing appear to have been intended by these language changes.

169. ALI Code, *supra* note 3, at 418. The Reporter's *Note* continues with the following illustration of the broad scope of the standing provision: "Thus if there is a constitutional basis to assert that 'large acreage zoning' results in economic or racial segregation, subsection (5) permits a person, who claims that he is thereby excluded, to litigate the validity of the restriction." *Id.*

170. 272 U.S. 365 (1926).

171. *See* Building the American City, *supra* note 117, at 53.

172. 67 N.J. 151, 336 A.2d 713 (1975), *appeal dismissed and cert denied,* 423 U.S. 808 (1975). Professor Williams, in his exhaustive survey of American land-use and planning law, Williams *supra* note 2, at addend. ch. 66, at 4–5 has termed *Mount Laurel* "the most important zoning decision since *Euclid*—and, indeed, supercedes *Euclid* on one-third of its holding having to do with residential building types."

173. *See* 1976 Growth Report, *supra* note 35, at 30.

examination of the underlying legal bases of the municipal power to regulate land uses and has given authoritative approval to new criteria by which to judge the validity of municipal exercises of that power. These criteria are likely to influence the course of municipal land-use law for the next half-century.

The New Jersey high court held that municipal land-use regulations must serve both the needs of the people living in the municipality and the general welfare of the population residing in the region in which the municipality is located. As applied to the Mount Laurel community, the court held that

> As a developing municipality, Mount Laurel must, by its land use regulations, make realistically possible the opportunity for an appropriate variety and choice of housing for all categories of people who may desire to live there, of course including those of low and moderate income.[174]

The many insights of the New Jersey court into the municipal land-use regulatory process and the decision's relationship to decisions in other states require further analysis in order to assess the importance of this decision for the future development of legal doctrine in this area.[175]

Facts in the Mount Laurel Case. Mount Laurel is a typical suburban community in a heavily urbanized state. Located near the older cities of Philadelphia and Camden, its 22 square miles have experienced a growth of population of from 2,817 in 1950, to 5,249 in 1960, to 11,221 in 1970, about doubling in each decade. The township had also adopted a system of land-use controls utilizing many of the exclusionary devices identified in Chapter 1, particularly

174. 336 A.2d at 731-32.

175. *Mount Laurel* has been the subject of extensive discussion in the legal literature. *See, e.g.,* Ackerman, *The Mount Laurel Decision: Expanding the Boundaries of Zoning Reform,* 1976 U. Ill. L.F. 1; Payne, *Delegation Doctrine in the Reform of Local Government Law: The Case of Exclusionary Zoning,* 29 Rut. L. Rev. 803, 805-19, 859-66 (1976); Mytelka & Mytelka, *Exclusionary Zoning: A Consideration of Remedies,* 7 Seton Hall L. Rev. 1 (1975); Rose, *The Mount Laurel Decision: Is it Based on Wishful Thinking?* 4 Real Estate L.J. 61 (1975); Williams, *supra* note 2, at adden. ch. 66; Williams & Doughty, *Studies on Legal Realism: Mount Laurel, Belle Terre, and Berman,* 29 Rut. L. Rev. 73 (1975); Rohan, *Property Planning and the Search for a Comprehensive Housing Policy—The View from Mount Laurel,* 49 St. John L. Rev. 653 (1975); Kushner, *Land Use Litigation and Low Income Housing: Mandating Regional Fair Share Plans,* 9 Clearinghouse Rev. 10 (1975); Note, *The Inadequacy of Judicial Remedies in Cases of Exclusionary Zoning,* 74 Mich. L. Rev. 760 (1976); Mallach, *Do Law Suits Build Housing? The Implications of Exclusionary Zoning Litigation,* 6 Rut.-Cam. L.J. 653 (1975); Rose & Levin, *What Is a "Developing Municipality" Within the Meaning of the Mount Laurel Decision?* 4 Real Estate L.J. 359 (1976).

an overallocation of vacant land exclusively for industrial uses, restrictions on residential development to single-family homes, and minimum acreage, floor-area, and lot-width requirements. The New Jersey Supreme Court found that Mount Laurel, in administering its land-use regulatory system, behaved characteristically for developing suburban communities:

> Almost every one acts solely in its own selfish and parochial interest and in effect builds a wall around itself to keep out those people or entities not adding favorably to the tax base, despite the location of the municipality or the demand for varied kinds of housing.[176]

The General Welfare of the State as the Justification for Municipal Exercises of the Police Fower. The municipal zoning power exercised by Mount Laurel was indisputably grounded on the inherent police powers of the state. Police powers are an essential element of sovereignty, which authorize government actions that will promote the public health, safety, morals, and general welfare.[177] Government actions that do not serve any of these purposes are invalid as contrary to the substantive due process and equal protection provisions of state constitutions, the requirements of which, as the New Jersey Supreme Court pointed out, "may be more demanding than those of the federal Constitution."[178] Since *Euclid* established a presumption of legal validity for municipal land-use regulations, questions as to whether these purposes have in fact been served have been only infrequently raised, and even when raised, the focus of inquiry has been limited to whether the regulations serve the welfare of the municipality itself. This limited inquiry is probably both a cause and a consequence of the restrictive notions of standing, examined earlier,

---

176. 336 A.2d at 723. A similar development pattern, eliciting a similar type of restrictive zoning ordinance, can be seen in Madison Township (now Old Bridge Township) in New Jersey. The zoning ordinance of that township was found invalid by the New Jersey Supreme Court in January 1977. Oakwood at Madison, Inc. v. Township of Madison, — N.J. —, 371 A.2d 1192 (1977).

177. 1 Williams, *supra* note 2, at 179–182.

178. 336 A.2d at 725. Specifically, the *Mount Laurel* court stated:

> It is elementary theory that all police power enactments, no matter at what level of government, must conform to the basic state constitutional requirements of substantive due process and equal protection of the laws. These are inherent in Art. I, par. 1 of our Constitution, the requirements of which may be more demanding than those of the federal Constitution. [Citations omitted.] It is required that, affirmatively, a zoning regulation, like any police power enactment, must promote public health, safety, morals or the general welfare. . . . Conversely, a zoning enactment which is contrary to the general welfare is invalid. [Citations omitted.]

Id.

since resident landowners would be expected to raise only issues relating to the effect of the regulation on their property.

The *Mount Laurel* decision broke new ground in providing a sophisticated doctrinal rationale for broadening the scope of the court's inquiry into municipal land-use regulations that radiate an influence beyond the municipal boundaries. This was explained by the court:

> The warning [of an earlier case] implicates the matter of *whose* general welfare must be served or not violated in the field of land use regulation. Frequently the decisions in this state . . . have spoken only in terms of the interest of the enacting municipality, so that it has been thought, at least in some quarters, that such was the only welfare requiring consideration. It is, of course, true that many cases have dealt only with regulations having little, if any, outside impact where the local decision is ordinarily entitled to prevail. However, it is fundamental and not to be forgotten that the zoning power is a police power of the state and the local authority is acting only as a delegate of that power and is restricted in the same manner as is the state. So, when regulation does have a substantial external impact, the welfare of the state's citizens beyond the borders of the particular municipality cannot be disregarded and must be recognized and served.[179]

The antecedents for this view, the New Jersey Supreme Court went on to explain, were established in 1926 in *Village of Euclid v. Ambler Realty Co.*, when the United States Supreme Court warned of "the possibility of cases where the general public interest would so far outweigh the interest of the municipality that the municipality would not be allowed to stand in the way."[180]

Twenty-three years after *Euclid* the New Jersey Supreme Court had looked to factors outside the municipality's boundaries, but for the purpose of upholding a municipality's total exclusion of industrial uses on the basis of finding that there was sufficient acreage of available industrially zoned land elsewhere in the region.[181]

New Jersey has also been one of the states permitting nonresident landowners and neighboring municipalities to sue to invalidate municipal land-use regulations affecting their property interests, again recognizing that the extramunicipal impacts of municipal zoning cannot be disregarded.[182] But these earlier New Jersey decisions had also approved such restrictive zoning features as minimum build-

179. *Id.* at 726.
180. 272 U.S. at 390, *cited in* Mount Laurel, 336 A.2d at 726.
181. *See* Duffcon Concrete Prods. v. Borough of Cresskill, 1 N.J. 509, 64 A.2d 347 (1949).
182. *See, e.g.*, Borough of Cresskill v. Borough of Dumont, 15 N.J. 238, 104 A.2d 441 (1954); Walker v. Stanhope, 23 N.J. 657, 130 A.2d 372 (1957).

ing[183] and lot sizes[184] and exclusion of mobile homes[185] because they served the municipality's perceived needs, often over forceful and widely discussed dissents pointing out the broader adverse implications of the regulations for the metropolitan area.[186]

By the end of the 1960s, several prominent national commissions and scholarly articles had documented the widespread extent of the various exclusionary zoning devices and the manner in which they contributed to the growing racial and economic polarization affecting metropolitan areas.[187] The federal housing subsidy programs enacted in 1968 for the first time provided a workable means to build quantities of privately sponsored suburban housing for lower-income families, thereby focusing increased public attention on suburban regulatory barriers to such housing.[188] There were also pathbreaking judicial precedents from the neighboring Commonwealth of Pennsylvania. Beginning in 1965, the supreme court of that state invalidated zoning ordinances in suburban communities that established four-acre lot minimums,[189] that established two- and three-acre lot minimums,[190] and that totally excluded multifamily development.[191]

183. *See, e.g.,* Lionshead Lake, Inc. v. Township of Wayne, 10 N.J. 165, 89 A.2d 693 (1952).

184. *See* Fischer v. Town of Bedminster, 11 N.J. 194, 93 A.2d 378 (1952) (five acres).

185. *See* Vickers v. Gloucester Tp., 37 N.J. 232, 181 A.2d 129 (1962), *appeal dismissed*, 371 U.S. 233 (1963).

186. *See, e.g.,* Justice Frederick Hall's famous dissent in Vickers, *id.,* a portion of which is quoted in Chapter 1 *supra* at text accompanying note 274. Lionshead Lake, Inc. v. Township of Wayne, 10 N.J. 165, 89 A.2d 693 (1952), was perhaps the first "exclusionary" case to generate substantial controversy in the legal literature. *See* Haar, *Zoning for Minimum Standards: The Wayne Township Case,* 66 Harv. L. Rev. 1051 (1953); Nolan & Horack, *How Small a House?—Zoning for Minimum Space Requirements,* 67 Harv. L. Rev. 967 (1954); Haar, *Wayne Township: Zoning for Whom?—In Brief Reply,* 67 Harv. L. Rev. 986 (1954). Other articles on Wayne Township are cited in 2 Williams, *supra* note 2, at 638.

187. *See, e.g.,* Building the American City, *supra* note 117, at 211–17; Decent Home, *supra* note 15, at 135–43. A partial listing of the more provocative and influential law review articles written in this period, in addition to those cited in note 186 *supra,* would include Sager, *Tight Little Islands: Exclusionary Zoning, Equal Protection, and the Indigent,* 21 Stan. L. Rev. 767 (1969); Williams & Wacks, *Segregation of Residential Areas Along Economic Lines: Lionshead Lake Revisited,* 1969 Wisc. L. Rev. 827 (1969); Babcock & Bosselman, *Suburban Zoning and the Apartment Boom,* 111 U. Pa. L. Rev. 1040 (1963); Davidoff & Gold, *Exclusionary Zoning,* 1 Yale Rev. L. & Soc. Act. 56 (1970). An exhaustive listing of articles on this subject can be found in the *Bibliography* to National Commission Against Discrimination in Housing & The Urban Land Institute, Fair Housing and Exclusionary Land Use 61–72 (1974).

188. Sloane, *supra* note 25; Falk & Franklin, *supra* note 19, at 9–14, 93–96.

189. National Land and Investment Co. v. Kohn, 419 Pa. 504, 215 A.2d 597 (1965).

190. Appeal of Kit-Mar Builders, Inc. 439 Pa. 466, 268 A.2d 765 (1970).

191. Appeal of Girsh, 437 Pa. 237, 263 A.2d 395 (1970).

Each case was brought by landowners seeking higher density development than permitted by the applicable zoning. In each case the predominant opinion of the divided court justified the invalidation of the ordinance on the grounds that a municipality cannot enact municipal land-use controls with the purpose or the effect of enabling it to avoid the responsibility of coping with the burdens of an increased population. For example, in *Appeal of Kit-Mar Builders, Inc.*, the court stated:

> The implication of our decision in *National Land* is that communities must deal with problems of population growth. They may not refuse to confront the future by adopting zoning regulations that effectively restrict population to near present levels. It is not for any given township to say who may or may not live within its confines, while disregarding the interests of the entire area. If Concord Township is successful in unnaturally limiting its population growth through the use of exclusive zoning regulations, the people who would normally live there will inevitably have to live in another community, and the requirement that they do is not a decision that Concord Township should alone be able to make.[192]

The example of these cases was valuable in creating a climate where courts would be willing to severely scrutinize exclusionary municipal land-use regulations, although the Pennsylvania Supreme Court failed to articulate a useful legal standard for judging the validity of particular municipal regulations or for fashioning remedial orders effective in inducing reform beyond the immediate controversy. Lower courts in New Jersey, however, picked up the general theme of the Pennsylvania Supreme Court to develop a doctrine that each New Jersey municipality had to exercise its land-use regulatory powers to develop a "balanced community."[193] The holding by the New Jersey Supreme Court in *Mount Laurel*, that the legal justification for the exercise of the municipal land-use regulatory power is found in the promotion of the general welfare of the people of the state, represents the culmination of these trends, stated by an authoritative court.

---

192. 268 A.2d at 768-69.

193. "The test must be whether it [the zoning ordinance] promotes reasonably a balanced and well ordered plan for the entire municipality." Oakwood at Madison, Inc. v. Township of Madison, 117 N.J. Super. 11, 283 A.2d 353, 357 (1971), *aff'd*, — N.J. —, 371 A.2d 1192 (1977) (invalidating ordinance restricting multifamily construction and imposing large lot requirements for single-family construction); Molino v. Borough of Glassboro, 116 N.J. Super. 195, 281 A.2d 401 (1971) (invalidating limits on number of bedrooms in multifamily developments).

Promotion of the Housing Opportunities of the Region as the Standard for Measuring the Validity of Municipal Land-Use Regulations. From the legal justification of the municipal power to regulate land uses can be derived a *legal standard* for determining the validity or invalidity of a particular municipal regulation or regulatory program. In other words, if a municipality has the power to enact and enforce land-use regulations for the purpose of promoting the general welfare, then a particularized land-use regulation can be justified only if it in fact does promote the general welfare. This presents a two-part question: By what indicia is the promotion of the general welfare measured, and in regard to what geographic area?

For the Supreme Court of New Jersey, the impact of the municipal land-use regulation on the provision of needed housing affords one measure for determining whether the general welfare is being served. The provision of housing is identified as a major component of the general welfare because, in the court's view, "shelter, along with food, are the most basic human needs."[194]

The relevant geographic area is, in the court's opinion, the "region" of which the municipality is a part.[195] This follows from the recognition that the spatial impact of municipal land-use regulations will not extend beyond its metropolitan area or even beyond a smaller area in a particularly large metropolitan area. Thus, if the validity of a municipal land-use regulation is to be measured by its impact on the provision of housing, a court need assess that impact only within the relevant region. The court in *Mount Laurel* deferred further definition of what constitutes the relevant region to later judicial or legislative development, noting that "the composition of the applicable 'region' will necessarily vary from situation to situation and probably no hard and fast rule will serve to furnish the answer in every case."[196] In its next decision, *Oakwood at Madison, Inc. v. Township of Madison,*[197] the court concluded that "in general, there is no specific geographical area which is necessarily the authoritative region as to any single municipality. . . ."[198] however, the court did seem to find acceptable for purposes of testing an ordinance under *Mount Laurel*'s regional needs requirement, "that general area

---

194. 336 A.2d at 727. The court supported this finding by pointing to state legislative programs designed to meet the housing needs of low-, moderate-, and middle-income families in the state, and to its opinions upholding the programs as serving a valid public purpose. *E.g.,* N.J. Mortgage Finance Ag. v. McCrane, 56 N.J. 414, 267 A.2d 24 (1970). Also see note 109 *supra.*

195. 336 A.2d at 732-33.

196. *Id.* at 733.

197. 117 N.J. Super. 11, 283 A.2d 353 (1971), aff'd——N.J.——, 371 A.2d 1192 (1977).

198. *Id.* at 1221.

which constitutes, more or less, the housing market area of which the subject municipality is a part, and from which the prospective municipality would substantially be drawn, in the absence of exclusionary zoning."[199] The relationship between the provision of housing in the region and the validity of municipal land-use regulations was summarized by the *Mount Laurel* court:

> It is plain beyond dispute that proper provision for adequate housing of all categories of people is certainly an absolute essential in promotion of the general welfare required in all local land use regulation. Further the universal and constant need for such housing is so important and of such broad public interest that the general welfare which developing municipalities like Mount Laurel must consider extends beyond their boundaries and cannot be parochially confined to the claimed good of the particular municipality.[200]

Having established the linkage between the provision of housing and the general welfare, the New Jersey Supreme Court proceeded to establish more particular standards, both to provide better guidance to municipalities seeking to meet their obligations and to assist New Jersey's courts in applying these general principles to concrete factual situations. The court thus set forth, for the first time by the highest court of any state, an inclusionary obligation for developing municipalities

> affirmatively to plan and provide, by its land use regulations, the reasonable opportunity for an appropriate variety and choice of housing, including, of course, low and moderate income housing, to meet the needs, desires and resources of all categories of people who may desire to live within its boundaries. Negatively, it may not adopt regulations or policies which thwart or preclude that opportunity.[201]

The requirement that the municipal regulations provide "an appropriate variety and choice of housing" to meet the needs of "all categories of people" has several meanings. One is that the regulations must allow for a mixture of building types, permit varying density levels, and enable housing to be built at a wide range of costs affordable by the entire income spectrum.[202] The second is described else-

199. *Id.* at 1223. The court expanded on those factors "which draw most candidates for residence to a municipality," stating that they include, inter alia, proximity to jobs, availability of transportation to jobs, and proximity to and convenience of shopping, schools, and other amenities. *Id.* at 1121.

200. 336 A.2d at 727–28.

201. *Id.* at 728.

202. The court recognized that providing housing for families at the lower end of the income scale would require federal subsidies and also that new con-

where in the opinion as an obligation to meet the "municipality's fair share of the present and prospective regional need therefore."[203]

The "fair-share" concept limits the quantities of different kinds of housing that the municipality must plan for and rests on the acknowledgment that each developing municipality is subject to the same general affirmative obligation to provide housing opportunities.[204] If each provides for its fair share, then the total housing needs in the region will be suitably accommodated. Conversely, if the region's housing needs are not being met because developing municipalities in the region have maintained restrictive zoning, it would be inequitable to saddle one municipality with an obligation of greater magnitude than its fair share because it is the first to be brought to judgment in court.[205]

The court in *Mount Laurel* was not required to determine how each developing municipality's fair share was to be calculated, and consequently left the matter to "the expertise of the municipal planning adviser, the county planning boards and the state planning agency."[206] In its subsequent decision in *Oakwood at Madison*, the Supreme Court of New Jersey—adhering to the *Mount Laurel* rule

---

struction would furnish housing for only a small part of the state's population. 336 A.2d at 732 n.21. So, while the impact of the new affirmative obligation on developing municipalities would "produce no mass or sudden emigration of those of low and moderate income from the central cities and older suburbs to the developing municipalities," this would not be an excuse for not affording suburban housing opportunities "at once." *Id.*

203. *Id.* at 724.

204. The court recognized that "[f]requently it might be sounder to have more of such housing, like some specialized land uses, in one municipality in a region than in another, because of greater availability of suitable land, location of employment, accessibility of transportation or some other significant reason." *Id.* at 732. But because under present legislation in New Jersey, zoning must be on an individual municipal basis rather than a regional basis, the court concluded that every municipality within the region "must bear its fair share of the regional burden." *Id.* at 733. Recognizing the difficulties implicit in dealing with such regional matters from a municipal level, the court expressed its view that "[a]uthorization for regional zoning—the implementation of planning—or at least regulation of land uses having a substantial external impact by some agency beyond the local municipality, would seem to be logical and desirable as the next legislative step." *Id.* at 733 n.22.

205. Some commentators have noted, drawing upon experience with fair-share housing, that as a practical matter voluntary compliance with the legal requirements announced by the court might be enhanced if the obligation to accept "undesirable" housing was numerically limited. One of the attractive features municipalities see in voluntary regional fair-share housing allocation plans is the usefulness of the plans in limiting the annual number of units of federally subsidized housing the municipality must accept. *See* Franklin, Falk & Levin, In-Zoning: A Guide for Policy Makers on Inclusionary Land Use Programs 145–46 (1974).

206. 336 A.2d at 733.

that a developing municipality must afford the opportunity for a fair share of the regional need for low- and moderate-income housing—invalidated the zoning ordinance of Madison Township, but also ruled that "no formulaic determination or numerical specification of such a fair share is required."[207] (The intricacies of fair-share plans are discussed in detail in Chapters 3 and 6).

Although using different words, the New York Court of Appeals, the highest court in that state, has followed the New Jersey Supreme Court in establishing that promoting needed housing opportunities in the region is a measure of the validity of municipal land-use regulations. *Berenson v. Town of New Castle*[208] was decided only nine months after *Mount Laurel*, and involved a similar suburban community experiencing heavy population pressure in an expanding New York region.

Deciding an action brought by a landowner attempting to develop his land with multifamily housing, which was not permitted by the zoning ordinance, the New York Court of Appeals began with a general statement of the purpose of zoning: "The primary goal of a zoning ordinance must be to provide for the development of a balanced, cohesive community which will make efficient use of the town's available land."[209] The court then set forth a two-part test for determining the validity of any municipal land-use ordinance. As the first part the ordinance must provide "a properly balanced and well ordered plan for the community."[210] This is not to be a mechanical test, for "what may be appropriate for one community may differ substantially from what is appropriate for another."[211] As one element of this judgment, the extent to which the municipality's zoning provides for an acceptable level of housing opportunities is dependent upon whether the existing housing stock in the municipality adequately meets the community's current housing needs and what additional housing might be required for its future needs.

As the second part, the court stated that "in enacting a zoning ordinance, consideration must be given to regional needs and requirements,"[212] and that "there must be a balancing of the local desire to maintain the status quo within the community and the greater public

207. 117 N.J. Super. 11, 283 A.2d 353 (1971), aff'd —— N.J. ——, 371 A.2d 1128 (1977). The *Oakwood at Madison* court qualified its view opposing precise numerical quantifications in determining "fair share" by stating that "we do not preclude it if the municipal planning advisors deem it useful." *Id.*

208. 38 N.Y.2d 102, 341 N.E.2d 236 (1975).

209. 341 N.E.2d at 241.

210. *Id.* at 242.

211. *Id.*

212. *Id.*

interest that regional needs be met."[213] Only if the regional needs are being adequately met by other municipalities can they be excluded from the municipality's ordinance. Then, adding a subjective factor not required by *Mount Laurel*, the court of appeals stated that it was also necessary to determine "whether the town board, in excluding new multiple housing within its township, considered the needs of the region as well as the town for such housing."[214] A conscious consideration by the municipality's decision-makers of the regional housing needs, and the impact of their municipal land-use regulations on them before the ordinance is adopted, now seems to be a requirement in New York.[215]

California may also be moving in this direction. In *Associated Homebuilders of Greater Eastbay, Inc. v. City of Livermore*,[216] decided in December 1976, the court held that a local ordinance governing the issuance of building permits could be upheld only if reasonably related to the public welfare. Where the ordinance in question had in fact an impact on "the supply and distribution of housing for an entire metropolitan region, judicial inquiry must consider the welfare of that region."[217] The court then instructed the trial court to develop a factual record that would reveal the actual impact of the ordinance, to identify the competing interests affected by the ordinance (including that of existing suburban residents as well as nonresidents seeking better housing), and then to determine whether the ordinance, in its effects, "represents a reasonable accommodation of the competing interests."[218] The court gave no further guidance as to how that balancing determination should be made.

The Burden of Proof. How the tests for judging the validity of municipal land-use regulations are actually utilized in cases turn in large part on the allocations of the burdens of proof between the plaintiff challenging the regulations, and the defendant municipality. The court in *Mount Laurel* was cognizant of this and of the need for guidance, which it provided:

213. *Id.*

214. *Id.* at 243.

215. The New York courts have not extended their concept of standing to include nonresidents seeking to challenge a municipality's exclusionary land-use regulations, nor have they authorized broad judicial supervision over a municipality's redrafting of its ordinances to meet the court's legal requirements. These questions did not have to be reached in the *Berenson* case, which was brought by landowners seeking a rezoning for a high-density condominium development, and where the court was setting forth the legal principles to govern the trial of the case.

216. 135 Cal. Rptr. 41, 557 P.2d 473 (1976).

217. *Id.* at 55.

218. *Id.* at 56.

> Procedurally, we think the basic importance of appropriate housing for all dictates that, when it is shown that a developing municipality in its land use regulations has not made realistically possible a variety and choice of housing, including adequate provision to afford the opportunity for low and moderate income housing or has expressly prescribed requirements or restrictions which preclude or substantially hinder it, a facial showing of violation of substantive due process or equal protection under the state constitution has been made out and the burden, and it is a heavy one, shifts to the municipality to establish a valid basis for its action or non-action.[219]

This quotation suggests that the plaintiff in New Jersey can prove a prima facie case primarily on the basis of an examination of the text of the municipality's land-use regulations. The plaintiff need establish only that the regulations either do not make "realistically possible a variety and choice of housing," including that for low- and moderate-income households, or that they contain restrictive features (such as those described in Chapter 1) that have the same effect.[220] The plaintiff will clearly not have to prove either an intent by the municipality to exclude, which is not a relevant factor,[221] or a causal relationship between the municipality's restrictive regulations and the unmet regional needs. The existence of such a causal relationship can be assumed.[222]

Other courts are not so ready to shift the burden of proof to the defendant municipality. In Pennsylvania, the state where manifestly exclusionary zoning ordinances were first invalidated, the courts have established a different set of evidentiary rules that limit the focus of the court's inquiry and could result in upholding municipal regulations that could not pass a stricter "regional general welfare" standard:

> A zoning ordinance is still presumed valid and constitutional and anyone challenging an ordinance has a heavy burden of proving otherwise. When an individual challenging a zoning ordinance proves a total prohibition of an otherwise lawful use, the burden shifts to the municipality to prove

219. 336 A.2d at 728.

220. In the *Oakwood at Madison* case, the New Jersey Supreme Court described these types of provisions as "cost-generating features" of the ordinances. The plaintiff in that case met his burden of proof by demonstrating both an inadequate amount of land zoned for small lots and multifamily uses and undue cost-generating features.

221. 336 A.2d at 725 n.10.

222. Since the New York court in *Berenson* did not articulate a fair-share requirement, it seems to require a particularized demonstration of the impact of the municipality's land-use regulations on possibly unmet regional housing needs. Both the New Jersey and the New York courts are seeking to limit a municipality's affirmative obligation to situations where there are unsatisfied housing needs in the metropolitan area.

that such prohibition bears a relationship to the public health, safety, morals and general welfare.[223]

The Pennsylvania courts operating under this rule have had to struggle in several cases with municipal regulations that exclude multifamily uses from all but a small fraction of the available municipal land.[224] Because the exclusion was not total, the burden of proof was not shifted to the municipality, but the regulations were invalidated anyway. In one of these cases the Pennsylvania Supreme Court fell back on fair-share notions in holding that, with an ordinance designating only 80 acres for multifamily uses out of 11,589 (that is, 0.6 percent), "the township continues to be 'exclusionary' in that it does not provide for a fair share of the township acreage for apartment construction."[225]

A subsequent case from the intermediate appellate court (where most Pennsylvania zoning cases are resolved) invalidated a similar ordinance allocating only 49 acres out of 5,250 for multifamily uses (that is, 0.9 percent), of which only 8 acres were actually suitable for that use.[226] For situations in Pennsylvania where no use has been completely or nearly completely excluded, the plaintiff must still prove that the zoning requirement "bears no reasonable relationship to the protection of the public health, safety, or welfare, and that it had an exclusionary purpose or effect."[227]

These evidentiary rules in Pennsylvania illustrate that the courts in that state have little concern for the special housing needs of low-income families. All the Pennsylvania cases that have invalidated zoning ordinances as exclusionary have focused on refusals to permit higher density development and the implications this has for not accommodating existing population pressures. The Pennsylvania courts have refrained from taking the next step—to analyze the real impact

223. Ellick v. Board of Supervisors, 17 Pa. Commw. Ct. 404, 333 A.2d 239, 243–44 (1975).

224. *See* Township of Williston v. Chesterdale Farms, Inc., 462 Pa. 445, 341 A.2d 466 (1975); Waynesborough Corp. v. Easttown Tp. Zoning Hearing Bd., 23 Pa. Commw. Ct. 137, 350 A.2d 895 (1976).

225. *See* Township of Williston v. Chesterdale Farms, Inc., 341 A.2d at 468. A dissenting judge criticized the majority's facile reliance on the fair-share idea: "The opinion does not state why this share is not 'fair,' does not vouchsafe what might be considered a 'fair share,' and does not indicate any criteria by which a fair share may be ascertained." 341 A.2d at 469.

226. Waynesborough Corp. v. Easttown Tp. Zoning Hearing Bd., 23 Pa. Commw. Ct. 137, 350 A.2d 895 (1976).

227. DeCaro v. Washington Tp., 21 Pa. Commw. Ct. 252, 344 A.2d 725, 728 (1975) (upholding three-acre lot zoning). *See* Russell v. Penn Tp. Planning Comm'n, 22 Pa. Commw. Ct. 198, 348 A.2d 499 (1976) (ordinance establishing minimum pad sizes for mobile home parks not held exclusionary for failure of proof).

of the municipality's land-use regulations on the region's population distribution, viewed separately by income and race. It would then be apparent that the exclusionary impact of the regulations bear more heavily on the low-income groups, a situation about which the Pennsylvania courts do not seem disposed to correct.

An alternative approach to that of the *Mount Laurel* decision was developed by the intermediate appellate courts in Michigan.[228] Recognizing the extensive unmet housing needs of low- and moderate-income households, and that housing is a fundamental value,[229] these courts held that housing for low-income families was a "preferred use," and that, if denied to any parcel of land because of a municipal regulation, the burden of proof would shift to the municipality to justify the regulation. This principle was applied to overcome municipal ordinances restricting multifamily housing[230] and mobile homes.[231] The "preferred use" approach was an innovative alternative, because it recognized the special unmet housing needs of low-income households and promised to be an effective method for obtaining more sites for such housing. Unfortunately, the Michigan Supreme Court disavowed the doctrine,[232] and the law in Michigan now closely resembles the law in Pennsylvania, where the presumption of validity of municipal regulations prevails except in cases of total exclusions of otherwise valid uses.[233]

Justification for Municipal Restrictions. The New Jersey Supreme Court in *Mount Laurel* had little difficulty in discounting the reasons asserted by Mount Laurel Township once the burden of proof had shifted to the town to justify the restrictive features of its land-use regulations. The municipality had argued that it had the right to permit only those land uses that would be likely to generate at least as much in increased tax revenues as they would cost in increased municipal expenditures. While agreeing that a developing municipality may properly zone for a better economic balance vis-à-vis educational and governmental costs engendered by residential

228. Bristow v. Cty of Woodhaven, 35 Mich. App. 205, 192 N.W.2d 322 (1971); Simmons v. City of Royal Oak, 38 Mich. App. 496, 196 N.W.2d 811 (1972).

229. "Citizens of the general community have a right to decently placed, suitable housing within their means and such right must be a consideration in assessing the reasonableness of local zoning prescribing residential requirements or prohibitions." Bristow v. City of Woodhaven, 192 N.W.2d at 327–28.

230. 196 N.W.2d 811 (1972).

231. 192 N.W.2d 322 (1971).

232. Kropf v. City of Sterling Heights, 391 Mich. 139, 215 N.W. 2d 179 (1974).

233. *Id.;* Nickola v. Township of Grand Blanc, 394 Mich. 589, 232 N.W.2d 604 (1975).

development (pursuant to a legitimate comprehensive plan), the court held that "no municipality may exclude or limit categories of housing for that reason or purpose."[234] The municipality also claimed that half-acre lots were necessary since sewer and water utilities were unavailable. The court replied by noting that the land was flat and readily amenable to utility installations, and that the municipality could require them as improvements by developers or install them under the special-assessment or other statutory procedures.[235]

A developing municipality will nevertheless be able to maintain restrictive provisions in its land-use regulations in many circumstances. It is implicit in the *Mount Laurel* decision that a municipality retains considerable latitude in the design of its municipal land-use regulations, enabling it to impose restrictions—such as large lots and minimum house sizes—so long as its affirmative obligations to meet regional needs are also satisfied. Thus a developer seeking to build a multifamily housing development on a parcel of land would not be able to complain because the sites are zoned for large lots if the municipality's zoning ordinance made suitable provision elsewhere for its fair share of multifamily housing.[236] Restrictive provisions are not per se unlawful.

There may also be an occasional situation where a developing municipality can assert a justification for restrictive provisions that a reviewing court should accept, even though the municipality is not contributing to meeting the regional housing needs.[237] The conservation of sensitive natural land-use resources, such as wetlands and beach areas, that make up a significant portion of the municipality's total land area, may provide it with reason for not permitting development in such ecologically fragile terrain. The ecological features of the municipality's land are thus elements that could enter into the court's evaluation of the municipality's overall policy. But, as the court in *Mount Laurel* observed, the ecological or environmental damages from development must be "substantial and very real," and "not simply a makeweight to support exclusionary housing measures or preclude growth."[238] It would, of course, give the court additional assurances if these special areas were identified by a state or regional agency concerned with environmental protection.

234. 336 A.2d at 730–31.
235. *Id.*
236. Paglee v. Township of Pemberton, 73 N.J. 64, 372 A.2d 329 (1977).
237. As discussed *infra, Mount Laurel's* affirmative obligation applies only to "developing municipalities." Thus the reasonableness of excluding multifamily housing or imposing other restrictive requirements depends on the nature and extent of development in the municipality in question. *See* notes 240–43 *infra*, and accompanying test.
238. 336 A.2d at 731.

Unresolved Questions in Mount Laurel. Several important questions were explicitly or implicitly left unresolved in the *Mount Laurel* decision.[239] The legal duties described in the opinion are imposed only on "developing municipalities." The court did not define what constitutes a "developing municipality."[240] In March of 1977, in *Pascack Association, Ltd. v. Mayor and Council of Washington Township*,[241] the Supreme Court of New Jersey ruled that the doctrine announced in *Mount Laurel* was authoritative only to *"fairly sizable developing, not fully developed municipalities—*particularly small ones—which may vary in character from . . . a tiny municipality . . . developed in a dense, moderate-income multifamily residential pattern, to one like the subject municipality, homogeneously and completely developed as a middle-upper income, moderate- to low-density, single-family community"[242] (emphasis added). Washington Township, a "bedroom community" comprising three and a quarter square miles of which 94.5 percent was developed for single-family residences, did not, in the court's view, fall into the category of a "developing municipality," and could reasonably exclude multifamily housing on its remaining 2.3 percent vacant land.[243] While refusing to extend the *Mount Laurel* rule to all municipalities or "developed" municipalities, it cannot be said that the court has yet announced an unambiguous and truly workable definition of developing municipalities that is capable of providing lower courts with necessary guidance. Consequently, continued litigation on this question can be expected.[244]

The question of the extent of a developing municipality's obliga-

239. *See generally* Williams, *supra* note 2, at addend. ch. 66; Falk & Franklin, *supra* note 19, at 112–13; and selected sources cited in note 175 *supra*.
240. *See* Rose & Levin, *What Is a "Developing Municipality" Within the Meaning of the Mount Laurel Decision?* 4 Real Estate L.J. 359 (1976).
241. No. A-130 (N.J. Sup. Ct., decided March 23, 1977).
242. *Id.*, slip op. at 21.
243. In a companion case, Fobe Associates v. Mayor and Council and Bd. of Adj., No. A-129 (Sup. Ct., decided March 23, 1977), the court held that Demarest, another "bedroom community" within the same county, was "developed" under the *Mount Laurel* rule because it contained only a few isolated parcels of vacant land within its two and a half square miles. Consequently it sustained the municipality's refusal to grant a variance for the proposed garden apartments.
244. In a strongly worded dissenting opinion, Justice Pashman characterized the practical effect of the majority's ruling in *Pascack* as "allow[ing] municipalities which have already attained "exclusionary bliss' to forever absolve themselves of any obligation for correcting the racial and economic segregation which their land use controls helped to create. . . . [R]emaining communities and inner cities will be required . . . to take more than their 'fair share' of low and middle income multi-housing [*sic*]; that specter can only encourage municipalities to avoid the label of 'developing.'" Pascack, slip op. at 14–15.

tion was expressly reserved by the *Mount Laurel* court.[245] What happens if the municipality's fair share of housing of all types is not built despite a land-use regulatory system that is unassailable because of the opportunities it provides? Will the New Jersey courts require a municipality to take more affirmative steps, particularly toward low- and moderate-income housing, such as offering zoning incentives to development or creating its own housing development capabilities? Will it make a difference if the municipality is trying to rectify past exclusionary regulations, as contrasted to a municipality that has never been exclusionary? The court's subsequent *Oakwood at Madison* decision indicated that municipalities would not be required to take actions outside of their legal controls over land uses.[246] The court, however, did make clear that nothing less than zoning for "least-cost" housing (that is, housing at the lowest cost feasible), consistent with minimum standards of health and safety, would satisfy the mandate of *Mount Laurel*.[247]

The final unresolved question in the *Mount Laurel* opinion is that of fashioning an appropriate remedy. The court in *Mount Laurel* ordered that the municipality be given ninety days to prepare a zoning ordinance that complied with the requirements of the opinion.[248] The court in *Oakwood at Madison* also ordered the municipality to amend its zoning ordinance in light of the requirements set forth in its opinion, including fairly specific demands for more acreage zoned for small lots and multifamily units and the elimination of undue cost-generating features that inhibit the development of least-cost housing.[249] Yet the situation in *Mount Laurel* remained unresolved almost two years later when the voters in the November 2, 1976 election voted down a municipal ordinance drawn up in response to the opinion.[250] In the following chapter, ways of fashioning effective judicial remedies and overcoming local intransigence are examined in detail.

245. 336 A.2d at 734.

246. The opinion approved the provision of density bonuses to encourage the development of multifamily housing for lower income families, but reserved judgment on the mandatory inclusion of lower income units. 371 A.2d 1210–1211, 1224–1225. The discussion of neither of these points was necessary to the decision of the case.

247. In advancing the concept of "least cost" housing, the court recognized that compliance with that directive "may not provide newly constructed housing for all in the lower income categories . . . , [but] it will nevertheless through the 'filtering down' process . . . tend to augment the total supply of available housing in such manner as will indirectly provide additional and better housing for the insufficiently and inadequately housed of the region's lower income population." *Id.*, at 1208.

248. 336 A.2d at 734.

249. 371 A.2d at 1228.

250. *See* Falk & Franklin, *supra* note 19, at 113.

Future Prospects. Other state courts have not yet followed the advanced lead provided by the New Jersey Supreme Court. New York, which has adopted the New Jersey court's legal reasoning, has not decided whether to similarly broaden its rules on standing to sue to include persons other than those with directly affected real property interests.[251] This may minimize the number of land-use cases brought in New York's courts and also enable the courts to limit their relief to site-specific orders. The Pennsylvania courts have already refused to broaden their concepts of standing[252] and have also refrained from following the logic of their initial anti-exclusionary zoning decisions. Most other states have not even gone as far as Pennsylvania in enunciating antiexclusionary principles.[253] While California has at last recognized that local land-use decisions must be judged on broader principles of the general welfare, the courts there have not yet applied the principle to invalidate local exclusionary actions.[254]

It would be appropriate to ask what factors might contribute to the state judiciary's caution in this field, besides the normal conservatism that makes judges reluctant to upset established precedents. Several factors might be mentioned. First, the reform attitude taken by the New Jersey courts is involving them in many difficult issues whose resolution will be widely felt within the state. What is the relevant region? What is "fair share" and how is it derived? What is "low-income" housing? How far does the affirmative duty of the municipality extend? The determination of these questions requires amassing vast amounts of data of a kind that courts are unaccustomed to using and requires them to make novel judgments on the basis of this data. Consequently, many judges feel that they lack the competence to deal with these complexities. It is a feeling summed up by the expression: The court is not a superplanning agency. These are questions for planners, not for lawyers and judges.

A related factor is the fear that the court might be treading on ground reserved to municipal legislative bodies. They are the bodies empowered by the state constitution and state legislature to write land-use regulations, and, if a regulation is unconstitutional, it is their obligation to enact a regulation that is not. The court's role is limited to evaluating what the municipal legislature has done. Some judges might also be concerned that the broad relief they are being asked to order will be unpopular in the community in which they live.[255] The very reason that the cases are in court is because the

251. *See* note 215 *supra*.
252. *See* text at note 165 *supra*.
253. *See* 3 Williams, *supra* note 2, at ch. 66.
254. *See* text accompanying notes 216–18 *supra*.
255. In Urban League v. Borough of Carteret, 142 N.J. Super. 11, 359

municipal legislatures have chosen not to make greater provision for housing for larger numbers of people, particularly lower income people and racial minorities. And state legislatures and state executives, who have shown a concern for housing low-income households through enactment of a variety of state housing programs, have also chosen not to interfere with municipal autonomy in this area. Land-use regulation is seen as too sensitive politically. It is thus left to the courts to assume the lead role in reform, even if it frustrates suburban residents who do not want to face problems they believe are brought by lower income and minority families. Many in the judicial system are unwilling to take this kind of unpopular stand.

Finally, these land-use cases frequently remain in the courts for years without reaching a final resolution. Many of the New Jersey cases have been in litigation for over five years, and no final solution has been reached even in *Mount Laurel*. This results from the complex nature of the facts, the lack of experience in making such judgments, and the resistance from municipalities in obeying remedial decrees. The delays inherent in this type of comprehensive land-use litigation might reinforce a court's determination not to become enmeshed in the first place.

The other side of the coin is that there are important principles at stake that most courts are not now addressing, but should be. When restrictive municipal regulations deny people what can be considered a fundamental right—that is, the opportunity to live in adequate housing in a pleasant surrounding and near their places of employment—an opportunity for redress is necessary, and the courts are the only forum open to them. The New Jersey Supreme Court in its *Mount Laurel* decision has furnished a persuasive logic, grounded on the fundamental obligation of government to serve the interests of all the people, for greater judicial activism in this area of the law, and judges should look carefully at the soundness of this view.

One of the purposes for which the Advisory Commission on Housing and Urban Growth was established was to determine whether it is proper for courts to undertake to remedy the social dislocations flowing from unreasonably restrictive municipal land-use regulations. Our conclusion has been that it is. By examining in this book the legal doctrines governing these questions, the types of remedies available to a court, and the proper utilization of planning data, we hope to help overcome the reluctance of courts to deal with this type of land-use litigation by providing guidance on which they can draw. Subsequent chapters are intended to do this.

A.2d 526 (1976), a court reviewed the zoning ordinances of 23 out of the 25 municipalities in Middlesex County and invalidated 11 of them as not meeting the standards of the *Mount Laurel* decision.

POLICY STATEMENTS

1. The "general welfare," as a basic state constitutional principle and the predicate for local policy power regulations, should be understood as being regional in context, and as including the fundamentally important state interest that the housing needs of all income groups of the state be promoted and enhanced.

2. In exercising their police power authority, local governments have an affirmative legal duty to promote the "general welfare." This affirmative duty has several parts: (a) to plan for present and prospective housing in a regional context; (b) to eliminate those local regulatory barriers that do not presumptively make it realistically possible to provide housing for persons of low-and moderate-income; and (c) to offer regulatory concessions and incentives to the private sector in this regard.

3. The obligations of communities to meet low- and moderate-income housing needs should be evaluated in terms of a determination of the local "fair share" of the region's housing needs. Preferably, legislatures should seek to establish standards and processes to aid in the measurement and allocation of such needs.

4. Under the police power doctrine presented in Policy Statements 1 through 3 above, local regulatory devices—such as requirements for minimum large lot size, floor area, and bedroom space; prohibitions on multifamily residential development; and growth-control ordinances without reasonable time limitations or inclusionary housing components—require careful judicial scrutiny. Upon the establishment of a significant relationship of one of these restrictive land-use controls and a negative impact on regional housing opportunities for all racial and income groups, the burden of going forward with evidence should shift to the local government[s] concerned.

5. In the Advisory Commission's view, recent federal court decisions have unduly limited access to federal courts to contest municipal land-use regulations and have failed to extend the protections of the equal protection clause of the Fourteenth Amendment to the claims of lower income families disadvantaged by municipal land-use regulations. The Commission firmly believes that these judgments should not be reflected in the decisions of state courts interpreting their own state constitutions and statutes. It is inherent in our system of federalism and in constitutional jurisprudence that decisions of the U.S. Supreme Court are not necessarily dispositive of questions regarding rights guaranteed by counterpart provisions of state law.

6. Contrary to recent federal judicial precedent, upon proof that a local land-use control ordinance—through such regulatory devices as minimum lot area, population density limitations, and interceptor sewer extension policy—has made "practically and economically impossible" the construction of sufficient numbers of low- and moderate-income housing, at least the following classes of plaintiffs should have standing to contest the validity of the restrictive land-use controls in federal and state courts: (a) former low- and moderate-income residents who were forced to move elsewhere in the region because of the absence of suitable residential opportunities within the municipality; and (b) low- and moderate-income residents living in substandard housing elsewhere in the region who desire to secure decent housing accessible to suitable employment, education, and neighborhood services in the locality. Assuming that these classes of plaintiffs have established that, as a result of the municipality's exclusionary practices, they incurred higher transportation costs for work-related activities, received poor residential services, and were not able to secure an adequate level of housing elsewhere in the regional housing market, sufficient proof has been presented to satisfy "prudential" and constitutional requirements that there exists "injury in fact," and that the alleged injury is directly related to the claims sought to be adjudicated.

Congress should give serious consideration to enacting legislation that would reduce procedural barriers in the federal courts, and reverse the current trend toward an elaboration of technical rules of standing, ripeness, sovereign immunity, and exhaustion of administrative remedies.

7. The achievement of "socioeconomic" objectives (*e.g.*, historic district preservation, growth-management schemes with an inclusionary housing component, and mandatory inclusionary zoning schemes in and of themselves) through local zoning legislation, as well as the classification of permitted land uses by physical characteristics, should be acknowledged as within the powers delegated to local governments by state enabling legislation, *i.e.*, under the "general welfare" purpose clause of typical state enabling legislation.

❋ *Chapter 3*

The Role of the Courts

JUDICIAL INVOLVEMENT

The Issue

The pattern of racial and economic class separation in metropolitan areas is not of judicial making. It has resulted from many forces: private preference, private discrimination, differences in income, developers' views of market pressures, federal programs, and local planning and zoning, among others. Courts can have little direct impact on many of the forces, such as private preference and income distribution; courts can, however, affect the substance and administration of laws. To date, there have been increasing appeals to the judiciary, based on statutory and constitutional grounds, to intervene against various local laws that are considered causally related to segregated residential patterns.[1] In addition, courts have been asked to strike down municipal growth plans that limit the number of new residents, thereby excluding, at least temporarily, persons of any class or race who might desire to move to the municipality.[2]

---

1. Local laws are the normal object of attack because most land regulation powers are exercised at the local level. Federal subsidies to local communities which allegedly discriminate are now also under attack. *See, e.g.,* Evans v. Lynn, 376 F. Supp. 327 (S.D.N.Y. 1975), *rev'd sub nom.,* Evans v. Hills, 537 F.2d 571 (2d Cir. June 4, 1976) (en banc), *cert. denied,* 97 S. Ct. 797.

2. *See* Construction Industry Ass'n. v. City of Petaluma, 375 F. Supp. 574 (N.D. Cal. 1973), *rev'd,* 522 F.2d 897 (9th Cir. 1975), *cert. denied,* 424 U.S. 934 (1976); Golden v. Town Planning Board of Ramapo, 30 N.Y.2d 359, 285 N.E.2d 291 (1971), *appeal dismissed,* 409 U.S. 1003 (1972).

At issue in this chapter is the proper role of federal and state courts in the management of urban growth, with special emphasis on the propriety of judicial review of local plans and regulations that inhibit persons of low income from being housed in many suburban communities.

A Brief Historical Excursion

Most land-use litigation of the past has involved conflicts between local regulatory bodies and property owners whose freedom to use their property in the most profitable manner has been constrained by regulatory decisions.[3] A lesser number of suits have been brought by neighbors protesting that regulations have been unduly relaxed. The United States Supreme Court played a brief role at the outset in *City of Euclid v. Amber Realty*,[4] laying down the basic constitutional ground rules for adjudicating these conflicts. But thereafter the federal courts in general, and the Supreme Court emphatically, withdrew from the field, leaving the balancing between private and public rights to state courts.

Generally speaking, there has been a sharp distinction in the attitudes of state courts. One group has tended to review regulatory decisions in fine detail and to overrule restraints on development after recalculating costs and benefits in its own terms.[5] The other group—the "pro-zoning" states, as Professor Williams calls them[6]—has tended to uphold land-use restrictions. These courts interfere only in cases where an unfair advantage or disadvantage has been given a particular landowner and no persuasive general reason is advanced for the discriminatory treatment, or where a regulation has imposed very onerous burdens on a landowner.

Current litigation concerning the validity of local legislative private-public balancing judgments, where a regulation seemingly frustrates housing choices of persons within a region, deals not with property rights but rather with claimed social and economic rights of the persons excluded.

Federal Court Response. Much of the new litigation has been brought in federal courts. Many of the cases have centered on racial discrimination. In one set, a federally subsidized developer has been refused permission by a local jurisdiction to go forward with a pro-

3. 1 N. Williams, American Land Planning Law 71-74 (1974).
4. 272 U.S. 365 (1922). *See also* Nectow v. City of Cambridge, 277 U.S. 183 (1928).
5. 1 Williams, *supra* note 3, at 74-75.
6. *Id.* at 77-78.

ject, and there was substantial evidence that the refusal was premised on racial discrimination.[7] Relief uniformly has been granted when plaintiff has established the presence and causal relation of the bias.[8] In a second set of cases, plaintiff has not established a racially discriminatory purpose, but rather has demonstrated that the effect of the regulation prohibiting the project has a disproportionate racial impact. In the past, some lower federal courts had held that such an effect renders the regulation presumptively invalid.[9] However, the U.S. Supreme Court recently has held otherwise. In *Village of Arlington Heights v. Metropolitan Housing Development Corporation*,[10] the Court ruled that "official action will not be held unconstitutional solely because it results in a racially disproportionate impact. . . . Proof of racially discriminatory intent or purpose is required to show a violation of the Equal Protection Clause."[11] The case involved denial of a zone change that would have allowed construction of a federally subsidized housing project. Plaintiffs had failed to prove a racially discriminatory purpose, although the Court conceded that the refusal resulted in a heavier impact on racial minorities. A number of criteria were suggested by the Court to determine whether the basis for the action was intentionally discriminatory. The case was remanded for this determination and also for consideration of plantiffs' allegation that the denial violated the

7. *See, e.g.,* Dailey v. City of Lawton, 425 F.2d 1037 (10th Cir. 1970); Kennedy Park Homes Ass'n v. City of Lackawanna, 436 F.2d 108 (2d Cir. 1970), *cert. denied,* 401 U.S. 1010 1971); Crow v. Brown, 332 F. Supp. 382 (N.D. Ga. 1971), *aff'd per curiam,* 456 F.2d 788 (5th Cir. 1972); Sisters of Providence v. City of Evanston, 335 F. Supp. 396 (N.D. Ill. 1971).

8. The burden of proof on the plaintiff, however, is not insubstantial. *See, e.g.,* United States v. City of Black Jack, 372 F. Supp. 319 (E.D. Mo. 1974), *rev'd,* 508 F.2d 1179 (8th Cir. 1974); Citizens Comm. v. Lindsay, 362 F. Supp. 651 (S.D.N.Y. 1973).

9. In Washington v. Davis, 426 U.S. 229, n. 12 (1976), discussed in text at notes 71–79 *infra,* the U.S. Supreme Court cited with disapproval the following cases, among others, in which lower courts had relied on the racial impact of effect, rather than the official purpose of particular actions to find a violation of the Equal Protection Clause:

Norwalk CORE v. *Norwalk Redevelopment Agency,* 395 F.2d 920 (CA2 1968) (urban renewal); *Kennedy Park Homes Assn.* v. *City of Lackawanna,* 436 F.2d 108, 114 (CA2 1970), cert. denied, 401 U.S. 1010 (1970) (zoning); *Southern Alameda Spanish Speaking Organization* v. *Union City,* 424 F.2d 291 (CA9 1970) (dictum) (zoning); *Metropolitan H.D. Corp.* v. *Village of Arlington Heights,* 517 F.2d 409 (CA7), cert. granted 423 U.S. 1030 (1975) (zoning); *Gatreaux* v. *Romney,* 448 F.2d 731, 738 (CA7 1971) (dictum) (public housing); *Crow* v. *Brown,* 332 F. Supp. 382, 391 (ND Ga. 1971), aff'd, 457 F.2d 788 (CA5 1972) (public housing); *Hawkins* v. *Town of Shaw,* 437 F.2d 1286 (CA5 1971), aff'd on rehearing en banc, 461 F.2d 1171 (1972) (municipal services).

10. 97 S. Ct. 555 (1977).

11. *Id.* at 4076.

Fair Housing Act of 1968 (42 U.S.C. § 3601 *et seq.*). It should be noted that the Court's ruling does not extend beyond a constitutionally based attack on local actions, and presumably a challenge based on statutory violations would be unaffected by this decision.[12]

The relative availability of federal courts to hear cases involving alleged exclusion on racial grounds led advocates of open housing, and some commentators, to predict intensive federal court intervention on behalf of both low-income plaintiffs and persons in general who were excluded by population limitations, timing controls, and other means imposed by local regulations and plans. Some lower federal court decisions fulfilled these expectations. Thus, in *Southern Alameda Spanish Speaking Org. (SASSO) v. City of Union City*[13] the court of appeals suggested that a city was subject to a constitutional duty to see that its general plan accommodates the needs of its low-income families. The district court, on remand, directed the city to take the steps necessary to accommodate within a reasonable time the needs of its low-income residents.[14] More sweepingly, a federal district court in *Construction Industry Ass'n of Sonoma County v. City of Petaluma*[15] struck down, on freedom-of-travel grounds, a municipal plan designed to limit new residential construction well below what would otherwise have been produced by the market. The importance of this development of the freedom-of-travel doctrine under the Equal Protection Clause, however, was significantly negated in a later decision of the Court of Appeals for the Ninth Circuit.[16]

The majority of Justices on the present U.S. Supreme Court seem inclined to the view that there is no federal court role, in the absence of a federal legislative directive, on behalf of persons, low-income or otherwise, whose housing opportunities in metropolitan areas are frustrated, unless the exclusion is linked to race. Two recent cases illustrate this attitude. In *Village of Belle Terre v. Boraas*,[17] the Court found no constitutional violation in connection with a sub-

12. See text accompanying note 70, *infra.*
13. 357 F. Supp. 1188 (N.D. Cal. 1970), 424 F.2d 291 (9th Cir. 1970).
14. The Housing and Community Development Act of 1974 extends the obligation of a city to house not only its own low-income residents but also those "expected to reside" within its borders, based on the community's existing or proposed employment opportunities (42 U.S.C. § 5304(a)(4) (1975 Supp.). *See* City of Hartford v. Hills, 408 F. Supp. 889 (D.Conn. 1976) *rev'd sub nom.* City of Hartford v. Town of Glastonbury, ——F.2d—— (2d. Cir. Aug. 15, 1977) (*en banc*).
15. 375 F. Supp. 574 (N.D. Cal. 1974), *rev'd*, 522 F.2d 897 (9th Cir. 1975), *cert. denied*, 424 U.S. 934 (1976).
16. Construction Industry Ass'n v. Petaluma, 522 F.2d 897 (9th Cir. 1975), *cert. denied*, 424 U.S. 934 (1976).
17. 416 U.S. 1 (1974).

urban zoning ordinance that permitted only single-family houses and prohibited occupation of a dwelling by more than two unrelated persons as a family. Six students from a nearby college had rented a home and sought injunctive relief against the ordinance on numerous grounds, including right to travel, freedom of association, and equal protection. The Court found no need for strict scrutiny and upheld the ordinance as neither unreasonable nor arbitrary.[18]

The *Boraas* case, of course, did not involve claims of exclusion on wealth grounds. The recent Supreme Court decision in *Warth v. Seldin*,[19] however, did involve such claims, and the Court refused to exercise jurisdiction on standing grounds. Various plaintiffs, described below, attacked the system of land-use ordinances and plans of a suburban town near Rochester, New York, claiming that the regulations effectively excluded persons of low and moderate income from living in the town. The case was dismissed below on standing grounds. The Supreme Court, assuming for purposes of the case that the regulations were unconstitutionally exclusionary, affirmed the determination that plaintiffs lacked standing. Plaintiffs, and others who sought to intervene as plaintiffs, included low-income residents of Rochester, developers of low-income housing, and an association representing, among others, residents of the defendant town.

The first category of plaintiffs (low-income residents of Rochester) failed because they did not—and presumably, in the view of the majority of the Court, could not—allege facts showing that judicial relief would personally benefit them in a tangible way, or, to put it negatively, that the ordinance in question concretely harmed them. They could not show the requisite causal connection because they had no interest in land subject to the regulations and they could not identify third parties specifically frustrated by the ordinances who otherwise would build low-income housing that would be available to them.

The second category of plaintiffs (developers of low-income housing in the region), failed because the complaint referred to no specific project that was currently precluded by the ordinances. "In short, insofar as the complaint seeks prospective relief, Home Builders has failed to show the existence of any injury to its members of sufficient immediacy and ripeness to warrant judicial intervention."[20]

---

18. Lower federal courts in California had come to a similar result in an analogous case. Palo Alto Tenants Union v. Morgan, 321 F. Supp. 908 (N.D. Cal. 1970), *aff'd*, 487 F.2d 883 (9th Cir. 1973).

19. 422 U.S. 490 (1975).

20. *Id.* at 516.

A third plaintiff (an association representing, among others, some residents of the defendant town), claimed injury because they were precluded from living in an integrated community. In the Court's view, prudential considerations (if not constitutional obstacles) counselled against affording them standing. Among these was that they were really seeking to raise putative rights of third parties.

Warth v. Seldin can be read either narrowly, to mean that a federal forum will be available to test land-use regulations that allegedly discriminate on an income basis if proper plaintiffs are found, or more broadly, to indicate that claims of this sort are not appropriate for federal cognizance. The latter is suggested by a number of factors. First, the Court implies in one passage that the questions in issue might better be addressed by other government institutions more competent to address them.[21] Second, standing doctrine is applied more narrowly than in analogous cases such as *United States v. SCRAP.*[22] Third, while it is possible to hypothesize a proper plaintiff to raise the issues in question, it might be hard to find one.[23] For instance, it is questionable, under the Court's approach, that a developer of low-income housing with an interest in property within a defendant's jurisdiction would have standing to raise the constitutional claims of third parties in interest who would occupy a completed project.

Analogous developers were denied the opportunity to raise the right-to-travel claims of prospective customers by the Ninth Circuit Court of Appeals in the *Petaluma* case,[24] which relied heavily on *Warth* in reversing the lower court decision discussed above. This might be cured by joining as plaintiffs those low-income nonresidents with contracts to lease upon the completion of the project, but a court might treat even such contracts as too ephemeral to show causally related injury in fact. In any event, in such a suit it is quite probable that the court would focus on the question of whether the

21. *Id.* at 500.

22. 412 U.S. 669 (1973).

23. *Cf.* Planning for People Coalition v. County of DuPage, (N.D. Ill. 1976), in which Warth was distinguished and individual plaintiffs were found to have standing in light of a record of overt actions on the part of defendants specifically aimed at discouraging the construction of low- and moderate-income housing.

24. 522 F.2d 897 (9th Cir. 1975). However, standing was granted prospective developers who challenged exclusionary zoning ordinances in Metropolitan Housing Development Corporation v. Village of Arlington Heights, 517 F.2d 409 (7th Cir. 1975), *rev'd on other grounds*, 97 S. Ct. 555 (1977). *See also* United States v. City of Black Jack, 508 F.2d 1179 (8th Cir. 1974), *cert. denied*, 422 U.S. 1042 (1975). The *Warth* position on standing is also contrary to state law in many instances, *e.g.*, *In re* Douglaston Civic Association v. Galvin, 36 N.Y. 1, 364 N.Y.S.2d 830, 324 N.E.2d 317 (1974), in which standing was granted a propertyowners' association of neighbors who contested the grant of a variance.

refusal to permit the particular development at the particular site in question was reasonable, and would avoid the larger question sought to be raised in *Warth*—that is, the permissibility of excluding all low- and moderate-cost housing from a suburb.

Even if the standing obstacle can be overcome, however, recent Supreme Court cases strongly suggest that no federal constitutional basis for relief will be found. The two cases most in point appear to be *Lindsey v. Normet*[25] and *San Antonio School District v. Rodriguez*.[26] Both reject claims that poor people are improperly deprived of equal protection rights by statutory arrangements that arguably impact more harshly on the poor than on more wealthy persons. In *Lindsey* the claim was made that tenants were denied equal treatment by a statute that precluded a tenant, in a landlord's action for eviction for nonpayment of rent, from offering in defense such facts as the existence of serious code violations in the rented premises. In *Rodriguez* plaintiffs were unsuccessful in establishing that children in school districts spending less per capita for educational programs than the statewide average were thereby denied equal protection of the law. In both cases the Court refused to find a "suspect classification" or the deprivation of a "fundamental interest." Thus in neither case was the burden of proof reversed with the state required to show a "compelling state interest" to sustain the legislation under attack.

A number of factors led to the results in the two cases. Two are of special importance in speculating on the future availability of federal courts as a sympathetic forum in non-race-related exclusion cases. First, a majority of the Court is unwilling to find in the Constitution judicial remedies for all maldistributions of income. In *Lindsey*, the Court finds no constitutional guarantee of dwellings of a particular quality.[27] In *Rodriguez*, the Court finds no constitutional demand that the spending levels for education must be equalized for all. Second, and of even greater importance, in response to concerns of federalism, a majority of the Court is unwilling to impose a single formula nationwide. This is most emphatic in *Rodriguez*, where the Court is quite disinclined to interfere with varying state approaches to the organization and financing of local government services, including education.[28]

State Court Responses.   If the foregoing establishes the probable unavailability of pervasive federal judicial intervention, the issue is

25. 405 U.S. 56 (1972).
26. 411 U.S. 1 (1973).
27. 405 U.S. at 74.
28. 411 U.S. at 40–44, 49–50.

left squarely with the state courts as to when, and to what extent, they will intervene. Only one state court system—New Jersey—has had extensive experience to date, although there have been some relevant cases elsewhere.[29] In 1960, Justice Hall of the New Jersey Supreme Court, in his famous dissent in *Vickers v. Gloucester Township*,[30] a case involving the total prohibition of mobile homes from a township with large areas of vacant land near the Philadelphia metropolitan area, argued that local legislation—which on analysis had little to justify it other than a desire to maintain the "character" of the township, to avoid service costs associated with lower cost housing, and to allow in as new residents only certain kinds of people—was invalid because it was antithetical to a proper definition of the "general welfare."

The Hall position rejected a strong exclusionary zoning tradition in New Jersey,[31] and eventually became that state's prevailing judicial view.[32] It has manifested itself in a number of cases in which a particular regulation or administrative action has come under attack. Thus, in *Molino v. Borough of Glassboro*,[33] the court, at the behest of a private developer, invalidated apartment regulations that significantly restricted multibedroom units and required expensive facilities such as swimming pools and air conditioning. In *DeSimone v. Greater Englewood Housing Corp. No. 1*,[34] the court, over objections of

29. The possibility that a trend may be developing along the lines of the New Jersey doctrine is illustrated by recent decisions in the highest courts of New York and Pennsylvania. Berenson v. Town of New Castle, 38 N.Y.2d 102, 341 N.E.2d 236 (1975) (validity of entire zoning ordinance excluding multifamily housing is dependent on whether it promotes "a balanced and integrated community" and considers "the needs of the *region* as well as the town for such housing"); Township of Willistown v. Chesterdale Farms, Inc., 341 A.2d 466 (1975) (zoning ordinance providing for apartment construction in only 80 of 11,589 acres in township is exclusionary in failing to provide a fair share of township acreage for apartment construction). Other jurisdictions have ruled against exclusionary zoning practices, but with a less advanced doctrinal rationale, including Connecticut, Illinois, Michigan, Rhode Island, and Virginia. *See, e.g.,* Kavanewsky v. Zoning Bd. of Appeals, 160 Conn. 397, 403-04, 279 A.2d 567, 571 (1971) (noncompliance with state statute); Lakeland Bluff, Inc. v. County of Will, 114 Ill. App. 2d 267, 274-75, 282, 252 N.E.2d 765, 768-69, 772 (1969); Tocco v. Atlas Tp., 55 Mich. App. 160, 166-67, 222 N.W.2d 264, 267-68 (1974); Town of Glocester v. Olivo's Mobile Home Court, Inc., 111 R.I. 120, 126-28, 300 A.2d 465, 469-70 (1973); Board of Supervisors v. Allman, 215 Va. 434, 446, 211 S.E.2d 48, 54-55 (1975); Board of County Supervisors v. Carper, 200 Va. 653, 662, 107 S.E.2d 390, 396-97 (1959). *And see* discussion of "exclusionary" cases in Chapter 2, *supra*.

30. 37 N.J. 232, 252, 181 A.2d 129, 140 (1960), *cert. denied*, 371 U.S. 233 (1963).

31. 3 Williams, *supra* note 3, at 5-6.

32. This history is traced in *id.*, at 16-18 *et seq.*

33. 116 N.J. Super. 195, 281 A.2d 401 (1971).

34. 56 N.J. 428, 267 A.2d 31 (1970).

neighbors in an attractive portion of town, upheld a variance for a multiple dwelling for displaced residents from an urban renewal area, in an opinion suggesting that the denial of a variance under the circumstances could not well be sustained under a proper interpretation of general welfare. In *Baskerville v. Town of Montclair*,[35] the court struck down a condition imposed upon rezoning that the resulting structures must be worth at least $35,000 on the ground that such a condition did not further the general welfare. In *Oakwood at Madison v. Township of Madison*,[36] the court struck down restrictions against large apartments and large-lot requirements.[37]

Analogous cases have been decided in Pennsylvania. These include, most importantly, *In Re Appeal of Kit-Mar Builders*,[38] invalidating two- and three-acre minimum-lot requirements, and *In Re Appeal of Girsch*,[39] holding invalid an ordinance totally prohibiting apartment houses within the jurisdication.[40]

In a New York case, *Berenson v. Town of New Castle*,[41] the plaintiff sought rezoning to permit multifamily housing. The state's highest court set out a test for determining whether a zoning ordinance may totally exclude multifamily housing that includes a consideration of the regional impact of the ordinance and the housing needs of those residing outside the zoning township.

All the foregoing cases involved particular projects. The recent New Jersey Supreme Court decision in *Southern Burlington NAACP v. Township of Mount Laurel*,[42] however, established, at least in New Jersey, the propriety of a much broader lawsuit—one testing the

35. Docket No. L-25287-68 (N.J. Super., Law Div. 1970), *aff'd*, No. A-1813-69 (App. Div. 1971), *cert. denied*, 58 N.J. 437 (1971).
36. 117 N.J. Super. 11, 283 A.2d 353 (Law Div. 1971), *aff'd*, —N.J.—, 371 A.2d 1192 (1977). *See* discussion of case in text accompanying notes 189-90 and 209-11 *infra*.
37. The case was remanded after the ordinance in question was changed during the pendency of the appeal. Again the ordinance was held invalid, 128 N.J. Super. 438, 320 A.2d 223 (Law Div. 1974), and the somewhat muddied basis of the original opinion was clarified. *See* Opinion of New Jersey Supreme Court, *supra* note 36, and 3 Williams, *supra* note 3, at 27-35.
38. 439 Pa. 466, 268 A.2d 765 (1970).
39. 437 Pa. 237, 263 A.2d 395 (1970).
40. Most of the New Jersey cases are squarely grounded on general welfare analysis—*i.e.*, that the ordinance provisions in question were inconsistent with a regional need for housing sites for low- and moderate-income families, among others. The Pennsylvania cases, however, required the concurrence of judges with distinctly different views. One group echoes the New Jersey type of analysis. The other premises invalidity on arbitrary interference with the property rights of the plaintiff landowners and developers. *See* discussion of these cases in Chapter 2 *supra*.
41. 38 N.Y.2d 102, 341 N.E.2d 236 (1975).
42. 67 N.J. 151, 336 A.2d 713 (1975), *appeal dismissed*, 96 S. Ct. 18 (1975).

validity of the entire system of land-use ordinances, plans, and policies of a local jurisdiction.

Plaintiffs representing resident and nonresident low-income persons attacked the township's system of land-use regulation on the ground that the system unlawfully excluded low- and moderate-income families from the municipality.[43] The court broadened the issue to include the effect of the regulation on various categories of persons (such as large, growing families not in the poverty class, but who still cannot afford relatively high-priced single-family dwelling or expensive apartments). It restricted its consideration to municipalities such as Mount Laurel—municipalities of sizable land areas outside central cities and older built-up suburbs which have shed rural characteristics, have recently undergone or are undergoing great population increase, are still not completely developed, and remain in the path of inevitable future growth.

Justice Hall, writing for a unanimous court, examined in detail the zoning ordinance and concluded that Mount Laurel "has exhibited economic discrimination in that the poor have been deprived of adequate housing."[44] The reason found for this was to keep down local taxes, and the township's policies were found to have disregarded the needs of people within the region. The court concluded that under New Jersey law a municipality like Mount Laurel "must, by its land use regulations, presumptively make realistically possible an appropriate variety and choice of housing. More specifically, presumptively it cannot foreclose the opportunity of the classes of people mentioned for low- and moderate-income housing and in its regulations must affirmatively afford that opportunity, at least to the extent of the municipality's fair share of the present and prospective regional need therefor."[45] The court rested this conclusion on the grounds that land-use regulations, to satisfy state constitutional requirements of due process and equal protection, must promote the general welfare; that when a municipality's regulations have a substantial external impact, the welfare of state citizens beyond its boundaries must be recognized and served; and that the proper provision of adequate housing for all categories of people is essential in promoting the general welfare.[46] This is satisfied by land-

43. A similar suit, it will be recalled, was dismissed by the federal courts on standing grounds. Warth v. Seldin, 422 U.S. 490 (1975).

44. 67 N.J. at 170, 336 A.2d at 723.

45. *Id.* at 174, 336 A.2d at 724.

46. *Id.* at 179, 336 A.2d at 727. A constitutional amendment to reverse or eliminate the basis for the *Mount Laurel* holding was introduced in the New Jersey Senate. The proposal would have amended art. IV, § VII, para. 11 of the New Jersey Constitution to authorize enactment and enforcement of zoning, planning, and land-use ordinances, otherwise valid, which may have the effect of

use regulations that provide reasonable opportunities for housing, including low- and moderate-cost housing. It is violated by regulations that thwart that opportunity.[47]

Detailed review of Mount Laurel's ordinances indicated failure to satisfy the standards enunciated, and the court was unpersuaded by the town's fiscal and environmental justifications to sustain them.[48] Finding that, in the absence of some authoritative regional planning agency, every municipality within a region[49] must bear its present and future fair share of the regional housing burden,[50] the court ordered Mount Laurel to quantify its fair share,[51] to translate this

---

limiting or restricting land use solely by reason of insufficient financial resources of an individual or group. 4 Hous. & Dev. Rep. 78 (June 28, 1976).

47. 67 N.J. at 179–80, 336 A.2d at 728.

48. 67 N.J., at 185–87, 336 A.2d at 730–31.

49. The composition of the applicable "region" will necessarily vary from situation to situation and probably no hard and fast rule will serve to furnish the answer in every case. Confinement to or within a certain county appears not to be realistic, but restriction within the boundaries of the state seems practical and advisable. (This is not to say that a developing municipality can ignore a demand for housing within its boundaries on the part of people who commute to work in another state.) Here we have already defined the region at present as "those portions of Camden, Burlington and Gloucester Counties within a semicircle having a radius of 20 miles or so from the heart of Camden City."

67 N.J. at 189–90, 336 A.2d at 733.

50. The concept of "fair share" is coming into more general use and, through the expertise of the municipal planning adviser, the county planning boards and the state planning agency, a reasonable figure for Mount Laurel can be determined, which can then be translated to the allocation of sufficient land therefor on the zoning map.

Id. at 190, 336 A.2d at 733. *See* discussion of fair share in Chapter 6, *supra.* *See also* the New Jersey Supreme Court's most recent view on the subject as expressed in Oakwood at Madison, Inc. v. Township of Madison, 117 N.J. Super. 11, 283 A.2d 353 (1971), aff'd —— N.J. ——, 371 A.2d 1192 (1977), and discussed in text accompanying notes 189–90 and 209–16, *infra.*

51. We have earlier stated that a developing municipality's obligation to afford the opportunity for decent and adequate low and moderate income housing extends at least to ". . . that municipality's fair share of the present and prospective regional need therefor." Some comment on that conclusion is in order at this point. Frequently it might be sounder to have more of such housing, like some specialized land uses, in one municipality in a region than in another, because of greater availability of suitable land, location of employment, accessibility of public transportation or some other significant reason. But, under present New Jersey legislation, zoning must be on an individual municipal basis, rather than regionally. So long as that situation persists under the present tax structure, or in the absence of some kind of binding agreement among all the municipalities of a region, we feel that every municipality therein must bear its fair share of the regional burden.

67 N.J. at 188–89, 336 A.2d at 732–33. In Oakwood at Madison, Inc. v. Township of Madison, 117 N.J. Super. 11, 283 A.2d 353 (1971), aff'd —— N.J. ——,

figure to the allocation of sufficient land to house this number, and to revise its zoning ordinances appropriately.

The Competency of Courts

The New Jersey court in *Mount Laurel* undertook what the United States Supreme Court eschewed in *Warth v. Seldin*[52] —it entertained an attack, on exclusionary grounds, against the entire system of land-use ordinances, plans, and policies of a jurisdiction. Thus, not only was it willing to deal with income-related barriers, but it also refused to limit the judicial role to one of testing the validity of a particular regulation applied to a particular proposed development. The latter factor is of considerable importance. A decree in such a suit, if it can be effectively implemented, results in systemic change that potentially benefits large numbers of people and not simply the immediate parties to the suit. Was this a proper choice of role? The answer to this question depends on the importance of the values at stake, the possibility of these values being vindicated without judicial intervention, and the ability of courts to deal competently and successfully with the conflicts at issue.

The values at issue are fundamental. They involve, among others, opportunities for decent living accommodations in more pleasant environments, freedom from law-imposed discrimination based on income (and income as a surrogate for race), and access to employment and educational opportunities. History indicates the unlikelihood that these values will be satisfactorily vindicated in the absence of judicial intervention. State legislatures have shown little willingness to fashion political structures that permit effective representation of the interests of nonresident regional population in land-use planning and regulatory decisions having to do with housing.[53] Rather, power has been vested, and remains, at the local level,[54] and

---

371 A.2d 1192 (1977), the New Jersey Supreme Court, in holding that the defendant municipality had failed to meet its regional housing needs, modified somewhat its earlier *Mount Laurel* view in finding that the defendant municipality need not specifically quantify its precise fair share with "formulaic" certainty unless municipal planning advisers deem such a numerical specification useful, 371 A.2d 1228 (1977). *See* discussion at text accompanying notes 189–90 and 209–16 *infra.*

52. 422 U.S. 490, 95 S. Ct. 2197 (1975).

53. *See* Heyman, *Legal Assaults on Municipal Land Use Regulation,* in Modernizing Urban Land Policy 153 (M. Clawson ed. 1973) [hereinafter cited as Heyman].

54. There have been some departures for the protection of physical environmental values, but successful regional or state intervention on behalf of excluded low-income persons has been rare. *Id.* The Massachusetts Zoning Appeals Law, 40B Mass. Gen. Laws Ann. § 20–23 (Supp. 1971), discussed in detail in Chapter 7 *infra,* is one such exception.

those adversely affected by parochial exclusionary decisions have little if any voice in their formulation and few effective political means to overturn them.[55]

The foregoing characterizations, as far as they are accepted, justify judicial intervention in behalf of those effectively disenfranchised to the degree that the courts are competent to handle resulting litigation successfully.[56] The question, thus, is whether a court can effectively entertain suits of the breadth involved in the *Mount Laurel* case. Professor Kurland, writing in 1968, suggested that the success of a fundamental decision based on equal protection considerations depends on the existence of at least two of three ingredients: that the constitutional standard is a simple one; that courts have adequate control over the means of effectuating enforcement; and that the public acquiesces in the principle and its application.[57]

There is much to be said for the Kurland formulation. Only the first two ingredients need be elaborated. A constitutional standard that seeks to balance a multiplicity of values yields results with little pervasive impact. Moreover, such a standard in an area requiring technical professional judgments—as in present-day land planning and regulation—rests on issues difficult to evaluate in an adversary context. Similarly, if no effective remedy can be fashioned to bring about the demanded outcome, the effort is largely pointless, and confidence in the judiciary—and thus the rule of law—is eroded.

At least the first two of Professor Kurland's ingredients seem satisfied by the *Mount Laurel* decision. The basic standard is that presumptively a municipality cannot foreclose the opportunity for low- and moderate-income housing, and in its regulations it must affirmatively afford that opportunity, at least to the extent of the municipality's fair share of the present and prospective regional need for such housing.[58] While, as the *Mount Laurel* court acknowledged,

55. Numerous federal programs have exacerbated the exclusionary problem. *See* National Commission on Urban Problems, Building the American City (1969); J. Stevens, Impact of Federal Legislation and Programs on Private Land in Urban and Metropolitan Development (1973).

56. Compare the reapportionment and school desegregation decisions collected and discussed in D. Bell, Racism in American Law (1973).

57. Kurland, *Equal Educational Opportunity: The Limits of Constitutional Jurisprudence Undefined*, 35 U. Chi. L. Rev. 53, 592 (1968).

58. 67 N.J. 151, 174, 336 A.2d 713, 724 (1975). *See* text at note 45 *supra.* The post-*Mount Laurel* decision of Oakwood at Madison, Inc. v. Township of Madison, 117 N.J. Super. 11, 283 A.2d 353 (1971), aff'd — N.J. —, 371 A.2d 1192 (1977), essentially reinforces the *Mount Laurel* regional fair-share standard, modifying it only to the extent of not requiring a "formulaic determination or numerical specification of such a fair share," but at the same time not precluding it (if the municipal planning advisors deem it useful." *Id.,* at 1228. *See* discussion of *Oakwood at Madison* at text accompanying notes 189–90 and 209–16 *infra.*

the definition of proper "region" is open to some debate, and estimations of present and prospective low- and moderate-income housing needs must be based on a respectable methodological approach, the standard is amenable to quantification and thus is in some respects analogous to the simple one-man–one-vote standard of the reapportionment cases. Similarly, if the courts so desire, acceptable methodologies do exist for translating the resulting numbers into dwelling units and thus, where necessary, into acreages. Moreover, as discussed in detail in Chapter 6, more sophisticated methodologies are available which can relate housing units to other important community concerns, such as employment opportunity, school capacity, public transportation, and other essential services.

None of the foregoing calculations is easy, and differing approaches are arguable, but professionally expert help is available to courts in making these judgments, and once the methodologies are chosen most of the outcomes follow relatively automatically. A judicial standard premised even on a relatively simple model—one that contemplates a relatively even distribution of low- and moderate-income housing throughout a region, without assessing other planning concerns—is not necessarily irrational.[59] First, such a standard does not compel such a distribution; it simply prohibits suburban localities from zoning out such a distribution should other incentives exist to bring it about. Second, such a standard is judicially administerable and does not invite deep judicial participation in sophisticated planning decisions, many of which are essentially political. Third, this approach invites an appropriate political response—the creation of a regional planning structure.

Considerable doubt has been expressed about the availability of effective judicial remedies to enforce the outcome of a *Mount Laurel* type of suit.[60] Curiously, many of the commentators have neglected to point out that the *Mount Laurel* court, recognizing that the remedy problems are by no means inconsequential, called upon the legislature to authorize some form of regional zoning as the preferred next step.[61] A substantial portion of the second part of this chapter

59. That the court in *Mount Laurel* had this model in mind is suggested by that passage in its opinion quoted in note 51 *supra. See also* Mass. Gen. Laws Ann. ch. 40B, §§ 20–23, discussed in Chapter 7 *infra.*

60. *See, e.g.,* Rose, *Exclusionary Zoning and Managed Growth: Some Unresolved Issues,* 6 Rut.-Cam. L.J. 689 (1975); Note, *The Inadequacy of Remedies in Cases of Exclusionary Zoning,* 74 Mich. L. Rev. 760 (1976). *But see* Ackerman, *The Mount Laurel Decision: Expanding the Boundaries of Zoning Reform,* 1976 U. Ill. L.F.1; Mytelka & Mytelka, *Exclusionary Zoning: A Consideration of Remedies,* 7 Seton Hall L. Rev. 1 (1976); Williams, *supra* note 3, at Addendum, ch. 66; Rubinowitz, *Exclusionary Zoning: A Wrong in Search of a Remedy,* 6 Mich. J.L. Ref. 625 (1973).

61. 67 N.J. at 191–92 n.22, 336 A.2d at 732–33. *And see* note 51 *supra.*

is devoted to the analysis of potential remedies. Despite the complexities, however, we conclude that courts can fashion effective remedies and thus help to bring about fundamental changes in metropolitan housing patterns.

We conclude that state courts have an important role to play in combating the exclusion of low- and moderate-income housing in the suburbs. Perhaps they should have a like role in assessing growth management plans in general. In this regard we note with approval a growing judicial trend to evaluate growth management regulations in the light of their impact on lower income housing.[62] We believe, however, that it is premature to address the broader question of judicial intervention in such cases.

At least three considerations lead us to this conclusion. First, normal market forces work in the interest of middle- and upper-income persons, and there is no persuasive showing to date that their needs will not be thus accommodated most readily in the absence of judicial intervention. Second, we cannot fashion simple standards upon which to premise effective and meaningful judicial intervention in cases beyond those involving low- and moderate-income housing. Third, judicial effort, in our view, should be concentrated where the deprivation is clearest. Perhaps repetitive litigation centered on the exclusion of low- and moderate-income housing will evolve principles transferable to growth management questions in general. But until that occurs, courts should avoid an involvement that is fraught with so many variables that the dangers of failure are greatly increased.[63]

JUDICIAL REMEDIES

The first part of this chapter discussed whether and under what circumstances courts should entertain challenges to exclusionary land-use regulations. This section discusses in much greater detail selected procedural obstacles and matters of remedy that are crucial to actual success in those cases where judicial intervention is warranted.

The complaints in exclusionary zoning challenges are roughly of

62. *See, e.g.,* Golden v. Planning Bd. of Ramapo, 285 N.E.2d 291, 334 N.Y.S.2d 138 (1972), *appeal dismissed,* 409 U.S. 1003 (1972); Construction Industry Ass'n v. City of Petaluma, 375 F. Supp. 574 (N.D. Cal. 1974), *rev'd,* 522 F.2d 799 (9th Cir. 1975), *cert. denied,* 424 U.S. 934 (1976).

63. For example, the right-to-travel standard employed by the district court in *Petaluma* (375 F. Supp. 574), while clear and "automatic," is too unsophisticated to be workable. If applied consistently, theoretically it could also invalidate any otherwise valid land-use regulation that increases construction costs.

two kinds. In one (for example in *Dailey v. City of Lawton*)[64] the plaintiff has an interest in particular land, and the legal action seeks a judicial order compelling the defendant to permit its development for low- or moderate-income housing. In the other, the suit challenges the validity of an entire scheme of land-use ordinances and policies. The plaintiff may be a landowner, an affected resident or nonresident, a developer, or an organization (usually representing a class of excluded individuals). The defendant may be a single city, as in *Southern Burlington County NAACP v. Township of Mount Laurel*,[65] or a number of cities within a region, as in the suit against 23 towns in Middlesex County, New Jersey.[66] The latter type of suit, while more difficult to attempt, if successful, can benefit the entire class of low- or moderate-income residents of the town or region, not merely future residents of a particular site, and thus is the major focus of attention below.

While it may be that the standard for determining whether the defendant has acted illegally by imposing exclusionary regulation is the same whether the lawsuit relates to a specific parcel or challenges an entire regulatory scheme, the complexity both of staging the lawsuit and constructing a remedy is so great in the latter instance that the distinction deserves emphasis. The discussion below will include cases concerning both land-use regulations, and public housing authorities and redevelopment agencies. While the obligations of a municipality may be different when a public agency rather than a private builder is involved, the latter cases cope with remedy problems that are similar to those in the regulatory instances.

Cases Involving Specific Parcels of Land

Selected Procedural Matters.

Standing. Standing to sue doctrine offers no problems of access to court when the plaintiff owns the subject land. This is true even in the federal courts under the restrictive doctrine of *Warth v. Seldin*,[67]

---

64. 425 F.2d 1037 (10th Cir. 1970).
65. 67 N.J. 151, 336 A.2d 713 (1975), *appeal dismissed*, 96 S. Ct. 18 (1975).
66. Urban League v. Carteret, 142 N.J. Super. 11, 359 A.2d 526 (1976).
67. 422 U.S. 490 (1975). The plaintiff can successfully allege an "injury in fact," and seek to protect an interest "arguably within the zone of interests to be protected or regulated by the statute or constitutional guarantee in question." *See* Ass'n of Data Processing Service Org. v. Camp, 397 U.S. 150 (1970); Barlow v. Collins, 397 U.S. 159 (1970). Courts also consider that an option-holder has sufficient interest to sustain "an injury in fact." *See* SASSO v. City of Union City, 424 F.2d 291 (9th Cir. 1970); Ybarra v. City of Los Altos Hills, 503 F.2d 250 (9th Cir. 1974).

discussed earlier in this chapter. However, restrictive federal standing doctrine, if followed by state courts, might make certain arguments unavailable to the plaintiff. In the recent *Petaluma* case,[68] the Ninth Circuit Court of Appeals refused to entertain the argument of an association of building contractors and two landowners that a growth-control plan denied the poor the right to travel and settle within the municipality of Petaluma, a ground found decisive by the lower court. The appellate court held that the plaintiffs had no standing to raise this argument in behalf of third parties, although they were competent to challenge the plan (unsuccessfully) on due process grounds and as a burden on interstate commerce.

Joinder of Parties. Site-specific cases do not involve multiple government defendants, although there may be a class of potential renters of the proposed housing for the site represented by the plaintiff. Class actions for such purposes seem to present no serious problems, at least under the Federal Rules of Civil Procedure.[69]

Burden of Proof. Practically every case involving a specific proposed project involves a refusal to rezone, or the denial of an administrative permit (for example, a special-use permit or a variance). It has been traditional to treat the refusal to rezone as legislative action and the denial of a permit as a quasi-judicial action. It has also been traditional in both instances to treat government action as presumptively valid, with the plaintiff having the burden of proving the contrary. This burden is especially heavy if the action is treated as legislative. Thus, under the usual rules, a developer of low- or moderate-income housing who has been denied rezoning is hard put to obtain judicial reversal unless irrational discrimination is proved.

Cases involving race, however, are treated differently. If racial discrimination is patent or if the plaintiff establishes a racial purpose to the action, the burden shifts to the defendant municipality. Then the action can be sustained only on the basis that it serves a compelling state interest, a test normally impossible to satisfy.[70]

68. Construction Industry Ass'n v. City of Petaluma, 522 F.2d 897 (9th Cir. 1975), *cert. denied,* 424 U.S. 934 (1976).

69. Prerequisites to a class action, Fed. R. Civ. P. 23, are that (1) the class is so numerous that joinder of all members is impracticable; (2) there are questions of law or fact common to the class; (3) the claims or defenses of the representative parties are typical of those of the class; and (4) the representative parties will fairly and adequately protect the interests of the class. *See* Dailey v. Lawton, 425 F.2d 1037 (1970).

70. *E.g.,* Kennedy Park Homes Ass.n v. City of Lackawanna, 436 F.2d 108 (2d Cir. 1970); Dailey v. City of Lawton, 425 F.2d 1037 (10th Cir. 1970).

However, in two recent cases the U.S. Supreme Court has ruled that disproportionate racial impact alone, without proof of discriminatory racial purpose, does not violate the Equal Protection Clause and thus does not shift the burden of proof to the defendant municipality to justify its action on the basis of a compelling public interest. In the first of the two cases, *Washington v. Davis,*[71] the Court upheld the validity of an employment test for municipal police department applicants, despite empirical findings that a disproportionate number of racial minority applicants failed the examination.

The second case, *Village of Arlington Heights v. Metropolitan Housing Development Corporation,*[72] followed the rule announced in *Washington v. Davis, supra.* The case concerned the refusal of Arlington Heights to make a zone change sought by plaintiffs to permit construction of multifamily subsidized housing under the Section 236 program. The Chicago-area suburb of over 60,000 was virtually all white, and the impact of the denial to rezone fell more heavily on blacks seeking residence within Arlington Heights than on whites. Nevertheless, while acknowledging this discriminatory effect of the local action, it was upheld by the Court because no discriminatory purpose had been proved.

The Supreme Court thus greatly has narrowed the test of whether a municipality's laws or official practices violate the Equal Protection Clause, and such practices thus must be justified by a compelling public interest to avoid being invalidated. However, these decisions relate only to constitutional challenges. This leaves open the question of whether the "effects test" is still valid to shift the burden of proof to defendants where a statutory violation is alleged. Although the Constitution, according to *Washington v. Davis,* is not violated when a law is passed which, neutral on its face, affects a greater proportion of one race than another,[73] a statute may be passed by Congress enlarging minority rights. While the Constitution may not give minorities the right to require more of a government than that it not

---

71. 426 U.S. 229, 96 S. Ct. 2040 (1976). In a concurring opinion in Washington v. Davis, Mr. Justice Stevens reserved his opinion on the merits of the cases disapproved by the Court (*see* note 9 *supra*), and cautioned that "the line between discriminatory purpose and discriminatory impact is not nearly as bright, and perhaps not quite as critical, as the reader of the Court's opinion might assume." *Id.* at 2054. Justice Stevens voted to sustain the test in question "on a ground narrower than the Court describes." *Id.* For an astute analysis of the implications of the *Davis* case, concluding, inter alia, that the disproportionate impact doctrine can continue to play a useful role in antidiscrimination litigation, *see* Brest, *The Supreme Court, 1975 Term, Forward: In Defense of the Antidiscrimination Principle,* 90 Harv. L. Rev. 1 (1976). *See also* discussion of *Washington v. Davis* in Chapter 2 *supra.*

72. 97 S. Ct. 555 (1977).

73. 426 U.S. 229, 242 (1976).

deliberately discriminate, Congress has passed statutes requiring, for example, that affirmative efforts to promote fair housing be made by all federal departments and agencies,[74] and providing that local laws permitting discriminatory housing practices are invalid.[75] The distinction between constitutional and statutory grounds of complaint is noted by the Court in its opinion in *Washington.*[76]

Resident Advisory Board v. Frank L. Rizzo,[77] a post-*Washington* district court case, maintains the use of the effect test by ruling that the affirmative action requirements of Title VIII and its legislative history require that proof of a racially discriminatory impact is sufficient to shift the burden of proof to the defendant government. In this case, the adverse impact stemmed from termination of a proposed public housing project by city agencies. In addition, the court found intentional discrimination, establishing a constitutional violation within the confines of the *Washington* decision, in the conclusion that the officials must have known that the consequences of their actions would impact adversely on the black community.[78]

Also, one pre-*Washington* case not included in the list of decisions disapproved in that case, *United States v. City of Black Jack,*[79] relied expressly on the effects test to find a violation of Title VIII. In *Black Jack* the court found that the defendant municipality had violated Title VIII in adopting a zoning ordinance that precluded approval of a proposed multifamily Section 236 housing project. While racial motivation might have been established, the court rejected it as a basis for its holding, and relied exclusively on the adverse impact of the action on black people living in the metropolitan area.

Thus, in cases demonstrating statutory violations, the effects test may remain a viable tool for making out a *prima facie* case to shift the burden of proof to the defendant. In the absence of some racial linkage, no federal case involving housing has shifted the burden of proof to the municipality where discrimination is established simply on the basis of wealth. The compelling state interest analysis is triggered only when two criteria have been met.[80] A desired benefit must be lost because of the "impecunity" of the class discriminated against, and the class must sustain "an absolute deprivation of a

74. Title VIII (Fair Housing) of the 1968 Civil Rights Act, 42 U.S.C. § 3601 *et seq.,* § 3608.
75. 42 U.S.C. § 3615.
76. 426 U.S. 229, 238–39, 248. *See also* Brest, *supra* note 71, at 22–26.
77. 425 F. Supp. 987 (E.D. Pa. 1976).
78. *Id.*
79. 508 F.2d 1179 (8th Cir. 1974), *cert. denied,* 422 U.S. 1042 (1975).
80. San Antonio School District v. Rodriguez, 411 U.S. 1 (1973) (inequalities in school financing).

meaningful opportunity to enjoy that benefit."[81] Thus, in *Ybarra v. City of the Town of Los Altos Hills*,[82] the plaintiffs failed to show "an absolute deprivation" since they could not show that adequate low-cost housing could not be obtained elsewhere in the county.

There are state cases to the contrary, of course. The New Jersey and Pennsylvania cases discussed earlier can be viewed as instances in which the burden of showing a compelling state interest is shifted to the municipality once discrimination on the basis of income is established. A recent Oregon case involving burden of proof, *Fasano v. Board of County Commissioners*,[83] might create difficulties for proponents of low-income housing. There the county had rezoned a large parcel to permit a mobile home park. The court treated the rezoning as an administrative action, thus removing from the case the presumption of validity attending a legislative action. Further, the court determined under Oregon law that the one seeking a change from established regulation had the burden of showing consistency with a prestated comprehensive plan. Thus the burden in the judicial hearing was on the developer and not on the plaintiffs, who were objecting neighbors. In the course of the opinion, the court stated

> The more drastic the change, the greater will be the burden of showing that it is in conformance with the comprehensive plan as implemented by the ordinance, that there is a public need for the kind of change in question, and that the need is best met by the proposal under consideration. As the degree of change increases, the burden of showing that the potential impact upon the area in question was carefully considered and weighed will also increase.[84]

This will entail, the court states, an explanation of why the change should take place in the particular location sought if other areas elsewhere are already zoned for the use.

The burden of proof noted in *Fasano* could substantially deter developers seeking to construct higher density low-income housing over the objections of neighbors, despite the willingness of local governments to approve the project. The development involved in *Fasano* in fact was low-cost housing. The zoning change sought was the location of a "floating zone" planned-unit development, authorized by the text of the zoning ordinance but not located on the map until approval of an application. Densities permitted in the under-

81. *Id.* at 20.
82. 503 F.2d 250 (9th Cir. 1974).
83. 264 Ore. 574, 507 P.2d 23 (1973).
84. 507 P2d. at 28, 29.

lying single-family zone were about the same as under the planned-unit development category. Therefore, the proposed change was not a large one.

The "problem" of *Fasano* can be obviated by a comprehensive plan that discusses low- and moderate-income housing, thus providing a solid referent for rezoning or a special permit that allows such a project to occur. The housing assistance plan (HAP), required by the Housing and Community Development Act of 1974 in order to qualify for a community development block grant, is an example of such a low-cost housing plan.[85] In the absence of such a plan, however, a "mischievous" result might obtain, as arguably occurred in the *Fasano* case.

Scope of Judicial Review in Cases Involving Specific Parcels. As the prior discussion indicates, it is commonplace to say that when local action amounts to the granting or denial of a change in applicable zoning, the scope of review is narrow because the action in question is legislative. Similarly, it is traditional to treat the granting or denial of permits by local administrative bodies as quasi-judicial, with judicial review of a somewhat broader, but still limited, scope. The *Fasano* case suggests that both types of action might be subject to deep judicial review in any instance where a change is permitted.[86] Low-cost housing projects often require an *ad hoc* change from underlying zoning regulation. Thus it is useful to examine the scope of review normally afforded such actions, be they quasi-judicial or legislative.

Quasi-Judicial Decisions. As stated above, if the local action is treated as administrative, judicial review typically is limited to whether there has been an abuse of discretion, or to a review of the evidence to determine whether it supports the findings made by the local agency. In practice, review is usually narrow, because courts apply both a presumption that findings were made and that they were supported by sufficient evidence. Thus, actions on special exceptions and variances by zoning administrators, zoning boards of adjustment, planning commissions, and by other agencies on such matters as construction permits and utility hookups, can be difficult to attack in court.

The relative unavailability of a judicial forum, however, might be changing. In this regard recent California decisions are of interest. A

85. 42 U.S.C. § 5304(a)(4) (1975 Supp.). *See also* discussion of housing plans in Chapters 5 & 6 *infra*.

86. Narrowly read, the *Fasano* rule is similar to the Maryland rule on zoning changes, discussed in Chapter 5 *infra*.

California statute provides for a mandamus proceeding to test "adjudicatory decisions" of administrative agencies.[87] Heretofore the scope of review was quite limited, as indicated above. Two 1974 California Supreme Court decisions, however, now require a more active role for the court in such proceedings. In *Strumsky v. San Diego County Employers Ass'n*,[88] the court applied to local agencies the rule as to scope of review that had been applicable to agencies with a statewide jurisdiction. "If the order or decision substantially affects a fundamental vested right, the court, in determining under § 1094.5 of the Code of Civil Procedure whether there has been an abuse of discretion because the findings are not supported by the evidence, must exercise its independent judgment on the evidence and find an abuse of discretion if the findings are not supported by the weight of evidence."[89] This weight of the evidence test requires the court to determine much more than whether the findings are supported by substantial evidence in light of the whole record.

The second case of importance is *Topanga Association for a Scenic Community v. County of Los Angeles*,[90] which involved the grant of a zoning variance to permit construction of a mobile home park. While the court found that the variance grant did not affect a vested right, it nevertheless required the reviewing court to "scrutinize the record and determine whether substantial evidence supports the administrative agency's findings and whether these findings support the agency's decision."[91] The administrative agency must "render findings sufficient both to enable the parties to determine whether and on what basis they should seek review and, in the event of review, to apprise a reviewing court of the basis for the board's action." Still to be decided is whether the denial of an exception or a variance affects a vested right. But whether or not it does, as the *Topanga* case makes clear, judicial inquiry into land-related "administrative decisions" is destined to be deeper than it has been before.

Rezoning.   As previously stated, courts generally have considered both zoning and rezoning to be legislative acts with only limited judicial review available. *Fasano*, of course, questions this where rezoning involves a specific proposal for development. It is not unlikely that, under one doctrine or another, other courts will rule similarly. It thus seems likely that the state judiciary is about to enter

87. Code Civ. Proc. § 1094.5.
88. 11 Cal. 3d 28, 112 Cal. Rptr. 308, 530 P.2d 29 (1974).
89. 112 Cal. Rptr. 805, 816.
90. 11 Cal. 3d 506, 113 Cal. Rptr. 836 (1974).
91. 11 Cal. 3d 506, 514, 113 Cal. Rptr. 840.

areas previously considered beyond their scope. As courts consider planning and zoning problems, they will gain an expertise and familiarity that will facilitate their active participation in exclusionary zoning cases.

Remedies. We are dealing here with instances involving proposed housing developments on specific parcels of land. For purposes of this section, we assume that the proposed development has been vetoed—that requisite permits (special exception, rezoning, building permit, and so on) have not been issued. We further assume that the local action has been improper and thus the plaintiff has an actionable cause. The question treated here is what judicial remedies are, or ought to be, available to vindicate the plaintiff's rights? The "best" solution from the plaintiff's viewpoint is a court order requiring that necessary actions be taken by the regulating government to permit the construction of the development; in other words, judicial rezoning of the parcel in question or judicial issuance of the administrative permit. But such relief raises serious questions. Should the court supersede the regulating authority? Or should it return the matter to the local government agencies with a direction to rezone or reconsider the denial of the permit under what the court conceives to be the proper standard?

In some cases the answer is clear. There are some instances where the plaintiff's case is based on one or more grounds that would lead a court to compel the issuance of development permission. If, for instance, the plaintiff showed that the development was thwarted for discriminatory reasons (for instance, that like development for white residents would have been approved), presumably the plaintiff would obtain direct relief, as in *Kennedy Park Home Ass'n v. City of Lackawanna*[92] and *United Farm Workers of Florida Housing Project v. City of Delray Beach.*[93] But the situation is not necessarily the same where the complaint is founded on a broader argument, such as the failure of the defendant jurisdiction to allow under its regulatory ordinance for a fair share of the regional housing need,[94] or the complete exclusion of apartment houses.[95] Plaintiffs' success in establishing such grounds for the suit does not necessarily mean that a court should order that plaintiffs must be allowed to devote

92. 436 F.2d 108 (2d Cir. 1970), *cert. denied,* 401 U.S. 1010 (1971).
93. 493 F.2d 799 (5th Cir. 1974).
94. *Cf.* Southern Burlington NAACP v. Township of Mount Laurel, 67 N.J. 151, 336 A.2d 713 (1975), *appeal dismissed,* 96 S. Ct. 18 (1975); Oakwood at Madison, Inc. v. Township of Madison, 117 N.J. Super. 11, 283 A.2d 353 (1971), aff'd — N.J. —, 371 A.2d 1192 (1977).
95. *E.g., In re* Appeal of Girsh, 437 Pa. 237, 263 A.2d 395 (1970).

the particular parcel of land involved in the suit to the otherwise proscribed use.[96]

The issue in question is not new. In scores of prior cases plaintiffs have established to the satisfaction of a court that a particular regulation is impermissible as applied to the land involved in the suit. The usual judicial response is to give declaratory and injunctive relief, but, by means of stay, to give the defendant jurisdiction a reasonable opportunity to adopt new regulations that would not be impermissible under the rule announced in the case. The basis for this approach is well exemplified in the recent statement of a New Jersey court in a fair share case:

> In holding the zoning ordinance under review invalid it must be noted that the court is not directing the municipality to rezone the plaintiff's property for multifamily use. While the experts who testified on both sides were in general agreement that the subject premises would be suitable for this type of land use and development, it is not the province of the court to specify zoning densities or to exercise any other control at this juncture over the manner in which the township must meet its obligation to provide for multifamily or rental-type housing within its borders.[97]

This approach, of course, can lead to extraordinary delay and frustration of the project. In *In re Appeal of Girsh*,[98] for instance, the Pennsylvania Supreme Court held that an ordinance making no provision for apartments (in this case luxury apartments) unconstitutionally prevented free entry into the township. While the township did rezone to create an apartment district, it did not include plaintiff's land within it, and Girsh's transferee had to come back to the

96. The potential difficulties of a plaintiff landowner in a fair-share suit are substantial. In the absence of a prior decision or an authoritative regional planning analysis, plaintiff must establish what the fair share is and how the defendant falls short. This can be a considerable burden (see text on remedies, *infra*). This burden can be minimized if the town has permitted *no* multifamily low-cost housing. In such case it will not be able to raise the defense that it is already permitting "enough," *i.e.*, its fair share of the regional need. Unless the proposed construction would provide a very large number of units—so many that it might exceed a hypothetical fair share—there would be no need to make the calculation for the first suit and the defendant city or county undoubtedly would bear the burden of establishing the existence of a sufficient amount of low-cost housing within its jursidiction as a defense. *Cf.* Zelvin v. Zoning of Appeals, 306 A.2d 151 (Conn. 1973), in which the court sustained a ban on further apartments in the town partly on the basis that 1,500 garden apartments, representing 19 percent of the total dwelling units, had been built in the prior fourteen-month period.

97. Pascack Association, Ltd. v. Township of Washington, 131 N.J. Super. 195, 329 A.2d 89, 91 (Law Div. 1974), *rev'd. on other grounds*, Docket No. A-3790-72 (App. Div. 1975), *cert. granted*, —— N.J.—— (1975).

98. 437 Pa. 237, 263 A.2d 395 (1970).

court again to obtain the building permit, after withstanding an effort by the township to condemn the land. After a five-year delay (1967–1972), conditions in the area rendered the proposed project unfeasible. This type of experience perhaps led the Pennsylvania court in a later case to affirm a lower court decision ordering that a building permit be granted to plaintiff to allow the construction of an apartment project.[99] Similarly, the Michigan Supreme Court has held that a court may give permission for construction which it finds to be "reasonable under all the circumstances," regardless of the existing zoning.[100]

Illinois courts have ordered defendant municipalities to permit the requested use where it has been concluded that the zoning regulation in question is invalid as applied.[101] This approach has been criticized on at least two grounds: (1) courts thereby exercise legislative and administrative functions; and (2) courts unfamiliar with the technical aspects of zoning regulation thereby render unwise decisions. The contrasting policy considerations are evident. On the one

99. Township of Willistown v. Chesterdale Farms, Inc., 462 Pa. 445, 341 A.2d 466 (1975). *See also* Casey v. Zoning Hearing Bd. 303 A.2d 535 (Pa. 1973). In this case the plaintiff sought a building permit to construct, by its own description, middle- to high-income apartments in a township whose zoning ordinance zoned only a token amount of land for apartments. The court held that the ordinance did not allow a fair share of housing and was exclusionary and invalid under its decision in *Girsh*. It therefore ruled that the plaintiff was entitled to a building permit as of right, and in order to bypass the delay in *Girsh*, granted the plaintiff the necessary building permit "to complete its apartment complex as planned." *Id.* at 537 Pennsylvania's Municipal Planning Code, Act 247 of 1968, *as amended by* Act 93 of 1972, 53 Purdon's Pa. Stat. Ann. 10101 *ff.*, authorizes a court to order approval of the "described development or use" if a constituional challenge succeeds as to a specific parcel.

100. Sabo v. Monroe Tp., 394 Mich. 458, 221 N.W.2d 303, 536–37 (1975).

101. The courts in Illinois have ordered municipalities to permit the requested use, in order to avoid the city's response of simply rezoning to a slightly less restrictive classification, yet too restrictive to permit plaintiff's development in that location. *See* Sinclair Pipe Line Co. v. Richton Park, 167 N.E.2d 406 (1968); Hartman, *Beyond Invalidation: The Judicial Power to Zone*, 9 Urb. L. Ann. 159 (1975) [hereinafter cited as Hartman]; and text accompanying note 104 *infra*. Similarly, Florida courts have shifted from enjoining enforcement of any classification more restrictive than that requested by the plaintiff, to directing rezoning in accordance with the landowner's request. Burritt v. Harris, 172 So. 2d 820 (Fla. 1965); City of Miami Beach v. Weiss, 217 So. 2d 836 (Fla. 1969); Davis V. Situs, Inc., 275 So. 2d 600 (Fla. Dist. Ct. App. 1973). In Virginia, the court enjoined the local government from "taking any action which would disallow the one use shown by the record to be unreasonable, subject to council's right under its charter to amend a permit ordinance and impose reasonable conditions not inconsistent with such use." City of Richmond v. Randall, 215 Va. 506, 211 S.E.2d 56 (1975); Board of Supervisors v. Allman, 215 Va. 434, 211 S.E.2d 48 (1975); and many other cases cited in Hartman, *supra*. These cases did not involve attacks on zoning as exclusionary; rather, the courts found that the existing restrictions were arbitrary and unreasonable as applied *to those particular sites.*

hand, judicial licensing of plaintiff's project at the location sought and in accordance with the plaintiff's design, solely on the grounds that the defendant's ordinance precludes reception of a fair share of regional needs, might result in an exceedingly unwise decision. The location, for instance, could be ill-suited to low-income housing needs if it were remote from public transportation, schools, or shopping areas. Plaintiff's parcel may be far removed from existing development, or be located on ecologically fragile (floodplain, steep slopes) or environmentally valuable (marsh or coastal zone) land.[102] On the other hand, the remedy of "remanding" for local reconsideration can be tantamount to no relief if the local government adamantly opposes such projects.[103]

There can be no wise or doctrinaire answer to this conflict. However, the procedure adopted by the Illinois courts exemplifies one possible resolution of the difficulty. Illinois trial courts are permitted to make two distinct but consistent determinations in these cases. First, the court decides whether or not the existing zoning classification is valid as applied to the plaintiff's property. If the court invalidates the zoning, the plaintiff, under the Illinois decisions, still has the burden of proving to the court that the proposed use is reasonable and in the best interest of the public and the community.[104] Note that the property owner also has the burden of proving the suitability of the site for the proposed housing under the *Fasano* rule discussed above.[105] Presumably, issues related to the suitability of the subject site for more intensive development, and availability of alternative locations for the proposed housing, would be included in the burden of proof the plaintiff must sustain. Depending on the outcome of the trial, the court might then decide to order the municipality to permit the plaintiff to proceed with the specific use contemplated during the trial.

102. *See, e.g.,* the dissent of Judge Fairchild in Metropolitan Housing Dev. v. Village of Arlington Heights, 517 F.2d 409 (7tn Cir. 1975), *rev'd,* 97 S. Ct. 555 (1977), in which he agrees with the majority as to the need for low-cost housing in the village, but points out that nine other suitable vacant sites exist in Arlington Heights, already zoned for such construction.

103. *See In re* Appeal of Girsch, 437 Pa. 237, 263 A.2d 395 (1970). In Kennedy Park Homes Ass'n v. City of Lackawanna, 436 F.2d 108 (2d Cir. 1970), the court, upon finding intentional racial discrimination, sought to insure that the defendant would interpose no further obstacles by enjoining the city from interfering with construction of the subdivision and ordering it to take affirmative steps necessary to allow construction to begin. Nevertheless, construction was barely begun on a few homes by 1975, and plaintiffs have had to resort to the court for continuing assistance in combatting obstructions imposed by the city. Telephone conversations with Michael Davidson and Will Gibson, attorneys for plaintiffs, Sept. 1975.

104. First National City Bank of Skokie v. Village of Morton Grove, 299 N.E.2d 570, 575 (Ill. App. 1973).

105. *See* text accompanying notes 83 and 84, *supra.*

This approach avoids two consequences of leaving the property unzoned that are considered undesirable by the Illinois Supreme Court.[106] Not only does it avoid further delay to the plaintiff, as mentioned above, if the city chooses to rezone to a less restrictive classification that still obstructs the use sought by the plaintiff, but it avoids unforeseen difficulties that could be created by the plaintiff. If the court broadly rezoned the subject property, as opposed to ordering only the specific use which induced the court to invalidate the former zoning, the property owner might thereafter put the property to a use entirely different from the one depicted in a favorable light during the trial.[107]

It should be noted that under both the Illinois and *Fasano* procedures, the plaintiff retains the burden of showing that development should be permitted on a particular site even after the existing zoning has been invalidated. However, once a court has determined that existing zoning or a permit denial has the effect of excluding a town's fair share of regional low-cost housing, it could be argued that the burden then shifts to the defendant government to justify denial of the subject low-cost housing development application. While such an approach was recently overruled by the Michigan Supreme Court,[108] no fair share allocation formula was employed by that court as a standard to establish the defendant's housing obligations.[109] Whether the court adopts the Illinois procedure, or rezones the property, or merely remands with limited directives to the locality, could depend on such factors as whether the local government authorities have been and are cooperative or obstructionist,[110] as well as the complexity and scale of the proposed project. Moreover, in appropriate cases the court can appoint independent planning consultants to advise on the wisdom of utilizing the particular parcel sought for such use by the plaintiff, as was done in *Pascack v. Washington Township.*[111]

The New Jersey Supreme Court recently weighed the pros and cons of the issues discussed herein, and it resolved them in a fashion

106. Sinclair Pipe Line Co. v. Richton Park, 19 Ill. 2d 370, 378, 167 N.E.2d 406, 411 (1960).

107. *Id.*

108. Kropf v. City of Sterling Heights, 391 Mich. 139, 215 N.W.2d 179 (1974).

109. *See* discussion accompanying notes 157–61 & 251 *infra*, regarding latitude that should be accorded a defendant government to deny low-cost housing development permission under a zoning ordinance prepared pursuant to a court order following invalidation of an exclusionary regulation.

110. *See* SASSO v. City of Union City, 424 F.2d 291 (9th Cir. 1970), 357 F. Supp. 1188 (N.D. Cal. 1970).

111. 329 A.2d 89 (N.J. 1974). In that case court-appointed consultants made such a recommendation and the court ordered the township to issue the plaintiff a building permit upon proper application.

not dissimiliar from the Illinois courts' approach. In *Oakwood at Madison v. Township of Madison*,[112] the court directed that, subject to stated conditions, the trial court allow the issue of a building permit to the plaintiff developer. The court's decision was based not on any confiscatory challenges made to existing zoning, but on the fact that plaintiff had borne the expense of the public-interest litigation for six years, and the court sought to provide continuing incentives for such socially beneficial activity. Safeguards against two of the dangers discussed above that have troubled the courts were imposed. The court directed that issuance of development permission be subject to two conditions: (1) the trial court must insure that the permit issued be only for the project as planned and proposed during the litigation, guaranteeing allocation of at least 20 percent of the units to low- or moderate-income families; and (2) the trial court must first determine whether the subject land is environmentally suited to the proposed development.[113]

The discussion above assumes that plaintiff has been frustrated by a local unwillingness to rezone a parcel to permit the desired development. The judicial dilemma is eased considerably, however, if the defendant government's ordinances provide for multifamily housing by such techniques as floating zones, special exceptions, or conditional uses. If the criteria for such special permissions are at all clear, the grant or denial is of a quasi-judicial nature, which is more comfortably subject to judicial review, and to a court order allowing the development if the court finds the criteria satisfied.

Two further points deserve mention. First, whether or not the court decides to rezone the parcel in question or to grant the special permit, it is crucial that jurisdiction be retained and the parties be instructed to follow a particular schedule, with reports back to the court. Such a process short-circuits the considerable delays that would be encountered if a new suit were necessary to test the alleged obstructionism. Second, it is particularly important that the initial judicial order be as precise as possible so that defendant is under a realistic threat of contempt for disobedience.

Cases Involving the Exclusionary Effects of Systems of Land Use Regulation

Types of Cases That Can Be Brought. The section immediately preceding dealt with lawsuits that concerned a particular parcel of land. We now turn to broader suits, where systems of plans and

112. Oakwood at Madison, Inc. v. Township of Madison, 117 N.J. Super. 11, 283 A.2d 353 (1971), aff'd —— N.J. ——, 371 A.2d 1192, 1226–1227.
    113. *Id.* at 1226.

ordinances of one or more local jurisdictions are attacked, often by plaintiffs who are not the owners of any of the land in question. The substantive principles in these suits often will be the same as those involved in cases where the litigation centers on a particular parcel. For instance, where state law permits, the gravamen of the complaint might be that the plans and regulations under attack preclude reception of a fair share of the region's low- and moderate-income residents. Suits of the breadth envisaged, however, are discussed separately because they raise much more complex procedural and remedial problems than ones centering on particular parcels of land.

A few examples suffice to illustrate the types of cases involved here. One is a suit by a representative plaintiff against a single municipality complaining that the defendant's plans and ordinances do not make adequate provision for that municipality's low-income residents.[114] Another is litigation brought by an organization representing affected individuals against a single municipality complaining that the defendant's plans and ordinances exclude a fair share of the region's poor.[115] A third is a similar suit that includes a number of municipalities within a region.[116] A fourth example is a suit by a representative plaintiff against federal or state agencies seeking discontinuance of subsidies to local jurisdictions that allegedly have exclusionary land-use regulations that are improper.[117] Suits of this nature, as indicated, can raise difficult issues of standing and joinder, as well as complex remedial problems.

Selected Procedural Matters.

Standing. We are dealing in the main here with cases where the plaintiff (or others represented by the plaintiff) has no interest in land or projects in the defendant municipality and thus can show no direct relationship between the alleged exclusionary pattern of land plans or regulations of the defendant, and the thwarting of the plaintiff's housing choices.

As discussed in the first part of this chapter, the United States

114. *Cf.* SASSO v. City of Union City, 357 F. Supp. 1188 (N.D. Cal.), 424 F.2d 291 (9th Cir. 1970).

115. *Cf.* Southern Burlington County NAACP v. Township of Mount Laurel, 67 N.J. 151, 336 A.2d 713 (1975), *appeal dismissed,* 96 S. Ct. 18 (1975).

116. *Cf.* Urban League v. Carteret, 142 N.J. Super. 11, 359 A.2d 526 (1976); Commonwealth of Pa. v. County of Buck, 302 A.2d 897 (Pa. Commwlth. Ct. 1973).

117. *Cf.* City of Hartford v. Hills, 408 F. Supp. (D.Conn. 1976) *rev'd sub nom.* City of Hartford v. Town of Glastonbury, —F.2d.— (2d. Cir., Aug. 15, 1977) *(en banc).*

Supreme Court in *Warth v. Seldin*[118] concluded that such a plaintiff had no standing to bring a constitutional challenge against such plans and regulations in the federal courts. This decision does not necessarily mean that the federal courts are unavailable in related cases where standing can be premised on federal statute.

In *Evans v. Hills*[119] the Second Circuit Court of Appeals reversed a previous decision *en banc*, and held that nonresident ghetto dwellers did not have standing to challenge the provision of federal sewer and recreation subsidies to a town within the county in which they dwelled. The plaintiffs alleged that the federal agencies involved had failed to perform affirmative duties to combat restrictive land-use controls that resulted in discriminatory land-use patterns. Applying *Warth*, the court held that the plaintiffs failed to demonstrate a close causal relationship between the town's regulations and their injury. The court also refused to recognize the plaintiffs' interests within the scope of the 1964 and 1968 Civil Rights Acts.

State courts, of course, need not find the *Warth* reasoning persuasive on the standing issue. The New Jersey court rejected it in the *Mount Laurel* case, finding that nonresidents of the township who lived in the region and who were in need of standard housing were appropriate plaintiffs.[120] The basic issue, as discussed previously,[121] is whether it '. appropriate for state courts to become involved with such problems. Respectable precedent exists for determining that nonresident plaintiffs suffer sufficient injury,[122] the fair share concept establishes a manageable standard, and, as discussed below,[123] feasible and effective remedies are available. The ultimate determination, then, should be based on a state court's perception of the importance of the values at stake and the possibility of their vindication without judicial intervention.[124] In our view, this should

118. 422 U.S. 490 (1975).

119. 536 F.2d 571 (2d Cir. 1976). *See also* Planning for People Coalition v. County of DuPage, 70 F.R.D. 38 N.D. Ill. 1976 which distinguished *Warth* on other grounds; Cornelius v. City of Parma, 374 F. Supp. 730 (N.D. Ohio 1974), *aff'd*, 521 F.2d 1401 (6th Cir. 1975), *cert. denied* 424 U.S. 955 (1976). (plaintiffs denied standing to challenge local zoning as exclusionary and violative of the Fair Housing Act of 1968, 42 U.S.C. § 3601).

120. 67 N.J. 151, 159, 336 A.2d 713, 717 n.3 (1975). The court cited N.J.S.A. 40:55-47.1 and Walker v. Borough of Stanhope, 23 N.J. 657, 130 A.2d 372 (1957) in support of this. *See also* Crescent Park Tenants Ass'n v. Realty Equities Corp., 58 N.J. 98, 101 (1971), which cites the *Stanhope* case; Urban League v. Mayor & Council of Carteret, 142 N.J. Super. 11, 359 A.2d 526 (1976); and Jaffe, Judicial Control of Administrative Action 542–43 (1965) for the proposition that "[t]he New Jersey cases have historically taken a much more liberal approach on the issue of standing than have the federal cases."

121. See text accompanying notes 52 to 62, *supra*.

122. *Cf.* United States v. SCRAP, 412 U.S. 669 (1973).

123. *See* discussion of remedies in text following notes 165 *et seq.*, *infra*.

124. *See* text accompanying notes 53–56, *supra*.

lead a state court to assume jurisdiction at the behest of nonresident plaintiffs (or organizations representing them). Federal court unwillingness to assume such a role should not be dispositive, because it is based in large part on considerations of federalism, which are not appropriate for state court cognizance.[125]

Joinder of Parties. Suits seeking the invalidation of exclusionary regulations and adoption of inclusionary policies seldom involve only a single plaintiff and defendant. The primary advantage of joining multiple plaintiffs, as in *Mount Laurel*,[126] is to facilitate pursuit of more than one theory of relief, thereby increasing the probability of success. If standing prerequisites are met, there are no other serious joinder problems on the plaintiff's side.

This section primarily concerns joinder of multiple defendants, for example, all the municipalities in the region which are allegedly enforcing exclusionary ordinances and policies. There are two primary advantages for plaintiffs in joining a number of defendants. First, joinder enlarges the reach and impact of the remedy, allowing the court to compel production of a regionwide housing allocation plan. Second, joinder saves expense and time for the plaintiff by avoiding multiple lawsuits where the same issues will be relitigated.

Urban League of Greater New Brunswick v. Mayor and Council of the Borough of Carteret[127] involved a class-action suit by five persons and an organization, who sued individually and as representatives of others similarly situated. Defendants who were joined were twenty-three of the twenty-five municipalities in the county whose zoning ordinances were attacked as unconstitutionally exclusionary. During the course of the trial, one municipality was granted an outright dismissal, and eleven were granted dismissals conditional upon their adoption of court-approved amendments so that their zoning ordinances would permit approval of more low-cost housing. Plaintiffs charged that the zoning ordinances of the defendant municipalities did not afford the opportunity for accommodating regional low-cost housing needs. The court did not discuss the propriety of the joinder of the multiple defendants.

Joinder rules differ from state to state. Many states, however, have rules that are reflected in the provisions of Rules 19 and 20 of the

---

125. *See* Brennan, *State Constitutions and the Protection of Individual Rights,* 90 Harv. L. Rev. 489 (1977); discussion in Chapter 2, *supra,* in text accompanying notes 37–39.

126. Southern Burlington County NAACP v. Township of Mount Laurel, 67 N.J. 151, 336 A.2d 713 (1975), *appeal dismissed,* 96 S. Ct. 18 (1975).

127. 142 N.J. Super. 11, 359 A.2d 526 (1976).

Federal Rules of Civil Procedure.[128] Rule 19 provides for compulsory joinder of certain parties where feasible. Rule 20 provides for permissive joinder. Only Rule 19 is examined here because, ironically, the permissive joinder rules are inapposite.[129]

Rule 19[130] requires joinder in a number of instances. Most relevant is the provision for joinder if "complete relief cannot be accorded among those already parties." The rule distinguishes between parties who are indispensable to the action (those parties in whose absence the litigation must be dismissed) and parties whose presence is merely desirable.[131] In the type of litigation under discussion, plaintiffs will rarely argue that the defendants are indispensable, but rather that their presence is desirable for a just adjudication.[132]

Repetitive judicial determinations stress that "pragmatic considerations are to be controlling" in interpreting the rule,[133] that "the rule should be employed to promote the full adjudication of disputes with a minimum of litigation effort,[134] that "although a court technically may not bind absent persons or those who are not in privity with the actual parties, the non-party's claim or defense may be impaired as a practical matter,"[135] and that "the real purpose of this rule is to bring before the court all persons whose joinder would be desirable for a just adjudication of the action."[136]

128. For example, in California, Cal. Code Civ. Proc. § 389 is virtually identical with Rule 19, as is § 379, insofar as it concerns defendants, with Rule 20.

129. Rule 20 provides for permissive joinder of a proper party when the right to relief arises out of the same transaction or occurrence. Because exclusionary zoning ordinances are adopted independently by each individual municipality, it is difficult to establish that the wrong (and thus the relief) arises out of the same transaction or occurrence. *See* Fair Housing Development Fund Corp. v. Burke, 55 F.R.D. 414 (E.D.N.Y. 1972).

130. Rule 19(a) provides in relevant part:

A person . . . shall be joined as a party in the action if (1) in his absence complete relief cannot be accorded among those already parties, or (2) he claims an interest relating to the subject of the action and is so situated that the disposition of the action in his absence may (i) as a practical matter impair or impede his ability to protect that interest or (ii) leave any of the persons already parties subject to a substantial risk of incurring double, multiple, or otherwise inconsistent obligations by reason of his claimed interest. . . .

131. Factors to be considered by the court in making the determination of indispensability are contained in Rule 19(b).

132. It is very doubtful, for reasons explicated *infra*, that additional municipalities would be considered indispensable within the meaning of Rule 19(a) without whose presence the suit could not proceed. This is important because some of the defendants might be able to object successfully to joinder on venue grounds.

133. 7 Wright & Miller, Federal Practice and Procedure 14 (1972).

134. *Id.* at 18.

135. *Id.* at 21.

136. *Id.* at 32.

As stated, the basis for joinder under Rule 19 (or a similar state rule) most applicable here is that unless the defendants in question are parties, complete relief cannot be accorded to the plaintiffs. The relief sought in exclusionary zoning cases involves both the invalidation of existing ordinances and the production by defendants of ordinances providing for a fair share of regional low-cost housing need. In the course of such litigation, the court must judge the adequacy of the defendants' plans and the number of housing units determined by each town to be its share of the regional need. One judge, in a concurring opinion, has advocated that joinder of all municipalities in the region be undertaken after judgment is entered against the defendant municipality and, if necessary, on the court's own motion, in order to allocate housing needs equitably and to avoid conflicting decisions in cases involving other communities in the region.[137] As elsewhere discussed,[138] the fair share determination can be based on a number of general methods.

The regional low-cost housing need can be distributed evenly among jurisdictions on some basis, such as existing land area. Or more sophisticated approaches can be used by taking account of a variety of planning considerations (such as employment, existence of public services, tax bases, or environmental limitations) in allotting the additional housing units among the jurisdictions. In either case, the plaintiffs and those defendants already before the court have a vital interest in joining all the municipalities in the region in the suit.

To illustrate, assume that the more simple method of calculating fair share is used (that is, a neutral mathematical division), and that in the future a second suit is brought against the absent regional municipalities. The numerical obligation in the later suit may turn out to be either higher or lower than in the original suit. If it is higher, the plaintiffs in the initial suit will insist that the number of housing units determined to be a fair share in the first suit was inadequate. If the number in the second suit is lower than in the first, the defendant in the first suit will be required to fulfill greater obligations than have been imposed on other regional municipalities.[139]

137. Oakwood at Madison, Inc. v. Township of Madison, 117 N.J. Super. 11, 283 A.2d 353 (1971), aff'd — N.J. —, 371 A.2d 1192 (1977), (Pashman, J., concurring and dissenting).

138. *See* text at notes 217 to 219, *infra; see gen.* Chapter 6 *infra.*

139. The other basis of joinder under Rule 19(a)(2)—see note 130 *supra*—might also be applicable. A fair-share methodology seeks to assign numbers on a uniform basis among multiple jurisdictions within a region. Assuming that the gross number is established, the portion of the whole assigned to one jurisdiction is dependent on the protions assigned to the other jurisdictions. Unless all of the jurisdictions are joined in a single suit, it is possible that one or more of the jurisdictions will be treated "unfairly" inter se, in successive suits. This is what both (i) and (ii) of Rule 19(a)(2) seek to guard against.

If more sophisticated, planning-oriented methodologies are used, there is even more reason for joining all municipalities in the region in the formulation of a plan, since each municipality undoubtedly will be assigned a different proportion of the total housing need. Authoritative regional planning cannot be undertaken at all unless all affected municipalities can participate.[140]

Arguments along the lines suggested above were unsuccessful in a federal district court in *Fair Housing Development Fund v. Burke.*[141] The suit was initially brought against the Town of Oyster Bay, New York, challenging the constitutionality of its zoning ordinance. One year later, plaintiffs sought to add as parties defendant twelve incorporated villages within the geographic boundaries of the town. Under New York law, the incorporated villages had zoning authority within their boundaries, and Oyster Bay had such authority in the unincorporated areas but no jurisdiction over lands within the villages. While stressing that the court "is bound by 'practical rather than rigid legalistic considerations'" in deciding joinder motions under Rule 19, and that "[t]he primary consideration . . . is whether any judgment that might be rendered will be adequate in the absence of the parties sought to be joined,"[142] joinder was denied because "[t]he Town and the villages are distinct, independent governmental entities, completely autonomous in their zoning powers, and any relief determined to be proper can be adequately fashioned with respect to the present defendant, the Town."[143] This led the court to conclude that there were no compelling reasons for joinder.

Plaintiffs' argument, which was rejected, was that discovery had shown that the villages and the town were "socially, economically, and otherwise interrelated into a functional whole and their policies collectively contribute to the overall pattern of racial segregation which prevails within the geographic boundaries of the Town."[144] Given this, plaintiffs contended, joinder is necessary because "if the equitable relief desired is to be meaningful, it will require court ordered cooperation between all governmental units within the Town's geographic boundaries."[145]

Whether the reasoning of the *Burke* case applies to a fair share suit of the sort discussed in this chapter depends on the precise remedies sought by plaintiffs in *Burke*. There is no suggestion in the opinion that a fair share remedy was being proposed. All that is mentioned is

140. *See* text accompanying note 137 *supra.*
141. 55 F.R.D. 414 (E.D.N.Y. 1972).
142. *Id.* at 418.
143. *Id.* at 418-19. The court thus only considered Rule 19(a)(1). Plaintiffs made no claim under 19(a)(2). *Id.* at 417 n.4.
144. *Id.* at 417.
145. *Id.*

a prayer for declaratory and injunctive relief and court ordered cooperation among all governmental units within the town's geographic boundaries. But as submitted above,[146] it is the quantification required by fair share analysis, together with the interdependency of the numbers assigned to the multiple jurisdictions within a regional area, upon which a Rule 19 joinder analysis is premised. Hence it is doubtful that the *Burke* case militates against a joinder result.[147]

Support for joinder under Rule 19 type provisions is found in *Bradley v. School Board of City of Richmond, Virginia,*[148] a school desegregation case. There, both plaintiffs and the defendant school board sought joinder of the school boards of the two counties adjacent to the city of Richmond, as well as the state board of education.[149] Joinder was ordered under 19(a)(1) over the objections of

146. *See* text accompanying notes 136–38 *supra.*

147. In Commonwealth of Pa. v. County of Bucks, 302 A.2d 897 (Pa. Commwth. Ct. 1973), plaintiff sought equitable relief against all 54 local municipalities in Bucks County, as well as the county itself. The complaint was dismissed, (but not for misjoinder), on the grounds that plaintiffs lacked standing, sought an advisory opinion, and would involve the court in a legislative matter. Most of the court's opinion addresses matters discussed in the first section of this chapter. *See* text at note 127, *supra.* Twenty-three towns in Middlesex County, N.J. were successfully joined as defendants. The court was asked to require the towns, "individually and collectively, to take reasonable steps to correct past discriminatory conduct by preparing and implementing a joint plan to facilitate racially and economically integrated housing. . . ." Complaint of Plaintiffs, Urban League v. Carteret, 142 N.J. Super. 11, 359 A.2d 526 (1976).

148. 338 F. Supp. 582 (E.D. Va. 1971), 51 F.R.D. 139 (E.D. Va. 1970), *rev'd on other grounds,* 462 F.2d 1058 (4th Cir. 1971), *aff'd by an equally divided court,* 412 U.S. 92 (1972).

149. The court's decision to join the state as a defendant was based on evidence of actual overall control of the school system by the state, state participation in causing the racial imbalance, and state action based on an agency theory, since the local units were acting as agents of the state. This holding was reversed by the court of appeals, 462 F.2d 1058 (4th Cir. 1972), on the ground that there was insufficient evidence of state participation. As one writer warns: "The court's disregard of the evidence presented, and its subsequent conclusion that the racial imbalance was caused mainly by a variety of unknown forces only peripherally related to state action, is indicative of the extremely high threshold level the court required for a determination of state action." Note, 58 Iowa L. Rev. 342 (1972). It should be noted that the *Bradley* case involved race discrimination, that an affirmative obligation to desegregate schools had already been well established by the U.S. Supreme Court, and that the district court had found evidence of overt invidious state action in a 200-page opinion largely devoted to this issue. If joinder of the state were sought in a case of wealth discrimination rather than racial discrimination, affirmative state obligations would be more difficult to establish. If the only theory to support a finding of state action was that local jurisdictions had acted as agents of the state in controlling land use, it might be impossible. A neutral act, such as establishment of local property taxes in a manner that has forced each locality to seek high "ratables," could be said to have the foreseeable effect of discouraging low-cost housing and thus might provide a stronger argument for joinder of the state, particularly if the forum were a state rather than federal court.

the adjacent counties on the ground that a potential judicially ordered remedy in the case, in order to give complete relief, was the creation of a unitary school system in the three districts which would permit racial balancing substantially impossible in Richmond alone. This was reversed on appeal[150] on the ground that no cause of action lay against the school boards of the adjacent counties because they were not alleged to have practiced de jure segregation or to have committed any acts that were related to de jure segregation in Richmond.[151] Had such allegations been possible, however, presumably joinder, as ordered by the district court, would have been upheld.

Such allegations—namely that de facto segregation in the suburbs perpetuates segregated housing in the central city in violation of the constitutional rights of central city residents are at the heart of the fair share housing suits under discussion in this chapter. State courts that have recognized an obligation on the part of suburbs to accommodate regional low-income housing needs thus find no objection to the joining of several suburbs as defendants in such a suit.

The U.S. Supreme Court, however, has found only limited authority in the Constitution to open up metropolitan educational or housing opportunities to racial minorities suffering discrimination within central cities. Two key decisions define the extent to which suburban governments may be required to participate in federal court remedies imposed for constitutional violations which have occurred entirely within the central city. These cases thus bear on the discussion of joinder of parties in this section.

In *Milliken v. Bradley*,[152] the Detroit Board of Education was found guilty of de jure racial segregation in its schools. After this finding was made, the district court announced that it would consider as a remedy the implementation of a multidistrict, metropolitan-area plan. Intervention by the suburban districts was then permitted, but only to advise the court of the propriety of such a remedy and to review preferred plans. Thereafter the court rejected arguments that the remedy was improper unless the suburban districts had committed violations, and adopted a metropolitan busing plan. On review, the U.S. Supreme Court reversed. It equated the scope of permissible remedy with the constitutional wrong. Finding that it was not unconstitutional to maintain separate school districts within a metropolitan area that had different racial balances, and that only Detroit has been found guilty of de jure segregation, it held that the remedy had to be restricted to Detroit. Restructuring of school districts on a

150. *See* note 148 *supra.*
151. *See* Milliken v. Bradley, 418 U.S. 717, (1974).
152. 418 U.S. 717 (1974).

metropolitanwide basis might be possible, but only involving suburban districts formed for discriminatory purposes or pursuing discriminatory activities related to Detroit.

The extent to which a federal court may impose an interdistrict remedy was further defined in the recent case of *Hills v. Gautreaux*,[153] where the U.S. Supreme Court restated and clarified its ruling in *Milliken*. The Court in *Gautreaux* stated that *Milliken* had not ruled out a metropolitan-area desegregation order whenever there had been no commensurate constitutional violation by the suburbs, but only that such an order may not restructure the operation of these local and state governmental entities:

> Nothing in the *Milliken* decision suggests a *per se* rule that federal courts lack authority to order parties found to have violated the Constitution to undertake remedial efforts beyond the municipal boundaries of the city where the violation occurred.[154]

In *Gautreaux* the Court accepted the plaintiffs' view that relief against HUD was not "interdistrict" but confined within the unitary housing market area that is the normal locus of HUD operations, and that this area was not confined to the central city. The way was thus opened for such a housing market areawide remedy to be imposed on remand to the trial court in the *Gautreaux* case.[155] That case involved the unconstitutional practices of the Chicago Housing Authority and HUD with respect to the location of public housing projects in Chicago. The Supreme Court also held that the federal district court could order the Chicago Housing Authority to seek to take remedial action outside the city limits (also within the area of its jurisdiction), since such an order would not necessarily interfere with local government operations because suburbs not implicated in the adjudicated violation would retain their statutory right to object to the imposition of publicly funded housing within their borders.[156] Furthermore, the suburbs have no obligation affirmatively to seek federal grants to meet those needs.

153. 425 U.S. 284 (1976).

154. 425 U.S. 284.

155. *See also* Rubinowitz & Dennis, *School Desegregation Versus Public Housing Desegregation: The Local School District and the Metropolitan Housing District*, 10 Urb. L. Ann. 145 (1975).

156. However, their Housing Assistance Plans in order to be approved by HUD for community development block grants, would have to reflect housing needs of the inner-city low-income residents "expected to reside" within their borders, including, presumably, those likely to seek such housing as a result of the court order. *But see* City of Hartford v. Hills, 408 F. Supp. 889 (D. Conn. 1976) *rev'd sub nom.* City of Hartford v. Town of Glastonbury, —F.2d— (2d. Cir. Aug. 15, 1977) *(en banc)*.

Burden of Proof. There are two aspects of burden of proof—the burden of going forward and the burden of persuasion. Plaintiff in a fair share suit has the burden of going forward. Plaintiff must produce evidence that at a minimum shows that defendant's ordinances thwart the location within the municipality of a fair share of the region's low- and moderate-income residential needs. This burden can be difficult to satisfy if, for instance, the local jurisdiction uses agricultural or low-density districts as "holding zones" that it is willing to rezone for more intensive residential uses upon proper application,[157] or if the zoning ordinance utilizes flexible regulatory techniques of which the exercise is largely unpredictable.[158]

In the *Mount Laurel* case, for instance, the plaintiff's burden of going forward was easy. The ordinance permitted no multifamily housing, except the limited amount designed for affluent small families permitted under a subsequently repealed planned-unit development ordinance. Restrictive minimum lot area, lot frontage, and building size requirements precluded single-family housing, except for middle- and high-income families. An overly large percentage of land was zoned for industry, removing it from residential use.

But more difficult cases can be envisaged where the ordinance in question permits a considerable amount of low- and moderate-income housing, and the question then is whether the amount is "enough."[159] Once plaintiff has established the facts over defendant's rebuttal—that is, the region, the needs in question, the numbers assigned to defendant, and ultimately the failure of defendant's ordinances to accommodate the assigned number[160]—clearly the burden of persuasion shifts to the defendant to justify its shortfall. And as suggested in *Mount Laurel*, the burden "is a heavy one."[161] The technique is similar to that employed in cases involving suspect classifications or the deprivation of a fundamental interest.[162]

In the *Madison Township* case,[163] the court emphasized that it did not regard it as mandatory for defendant municipalities "to devise specific formulae for estimating their precise fair share of the lower income housing needs of a specifically demarcated region. Nor do we

157. Wait-and-see zoning can be used as an inclusionary device as well as for exclusionary purposes. *See* R. Babcock & F. Bosselman, Exclusionary Zoning, Land Use Regulation and Housing in the 1970s (1973); and Chapter 4 *infra*.

158. *See* discussion in text accompanying notes 226 *et seq., infra*.

159. *Cf.* Zelvin v. Zoning Bd. 306 A.2d 151 (1973).

160. All of these factors are explored in detail in the section on Remedies, *infra*.

161. 336 A.2d 713, 728 (1975).

162. *See* discussion of equal protection in Chapter 2 *supra*.

163. 117 N.J. Super. 11, 283 A.2d 353 (1971), aff'd —— N.J. ——, 371 A.2d 1192 (1977).

conceive it as necessary for a trial court to make findings of that nature in a contested case."[164] Rather, concern should be directed toward the *substance* of the ordinance and the *bona fide* efforts toward minimizing defendant's exclusionary regulations.[165]

Scope of Judicial Review. In the prior section dealing with cases involving specific parcels of land, the questions addressed concerned the intensity with which courts should review local legislative and administrative decisions denying permission for the development of a low- or moderate-income housing project on a particular parcel of land. The question is how intensively should courts involve themselves in the review of systems of land-use planning and regulation employed by municipalities? This question raises all the issues addressed in the first section of this chapter—the role of the courts in the management of urban growth and the protection of low- and moderate-income persons against exclusionary practices of suburban municipalities—and need not be reiterated here.

Remedies. In this section it is assumed that a court has invalidated all or portions of the zoning ordinance of a defendant government because its regulations preclude entry of any, or a fair share of, low-income persons. What are the remedies available to a court for restructuring the ordinances to assure that they do not obstruct such entry? And further, are there judicious means at hand to prompt localities to foster the production of low-income housing? The task of fashioning effective remedies is burdened with twin difficulties: (1) the assembly of data and the design of a regional housing allocation plan to rectify present deficiencies; and (2) the skillful employment of various techniques to deter reluctant defendants from stalling and obstructing the necessary changes. Experience has shown considerable difficulties in solving the latter problem.

Constructing a remedy in an exclusionary zoning case is a complex process in which the court compels the defendant government to amend its ordinances, to change its policies and practices, and to allow low-cost housing within its borders. There is no single court order that can accomplish all these steps, as is often the situation in public housing and relocation cases. In the latter, relief usually involves fewer political issues than are encountered in mandating a town plan that will include low-income (usually multifamily) housing. But substantial local resistance to court orders in public housing and relocation cases has often been encountered; thus the methods

---

164. *Id.*, at 1220.
165. *Id.*, at 1220.

used by courts to induce compliance in such situations provide useful precedents for exclusionary zoning cases.

Other cases of relevance include those involving school desegregation and legislative reapportionment, where courts have compelled local governments, in highly political contexts, to change detailed existing administrative and legislative arrangements to accord with a constitutional norm. Most of the discussion that follows involves remedies designed to require local governments to make possible the opportunity for the location and construction of low-cost housing. This is followed by a brief discussion of potential court orders requiring towns to foster affirmatively the production of low-cost housing.

Affording the Opportunity for Low-Income Housing. There are a number of stages in the process by which a court compels changes in plans and ordinances to afford the opportunity for low-income housing in a jurisdiction. They can be conveniently grouped under two headings: (1) the court orders resulting in the plan; and (2) continuing jurisdiction to compel compliance with the orders. The court orders in these cases will require that the defendant town (or towns) produce a plan found by the court to be adequate to permit a proper amount of low-cost housing. A court-appointed consultant or special master may be useful in judging the adequacy of the plans that are produced and monitoring compliance. During all stages of the process, the court must stand ready to amend its orders as new information or circumstances are brought to its attention, and to monitor and require the defendants to comply. The following discussion includes recommendations designed to optimize the achievements at each stage and, ultimately, the final result.

Initially, the court must decide who should prepare the new zoning provisions and policies, the court or the defendant government. The local legislature is better suited to this task than a court, and there should be compelling reasons to alter these traditional roles.[166] One such reason would be substantial intransigency by the town, for whatever reasons, to proceed in a timely and reasonable manner. Courts in the reapportionment and school desegregation cases, even

---

166. This view—that courts ordinarily should not be making the political decisions involved in land-use planning and regulation even if it is necessary to engage consultants to assist the local government—seems widely shared even by those who have assisted courts in fashioning such plans. Telephone conversation with Professor Melvin Levin, Department of Urban Planning, Rutgers University, Sept. 5, 1975. Professor Levin was an advisor to the court in drafting amendments to allow multifamily housing in a defendant municipality in the *Pascack* case.

when faced with initial inaction on the part of defendant governments, have been hesitant to enter the political arena by fashioning plans in the first instance. In neither arena has a court written a plan for a local government until the local government has failed to exercise the opportunity to do so or has acted in bad faith.[167]

It should be noted, however, that neither the court nor the local government is necessarily starting with a clean slate in writing such a plan. The Housing and Community Development Act of 1974 requires preparation of a HAP by all applicants for community development block grants.[168] The plan must reflect the low-income housing needs of those residing in, or "expected to reside" in the community.[169] Since regional needs are thus a required consideration, such a plan could serve as the basis for the fair share housing plan ordered by the court. Furthermore, regional housing allocation plans are already in existence in some metropolitan regions. At a minimum, such a plan would allot low-cost housing goals to the defendant community, but might also contain minimum standards for the location and size of housing units.

In most instances, the parties should be required to submit proposed court orders, on notice, and they should be evaluated at a hearing. Such orders might cover the procedures to be utilized in fashioning a new plan or, at the other extreme, the new plan itself. In many instances, of course, there will be a series of orders related to steps in the planning process culminating in a final order sanctioning a particular plan. For example, in *Gautreaux v. Chicago*

---

167. Whether a court draws up a plan by itself, with a special master or blue-ribbon commission, or insists that the local government replan, depends in great part on the good faith demonstrated by the local government. Do minority members serve on the local governing body, on the planning commission, or other authoritative posts? Is there any multifamily low-cost housing in the town at all? How has the city dealt with past attempts to integrate housing and how long has it been since the present attempt was begun? What is suggested by evidence of public sentiment? *See, e.g.,* Southern Alameda Spanish Speaking Organization v. City of Union City, 357 F. Supp. 1188, 1190 (N.D. Cal. 1970) (where Mexican-, Spanish-, Portuguese-, and Japanese-Americans held all the seats on the city council and were a majority of the planning commission and park and recreation commission). It is to be expected that courts in most forthcoming exclusionary zoning cases will decide to order the local jurisdiction to prepare a plan, but will review it for adequacy and monitor the town's responses to secure compliance.

168. 42 U.S.C. § 5304(a)(4) (1975 Supp.).

169. *Id.* Elements that must be contained in the Housing Assistance Plan are a survey of the housing stock of the community, an assessment of its housing needs, a goal for the provision of assisted housing, and a description of the location of existing and proposed low-income housing. These provisions seem to follow closely the requirements for developing a housing plan ordered by the lower court in the *Mount Laurel* case.

Housing Authority,[170] Judge Austin requested the parties to formulate plans for new site-section and tenant-assignment procedures to remedy constitutional infirmities. If agreement between the parties proved impossible, they were each ordered to submit a proposed judgment order.[171]

In *Garrett v. Hamtramck,*[172] the court also ordered the parties to submit proposed programs. The comprehensive and detailed proposal of the plaintiff was accepted almost verbatim by the court. Consultant reports, if any, should also be circulated to the parties for comment prior to hearing, as in *Pascack v. Washington Township.*[173] The principal advantage of these procedures is to give the parties an opportunity to challenge opponents' proposals prior to and during hearings, and to provide an opportunity for detailed analysis before the final formulation of the order in question. Moreover, such procedures provide the opportunity for any further fact-finding necessary for the formulation of the order. Finally, the pre-order hearing can be used to test the feasibility of possible attainable remedies.

There are presently very few court orders requiring that defendant governments amend their zoning ordinances to permit low-cost housing.[174] Most exclusionary zoning cases concern the denial of a specific proposal, and not the rewriting of local regulations. Certain features of carefully drawn court orders in public housing and relocation cases, however, serve as useful examples. The defendants in these cases were required to submit plans in response to court orders, though not land-use plans and zoning ordinances.

It can safely be assumed that the defendant will often be uncooperative, if not intractable. Since the process of producing an adequate housing plan will take time, it is important that necessary court orders remain flexible and capable of being modified or supplemented

170. 304 F. Supp. 736 (N.D. Ill. 1969), *aff'd*, 436 F.2d 366 (7th Cir. 1970), *cert. denied*, 402 U.S. 922 (1971).

171. The response from Chicago Housing Authority was only minimal, and the court relied heavily on the proposal from the plaintiff, written in consultation with Professor Philip Hauser of the University of Chicago. Conversation with A. Polikoff, attorney for plaintiffs, Sept. 10, 1975.

172. 335 F. Supp. 16 (E.D. Mich. 1971) (plan ordered), 357 F. Supp. 925 (E.D. Mich. 1973), *aff'd in part*, 503 F.2d 1236 (6th Cir. 1974), *amended in part*, 394 F. Supp. 1151 (E.D. Mich. 1975).

173. 131 N.J. Super. 195, 329 A.2d 89 (L. Div. 1974), *rev'd on other grounds*, Nos. A-3790-72, A-1841-73 (N.J. Super. Ct., App. Div., June 25, 1975), *cert. granted*, No. 11754 (N.J. Oct. 14, 1975).

174. *But see* Southern Burlington County NAACP v. Township of Mount Laurel, 67 N.J. 151, 336 A.2d 713 (1975); Oakwood at Madison, Inc. v. Township of Madison, 320 A.2d 223 (N.J. 1974) *aff'd*, —— N.J. ——, 371 A.2d 1192; Pascack Ass'n, Ltd. v. Washington Tp., 329 A.2d 89 (N.J. 1974) Nos. A-3790-72, A-1841-73 (N.J. Super. Ct. App. Div., June 25, 1975); Urban League v. Carteret, 142 N.J. Super. 11, 359 A.2d 526 (1976).

as circumstances require. It is interesting to note that the court in *Gautreaux v. Chicago Housing Authority*[175] visualized its original judgment order only as a starting guideline for the preparation of a final plan, and encouraged the parties to propose amendments as experience would subsequently suggest.[176] While there were five subsequent orders in the months following, these were simply technical modifications of the original provisions. The defendant did not make the most of its opportunity to propose serious changes.[177]

Court orders should be written with sufficient specificity so that the defendant knows exactly what it is expected to do, and so the court can judge whether there has been compliance or default. In *Gautreaux v. Chicago Housing Authority*[178] the first order sought to prevent further construction or leasing of public housing in predominantly black neighborhoods in Chicago. The court required that the next 700 units of public housing and 75 percent of all units thereafter be located in white neighborhoods, and included a number of detailed additional limitations. This order, and the one that followed it a year later (requiring that proposals for 1,500 sites be submitted to the city council within two months)[179] are good examples of orders that are definite and precise, and thus facilitate the job of monitoring for compliance. (This order should be contrasted with the later decisions in the *Gautreaux* litigation in the Seventh Circuit Court of Appeals and the U.S. Supreme Court, mandating a general "metropolitan area remedy.")[180]

In *Garrett v. Hamtramck*[181] the trial court issued an order so detailed and complete that it is reminiscent of an agency manual of regulations. The case dealt with Hamtramck's obligation to furnish relocation housing for those displaced by urban renewal projects. The city was required to locate the displaced residents, determine how many would like to return, and then provide low-cost housing and assistance to relocatees in resettling in Hamtramck. The order setting forth the relocation procedures on an instructive step-by-step basis was more likely to promote the desired result, than if numerous decisions as to how to proceed to satisfy the general requirements of the decision were left to the local government. The

175. 304 F. Supp. 736 (N.D. Ill. 1969).
176. 304 F. Supp. 736, 741 (N.D. Ill. 1969).
177. Conversation with plaintiff's attorney, A. Polikoff, Sept. 10, 1975.
178. 304 F. Supp. 736 (N.D. Ill. 1969). *See* Appendix A *infra* for a summary of the court's orders and appeals.
179. 342 F. Supp. 828 (N.D. Ill. 1970).
180. *See* Appendix A *infra*.
181. 335 F. Supp. 16 (E.D. Mich. 1971) (plan ordered), 357 F. Supp. 925 (E.D. Mich. 1973), *aff'd in part*, 503 F.2d 1236 (6th Cir. 1974), *amended in part*, June 4, 1975, 394 F. Supp. 1151 (E.D. Mich. 1975).

detailed order permitted the defendant to know what it should be doing at each step, and provided the court with a good basis to determine whether there had been compliance. In this extreme example, the court chose detail, rather than flexibility, in its attempt to force a seemingly obstinate defendant city government to change.

A school desegregation case, *Morgan v. Kerrigan et al.,*[182] concerned the formulation of a plan to integrate the Boston public schools. In an effort to compel the defendant Boston School Committee to prepare a satisfactory plan, the court prescribed the general contents and set the standards for a plan to be filed by the defendant, specified dates for filing progress and final reports, and required that the school committee approve the plan before its submission to the court.

In other cases, court orders have been issued which lack specificity. In *Crow v. Brown*[183] the court required that the defendant compile and submit a list of site selections within the metropolitan area of Atlanta for dispersal of future low-rent public housing. The court, however, failed to impose a minimum or maximum number of units or to specify criteria as to location, except that the sites be dispersed. No timetable was set for housing construction. This vagueness would have made difficult any future resort to the court by the plaintiff. While the order did produce recommended sites, no housing was ever built. This failure was largely due to the federal moratorium on housing subsidies in January 1973.[184]

Hawkins v. Town of Shaw[185] points up the wisdom of plan preparation with caveats about the specification of contents. There the appellate court reversed a lower court decision for the defendant, and prescribed as a remedy that the district court receive and consider a plan prepared by the town of Shaw for the equalization of community services. The case concerned a charge by the plaintiffs that the town had adopted a discriminatory policy in provision of municipal services that had the effect, if not the intent, of discriminating against black neighborhoods. The circuit court made a persuasive statement in favor of requiring such a plan for defendants:[186]

---

182. Morgan v. Hennigan, 379 F. Supp. 410 (D. Mass. 1974), *aff'd sub nom.* Morgan v. Kerrigan, 509 F.2d 580 (1st Cir. 1974), *cert. denied,* 95 Sup. Ct. 1950 (1975).

183. 332 F. Supp. 382 (N.D. Ga. 1971), *aff'd per curiam,* 457 F.2d 788 (5th Cir. 1972). *See* text accompanying notes 198–99 *infra.*

184. Telephone conversation with Moreton Rolleston, Jr., attorney for plaintiffs, Sept. 16, 1975.

185. 461 F.2d 1171 (5th Cir. 1971).

186. *Id.* at 1176.

[T]he planning concept represents a useful tool in situations such as this case. The district court will have the benefit of the ideas and abilities of those who draft the plan as well as those who criticize it. Submission of a plan puts a concrete proposal before the Court and the parties as a focus for discussion and development. More importantly, the plan as adopted will provide the district court with a device for control of the remedy as well as a standard for measuring compliance. It will also facilitate appellate review. The planning concept is well suited to this case.

However, the dissent objected that the court had ordered the city to write a plan without giving sufficient guidelines: "Hard reality fore-ordains that no plan can be devised which will solve the complex variables of 'equalizing' municipal services. This court's broad-brush approach to this case guarantees such a fruitless result."[187] Even where the local government is acting in good faith, if court guide-lines are unclear the plan produced may not be found valid by the court.[188]

The Supreme Court of New Jersey recently declared that, though defendant municipality was obligated to create a plan that would provide the opportunity for a fair share of the housing needs of its region, "no formulaic determination or numerical specification of such a fair and reasonable share is required . . . [but is not precluded] if the municipal planning advisors deem it useful."[189] The stand of the court was criticized in a dissenting view: "Because this approach gives the trial court no reliable way of measuring local compliance with the Court's remedial order, I fail to see how it will encourage implementation of an effective remedial plan."[190] The court's reluc-tance to require precise numerical quotas and regional boundary delineation was based on the technical difficulties and the controver-sial political nature of translating data into formulas. However, the resulting uncertainties may weaken the court's power of en-forcement. Without a hard and fast rule of equal sharing of the hous-ing burden, courts may find themselves in an enlarged policy-making role, rather than a diminished one.

187. *Id.* at 1186. By 1976—five years later—the city had expended approxi-mately $300,000 in revenue-sharing and other surplus funds in compliance with the court's order. All improvements that were the subject of the order have been completed except the required street paving. The city attempted to raise the amount needed for this project, about $350,000, through a bond issue, which was defeated by the voters, and is seeking federal financing for the re-quired sum. Telephone conversation with Ancil L. Cox, Jr., city attorney for the Town of Shaw, Mississippi, Feb. 18, 1976.

188. *See, e.g.,* Holt v. Richardson, 240 F.Supp. 724 (D. Haw. 1965) (legis-lative reapportionment).

189. Oakwood at Madison, Inc. v. Township of Madison, 117 N.J. Super. 11, 283 A.2d 353 (1971), aff'd —— N.J. ——, 371 A.2d 1192, 1228 (1977).

190. *Id.* at 47 (Pashman, J., concurring and dissenting).

Another device used by the court in *Gautreaux v. Chicago Housing Authority*[191] to encourage compliance by the defendant was the setting of a short-range timetable (30 days for evidence that the tenant assignment policy had been modified, for example), and reports to the plaintiffs, HUD, and the Civil Rights Division of the Department of Justice regarding tentative site selections. Semiannual reports were required to demonstrate conformity with site-selection requirements. Others beside the court were thus enabled to act as watchdogs, and the defendant was brought into court again a year later because no sites had been acquired. The court then ordered submission of 1,500 sites for city council approval within two months. This short timetable should have left greater control in the hands of the court.[192]

Subsequent to the decision of the U.S. Supreme Court in *Hills v. Gautreaux* (1976),[193] an agreement between the plaintiffs and HUD specified a one-year development program for the housing of approximately 400 minority families throughout the Chicago SMSA, with the requirement that 75 percent of the beneficiary families reside outside of the city of Chicago and outside of other geographic areas with a concentration of minority residents.[194]

The court in the *Mount Laurel*[195] and *Madison Township*[196] cases set a short timetable (90 days) for the city to amend its ordinance. Setting a definite date requires the defendant either to comply or to come into court and request an extension, thereby alerting the court to the lack of progress. Thus, in *Mount Laurel* the court was alerted to the city's inaction when the city had to ask for an extension just before the 90-day period expired. Following a hearing at which both parties were represented, the court granted a three-month extension, and required monthly reports thereafter.[197]

191. Gautreaux v. Chicago Housing Authority, 304 F. Supp. 736 (N.D. Ill. 1969).

192. Even these techniques for compliance were too feeble in view of the result: there is still no public housing in white areas in Chicago. In fact, no public housing has been built since the *Gautreaux* litigation began in 1967. The moratorium on federally sponsored public housing and repeated appeals to the United States Supreme Court seemingly explains the delay. See Appendix A *infra*.

193. 96 S. Ct. 1538 (1976).

194. The text of the agreement between plaintiff and HUD is in Appendix A *infra*.

195. 67 N.J. 151, 336 A.2d 713 (1975), *appeal dismissed*, 96 S. Ct. 18 (1975).

196. Oakwood at Madison, Inc. v. Township of Madison, 117 N.J. Super. 11, 283 A.2d 353 (1971), aff'd — N.J. —, 371 A.2d 1192 (1977).

197. Docket No. L-25741-70, July 11, 1975. The extension was necessitated originally by a late petition for rehearing of the appeal to try to raise a federal question, which was denied, and by the subsequent appeal to the U.S. Supreme Court, which was dismissed. Communication from Justice Frederick W. Hall, New Jersey Supreme Court (retired), the author of the *Mount Laurel* opinion.

There are several methods a court can use to encourage or compel a town to comply with the court-mandated planning schedule. One technique is the appointment of a committee with responsibility to accomplish the steps in the remedial process. A major difficulty is linking default with an official in charge. Presume that in a particular case a court overturns a local decision to bar a proposed low-income housing project. Under the local processes, the developer must then present plans to the planning commission for approval, to the zoning board of appeals for a variance, to the health department and the fire chief for requisite permits, and finally to the inspection department for a building permit. The project may falter at any step, and the court will find it difficult to pin responsibility for delay or frustration of the project on a particular agency. To ameliorate this, it might be wise to require the designation of an official whose responsibility is to organize compliance with the court order, and who must answer if there is a default in performance. The defendant city should not be able to deflect responsibility for compliance to an assortment of state, county, and municipal planning and permit-issuing agencies.

The court in *Crow v. Brown*[198] required formation of such a committee. In that case, which involved the denial of turnkey housing projects, no low-rent public housing projects had been built in Fulton County, outside Atlanta, although cooperation agreements had been entered into between the county and the Atlanta Housing Authority. The court ordered relief for the plaintiffs, and formation of a joint committee composed of officials of the county and the housing authority to draw up a list of areas appropriate for low-rent housing that lay within the jurisdiction of the housing authority in the unincorporated portion of the county. Sixty days after the general list was compiled, detailed site selections were to be made, and copies of the list given to the housing authority, HUD, county officials, and the court. Recommendations of the joint committee were then to be implemented by the county and the housing authority. The committee was formed, met, and made the requisite site recommendations. Public housing was never built on the sites, however, due to a federally imposed moratorium on funds.[199]

Another method of compelling a town to comply with the timetable is for the court to impose a moratorium on any other residential

198. 332 F. Supp. 382 (N.D. Ga. 1971), *aff'd per curiam*, 457 F.2d 788 (5th Cir. 1972). *Cf.* the order in James v. Wallace, 406 F. Supp. 318 (N.D. Ala. 1976) (directs comprehensive reformation of Alabama's prison system; judge appointed a 39-member human-rights committee composed of lawyers, doctors, clergymen, and other citizens across the state to monitor implementation of his order for prison reform).

199. Telephone conversation with Morton Rolleston, Jr., attorney for plaintiffs, Sept. 16, 1975.

construction (or perhaps on *all* other construction) in the town pending compliance with the order. The most obvious examples of such moratoria are those imposed by a local government in growth-control and environmental protection cases, where cities impose a temporary halt on construction for legitimate public purposes. For example, all construction can be temporarily halted pending completion of a general plan,[200] or pending installation of needed sewer or water facilities.[201] Just as it is within the government's police power to curb construction in order to regulate growth, as in *Golden v. Town of Ramapo*,[202] a court should be able to suspend residential construction for the public purpose of accommodating low-cost housing and insuring compliance with the court's order.[203]

Examples of moratoria can be found in some of the cases previously discussed. In *Gautreaux v. Chicago Housing Authority*[204] the court suspended construction of all public housing within black neighborhoods until 700 units had been built elsewhere. In *Kennedy Park Homes v. City of Lackawanna*[205] the court enjoined the city from issuing building permits for any construction in two wards, which would contribute additional sewage to the municipal system, until the plaintiff had been granted permission to tap into the sewer sys-

200. A 26-month interim zoning regulation, which permitted no construction, was upheld pending completion of a master plan to protect the Hackensack Meadowlands. Meadowland Regional Dev. Agency v. Hackensack Dev. Comm'n, 119 N.J. Super. 572, 293 A.2d 192 (1972), *cert. denied*, 62 N.J. 72, 299 A.2d 69 (1972).

201. Steelhill Dev., Inc. v. Town of Sanbornton, 469 F.2d 956 (1st Cir. 1972).

202. 30 N.Y.2d 359, 285 N.E.2d 291, 334 N.Y.S.2d 138, *appeal dismissed*, 409 U.S. 1003, 34 L. Ed. 2d 294 (1972).

203. Borrowing from land-use law in which towns impose holding zones to freeze development pending completion of general plans or installation of facilities, it is seen that courts have sanctioned moratoria of two or three years. *See* Mang v. County of Santa Barbara, 182 Cal. App. 2d 93, 5 Cal. Rptr. 724 (1960) (very large areas temporarily zoned for agricultural use only to allow county to meet problems related to large population increases); Golden v. Town Board of Ramapo, 30 N.Y.2d 359, 285 N.E.2d 291, 334 N.Y.S.2d 138, *appeal dismissed*, 409 U.S. 1003, 34 L. Ed. 2d 294 (1972) (upheld town ordinance enacted to control growth pending installation of adequate public facilities; land could conceivably be kept undeveloped for as long as 18 years after ordinance adopted); 334 N.Y.S.2d 138, 30 N.Y.2d 359, 285 N.E.2d 291, *appeal dismissed*, 409 U.S. 1003, 34 L. Ed. 2d 294 (1972). The California Government Code permits cities to adopt interim zoning measures pending completion of comprehensive plans, which may last for as long as two years. Cal. Govt. Code § 65858. *See also* Oakwood at Madison, Inc. v. Township of Madison, 17 N.J. Super. 11, 283 A.2d 353 (1971), aff'd — N.J. —, 371 A.2d 1192 (1977) (J. Pashman, concurring and dissenting).

204. 304 F. Supp. 736 (N.D. Ill. 1969).

205. 318 F. Supp. 669 (W.D.N.Y. 1970), *aff'd*, 436 F.2d 108 (2d Cir. 1970), *cert. denied*, 401 U.S. 1010 (1961).

tem for its proposed housing project. One ground for permit denial had been the alleged lack of sewer capacity. The order in *Garrett v. City of Hamtramck*[206] included a provision enjoining any rezoning, granting of variances, building or demolition permits, or property acquisition for nonresidential use in one area of the city, until there had been compliance with provisions of the order to produce relocation housing. The plaintiff's complaint in the pending case, *Accion Hispana v. Town of New Canaan,*[207] requests that in the 45-day period given defendant to submit a new zoning law for the court's approval, the town not be permitted to grant rezonings or issue building permits or certificates of occupancy.

Another method of pressuring the defendant government to produce an acceptable plan on schedule is the threat of imposing a court-created plan, with features that may not be ideal to the city. For example, a court plan might include the zoning of land for mobile home parks to meet low-cost housing needs, which shall be put into force unless a prompt and satisfactory alternative is proposed by the defendant. In reapportionment cases, courts have been faced with the need to rapidly establish fair apportionment plans before the next elections, yet defendants provoked the courts with long delays. One court[208] overcame delays by adopting a back-up plan for the redistricting of Los Angeles County that would go into effect if the legislature failed to meet the court-imposed deadline.

The premise of this section on remedies is that the court has determined that the defendant's plans and ordinances do not permit the location within it of a fair share of the region's low-income housing and that this failure is actionable. The new plans and ordinances that are called for will have to quantify the fair share and deal with their location and associated planning conditions.

However, the complexity, difficulty, and political nature of formulating exact numerical housing goals and precise regional boundaries have led the New Jersey Supreme Court to draw back from such mandates, either for the trial courts or the municipalities.[209] Rather, the court said, it is sufficient for the trial court to study the *substance* of the zoning ordinance, and determine whether *bona fide* efforts have been made to eliminate exclusionary requirements.[210] On the

206. 335 F. Supp. 16 (E.D. Mich. 1971), *plan ordered,* 357 F. Supp. 925 (E.D. Mich. 1973), *aff'd in part,* 503 F.2d 1236 (6th Cir. 1974), *amended in part,* 394 F. Supp. 1151 (E.D. Mich. 1975).
207. Civ. No. B312 (D. Conn., filed June 14, 1971).
208. Brown v. Silver, 63 Cal. 2d 270, 405 P.2d 132, 46 Cal. Rptr. 308 (1965).
209. Oakwood at Madison, Inc. v. Township of Madison, 117 N.J. Super. 11, 283 A.2d 353 (1971), aff'd — N.J. —, 371 A.2d 1192, 1200, 1213, 1216-1223, 1228 (1977).
210. *Id.* at 15.

other hand, the court did offer methods for making more quantitative measurements of both fair share and region. Although *Mount Laurel* devised no formula for estimating fair share, leaving this matter to the defendant municipality, the court in the *Madison Township* case suggests that the formula specified by the *Madison Township* trial court was *prima facie* fair under the facts of this case.[211] The trial court had held that the defendant was obligated to provide the same proportion of additional low- and moderate-income housing unit capacity within its borders as its present proportion of low- and moderate-income population, about 12 and 19 percent, respectively. The New Jersey Supreme Court found that this formula would be a fair one "if the existing municipal proportions correspond at least roughly with the proportions of the appropriate region."[212] This formulation furnishes a rough guideline for calculating fair share obligations, even though the court cautions against requiring formulaic determinations or numerical specifications. The court also cautions that sound planning would require that the amended zoning ordinance overzone for the number of low-cost units in order to help insure actual construction of the target number. Overzoning is necessary because all the land zoned for low-cost housing probably will not be used exclusively for this purpose.[213]

An appropriate region, according to the court, "is that general area which constitutes, more or less, the housing market area of which the subject municipality is a part, and from which the prospective population of the municipality would substantially be drawn, in the absence of exclusionary zoning."[214] The court implies this would probably include the broader region of northeastern New Jersey and the New York metropolitan area.

The *Madison Township* case defined the *quality* of housing that must be planned for, as well as the *quantity*.[215] Providing the opportunity for construction of low-cost housing may result in no housing if governmental subsidies necessary to make such projects economically feasible fail to materialize. Therefore, the zoning must accommodate what the court terms "least cost housing" in order for vacant low-cost housing, which becomes available as families move up, to filter down as quickly as possible. The less expensive the recently constructed housing, the sooner dwellings that are vacated will filter down to the poorest families.[216]

211. *Id.* at 80.
212. *Id.*
213. *Id.* at 46.
214. *Id.* at 81.
215. *Id.*, 8 V, at 33–39.
216. *Id.* at 36-38.

In arriving at the number of additional units the town must make possible through its regulations, the town and the court will be making judgments related to the housing needs of the region, what area comprises the region, who qualifies as the low- and moderate-income residents, and how to allocate the housing among the cities of the region. These issues are dealt with in detail in Chapter 6, so only a few matters are noted here.

The allocation decision is perhaps the most difficult. On the one hand, a simple mathematical approach, premised perhaps on the comparative amounts of vacant and developable land, is easier to administer.[217] On the other hand, it is evident that equal distribution ignores important planning considerations, such as employment opportunity and availability of public transportation, social services, and shopping centers. Moreover, it does not take into consideration the suitability of the vacant land for intensive use, or the fiscal and other resources (for instance, classroom space) in the various towns.

As discussed in Chapter 6, there are a number of sophisticated mathematical models for allocating low-income housing on a regional basis (San Bernadino County, California; metropolitan Washington, D.C., for instance). Each seeks to quantify a number of factors—such as additional school capacity, employment opportunities, and availability of undeveloped land—and thus to minimize subjective or politically motivated judgments.[218]

Whether or not a self-executing formula is utilized, the regional nature of the fair share approach highpoints the utility of having all the local political jurisdictions in the region before the court rather than simply a particular city chosen out as a sole defendant. If a formula approach is used it should be devised through the joint action of all cities affected by it (or at least subject to their scrutiny). If a formula approach is not feasible it becomes even more important

217. In *Urban League v. Carteret*, 142 N.J. Super. 11, 359 A.2d 526 (1976), the court first allocated low-cost housing needs among the eleven defendants in proportion to the number of units needed to correct existing imbalances in order to bring each municipality up to county averages of low- and moderate-income housing. Then the remaining units, roughly 14,700 out of the total need for an additional 18,700, were distributed equally among the eleven defendant municipalities. The court noted, "Each municipality has vacant suitable land far in excess of its fair share requirement without impairing the established residential character of neighborhoods." *Id.* at 32 of slip op.

218. Another approach suggested is that the variables are so great and the political considerations so important in determining the actual allocation that so long as a housing allocation formula meets minimal standards of rationality, it can be used by a court that decides to attempt such a regional allocation. A number of housing allocation plans are in existence already that courts may look to as guides in this regard. *See* discussions of housing allocation plans in H. Franklin, D. Falk & A. Levin, In-Zoning: A Guide for Policy-Makers on Inclusionary Land Use Programs (1974) [hereinafter cited as In-Zoning]; and Chapter 6 *infra*.

to strive for a political compromise among the local jurisdictions, which can best be stimulated by a court that has all the local governments before it.

As has been noted,[219] data collection to make calculations for housing obligations can be expensive, and if the plaintiff is to undertake the project, either to offer evidence of invalid regulations or to propose a remedy, there are few plaintiffs who can afford the cost. It is therefore worthwhile to explore briefly the sources of data that already exist in many communities.[220] A word of caution is needed at the outset. Since the purpose of the data collection is to allocate housing among communities, only data that are uniformly accurate for every city within the selected region can be used. There are at least four major sources of such data.

First are data from the United States Bureau of the Census. Every decade the Census Bureau makes a nationwide count of population and building structures, and procures information about income level and overcrowding. Even though this data becomes outdated as the decade proceeds, it has the virtue of uniform applicability throughout a jurisdiction. Moreover, a special census during the decade may be requested within a selected area.

The second source is information provided to the Department of Housing and Urban Development for housing assistance plans. Such plans, on a local basis, involve the same topics as are relevant in formulating regional housing allocation plans. However, 1975 is the first year of reporting, and the data are not yet completely reliable. These figures lack the cross-comparability needed to make interjurisdictional comparisons. Housing need, for example, must be demonstrated, but only for the reporting entity itself, and entities may define need differently.[221]

219. Bosselman, *Growth Management and Constitutional Rights—Part I: The Blessings of Quiet Seclusion,* 8 Urb. L. Ann. 3, 25 (1975).

220. In *Mount Laurel,* the first case in which a court has ordered determination of "regional fair share," the planners, initially estimating *local* moderate- and low-cost housing need, are utilizing the following sources already in existence: U.S. Census 1970 data, town master plan, records of the building inspector, regional housing studies, reports of the County Planning Board and State Department of Community Affairs, and the HUD Community Development application submitted by the county. *See* Affidavit of Louis Glass, Land Planner for Mount Laurel Township, Docket No. L-25741-70-P (Aug. 21, 1975).

221. Conversation with James Lester, economist for HUD, San Francisco Regional Office, Sept. 21, 1975. Sources of data available for preparation of the estimated housing needs of those "expected to reside" in a community, in preparation of the Housing Assistance Plan, were reviewed by the district court in City of Hartford v. Hills, 408 F. Supp. 889 (D. Conn. 1976) The court said:

For example, HUD's own instructions suggest the use of census materials; code enforcement records; local agency records; 701 plans; or studies done by reputable research, community service, or planning organizations,

A third source of data is state agencies. For example, nearly all states contribute a portion of local school budgets based on the average daily attendance in the district. Therefore, the school age population is known. The license division of the motor vehicle department can give information on car registrations and on in-migration of car owners based on new car registrations from out of state. There may be, as there is in California, a requirement that cities report to the state the number of new dwellings and mobile home parks each year. Also, although this may be unique to California, the state department of finance has established a procedure for making an annual population estimate for every city in the state. These data are used in determining the size of subventions returned to cities under various tax programs, and in determining if a locality can increase property taxes. The department also undertakes a mid-decade census (based on sampling techniques) upon the request of local governments at a relatively low cost, which may include information on ten items selected by the locality.[222]

A fourth source of information is data gathered regularly by regional and local planning agencies, councils of governments, and A-95 review agencies. Care must be used, however, as there are often serious questions about their completeness and the consistency of the data as they apply throughout the region. The consultants who examined the zoning ordinance of Washington township in the *Pascack* case[223] used data from the county planning board to assess the housing shortage in the county. From this source they were able to compile accurate figures on the amount of private rental housing needed to meet current and future needs, and the projected housing

such as private consulting firms. (Instructions for Form HUD-7015.8 thru 11.) The proposed HUD regulations also list several data sources, such as approved development plans; building permits; and major contract awards. (24 C.F.R. § 570.303(c)(2)(i)(A); 41 Fed. Reg. 2347, 2349 (Jan. 15, 1976.) One of the plaintiff's expert witnesses, Mr. Paul Davidoff, also listed a number of other possibilities, including studies conducted by or for state agencies; plant or shopping center surveys; zip code information from the payroll records of local companies; or data gathered by the local chamber of commerce. 408 F. Supp. at 905.

The district court was reversed on standing grounds in City of Hartford v. Town of Glastonbury, ——F.2d —— (2d. Cir. Aug. 15, 1977) (*en banc*).

222. Some states may have agencies similar to the Department of Planning and Community Affairs in New Jersey. Such departments collect considerable information. (*See* Report of Advisors to the Court in the *Pascack* case, *supra* note 173, which relied on data provided by the New Jersey department on the percentage of developable land set aside for multifamily dwellings, by county.) State boards of equalization are an obvious source of information on per capita assessed valuations, which can be critical in judging service capacities of various communities in the region.

223. Report of Advisors to the Court, Jan. 9, 1974, Pascack Ass'n, Ltd. v. Township of Washington, No. L-36048-70, *supra* note 173.

requirements of the population by age and income level.[224] In allocating housing assistance funds in the Bay Area, however, the regional office of HUD has not found this kind of information sufficiently complete to be usable.[225]

Although the above material discusses means by which a planning effort arrives at the number of low-income housing opportunities that should be afforded in the fair share effort, simple numbers are not a plan or a land-use regulatory ordinance. The numbers must be translated into reasonable potential sites—locations that are reasonably appropriate and attractive for low-income housing sponsors.[226]

There are a number of methods available for approaching the location problem. None is exclusive. One is to specify on a map the particular locations where low-income housing[227] is a permissible development. A second approach is a similar mapping where low-income housing is the sole permitted use. A third approach is through flexible regulatory techniques, such as floating zoning or special-permit devices. A fourth approach is through the use of inclusionary techniques,[228] such as a requirement that a certain percentage of units in new residential projects be devoted to low-income residents, or through some public housing variant such as the provision of subsidized leaseholds in existing or newly constructed buildings. The first three approaches are discussed here.

The first approach is the most conventional. A portion of the juris-

---

224. *Id.* The consultants in *Pascack* also utilized information in a report issued by Rutgers University, Center for Urban Policy, *Housing Development and Municipal Costs.* Those seeking available data should be in contact with urban studies centers at local universities.

225. Conversation with James Lester, *supra* note 221.

226. Since some cities have sought to meet their obligations to furnish low-income housing by offering undesirable sites near industry or commerce, the court should require that sites chosen be appropriate for residential purposes. Moreover, sites should not endanger fragile environmental areas, such as flood plains, marsh areas, or steep slopes. Topographic conditions of selected sites should not entail costly site preparation, as where there is a high water table or need for an unusual amount of grading. In addition, low-cost housing sites should normally be dispersed to avoid the creation of a ghetto in suburbia. Finally, of course, provisions found to constitute arbitrary limitations (*e.g.*, bedroom restrictions, large-lot or setback requirements, and similar cost-elevating limits) should be barred. In *Mount Laurel* the court required that exclusionary provisions of the zoning ordinance be amended to provide for multifamily housing, small houses on small lots, a reasonable amount of low-income housing included in any PUDs authorized, and a scaled-down percentage of land zoned for industrial and commercial uses. It should be noted that invalid provisions cannot be amended until the necessary target numbers have been determined, to quantify, for example, *how much* small, inexpensive, or multifamily housing is needed.

227. In this context low-income housing normally means high-density, multifamily, minimum-code buildings.

228. *See* discussion of such inclusionary techniques in Chapter 7 *infra*.

diction is zoned to permit high-density development (with perhaps some liberalized performance standards for defined low-income housing).[229] In some instances this approach will suffice to provide real opportunities for low-income housing developments. In many instances, however, as where there is a substantial demand for middle- and upper-income apartments, the new zoning will simply drive up the price of affected land, thereby reducing access for low-income housing developers. Moreover, given such demand, it is predictable that the new zone will be developed largely by the more remunerative upper-income developments.

The second approach—the creation of a zone where low-income housing is the sole permitted use—is quite novel and probably unfeasible. First, unless such zones were quite small, such an approach would invite the creation of ghettoes; and second, the device is fraught with legal problems. Even assuming that exclusive-use zones of this sort are permissible,[230] owners of land within such zones would be able to raise substantial constitutional challenges.[231]

229. *See* Babcock & Bosselman, *supra* note 157, who comment:

The initial impulse of most local decision makers who wish to provide for increased densities may be to take a look at the zoning map, pick out a few sites, and propose that they be reclassified for higher densities. This is probably ineffective as well as unwise.

In the first place it injects locational disputes into the debate over policy at the outset. Apart from the awkward public relations, such a move is based on the dubious premise that local planners or legislators can see through the vagaries of the market and identify with precision on what parcel or parcels the confluence of the desires of a willing seller and an eager developer will occur. This is highly unlikely. On the contrary, although sound planning should be the basis of housing goals it is essential that the goals *not* be expressed in the form of premapped areas designated for higher-density housing. Recent experience with land use regulation shows that this type of premapped planning would be counterproductive.

Id. at 63.

The New Jersey Supreme Court, in the recent case Oakwood at Madison, Inc. v. Township of Madison, 117 N.J. Super. 11, 283 A.2d 353, (1971) aff'd — N.J. —, 371 A.2d 1192, (1977), envisioned the use of a "least-cost housing zone" in the revised zoning ordinance required of the defendant to remedy exclusionary practices. The court, contemplating the likelihood that all land zoned for least-cost housing would not actually be so used, called for overzoning the amount of land in this category in order to help ensure construction of the target number of low-cost units. *Id.* at 1210–1211.

230. Exclusive residential zoning has been permissible since the early days of Village of Euclid v. Ambler Realty Co., 272 U.S. 365 (1926), but its early acceptance was premised on nuisance analogies—*i.e.*, that the intrusion of any other use could create conditions a legislature deemed harmful. Exclusive-use zoning for other purposes, such as industrial uses, has normally been permitted under similar reasoning, *e.g.*, Lamb v. City of Monroe, 358 Mich. 136, 99 N.W.2d 566 (1959) (the court quoted Rathkopf and Rathkopf, The Law of Zoning and Planning [3rd ed. 1972] with a list of 16 areas where exclusive industrial zoning had been established); People *ex rel.* Skokie Town House Builders, Inc. v. Village of Morton Grove, 16 Ill. 2d 183, 157 N.E.2d 33 (1959).

The third approach—an alternative to locational mapping—is the use of a flexible regulatory technique that incorporates in the text of the zoning ordinance standards whereby the required amount of low- and moderate-cost housing could be permitted, but postpones designation of actual sites until a developer applies for permission to construct such housing. Ultimate compliance with the court order would require the municipality to grant requisite permission upon application, unless it could show a justifiable reason for refusing permission on the specific site. Refusal would only be justified if the proposed housing project did not meet the standards set forth in the court-approved ordinance.

One flexible device is the floating zone. A floating zone is a district defined in the text of a zoning ordinance which is established on particular property only after legislative approval of an application. The zoning map is then amended and only the use so provided (defined low- or moderate-income housing, for example) is thereafter permitted on a rezoned parcel. The text portion of the ordinance sets out the criteria approved by the court order regarding location and other conditions. Since no property is affected until application is made, the technique avoids the inflation of land values that might result from the first approach and the legally vulnerable deflation that might result from the second.

Arguably, exclusive-use zoning, primarily to stimulate activities deemed socially beneficial, is within the police power, *e.g.*, zoning for agricultural uses only (D. Hagman, Urban Planning and Development Control Law 108 [1971]), although this is debatable. *Cf.* Board of Supervisors v. DeGroff Enterprises, Inc., 214 Va. 235, 198 S.E.2d 600 (1973) (voiding an "inclusionary" ordinance requiring that new residential developments of over 50 units include from 10 to 15 percent of its units for lower income families, partly on grounds that is a form of socioeconomic zoning), *with* Maldini v. Ambro, 36 N.Y.2d 481, 369 N.Y. Supp. 2d 385, 330 N.E.2d 403 (1975), *appeal dismissed and cert. denied*, 96 S. Ct. 419 (1975) (sustaining establishment of "a zoning district which allowed, among other things, residences designed for, but not necessarily limited to aged persons") (369 N.Y. Supp.2d 385, 391); Taxpayers Ass'n v. Weymouth Tp., No. A-105 (Sup. Ct. N.J., September 28, 1976) (upholding creation of a zoning district in which one of the permitted uses is a mobile home park for exclusive use of elderly); Shepard v. Woodland Tp. Committee, No. A-91 (Sup. Ct. N.J., September 28, 1976 (upholding an ordinance permitting "senior citizen communities" in a residential-agricultural district). In any event, a characteristic limitation on such zoning is that there be a reasonable prospect for an economic use to be made of the land so zoned. *See generally* Williams, *supra* note 3.

231. The basic challenge is that the cost imposed by the regulation should be shared and not borne by the landowners so zoned. The environmental cases, *e.g.*, Just v. Marinette County, 201 N.W.2d 761 (Wisc. 1972); Candelstick Properties, Inc. v. San Francisco Bay Conservation and Dev. Comm'n, 11 Cal. App. 3d 577, 9 Cal. Rptr. 897 (1970), are arguably distinguishable because alternative uses on the fragile lands involved in them would cause ecological harm. In any event, the law is quite unsettled on the question.

An analogous technique is a special-use permit granted by administrative, rather than legislative, action. Presumably the same type of criteria would be written in the ordinance governing the grants or denials of such permits for low- and moderate-income housing projects as would govern applications for rezoning to a floating zone. Another flexible approach is some form of "holding zone." Many communities zone large amounts of land for agricultural or other low-density uses, with the intention to rezone parcels upon application. If the town has indicated by resolution that rezoning for low-cost housing under liberal conditions is a planning policy, and demonstrates in an appropriate manner its willingness to rezone in this way, such an approach can be considered an appropriate flexible technique.[232]

A court-approved plan that relies heavily on flexible techniques for implementation leaves open the possibility of evasion through maladministration. Skeptical judicial scrutiny of decisions denying appropriate rezoning or permit issuance to applicants seeking to develop low-cost housing would be the only recourse. There are a number of ways, however, for minimizing the needs for repetitive lawsuits. First, the court may appoint a special master to supervise the administration of the plan and ordinances.[233] The existence of a special master with detailed knowledge of the plan and policies, to whom a disappointed applicant can turn, will be a powerful stimulant to good-faith administration.

The court should also insist that the plan and ordinances contain a detailed statement of policy indicating the municipality's intention to administer its ordinances to include low-cost housing within its boundaries. This will provide a referent for rezoning or permit decisions and a solid basis for judicial review. Moreover, its existence will advertise the town's willingness to comply with the court order to prospective builders, and thus invite applications to develop. Such a statement, at a minimum should contain such provisions as:

(a) a declaration that the municipality intends to encourage new housing with a variety of type and cost through revision of its codes,
(b) a schedule of the pace and extent of such development that the municipality regards as reasonable, and
(c) the types of area or areas where proposals for such development will be sympathetically considered, and why those areas have been selected.[234]

232. *See* discussion of flexible techniques in Chapter 4, *infra; see also* Babcock & Bosselman, *supra* note 157, at ch. 5; and In-Zoning, *supra* note 218, at Pt. IV.

233. This was done by the trial court in Association of Contractors v. City of Petaluma, 375 F. Supp. 574 (1974).

234. See Babcock & Bosselman, *supra* note 157, at 61-62.

As the previous discussion indicates, courts involved in fair share cases must often cope with complicated technical and planning issues. At the least, a court must be able to conclude on the basis of disputed testimony whether municipal plans and ordinances provide housing development opportunities for a fair share of a regional low-cost housing need and whether new plans and ordinances proferred by the defendants adequately address shortages, if any. But courts must also be prepared to undertake the more strenuous burden of providing guidelines and, in some instances, supervising preparation of substitute plans. Obviously, aid in these tasks will be forthcoming from the parties, especially the plaintiff. But in many cases, the court will find it desirable to rely on court-appointed experts to alleviate time pressures and to provide specialized knowledge beyond the traditional competence of the court.[235]

Special masters have been helpful to courts in analogous cases. In legislative reapportionment disputes, for instance, such masters have been appointed to prepare nonpartisan redistricting plans for submission to the parties prior to court consideration.[236] Court-designated masters have also prepared plans in school desegregation cases where school boards were unwilling or unable to do so.[237] A special master

235. Courts, of course, can amass specialized knowledge in socio-political areas. *See, e.g.,* the school desegregation cases, such as Bradley v. School Bd. of Richmond, 338 F. Supp. 67 (1972), in which Judge Mehrig's 200-page opinion is a textbook of social history. Fair-share cases, however, can abound with technically difficult and time-consuming fact questions (*e.g.,* the fair-share number) and issues involving skilled professional judgments (*e.g.,* whether particular flexible regulatory devices are well suited in the context to provide adequate low-cost housing opportunities. In Oakwood at Madison, Inc. v. Township of Madison, 117 N.J. Super. 11, 283 A.2d 353 (1971), aff'd — N.J. —, 371 A.2d 1192 (1977), the Supreme Court of New Jersey gave the trial court, on remand, the discretion to appoint a zoning and planning expert in the event of defendant's undue delay or failure to comply with the court's opinion. *Id.,* at 1228. In Morgan v. Hennigan, 379 F. Supp. 410 (D. Mass. 1974), *aff'd sub nom.* Morgan v. Kerrigan 509 F.2d 580 (1st Cir. 1974), *cert. denied* 95 S. Ct. 1950 (1975) a school integration case, the court appointed two professors of the Boston University School of Education as experts, in part to help the court evaluate the work of a panel of masters also appointed by the court to formulate a school desegregation plan.

236. In one case the deans of three law schools were appointed to serve as a panel to draft such a plan. Stout v. Bottorff, 246 F. Supp. 825 (S.D. Ind. 1965). The director of the Yale Computer Research Center prepared a computer-generated reapportionment plan in an attempt to attain a politically neutral result. *See* Butterworth v. Demsey, 237 F. Supp. 302 (D.Conn. 1965). In California a reapportionment plan was formulated by three retired judges who were appointed as special masters by the state supreme court. They employed law professor Paul L. McKaskle as staff supervisor. Legislature v. Reinecke, 10 C.3rd 396, Appendix A n.1 at 408, 110 Cal. Rptr. 718, 516 P.2d 6 (1973).

237. *See* Swann v. Charlotte-Mecklenburg Bd. of Education, 91 S. Ct. 1267 (1971). In Morgan v. Kerrigan, *supra* n. 235, the court appointed a panel of four masters to draft a school desegregation plan. The panel, composed of a retired state supreme court justice, a former U.S. commissioner of educa-

acts as an arm of the court, holds hearings, gathers evidence, and makes a recommendation or report to the court. The findings of a special master are considered the findings of the court, to the extent that the court adopts them. Consultants, on the other hand, normally have more restricted duties and are usually engaged solely to answer specific questions within their expertise asked by the court.[238] The court may employ expert assistance at any point in the lawsuit for a variety of purposes, such as determining the fair share obligations, judging the adequacy of the defendant's proposed plans and ordinance amendments, assisting the defendant to prepare an adequate plan and ordinance, or monitoring compliance with an amended ordinance.

Having the services of a consultant available may also give the court the same kind of leverage with the defendant that is produced by a prepared backup plan. Should the town fail to comply with the court's orders on schedule, the court can employ the consultant to work for the court or with the town to complete the task in a reasonable time. In this way, the court will act only after the town has relinquished its opportunity to do so. In the *Pascack* case,[239] for example, the court engaged the services of consultants to determine whether or not the town's amended ordinance complied with the court order to provide adequate multifamily housing, and if not, what amendments were needed. In *Gautreaux v. Chicago Housing Authority*[240] the court appointed a special master to investigate the causes of the housing authority's five-year delay in complying with the court's orders, and to recommend a plan for prompt execution of these orders and judgments.

Special masters or consultants may be experts in relevant fields, or widely respected public figures, such as retired judges or government officials.[241] It is important that the special master or

tion, a former state attorney general, and a professor of education at Harvard University, held evidentiary hearings, and evaluated plans submitted by the parties. The plan they recommended to the court incorporated elements of these plans, and also proposals of their own. The court modified the plan, based on objections by the parties and updated data provided by the court-appointed experts (see note 235 *supra*).

238. See, however, Report to the Court of the Advisors, Jan. 9, 1974, Pascack v. Township of Washington, No. L-36048-70, *supra* note 173, in which the consultants actually made a recommendation for a new zoning ordinance, which was adopted by the court.

239. *Id.*

240. 384 F. Supp. 37 (N.D. Ill. 1974).

241. Retired Governor Edmund G. Brown of California served as a special master for the court in the relocation housing controversy surrounding clearance of land for the proposed Yerba Buena Convention Center in San Francisco. In the *Petaluma* case the court appointed as special master a professor of law and city planning at the University of California, Berkeley. In *Pascack* two Rut-

consultant be a neutral and qualified person who can lend personal prestige to the report submitted. Expert witnesses, of course, are normally expected to take partisan stands. But it is essential that the stature of the person selected as special master or consultant merit the confidence of all parties in order to maximize the legitimacy, and thus the acceptability, of the report.[242]

The appointment, powers, and procedures of a special master are guided by statute.[243] Some representative provisions are as follows. Rules of evidence are normally applicable at hearings. The master is normally empowered to compel production of evidence, put witnesses under oath, and the like. The master's report is submitted to the court for approval. The parties may object to findings of fact, conclusions of law, or sufficiency of the evidence to support the findings, and they have a right to be heard by the court before action is taken. A draft of the final report may be submitted to the parties for their suggestions before it is filed with the court. Following the hearing, the court may adopt, modify, reject, or recommit the report to the master. Under federal rules, compensation and determination of which party is to pay is within the discretion of the court. Courts often have divided the fee between plaintiff and defendant. In some instances, the entire cost has been assigned to the losing party, the party who sought the reference, or the party whose conduct necessitated it.[244]

Once the municipality has completed necessary amendments to its zoning ordinance, the court, which presumably retained jurisdiction, reviews it for compliance with judicial directives. If it is found to be satisfactory, the ordinance can become part of the court's judicial decree. If not, the defective portions must be remedied by the court or the defendant in line with the court's original or amended mandates.

At this point, the plaintiff may be permitted to file an amended complaint if it feels the ordinance fails to correct exclusionary provisions. In the *Mount Laurel* case, the New Jersey Supreme Court

gers University professors were appointed consultants: Jerome Rose, a professor of urban planning, and Melvin Levin, chairman of the Graduate Department of Urban Planning. In *Gautreaux*, while the plaintiff requested the appointment of a specialist in the field of public housing, the court appointed a U.S. magistrate.

242. Conversation with Melvin Levin, consultant in the *Pascack* case and chairman of the Graduate Department of Urban Planning, Rutgers University, Sept. 5, 1975. In Morgan v. Hennigan, a school desegregation case, the court first proposed names of a panel of masters, and gave the parties an opportunity to object to the selections and to terms of the proposed order of reference before issuing an order appointing the panel.

243. *See* Fed. R. Civ. P., Rule 53; and for an example of state statutes, Cal. Code C.U. Proc. §§ 638 to 645.

244. *See generally,* Moore's Federal Practice, § 53.04(1).

provided that plaintiffs should initially proceed by supplemental pleading if they wanted to challenge the defendant's response to the court's directives.[245] Plaintiffs filed an amended complaint in superior court, charging that the amended zoning ordinance was inadequate on a number of grounds related to amount of land and number of units provided for low-cost housing, lack of incentives to attract low-cost housing developers, insignificant elimination of industrial overmapping, failure to provide for mobile homes, and retention of costly restrictions on new construction.[246]

As can be seen from the foregoing, substantial time can pass between a judgment that existing ordinances are improperly exclusionary and the confirmation of a valid new plan. In appropriate cases a minimum amount of housing can be made possible by an interlocutory court order without waiting for the comprehensive planning needed to establish maximum obligations. Evidence in the suit will normally provide an approximation of fair share, and the immediate imposition of a small percentage of this number on the jurisdiction, to be located on clearly appropriate sites, will permit waiting developers, or those who could be solicited by advertising, the chance to begin building at once. Clearly, if the town has excluded all low-cost housing, as was the case in *Mount Laurel*,[247] the court can act immediately and require that permission be granted for numbers well below projected thresholds. This would quickly allow at least a modest amount of low-cost housing into the town.

An example of this approach is *Oakwood at Madison v. Township of Madison*,[248] where the court held that the town's zoning ordinance was exclusionary and thus invalid, but did not require that planning and data gathering be completed before establishing minimum fair share numbers. The court held, on the basis of data before it, and "without the rigidity of a mathematical formula,"[249] that fair share needs would not be met unless the town's zoning ordinance "approximates in additional housing unit capacity the same proportion of low-income housing as its present low-income population, about 12 percent, and the same proportion of moderate-income housing as its present moderate-income population, about 19 percent."[250]

245. Southern Burlington County NAACP v. Township of Mount Laurel, 67 N.J. 151, 336 A.2d 713 (1975), *appeal dismissed*, 96 S. Ct. 18 (1975).
246. *Id.*, Docket No. L-25741-70-PW, filed May 6, 1976.
247. 67 N.J. 151, 336 A.2d 713 (N.J. 1975).
248. 117 N.J. Super. 11, 283 A.2d 353 (1971), aff'd — N.J. —, 371 A.2d 1192 (1977).
249. 320 A.2d at 227.
250. This remedy, sought by plaintiffs, was calculated so as to maintain the township's present housing balance into the future. The town has less low-income housing now than other communities. Telephone conversation with Lois

It is assumed here that the defendant has complied with the court order to prepare a nonexclusionary plan and zoning ordinance, and that the court has found them to be adequate to meet the municipality's obligations to provide adequate opportunities for low-cost housing. This section deals with monitoring the town's adherence to its newly adopted policies and ordinances. Additional low-cost housing will not be built if developers are refused permission when they apply for permits and zone changes. For this reason, it is essential for the court to retain jurisdiction of the case for the period necessary to assure compliance.[251]

The court may have to determine whether or not refusals to grant permits or rezonings are consistent with the new ordinance and plan. Difficult evidentiary problems will be presented, and a special master would be of great help in making the necessary factual determinations. One can hypothesize a variety of possible defenses in particular instances. For example, a town may argue in a particular case that needed facilities to service the proposed project, such as sewer and water facilities or roads, are regional facilities that should be financed and constructed on a regional basis, not solely by the defendant government. Relatedly, it may be argued that installation of such facilities, although admittedly a local responsibility, would be unwise at the particular time on efficiency grounds or because wasteful scatteration and leap-frog development would ensue. In a particular instance, a town might refuse to comply with expanded low-cost housing opportunities according to the approved plan on the ground that regional demand has fallen, that such development has shifted to other towns within the region, or that data relied on are no longer applicable or accurate. In such a case the town actually would be arguing for a recalculation of fair share.

If the court, probably with the help of a special master's recommendations, concludes that the town is not acting in good faith, how can it exert pressure on the defendant to comply? The discussion that follows assumes applications for permits, and thus, in the usual case, the existence of federal or state subsidies for low-cost housing.

There is some potential support in present case law for suspending

<hr/>

Thompson, attorney for plaintiffs, Sept. 1975. *See also* Crow v. Brown, where courts ordered housing units without requiring comprehensive planning and detailed data gathering. 332 F. Supp. 382 (N.D. Ga. 1971), *aff'd per curiam*, 457 F. 2d 788 (5th Cir. 1972).

251. A notorious example of the need to retain extended jurisdiction of a case is in the field of school desegregation. Here courts found themselves enmeshed in coercing, reviewing, rejecting, and rewriting plans for integrating school systems, with many of the same sociopolitical issues that occur in housing. To ensure implementation of their decrees, they sometimes retained jurisdiction for years. *See*, for example, the six-year desegregation attempt in Wright v. City Council of the City of Emporia, 407 U.S. 451 (1972).

various federal grants as long as discriminatory housing programs are maintained by the subsidized local government. In *Evans v. Hills*[252] the Court of Appeals for the Second Circuit denied standing to plaintiffs to challenge a HUD grant for construction of a sanitary sewer and a Bureau of Outdoor Recreation (BOR) grant for acquisition of recreational land. The plaintiffs alleged that the town of New Castle was maintaining a housing and community development program that discriminated on racial and economic grounds. The court applied a strict scrutiny analysis to the alleged causal relationship between the agency actions and the pattern of residential development, and thereby refused to recognize a violation by HUD and BOR of Title VIII of the 1968 Civil Rights Act[253] or of Title VI of the 1964 Civil Rights Act.[254] Recently, in *Gautreaux v. Hills*,[255] the U.S. Supreme Court applied Title VIII of the 1968 Act to invalidate a HUD administered public housing program in the Chicago SMSA.

In *City of Hartford v. Hills*,[256] the city of Hartford, Connecticut charged HUD with improperly making community development grants to seven suburbs in the Hartford area which had submitted inadequate HAPs under the Housing and Community Development Act of 1974.[257] The plaintiffs obtained a permanent injunction in the district court restraining expenditure of the grants already paid to the suburbs, but were denied standing by the Court of Appeals.[258]

The approach suggested by these federal cases, however, was rejected by a state court decision which refused to enjoin a grant of state park funds to a city which allegedly excluded low-cost housing. In *Upper St. Clair Township v. Pennsylvania Department of Community Affairs*[259] the court held that the state agency was without authority to deny funds for a park merely because the town was asserted to exclude the poor and minorities through its land-development policies. While the court found that the town's policies were not unconstitutionally exclusionary, it also stated that even assuming the contrary, no injunction would lie absent some causal connection between terminating funding of the public park and fostering integrated housing.[260] The court also questioned whether forthcoming state

252. 537 F.2d 571 (2d Cir. 1976) (en banc), *cert. denied*, 97 S. Ct. 797 (1977).

253. 42 U.S.C. § 3601.

254. *Id.*, § 2000d.

255. 425 U.S. 284 (1976).

256. 408 F. Supp. 889 (D. Conn. 1976), *rev'd sub nom.* City of Hartford v Town of Glastonbury,—F.2d— (2d Cir., Aug. 15, 1977) (*en banc*).

257. 42 U.S.C. § 5304(c)(1).

258. This case is discussed in greater detail in text accompanying note 71, in chapter 2 *supra*.

259. 312 A.2d 906 (Pa. Commw. Ct. 1974).

260. *Id.* at 912.

administrative regulations would be valid.[261] The basis for the court's doubts is whether the state agency had been delegated authority to adopt regulations discouraging exclusionary zoning by the relevant state statute. There is no suggestion in the case that such a delegation, if made, would be unconstitutional, despite the lack of a causal relation between the facility subsidized and exclusionary practices.

Another method of obtaining compliance with the court's order entails suspension of the operation of local ordinances or statutes that are the bases for a municipality's refusal to grant development permission for a low-cost housing project. In *Gautreaux v. Chicago Housing Authority*[262] the court suspended the operation of an Illinois statute[263] as it applied to the housing authority's actions. The statute required city council approval for acquisition of sites for public housing. The Chicago City Council had failed to approve public housing sites submitted by the housing authority, and this inaction prevented the authority from complying with the court's prior order to provide 1,500 public housing units in white areas of the city.[264]

The Massachusetts "anti-snob" zoning statute[265] is a statutory example of suspending the operation of particular laws in particular circumstances. It provides for a one-stop, single hearing process in the case, as part of the remedy to provide adequate housing for relocatees, the district court ordered that "to the extent that the Wyandottee renewal plan may conflict with any zoning ordinances, those standards. In *Garrett v. City of Hamtramck*,[266] a relocation housing case, the district court, as part of the remedy to provide adequate housing for relocatees, ordered that "to the extent that the Wyandottee renewal plan may conflict with any zoning ordinances, those ordinances shall be deemed inapplicable to the extent of any such inconsistency."[267]

It should be noted that these cases do not invalidate otherwise valid laws, but suspend their application to the controversy within the court's jurisdiction so as to permit compliance with the court's order. One writer, Professor Leonard S. Rubinowitz, who advocates

261. These proposed regulations indicate that municipalities engaging in exclusionary development practices may be found ineligible for grants under the state Land and Water Conservation Act until the state is assured that actions to eliminate discriminatory practices have been initiated.

262. 480 F.2d 210 (7th Cir. 1973).

263. Ill. Rev. Stat. ch. 67½, § 9.

264. 342 F. Supp. 828 (1972), *aff'd*, 480 F.2d 210 (7th Cir. 1973).

265. Mass. Ann. Laws ch. 40B, § 2-23 (Supp. 1975). *See* discussion in Chapter 7 *infra*.

266. 357 F. Supp. 925 (E.D. Mich. 1973).

267. *Id.* at 928.

use of this "set-aside technique,"[268] suggests how the court could use it as a remedy:

> A hearing would be held which would be limited to establishing that the developer had made a good faith effort to secure necessary approvals, the locality had denied the approvals, and the denial frustrates effective relief for the plaintiffs. The reasons for the denial and the merits of those reasons would not be at issue, for the set-aside principle provides for the court-ordered bypass of local regulations if they frustrate constitutionally required relief, even if they are otherwise valid. The supplemental order in this situation would enjoin the community from impeding the building of the development in any way, thus permitting the developer to commence construction of the particular project without securing further local approvals.[269]

If a court is forced to the conclusion that the town is acting in bad faith and is determined to maintain its exclusionary policies as long as possible, it can always take the draconian step of negating all or portions of the municipality's regulatory ordinances, leaving the jurisdiction's land unzoned in whole or part until a conforming scheme is proffered. Obviously this is to be avoided, but the threat of its use might provide considerable judicial leverage.

As a last resort, the court may determine that participants in the defendant government have so persistently disobeyed its orders that they will never comply without being charged for contempt of court. A successful contempt action, however, requires that the court be able to determine precisely which official was responsible for the failure to obey the order, and which provisions of the order have been disobeyed. This is one important reason that the court order be written in as detailed and precise manner as pos-

268. Rubinowitz, *Exclusionary Zoning: A Wrong in Search of a Remedy*, 6 Mich. J.L. Ref. 625, 645, 662 *ff.* (1973).

269. *Id.* at 663. Rubinowitz contends that legitimate local concerns that prompted the denial in the first place may be assuaged by high standards for construction and environmental quality set by HUD (if it is subsidizing the project) and which guarantee a minimum threshold of quality. The Housing and Community Development Act of 1974, 42 U.S.C. § 5304(a)(4), requires that any proposed housing projects be located in areas where adequate public facilities and services are available. 24 C.F.R. 1273.103 specifies required standards for types of housing sites and neighborhoods in order for new construction to qualify for the Section 8 Housing Assistance Program. Also, the developer may be presumed to have an incentive to build sound projects. Lastly, the court might keep a record of any problems created by this method so that it could impose necessary additional requirements on future developers. Rubinowitz, *supra* at 663, 644.

sible,[270] and that particular officials be identified in the court order as having cognizant responsibility.[271]

Fostering the Production of Low-Income Housing. The preceding analysis of remedies is premised on the existence of a municipal duty to utilize planning and regulatory authorities in such a manner that the opportunity exists for the presence within the municipality of a fair share (however calculated)[272] of the region's low- and moderate-income households. Much of what has been said, however, assumes the existence of a developer of housing for such households—a nonprofit or limited dividend entity, or a public housing authority, for instance—that takes the initiative in seeking suburban sites. Arguably, however, the municipal duty is broader than indicated and includes taking all reasonable actions to foster low- and moderate-income housing.[273]

While this chapter explores judicial roles and remedies and not the sources of substantive legal principles, brief reference to the possible bases for this expanded duty is useful. There are at least two possible sources for a municipality's obligation to foster within its boundaries a fair share of regional low- and moderate-income housing: specific statutes, and constitutions.

California's planning statute requires that a general plan include a housing element defined as follows:

> A housing element consisting of standards for the improvement of housing and for provision of adequate sites for housing. This element of the plan shall endeavor to make adequate provision for the housing needs of all economic segments of the community.[274]

As California mandates general planning,[275] it is arguable that the policy statement implicit in the section dealing with the housing element creates a municipal obligation to provide, to the extent feasible, adequate low- and moderate-income housing for at least those resi-

---

270. *See* text at notes 178–88 *supra.*

271. Even where the order is detailed and the officials identified, however, the court or the parties might hesitate to bring a contempt action. None has been brought to date in the exclusionary zoning field. For example, in *Gautreaux*, where the court has been unable, through any court order, to extract compliance from the defendant, the attorney for the plaintiff has refrained from asking for the contempt charges in part, at least, because he "preferred to get things moving practically and not to threaten to put people in jail." Conversation with A. Polikoff, attorney for plaintiffs, Sept. 10, 1975.

272. See Chapter 6 *infra*, and text in this chapter at notes 217 to 234 *supra.*

273. *See* 3 Williams, *supra* note 3, at 50–51 *et seq.;* and discussion *infra* at notes 282–83.

274. Cal. Gov't Code § 65302c.

275. *Id.* § 65301, 02.

dents in the community who are in those economic segments. Analogous statutory provisions in other jurisdictions can provide a similar basis for courts to find an affirmative municipal obligation.

Statutes providing for various government subsidies might also be important. Reference was previously made to suits challenging the propriety of federal grants to municipalities which allegedly use planning and regulatory authority to exclude minorities and lower income persons.[276] The Housing and Community Development Act of 1974[277] mandates an affirmative duty to plan for the community's low-cost housing needs. Applications for community development block grants must contain a HAP. This plan must survey the condition of housing stock and assess housing assistance needs of lower-income persons residing in or *expected to reside* in the community. According to HUD regulations, this number should be based on planned or existing employment facilities, and thus should include a fair share of the region's housing needs.[278] The HAP must also specify realistic annual goals for the number of units or persons to be assisted, and indicate the general location of proposed housing for lower income persons. The application must be denied if the description of housing needs is plainly inconsistent with facts and data "generally available."[279] Thus, if needs are misrepresented (for example, the estimate is set too low), the application can be denied.

Fair housing groups have begun to litigate to compel HUD to deny community development grants to cities with allegedly inadequate HAPs. A federal district court issued a permanent injunction against expenditure of block grants by seven suburbs in the metropolitan area adjoining Hartford, Connecticut.[280] In that case, the city of Hartford and other plaintiffs charged that the suburbs in question (which are seeking to use $4 million in block grants for nonhousing-related projects) underestimated housing needs for low-income groups "expected to reside" within their borders and refused to shoulder their fair share of regional housing needs. The court found that the defendant, HUD, had acted contrary to its statutory duty to make an independent assessment of housing need based on data currently defined as generally available. Parma, Ohio,

276. *See* text at notes 252-61 *supra.*
277. 42 U.S.C. § 5304(a)(4)(A).
278. 24 C.F.R. § 570.303(b)(2).
279. 42 U.S.C. § 5304(c)(1).
280. City of Hartford v. Hills, 408 F. Supp. 889 (D. Conn. 1976). While the book was at press, the Second Circuit reversed finding plaintiffs lacked standing. City of Hartford v Town of Glastonbury, —F.2d— (2d. Cir., Aug. 15, 1977) (*en banc*).

is also being challenged for submitting to HUD an inadequate HAP. The United States Justice Department and the National Committee Against Discrimination in Housing are the plaintiffs in this suit.[281] Administrative challenges are being brought against Burlington County, New Jersey (in which the township of Mount Laurel is located) and against twenty-five metropolitan Detroit suburbs to compel denial of community development grants unless regional low-income housing needs are addressed by these communities.

It might also be argued that communities have an affirmative obligation to implement the HAP they have submitted to HUD. In the event that private sponsors do not supply the specified amount of low-cost housing, the question arises whether the local government has an affirmative obligation to implement the plan by constructing low-rent or subsidized housing through its housing authority. Unfortunately, HUD's instructions for preparing the HAP and its regulations are silent on this question.

A related issue concerns the authority given the secretary of HUD by the act[282] to adjust the amount of the annual grant based on a required annual review of the program to determine whether, among other things, the grantee has carried out a program substantially as described in the application. If the HAP is unimplemented at year's end, it could be argued that this constitutes nonperformance of the program as described in the application, and therefore that the block grant funding must be reduced or withheld. The legislative history of the 1974 Act and the statutory language may well create an affirmative obligation to carry out a HAP or risk loss of community development funds, following annual review. Inaction on the part of a municipality to provide low-cost housing in the absence of private builder response is only one example of possible failure to implement a HAP. A clear example of such failure would seem to be the denial of permission to a private builder who sought to construct low-cost housing consistent with HAP provisions. The obligation of the local government to implement the plan in this case would seem to furnish grounds both for action by the Secretary of HUD to reduce or deny community development block grant funds and also possible recourse to the courts to enforce the HAP.[283]

It is doubtful, in the absence of racial discrimination, that the federal Constitution will be interpreted in the near future to provide a basis for either negating plans and regulations which exclude regional low-income population from a locality, or imposing an affirmative-

281. *See* 27 Land Use L. & Zoning Dig. 2 (1975).
282. 42 U.S.C. § 5304(d) (1975 Supp.).
283. *See* discussion in text accompanying notes 277–80 *supra*.

action obligation on municipalities with respect to such persons.[284] Where racial discrimination is involved, however, the Constitution clearly applies, and a showing of a consistent municipal practice of excluding minorities from all or portions of a municipality could support affirmative remedial action to redress the governmentally caused discrimination.[285] A similar determination might well follow in a state court where there has been a pattern of exclusion on the basis of income, if the state constitution is interpreted to bar such discrimination.[286]

If the court determines that the municipality has an affirmative obligation to foster and encourage construction of low-cost housing, the plan resulting from the court's orders should specify means for accomplishing the aim. Four major possibilities suggest themselves: (1) promoting subsidized housing by private developers; (2) forming a local housing authority and constructing public housing; (3) mandating a stipulated percentage of low-cost housing units in all new multifamily residential projects built by private developers; and (4) permitting mobile homes within the jurisdiction.[287]

Subsidized housing assumes the existence of rent assistance or federal, state, or local subsidy programs, whereby the costs of development can be lowered, resulting in significantly lower rental or purchase prices. Typically, such programs have been designed to aid lower income persons who are above the income levels of those eligible for public housing. Programs of the recent past have been designed to induce the private sector to undertake such development through either nonprofit or limited dividend organizations.[288] Most subsidy programs for such development are not presently operating.

284. *See* text accompanying notes 7–18 *supra. But see* SASSO v. Union City, 424 F.2d 291 (9th Cir. 1970), (which suggests a municipal obligation under the Equal Protection Clause to make reasonable provision for housing for low-income residents of the community itself); Williams, *supra* note 3, at §§ 66.15 to 66.16.

285. In Hills v. Gautreaux, 425 U.S. 284 (1976), the U.S. Supreme Court emphasized that local governments retain their statutory power to withhold approval of federally subsidized housing within their borders, even though the Chicago Housing Authority may be ordered to build within the metropolitan area in order to remedy the discriminatory practices of HUD and the Chicago Housing Authority. *Cf.* United Farmworkers v. City of Delray Beach, 493 F.2d 799 (5th Cir. 1974); Gautreaux v. Chicago Housing Authority, 503 F.2d 930 (7th Cir. 1974); Crow v. Brown, 457 F.2d 788 (5th Cir. 1972).

286. Southern Burlington County NAACP v. Township of Mount Laurel, 67 N.J. 151, 336 A.2d 713, 743 (1975) (concurring opinion of Judge Pashman); Urban League v. Carteret, 142 N.J. super. 11, 359 A.2d 526 (1976). *See also* Brennan, *supra* note 125.

287. *See* 3 Williams, *supra* note 3, at 111–119.

288. *See* Burke & Heyman, *Federally Assisted Housing and the Private Sector*, 1970 Bus. Law. 381–95.

The probabilities of reactivation, however, are good because the need is clear.[289] Even now, federal revenue-sharing funds could be devoted to locally subsidized programs. In his concurring opinion in the *Mount Laurel* case, Judge Pashman wrote: "Failure to actively cooperate in the implementation of such [subsidized] programs as effectively thwarts the meeting of regional needs for low and moderate income housing as does outright exclusion."[290]

An order requiring a city to seriously explore the development of subsidized housing was issued in at least one case, *SASSO v. City of Union City*.[291] The case involved a city referendum, held by objecting residents, to nullify a zone change for a proposed low-cost housing project. Both the trial and appellate courts refused to overturn the referendum, but on remand the district court invoked a remedy which imposed rigorous affirmative duties on the defendant city to take necessary steps to accommodate needs of its low-income residents. Such steps were to include encouragement and, if possible, implementation of programs dependent on private initiative subsidized by federal and state funds, as well as publicly built housing programs "in the event that private initiative and landowner cooperation (over which admittedly the City has no control) are insufficient to reasonably accommodate the housing needs of low income residents."[292] The court set a six-month deadline for accommodating the housing needs of low-income residents and required regular progress reports to the court every three months. As a result, the city council appointed a citizens' committee composed of both supporters and opponents of the plaintiff's housing project.[293] This committee recommended that turnkey projects be solicited. The Union City Housing Authority advertised widely throughout the Bay Area, and some 200 units have now been either approved or submitted for

289. HUD has agreed to release the entire $264.1 million in Section 235 (subsidized homeownership) funds impounded in 1972. Program requirements have been modified to serve the needs of families with higher incomes than in the past. 3 Hous. & Dev. Rep. 470 (Oct. 20, 1975). More recently the Carter Administration has indicated a disposition to revive and reform some of the former production-oriented programs, such as to additional public housing. 4 Hous. & Dev. Ref. 780 (February 7, 1977), 868 (February 21, 1977).

290. 67 N.J. 151, 336 A.2d 713, 744 (1975). Accord, Urban League of Greater New Brunswick v. Mayor of Carteret, et al. 142 N.J. Super. 11, 359 A.2d 526 (1976).

291. 347 F. Supp. 1188 (N.D. Cal. 1970). The case is frequently cited for the court of appeals's opinion, 424 F.2d 291 (9th Cir. 1970), in which a municipal duty to house low-income groups is implied.

292. 347 F. Supp. at 1199.

293. Telephone conversation with Richard Arjo, director of planning for the City of Union City, September 16, 1975.

approval. Subsidy scarcities have prevented actual construction of such turnkey units to date.[294]

While the defendant government sought to comply with the court order in this case, an obvious difficulty with a remedy of this type is monitoring compliance. Requiring that a city "encourage and if possible implement" subsidized housing programs is indefinite; the words too rubbery to be easily enforceable.[295] A court faced with a reluctant defendant will find it difficult to gauge the amount of effort that should be expended to secure private developers in order to satisfy the order. Moreover, lack of success is not necessarily proof of bad faith if, for instance, no subsidy funds are available. Flagrant instances of failure to pursue subsidies would be detectable. However, more thorough investigative techniques would have to be developed in many borderline instances. If a special master assisted the court, for example, he or she might determine whether the town had undertaken efforts such as identifying packagers of subsidized housing, contacting a number of them, and mounting an aggressive campaign to attract them. Efforts to secure such developers could be measured by actions such as municipal assurances of cooperation in granting necessary permits, locating suitable sites, and promoting local financing assistance.

There might also be circumstances in which the court decides that the defendant government, in the words of Judge Pashman, "has an affirmative duty to provide housing for persons with low and moderate incomes through public construction, ownership, or management."[296] This would mean that the court would order the formation of a local housing authority,[297] the signing of any necessary coopera-

294. The SASSO development, scaled down to half size, was resubmitted to the city; rezoning was obtained in 1971. No objecting landowners sought a referendum to nullify the zone change, and the housing project has been completed. *Id.*

295. *See* Order of Judge Furman in Urban League v. Carteret, 142 N.J. Super. 11, 359 A.2d 526 (1976). The "municipalities should pursue and cooperate in available federal and state subsidy programs for new housing and rehabilitation of substandard housing, although it is beyond the issues in this litigation to order the expenditure of municipal funds or the allowance of tax abatements." *Id.*, slip op. at 35

296. 336 A.2d 713, 745 (1975). *But see* Oakwood at Madison, Inc. v. Township of Madison, 117 N.J. Super. 11, 283 A.2d 353 (1971), aff'd — N.J. —, 371 A.2d 1192, 1224 (1977), where the court says that although there may be a moral obligation for municipal sponsorship of public housing projects, there is no lawful basis for a court to impose such action as obligatory.

297. The formation of a housing authority is less important under the Housing and Community Development Act of 1974 than previously. The act relies more on housing assistance payments, which supplement rental payments of low-income persons (Title 8 of the act, P.L. 93-383, § 201(a)(8), 42 U.S.C. § 1437f) than on constructing new publicly owned housing. HUD regulations

tion agreements, the making of applications for state and federal funding, and the construction, where necessary, of publicly owned low-rent housing.[298]

Local government for many years has had the right to determine the need for federally assisted public housing within its jurisdiction, and no contract for such housing could be signed with HUD until the local government had shown such a need and also signed a cooperation agreement.[299] Thus a suburb would veto public housing sponsored either by a regional or local housing authority by refusing to sign such an agreement.[300] The Housing and Community Development Act of 1974 retains the requirement of a determination of need for low-rent housing by the local governing body before contracts for conventional public housing are signed.[301]

There is a second, weaker provision for local approval of federally assisted housing within a locality which applies to conventional public housing and, for the first time, to subsidized housing such as the Section 8 leased housing assistance program, Sections 235 and 236 subsidy programs, and certain other housing assistance programs.[302] HUD must notify the local government of each application received for these programs, and the local government may object to the application, but only on one ground: namely, that it is inconsistent with the HAP, which is required by the 1974 Act in applying for community development block grants.[303] However, since a showing of inconsistency would probably be difficult for the local government to make, this provision for local approval probably has no teeth. Furthermore, HUD may override the objection if it determines

---

provide that new housing is to be built only when the existing housing supply is inadequate (24 C.F.R. 1273.103). Furthermore, HUD may enter into contracts directly with owners of housing when no public housing agency exists. P.L. 93-383, § 201(a)(8)(b)(1), 42 U.S.C. 1437f(b)(1).

298. State enabling legislation ordinarily provides for expeditious creation of housing authorities and commissions. Such authorities are usually created by resolution or ordinance, in some states subject to local voter approval. Antieau, *Local Government Law* § 30F.01.

299. 42 U.S.C. § 1415(7)(a)(b), reenacted in the 1974 act as 42 U.S.C. § 1437c(e)(1)(2).

300. *See, e.g.*, Mahaley v. Cuyahoga Metropolitan Housing Authority, 500 F.2d 1087 (6th Cir. 1974). A federal court may not impose federally assisted housing over the objections of a nonimplicated suburb in an order directing metropolitanwide relief. Hills v. Gautreaux, 425 U.S. 284 (1976).

301. 42 U.S.C. § 1437c(e)(1)(2). However, the Section 8 leased housing assistance program, 42 U.S.C. § 1437f, is now excluded from this provision for local determination of need, P.L. 93-383, § 201(a)(8)(h), 42 U.S.C. § 1437f(h), and these rental assistance payments now constitute the central thrust of federally assisted housing.

302. 42 U.S.C. § 1439.

303. 42 U.S.C. § 1439(a)(5).

that the application *is* consistent with the municipality's HAP. Arguably, an applicant who has been denied permission to build subsidized housing on the ground that such construction would be "inconsistent with the local housing assistance plan" could appeal to the court as well as to HUD for a determination that the denial rather than the permission would be inconsistent with the policies of the HAP.

These federal statutory requirements for local approval of federally assisted housing would not necessarily block imposition by a state court, as a remedy for past discriminatory practices, of the provision of conventional public housing by a municipality. The state court could order the local government to sign a cooperation agreement in conformity with the federal statute.[304] Such an order would be required in a situation where the court found the municipality had failed to provide its regional fair share of low-cost housing, and that the best method to remedy this past discrimination was actual provision, under government sponsorship, of low-rent conventional housing. The state court would, in effect, make the determination of need for the local government, and withdraw the power of a locality to veto needed housing after the court had made a finding of unconstitutionally discriminatory action. Thus, no apparent supremacy problem exists, since the court, as an arm of the state, would be making the determination of need.

Where state statutes require local approval of public housing, state courts could suspend operation of the statute as it applies to the defendant municipality until the municipality had provided the quantity of low-rent housing required by the court order.[305] Suspension of the statute requiring or permitting local approval would be an effective remedy for the court to impose, since the court would have no control over the outcome of an election.

There is substantial literature that describes inclusionary land regulation.[306] Such regulation generally consists of granting special permits for low- or moderate-income residential projects consistent with a housing allocation plan.[307] One technique of inclusionary

---

304. 42 U.S.C. § 1437c(e)(1)(2).

305. *See* Gautreaux v. Chicago Housing Authority (342 F. Supp. 828 (N.D. Ill. 1972), *aff'd*, 480 F.2d 210 (7th Cir. 1973), in which the district court suspended application to the Chicago Housing Authority of an Illinois statute requiring local approval for public housing.

306. *See* In-Zoning, *supra* note 218; and Chapter 7 *infra*.

307. The special permit can be a variance, a conditional-use permit, the placement of a floating zone, or permission might be granted pursuant to conditional contract, or site-specific zoning, or some analogous flexible technique. *See id.* at 116-22.

regulation might be especially useful to satisfy affirmative obligations—inclusion of a percentage of low- and moderate-income units in new multifamily residential projects. At least three local jurisdictions have adopted ordinances requiring that a set percentage of lower income housing be included in all new multifamily residential projects greater than a particular size.[308] There has been little experience to date under the ordinances. One was held invalid, however, in *Board of Supervisors of Fairfax County v. DeGroff Enterprises.*[309] There the Virginia Supreme Court determined that the ordinance was both beyond the authority granted under the state enabling act and would constitute a "taking" of private property. Commentators are optimistic, however, that such mandatory ordinances will survive legal attack in other states.[310] They also point out that such ordinance requirements mesh well with the new Section 8 leased housing program authorized under the Housing and Community Development Act of 1974, which provides for mixing subsidized leased units in the same building with unsubsidized units.[311]

Another approach is to create incentives by ordinance for the inclusion of lower income units in multifamily residential projects. Such bonuses usually take the form of granting additional densities and relaxing other requirements in order to eliminate or ameliorate economic loss resulting from the inclusions.[312]

Mandating Provision of Public Utilities. A local government, by failing to provide adequate utility services,[313] may exclude new hous-

308. Fairfax County, Virginia; Montgomery County, Maryland; Los Angeles, California. A detailed analysis of the three ordinances appears in Klevin, *Inclusionary Ordinances. Policy and Legal Issues in Requiring Private Developers to Build Low Cost Housing* 21 U.C.L.A. L. Rev. 1432 (1974). *See also* In-Zoning, *supra* note 218, at 131–41; and Chapter 7 *infra.*

309. 214 Va. 235, 198 S.E.2d 600 (1973). This case is discussed in the section "Mandatory Inclusionary Ordinances" in Chapter 7 *infra.*

310. In-Zoning, *supra* note 218, at 138–40.

311. *Id.* at 134.

312. *See generally id.* at 122–24, 140; and Chapter 7 *infra.* The New Jersey Supreme Court distinguished between density bonuses keyed to quantitative or bulk concessions by the builder—such as added bedrooms—or bonuses keyed to sale price concessions, in providing a percentage of low-cost housing. Of the former, the court said such bonuses are "both valid and mandatory where necessary to achieve sufficient suitable least-cost housing," but refused to pass on the validity of the latter. Oakwood at Madison, Inc. v. Township of Madison, 117 N.J. Super. 11, 283 A.2d 353 (1971 aff'd — N.J. —, 371 A.2d 1192, 1210, 1225 (1977). *See also id.* (Pashman, J. concurring and dissenting), 1258–1259.

313. The term public utilities covers a wide range of capital-intensive municipal activities that must be extended to newly developed neighborhoods. For simplicity, we will refer merely to water and sewage systems in the accompany-

ing as effectively as by enforcing exclusionary land-use regulations. If a court concludes that a locality[314] is improperly excluding new housing opportunities, especially for low-income families and racial minorities, it may find it necessary to order the municipality to provide requisite services. This section discusses how this might be done.

Conflict may arise in one of several contexts. First, a city's refusal to extend services or to enlarge the capacity of utilities, such as water or sanitary sewage, might be challenged with regard to a specific site. Thus, a complainant might be refused a permit for a hookup or extension of public utilities to a project, or a building permit might be withheld on the ground that public services in the locality are inadequate to service the project. Second, a complainant, in a representative capacity or otherwise, might seek to attack a particular policy toward the provision of services, such as a moratorium on building permits or sewer hookups, with no specific development as a focus of the challenge. Finally, necessary extension or enlargement of public services might become an issue in connection with a general challenge to a city's exclusionary regulatory policies, if inadequate facilities seemingly create an obstacle to providing the opportunity for low-cost housing.

---

ing discussion because they are essential to new development, require large capital expenditures, yet their extension is subject to municipal discretion. Capital outlays have increased 50 percent in the nation's cities in the past decade. The following figures are a summary of all municipal expenditures for public services in 1970/71, rounded to the nearest million dollars.

Police protection	$3,500	Education	$5,200
Fire protection	$2,000	Libraries	$ 450
Highways	$2,700	Health and hospitals	$2,300
Sanitation	$3,000	Recreation	$1,400
Public Welfare	$2,700	Housing and Urban Renewal	$1,400

International City Management Association, 1973 Municipal Yearbook, Table 1/1 at 92.

314. The discussion herein is confined to governmentally managed facilities because the subject of this chapter includes the practices and policies of local governments with regard to low-cost housing. It is probable, however, that a court would find that these obligations can also be imposed on privately owned utility companies if their practices are creating obstacles to dispersed housing. In that case the court might join the state public utility commission, which regulates actions of private utilities.

Public utilities are also furnished by special-purpose districts, established pursuant to state laws. These may be organized on a regional basis, with their own governing boards, and are not subject to the direction of city or county legislatures. Plaintiffs objecting to the exclusionary effects of their policies would have to bring an action directly against such districts. In an action against a local government the private utility company or the special district could be joined as defendants, since the local government has no control over their policies. The issue of extension of services beyond city limits is not discussed here.

The organization of this section follows the stages at which requisite actions may or may not be taken by a municipality for the provision of utilities. These actions may encourage or discourage increased urban development. At one stage a municipality gives or withholds permission to individual applicants to hook up to lines and mains already installed. At another stage, a municipality extends or refuses to extend supply lines and mains to undeveloped sections within the service area upon reasonable demand. At a third stage, a municipality decides whether or not to improve or enlarge inadequate facilities or sources of supply for its entire service area. The legal obligations to comply with development demands, and the financing of each stage of service differ; therefore, each is discussed in turn.

There is no serious problem confronting a court where an applicant is denied permission to hook up to existing facilities (as with water mains and sewer lines) that have adequate capacity to service the new project. The universal rule governing provision of utility services by a public service company, or a municipality performing the duties of a public service company, is that all applicants must be served equally. If facilities are installed and capacity is adequate, the duty to permit hookups is ministerial and may be compelled by an appropriate action, such as one in mandamus.[315] The cost of connecting to existing lines is considered an operating expense, not a capital outlay, and is usually financed either by the developer or from operating revenues. Since the city ordinarily has no discretion to refuse service, and there are no financing problems posed given the existence of capacity, a court should have no problem ordering that the requisite permits be issued.

More extensive problems arise when construction of projects, such as low-income housing developments, is proposed in outlying sections beyond the developed portion of the service area. In such a situation the city must make a determination whether or not to extend lines or mains. The baseline doctrine here is similar to that already mentioned: when a city is the sole supplier of services in an area, it is governed by the same obligations as a privately owned utility,[316] and it must extend service to all who make reasonable demands.[317]

315. Delmarva Enterprises, Inc. v. Mayor and Council of Dover, 282 A.2d 601 (Del. 1971).

316. Robinson v. City of Boulder, 547 P.2d 228 (1974) *aff'd*, Colorado Supreme Court, No. 26720 (Mar. 15, 1976); Reid Development Corporation v. Parsipanny Troy Hills, 89 A.2d 667, 670 (N.J. 1952). *See also* Note, *Control of the Timing and Location of Government Utility Extensions*, 26 Stan. L. Rev. 945 (1974) [hereinafter cited as *Control of Government Utility*

The standard of "reasonableness" permits the exercise of some discretion.[318] Examples of reasonable bases for refusal to extend utilities to previously unserviced areas have been that the proposed development is too remote from developed sections of the service area,[319] that the economic return from new customers probably will not justify the expenditure,[320] that expected demand will be light compared to the cost of extending service,[321] and other utility-related reasons.[322]

Refusals to extend utilities premised on other reasons, however, have been invalidated in a number of instances. Thus, when Boulder, Colorado, to effectuate a land plan, vetoed a utility extension to control residential development on the urban fringe, the veto was overturned[323] in an opinion stressing the impermissibility of denying extensions for non-utility-related reasons:

> The City has not cited, nor has the Court been able to locate, any case which permitted a city holding an exclusive franchise for utility services to deny extension of those franchise services for non-utility related reasons, such as growth control, where the city had the capacity to provide the services. . . .[324]

Courts in other jurisdictions, of course, might view this method of regulating growth with more favor.[325] Courts have also invalidated

---

Extensions] for an argument that important differences should be recognized between government and privately owned utilities.

317. See authorities cited in note 316 *supra.*

318. Lawrence v. Richards, 88 A. 92 (Me. 1913); Rose v. Plymouth Town, 173 P.2d 285 (Utah 1946). *See generally* 12 E. McQuillen, Municipal Corporations, § 35.35 (R. Smith ed. 1970); Annotation: Municipal Water System— Extension, 48 A.L.R. 2d 1188 (1956); *Control of Government Utility Extensions, supra* note 316. For a discussion of the obligation of private utility companies to extend service, see Lukrawka v. Spring Valley Water Co., 169 Cal. 318, 146 P. 640 (1915), still the leading case. *See generally* Am. Jur. Pub. Util. § 16; Note, *Duty of a Public Utility to Render Adequate Service: Its Scope and Enforcement,* 62 Col. L. Rev. 312 (1962).

319. Lawrence v. Richards, 88 A. 92 (Me. 1913).

320. Rose v. Plymouth Town, 173 P.2d 285 (Utah 1946).

321. Reid Dev. Corp. v. Parsippany-Troy Hills Tp., 107 A.2d 20 (N.J. App. Div. 1954).

322. *See* cases cited in *Control of Government Utility Extension, supra* note 316, n. 26 at 949.

323. Robinson v. City of Boulder, 547 P.2d 228 (1974), *aff'd* Colorado Sup. Ct. No. 26720 (Mar. 15, 1976).

324. *Id.* at 246. *See also* Reid Dev. Corp. v. Parsipanny-Troy Hills Township, 107 A.2d 20 (N.J. App. Div. 1954).

325. *Cf.* Construction Industry Ass'n v. City of Petaluma, 375 F. Supp. 574 (N.D. Cal. 1973), *rev'd,* 522 F.2d 897 (9th Cir. 1975), *cert. denied,* 424 U.S. 934 (1976).

refusals to extend service when it is clear that such refusals were based on racial discrimination.[326]

An unanswered question is whether a court would order the extension of utility services where the effect of a refusal is exclusion of low-cost housing, even though the refusal is based on reasonable utility-related grounds. To put it another way, is there an affirmative duty to provide utilities in order to make possible the opportunity for a larger share of low-cost housing? As was discussed earlier,[327] there are possible statutory and constitutional sources for a municipal obligation to foster the production of low-income housing. This obligation could easily include the extension of utilities. In fact, utility extension probably raises fewer questions than production of housing, because, for reasons explored below, a financial base is better assured.

Affirmative action to extend utilities was proposed, but not ordered, in the *Mount Laurel* case.[328] The city claimed that its requirement of a 20,000-square-foot minimum lot size, found by the court to be exclusionary, was required for safe sewage disposal and water supply. The court concluded that the land was amenable to utility installations, and that "the township could require them as improvements by developers or install them under the special assessment or other appropriate statutory procedure."[329] In effect, the court was suggesting that the city was obligated to extend its sewage and water lines if their absence required imposition of exclusionary land-use controls.

Financing court-ordered extensions of utility services should not raise serious problems. Provisions for financing could be included in the court order, but it would seem reasonable to permit the city to select an appropriate method. Normally, voter approval need not be sought, because extensive capital outlays, which often mean voter-approved bonds, are not usually required for the extension of lines or mains and attendant facilities.[330] Rather, water and sewer extensions

326. Kennedy Park Homes Ass'n v. City of Lackawanna, 318 F. Supp. 669 (W.D.N.Y. 1970), *aff'd*, 436 F.2d 108 (2d Cir. 1970), *cert. denied*, 401 U.S. 1010 (1971); United Farm Workers v. City of Delray Beach, 493 F.2d 799 (5th Cir. 1974).

327. *See* text accompanying notes 274–86 *supra. Cf.* Metropolitan Housing Corp. v. Village of Arlington Heights, 517 F.2d 409 (7th Cir. 1975), *rev'd*, 97 S. Ct. 555 1977.

328. Southern Burlington County NAACP v. Township of Mount Laurel, 67 N.J. 151, 336 A.2d 713 (1975), *appeal dismissed and cert. denied*, 423 U.S. 808 (1975).

329. *Id.* at 731.

330. For example, an additional water reservoir might cost roughly $100,000; a sewage pumping plant between $40,000 and $70,000 (estimates given by

are generally paid for by the abutting property owner or subdivision developer, by the utility, or by some combination of these, and no apparent reason exists for a court to order a city to alter its customary financing equations so as to excuse the low-cost builder from the same fraction of financial burden imposed on other developers.

In new subdivisions, a majority of cities require developers to install sewers at their own expense.[331] The developer may be repaid some or all of these costs over time by the utility to the extent justified by receipts.[332] Alternatively, a municipality may make the improvements and assess the property owner for the cost,[333] or impose an impact fee to defray a portion of the costs.[334] Special assessment districts are often formed, which allow repayment over a number of years[335] to ease the burden of large outlays by homeowners and developers. The utility finances the assessment by issuing long-term obligations paid for out of revenues. The assessment becomes a lien against abutting properties. The total assessment normally is roughly related to benefits received, and is allocated on the basis of lot frontage, consumption or use, or increase in market value due to the presence of the utility.

Where a city imposes a substantial portion of the cost of extending facilities on the developer, a low-income housing developer may find

Frank Howard, attorney for East Bay Municipal Utilities District, a Bay Area, California special district). Main extensions above six inches are paid for by the district, financed out of water charges and ad valorem taxes.

331. Institute of Urban Research, University of Connecticut, Financing the Hartford Metropolitan District: With Special Reference to the Extension of Sanitary Sewers XXIV (Connecticut Urban Research Report No. 6, Aug. 1964) [hereinafter cited as Connecticut Urban Research Report].

332. Deerfield Estates, Inc. v. Township of E. Brunswick, 286 A.2d 498, 507 (N.J. 1972); Lakewood v. Lakewood Water Co., 102 A.2d 671 (N.J. App. Div. 1954) (private utility company); Connecticut Urban Research Report, *supra*, note 331. The report contains figures showing that in financing new subdivisions the developer pays the total cost of financing sewer extensions in 79 percent of the cities reporting. The figures applied to 76 cities with populations between 100,000 and 500,000. In 18.5 percent of these cities the developer shared the costs with the city.

333. 1975 amendment to New Mexico subdivision law, reported in 27 Zoning Dig. 328 (1975).

334. City of Dunedin v. Contractors and Builders Ass'n, 312 So.2d 763 (Fla. 1975). The court approved an impact fee of $325 for each water connection and $375 for each sewer connection, an amount in excess of the cost of connection, for use in future expansions. A utility's share of extension costs are usually recaptured from user charges based on consumption and ad valorem taxes. Half the cities in the country use sewer service charges to finance construction of trunk and interceptor sewers. Connecticut Urban Research Report, *supra* note 331, at 49.

335. *Id.* Special assessments are the most common method of financing utility extensions, though larger cities tend to share the cost with the developer or homeowner.

that the resulting housing units are priced out of the low-cost market. This can be minimized, however, under various subsidy programs. Under the Section 235 and 236 federally subsidized programs, some of these costs have been includable as off-site costs, if other construction costs have not exhausted the project ceiling. And it is possible that such costs may be absorbed as off-site project costs in some low-rent public housing programs, such as turnkey projects. In any event, the costs incurred are not usually substantial when viewed as amortized payments over the life of the mortgage or the period of long-term debt obligation of a special assessment district.

The most difficult situations arise where a municipality refuses or delays permission for connections to existing lines, or for extension of service, because there is a lack of capacity in its sewage treatment plant or its water supply works, and this frustrates the provision of fair share housing.[336] Under what circumstances is it appropriate for a court to order the municipality to enlarge or improve these utilities?

Presumably in a jurisdiction such as New Jersey, that enforces a fair share obligation, or perhaps in any jurisdiction under equal protection reasoning, it would be illegal to turn down a low-income project because of inadequacy of utilities where comparable upper-income projects are permitted despite the inadequacies. In a leading analogous case involving racial minorities, *Kennedy Park Homes Association v. City of Lackawanna*,[337] the court found that although the city's "sewer crisis" actually existed, inadequate sewage facilities were not the real reason for the city's opposition to the proposed housing project. Plaintiffs sought to construct housing for blacks in a virtually all-white ward of the city. During the ten-year period when it was recognized that the sewage facilities were inadequate, the city nevertheless continued to issue subdivision and building permits, and failed to take even preliminary steps to remedy the sewage-treatment problem. The court found for the plaintiffs and ordered the city to apply to the county health department for permission to discharge sewage from the proposed project into the city's system. The court also ordered that if the county disapproved the application, the city was to "take whatever action is necessary to provide

---

336. "Water supply works for metropolitan areas consist generally of wells, raw and/or filtered water pumping stations, watershed lands, dams, reservoirs, treatment works, main supply lines to the metropolitan area, and filtered water storage structures of various kinds." Financing Metropolitan Government 97 (Symposium Conducted by the Princeton Tax Institute 1955).

337. 318 F. Supp. 669 (W.D.N.Y. 1970), *aff'd*, 436 F.2d 108 (2d Cir. 1970), *cert. denied*, 401 U.S. 1010 (1971).

adequate sewage service to the Kennedy Parks Homes Association subdivision."[338]

Site-related challenges to a city's refusal to enlarge its utility capacity might also be based on exclusionary effect rather than exclusionary intent. The issue arises in cases dealing with obligations of a city to continue expansion of capacity in the face of increasing population pressures. The plaintiff is usually contesting restrictive land-use controls, such as large-lot requirements[339] or limits on multifamily housing.[340] Most recently, a Pennsylvania court wrote: "Suburban municipalities within the area of urban outpour must meet the problems of population expansion into [their] borders by increasing municipal services, and not by the practice of exclusionary zoning."[341] Although in this case the court was not being asked to order increased municipal services, the quoted language indicates probable judicial receptivity to such a plea in an appropriate case.

A general challenge to a city's lack of public utility capacity could arise obliquely in connection with an attack on its land-use regulations,[342] or directly in connection with a moratorium on services or a failure to enlarge facilities.[343] A number of cities have imposed moratoria on further utility connections or on the issuance of building permits to solve the problem when service capacity falls behind the continuing pressure from developers. Courts in some instances have been sympathetic where the city is making efforts to rectify the inadequacy during the breathing spell provided by the moratorium.[344]

---

338. 318 F. Supp. 669, 697 (W.D.N.Y. 1970). The court was silent as to the necessary means to finance the needed construction.

339. Appeal of Kit-Mar Builders, Inc., 439 Pa. 466, 268 A.2d 765 (1970).

340. Appeal of Girsh, 437 Pa. 237, 263 A.2d 395 (1970).

341. Township of Willistown. v. Chesterdale Farms, Inc., 462 Pa. 445 341 A.2d 466 (1975); *accord*, Smookler v. Tp. of Wheatfield, 207 N.W.2d 464 (1973). In this case the zoning ordinance provided for mobile home parks, but no land had been designated for such use. When plaintiff sought rezoning to permit such construction, the application was denied on the basis of the increased fiscal and population impact on the town. The court held that increased burdens on the town for future services that would be required was not sufficient justification for exclusionary zoning.

342. Southern Burlington County NAACP v. Township of Mount Laurel, 67 N.J. 151, 336 A.2d 713, *appeal dismissed and cert. denied*, 423 U.S. 808 (1975).

343. While one case holds that a utility may be permitted to act defensively and to refuse to expand in order to prevent urbanization of the service area, this is the sole authority to this effect. *See* Wilson v. Hidden Valley Municipal Water District, 125 Cal. 2d 271, 63 Cal. Rptr. 889 (1967).

344. Smoke Rise, Inc. v. Washington Suburban Sanitary Comm'n, 400 F. Supp. 1369 (1975), Growth Control Monitor 458; *In re* Belle Harbor Realty Corp., 35 N.Y.2d 507, 364 N.Y.S.2d 160 (Dec. 1974).

In fact, it is arguable that where a city imposes such a moratorium it assumes an enforceable obligation to complete the remedial action.[345]

In the *Ramapo* case, control of building permits for a period up to 18 years, pending scheduled provision of adequate public services, was found valid in the face of due process claims, largely because of the undertaking to provide services in accordance with a plan.[346] It is not clear, however, that a court would sustain such a moratorium where there is no showing of the intention or the means of enlarging utility capacity.[347] It is instructive to note that courts have ordered

345. Letter from Commission member Robert Freilich, Professor of Law, University of Missouri-Kansas City School of Law, and former counsel, City of Ramapo, New York.

346. Golden v. Planning Bd. of Ramapo, 30 N.Y.2d 359, 285 N.E.2d 291, *appeal dismissed,* 409 U.S. 1003 (1972).

347. A water hookup moratorium was declared in Marin County, California, following defeat at the polls of a bond issue to finance an increased water supply. Several cases challenged the necessity for the moratorium; none successfully. *See* Swanson v. Marin Municipal Water District, 56 Cal. App. 3d 512 (1976). Voters approved a $19 million bond issue in 1976 to bring water from a closer source. However, a statewide drought has necessitated water rationing by the district averaging 46 gallons per person per day. Conversation with Thomas Thorner, attorney for the district, Feb. 1, 1977.

An initiative banning residential building permits in Livermore, California, was recently validated by the California Supreme Court in Associated Homebuilders v. City of Livermore, 135 Cal. Rptr. 41 (1976). The ban is to be enforced until problems of overcrowded schools, water shortage, and inadequate sewer facilities can be met. First, the court held that ordinances enacted by initiative need not comply with statutory requirements of notice and hearing to be valid. The court went on to find the ban a valid exercise of the police power, despite the fact that the measure specified no timetable and no individual or agency to complete needed improvements. Charges of vagueness of standards by which eventual adequacy of expanded facilities could be judged were rejected by the court. The ordinance standards were rendered sufficiently specific by incorporating by reference the standards established by other state and local agencies. Finally, the court held that even land-use ordinances that substantially limit immigration into a community do not call for strict judicial scrutiny. Cases from other states, the court ruled, which hold that communities lack the authority to adopt such exclusionary ordinances, rest on principles of state law inapplicable to California, which has a strong tradition of deferring to legislative judgment. According to the court's reasoning, since the Livermore ordinance banned *all* residential building permits temporarily, rather than impeding only low- and moderate-cost housing, the question of denial of equal protection did not arise. However, the California court did observe that the external impact of such restrictions is relevant to determining its relationship to the public welfare, referring to the "regional general welfare" doctrine articulated in *Mount Laurel* for the basis of this principle, *id.* at 64. Consequently, the court sent the case back for trial to determine whether the Livermore policy was reasonably related to the welfare of the *region,* rather than the city, stating: "For the guidance of the trial court we point out that a restriction must be measured by its impact the surrounding region." *Id.* at 55. *See also* the sharply worded dissent of the surrounding region." Slip op. at 28. *See also* the sharply worded dissent of Judge Mosk, who would have invalidated the ordinance on the ground that the "total exclusion of new residents" cannot be constitutionally accomplished under a city's police power.

municipalities to enlarge or to improve utilities to insure health and environmental protection where other public agencies have noted substantial departures from statutory standards.[348] While the remedies in these cases are often statutorily mandated, the cases demonstrate that such court orders are considered feasible and proper in the health and environmental contexts, even though they may raise enforcement difficulties. The same remedies would seem similarly propitious in remedying the exclusion of fair share housing.

Large capital expenditures are often required to increase the capacity of municipal utility services. Unlike the financing of service extensions, enlargement of a system can entail great expense, long-range financial planning, and, in many instances, some form of debt financing. There are various means by which a municipality may raise the necessary capital. While general obligation bonds may seem at first to be the principal source of funds, a municipality has other options not subject to voter-approval restrictions. The existence of these alternative methods of financing creates more opportunities for judicially imposed relief than is generally presumed. Some of these alternatives are considered here.

At present, established utilities often finance extensions and some enlargements from capital-improvement funds that have been accumulated from service charges and *ad valorem* taxes.[349] These funds, however, take years to accumulate unless unacceptably high rates are charged. Taxes can be increased to swell the fund at a more rapid pace. For "young" suburbs, however, this source of financing probably is not yet available.

A number of techniques have been developed to avoid debt limitations imposed by state statutes or constitutions.[350] In general, these methods are based on the formation or use of some entity not subject to these limitations. In California, as an illustration, public employee retirement funds have been used, or nonprofit corporations have been formed for the purpose of constructing a particular project. The local government rents the facilities for an extended period, at the end of which time they are purchased. The ingenuity

---

For an argument that a good-faith effort must be made to augment water shortages by all means, including rationing, before a moratorium is permitted under California law, *see* Note, *The Thirst for Population Control: Water Hook-up Moratoria and the Duty to Augment Supply,* 27 Hastings L.J. 753 (1976).

348. Commonwealth *ex rel.* Alessandroni v. Borough of Confluence, 234 A.2d 852 (Pa. 1967); Ramey Borough v. Commonwealth, 327 A.2d 647 (Pa. 1975); Charles v. Diamond, 345 N.Y.S.2d 764 (1973).

349. Conversation with D. Ballentine, Director, California Municipal Utilities Association, December 19, 1975.

350. *See generally,* J. Beebe, D. Hodgman, & F. Sutherland, *Joint Powers Authority Revenue Bonds,* 41 So. Cal. L. Rev. 19 (1967).

of these lease-purchase devices testifies to the ability of local governments to invent financing methods when circumstances require new solutions.

In many instances, however, the local government will find it necessary to resort to some form of debt financing to raise necessary capital. There are two principal categories of municipal bonds—general obligation bonds and revenue bonds. The former are more attractive in many respects because they are more marketable. General obligation bonds are secured by the full faith, credit, and taxing power of the issuing jurisdiction, so they offer a lower risk to investors. They therefore bear a lower interest rate than revenue bonds, which are payable solely from the proceeds derived from whatever operation is being financed. In either case the bonds may be repaid with income derived from the utility.

In a few states, such as California, however, there is a requirement that a higher percentage of voters approve general obligation bonds than revenue bonds. The California Constitution requires that two-thirds of the voters approve such bonds,[351] while a statute requires a simple majority for the adoption of revenue bond proposals.[352] Furthermore, in home rule jurisdictions such as California, some types of cities may be permitted to issue revenue bonds without a vote unless the charter forbids such action.[353] Finally, while general obligation bonds are often subject to constitutional or statutory debt limitations, revenue bonds generally are not. However, if the amount sold reaches an unfavorable balance with anticipated revenues, the marketability of revenue bonds would be adversely affected. In light of the comparative advantages of each type of bond, a local government may find it more practical to borrow for capital expansions by using revenue bonds, even though they are more expensive.

If a court orders a municipally managed utility to improve or expand its plant, the selection of the most desirable financing arrangement probably should be left initially to the defendant. The court order would be limited to requiring enlargement of facilities. The defendant would be expected to solve the many problems attendant on compliance, perhaps making regular reports to the court on progress made.

Courts have taken this approach when they found it necessary to order municipalities to improve or construct sewage-treatment plants

351. California Constitution, § 18, art. 16 (West Supp. 1975).

352. Cal. Gov't. Code § 4386 (West 1966).

353. City of Santa Monica v. Grubb, 245 Cal. App. 2d 718, 54 Cal. Rptr. 210 (1966); Redwood City v. Moore, 231 Cal. App. 2d 563, 42 Cal. Rptr. 72 (1965).

in environmental cases. The financial inability of the defendant cities was held to be no defense to compliance.[354] Instead, the courts indicated that economic impossibility, if proved, would be a factor to be considered in a later action to enforce the judgment. In one such case, the Pennsylvania Supreme Court said:

> There is no indication in the pleadings that appellants have exhausted every possible avenue in an effort to find some way of financing this sewage construction. . . . [T]here have been and will continue to be a number of governmental programs designed to alleviate these conditions. New methods of financing in this area are being developed constantly for those who heretofor have been unable to raise the necessary funds.[355]

Should the city refuse to comply with the court's order and fail to secure the necessary financing, only then would the court be faced with the difficult problem of how to enforce its order. While there are no examples of judicially ordered bond issues to finance utility expansions, such a course of action is not impossible. Presumably, the court can compel the local governing body to take any steps within its control toward attaining needed funds. Some resources may already be on hand, such as authorization to issue bonds still remaining unused from some previous referendum. There may be some reserves accumulated in a capital improvement fund. But if these sources prove inadequate, the city will have to borrow money through a new bond issue. While the city government will need to approve the issuance of the bonds, or, if the bonds must first be approved by the voters, approve placing them on the ballot, a court can order these steps to be taken. But what happens if the electorate fails to approve?[356] Anticipating this possibility, one court wrote: "Neither Petaluma city officials, nor the local electorate may use their power to disapprove bonds at the polls as a weapon to define or destroy fundamental constitutional rights."[357] This court was never called upon to demonstrate how it could compel issuance of the needed bonds, since its decision was reversed on appeal.[358]

354. Commonwealth *ex rel.* Allesandroni v. Borough of Confluence, 234 A.2d 852, 854 (Pa. 1967); Ramey Borough v. Commonwealth, 327 A.2d 647, 650 (Pa. 1975).
355. Commonwealth *ex rel.* Alessandroni v. Borough of Confluence, 234 A.2d 852, 853-54 (Pa. 1967).
356. *See* Rose v. Plymouth Town, 173 P.2d 285 (Utah 1946).
357. Construction Industry Ass'n v. City of Petaluma, 375 F. Supp. 574, 583 (N.D. Cal. 1974), *rev'd*, 522 F.2d 897 (9th Cir. 1975).
358. *Id.* at 899. The appellate court upheld a growth-control ordinance invalidated by the trial court so the need to increase public services was at least temporarily mooted.

If voters should fail to give the necessary approval to a proposed bond issue, is the municipality relieved of its obligation to enlarge its capital facilities? If so, a court would be permitting the electorate of a municipality to evade the order of the court, although evasion by municipal officials could result in an action for contempt of court.

Under the circumstances it would seem appropriate for a court to suspend the applicable state requirement for voter approval on the ground that the electorate of a municipality has no greater authority to deny state or federal constitutional rights of aggrieved persons than is possessed by municipal officials. One court suspended a state statute which had the effect of thwarting compliance with its order and "correction of federal constitutional wrongs."[359] While the court in this case was protecting a federal constitutional right against operation of a state statute,[360] it would seem that a state court could also suspend a state statute the effect of which is to prevent correction of a constitutional wrong.

The "utility problem" vexes those seeking to define the proper role of courts in dealing with the use of land-regulatory powers for exclusionary ends. The vexation arises principally because the mind too soon contemplates the judicial dilemma created where financing depends on voter-approved bonds and the electorate is negative. This section seeks to illustrate that this ultimate dilemma should only rarely arise, and that effective remedies short of suspension of referendum requirements will normally be available to courts to assure requisite financing. Only in the most extreme case will this ultimate confrontation occur, and if it does there is an appropriate path available.

POLICY STATEMENTS

1. The appropriateness of judicial intervention on behalf of those adversely affected by local land-use decisions depends on: (a) the importance of the values at stake; (b) the possibility of these values being vindicated without judicial intervention; and (c) the ability of courts to deal competently and successfully with the conflicts at issue.

---

359. Gautreaux v. Chicago Housing Authority, 342 F. Supp. 827, 829 (N.D. Ill. 1972), *aff'd,* 480 F.2d 210 (7th Cir. 1973). In this case an Illinois statute requiring the approval of public housing sites by the local government prevented acquisition of any sites when the Chicago City Council failed to act on all proposals submitted to it.

360. *See* discussion of the court's action in Note, *Desegregation and Public Housing,* 8 Urb. L. Ann. 265 (1974).

The Advisory Commission views opportunities for decent living accommodations in decent environments, freedom from law-imposed discrimination based on income (and income as a surrogate for race), and access to employment and educational opportunities as fundamental values. Moreover, history indicates the unlikelihood that these values will be satisfactorily vindicated in the absence of judicial intervention, since those adversely affected by parochial exclusionary decisions have little, if any, voice in their formulation and few effective political means to overturn them. Consequently, the Advisory Commission advocates judicial intervention to the extent that the courts are competent to handle successfully the resulting litigation.

Suggested criteria for evaluating judicial effectiveness in this area include: (a) the existence of a constitutional standard; and (b) adequate control by the courts over the means of effectuating enforcement. In the landmark case of *Southern Burlington County N.A.A.C.P. v. Township of Mount Laurel*, 67 N.J. 151, 336 A.2d 713, *cert. denied*, 423 U.S. 808 (1975), the New Jersey Supreme Court held that presumptively a municipality cannot foreclose opportunities for low- and moderate-income housing and "in its regulations must affirmatively afford that opportunity at least to the extent of the municipality's fair share of present and prospective regional need therefor." For the following reasons, the above criteria are substantially satisfied by the standard articulated in the *Mount Laurel* decision: (a) the concept of regional "fair share" can be reasonably ascertained with one of several readily available methodological frameworks; (b) such a standard does not compel a relatively even distribution of low- and moderate-income housing throughout a region, it simply prohibits suburban localities from zoning out such a distribution should other incentives expect to bring it about; (c) such a standard is judicially administrable and does not necessarily require judicial participation in sophisticated planning decisions, many of which are essentially political; and (d) this approach invites an appropriate political response, *e.g.*, creation of a regional planning structure.

The Advisory Commission concludes that courts can fashion effective remedies and thus help to bring about fundamental changes in metropolitan housing patterns. In addition the Advisory Commission notes with approval a growing judicial trend to evaluate growth-management regulations in light of their impact on lower income housing. (It is not necessary that the courts specify a precise number for a locality's "fair share.") It is premature, however, to address the broader question of judicial intervention in such cases. At least three considerations lead us to this conclusion. First, normal market forces work in the interest of middle- and upper-income persons, and there is no persuasive showing to date that their needs will not be thus accommodated most readily in the absence of judicial intervention. Second, we cannot fashion simple standards upon which to premise effective and meaningful judicial intervention in cases beyond those involving low- and moderate-income housing. Third, judicial effort should be concentrated where the deprivation is clearest. Perhaps repetitive litigation centered on the exclusion of low- and moderate-income housing will evolve principles transferable to growth-management questions in general. But until that occurs courts should avoid an involvement that is fraught with so many variables that dangers of failure are greatly increased.

2. In exclusionary zoning litigation involving specific parcels of land, factors that should affect a court's decision whether to remand for local reconsideration or to rezone the parcel itself—where it has been concluded that the zoning regulation in question is invalid as applied—include: (a) whether or not local government authorities have been and are cooperative or obstructionist; and (b) the complexity and scale of the proposed project. Once a court has determined that existing zoning or a permit denial has the effect of excluding a town's fair share of regional low-cost housing, the burden should then shift to the defendant government to justify denial of the subject application for a permit or zoning change.

3. Ordinances that provide for multifamily housing by such techniques as "floating zones," special exceptions, or conditional uses could facilitate the judicial administration of land-use disputes. If the criteria for such special permissions are at all clear, grant or denial of the proposed development will be of a quasi-judicial nature, which is more comfortably subject to judicial review.

4. Whether or not a court decides to rezone a parcel in question or to grant a special permit, it is crucial that jurisdiction be retained and parties be instructed to follow a particular schedule, with reports back to the court. Such a process short-circuits the considerable delays that would result from a new suit to test the alleged obstructionism. It is particularly important that the initial judicial order be as precise as possible so that the defendant is under a realistic threat of contempt for disobedience.

5. When a court has invalidated all or portions of the zoning ordinance of a defendant government because its regulations preclude entry of any or a "fair share" of low-income persons, the local legislature initially is better suited than a court to the task of preparing

the new zoning provisions and policies. Compelling reasons must exist to alter these traditional roles. One such reason would be substantial intransigency by the town, for whatever reasons, to proceed in a timely and reasonable manner.

6. In most instances the parties should be required to submit proposed court orders, on notice, and they should be evaluated at a hearing. Such orders might cover the procedure to be utilized in fashioning a new plan, or, at the other extreme, the new plan itself. In many instances there will be a series of orders related to steps in the planning process, culminating in a final order sanctioning a particular plan. Consultant reports, if any, should also be circulated to the parties for comment prior to the hearing.

[The principal advantage of these procedures is to give the parties the opportunity to respond prior to and during hearings and to provide an opportunity for detailed analysis before the final formulation of the order in question. Such procedures provide the basis for further fact-finding, if any, necessary for the formulation of the order. Finally, pre-order hearing can be used to test the feasibility of possible attainable remedies.]

7. To assure the preparation of an acceptable plan or to facilitate the defendant government's task in amending its zoning ordinances to permit low-income housing: (a) court orders should be written with sufficient specificity so that the defendant knows exactly what it is expected to do and so the court can judge whether there has been compliance or default; (b) a short-range timetable (*e.g.*, 30–90 days) should be set by the court, with a concomitant requirement for status reports at regular intervals; (c) a committee should be appointed with the responsibility to accomplish the steps in the remedial process necessary for compliance with a court-mandated planning schedule; (d) the defendant city should not be able to deflect responsibility for compliance to an assortment of state, county, and municipal planning and permit-issuing agencies; and (e) the court, to compel a town to comply with a timetable, could either impose a moratorium on any other residential construction in the town pending compliance with the order, or impose a court-created plan. In some instances the court may choose to appoint a master to propose a plan.

8. Due to the complexities and number of stages involved in the process by which the court compels changes in plans and ordinances to afford low-income housing opportunities in a jurisdiction, the court must stand ready to amend its orders as new information or circumstances are brought to its attention, and to monitor and require the defendants to comply.

9. A court-appointed special master or consultant may be useful in judging the adequacy of the plans that are produced and in monitoring compliance.

10. Assuming the court has determined that the defendant's plans and ordinances do not permit the location within it of a "fair share" of the region's low-income housing, and that this failure is actionable, numerous sophisticated methodological approaches exist for the quantification of the "fair share," the determination of the locational structure of the planning scheme, and the establishment of the procedural framework for the implementation of the plan.

[A strict equal distribution of the required housing among the communities would ignore important planning considerations, *e.g.*, employment opportunity and availability of public transportation, essential services, and shopping centers. Moreover, it fails to take into consideration the suitability of the vacant land for intensive use, and fiscal and other resources (for instance, classroom space) in the various towns.]

Whether or not a self-executing formula is utilized, the regional nature of the "fair-share" approach highpoints the utility of having all the local political jurisdictions in the region before the court, rather than simply a particular city singled out as a sole defendant. If a formula approach is used, it should be devised through the joint action of all cities affected by it (or at least subject to their scrutiny). If a formula approach is not feasible, it becomes even more important to strive for a political compromise among the local jurisdictions, which can best be stimulated by a court that has all of them before it. Joinder of multiple-defendant localities within the region is permissible under the provisions of Federal Rule of Civil Procedure 19, and similar state rules.

11. In writing a court-ordered plan, it should be noted that neither the court nor the local government is necessarily starting from a clean slate. The Housing and Community Development Act of 1974 requires preparation of a Housing Assistance Plan by all applicants for community-development block grants. The plan must reflect the low-income housing needs of those residing in, or "expected to reside" in, the community. Since regional needs are thus a required consideration, such a plan could serve as the basis for the "fair-share" housing plan ordered by the court. Furthermore, regional housing allocation plans are already in existence in some metropolitan regions. At a minimum, such a plan would allot low-cost housing goals to the defendant community, but might also contain minimum standards for the location and size of housing units.

12. A number of methods are available for approaching the location problem in a "fair-share" effort, including: (a) specification on a map of particular locations where low-income housing is a permissible development; (b) implementation of flexible regulatory techniques such as "floating zones" or other zoning devices; and (c) implementation of inclusionary land-use control techniques, *e.g.*, requirements that a certain percentage of units in new residential projects be devoted to low-income residents, or through some public housing variation such as the provision of subsidized leaseholds in existing or newly constructed buildings.

13. A court-approved plan that relies heavily on flexible techniques for implementation leaves open the possibility for evasion through maladministration. Skeptical judicial scrutiny of decisions denying appropriate rezoning or permit issuance to applicants seeking to develop low-cost housing is the ultimate remedy. Ways for minimizing the need for repetitive lawsuits include: (i) court appointment of a special master to supervise the administration of the plan and ordinances; and (ii) court insistence that the plan and ordinances contain a detailed statement of policy indicating the municipality's intention to administer its ordinances to include low-cost housing within its boundaries. (This will provide a referent for rezoning or permit decisions and a solid basis for judicial review, as well as a promotional mechanism for the expression of the town's willingness to comply with the court order and thereby invite applications to develop.) Such a statement, at a minimum, should contain such provisions as: (a) a declaration that the municipality intends to encourage new housing with a variety of type and cost through revision of its codes; (b) a schedule of the pace and extent of such development that the municipality regards as reasonable; and (c) the types of area or areas where proposals for such development will be sympathetically considered, and why those areas have been selected.

14. Since substantial time can pass between a judgment that existing ordinances are improperly exclusionary and the confirmation of a valid new plan, in appropriate cases some housing can be made possible by court order without waiting for the comprehensive plannning needed to establish maximum obligations. Evidence in the suit will normally provide an approximation of "fair share," and the immediate imposition of some percentage of this number on the jurisdiction to be located on clearly appropriate sites will permit waiting public or private developers, or those who could be solicited by advertising, the chance to begin building at once. Clearly, if the town has excluded all low-cost housing, the court can act immediately

and require that permission be granted for numbers well below projected thresholds. This would expeditiously allow at least a modest amount of low-cost housing into the town.

15. Assuming that the defendant has complied with the court order to prepare a nonexclusionary plan and zoning ordinance, and that the court has found them to be adequate to meet the municipality's obligations to provide adequate opportunities for low-cost housing, if the town fails to adhere to its newly adopted policies and ordinances and developers are refused permission when they apply for permits and zone changes, additional low-cost housing will not be built. For this reason it is essential for the court to retain jurisdiction of the case for the period necessary to assure compliance.

The court may have to determine whether or not refusals to grant permits or to rezone are consistent with the new ordinance and plan. Difficult evidentiary problems will be presented, and a special master would be of great help in making the necessary factual determinations. If the court concludes that the town is not acting in good faith, pressure can be exerted on the defendant to force compliance through: (a) suspension of other federal or state grants; (b) suspension of local laws that obstruct compliance; (c) negation of all zoning; and (d) contempt. (Resort to any of these rather drastic court actions assumes applications for permits and thus, in the usual case, the availability of federal or state subsidies.)

16. Assuming that under the circumstances the court determines that the municipality has an affirmative obligation to foster and encourage construction of low-cost housing, the plan resulting from the court's orders should specify means for accomplishing the aim. Major possibilities include: promoting subsidized housing by private developers; forming a local housing authority and constructing public housing; mandating a stipulated percentage of low-cost housing units in all new multifamily residential projects built by private developers; and permitting mobile homes within the jurisdiction.

17. When extension or enlargement of public utilities is necessary to permit low-cost housing, a court may find it necessary to order a municipality to provide required services. Effective remedies, short of suspension of voter approval for bonds, are normally available to courts to assure adequate financing. However, if this ultimate confrontation should arise, there is legal precedent for a court to suspend state statutes to the extent that they obstruct compliance with judicial orders.

Appendix to Chapter 3

A Summary of the Litigation in Hills v. Gautreaux

INTRODUCTION

In *Hills v. Gautreaux*[1] the U.S. Supreme Court in 1976 culminated almost a decade of efforts by the federal courts to "prohibit the future use and to remedy the past effects of the defendant Chicago Housing Authority's unconstitutional site selection and tenant assignment procedures."[2] In affirming a lower federal court decision mandating a metropolitan remedy for the dispersal of federally subsidized housing units, the Court structured the basis upon which the District Court for the Northern District of Illinois would develop an appropriate remedy. Subsequent to the *Hills v. Gautreaux* decision, an agreement between the plaintiffs and HUD about the implementation of the decision was finalized. Included in the agreement is the obligation by HUD to develop within a year a program for the housing of 400 plaintiff class families throughout the Chicago SMSA, with no more than 100 of the families being located within the city of Chicago or in other areas of minority concentration.[3]

While scattered references to the Supreme Court decision in *Gautreaux* are made in this book, especially in Chapters 2 and 3, it is also helpful to look at the litigation as a block. In testing the various aspects of remedial techniques, other courts can learn from the experience gained in this lenthy litigation. This summary will therefore

1. 96 S. Ct. 1538 (1976).
2. 304 F. Supp. 736, 737 (N.D. Ill. 1969).
3. *See* text of the agreement between plaintiffs and HUD in text accompanying note 36, *infra.*

emphasize the techniques and methods the court used to gain compliance with its orders, rather than the substantive content of the decisions. The 1976 Supreme Court decision will not be discussed. Rather, pertinent parts of the text of the agreement between the plaintiffs and HUD over implementation of the decision will be presented at the conclusion of this appendix.

The *Gautreaux* litigation was directed against both the Chicago Housing Authority and the Department of Housing and Urban Development, although the two actions were consolidated in 1974.[4] Certiorari was denied by the U.S. Supreme Court in 1971,[5] but was granted in 1975.[6] A number of law review articles on the *Gautreaux* litigation have appeared and will be briefly mentioned where appropriate.

1966-1969

The plaintiffs first filed their complaint in 1966. They charged that the site-selection and tenant-assignment practices of the Chicago Housing Authority violated constitutional and sta.,itory safeguards against further racial impaction of public housing.[7] Finding for the plaintiffs, District Judge Richard Austin issued the first judgment order in 1969, from which no appeal was taken.[8] In this order, a comprehensive plan was entered in which the next 700 units of public housing to be built in Chicago were to be located in predominantly white areas, and three-fourths of the public housing thereafter. Certain restrictions were imposed on the size of units and concentrations within neighborhoods in order to promote the integration of the black tenants within white neighborhoods. Formulation of a new tenant-assignment plan was also ordered. The housing authority was ordered to "use its best efforts" to increase the supply of housing units as rapidly as possible.

The precision of the order has been praised as making circumvention more obvious and difficult.[9] It has been criticized on several grounds, but principally because its effect has been to halt all public housing construction in Chicago, causing great hardship among those on the housing authority's long waiting lists.[10]

4. 363 F. Supp. 690 (N.D. Ill. 1974).
5. 402 U.S. 922 (1971).
6. 503 F.2d 930 (7th Cir. 1975), *cert. granted sub nom.*, Hills v. Gautreaux, 421 U.S. 962 (1975).
7. 265 F. Supp. 582 (N.D. Ill. 1967).
8. 304 F. Supp. 736 (N.D. Ill. 1969).
9. 6 Colum. J. L. & Soc. Prob. 253 (1970).
10. *See* 79 Yale L.J. 712 (1970); 83 Harv. L. Rev. 1443 (1970); 122 U. Pa. L. Rev. 1330 (1974); *See also* 118 U. Pa. L. Rev. 436 (1970) (some requirements

Useful techniques included in the order are as follows:

1. Detailed reporting requirements were included, with relatively short timetables for compliance. The reports were to be circulated not only to the court, but also to the counsel for the plaintiffs. Information about tentative site selections, to show whether their locations complied with criteria contained in the order, was to be provided counsel for plaintiffs as well as the Justice Department and HUD.

2. The court retained jurisdiction of the case for purposes of enforcement and modification of the order when relevant information was presented. In this way the court coupled precision and detail in the order with flexibility to make needed changes when developments warranted amendments.

3. The order was made binding upon the Chicago Housing Authority, its officers, agents, servants, employees, attorneys, and their successors, and upon those persons—including the members of the City Council of the City of Chicago—in active concert or participation with them who received actual notice of the order by personal service or otherwise.[11]

According to remarks made by a Chicago Housing Authority Commissioner, this binding effect could include suburban zoning boards, the county housing authority, and the Illinois Housing Board.[12] If a court order could be made binding on other local agencies, a plaintiff's attempt to secure all necessary approvals for a housing project would be greatly expedited.

1970

A year later, no housing sites had been submitted by the Chicago Housing Authority to the Chicago City Council. The authority had informed plaintiffs that they did not intend to submit any housing sites to the Chicago City Council prior to the Chicago mayoralty election of April 1971.[13] The district court modified its previous order to the Chicago Housing Authority and required submission

---

of the order were superfluous and inconsistent with the legal theory of the decision).

11. 304 F. Supp. 736, 741 (N.D. Ill. 1969) *See* Fed. R. Civ. P. 65(d), which provides that "every order granting an injunction . . . is binding upon the parties to the action, their officers, agents, servants, employees, and attorneys, and upon those persons in active concert or participation with them who receive actual notice of the order by personal service or otherwise."

12. 6 Colum. J. L. & Soc. Prob. 253, 273 (1970).

13. 436 F.2d 306, 308 (7th Cir. 1970).

of proposals for 1,500 dwelling units to the Chicago City Council within two months.[14]

1971

Another year passed without approval of proposed sites by the Chicago City Council. A letter of intention had been signed by the housing authority, HUD, and the mayor of Chicago, indicating how the housing deficit would be met. In return, HUD released $26 million in Model Cities funds it had previously refused to approve. However, the city and the authority failed to comply with the intended schedule. Therefore, in the suit *Gautreaux v. Romney*,[15] the court sought to compel compliance by enjoining HUD from making available the Model Cities funds until Chicago had approved sites for 700 of the 1,500 units previously ordered by the court. The injunction was reversed on appeal[16] on the ground that the federal statute[17] under which the district court acted only allows termination of funding for the particular program where discrimination has occurred, which would not include the Model Cities Program in this case.[18]

1973

By 1973, with no sites yet approved by the Chicago City Council, the district court[19] suspended application to the Chicago Housing Authority of the Illinois statute that required local approval for public housing.[20] The court distinguished its ruling from the Supreme Court decision in *James v. Valtierra*[21] on the basis that the California law in *Valtierra* was seemingly neutral on its face, while only racial considerations could explain the defendant's actions in *Gautreaux*. The City of Chicago was joined as a defendant in this particular case.

One writer suggests that the order which suspended site approval by the city council would have been even more effective if it had imposed affirmative obligations on the city rather than merely relieving it of its duty to act. The city council could have been required to

---

14. (Unreported decision), *aff'd*, 436 F.2d 306 (7th Cir. 1970), *cert. denied*, 402 U.S. 922 (1971).
15. 332 F. Supp. 366 (N.D. Ill. 1971).
16. 456 F.2d 124 (7th Cir. 1972).
17. Civil Rights Act of 1964 § 602, 42 U.S.C. § 2000(d).
18. *See* Comment, 58 Iowa L. Rev. 1283 (1973), supporting Judge Sprecher's dissent on the issue of the court's power to terminate funding of the Model Cities Program.
19. 342 F. Supp. 827 (N.D. Ill. 1972), *aff'd*, 480 F.2d 210 (7th Cir. 1973).
20. Ill. Rev. Stat. ch. 67½ § 9.
21. 402 U.S. 137, 91 S. Ct. 1331, 28 L. Ed. 2d 678 (1971).

take all steps necessary to free the local housing authority to proceed.[22]

1973-1974

The court then ordered all parties to submit plans for integrating public housing sites, indicating that remedies need not be limited to the city.[23] The district court refused to adopt plaintiff's plan, which called for placing public housing outside the city (a so-called metropolitan solution). Plaintiffs requested metropolitan relief similar to that granted by the Court of Appeals for the Sixth Circuit in *Bradley v. Milliken*.[24] The request was based on expert testimony that by the year 2000, virtually all of Chicago would be predominantly black. A metropolitan public housing plan was approved on appeal.[25]

The court of appeals reconciled its intercity housing solution with the Supreme Court decision in *Milliken v. Bradley*,[26] which had reversed the decision of the court of appeals. *Milliken* invalidated a metropolitan solution to school segregation in Detroit. A plan to bus black students out of Detroit's almost totally black school system to schools in white suburbs was invalidated on the basis that de jure racial discrimination had occurred solely within Detroit, and therefore the remedy must necessarily be confined within Detroit.

According to the court of appeals in *Gautreaux*, the law has always been that "political subdivisions of the States may be readily bridged when necessary to vindicate federal constitutional rights,"[27] and this is still the law. According to the court in *Gautreaux*, *Milliken* did not intend to change this basic substantive right by ruling on an appropriate remedy. The remedy of an interdistrict solution does not follow automatically when racial imbalances between districts are discovered. The difficulties of providing an interdistrict remedy among the 54 school districts outside Detroit (logistics, finance, administration, and policy legitimacy) were so great, that such relief would "be an impractical and unreasonable over-response to a viola-

---

22. 8 Urb. L. Ann. 265 (1974). *Cf.* Kennedy Parks Homes Ass'n v. City of Lackawanna, 318 F. Supp. 669 (W.D.N.Y. 1970), *aff'd*, 436 F.2d 108 (2d Cir. 1970), *cert. denied*, 401 U.S. 1010 (1971) (defendant required to take all necessary steps to enable plaintiff to proceed with housing project).

23. 363 F. Supp. 690 (N.D. Ill. 1973).

24. 484 F.2d 215 (6th Cir. 1973).

25. 503 F.2d 930 (7th Cir. 1974).

26. 418 U.S. 717 (1974). *See* Rubinowitz & Dennis, *School Desegregation Versus Public Housing Desegregation: The Local School District and the Metropolitan Housing District*, 10 Urb. L. Ann. 145 (1975).

27. 503 F.2d 930 (7th Cir. 1974).

tion limited to one school district.[28] Only an interdistrict violation would justify incurring these massive difficulties.

The court of appeals in *Gautreaux* found that an intercity remedy was not precluded by *Milliken* on several grounds. First, for reasons enumerated in the decision,[29] the difficulties of establishing intercity public housing are not so great as those of unifying intercity school districts, and thus the intolerable administrative burden of a metropolitan solution did not exist.

Second, the intercity violation the court in *Milliken* had been unable to find in the Detroit-area school systems was found to have taken place in Chicago-area public housing. Not only had the suburbs limited their public housing projects to their black areas, but the Chicago Housing Authority's discriminatory policy also had an impact on the suburbs by exacerbating white flight. Third, the court noted that all the parties were in agreement that the Chicago metropolitan area constitutes a "single relevant locality for low-rent housing purposes and that a city-only remedy will not work."[30]

The fact that the suburbs had not signified their assessment of a need for low-rent housing by signing the necessary cooperation agreements was not mentioned by the court of appeals.[31] In an aside to the district court, the court of appeals suggested that "a Court order directing that those [suburbs] not volunteering were to be made parties might help."[32]

1974

In November 1974 the district court appointed a U.S. magistrate to serve as special master. He was to make a study of the existing patterns of racial segregation in Chicago, determine the precise causes of the five-year delay in implementing the orders of the court, and recommend a plan that would expedite compliance with these orders.[33] Copies of the master's report were to be furnished to the Chicago Housing Authority, HUD, and the plaintiff's counsel. The special master was then to meet with the parties in executive session to discuss their suggested revisions before the plan was presented to the court.

28. *Id.* at 936.
29. *Id.* at 935.
30. *Id.* at 937.
31. In Mahaley v. Cuyahoga Metropolitan Housing Authority, 500 F.2d 1087 (1974), the Sixth Circuit Court of Appeals accorded suburbs the right to refuse public housing if they determine no need exists within their own jurisdictions.
32. 503 F.2d at 936.
33. 384 F. Supp. 37 (N.D. Ill. 1974).

Observations on Pre-1976 Remedial Actions

With the benefit of almost ten years of hindsight, it is perhaps possible to extract some lessons from the arduous efforts of the courts in dealing with a nearly intractable situation. The court of appeals referred to the eight years of resistance by Chicago to integrated public housing as "a callousness on the part of the appellees toward the rights of the black, underprivileged citizens of Chicago that is beyond comprehension."[34] Of the district court's orders they said:

> We are fully aware of the many difficult and sensitive problems that the cases have presented to the able District Judge and we applaud the care, meticulous attention and the judicious manner in which he has approached them. With his orders being ignored and frustrated as they were, he kept his cool and courageously called the hand of the recalcitrant.[35]

Given the degree of obstinancy on the part of the Chicago City Council and the housing authority to providing additional housing sites in accordance with the court's directives, it is at least arguable that the court could have acted in a coercive fashion earlier in the proceedings than it did. For example, an affirmative order was eventually issued that a specific number of housing units be provided on a set timetable. Perhaps these units should have been required at the very outset. The state statute requiring city council approval of public housing sites was suspended when it prevented compliance with the court order. The Chicago City Council's policies and practices were well known to the court.[36] It would have been reasonable for the court to have suspended or threatened to suspend the Illinois statute much earlier.

Auxiliary kinds of leverage, such as terminating funds of other grant programs, could have been invoked as a remedy in the first instance. Joinder of the city as a defendant and requiring submission by the parties of additional suggestions and plans to aid in carrying out court orders also should not have been delayed. Earlier appointment of a special master would have helped. While acknowledging the possible value to a court of earlier enforcement of these techniques, however, it is necessary to make two observations.

First, much of the long delay by the agencies involved is explainable by circumstances beyond the court's power to change. For example, the federal moratorium on public housing funds was imposed

34. 503 F.2d at 932.
35. *Id.*
36. 296 F. Supp. 907 (N.D. Ill. 1969).

during the course of this case.[37] The moratorium was later lifted for the 1,500 housing units the authority had agreed to build. For much of this time, however, there was no final, nonappealable order requiring defendants to proceed. Other delays were explained by the operational difficulties of the housing authority, such as locating suitable sites in the scarce vacant land left in white neighborhoods, preparing environmental reviews, and the like.

Second, and more important, we must remember that several of these techniques were being utilized for the first time in the *Gautreaux* litigation. Many of the orders went through the appellate mill before becoming final. As a consequence, we have all benefited from the trail-blazing attempts of this court. To question whether they might have been employed at an earlier stage in the proceedings is not to question the instructive value of these innovative efforts in an extremely complex undertaking.

1976

The text of the agreement between plaintiffs and HUD concerning implementation of the Supreme Court decision in *Hills v. Gautreaux* reads, in part, as follows:

This letter will confirm the understandings which, subject to submission for consideration by the District Court, HUD and the plaintiffs intend to carry out. It is intended that the steps set forth in this letter will enable the Court and the parties to the litigation to consider metropolitan-wide relief at a future point in time on a more informed basis. Neither the plaintiffs nor HUD make any representations as to what their respective positions ultimately will be regarding metropolitan-wide relief.

The said understandings are as follows:

1. HUD will develop a one year Section 8 demonstration program intended to house approximately 400 plaintiff class families in existing housing throughout the Chicago Standard Metropolitan Statistical Area (SMSA) along the following lines:

a. Not more than 25% of the families to be housed under this demonstration may locate in any portion of the City of Chicago or in minority areas (to be designated by agreement between HUD and the plaintiffs) of the Chicago SMSA outside of the City of Chicago. To the extent that any such families locate in the City of Chicago, it is understood that the units in which such families would be housed will be subject to existing court orders and should be treated as a separate category of units under those orders.

b. HUD will enter into a contract with the Leadership Council for Met-

37. The Nixon Administration announced its suspension of all programs for federally subsidized, newly constructed, lower income housing in January 1973. It was upheld in Commonwealth v. Lynn, 501 F.2d 848 (D.C. Cir. 1974).

tropolitan Open Communities under which the Leadership Council will provide the services of approximately six professional and three clerical employees to locate, counsel and assist members of the plaintiff class to find existing units, and locate owners of housing willing to participate in the demonstration program. It is intended that the Leadership Council's activities will commence on or about July 1, 1976.

c. The Leadership Council will contact members of the plaintiff class in numbers and pursuant to a method to be determined, and will counsel and assist families who respond. These activities will be designed to house approximately 40 new subsidized families per month after the first few months.

d. The 400 units will not be allocated among the counties, but tentative goals for distribution of such units among the counties are: approximately 100 to 150 units for Cook County, approximately 25 to 40 units for each of the other 5 counties in the Chicago SMSA and 0 to 100 units for Chicago plus designated minority areas outside Chicago. It is intended that families be located in each county in a dispersed fashion.

e. All housing authorities in the SMSA will be given the opportunity to participate. Participating housing authorities will inspect units prior to occupancy, assist in initial occupancy, execute and administer the subsidy contract with owners, and perform the other functions of housing authorities under the Section 8 existing housing program. Housing authorities will receive the established 8½% fee. The initial occupancy fee will be set at $100, subject to adjustment by HUD, in view of the fact that services funded by HUD will be provided by the Leadership Council as referred to above. In areas where no housing authority has been organized or where an existing housing authority declines to participate, HUD will perform or cause to be performed the functions assigned to housing authorities under the Section 8 existing housing program.

f. HUD will amend annual contribution contracts with participating housing authorities to add the contract authority necessary to fund in full the additional number of units which each housing authority administers pursuant to the demonstration program

* * *

8. Plaintiffs agree to postpone seeking a metropolitan-wide relief order from the District Court for nine months from July 1, 1976, while the foregoing steps are implemented. After the expiration of the said nine month period, plaintiffs will be free to file pleadings in the Gautreaux litigation seeking metropolitan-wide relief or relief preliminary to metropolitan-wide relief, provided that in the event such a pleading is filed between April 1, 1977, and June 30, 1977, HUD shall be entitled to terminate the operation of the demonstration program under paragraph 1 above, and HUD's encouragement efforts under paragraph 4 above. Nothing in this paragraph 8 shall prevent plaintiffs from filing pleadings at any time seeking any type of relief from the Chicago Housing Authority, provided that any motion or pleadings seeking judicial relief to require the Chicago Housing Authority to seek authorization to operate housing programs out-

side of the City of Chicago and filed prior to June 30, 1977, shall be delivered in final draft to HUD at least 60 days prior to filing to enable HUD to determine what action to take in the Gautreaux litigation and under this letter, and provided further, that the subsequent filing by plaintiffs of such pleadings prior to June 30, 1977, shall relieve HUD of any obligation to continue operation thereafter of the demonstration program under paragraph 1, above, or to continue encouragement efforts under paragraph 4, above, but shall not limit or terminate any rights of HUD under this letter. Any unobligated Section 8 authority for new construction or substantial rehabilitation under paragraph 4 shall continue to be exempt after June 30, 1977, from plaintiffs' efforts in litigation to obtain metropolitan-wide relief, but only to the extent that such unobligated Section 8 authority is subsequently obligated pursuant to advertisements or readvertisements made prior to June 30, 1977. Commencing July 1, 1977, or the date on which HUD terminates the demonstration program or encouragement efforts pursuant to this paragraph 8, based upon a pleading filed by plaintiff on or after April 1, 1977, unobligated Section 8 authority for existing housing under paragraph 3 shall not thereafter be exempt from plaintiffs' efforts in litgation to obtain metropolitan-wide relief.[38]

38. Letter from Robert R. Elliott, General Counsel to the U.S. Department of Housing and Urban Development, to Alexander Polikoff, counsel for plaintiffs in *Gautreaux,* dated June 7, 1976, is printed in full in 4 Hous. & Dev. Rep. 40 (June 14, 1976).

✳ *Chapter 4*

Improving the Administration of Land-Use Controls

The indictment of zoning to which all critics subscribe is that its administration is arbitrary and capricious. Procedural due process is continually flaunted in our medieval hearings, our casual record keeping and our occult decision-making.—R. Babcock, *The Zoning Game.*

New forms of land development, social and economic concerns, and the desire to preserve the natural environment have strained the traditional mechanisms for implementing land-use policy. As a result, the administrative system has become more complex and requires continual adjustment.[1] Of particular concern in achieving more rational and equitable urban growth is the extent to which our traditional system of land-use controls has evolved into a highly discretionary administrative process. While this development has its salutary aspects—particularly in permitting local government to respond to the increased complexities of land-use decisionmaking—it has also strained the fairness and rationality of the entire land-use regulatory process. As the National Commission on Urban Problems (the Douglas Commission) reported in 1968 in its nationwide survey of land-use controls:

[T]he system is too often "unfair" in its day-to-day administration.

1. The shortcomings of the administrative system have been widely recognized. *See, e.g.,* D. Mandelker, The Zoning Dilemma (1971); N. Marcus & M. Groves, The New Zoning Legal, Administrative and Economic Concepts and Techniques (1970); Report of the National Commission on Urban Problems, Building the American City (1968) [hereinafter cited as Building the American City]. *See* R. Babcock, The Zoning Game (1966).

Arbitrariness—the failure to relate regulations to discernible public objectives and to apply them evenhandedly to all comers—is commonplace in many localities.

The greatest abuses arise in enforcement and in the handling of discretionary decisions. . . .[2]

The high degree of discretion that has emerged as an integral part of the land-use administrative process was not foreseen in 1924 by the drafters of the Standard State Zoning Enabling Act (SZEA).[3] As envisioned at the time, the local legislative body would adopt regulations that specified, in advance and in detail, development standards ranging from land-use classifications to maximum building heights and setbacks. Districts were crudely drawn and cumulative in nature. Industrial zones, for example, were open to almost any use without need for adjustment. Residential districts were to be protected from other incompatible uses, with zoning changes viewed as unacceptable encroachments. The entire city was to be regulated according to what one prominent commentator on the history of the early zoning movement described as a "fixed, developmental pecking order for every square inch of city land. . . ."[4]

A potential developer had only to look at the map and read the regulations to know exactly what could or could not be done with the property. The public debate and legislative adoption of the regulations was to reduce the need for discretionary judgments in the administration of land use controls. Enforcement was left in the hands of a building inspector or similar administrative official. Provisions were made for a board of adjustment to hear and decide appeals of the building inspector's decision, grant special exceptions when provided for in the regulations, and grant variances in cases of hardship. Any need to amend the regulations or revise the zoning map (which was expected to be infrequent) would be accommodated by the legislative process.

But almost from the beginning, zoning did not operate in that fashion. In most communities the adoption of zoning preceded the adoption of a master plan—sometimes by years. The U.S. Department of Commerce did not issue the Standard City Planning Enabling Act until 1928, four years after it had issued SZEA.[5] Moreover, the

2. Building the American City, *supra* note 1, at 226.

3. U.S. Dept. Commerce, A Standard State Zoning Enabling Act (rev. ed. 1926); *reprinted in* H. Rathkopf, The Law of Planning and Zoning 100–01 (1956).

4. S. Toll, Zoned American 183 (1969).

5. U.S. Dept. Commerce, A Standard City Planning Enabling Act (revised ed. 1928); *reprinted in* E. Roberts, Land Use Planning 3–15 (1971).

system of dividing a community into broad compatible use districts was simply not adequate for a changing urban environment that required delicate adjustments among competing land uses. Zoning—which was intended to be a comparatively simple system of pre-regulating land use—has therefore been contorted into a system for the administrative control of land development in which decisions are made on a case-by-case basis.

Increasingly, communities are adopting what the Douglas Commission has characterized as "wait and see" techniques. Under this approach, a community affords itself an opportunity to delay final development decisions (usually by planning an area in a highly restrictive zoning classification) until a particular development is proposed that is to the community's liking. Typically, the "old" flexible techniques—variances, special permits, rezonings—are utilized; more recently they have been supplemented by an array of new devices designed to accommodate special development considerations. Such techniques include floating zones, planned-unit developments, overlay zones, and conditional rezoning.

Each of these devices allows the community to postpone its decisions until development is about to occur, and then, in response to a proposal, establish in detail the manner in which the land is to be developed. The key ingredient of this approach is its flexibility; the regulations do not specifically state what can and cannot occur on the land. Instead, they establish varying criteria and standards for development that permit, at the planning and design stage, wider options in use, location, site design, and building design. No longer can a person merely look at the text of a zoning ordinance or the zoning map in order to ascertain the community's policies toward land use.[6] As described by Professor Jan Krasnowiecki, "the community's new land use policy comes to be expressed in the zoning amendment."[7]

The increasing reliance on discretionary land-use controls can be attributed to many factors, including the following:

1. Disillusionment with Traditional Techniques that Limit Development Options. Specification of permitted or prohibited uses and specific development standards enable communities to predict with greater certainty what is likely to occur on a given piece of land. At

6. American Law Institute, A Model Land Development Code 176 (Adopted May 21, 1975) (1976) [hereinafter cited as ALI Code].

7. Krasnowiecki, *The Basic System of Land Use Control: Legislative Pre-regulation v. Administrative Discretion*, in Marcus and Groves, *supra* note 1, at 316, *cited in* ALI Code at 176.

the same time, however, it inhibits innovation and good design. Wait-and-see approaches, on the other hand, allow the local agency to review and specify density and appropriate mixture of uses, as well as individual design features such as landscaping, building orientation, and vehicle storage, thus achieving an even greater degree of control over the character of the development.[8] Of course, these techniques can work to the developer's advantage as well, if, through the negotiation process, one is able to obtain concessions on one's site plan that result in cost reductions for streets and sidewalks, utility lines, and the like.

2. Larger Scale of Land Development. Traditional methods worked fairly well when development occurred mostly on a lot-by-lot basis. Since World War II, however, most development has been on a much larger scale. Major subdivisions, regional shopping centers, industrial parks, new towns, mixed developments, and large high-rise complexes are now the rule rather than the exception. As a result, the whole development process has become more complex, with rapid shifts in the housing market, changes in consumer preferences, complicated financing arrangements, and rapid increases in development costs. The old methods resulted in "little boxes all in a row"; the new flexible devices permit staging of development, lower development costs, improved site design, consideration of localized site variations, and more marketable developments.

3. Land Use Controls are Expected to Meet Wider Public Objectives. Interpretation of the "health, safety, morals, and general welfare" objectives on which zoning and other regulatory devices are based have been vastly expanded in recent years. Regulations based upon the police power are increasingly tested by objectives related to social equity (including expanded housing opportunity), environmental quality (including esthetics), governmental fiscal responsibility, and fair process, as well as general order and efficiency. The more sophisticated tools permit consideration and balancing of often conflicting objectives as the need arises.

These increased demands on the police power can threaten the fairness of the process. For instance, a rezoning for a low-income housing development raises issues before the local decision making body that go well beyond the usual questions of site and building design, density, utilities, impact on schools, and traffic systems. Local officials may be asked to evaluate the virtues of racial and economic

8. Building the American City, *supra* note 1, at 207.

integration, to balance the need for additional low-income housing against the possible inappropriateness and inadequacy of a particular site from an environmental point of view, or to determine whether low-income families can realistically be expected to afford the costs of home ownership. Moreover, the policy framework in which such decisions are made often is contained in a "master plan" produced years ago, before many people were concerned with issues of racial and economic integration or environmental protection and their relationship to land-use controls.

4. Greater Sophistication of All Actors in the Development Process. This can be considered both a cause and a result of the use of more elaborate tools. The larger scale and greater complexity of land development have produced sophisticated private builders, lawyers, lenders, and others able to package and market such development and deal with the new regulations. Similarly, on the public side many legislators, administrative officials, planners, and attorneys have learned the approaches to new development and have been able to develop and administer new regulatory and management systems.

Private citizens—as neighbors, consumers, members of pressure groups, or voters—have also become more aware of the development process. The timing and effectiveness of their involvement varies widely, as does the willingness of both the public and private sectors to seek citizen involvement. In fact, greater use of flexible negotiation can be designed to shield development decisionmaking from citizens' scrutiny. Nevertheless, citizen groups have increasingly demonstrated their ability to affect the process, even if they enter at a late stage. (The broader issue of citizen participation in the land-use process is discussed later in this chapter.)

5. Developing A Multi-Tier System of Land-Use Control. Land-use control no longer is the exclusive domain of local government. States, and to some degree regional agencies and the federal government, are increasingly intervening in local land-use matters by setting standards, rules, and procedures aimed at meeting wider public objectives. State involvement in land-use controls takes many forms, from adoption of planning and zoning enabling legislation to direct state participation in the planning and development process.[9] The types of state involvement already in effect include:

9. *See* F. Bosselman & D. Callies, The Quiet Revolution in Land Use Controls (1972); American Society of Planning Officials, Increasing State and Regional Power in the Development Process (Planning Advisory Service Report No. 255, 1970) [hereinafter cited as ASPO].

1. State preemption of land-use planning and control (e.g., Hawaii).
2. State development permits for projects of unique state concern, such as coastal areas, lower income housing, major industrial development, and power plants (e.g., Florida, California, Oregon, Massachusetts, Maine, and Vermont).
3. State planning legislation specifying criteria and elements for local and regional plans (e.g., California, Florida, Oregon).[10]

Federal legislation and administrative regulations, sometimes implemented through state and regional agencies, have steadily added to the levels of decisionmaking in the development process. Coordination of the multiplicity of federal air, water, and noise pollution laws, solid-waste legislation, the National Environmental Policy Act,[11] and the National Coastal Zone Management Act,[12] requires an extraordinarily effective administrative process. All these laws demand greater flexibility and discretion at many levels, and the need for fairness and rationality increases proportionately.

Major commissions and leading commentators have analyzed various aspects of the situation and have recommended changes. The National Commission on Urban Problems, in its highly acclaimed study *Building the American City*, reported on the growing use and potential abuse of administrative discretion through wait-and-see techniques, and recommended that those techniques be refined, tied more closely to stated public objectives, and administered by qualified professionals.[13] The American Law Institute's *Model Land Development Code* is an important effort to accomplish many of these goals. The American Law Institute (ALI) is a prestigious association of lawyers, judges, and law professors, founded over a half-century ago to restate and reform the common law and to formulate model legislation.

Over the past twelve years the ALI has drafted a comprehensive code concerned with planning and land-use controls, which constitutes the first major revision of development legislation since publication of the Standard City Planning Enabling Act almost fifty years ago.

This chapter will explore in more detail the matter of discretion in land-use decisions and will evaluate the procedural and legislative implications of various attempts to balance the positive aspects of

10. *See* discussion in text accompanying notes 307–362 *infra* and Chapter 3, *supra*.

11. Pub. L. No. 90-190, 83 Stat. 852, 42 U.S.C. § 4321 *et seq.* (1970).

12. Pub. L. No. 92-583, 86 Stat. 1280, 16 U.S.C. § 1451 *et seq.* (Supp. II, 1972).

13. Building the American City, *supra* note 1, at 223.

flexibility with the need for a process that is fair and amenable to the interests of all parties. It will survey the development and range of discretionary land-use controls, the techniques employed, and the problems created by their uneven application at various levels of government.

The following pages also examine the implications of certain procedural and legislative reforms, including the shift in judicial attitudes toward individual requests for development permission, the use of hearing examiners, increased citizen participation, and higher level administrative reviews of local decisions, in terms of both their practical effect on land use administration and their relationship to other major issues addressed in this book. For instance, administrative delays, arbitrary denials of development permits, and failure to meet minimal standards of due process can have a significant impact on housing costs and availability. Furthermore, legislative and judicial insistence on conformance between comprehensive plans and land-use decisions will increase the importance of the process by which such decisions are made. As courts look more closely at the actions of government agencies, the degree to which the record of such actions reflects a fair and rational process will weigh heavily in a decision on their validity.

In one sense, the ALI Code could exacerbate the problems of discretion discussed in this chapter by expanding the discretionary powers of local government. However, the code is certain to have a major impact in promoting greater fairness and predictability in our land-use control process by proposing explicit standards and detailed procedures for making rules and granting permits.

Of particular relevance to this chapter is Article 2 of the Code, "Local Land Development Regulation." Among its general features it provides for the following: (1) it consolidates the traditionally separate zoning and subdivision ordinances into one "development ordinance"[14] to be administered by a single "land development agency;"[15] (2) it establishes specific procedures for the administration of the development ordinance that differ for the various functions of the land development agency;[16] (3) it establishes a joint hearing process for developments requiring multiple permits;[17] and (4) it authorizes the land development agency to issue "special development permits" for specified activities such as special exceptions and planned unit development.[18] The *Model Land Development Code*

14. ALI Code, *supra* note 6, at § 2-101.
15. *Id.* at § 2-301.
16. *Id.* at § 2-301 *et seq.*
17. *Id.* at § 2-401 *et seq.*
18. *Id.* at § 2-201 *et seq.*

also provides a legislative context for some of the issues raised in the following pages. Where specific sections of the Code are applicable, they will be noted.[19]

This chapter will explore in more detail the matter of discretion in land-use decisions and will evaluate the procedural and legislative implications of various attempts to balance the positive aspects of flexibility with the need for a process that is fair and amenable to the interests of all parties. It will survey the development and range of discretionary land-use controls, the techniques employed, and the problems created by their uneven application at various levels of government.

The following pages also examine the implications of certain procedural and legislative reforms, including the shift in judicial attitudes toward individual requests for development permission, the use of hearing examiners, increased citizen participation, and higher level administrative reviews of local decisions, in terms of both their practical effect on land use administration and their relationship to other major issues addressed in this book. For instance, administrative delays, arbitrary denials of development permits, and failure to meet minimal standards of due process can have a significant impact on housing costs and availability. Furthermore, legislative and judicial insistence on conformance between comprehensive plans and land-use decisions will increase the importance of the process by which such decisions are made. As courts look more closely at the actions of governmental agencies, the degree to which the record of such actions reflects a fair and rational process will weigh heavily in a decision on their validity.

THE TRADITIONAL TOOLS AND THE IMPLICATIONS OF FLEXIBILITY AND DISCRETION

The use of discretionary land-use controls involves a number of variations on familiar devices of zoning and subdivision regulation. The most typical devices are variances, rezonings, and special permits. The SZEA provided for the issuance of a variance by a board of zoning appeals in order to permit discretionary relief in situations in which conditions unique to a site made the strict application of the zoning ordinance a cause of "unnecessary hardship."

Problems have arisen over the appropriate use of the variance

19. For an overview of the Code *see* Fox, *A Tentative Guide to the American Law Institute's Proposed Model Land Development Code*, 6 Urb. Law. 928 (1974).

power. While minor adjustments of yards or building height may not contradict general policy, variances of use may actually be characterized as rezonings and are therefore not within the scope of authority of a board of appeals. The frequent misuse of the variance power is probably due to the lack of a standard definition of "unnecessary hardship," and also to the functional separation of the board of zoning appeals from the planning agency in many localities.[20] As a result, the board has neither its own internal standards upon which to base a decision to grant a variance nor the assistance of a professional planning staff.

Due to its traditionally administrative function, however, variance hearings are usually conducted in a more structured manner than rezoning hearings. The enabling statute and local ordinance usually require the swearing of witnesses, recorded proceedings, findings, and appeal procedures. The presence of additional procedural safeguards reduces opportunities for abuse of administrative discretion. Moreover, the complexities of today's land-use issues and the increased visibility of the process have made it more difficult for boards of adjustment to indulge in the excessive granting of use variances that were more common in previous years. As a result, "the variance has become a rather small–bore weapon in the arsenal of the municipality."[21]

Another traditional discretionary technique is rezoning, which can take three forms: (1) a comprehensive revision or modernization of the zoning text and map; (2) a textual change in zone requirements; or (3) a change in the zoning designation of a particular parcel or parcels. It is the last, the so-called single-parcel rezoning, that has been widely used in responding to development initiatives and in adding flexibility to the zoning process. Current use of rezonings includes floating zones, conditional and contract zoning, and planned unit development.

Site plan review, long used in connection with subdivision regulations, is another conventional administrative device. General rules and standards are prescribed for submitting the site plans that are reviewed and passed upon by local officials. A planned unit development is normally accompanied by a site plan review process. Many of

20. *See generally* Anderson, *Board of Zoning Appeals-Villain or Victim?* 13 Syracuse L. Rev. 353 (1962); Dukenheimer & Stapleton, *The Zoning Board of Adjustment: A Study in Misrule*, 50 Ky. L.J. 273 (1962); Ford, *Guidelines for Judicial Review in Zoning Variance Cases*, 58 Mass. L.Q. 15 (1973); Note, *Zoning: Variance Administration in Alameda County*, 50 Cal. L. Rev. 101 (1962); Note, *Variance Administration in Indiana—Problems and Remedies*, 48 Ind. L.J. 240 (1973).
21. Babcock, *supra* note 1, at 7.

the "newer" techniques, such as floating zones and conditional and contract zoning, may also require site plan review since they offer, through negotiation, a direct opportunity for tailoring development proposals to community objectives. Because site plan review involves considerations of physical design and layout, professional staff review as well as that of the planning commission and the governing body is normally prescribed.

In this manner the "new" flexible techniques have built on and substantially expanded earlier methods. The traditional devices— variances, special permits, rezonings—were not intended to be used as the mainstay of the development process; they were expected only to serve as safety valves. However, such devices frequently have been misused. Again, as the National Commission on Urban Problems has observed:

> From the beginning, variances and exceptions have afforded an opportunity for abuse of discretion. And as more communities have come to rely (overtly or covertly) on the "wait and see" approach, the opportunity has grown. Rezoning is peculiarly susceptible to this abuse.
>
> Variances, special exceptions, and rezonings today occupy a substantial part of the time of planning and zoning boards. In theory, such decisions are made within the framework of general guidelines set out in State enabling acts and local ordinances. In practice, such guidelines are difficult to apply, and action purportedly taken under them is difficult to evaluate, if only because of the array of conflicting public objectives that could be properly applied in many such cases.[22]

By responding to development proposals on an ad hoc basis, with no policies or plan for support, odd and often random development mixtures have been created that bear little resemblance to the patterns indicated by the zoning map, thus leading to further rezoning requests. Many communities have found it increasingly difficult to turn down rezoning requests when previous rezonings have violated the uniformity of the original map.[23]

Each of the techniques discussed in this chapter involves something more than the traditional administrative determination of compliance. While they vary in procedural complexity, each demands some evaluation by local officials before approval is granted; a number require extended negotiations. Flexible techniques complicate the administrative process. Self-executing techniques require

22. Building the American City, *supra* note 1, at 226.
23. *See, e.g.,* Marca v. Dade County, 304 So. 2d 461 (1974); Board of Supervisors v. Williams, 216 S.E.2d 33 (1975).

far less time, effort, and skill. Typically the permitted (or prohibited) uses and the development standards are spelled out in the ordinance and the community's buildings or zoning enforcement officer can readily determine from plans whether the proposed development is in compliance. When discretion is involved, however, more steps are added, more substantial professional skills are needed, and more public bodies become involved in making decisions. And, because there often is negotiation over specific plans, the process usually takes more time than administration of conventional regulations.

Most of the flexible techniques discussed here involve some negotiation. Planned unit developments, because they encompass elements of most of the other techniques, often involve considerable negotiation. Negotiation is a bargaining process; because both the developer and the public officials think they have something to gain, they are willing to sit down and swap. The community can offer higher densities to increase developer profits. In exchange, developers may offer such amenities as additional open space, increased landscaping, school site dedications, or a type or size of housing unit desired by the community or its officials.

A key issue in the negotiation process is the need to maintain an open process within defined guidelines. The give-and-take of bargaining may lend itself to one side's trying to take advantage of the other: "It is a human process which pits personalities against one another, and the stronger party usually wins."[24] The developer's bargaining team may include people with strong bargaining skills who can overwhelm a community and its officials with rhetoric and information. Conversely, developers may be taken advantage of by heavy-handed local officials who have density bonuses, site plan approval, and, usually, time on their side. Unreasonable demands not specifically authorized by local ordinance may be made of developers. These demands frequently go unchallenged because their cost to developers in time and money is less than the cost of litigation. However, it should be noted that some courts show an increasing willingness to allow the local governing body to require developers to share some of the burden created by their projects.[25]

This negotiation process may be inherent in the administration of

24. F. So, D. Mosena, & F. Bangs, Planned Unit Development Ordinances 7 (Planning Advisory Service Report No. 291, 1973).

25. *See, e.g.,* Gerla v. Tacoma, 533 P.2d 416 (1975); Transamerica Title Insurance v. City of Tuscon, 533 P.2d 693 (1975); Kuzer v. Adams, 88 Cal. Rptr. 183 (1970). *See also* the discussion of subdivision regulations in text accompanying notes 101–123, *infra.*

flexible controls, but it may also jeopardize procedural due process.[26] Sensitive negotiations do require some privacy. Personnel and labor management negotiations, for example, normally are permitted to be held in private even in states that have open meeting or "sunshine" laws. But privacy can go too far. Deals that are worked out in secret between developers and public officials can frustrate and render meaningless the public-hearing process, and further disillusion the public.

It should also be noted that while the techniques described here permit the community to make final development decisions in response to landowner applications, they do not prescribe all land uses or development conditions in advance. At the same time, all decisions cannot be ad hoc; objectives, policies, criteria, and standards are needed to preclude arbitrariness in decisionmaking and to form a basis for efficient management of growth and development. The discretionary exercise of development-control authority takes place between the extremes of the more rigid traditional zoning schemes on the one hand, and the total absence of development regulation on the other. In other words, discretion cannot be total; landowners need to have some reasonably clear notion of what the community is likely to do.

An important objective of public review of the development process is to minimize adverse external impacts, whether economic, physical, fiscal, esthetic, environmental, or social. Earlier forms of zoning gave little attention to the measurement of other than the most crude off-site effects and rarely sought to establish satisfactory levels of public acceptability. They relied instead on enumerated activities felt to be compatible, and permitted their congregation within specified zoning districts. These specification standards worked satisfactorily as surrogates for the objectives intended by the regulations, in the absence of better measures of compatibility.

With improving technology, however, it became possible to calculate and measure many external effects and to develop regulatory performance standards. During the 1950s and 1960s, performance-standard zoning, primarily for industry, came into fairly wide use with regulations based on permissible levels of physical effects such as noise, air pollution, vibration, glare, and heat. As measurements became more sophisticated, land use compatibility, at least for some effects, could be defined directly and written into regulations. Consequently, landowners' use of their property was not strictly limited by a list of permitted uses.

26. *See generally* Peterson, *Flexibility in Rezonings and Related Governmental Land Use Decisions*, 36 Ohio St. L.J. 499 (1975).

Performance standards broadened the range of options. If the landowner was able to keep the performance of activities on the land within the permitted range, he or she could conduct many activities not previously permitted. The concept of performance standards underlies most of the flexible regulatory techniques of modern development controls. In fact, the entire movement toward flexible zoning can largely be characterized as a movement away from listing the uses permitted on every piece of land toward listing the regulatory objectives and determining the actual use at the time application for development permission is made.

As many communities relied less on use lists and explicit development standards, the lists and standards were not always replaced with criteria sufficient to enable landowners to know what the community would be willing to accept. Vague, general statements often were substituted for standards, and the limits of discretion sometimes approached arbitrariness. The exercise of administrative discretion in land-use controls presents no particular legal problem per se. Site plan review requirements of subdivision regulations have typically involved some discretion, and few regulations have been challenged as to their discretionary nature.

Court intervention is promoted when excessive leeway is exercised by public authorities. The courts have consistently demanded that local actions be based on standards stated in the regulations.[27] This is most notably the case with special permits (special exceptions).

> [S]imply allowing a board of adjustment to grant special exceptions, without establishing standards to guide the board in the exercise of that authority, quite possibly might raise legal questions in some jurisdictions about invalid delegation of legislative power.[28]

In such a process, when important development issues are at stake, administration and management questions are paramount. The first question is, How can the negotiation process be made fair to all parties? Other questions involve governmental management: What

27. *See, e.g.,* Bauer v. City of Wheatridge, 513 P.2d 203 (1973); City of Petersburg v. Schweitzer, 297 So. 2d 74 (1974); Jackson v. Abercrombie, 194 S.E.2d 473 (1972); Summerell v. Phillips, 282 So. 2d 450 (1973); Town of Windham v. La Pointe 308 A.2d 286 (1973); Doran Investments v. Muhlenburg Township, 309 A.2d 450 (1973); Town of Westford v. Kilburn, 300 A.2d 523 (1973).

28. American Society of Planning Officials, New Directions in Connecticut Planning Legislation: A Study of Connecticut Planning, Zoning, and Related Statutes 42–43 (1967); Mandelker, *Delegation of Power and Function in Zoning Administration,* 1963 Wash. U. L.Q. 60.

actions are administrative and thus can be delegated to administrative agencies? To what degree should the governing body participate? When does excessive discretion amount to legislative decisionmaking and require formal action by the governing body? How much authority can be delegated to an administrative official rather than to a public body?

There are three basic interest groups involved in this process: (1) the applicant developer (including site planners, lawyers, and architects retained by the developer); (2) the public review authority, which is generally represented by the professional planning staff, the planning commission, legislative bodies, and other agencies and departments of local government; and (3) the general public—those people who reside in the area of the proposed development, potential consumers, and other interested citizens. Representatives of the first two groups directly participate in the negotiations; the general public usually must air its views at subsequent public hearings.

The Plan

Early development of zoning in this country foresaw the need for coordination between controls on land use and a process of long-range consideration of the community's future development. The Standard Zoning Enabling Act required that the zoning ordinance "be made in accordance with a comprehensive plan," though the "in accordance" requirement has not been consistently applied as a test of the validity of a zoning ordinance. With increasing reliance on discretionary controls, however, there has been more discussion of the use of the plan as a policy base for development decision-making. The nature and form of the comprehensive plan as it relates to land development regulations has been the subject of persistent debate among planners and lawyers, a debate that began even before the drafting of the two model acts. Despite the failure of most courts to require a relationship between the zoning ordinance and the "planners' plan," many are increasingly finding that the study and policy-making process that goes into formulating a plan offers a sound foundation (indeed, some say a prerequisite) for the achievement of public objectives in the exercise of land-use controls.[29]

The relatively obscure process of preparing a zoning ordinance seldom permits the public (or the courts) to understand the intent or purposes of the zoning regulations. The preparation of a comprehensive community plan, on the other hand, typically involves detailed study and analysis and reaching a consensus about the kind

29. *See* discussion in text accompanying notes 156–62 *infra* and *generally,* Chapter 5 *infra.*

of community desired. The zoning ordinance that follows from this planning process has a much more solid and visible policy base.

In Chapter 5 the Advisory Commission urges that the local exercise of land-use control powers be contingent on adoption by the local governing body of a comprehensive plan for development. This recommendation is consistent with that of the report of the National Commission on Urban Problems, which proposed that

> State governments enact legislation denying land-use regulatory powers, after a reasonable period of time, to local governments that lack a "development guidance program" as defined by State statute or administrative regulations made pursuant to such statute. Powers denied would be exercised by the State, regional, or county agencies as provided by the statute. The existence and enforcement by program requirements should, after a reasonable period of time, be made a condition of state participation in the federal 701 planning assistance program.[30]

The American Law Institute, in drafting its *Model Land Development Code*, debated the proper relationship between zoning and planning. The Code authorizes but does not require local governments to adopt a land development plan.[31] As an incentive to planning, however, the Code would grant special powers to local governments which had adopted a land development plan. Only those governments would be empowered, *inter alia*, to: adopt special procedures for regulating planned unit development;[32] designate specially planned areas and prepare "precise plans" for development within these areas;[33] incorporate criteria for development permission in its development plan;[34] adopt special preservation districts.[35] A number of these powers increasingly are being used by communities that have developed systematic and unified growth management systems.[36]

Most communities are bound by present state zoning and planning enabling legislation and its interpretation by the courts.[37] Because many cases have narrowly construed the "in accordance" requirement, communities wishing to strengthen the relationship between development controls and planning may find a difficult path

30. Building the American City, *supra* note 1, at 237–38.
31. ALI Code, *supra* note 6, at § 3-101.
32. *Id.* at § 2-210.
33. *Id.* at § 2-211.
34. *Id.* at § 2-212.
35. *Id.* at § 2-209.
36. *See, e.g.*, McQuail v. Shell Oil Co., 40 Del. Ch. 396, 183 A.2d 572 (1962); Nelson v. South Brunswick Planning Bd., 84 N.J.2d 265, 201 A.2d 741 (1964); Golden v. Planning Bd. of Ramapo, 30 N.Y.2d 359, 334 N.Y.S.2d 138, 285 N.E.2d 291 (1971).
37. *See* Chapter 5 *infra*.

ahead. However, the formal adoption of a comprehensive plan by a governing body gives that plan far greater credibility, establishes the community's commitment to planning, and forces the members of that body to examine the plan and make decisions in light of it.[38] Requiring a written statement of reasons supporting a decision whenever a rezoning is made would also lead to more honest and open actions.[39] Finally, a growing number of courts are beginning to give greater credence to discretionary decisions by governing bodies when those decisions bear a direct relationship to stated community policies as embodied in a plan.[40]

In a New Jersey case upholding an innovative regulatory approach that combined individualized treatment and discretionary review with requirements for particular types of development desired by the township, the court stated:

> [T]here has been a definite and continuing close correlation of planning and zoning in this township, and the zoning amendment under attack must be considered with that fact always in mind. When such close correlation exists, zoning is peculiarly a tool and implementation of planning. . . . The latter always embraces or should embrace the former, but it is much broader and has been defined in a leading case as "a systematic development contrived to promote the common interest in matters that have from the earliest times been considered as embraced within the police power."[41]

The lesson here is that where planning provides a sensible and detailed basis for regulation, innovative regulation is more likely to be sustained on the ground that it not only prevents identified ills but also promotes desired public objectives, as well as better insuring fair treatment among the interested parties.

FLEXIBLE TECHNIQUES FOR CONTROLLING LAND DEVELOPMENT

In the following pages a variety of techniques available to control land development are analyzed. The techniques were selected be-

38. The ALI Code, note 6 *supra*, does call for adoption of the plan by the governing body, at § 3-106.
39. *See, e.g.*, Robey v. Schwab, 307 F.2d 198 (D.C. Cir. 1962); Dietrich v. District of Columbia Bd. of Adj., 293 A.2d 470 (D.C. App. 1972); Roseta v. County of Washington, 254 Or. 161, 458 P.2d 405 (1969); West v. City of Astoria, 524 P.2d 1216 (Or. App. 1974).
40. *See, e.g.*, Hines v. Pinchback-Halloran Volkswagen, Inc., 513 S.W.2d 492 (1974); Baker v. City of Milwaukie, 271 Or. 500, 533 P.2d 772 (1975).
41. Newark Milk and Cream Co. v. Parsippany-Troy Hills, 47 N.J. Sup. 306, 324, 135 A.2d 682, 692 (1957).

cause of their tendency to involve some degree of administrative discretion in the granting of a right to develop, and because of their operation within the traditional framework of land use regulations.

Planned Unit Development

Planned unit development (PUD) is the name most commonly given to a group of techniques that has come into widespread use in the last ten to fifteen years.[42] PUD is a regulatory tool, combining elements of zoning and subdivision regulations, which permits large-scale developments to be planned and built as a unit, and allows (but not necessarily requires) greater flexibility in siting buildings, mixing of housing types with other land uses, arrangement of open spaces, and the preservation of natural features. Its two key elements are the application of controls to the entire development rather than to individual lots (which permits clustering of buildings), and the requirement of discretionary public review to assure that site designs are consistent with public objectives.

Some observers feel PUD is not an innovative concept at all, but merely a repackaging of some of the better zoning devices: general residence districts (in which density is limited but housing type is not), clustering, regulating the timing of development, and site plan review. They assert that any community whose regulations include such techniques can accomplish PUD's objectives without raising many of the problems that attend the PUD bargaining process.[43]

PUD is typically included within the district regulations of the zoning ordinance. While there is little consistency in the way PUD regulations are implemented, two basic approaches have emerged: districting and special permits.[44] The first approach has two common variations. In the floating-zone method the requirement of the PUD zone are enumerated in the zoning ordinance but are affixed to particular parcels only after application by a developer and approval by a designated public body. The principal identifying characteristic of this procedure is that public approval of the PUD takes the form of an amendment to the zoning ordinance. Another variant of the PUD districting approach is the "overlay zone," which is located on the zoning map as a development option for that particular site (an alternative to the permitted uses under the existing zoning).

The second major approach to implementing PUD regulations is the special permit, in which PUDs are permitted as special uses in

42. *See Symposium: PUDs,* 1965 U. Pa. L. Rev. 114; *see also* Frankland v. City of Lake Oswego, 267 Or. 452, 517 P.2d 1042 (1973).

43. 2 N. Williams, American Land Planning Law: Land Use and the Police Power 226-227 (1974) [hereinafter cited as Williams].

44. F. So *et al., supra* note 24, at 9-10.

designated zoning districts by including PUD provisions along with other special uses listed in the district regulations.[45] Thus a developer can consult the zoning ordinance and then determine on the zoning map where, subject to public approval, PUDs might be located. In such cases, no zoning amendment is required, although many governing bodies have retained their authority to grant final approvals.

While PUD requirements are usually applied to sizable developments, there is no typical or minimum size: PUDs can range from 2 to 3 acres to 500 acres or more. The key ingredient is not size but the willingness of communities to grant developers the flexibility and freedom in design and siting that is most profitable for the development and in keeping with public objectives. Occasionally PUD regulations allow a bonus of a density greater than that permitted in the underlying district, if the developer meets stated objectives such as the preservation of natural features, enclosed or screened parking areas, provision for extra open space, and the incorporation of preferred housing types such as multifamily or housing for lower income families. In this way, communities can obtain from developers desired amenities not required if the developer opts to proceed in accordance with the underlying regulations.

Despite their wide use, PUDs rarely have been specifically authorized in state enabling legislation. According to a 1973 study by the American Society of Planning Officials (ASPO), "In the eight years since the model act was published [by the Urban Land Institute and the National Association of Home Builders], only six states have passed laws based on it. An equal number of other states have some form of PUD or cluster subdivision enabling legislation. . . ."[46] Yet many communities have adopted such regulations without express enabling legislation and apparently with no legal challenge.

The validity of the PUD concept as a regulatory tool seldom has been litigated. Challenges usually are aimed at arbitrary standards or abuses of required procedures by official agencies, or (as permitted under some enabling acts), whether the power of decision can be delegated to the planning commission.[47] When neighbors challenge a municipality in its granting of a PUD, they, too, focus on discrete

45. *See* discussion accompanying text at notes 63–69 *infra.*

46. F. So *et al., supra* note 24, at 47.

47. *See, e.g.,* Dover Tp. Homeowners & Tenants Ass'n v. Township of Dover Planning Bd., 276 A.2d 156 (1971); Marshall v. Village of Wappinger Falls, 28 App. Div. 2d 542, 279 N.Y.S.2d 654 (1967); Haar & Hering, *The Lower Gwynedd Tp. Cases: Too Flexible Zoning or an Inflexible Judiciary?* 74 Harv. L. Rev. 1552 (1961). *But see* Rodgers v. Village of Tarrytown, 302 N.Y. 115, 96 N.E.2d 731 (1957); Cheney v. Village 2 at New Hope, Inc., 429 Pa. 626, 241 A.2d 81 (1968).

actions—such as increasing densities, permitting objectionable uses, approving a special permit—rather than on the entire ordinance. Consequently, the case law is of little assistance in defining the necessary standards and bounds of PUD provisions, and we are left with the reasonable conclusion that the concept itself is valid.

Basic Elements of the PUD Process. There is no such thing as a typical PUD ordinance. Some enactments establish few, if any, substantive requirements for the entire project, leaving great discretion to developers and administrative authorities. Others establish specific requirements related to permitted uses, maximum densities, required open space, and so on, for entire projects. Some provide for great flexibility in selecting building types, building locations, and uses within projects; others allow very little.[48] The one feature common to virtually all PUD ordinances is the requirement for a site plan review. It is here that development flexibility, negotiation, and discretionary application of standards come into play.

Considerable negotiation often takes place at each of the three customary steps in the application approval process—preapplication conference, preliminary development plan, and final development plan.[49] The preapplication conference is the point of first contact between developer and community officials and, perhaps, interested neighborhood groups. Here the developer will confer informally with members of the planning staff, department heads, and other interested parties, and perhaps learn (based on preliminary proposals) what attitude the community is likely to have regarding on the proposed development.

The preliminary development-plan stage is most important, because this is when the basic agreement is reached between developer and staff. The public can express its views at a public hearing held at this stage. Following formal application for a PUD permit, the developer will submit the preliminary development plan with specified documents and maps that provide a legal description of the project and a detailed site plan with supporting drawings. The planning commission then holds a public hearing within a specified period, usually 30 to 90 days, at which time the developer will present the proposal, the planning staff or consultant's recommendations are made available, and the public can express its views. If approved and a zoning change is required, it is transmitted to the governing body for final action. The result of this process is the culmination of negotiations on the site plan and other aspects of the proposal.

48. Building the American City, *supra* note 1, at 207.
49. F. So *et al.*, *supra* note 24, at 15.

The final development plan is the detailed engineering drawing of the site, sufficient for recording. No new negotiations occur at this stage since it involves merely the formalization of preliminary plans that have already been approved. Moreover, unless there is substantial deviation from the preliminary plans—and this should be defined in the ordinance—no further public hearing is required. The planning commission at this point approves the recording of the plat; the governing body need only to accept and record site plans and plats, and accept any dedicated properties, streets, rights of way, and so forth. Final approval by the governing body is desirable, since the plan may constitute the only legal control over the use of the property. Provision is usually made for amending the final development plan in case of unforeseen conditions. Minor alterations are permitted administratively, while major alterations, which might have a considerable effect on the basic plan, should be subjected to the same approval process as the final plan, including, when necessary, governing body action.[50]

Provisions that assure that the developer will carry out the approved plan are essential. Some ordinances include clauses requiring developers to begin construction within a specified time period—typically 12 to 18 months—or the parcel reverts to its original zoning. Similarly, ordinances often require that the entire development, as proposed, be completed, and in the order specified in the plan. Since a unitary development is fundamental to the PUD process, the omission of one element or delay in construction may considerably alter the entire project, its effect on surrounding areas, and public costs. Requirements for posting bond or depositing funds in escrow accounts can serve as protection against unsatisfactory or incomplete performance.

Substantive Standards. The issue of specification of detailed PUD standards represents a fundamental tension between assuring compliance with community objectives and stifling innovation and creativity. In effect, incorporating standards in PUD provisions is arguably a contradiction of the basic purpose of the concept. Neither the extreme of detailed standards for all PUD elements nor that of complete flexibility is desirable. Some design elements—including those of density, open space, parking, air-pollution levels, and run-off requirements—can and should be controlled through numerical standards. Other elements, even those easily quantifiable such as minimum lot sizes, need not be subject to numerical standards since there are better and more flexible ways to achieve the desired results.

50. *Id.* at 21-22.

Where numerical performance standards are neither possible nor desirable, performance criteria or statements of intent can serve as guides to developers and administrators. In such instances, considerable negotiation takes place. Since the design standards must offer wide options, it is essential that qualified professionals be involved on both the private and public sides. Regulations can only permit good development; they cannot assure it. Without solid design skills, flexible standards may result not only in a lower quality design but also in a lower level of amenity. Thus, both clear statements of objectives and qualified professionals are essential to assuring good design.

PUDs and Comprehensive Planning. Like most of the flexible techniques discussed in this chapter, PUDs offer many opportunities for carrying out policies enunciated in a community's plan—opportunities not readily available through the more traditional techniques. A variety in housing types, designs, and densities; more complete neighborhood-scale planning; preservation of desirable natural features; and attainment of such other public objectives as increasing the availability of lower cost housing units are thereby possible. These results can be accomplished primarily because of the larger scale at which most PUDs are built, their clustering provisions, and the negotiation process attending site plan review.

Since PUDs offer opportunities that are more difficult to obtain through traditional techniques, it has been proposed that in some situations, especially in the conversion of outlying undeveloped land, large-scale PUD development should be made mandatory.[51] Given the constitutional issues that mandatory PUDs might raise, there has been no legislative action in this direction at the state level, and PUDs have not been mandated to any significant degree at the local level. Rather, communities that find PUDs a more desirable way to accomplish planning objectives will offer incentives to developers intended to increase their profit.

The ALI Code specifically ties PUD authorization to the adoption of the local land-development plan. It would authorize the granting of "special development permission" for a PUD if the project:

(a) will be consistent with the currently effective Land Development Plan; and

(b) is likely to be compatible with development permitted under the general development provisions of the ordinance on substantially all land in the vicinity of the proposed development; and

51. Building the American City, *supra* note 1, at 246.

(c) will not significantly interfere with the enjoyment of other land in the vicinity.[52]

These criteria in turn can be translated by the PUD ordinance into more specific standards capable of harmonizing the entire development, but primarily its periphery, with surrounding areas.[53]

PUDs and Housing Opportunity. The PUD process, when utilized in conjunction with various density bonuses or other incentives, is well suited to promoting greater housing opportunity for low- and moderate-income families, especially in the suburbs.[54] While the PUD process itself may be neutral, the inclusion of specific standards and the bargaining process can make it a strong instrument for achieving an inclusionary housing policy. At the same time, in giving an appearance of flexibility and willingness to "open up," PUDs may be utilized as a cloak merely to hide resistance to change.[55]

Professor Norman Williams has expressed such reservations about this potentially exclusionary aspect of the PUD process.[56] For one thing, PUDs typically have not been used to lower the cost of housing.[57] PUD projects usually have higher front-end costs for land assembly and design, and longer processing time may add carrying costs that are passed on to buyers. For another, the bargaining process allows communities seeking to be exclusionary the opportunity to do so by negotiating more amenities and facilities at the expense of the developer, hence effectively driving up the cost of housing while maintaining an expansive public posture toward opening up housing opportunity.

52. ALI Code, *supra* note 6, § 2-210.
53. F. So *et al., supra* note 24, at 40–41.
54. *See* R. Babcock & F. Bosselman, Exclusionary Zoning 69–77 (1973).
55. In Southern Burlington County NAACP v. Township of Mount Laurel, 67 N.J. 151, 336 A.2d 713 (1975), the court stated at 729:

> As previously indicated, Mount Laurel has allowed some multi-family housing by agreement in planned unit developments, but only for the relatively affluent and of no benefit to low and moderate income families. And even here, the contractual agreements between municipality and developer sharply limit the number of apartments having more than one bedroom. . . . Such restrictions are so clearly contrary to the general welfare as not to require further discussion.

See also Note, *Exclusionary Use of the Planned Unit Development: Standards for Judicial Scrutiny,* 8 Harv. Civ. Rts.–Civ. Lib. L. Rev. 384 (1973).
56. 2 Williams, *supra* note 43 at 228–229.
57. F. So *et al., supra* note 24, at 8. The problems of obtaining reasonable bank financing and subcontractors' bids for a new type of development is discussed from the contractor's perspective in *Symposium: PUDs,* 1965 U. Pa. L. Rev. 114.

Few communities on their own initiative will encourage the development of lower income housing. As long as property taxes are the primary local revenue source, it is highly unlikely that communities will seek out such low tax ratables as low income housing, especially when bargaining rather than specified standards governs the process. Since the Advisory Commission takes the position that it is in the wider public interest to allocate housing responsibility throughout a region, the accomplishment of this objective may require solutions either mandating or providing incentives for a proportion of low- and moderate-income housing units in specified sizes or types of PUDs, or exacting payments from developers for the publicly-supported construction of such housing.[58] Such actions necessarily would diminish the flexibility aspect of PUDs in favor of the higher public objective of promoting housing opportunity.

No state currently has mandated such a housing requirement in conjunction with PUDs. A few communities offer developers density bonuses as an incentive for building lower income housing.[59] Also, some communities have enacted ordinances requiring all new housing development, under certain conditions, to include a minimum number of units for sale or rent to low- and moderate-income families. In Fairfax County, Virginia, a mandatory "inclusionary" ordinance was overturned by the Virginia Supreme Court.[60] This decision has not, however, prevented other communities such as Montgomery County, Maryland; Los Angeles, California; Cherry Hill, New Jersey; and Lewisboro, New York,[61] from attempting such schemes.

By tying the operation of such ordinances to the availability of federal subsidies, or by using suitable density bonuses or lower amenity standards to reduce the cost of housing, it may be possible to avoid the "takings" issue that was relied upon, in part, to invalidate the Virginia scheme. The general unavailability of federal housing subsidies, however, has made it difficult to evaluate the viability of such an approach. In light of the lack of experience to date, it is reasonable to conclude that a voluntary density bonus approach

58. *See* discussion of mandatory inclusionary ordinances in Chapter 7 *infra.*
59. New Castle County, Delaware, is one such example. M. Brooks, Lower Income Housing: The Planners' Response 51 (1972).
60. Board of Supervisors v. DeGroff Enterprises 214 Va. 235, 198 S.E.2d 600 (1973), discussed in Chapter 7 *infra.*
61. *See* H. Franklin, D. Falk, & A. Levin, In-Zoning: A Guide for Policy Makers on Inclusionary Land Use Programs (1974) for discussion of Fairfax County, Montgomery County, and Los Angeles; Erber & Prior, *The Trend in Housing Density Bonuses*, 41 Planning 14 (No. 10, 1974) for reference to Cherry Hill and Lewisboro.

will likely be more acceptable to the courts than mandatory percentage requirements.[62]

Many planners and developers have tended to view the PUD as a panacea, holding the key for solving many of the problems of conventional techniques. They have often ignored the very serious risks and dangers in its potential misuse. In fact, the prudent use of the PUD technique can improve the quality of development—when the process is accompanied by appropriate public scrutiny.

Special Permits

The special permit (sometimes called a special exception or a conditional use) is a zoning device that singles out for special treatment

> [T]hose types or aspects of development which might or might not be compatible with development permitted as of right by the zoning ordinance. An owner desirous of carrying out the development must go through the special permit process which gives the administering agency opportunity to determine whether that development, in the particular location contemplated, will create special problems which can be ameliorated by specially devised conditions or which call for denial of permission.[63]

Special permits most commonly are required for uses that the community feels are generally in keeping with the character of the zone but, because they possess characteristics different from the zone's major land uses, require special conditions to be made compatible. For example, utility substations, halfway houses, schools, and sometimes churches are often permitted as special uses in residential zones, however, due to their potential impact on a residential area, additional regulations may be applied for setbacks, parking, screening, minimum lot size, or perhaps proximity in relation to other uses. Other communities, as discussed below, may make the special permit the central feature of their land-use control system, thereby removing its "special" characteristics.

Discretion in granting the permit normally is circumscribed by two key factors: (1) only those uses identified in the text of the zoning ordinance as entitled to special permit treatment may be so processed; and (2) the ordinance includes criteria that are intended to be used

---

62. *See* H. Franklin *et al.*, *supra* note 61, at 140; and discussion in Chapter 7 *infra*.

63. Heyman, *Innovative Land Regulation and Comprehensive Planning*, in N. Marcus & M. Groves, *supra* note 1, at 33-34, *updated in* 13 Santa Clara Law. 183 (1972).

by administrators in deciding whether to grant the license. The legal rationale for special permits is distinct from that underlying variances. With the latter, the grant is made because a unique hardship is encountered under provisions of the zoning ordinance.[64]

Special permits have been used widely by communities that seek greater flexibility in the administration of land-use regulations. In many zoning ordinances the special permit provides the main component of flexibility. For example, one of the prerequisites to a grant of a special permit may be the existence of specified public facilities, such as the availability of public water and sewers. This condition has the same effect as would the enactment of an adequate public facilities ordinance.

The result of such a precondition is to expand significantly the amount of development that requires a special permit. For example, Clarkstown, New York, zoned most of the town for large lots, with higher intensity uses permitted by special permit after a finding that facilities were adequate. The court upheld this broadened application of the process, stating that a municipality can regulate intensity of use if the action is reasonable and if the community is making a good faith effort to provide the facilities.[65] But in a similar New Jersey case the court expressed concern over the vague criteria on which the discretionary action was based, and invalidated a scheme in which most development was by special permit.[66]

The special permit process is usually administered through the local board of appeals, and is subject to judicial review. Some communities vest the authority in the planning commission or in the elected governing body. The latter is frequently the case in New York State. A well known example is the Ramapo growth management scheme, which makes special permits a key element of its sequential timing systems.[67] Other jurisdictions apply special permits through zoning administrators or hearing examiners.[68]

Standards: When Should a Special Permit Be Granted? Two central issues have characterized the growth of the special permit device: (1) the limitations that should be placed on the permissible uses; and (2) the specificity of the governing criteria. As with other flexible techniques, opportunities for abuse of special permit au-

64. *See* R. Anderson, American Law of Zoning, §§ 6.01, 14.02 (1968).
65. Joseph v. Town Bd. of Clarkstown, 198 N.Y.S.2d 695 (1960).
66. Rockhill v. Chesterfield Tp., 23 N.J. 117, 128 A.2d 473 (1950). *See also* Rhode Island legislation that permits local boards to make special exceptions, R.I. Gen. Laws Ann. § 45-24-13.
67. *See* discussion of *Ramapo* system in Chapter 5 *infra*.
68. *See* discussion of hearing examiner, in text accompanying notes 265–293 *infra*.

thority exist when standards are vague. Accordingly, the degree of discretion needs to be circumscribed in the ordinance by conditions governing its use. When such provisions are quite specific, it is possible to know in advance when the conditions have been met and the permit must be granted. More commonly, the provisions lack specificity. Broader discretion is necessary and, because the standards themselves are open to interpretation, the applicant may have difficulty in demonstrating compliance. The point, of course, is that communities need to determine a proper balance between flexibility and prescription. The more discretion permitted, the greater the likelihood of court challenge on grounds of arbitrariness, vagueness, and lack of uniformity.

A basic checklist of special permit standards might include such items as ingress and egress to the site and structures; parking and loading; refuse and other service areas; utility connection; appropriate screening and buffering; yards and open space; and compatibility with surrounding uses.[69] The preceding are general criteria to which specific standards would be applied.

Special Permits and Comprehensive Plans.   Another standard for the special permit is the comprehensive plan. Excessive use of special permits can vitiate the policies of a comprehensive plan. One of the purposes of standards is to maintain generally cohesive neighborhoods. A proliferation of special uses will make it difficult to determine what is and is not compatible. As a result the plan itself may be rendered obsolete. Permit granting agencies should be aware of these cumulative effects and control the issuance of permits accordingly. Similarly, the planning process must be cognizant of new demands brought by special permit applications, and plans should be revised as necessary to fit changing conditions.

Special Permits and Housing Opportunity.   Special permits can be useful devices in encouraging preferred treatment for multifamily low- and moderate-income housing in areas zoned for single-family homes. Economically, however, they probably offer little incentive for the development of such housing, and may in fact be used to obstruct such projects by making conditions unrealistic, while at the same time giving the impression of "allowing" lower income housing in the community. The courts, on the other hand have little difficulty in upholding zoning for multifamily low- and moderate-income housing if it is accomplished by special permit, particularly

69. F. Bair & E. Bartley, Text of a Model Zoning Ordinance, with Commentary 57 (3d ed. 1966).

where the ordinance provides sufficient governing criteria that assure predictability and uniformity of application.[70] Policy support for preferred treatment of low- and moderate-income housing through the use of special permits could be found in the community's federally required housing assistance plan or in a regional housing plan for the area.[71]

In conclusion, special permits—when bound by officially adopted policies and criteria for their application—can be a valuable tool in promoting heterogeneous development, housing opportunity and creativity in design; in timing development (when tied to standards of adequate public facilities) as part of a managed growth policy; and in inviting greater public scrutiny of selected proposals. On the other hand, when used as a wholesale delegation of legislative responsibility to administrative bodies (thereby precluding predictability and uniformity), the extreme use of special permits can turn zoning into a system of licensing and lead to arbitrary decisionmaking. Insistence on a fair and rational process, implemented through adequate standards and grounded in sound planning, makes the special permit a useful technique to mediate between the two extremes of arbitrariness and rigidity in land-use controls.

Overlay Zoning

An overlay zone is a mapped zone that imposes an additional set of requirements upon those of the underlying zoning district. In an area where an overlay zone is established, the land may be developed under the conditions and requirements of both zones. An overlay zone might occasionally cover two or more underlying zones, as in the case of an historic area that includes single-family, multifamily, and commercial districts. The overlay zone would deal with architectural controls, while the underlying zones continue to regulate densities and uses.

Overlay zones are typically applied when there is a special public interest in a geographic area that does not coincide with underlying zoning district boundaries. Some of the more common uses for such zones relate to special environmental features that restrain development; floodplain zones and wet-soils overlay zones are examples. Other uses include maintaining the integrity of historic areas, preserving views, restricting areas to public uses, and limiting building heights and densities in certain parts of a city.

Overlay zones are described in the zoning text, mapped, and

70. *See* H. Franklin *et al.*, *supra* note 61, at 117; D. Mandelker, *supra* note 28, at 70-77; *see also* Maldini v. Ambro, 36 N.Y.2d 481 (1975).
71. *See* Chapter 7, *infra*.

adopted by the governing body in a manner similar to conventional zoning. Provisions are administered through the usual zoning process, with flexibility a factor when permission for development to overlay zones is granted through a special-permit process. When permission is granted in this manner and the overlay zone is anchored to the particular parcel, the process is analogous to that of a floating zone.[72] An overlay zone, however, is distinct from a floating zone in that the latter, when anchored, replaces the underlying district on the zoning map. Because of the more restricted nature of the overlay zone, its use avoids some of the objections directed at floating zones with regard to predictability and arbitrariness in application.

Applicable standards for overlay zones are determined by the manner in which they are administered—that is, whether development is permitted by right or by special permits. When special permits are used, their issuance should be limited to minimize potential abuse. In regard to housing opportunity, an overlay zone might be applied to all residentially designated areas of a defined density or size, and might thereby permit low-income or subsidized housing at a higher than usual density. Realistically, however, in an "inclusionary" zoning system other flexible techniques, particularly special permits combined with incentives, are more likely to achieve inclusionary objectives.

The major advantage of overlay zoning is that in adding a small element of flexibility to traditional zoning, it offers an opportunity to implement specific public policies (as enumerated in the local comprehensive plan), particularly toward environmental protection and cultural preservation. Moreover, because of its limited degree of flexibility and greater degree of predictability (as it is specifically tied to the zoning map), an overlay zone is less likely to be invalidated by the courts than other more flexible devices. This assumes, of course, that the initial determination of allowable uses was reasonable. Yet, overlay zoning is capable of achieving many of the same objectives.

Floating Zones

A floating zone is a district, the requirements for which are described in detail in the text of the ordinance but which is not specifically located on the zoning map. An applicant for development permission under provisions of the floating zone is granted governing body approval if the conditions spelled out in the ordinance are

72. *See* discussion of floating zones, in text accompanying notes 73–81 *infra*.

satisfied. The floating zone is then anchored to the particular parcel
—*replacing* the preexisting zoning—by an amendment to the zoning
text. The floating zone technique is commonly employed in instances in which the community wishes to limit specific uses but
does not wish to map their location in advance of application. These
uses might include general industrial facilities, PUDs, shopping centers, or some particular problem developments over which the community wishes to retain a significant degree of control.

The legal status of floating zones tends to be grounded not so
much on the concept per se but on the permissible conditions under
which it can be applied. Courts in a number of states have upheld the
validity of floating zones. The Maryland cases are perhaps the most
prominent, both in terms of the number of cases decided and the variations in the use of floating zones involved.[73] An explanation for
Maryland's pronounced disposition toward floating zones is in part
attributable to that state's judicial reluctance to uphold rezonings
in regular districts permitting more intensive uses under the rigorous
Maryland "change or mistake" rule.[74] In other states, such as Colorado,[75] New York,[76] Kentucky,[77] and Connecticut,[78] floating
zones have met with a generally favorable response, while in Pennsylvania the courts have vacillated.[79] The common argument that
floating zoning constitutes spot zoning has been overcome in most
states by the rationale that the governing body has conditioned its
usage on the satisfaction of certain standards specified in the ordinance.

The process for anchoring a floating zone has some of the same
elements as a conventional rezoning. There are, however, some important distinctions. Customarily, a rezoning application can be
denied if the existing zoning for the particular parcel is reasonable
and has been properly adopted. Under a floating zone application,
the question is not whether the existing zoning is reasonable, but
whether the conditions for granting rezoning, as spelled out in the
ordinance, have been met. The legislative body in this case is acting
much like an administrative agency considering an application for
a special permit, particularly where the zone floats over only a part

73. *See esp.* Huff. v. Board of Zoning App., 133 A.2d 83 (1957); Beall v.
Montgomery County Council, 212 A.2d 751 (1965).
74. *See note* 153, *infra.*
75. Moore v. City of Boulder, 29 Colo. App. 248, 484 P.2d 134 (1971).
76. Rodgers v. Village of Tarrytown, 302 N.Y. 115, 96 N.E.2d 731 (1951).
77. Bellemeade v. Priddle, 503 S.W.2d 734 (Ky. App. 1974).
78. Hawkes v. Town Plan & Zone Comm'n, 240 A.2d 914 (1968).
79. *Compare* Cheney v. Village 2 at New Hope, Inc., 429 Pa. 626, 241 A.2d
81 (1968), *with* Eves v. Board of Zoning Adjust., 401 Pa. 211, 164 A.2d 7 (1960).

of the community. Denial of the rezoning would be based on an applicant's failure to show that specified conditions would be satisfied.

Some ordinances allow the floating zone to be anchored or actually mapped by an administrative body such as a board of appeals or hearing officer. This procedure might raise problems of improper delegation of legislative authority in some jurisdictions. If, as some cases suggest, any ad hoc rezoning will be considered an administrative or quasi-judicial action, this problem, over the long run, may become less significant.

Standards and the Comprehensive Plan.   Because the floating zone becomes anchored only through a discretionary process, it is important that precise standards be established. The text of the zoning ordinance should provide the minimum standards that must be met prior to rezoning. For example, the community might adopt a general policy that it desires a regional shopping center within its boundaries, specifying standards in the ordinance about size, location of major streets, and site development. This would give a potential developer a clear notion of what local officials want. With these guidelines the developer could propose a regional shopping center on an appropriate site.

Even a liberal interpretation of the "in accordance with a comprehensive plan" requirement, however, does not overcome the attitude of some commentators that the floating zone is the antithesis of planning. Yet some courts view the process of writing the floating zone's requirements into the text of the ordinance, identifying the developments that will be permitted, and enumerating the conditions that must be satisfied, as meeting the "in accordance" test.[80] The rational consideration of alternatives and the provision for adequate review by a professional planning staff will further enhance the credibility of the floating zone technique. In fact, it has been suggested that "a persuasive case can be made that the floating zone technique is more apt to guard against discrimination and irrationality than is reliance on traditional small parcel reclassification even if subject to judicial review."[81]

Housing Opportunity.   The floating-zone device may have some potential value in an inclusionary land-use program. A community might, for example, define a low-income housing development as a

80. *See* Huff v. Board of Zoning App., 133 A.2d 83 (1957); Rodgers v. Village of Tarrytown, 302 N.Y. 115, 96 N.E.2d 731 (1951).
81. Heyman, *supra* note 63, at 39–40.

floating zone. Lot sizes, densities, and location of public transportation, employment, and shopping areas would be prescribed, and a site-plan review process would be incorporated into the ordinance. The ordinance might specifically tie the utilization of the floating zone to the availability of housing subsidy programs under which low-income housing could be built. Enumerating such conditions in the ordinance, preferably with reference to a local Housing Assistance Plan or other expression of public policy, would increase the likelihood of the ordinance being sustained. Moreover, delaying the identification of the site for a potential lower income development could help to avoid the problem of spiralling land prices when parcels are specifically zoned for multifamily use.

Conditional and Contract Zoning

Communities continue to seek ways to bind landowners to the terms under which a rezoning is granted. One of the reasons for this is the constraint placed on the rezoning process by the requirement that similar parcels be treated uniformly. Many rezonings have been granted on the strength of presentations showing attractive site plans, architectural renderings, and elaborate promises for amenities—all of which indicate that the proposed development would be highly desirable and advantageous to the community, and none of which is required by the ordinance.

After the rezoning is granted, the actual development may bear little resemblance to the original proposal if the developer reverts to the minimum requirements of the new district regulations.[82] Sometimes the new development does not even take place, and the rezoned land is held for speculative purposes awaiting development by a prospective developer-purchaser for a use different from that originally proposed but permitted under the new zoning classification. Consequently, communities have been concerned that by merely granting a rezoning they have no assurance that the anticipated development will be built or, if built, that it will have the promised amenities.

Over the years many techniques have been developed to address this problem. Under one scheme, the community requires the applicant to execute and record covenants that limit by deed the use that can be made of the property. Another—conditional rezoning—secures the property owner's agreement that in exchange for the rezoning, the use of the property will be limited, irrespective of the otherwise

82. *See, e.g.,* Frankland v. City of Lake Oswego, 267 Or. 452, 517 P.2d 1042 (1973).

applicable provisions in the zoning district.[83] A more common device —contract zoning—involves a reciprocal agreement. Not only is the land rezoned under the terms of the developer's agreement, but the community agrees to limit, at least for a period, its power to reclassify the land.[84]

In cases where the community has gone beyond conditional zoning to "contract away" its future zoning power, the courts have often invalidated such action on two general grounds. First, the community cannot contract away its future right to exercise the police power, and second, the contract is prima facie evidence of spot zoning and in direct violation of uniformity requirements of the comprehensive plan. The latter carried to its logical conclusion might result in all similar parcels of land being zoned differently.[85]

While most state courts have consistently disapproved contract zoning on these grounds,[86] New York,[87] Massachusetts,[88] and California[89] have cases reaching the opposite conclusion. Two other states, Maryland and Washington, have also shown a positive trend in favor of contract zoning.[90] There is little consistency to the reasoning presented by the cases upholding contract zoning. Most rely on the uniqueness of the particular situation—that the bargain was between the developer and the planning commission rather than the governing body, or that the contract protected the interests of the neighbors as well as the developer, or that the contract was for good purpose (that is, the ends justify the means). Most commentators shoot holes in these arguments, pointing out that few courts, even when the technique was upheld, have directly confronted the basic issues of bargaining away the police power and of spot zoning.[91]

83. *See* Miller, The Current Status of Conditional Zoning, Institute on Planning, Zoning, and Eminent Domain 121 (1974).

84. *Id.*

85. Schaffer, *Contract Zoning and Conditional Zoning*, 17 Zoning Dig. 345 (1965).

86. Illinois, a jurisdiction where courts have held contract zoning illegal, is the only state where, by statute, a municipality may enter into a pre-annexation agreement that may modify otherwise applicable zoning regulations.

87. Church v. Town of Islip, 8 N.Y.2d 254, 168 N.E.2d 680, 203 N.Y.S. 866 (1960).

88. Sylvania Elect. Prods. v. City of Newton, 344 Mass. 428, 183 N.E.2d 118 (1962).

89. Scrutton v. County of Sacramento, 275 Cal. App. 2d 412, 79 Cal. Rptr. 872 (1969).

90. Funger v. Mayor and Council, 244 Md. 141, 223 A.2d 168 (1966); Town of Somerset v. County Council, 229 Md. 42, 181 A.2d 671 (1962); Myhre v. City of Spokane, 70 Wash. 2d 207, 422 P.2d 790 (1967).

91. R. Anderson, American Law of Zoning, at § 8.21 (1969); 1 Williams, supra note 43 at ch. 29; Comment, *Toward a Strategy for Utilization of Contract and Conditional Zoning*, 51 J. Urb. L. 94 (1973).

Conditional zoning has had a similarly checkered legal history. Disapproval by the courts on the basis of lack of uniformity or spot zoning has given way, in some states, to the view that special conditions attached to a rezoning are beneficial in minimizing harms that might otherwise result from the change.[92] In any event, the process and implications of these two devices are similar and can be discussed in the same context. Since the process is that of piecemeal rezoning, the terms are not spelled out in the zoning ordinance but are applied on a case-by-case basis. It is, in that sense, an extreme discretionary process, involving considerable ad hoc bargaining between the developer and the community. In most instances, such a process occurs without authorizing legislation. Developers seem willing to accept additional restrictions as a quid pro quo for development permission.

Standards and the Comprehensive Plan. The failure to control conditional rezonings by procedural or substantive standards has given the courts the greatest amount of concern in dealing with the technique. The key question is whether the community can require developers to meet conditions that are not imposed on other property owners in the same zone. Can the community demand concessions from the developer through negotiation that they cannot obtain under terms of the ordinance?

One suggestion is to provide general guidelines for conditional and contract zoning by means of state enabling legislation.[93] Short of this approach, the local comprehensive plan, if sufficiently specific in the policies applicable to a rezoning, could provide some guidance for conditional or contract zoning situations. While conditional rezoning often has been equated with spot zoning, it offers the opportunity, at least in theory, to provide legislative flexibility and to reconcile the various interests affected by land reclassification. It may, for example, permit the development of property that is suitable for development but that has been passed over as a result of inadequate zoning.

Housing Opportunity. A number of writers have pointed out the potential value of conditional rezoning for expanding housing opportunity.[94] As a condition for rezoning to a multifamily zone, for example, the community could require construction of a certain

92. *See* cases at note 90 *supra*, and Miller, *supra* note 83.
93. In 1973 Virginia passed legislation authorizing conditional zoning. Va. Code Ann. § 15.1-491 (1973). *See* Comment, *supra*, note 91 at 110–11.
94. H. Franklin *et al.*, *supra* note 61, at 118–19. *See esp.* Shapiro, *The Case for Conditional Zoning*, 41 Temp. L.Q. 267 (1968).

proportion of low- and moderate-income units. However, given the variable attitude of the courts to these techniques, their use in this regard would be necessarily selective. Finally, though recent court decisions indicate greater receptivity to explicit discretionary techniques, there remain opportunities for abuse by all parties. A relatively private agreement, adhered to by both sides, is not likely to produce litigation, except by disgruntled neighbors. The need therefore, is clear for both procedural safeguards and substantive criteria for decision-making.

Incentive Zoning

Zoning generally places restrictions on individuals' use of their property. One of the more interesting zoning developments in recent years has been the utilization of the incentive or bonus device to permit owners more intensive use of their property and to enhance their opportunity for greater economic return. Essentially, incentive zoning represents a tradeoff between the community and the property owner. In exchange for providing something that the community views to be in its interest, but which it might otherwise not be able to require (open space, direct access to public transportation or parking, an arcade or building walkthrough, or cluster development rather than conventional lot-by-lot development), the developer is given a bonus, usually in the form of permission to build at a higher density.

Bonus provisions have been utilized most frequently either in high-density districts of central cities or in connection with PUDs. Examples of the former include San Francisco's use of density increases for buildings with direct access to transit stations, with open plazas, or with high-level observation decks; and Milwaukee's use of floor-area increases for owners providing plazas, arcades, and extra rear and side yards. New York has an elaborate system that provides special bonuses for, among other things, building theaters in the downtown theater district.[95] PUD ordinances commonly permit developers to build more housing in exchange for clustering the units, for providing common open space or other design features, or simply for making use of the PUD process.[96]

There has been little litigation on the use of incentive or bonus zoning,[97] in large part because developers usually are not being re-

95. The San Francisco, Milwaukee, and New York ordinances are discussed in M. Brooks, Bonus Provisions in Central City Areas (Planning Advisory Service Report No. 257, 1970).

96. *Id.*

97. *But see* Chrinko v. So. Brunswick Tp. Planning Bd., 187 A.2d 221 (1963) for a case involving density transfer. *See also* J. Costonis, Space Adrift (1974) for a discussion of the legal background for such controls.

stricted; to the contrary, they generally are being offered an opportunity to increase their economic return. In instances in which a developer views an ordinance as imposing burdens that are not outweighed by the benefits received, a "taking" question might thus be presented—in which case litigation would be more likely. For example, some communities deliberately skew downward the zoning allowed as of right in order to create a market for the bonus being extended. In this case the developer is being surcharged rather than receiving a gift. Challenges might also be brought by disgruntled neighbors, on equal protection grounds, arguing that they were unable to avail themselves of similar benefits (a tenuous challenge at best). Neighbors might also argue that because of the availability of such incentives they must bear additional public-service costs resulting from higher density development.

Bonus provisions can be administered as of right or through a special permit process, with or without review of the site plan PUDs, regardless of bonus provisions, are accompanied by site plan review. Provisions requiring more complicated calculations and greater judgment (and hence some negotiation) might also involve special permits and site plan review. Relatively straightforward provisions require no more than the usual zoning permission process.

Standards and Comprehensive Plans. Incentive or bonus zoning is an example of the performance approach to zoning. A major impediment to the effective exercise of other flexible techniques is the vagueness of the criteria employed in measuring acceptability—in most instances, general policies and guidelines, that are not quantifiable. In incentive zoning the standards are usually expressed numerically, as they are for industrial performance. The requirements are spelled out with little room for arbitrariness in their application; the developer can accurately assess the costs and benefits and be guided accordingly.

Developers will likely respond favorably to bonuses that offer greater profit opportunities: those that provide more rentable or salable space, or combine residential with commercial uses. Similarly, opportunities for saving money may come from: (1) clustering or concentrating structures and lowering the costs of utility lines and streets; (2) faster processing time, which gives developers a chance to build and sell more quickly; and (3) lowering physical design standards—such as narrower streets, thinner pavements, fewer sidewalks, or septic tanks instead of sanitary sewers in some subdivisions.

Density bonuses work best where land costs are high, mainly in central cities and in rapidly growing suburbs. However, it should be noted that in large cities incentive zoning will have little attraction if, as a matter of right, developers can do as they please under existing regulations. Most central business districts are overzoned for high density and would require a ruthless downzoning, perhaps to a "constitutional floor," to make incentives work. In fringe areas, where land is relatively inexpensive, consumers and hence developers are not particularly interested in higher density; bonuses that permit mixing of uses and lower construction costs may be more attractive. A bonus could also result from a priority review system for proposed developments providing desired amenities. In return the public could receive a wide range of other benefits, such as preservation by dedication of wetlands, wooded areas, and steep slopes; a mix of housing costs and types; or a building process staged in conjunction with the community's capital-improvement program. Sufficiently attractive bonuses may motivate developers to further absorb development costs, (which subdivision exactions currently may require).

Housing Opportunity. Bonus arrangements have great potential value in increasing the supply of low- and moderate-income housing. A developer might be granted a density bonus for building subsidized housing units. The communities of Arlington County, Virginia, and Bellingham, Massachusetts, have encouraged low-income housing through incentive zoning.[98] New Castle, Delaware, permits an additional, conventional, unsubsidized unit to be built along with each low-income unit, thereby potentially doubling density on a tract.[99]

The complex legal questions about uniformity of treatment, balance of costs and benefits to both developer and the public, and the relationship of incentives to the comprehensive plan, have rarely been raised because of the rather limited use of incentives to date. Clearly the discretionary nature of the incentive process and the significant economic consequences of bonus provisions make procedural due process a necessity. Nevertheless, the tentative steps taken thus far have shown incentives to be among the more manageable and productive of the flexible techniques that deserve further exploration.[100]

Subdivision Regulations

How should public facility costs be apportioned among old residents of a new subdivision, and future residents? This issue has

98. H. Franklin *et al.*, *supra* note 61, at 122-23.

99. 2 Williams, *supra* note 43 at 246-251.

100. However, in declaring the Fairfax County inclusionary ordinance invalid, the Virginia Supreme Court apparently ignored the density bonuses in that ordinance. *See* Board of Supervisors v. Degroff Enterprises, 214 Va. 235, 198 S.E.2d 600 (1973).

been the subject of controversy and litigation for many years.[101] Subdivision regulations have traditionally required developers, at their own expense, to construct to defined specifications the streets, water supply, sewage, and drainage systems. This was originally done both to discourage speculation in land development and to gain some control over land-development practices that sometimes resulted in subdivisions lacking in the basic necessities of residential development. Subsequent regulations have required developers to dedicate land for recreation and schools, or to pay a fee under specified conditions to the local treasury in lieu of such dedication. The objective is to impose upon the new development as much of the capital facility costs as possible.

More recently, communities have required developers to bear the cost of off-site improvements generated by new development such as a street widening to accommodate more traffic or an addition to an existing school building. Dedication of on-site streets and utilities is no longer seriously questioned. Yet the legal standing of more onerous exactions that communities seek to impose in their efforts to shift the burden of development costs is far less clear. A number of states have amended their subdivision enabling acts to authorize such exactions.[102]

Early challenges to park and school site dedication requirements were successful mainly because of a lack of enabling legislation.[103] Later cases seemed to be less concerned with enabling legislation than with showing that the exactions bore a direct relationship to the costs generated by the subdivision.[104] More recently, however, the courts, in evaluating exactions, have begun to apply a reasonableness test, which asks whether there is a reasonable relationship between the exactions and costs generated by the development. Where it is found that the exactions imposed do not result from the subdivision's own actions but from those of the entire community, they will be invalidated as an unconstitutional taking.[105]

101. *See* Comment, *Subdivision Exactions: The Constitutional Issues, the Judicial Response, and the Pennsylvania Situation*, 19 Vill. L. Rev. 782 (1974).

102. M. Brooks, Mandatory Dedication of Land or Fees-in-Lieu of Land for Parks and Schools 3 (PAS No. 266, 1971).

103. Heyman & Gilhool, *Constitutionality of Imposing Increased Community Costs on New Suburban Residents Through Subdivision Exactions*, 73 Yale L.J. 1119 (1964).

104. *See* cases cited in note 106 *infra;* and Johnston, *Constitutionality of Subdivision Control Exactions: The Quest for a Rationale*, 52 Cornell L. Rev. 871 (1967).

105. *See generally* Associated Home Builders v. City of Walnut Creek, 94 Cal. Rptr. 630, 484 P.2d 606 (1971); Ryers v. City Council of L.A., 207 P.2d 1 (Cal. 1949); Jenad, Inc. v. Village of Scarsdale, 18 N.Y.2d 78, 218 N.E.2d 673, 271 N.Y.S.2d 955 (1966); Gulest Associates v. Town of Newburgh, 25 Misc. 2d 1004, 209 N.Y.S.2d 729 (1961); Haugen v. Gleason, 226 Or. 99, 359 P.2d 108 (1961).

Such cases require the courts to decide how much can be required and what formula or set of criteria should be used. One line of cases has established that the costs imposed must be "specifically and uniquely attributable" to the needs of the new subdivision.[106] The Wisconsin case of *Jordan v. Village of Menomonee Falls*[107] approved a fee-in-lieu of dedication, and recognized that the cumulative effects of new residents could be considered in determining exaction requirements. Another line of cases appears to judge the validity by whether the residents of the new subdivision will benefit directly from imposition of the fee-in-lieu requirement.[108] This test substitutes a "reasonably related" stand for the "uniquely attributable" criterion. These decisions suggest that the provisions must contain statements limiting the use of the funds collected to the particular subdivision and that they be used only for the facilities for which the funds were collected.

Arguments based on the limits of police power for the protection of health, safety, and morals have emphasized the need to prevent neighbors from harming each other. In recent years, greater reliance on protection of the general welfare has led to stricter requirements, not just for prevention of harm but for the enhancement of the physical, social, and economic environments. Reliance on general-welfare arguments has significantly strengthened the case for subdivision exactions. While primarily used to support requirements for streets, utilities, and drainage, the same argument has validated requirements for open space and school sites. The courts have found the prevention of overcrowding of recreation facilities and schools to be in the interest of the entire community.

The logical extension of these arguments is to place the burden of all new development costs within a new subdivision—in other words, the community at large should not incur any additional costs as a result of development activity. Several communities have moved in this direction. In 1971, the circuit court of Loudon County, Virginia, approved a denial of a rezoning application on the grounds that the new development would cost the county more than it would generate in taxes.[109] As a result, the county amended its zoning regulations

106. Rosen v. Village of Downers Grove, 19 Ill. 2d 448, 167 N.E.2d 230 (1960); Pioneer Trust and Savings v. Village of Mount Prospect, 176 N.E.2d 799 (1961).
107. 28 Wis. 2d 608, 137 N.W.2d 442 (1965).
108. Jenad, Inc. v. Village of Scarsdale, 18 N.Y.2d 78, 218 N.E.2d 673, 271 N.Y.S.2d 955 (1966); Gulest Associates v. Town of Newburgh, 25 Misc. 2d 1004, 209 N.Y.S.2d 729 (1961).
109. Lee Jackson Development Corp. v. Board of Supervisors (Cir. Ct. No. 3839, 1972).

to specify that as a precondition to rezoning approval, developers would agree either to provide all new public facilities required by the development or to reimburse the county for them. This provision has been interpreted to include not only streets, utilities and drainage, and sites for open space and schools, but also the cost of school construction and such other public buildings as fire stations and civic offices. To date this regulation has not been tested.[110]

As an alternative to the exercise of this police power, developers in some communities are charged a development-impact tax determined by a formula based on the public costs of the development.[111] Several communities in Florida and Arizona have attempted to impose such taxes, with mixed success.[112] California has enacted legislation to authorize communities to impose such a tax calculated on the number of bedrooms in the new development.[113] Many California communities have enacted such ordinances, and these have withstood court challenge.[114] The result of these taxes is to carry the shifting of costs a step further. Developers, and hence new residents, are charged not only for the direct costs resulting from development, but also for the indirect costs, even when they occur off the site. The formula provides that the costs of, say, street widening, or a new traffic light, or a bigger sewer main, would be borne by new development.

Subdivision regulations normally contain a formula for determining the amount and character of land to be dedicated for various public uses, and they may provide for the alternative of payment in lieu of dedication under specified circumstances.[115] Such a formula seems to offer little room for negotiation, yet negotiation is in reality an integral part of the subdivision approval process. The vehicle usually is site plan review and authority often comes from a request for rezoning.

110. Ducker, *Loudon County's Pay-As-You-Grow Plan*, 26 Land Use L. & Zoning Dig. at 3 (1974).

111. *See* Lowenburg *et al.*, Windfalls for Wipeouts: An Annotated Bibliography on Betterment Recapture and Worsement Avoidance in the United States, Australia, Canada, England, and New Zealand (Exchange Bibliographies No. 618, 619, 620, 1974), esp., ch. 6: *Business License Tax on Developers (Bedroom or Construction Tax).*

112. City of Mesa v. Home Builders Ass'n 523 P.2d 57 (1974) (license tax on residential development valid); City of Dunedin v. Contractors & Builders Ass'n, 312 So. 2d 763 (Fla. App. 1975) (impact fee valid). *But see* Broward County v. Janis Dev. Corp., 311 So. 2d 371 (Fla. App. 1975) (land use fee a form of taxation and therefore invalid).

113. Cal. Gov't Code § 37101 (West. Supp.).

114. Associated Home Builders v. City of Newark, 18 Cal. App. 3d 107, 95 Cal. Rptr. 648 (1971).

115. *See esp.* R. Freilich & P. Levi, Model Subdivision Regulations: Text and Commentary 118-29 (1975).

With or without specific authority or formulae, communities have been able to obtain land or money contributions from developers simply because of their power to deny approval or to delay almost endlessly. Developers have been willing to contribute land or money as sweeteners to help assure quick approval of their plans.[116] The use of a term such as "suitable" offers considerable room for dickering and often cannot be avoided, especially when more flexibility is desired. If the community wishes, precise guidelines for determining suitability can be specified, setting forth provisions for unity of open space, shape, location, access, and relationship to community plans.[117]

Standards and the Comprehensive Plan. There are two principal methods for calculating the amount of land to be dedicated: a fixed percentage based on the total amount of land in the subdivision, and a density formula based upon the number of dwellings or lots. Under the latter method, there are two types of density formulae: one is based on the number of dedicated acres per dwelling units in the subdivision, and the other is based on the density of the subdivision in terms of dwelling units per acre, size of lots in square feet, or type of residential district.[118] *Model Subdivision Regulations*, published by the American Society of Planning Officials (ASPO), recommends the density method because a formula based on the number of people to be served is viewed as more equitable than one based on the number of acres.[119]

If a fee in lieu of dedication is required, the amount of the payment must be authorized in the ordinance. ASPO's *Model Subdivision Regulations*, for example, authorize a cash contribution when the community's plan shows a park outside the boundaries of the subdivision, when the subdivision is too small to sustain its own park, or when land or topography is ill suited for a park.[120] Fees for such purposes should be placed in a special fund and be drawn upon to purchase and develop appropriate sites for the benefit of residents of the particular subdivision.

There are three major bases for determining the amount of money to be paid: (1) the assessed or fair market value of the land or a percentage thereof; (2) a fixed dollar amount per lot or dwelling unit;

116. Ducker, *supra* note 110, at 5, quotes a member of the Loudon County Board of Supervisors: "I see no reason for us to approve any development unless it happens to be to our liking. If that means a developer has to make special efforts to please us, so be it."
117. M. Brooks, *supra* note 102, at 21–22.
118. *Id.*, at 11.
119. *See esp.* Freilich & Levi, *supra* note 115.
120. *Id.* at 121.

and (3) a variable amount of the fair market value based on the density of the subdivision. The lack of a formula for determining a fee and the uncertainty as to whether the subdivision residents will receive some benefit are both likely to give the courts some difficulty. The deposit of fees to meet future needs does not present the same problem.[121]

Subdivision exactions can be a useful way to implement objectives of a comprehensive plan or growth-management policy. Where specific sites or general locations of parks or schools are indicated, the land to be dedicated can be required to conform to these plans, or the fund into which moneys are placed can be used to buy desired sites. On a more general level, subdivision exactions can be used to implement a growth-management policy that calls for restricting new development costs to the newest residents, thereby holding down taxes. In either case, well-defined policies and procedural safeguards are essential for the protection of all parties involved.

Housing Opportunity. A criticism sometimes leveled at the imposition of special fees or dedications for new subdivisions is that they restrict opportunities to develop low-cost housing. These concerns make sense intuitively, though there is little evidence to indicate that exactions have been utilized as an exclusionary device. On the other hand, excessive physical design and amenity requirements have been cited as having a potentially more discriminatory impact than do zoning regulations.[122]

A counter to this criticism is that the costs involved are marginal, the amenities required are needed to assure a decent environment, and that it is better to amortize the costs over the long life of a mortgage than to pay them in an initial lump sum through property taxation or special assessment.[123] It can be argued that subdivision exactions, when compared with other flexible tools, have neither a serious discriminatory effect nor offer much opportunity for promoting low- and moderate income housing. Nevertheless, the extent to which bargaining over subdivision costs is carried on in private, and public officials are thus able to shield the reasons for their actions behind vague recitations of language in the regulations, can have adverse implications for a project already vulnerable to discretionary abuse.

121. Divan Builders, Inc. v. Planning Bd. of Wayne, 334 A.2d 30 (1975); Frank Ansvine, Inc. v. City of Cranston, 264 A.2d 910 (1970); Jordan v. Village of Menomonee Falls, 28 Wis. 2d 608, 137 N.W.2d 442 (1965).

122. Comment, *supra* note 101, at 807-10; Comment, *Interrelationship Between Exclusionary Zoning and Exclusionary Subdivision Control*, 5 U. Mich. J. L. Ref. 351 (1972).

123. R. Freilich & P. Levi, *supra* note 115, at 105-07.

An alternative approach, as yet untested, is to use variable subdivision standards as a way of promoting housing opportunity. While design standards in subdivision regulations are presumed reasonable, they are not immutable. Under special circumstances some standards (such as screening, pavement width, off-street parking) might be relaxed as a way to reduce costs and make lower cost housing economically feasible. The application of performance standards might permit developers to meet ordinance requirements at the lowest cost.

Law and practice on subdivision exactions remain cloudy. Communities are on solid ground when they require the developer to pay for streets, utilities, and sewers. Dedication of land for parks and schools is permitted in most states. Fees in lieu of land dedication also are generally valid, though the determination of the permissible amount and use of such fees needs further clarification. The closer one moves toward the objective of imposing the full burden of additional capital costs on each new development, the cloudier the policy becomes.

As standards become clearer in ordinance provisions, there remains a potential for abuse through excessive and extralegal demands.[124] Developers have been willing to comply with such demands, and in fact have been known to offer further contributions to expedite the speed of application approval. There is need for continued judicial scrutiny as well as for further safeguards through clearer standards, objectives, and prescribed review procedures.

Transfer of Development Rights

Transfer of development rights (TDR) is a relatively recent innovation in land-use controls that has perhaps received more attention in scholarly journals than it has in city halls.[125] The concept has been variously offered as a way to preserve agricultural land in the face of urban development, to prevent destruction of historic areas, to promote construction of low- and moderate-income housing, to protect ecologically sensitive areas, and to recover some of the benefits of

---

124. A series of case studies of the various techniques used by Illinois communities to obtain desired open space is contained in Platt & Moloney-Merkle, *Municipal Improvisation: Open Space Exactions in the Land of Pioneer Trust*, 5 Urb. Law. 706–28 (1973).

125. *See generally* Costonis, *The Chicago Plan: Incentive Zoning and the Preservation of Urban Landmarks*, 85 Harv. L. Rev. 574 (1972); Costonis, *Development Rights Transfer: An Exploratory Essay*, 83 Yale L.J. 75 (1973); *Costonis*, Space Adrift (1974); American Society of Planning Officials, (ASPO), Transferable Development Rights (1975); J. Rose, ed., Transfer of Development Rights (1975 [hereinafter cited as TDR]). *Cf.* Comment, *Unconstitutionality of Transferable Development Rights*, 84 Yale L.J. 1101 (1975).

public investment. Empirical evidence, however, is so limited that we must rely more on theory than on experience.

TDR is based on the premise that the right to use or develop land can be separated from ownership of the land itself. This right, usually expressed as potential intensity of use (units per acre, floor/area ratio, for example), is regarded as capable of transfer from one landowner to another. The transfer may be accomplished through private sale or under government regulation, the latter establishing the "amount" of transferrable right on a specific site through traditional land-use controls.

The TDR idea arises from a concern that the imposition of zoning controls confers substantial economic benefits on some owners and severely restricts others. Where zoning permits intense development, land values increase and hence pressure for replacement of low intensity uses with higher income-producing uses becomes great. The result may be the loss of historic structures and agricultural land, or the replacement of lower cost housing stock with upper income high-rise structures.

By transferring rights, property owners will be able to build at lower intensity (or not at all), sell the unused development rights, and thereby realize an economic return. The recipient or buyer in turn can make use of the newly conferred rights to build at higher intensity on a different site. Once the rights are transferred and used, they no longer can be negotiated. The municipality benefits from the transfer because land-use restrictions may be sustained which, absent such "compensation," might constitute "inverse condemnation" or an invalid "taking" of the property without compensation.

The TDR intensity within a single ownership unit is a common feature of cluster subdivisions, PUDs, and zoning bonus provisions designed to create incentives for the creation of more open space in high-density areas. Each time a developer of a PUD is allowed to cluster units in return for open space, a form of TDR is occurring. Each time a downtown bank is allowed to build an additional five stories in return for a street-level plaza, TDR takes place. Transfer between ownership units is a more recent phenomenon. TDR is particularly relevant to the urban fringe, where one landowner's development rights in unique natural areas might be transferred to other owners not necessarily in the immediate vicinity.

One proponent of TDRs has suggested that the system offers the following positive features:

1. Reduction of arbitrary and inequitable "windfalls" and "wipeouts" which frequently accompany governmental use of the police power to regulate land use.

2. More effective preservation of environmentally sensitive areas, open space, and agricultural lands, and more efficient use of land earmarked for development.
3. Unification of plans and programs for development and environmental protection.
4. A shift of the larger share of the total social cost of new development to the developer and ultimate consumer.
5. Recoupment of a portion of private gains created by public investment.[126]

Legal analysis of the TDR concept is expanding rapidly. One commentator has summarized TDRs' current legal status as follows:

Legal precedent exists in sufficient breadth and strength to provide strong encouragement to those considering development rights systems as methods of widespread land-use control. Judicial approval is not assured but can realistically be hoped for if the systems are well considered and well structured, if they are clearly responsive to the major short- and long-term wastes of land and other resources that occur under the present systems of land-use controls, and if their impact on the rights of individual land-owners is in clear furtherance both of demonstrable public interests and of the correlative rights and entitlements of individual owners.[127]

State enabling legislation for TDRs would also provide a helpful legal foundation. Another writer has suggested six essentials for a TDR system:

1. The system must be legally defensible.
2. The formula for issuing development rights must (a) fully reflect the loss in land values of those who are denied the right to develop their lands, and (b) be easily administered.
3. The supply of development rights and the demand for them must be such that (a) their value does not fall below their value when issued, and (b) developers will be encouraged to or can be required to make use of them because they can make reasonable profit from doing so.
4. The TDR system must have safeguards against fraudulent issues and transfers, hoarding, dumping, etc.
5. The establishment of a TDR system must not result in an overall loss in tax revenues.
6. The TDR system must be politically acceptable.[128]

126. ASPO, *supra* note 125, at 49.
127. Carmichael *Transferable Development Rights as a Basis for Land Use Control*, Fla. St. U. L. Rev. 107 (1974).
128. D. Heeter, *Six Basic Requirements for TDR System*, in ASPO, *supra* note 125, at 43–46.
129. *See* ASPO and TDR, *supra* note 125.

There are a number of TDR proposals in various stages of consideration, but only a few have been enacted. Major proposals include:[129]

For Historic Preservation	New York City (enacted)
	Chicago
For Open-Space Preservation	New Jersey
	Puerto Rico
As the Basic Land-Use Control Mechanism	Fairfax County, Va.
	Colorado
	Marin County, Calif.
	Maryland
	Sonoma County, Calif.
As a Method of Encouraging the Construction of Low- and Moderate-Income Housing	Southampton, N.Y.
As a Method of Regulating the Location and Timing of Urban Development	St. George, Vt. (enacted)
For Preservation of Prime Agricultural Land	Sunderland, Mass.[130]
	Suffolk County, N.Y.

The process used in the transfer of development rights proposals varies considerably. Particularly problematic is the determination of the value of the rights and the incorporation of those values into the TDR system. Market demands for land within a TDR district must be accurately projected; any substantial subsequent change in demand may destroy the market for the rights and abort the system.[131]

Standards and the Comprehensive Plan. A discussion of standards in connection with flexible land-use control devices involves the question of the degree to which administrative discretion is constrained. There is no clear parallel for TDRs because little administrative discretion is involved. The distribution of development rights throughout a jurisdiction must be determined at the outset. Administrative flexibility occurs when the sale of rights is negotiated between landowners. Policing the operation of the marketplace and recording each parcel's rights is the critical issue. The ultimate success of a TDR scheme, however, depends upon sound planning: "The problem

129. *See* ASPO and Rose, *supra* note 125.

130. *See* L. Susskind, ed., The Land Use Controversy in Massachusetts (1975).

131. *See* Niesmand & Chavoosian, The Transfer-of-Development Rights Game 1.9 to 1.10 (1974).

that can be solved with TDR still requires good planning first. If the planning solutions that are to be implemented by TDRs are not appropriate, then the TDRs are not going to accomplish desired ends."[132]

The desired ends sought by the utilization of TDRs have varied substantially in scope. Most TDR proposals have been intended to protect a vulnerable resource: farmland, natural areas, historic buildings. A few proposals have attempted to use TDRs to regulate the location and timing of new development. This is the primary intent of the TDR program in St. George, Vermont. Location can be easily controlled by restricting development to some areas and permitting it in others. Timing, however, requires the issuance of development rights by a governmental authority at a predetermined rate, which may be more difficult to establish, and requires at a minimum a sophisticated planning base.

Housing Opportunity. A determination of TDR utility in aiding the production of lower cost housing awaits more extensive experience with the technique. Professor Kevin Lynch suggests one possible method for achieving this end. A jurisdiction would determine its growth rate in terms of anticipated new dwelling units. Development rights for these units would then be apportioned among landowners. The government, however, would retain some of these rights for itself in a "development rights bank" and then make them available to developers specifically to build lower cost housing.[133] Creative use of TDR could have a positive effect on housing availability, provided the concept is grounded on sound economic analysis and intelligent planning.

Conclusion

The preceding discussion of flexibility and discretion in land-use controls is designed neither as an exhaustive catalog of all available techniques nor as a comprehensive analysis of all their numerous permutations and implications. Rather, it is designed to highlight a number of versatile techniques that are still relatively "unused" in many jurisdictions and that are likely to be adopted for local use in the foreseeable future; and to emphasize to policy-makers that because of the inherently discretionary nature of these techniques, they must be supported by a sound planning base, a fair and open system of administration, and need to be constantly related to the housing needs of the community and region.

132. Gruen, *The Need for Continued Sound Planning*, in ASPO, *supra* note 125, at 47.
133. TDR, *supra* note 125, at 259-64.

To the extent that the techniques discussed herein involve individual requests for development permission and require the application of existing land-use plans and regulations to specific parcels of property, the administrative and judicial review of such decisions may take on a character different from the one traditionally associated with the zoning process. The evolution of this new concept of administrative and judicial review is the subject of the remaining sections of this chapter.

IMPLICATIONS OF FLEXIBILITY: PROCEDURAL AND ADMINISTRATIVE REFORMS

As indicated earlier in the chapter, there is a growing concern over the process by which decisions are made on individual applications for development permission. This concern is an outgrowth of the greater use and abuse of flexible or discretionary land-use controls, more intense judicial scrutiny of the land-use control process, increased sophistication by the participants, and the greater complexity of the substantive regulations themselves. The procedural innovations fostered by these developments are the subject of the remainder of this chapter. Topics discussed will include the need for judicial recharacterization of the process, the use of hearing examiners to improve local procedure, the role of neighborhood organizations in local decision-making, and the additional layers of regional, state, and federal involvement in land-use decisions, as well as the need for greater coordination of these elements.

It should also be noted that some of the following discussion attaches great significance to the distinction between "legislative" and "administrative" or "quasi-judicial" actions by the local governing body. While this distinction is important in its legal implications, it should not distract from the underlying thrust of this chapter—the critical need for a system of land-use controls that is fair, rational, and equitable, and that offers some predictability for the expectations of landowners, neighbors, developers, and public officials.

Judicial Characterization
of Local Zoning Actions

While all courts uphold land-use regulation in theory, judicial attitudes toward changes in those regulations that affect individual parcels of property have varied sharply. The nomenclature accorded such changes is often dispositive of the result. For example, if the court views single-parcel rezonings[134] as "legislative," as most courts do, this characterization will place a heavy burden on an opponent of that regulation to prove a negative—that is, that the regulation has no connection with public health, safety, morals, or general welfare. On the other hand, if the court applies "spot zoning" terminology,[135] there is at least a mental tendency to require the proponent to prove the necessity for the regulation.

In 1926, when the United States Supreme Court first upheld zoning as a valid exercise of the police power, it expressed a deference to local legislative action subject only to constitutional limitations. In the landmark case of *Euclid v. Ambler*, the Court stated:

> The ordinance now under review, and all similar laws and regulations, must find their justifications in some aspect of the police power, asserted for the public welfare. The line which in this field separates the legitimate from the illegitimate assumption of power is not capable of precise delimitation. It varies with circumstances and conditions. . . . If the validity of the legislative classification for zoning purposes be *fairly debatable*, the legislative judgment must be allowed to control. [Emphasis added.][136]

Under the traditional rule that a decision of the local legislature is presumed valid, challenges to the validity of a zoning ordinance or an amendment have been required to demonstrate that the action or decision is arbitrary, capricious, or unreasonable, and that it has no relation to the public health, safety, and welfare. When the challenger fails to carry this burden of proof, the challenge fails. Moreover, when the evidence on balance is "fairly debatable," the question is resolved in favor of the local zoning action.[137]

The doctrine of presumption of validity rests in large part on judicial concern for the separation of judicial and legislative functions. The judiciary did not wish to be involved with the formulation of legislative policy when that policy did not palpably conflict with constitutional standards. As we shall see, in the application of this doctrine to local zoning decisions, the courts tended to equate the local exercise of the police power to that of a state legislative body. In some situations this analogy was inappropriate and ultimately led to some confusion on the part of the courts. For example, conceptual problems arose when the local legislature wished to change the land-use classification of only one parcel of property, rather than a large part

134. *See* discussion of rezonings in text following note 21 *supra*.
135. *See* text accompanying note 150 *infra*.
136. Euclid v. Ambler Realty Co., 272 U.S. 365, 387 (1926).
137. *Id.*

or all of the community. The courts for many years treated such a change as they did the original formulation of policy—as a legislative act.[138]

The effect of characterizing both the original regulations and changes to them as legislative acts was that the courts abstained, at least formally, from inquiring into the procedural[139] and substantive[140] aspects of such decisions. As a result, the local government's decision was usually upheld on review because of the legislative characterization. The Standard State Zoning Enabling Act and the Standard City Planning Enabling Act did nothing to disabuse the courts that changes in land-use regulations were anything less than legislative acts—both the original comprehensive regulations and subsequent piecemeal amendments were enacted as ordinances by the local legislature; therefore, each was a legislative act.

Other individual changes, such as special permits and variances, were not viewed in the same light as a complete change of the regulations. There were standards within the ordinance against which these actions could be judged by a court,[141] and the actions were undertaken not by the local legislative body, but by an inferior, appointed body most frequently called a board of appeals. Finally, the board had some procedural requisites to follow, and failure to do so or failure to abide by the standards for grant or denial became the basis for a court to overturn the decision upon review.[142]

These actions—because they were not legislative and because the board of appeals sat as an administrative or quasi-judicial body applying the law in specific cases—became known as quasi-judicial actions. The effect of this appellation was the application of stricter procedural and substantive standards and a modification of the burden upon the party attacking the result. Because of the legislative or quasi-judicial label, the courts often gave different treatment to matters that were essentially identical.[143] The problems inherent in the legislative characterization remained, however, and the courts

138. City of Phoenix v. Beall, 22 Ariz. App. 141, 524 P.2d 1314 (1974); Sun Oil Co. v. Village of New Hope, 220 N.W.2d 256 (Minn. 1974); Dexter v. Town Bd., 43 App. Div. 2d 899, 351 N.Y.S. 2d 237 (1974); Clawson v. Harborcreek Tp. Zoning Hearing Bd., 9 Pa. Comm. Ct. 124, 304 A.2d 184 (1973).

139. Sullivan, *Araby Revisited: The Evolving Concept of Procedural Due Process Before Land Use Regulatory Bodies*, 15 S.C. Law. 50, 54–57 (1974).

140. This was due to the scope and nature of review of "legislative acts." *See* cases cited in note 138 *supra*.

141. Mandelker, *Delegation of Power and Function in Zoning Administration*, 1963 Wash. U. L. Q. at 71–80.

142. Daly v. Town Planning and Zoning Comm'n, 150 Conn. 495, 191 A.2d 250 (1963); Hopf v. Board of Review, 102 R.I. 275, 230 A.2d 420 (1967).

143. D. Mandelker, The Zoning Dilemma 70–77, 83–84 (1971).

were troubled by the number of decisions that were affirmed because of the judicially created legislative barrier.[144] The judges were also aware of the realities of the functioning of local legislatures, where the decision-making process was hardly equivalent to that at the state level, but whose acts were nonetheless deemed to be presumably valid and rational.[145]

Faced with the need to balance the traditional presumption of validity accorded legislative actions against the knowledge of abuses in the local process, the courts began to devise methods of dealing with this conundrum. The earliest was an attempt to balance the hardship of the property owner or the community with the public good promoted by the regulations.[146] This "substantive due process" test was in its heyday in the first few decades of this century,[147] but has largely fallen into disuse.[148] In the field of land use, however, the test still has some utility.[149]

Another more widely used (but little understood) construct is spot zoning[150] —a term adopted by the courts to describe a rezoning in which a parcel has been uniquely designated for a use that appears to be unrelated to the surrounding land uses in the area. It has more often served as a convenient hook upon which to hang an undesirable

144. As Richard Babcock describes the situation:

The roots of this judicial restlessness lie in the mess of local zoning administration. In those jurisdictions where the final local zoning decisions are "legislative," that is, are made by the city council, the courts are torn between their traditional reluctance to explore the motives of legislators and their suspicion that, as one appellate judge put it, "there's a lot of hanky-pank that we suspect but cannot find in the record."

It is apparent in many instances that the judge would prefer that these land-use matters came to him through administrative channels (such as the Board of Zoning Adjustment) rather than through the local legislature so that his inquiry would not be inhibited by the alleged separation-of-powers doctrine that purports to forbid judicial inquiry into legislative motives.

R. Babcock, The Zoning Game 104 (1966).

145. Ward v. Village of Skokie, 26 Ill. 2d 415, 186 N.E.2d 529, 523 (1962) (Klingbiel, J., specially concurring).

146. Nectow v. Town of Cambridge, 277 U.S. 183 (1927). The cases that follow the *Euclid* rationale generally employ this balancing test through the use of the "fairly debatable" rule. *See* Selby Realty Co. v. City of San Buenaventura, 10 Cal. 2d 109, 110 Cal. Rptr. 799 (1973); Arverne Bay Construction Co. v. Thatcher, 278 N.Y. 222, 15 N.E.2d 587 (1938).

147. Lochner v. New York, 198 U.S. 45 (1905); Allgeyer v. Louisiana, 165 U.S. 578 (1897).

148. *See, e.g.*, Nebbia v. New York, 291 U.S. 502 (1934).

149. The more recent cases, such as *Selby Realty Co.* and Goldblatt v. Hempstead, 369 U.S. 590 (1962), all employ a "balancing test" but seem to place the balance in such a way that the challenger must prove the ordinance has no conceivable public welfare basis.

150. Anderson, American Law of Zoning §5.04, (1969); Platt, *Valid Spot Zoning: A Creative Tool for Flexibility of Land Use*, 48 Ore. L. Rev. 245 (1969).

rezoning,[151] although it is difficult to explain how a true legislative act may become less legislative by reason of the judicial characterization accorded it.[152]

A third check on abuse is the Maryland rule of "change or mistake," a judge-created rule wherein original regulations are seen as legislative acts, but later legislative acts amending those regulations somehow do not attain such dignity unless there is shown to be a change in neighborhood circumstances or a mistake in the original regulations.[153] A more recent attempt at rationality is the Washington "appearance of fairness" rule,[154] which is based upon a judicial desire for procedural reform in hearings before land-use regulatory bodies. Briefly stated, the rule requires "that not only must such hearings be fair but *appear* so to the parties and disinterested persons."[155] Again, the rule is judge-created and -maintained.

Finally, an attempt was made to move beyond the "public health, safety, morals, and general welfare" standard to the SZEA requirement that zoning regulations be "in accordance with a comprehensive plan."[156] That requirement was unclear, as most cities did not

151. *See, e.g.,* Roseta v. County of Washington, 254 Or. 161, 458 P.2d 405 (1969); Smith v. County of Washington, 241 Or. 380, 406 P.2d 545 (1965).

152. *Id.* In the latter case, despite the assertion that the rezoning was in accord with the local comprehensive plan, the court accomplished the task by the use of presumptions which were at once constructed and overcome.

153. The rationale and a criticism of this rule is ably treated in the opinion of the court and the dissent in McDonald v. Board of County Comm'rs, 238 Md. 549, 210 A.2d 325 (1965). *See also* Linowes & Delaney, *The Maryland Change or Mistake Rule: A Mistake Which Should Be Changed,* 1971 Land Use Controls Ann. 117; Colwell v. Howard County, 354 A.2d 210 (Md. App. 1976) (court analogizes the change-mistake rule to a *pons asinorum* or bridge of asses that is too difficult for asses, or for stupid boys, to get over).

154. *See* Fleming v. City of Tacoma, 81 Wash. 2d 292, 502 P.2d 327 (1972); Anderson v. Island County, 81 Wash. 2d 312, 501 P.2d 594 (1972); Buell v. Bremerton, 80 Wash. 2d 518, 459 P.2d 1358 (1972); Chrobuck v. Snohomish County, 75 Wash. 2d 858, 480 P.2d 489 (1972); Smith v. Skagit County, 75 Wash. 2d 715, 452 P.2d 832 (1969). In Glaspey & Sons v. Conrad, 83 Wash. 2d 707, 521 P.2d 1173 (1974), the Washington Supreme Court extended the appearance-of-fairness rule to cover the legislative act of adoption of a zoning ordinance.

155. In Smith v. Skagit County, 75 Wash. 2d 715, 733, 453 P.2d 832, 842 (1969), the court said:

> The public hearings, therefore, must not only be fairly undertaken in a genuine effort to ascertain the wiser legislative course to pursue, but must also *appear* to be done for that purpose. In short, when the law which calls for public hearings gives the public not only the right to attend but the right to be heard as well, the hearings must not only be fair but must *appear* to be so. It is a situation where appearances are quite as important as substance. [Emphasis in original.]

156. U.S. Dept. Commerce, A Standard State Zoning Enabling Act (rev. ed. 1926), *reprinted in* H. Rathkopf, Law of Planning and Zoning 100–01 (1956).

adopt a plan and were not required to do so.[157] Due to several considerations—chief among them the undesirable effect of voiding zoning regulations of cities which lacked a plan—some courts found the "comprehensive plan" to be the zoning regulations themselves.[158]

In recent years the comprehensive plan requirement is being reconsidered. In most states the plan is still an advisory, optional document.[159] In a growing number of states, however, the plan is given great weight in review of local land-use decisions.[160] In a few states the plan is given controlling status.[161] Given these developments it seems that the comprehensive plan will be given increasing weight by the courts in the course of future decisions.[162]

The result of these judicial efforts to offset the legislative label has been the blurring of the distinction between both legislative and quasi-judicial activities and the scope and nature of judicial review. The need for procedural and substantive standards is resulting in a gradual shift in the judicial appellations given the processes. Procedural standards for small-tract rezonings have been recognized as similar to those for granting a special permit or a variance, and the comprehensive plan has assumed greater importance for courts in their view of all land-use decisions. These developments could lead to greater predictability of review of the land-use decision-making process. Moreover, the court would be left within its traditional role, respecting the functions of another branch of government, while still providing for active review and enabling the weight of precedent to replace judicial gut reaction to local decisions.[163]

The case of *Fasano v. Board of County Commissioners*[164] is a prominent example of this trend toward a convergence of procedural

157. *See* Haar, *In Accordance with a Comprehensive Plan*, 68 Harv. L. Rev. 1154 (1955); Haar, *The Master Plan: An Impermanent Constitution*, 20 Law & Contemp. Probs. 353 (1955); Perry, *The Local General Plan in California*, 9 San Diego L. Rev. 1 (1971); Note, *The Comprehensive Plan Requirement in Zoning*, 12 Syracuse L. Rev. 342 (1961). *See also* Wheeler v. Gregg, 90 Cal. App. 2d 348, 203 P.2d 37 (1949) (finding the "comprehensive plan" and the "master plan," as those concepts are understood under the standard acts, to be one and the same).

158. Haar, *In Accordance with a Comprehensive Plan*, 68 Harv. L. Rev. 1154 (1955).

159. *See, e.g.*, Kozesnick. V. Township of Montgomery, 24 N.J. 134, 131 A.2d 1 (1957).

160. *See, e.g.* Udell v. Haas, 21 N.Y.2d 463, 288 N.Y.S.2d 888, 235 N.E. 897 (1968).

161. *See, e.g.*, Baker v. City of Milwaukie, 533 P.2d 772 (1975).

162. *See* Chapter 5 *infra;* Sullivan & Kressel, *Twenty Years After: Renewed Significance of the Comprehensive Plan Requirement*, 9 Urb. L. Ann. 33 (1975).

163. Sullivan, *From Kroner to Fasano: An Analysis of Judicial Review of Land Use Regulation in Oregon*, 10 Willamette L.J. 358, 370-74 (1974).

164. 264 Or. 574, 507 P.2d 23 (1973), *noted* 10 Will. L.J. 95 (1973).

and substantive concerns. The case involved a contested rezoning for a mobile-home subdivision in a suburb of Portland, Oregon. The lower courts relied on a combination of the change-or-mistake rule and the comprehensive plan to overrule the change in zoning. In affirming the lower courts, the Oregon Supreme Court went far beyond the immediate issues to make some definitive pronouncements about its view of the land-use regulatory process.

The court found that Oregon's enabling legislation[165] required that the comprehensive plan be the operative basis for land-use regulations adopted by counties, as well as the yardstick by which the validity of such decisions should be judged.[166] The court also held that all small-tract changes, whether accomplished by an elected or appointed body, whether done by ordinance or resolution, and whether called a rezoning or a conditional use permit, were quasi-judicial acts.[167]

Tracing the background of the presumption of validity in rezoning cases and distinguishing for this purpose between legislative and quasi-judicial acts, the court stated:

> At this juncture we feel we would be ignoring reality to rigidly view all zoning decisions by local governing bodies as legislative acts to be accorded a full presumption of validity and shielded from less than constitutional scrutiny by the theory of separation of powers. Local and small decision groups are simply not the equivalent in all respects of state and national legislatures.[168]

The extent to which the traditional presumption has been eroded is not entirely clear in Oregon. In fact, it is possible that a limited presumption of validity is still accorded to a quasi-judicial action, in the sense that parties seeking judicial review must still demonstrate error that harmed their interests.[169]

165. Or. Rev. Stat. §§ 215.010 to 215.422 (1973). This legislation was initially adopted in 1947, substantially revised in 1963, and was based on neither of the standard acts. Except for temporary or interim zoning, all such regulations had to be preceded by a comprehensive plan which those regulations were to carry out. Or. Rev. Stats. § 215.110.

166. The court in *Fasano* stated:

> We believe that the state legislature has conditioned the county's power to zone upon the prerequisite that the zoning attempt to further the general welfare of the community through consciousness, in a prospective sense, of the factors mentioned above. (*I.e.*, the statutory standards for comprehensive planning and land use regulation.)

507 P. 2d at 28.

167. The court relied on the distinctions drawn between legislative and quasijudicial acts in Comment, *Zoning Amendments: The Product of Judicial or Quasi-Judicial Action*, 33 Ohio St. L.J. 130 (1972).

168. Fasano v. Board of County Comm'rs, 507 P.2d at 26.

169. Dickinson v. Board of County Comm'rs, 533 P.2d 1395 (Or. App.

The question of burden of proof also arose in *Fasano* because in legislative matters the opponent of the legislative action must prove that no relationship exists between the act and the public welfare and must also overcome every possible reason for the action.[170] In a quasi-judicial matter it is necessary to distinguish the burden of persuasion from the burden of proof. If one likens a quasi-judicial proceeding to a trial, there the burden of persuasion shifts as each side puts on its case. However, the burden of proof remains throughout upon the moving party. This same analogy can be—and has been—made in land-use cases:[171] the burden of persuasion may shift from side to side, but the applicant has the burden of proof throughout the administrative proceeding.[172]

Fasano goes beyond the use of a quasi-judicial model by the inclusion of artificial, judge-created burdens, perhaps arising out of a judicial concern over (or distrust of) the current state of the art of planning. While emphasizing the comprehensive plan as the standard of judicial review, the court also requires that the applicant bear the burden of showing by "reliable, probative and substantial" evidence[173] that: "(1) there is a 'public need' for the proposal; and (2) that need is best satisfied by this proposal as compared with other available property."[174] This can be an extremely onerous burden. Courts in other jurisdictions have not gone as far as *Fasano* in this respect,

---

1975) was the first post-*Fasano* case to inquire into the sufficiency of proof. In that case the Oregon Court of Appeals said that it did not see its function as one of re-weighing the evidence, but of searching the record for substantial evidence to uphold necessary findings.

170. Lehnhausen v. Lake Shore Auto Parts Co., 410 U.S. 356 (1973); Madden v. Kentucky, 309 U.S. 83 (1970).

171. *See* Bronstein & Erickson, *Zoning Amendments in Michigan—Two Recent Developments*, 50 J. Urb. L. 729, 742 (1973).

172. The *Fasano* notion of burden is set forth:

> Because the action of the commission in this instance is an exercise of judicial authority, the burden of proof should be placed, as is usual in judicial proceedings, upon the one seeking change. The more drastic the change, the greater will be the burden of showing that it is in conformance with the comprehensive plan as implemented by the ordinance. . . . As the degree of change increases, the burden of showing that the potential impact upon the area in question was carefully considered and weighed will also increase.
>
> 507 P.2d at 29.

This graduated-burden-of-proof standard has not been tested by an Oregon appellate court since *Fasano*.

173. Or. Rev. Stat. § 34.040.

174. Fasano v. Board of County Comm'rs, 507 P.2d at 28. The public-need standard probably arose out of a portion of the Oregon county planning and zoning enabling legislation, Or. Rev. Stat. § 215.055(1), which requires consideration, inter alia, of the "public need for healthful, safe and aesthetic surroundings and conditions."

nor need they do so, as these two aspects of *Fasano* are not central to the concept of the quasi-judicial nature of particular acts by the legislature.

The impact of applying the *Fasano* model to public bodies would be considerable. In Oregon it is likely that planning commissions will be required: (1) to allow all parties to adequately present their cases;[175] (2) to act relatively free of outside interest, pressure, and contact;[176] (3) to provide for a record of their proceedings;[177] and (4) to base their orders on findings applicable to the case under consideration.[178] The staff of the planning commission may also have to alter its practices. As there are limitations on prehearing contacts with the decision-makers by the parties, so too are there limitations on lobbying by staff outside their normal report and presentation functions.[179]

Perhaps the most formidable changes are reserved for members of the local governing body. As quasi-judges they must weigh the evidence; conduct a fair and orderly hearing—with due process requirements, including the right of parties to present and rebut evidence, to examine and cross-examine witnesses, and to base their conclusions on a written record supported by substantial evidence. In Oregon, *Fasano* prohibits any local decision-maker[180] from listening to prehearing comments from any party.[181]

Initially, a shift from the legislative to the quasi-judicial model may have certain negative implications for developers. For example, it is possible, after *Fasano*, for opponents of development to arm themselves with trial techniques (such as cross-examination, rebuttal,

175. Sullivan, *supra* note 139, at 68–70. *See also* the discussion of this point in 36 Ops. Or. Atty. Gen. No. 7062, at 986–95.

176. Sullivan, supra note 139, at 69; 36 Ops. Or. Atty. Gen. No. 7062, at 983–85.

177. Sullivan, *supra* note 139, at 70; 36 Ops. Or. Atty. Gen. No. 7062, at 995–96.

178. Sullivan, *supra* note 139, at 71; 36 Ops. Or. Atty. Gen. No. 7062, at 997–99. *See also* Dickinson v. B.B.C. of Clackamas County, 533 P.2d 1395 (Or. App. 1975); West v. Astoria, 524 P.2d 1216 (Or. App. 1974); Bennett v. Lincoln City, 12 Or. App. 72, 503 P.2d 724 (1972); Sammons v. Sibarco Stations, 10 Or. App. 43 497 P.2d 862 (1972); Erickson v. Portland, 9 Or. App. 256, 496 P.2d 726 (1972).

179. *See* 34 Op. Or. Atty. Gen. No. 7062, at 984 (1974).

180. The specially concurring opinion of Schwab, C.J., in West v. Astoria, 524 P.2d 1216 (Or. App. 1974), strongly suggests this result. In Tierney v. Duris, 536 P.2d 431 (Or. App. 1975), the Oregon Court of Appeals modified the rule on prohibition of prehearing contacts with a "rule of reason" approach.

181. Fasano v. Board of County Comm'rs, 507 P.2d at 30. This rationale would not prevent a member of a decision-making body from reviewing or receiving a report from staff; however, that report must be a part of the record and available to all parties.

requiring findings, and so on), and thereby delay and ultimately prevent particular projects. Indeed, it may be argued that costly legal and planning expertise is needed now where none was necessary before.[182]

The *Fasano* procedural reforms also have the potential to benefit controversial proposals; the fact is that *Fasano* did prevent a mobile-home development from proceeding. The combination of insisting on conformance with a comprehensive plan and increasing the burden of showing such conformance in direct proportion to the extent of the change, the degree of public need, and the availability of other sites, could actually work to preserve the status quo. However, as with other techniques discussed in this chapter, a shift to the *Fasano* rationale must be accompanied by an altered view of the role of the comprehensive plan. If the plan contains a housing element that considers the needs of lower income households[183] then that part of the plan can serve as the basis for the planning and public need requirement.

The transition from a legislative to administrative type of hearing can be made without undue burdens. Those who desire changes will have some assurance from the plan that those changes will be made. Administrative bodies and courts should oppose dilatory tactics, and administrative decisions, firmly grounded in fact and supported by an adequate record, will more frequently withstand the scrutiny of judicial review.

The private citizen probably stands to gain the most from the quasi-judicial approach. As a party, a citizen has the right of full participation in the hearing—to present evidence, cross-examine, and seek administrative and judicial review.[184] Well armed with facts, the citizen can be quite effective against the most sophisticated developer. Finally, the quasi-judicial model also provides the opportunity for supra-local interests to be heard. Other municipalities or regional bodies may participate by regional review of local actions.[185] Allow-

182. In Oregon, *Fasano* is (only half-jokingly) referred to as the planners and attorneys "full crew law." Nevertheless, if the quasijudicial form is followed and review limited to traditional administrative law principles relative to "contested cases," the cost of litigation should be lowered significantly. Sullivan, *supra* note 163, at 370–75.

183. *See also* Chapter 6 *infra*.

184. *See* text following note 230 *infra*.

185. In Oregon, either the state or local governments may ask that a comprehensive plan, implementing an ordinance or an "action" that affects land conservation and development, be reviewed by a statewide body for fidelity to statewide criteria. That body, the Land Conservation and Development Commission, is empowered to revise and amend the plan, ordinance, or action. Or. Rev. Stat. 197.300 to 197.330. *See*, also, Cal. Pub. Res. Code §§ 27400 to 27424

ing other interests to intervene or to join as parties in a mini-trial setting (as opposed to a local legislative tribunal) is much more conducive to meaningful regional participation.

The characterization of rezonings as quasi-judicial instead of legislative has had an independent and rather confused development in other states. Before *Fasano,* courts in Nebraska,[186] New Jersey,[187] Utah,[188] and Washington[189] had adopted the quasi-judicial or administrative approach.[190] One of the earliest of these cases, *Kelley v. John,*[191] has produced a particularly confusing pattern of judicial citation. *Kelley,* decided by the Nebraska Supreme Court, involved the rezoning of a parcel from residential to commercial, an action that was termed "administrative" by the court. In the same year, in *Minneapolis-Honeywell Regulator Co. v. Nadasdy,* the Minnesota Supreme Court invalidated a referendum on a rezoning, holding that a referendum is available only for a "comprehensive type of zoning ordinance and does not apply to an altering or amending ordinance."[192]

In a 1969 case *In re Frank,* the Nebraska Supreme Court, with no mention of its earlier decision in *Kelley,* described rezoning as legislative, citing cases in California, Washington, Delaware, Rhode Island, Ohio, and Illinois as authority for its position.[193] This case subsequently led the Minnesota Supreme Court—in a case holding rezoning to be legislative and subject to a referendum[194]—to question the validity of *Kelley* while also distinguishing its decision

(relating to coastal areas); 18 N.Y. Stats. Ann., Tit. 27, §§ 800 to 819 (relating to the Adirondack areas).

186. Kelley v. John, 162 Neb. 319, 75 N.W.2d 713 (1956) (city ordinance rezoning specific property from residential to business use an administrative act).

187. Smith v. Town of Livingston, 54 N.J. 525, 257 A.2d 698 (1969), *aff'd per curiam,* 106 N.J. Super. 444, 256 A.2d 85 (1969) (while restating the New Jersey position that rezoning is legislative, the lower court applied language in *Kelley,* 75 N.W.2d at 716, and Bird v. Sorenson, 16 Utah 2d 1, 394 P.2d 808 (1964), to the denial of rezoning by initiative; Vickers v. Township Committee of Gloucester Tp., 37 N.J. 232, 181 A.2d (1962) (Hall, J., dissenting); Aldom v. Borough of Roseland, 42 N.J. Super. 495, 127 A.2d 190 (1956) (zoning amendment by local governing body not exclusively legislative, but partly quasi-judicial).

188. Bird v. Sorenson, 16 Utah 2d 1, 394 P.2d 808 (1964) (zoning amendment an administrative act and not referrable).

189. Barrie v. Kitsal County, 527 P.2d 1377 (1974); Buell v. Bremerton, 495 P.2d 1358 (1972).

190. *See also* discussion of distinction between legislative and quasi-judicial zoning actions in a special concurring opinion by Justice Klingbeil in Ward v. Village of Skokie, 26 Ill. 2d 415, 186 N.E.2d 529 (1962).

191. Kelley v. John, 162 Neb. 319, 75 N.W.2d 713 (1956).

192. 247 Minn. 159, 76 N.W.2d 670 (1956).

193. *In re* Frank, 183 Neb. 722, 164 N.W.2d 215, 216 (1969).

194. Denney v. City of Duluth, 202 N.W.2d 892 (1973).

in the *Nadasdy* case[195] because it merely involved the interpretation of a specific statute.

These developments have been paralleled by a curious usage of *Kelley* by the Ohio Supreme Court. *Donnelly v. City of Fairview Park*[196] involved the denial of a subdivision application which the court appropriately characterized as administrative. However, in discussing the distinction between legislative and administrative acts, the Ohio court cited *Kelley* (a rezoning case), going on to state the Ohio and majority position that rezonings are to be viewed as legislative. More recently, in *Forest City Enterprises, Inc. v. City of Eastlake*,[197] the Ohio Supreme Court struck down, on state and federal constitutional grounds, a city charter amendment requiring any land-use change to be approved in a referendum. In this rezoning case the Ohio court stated the Ohio position that rezonings are legislative, concluding:

> On its face, the charter provision makes no distinction between those changes made by council in an administrative capacity, and those made by council in a legislative capacity. Thus, the requirement of a mandatory referendum falls upon all changes with equal weight. Insofar as this purports to mandate a referendum as to an administrative determination, it is clearly invalid.[198]

The court again cited *Kelley* as authority for its position, even though that case characterized rezonings as administrative acts.

However, the Ohio decision was reversed by the U.S. Supreme Court, which held that the Eastlake charter amendment did not violate the due process clause of the Fourteenth Amendment. The Supreme Court majority reasoned that there is no delegation of legislative power in a referendum, because that power derives from the people in the first place, and "here, rather than a delegation of power, we deal with a power reserved by the people to themselves."[199] The Court quoted *James v. Valtierra*[200] for the proposition that the referendum procedure is a classic demonstration of devotion to democracy.[201]

The outcome of *Eastlake* has considerable significance for a range of problems addressed in this book. It is of particular importance

195 247 Minn. 159. 76 N.W.2d 670 (1956).
196. 13 Ohio St. 2d 1, 233 N.E.2d 500 (1968).
197. 41 Ohio St. 2d 187, 324 N.E.2d 740, rev'd 426 U.S. 668 (1976).
198. 324 N.E.2d at 744.
199. 426 U.S. 668, 675 (1976).
200. 402 U.S. 137 (1971). Both Valtierra and Eastlake are discussed in Chapter 2 *supra*, under the subtitle "The Unequal Burden of Voter Referenda."
201. 426 U.S. at 678-79.

for its practical impact on the administration of land-use controls. Two issues in particular stand out:

1. Are all rezonings, regardless of the size of the parcel or its *com-munitywide* significance, to be treated as legislative, both for purposes of judicial review and for inclusion within the scope of a referendum process?
2. What effect will a *mandatory* referendum for all land-use changes have on rational planning and the administration of land-use controls, on the development process and project costs, and on the potential for continued segregation of our urban areas?

The legislative/administrative issue apparently did not come up in *Eastlake* until the oral argument before the Ohio Supreme Court.[202] In its opinion the Ohio court stated unequivocally: "In Ohio, the power to zone or rezone, via the passage or amendment of a comprehensive zoning ordinance, is clearly a legislative function. . . . As such, the zoning or rezoning of property is subject to the referendum process."[203] Chief Justice Burger echoed this conclusion in his opinion. The Burger opinion, however, appears to turn more on the delegation of power issue than on the legislative/administrative distinction.

While some state courts have held that rezoning of individual parcels is a quasi-judicial or administrative act and not referable,[204] none of these courts has clarified the problem left by *Eastlake* and *Fasano*, which did not involve a referendum, that is, are there some situations in which, because of the magnitude of the rezoning or because of public policy in favor of referenda, that a rezoning of a *single* parcel might be characterized as quasi-judicial for purposes of judicial review but still legislative for purposes of a referendum? For example, the rezoning of a few acres in a central-city redevelopment area for a convention center could be properly handled under the *Fasano* guidelines for administrative and judicial review. However, its impact on the community may be of such magnitude as to properly allow a referendum.

There are some additional points to be made about the *Eastlake* case that follow from the background of cases referred to earlier. The

202. Conversation with Michael Hughes, co-counsel for Forest City Enterprises, Oct. 15, 1975.
203. Forest City Enterprises v. City of Eastlake, 41 Ohio St. 2d 87, 324 N.E.2d 740, 743 (1975).
204. *See, e.g.*, West v. City of Portage, 392 Mich. 458, 221 N.W.2d 303 (1974); Bird v. Sorenson, 16 Utah 2d 1, 394 P.2d 808 (1964).

confusing way in which the Ohio court cited cases from other states to arrive at its conclusion—that rezonings are legislative acts—is repeated in the Supreme Court opinion. One could easily dismiss the significance of such picayune analysis if it were not for the fact that the confusion about land-use controls and their terminology has such important effects on day-to-day land-use administration and on ultimate cost to the consumer.

At several points in Chief Justice Burger's opinion the lack of clarity persists. Two footnotes suggest that "administrative relief" in the form of a variance is still available and not subject to the referendum process.[205] This may come as a surprise to practitioners in the planning and zoning field who for years have heard diatribes against the "use variance." Another footnote cites a treatise on municipal corporations to the effect that the initiative and referendum process may be made available for any local matter, whether legislative or administrative.[206] However, the following section in the treatise points out that the "power of initiative or referendum usually is restricted to legislative ordinances, resolutions, or measures, and is not extended to executive or administrative action. . . ."[207]

Of course, it is the law of the state or the city charter in question that is controlling, and the argument for a change in characterization of local rezoning actions can be better made in the state courts where experience and proximity, with adequate information, might produce a more enlightened approach.

In fact, an attempt was made by Forest City Enterprises to obtain a rehearing before the Ohio Supreme Court. There was some hope that the court might reconsider its holding that a rezoning is a legislative function. This hope was fueled by the discussion in a later Ohio case, *State ex rel. Srovnal v. Linton*,[208] involving the adoption by a city council of a resolution confirming the planning commission's decision to grant a special exception. An attempt to require a

205. Forest City Enterprises v. City of Eastlake, 41 Ohio St.2d 187, 324 N.E.2d 740, rev'd 426 U.S. 674, 679 (1976). at nn. 9 & 13. Chief Justice Burger goes on to make a very clear statement that highlights the confusion noted in the text above:

> The situation presented in this case is not one of a zoning action denigrating the use or depreciating the value of land; instead, it involves an effort to *change* a reasonable zoning restriction. No existing rights are being impaired; new use rights are being sought from the City Council. Thus, this case involves an owner's seeking approval of a new use free from the restrictions attached to the land when it was acquired.

Id. at n.13.

206. *Id.* at n.9, *citing* 5 McQuillan, Municipal Corporations § 16.54, at 208.
207. 5 McQuillan, Municipal Corporations § 16.55.
208. 346 N.E.2d 764 (1976).

referendum on that action was denied by the Ohio Supreme Court because the resolution was an administrative action and not subject to referral.

While the *Srovnal* court stated at the outset that a "zoning use exception" is administrative and therefore distinct from a "use classification change," which is legislative, its discussion of the distinction was revealing:

> If the action of the legislative body creates a law, the action is legislative; if the action consists of executing or administering an existing law, the action is administrative.[209]

The court went on to refer to a zoning use exception as "applicable only to a specific set of facts involving a specific parcel of land in a use district."[210] Both of these comments are at least arguably applicable to typical rezonings, affording some hope to a shift in position by the court if the issue were properly presented and briefed, but unfortunately the application for rehearing was denied.[211]

The Supreme Court's majority opinion in *Eastlake* avoided two matters of great practical importance. Where the Court concerns itself with the referendum issue in general it shows little concern for the impact of a mandatory rather than a permissive referendum, the latter being generally available if the rezoning process is still characterized as legislative. Judicial observers not charged with either administering such a system or with shepherding a development proposal through such an ordeal do not seem cognizant of the implications of requiring "any change to the existing land uses" to be referred, at the cost of the applicant. The exclusionary motivation was quite apparent to members of the Ohio Supreme Court who concurred in a separate opinion:

> There can be little doubt of the true purpose of Eastlake's charter provision—it is to obstruct change in land use, by rendering such change so burdensome as to be prohibitive. The charter provision was apparently adopted specifically, to prevent multi-family housing, and indeed was adopted while Forest City's application for rezoning to permit a multi-family housing project was pending before the City Planning Commission and City Council.[212]

209. *Id.* at 767.
210. *Id.*
211. 346 N.E.2d 764 (1976) rehearing denied.
212. Forest City Enterprises v. City of Eastlake, 41 Ohio St. 2d 87, 324 N.E.2d at 748.

In the U.S. Supreme Court the dissenters noted this possibility as well.

The other matter avoided by the majority is that of the relationship between planning and zoning. If, as has occurred in some states, the courts will require a more direct relationship between an adopted plan and zoning actions implementing that plan,[213] one can only wonder what a mandatory referendum will do to that relationship, particularly in communities engaged in rezoning to implement a revised plan. It seems that "sensible growth," augmented by "rational planning and zoning," stands little chance of becoming a reality in a judicial climate that ignores the basic mechanisms upon which the land-use controls of most communities are based.

Nevertheless there are two positive notes on which to conclude this discussion. In communities that approach their land-use problems with some degree of intelligence and wish to do something other than terminate the development process entirely, a mandatory referendum as adopted in *Eastlake* will be quickly seen as a short-sighted and unworkable solution to the problems a community might face. The second hopeful development emerging from the *Eastlake* case is the sensitive and perceptive dissenting opinion by Justice Stevens, the newest member of the Supreme Court.[214]

Justice Stevens quickly traces the general background of zoning, noting the experience of the state courts:

> Although this Court has decided only a handful of zoning cases, literally thousands of zoning disputes have been resolved by the state courts. Those courts have repeatedly identified the obvious difference between the adoption of a comprehensive citywide plan by legislative action and the decision of particular issues involving specific uses of specific parcels. In the former situation there is generally great deference to the judgment of the legislature; in the latter situation state courts have not hesitated to correct manifest injustice.[215]

After quoting from leading cases in other states that have dealt with the legislative/administrative distinction, Justice Stevens concluded:

> The courts thus may well differ in their selection of the label to apply to this action but I find substantial agreement among state tribunals on the

213. *See* discussion in Chapter 5 *infra*.
214. Justice Stevens's dissenting opinion, 426 U.S. at 685 at n. 7, refers to Staszcuk v. United States, 517 F.2d 53, 56 (7th Cir. 1975), a zoning bribery case in which he wrote the opinion for the Court of Appeals for the Seventh Circuit.
215. 426 U.S. at 683-84.

proposition that requiring a citywide referendum for approval of a particular proposal like this is manifestly unreasonable.[216]

Among the courts that have elaborated the quasi-judicial analysis following the *Fasano* approach are those in Oregon,[217] Colorado,[218] Montana,[219] and Nevada.[220] A series of Michigan cases has also directly adopted the *Fasano* rationale, but in a manner that has resulted in considerable controversy. In a concurring opinion in *Kropf v. City of Sterling Heights*,[221] Justice Levin traced the developments leading to *Fasano*, and concluded:

> When a local legislative body decides to grant a change in zoning, it has in fact determined the merits of the individual grounds. So, too, unless the local body in fact rejects all applications for a change in zoning without reaching the merits, when it denies an application after entertaining the merits, it also in fact decides the merits of the individual grounds advanced. Such a determination on individual grounds is administrative, not legislative.[222]

Justice Levin expanded on this analysis in a subsequent case, holding that a zoning change is not referable.[223] That opinion, however, came from a divided court in which two members concurred with Justice Levin, one concurred only in the result, and three dissented. The Michigan Supreme Court has since decided three cases involving the rezoning of land for mobile-home parks.[224] In *Sabo v. Monroe Township*, on which the other two decisions are based, Justice Levin, in addition to following his earlier position on rezonings, added that a proposed use found to be "reasonable under all the circumstances" will be permitted, regardless of the existing zoning.[225] Nevertheless,

216. 426 U.S. at 692.

217. Culver v. Dagg, 532 P.2d 1127 (Or. App. 1975); Margii v. Ruecker, 533 P.2d 1372 (Or. App. 1975); West v. City of Astoria, 524 P.2d 1216 (Or. App. 1974); Tatum v. Clackamas County, 529 P.2d 393 (1973).

218. Snyder v. City of Lakewood, No. 26747 (Colo. Sup. Ct., Oct. 20, 1975); City of Colorado Springs v. District Court, 519 P.2d 325 (1974); Dillon Companies v. Boulder, 515 P.2d 627 (1973); Corper v. City and County of Denver, 536 P.2d 874 (Colo. App. 1975). *Compare* Witkin Homes, Inc. v. City and County of Denver, 31 Colo. App. 410, 504 P.2d 1121 (1973).

219. Lowe v. City of Missoula, 525 P.2d 551 (1974).

220. Forman v. Eagle Thrifty Drugs and Markets, Inc., 89 Nev. 533, 516 P.2d 1234 (1973).

221. 391 Mich. 139, 251 N.W.2d 179 (1974).

222. 391 Mich. at 169.

223. West v. City of Portage, 392 Mich. 458, 221 N.W.2d 303 (1974).

224. Sabo v. Monroe Tp., 394 Mich. 531, 232 N.W.2d 584 (1975); Nickola v. Grand Blanc Tp., 394 Mich. 589, 232 N.W.2d 604 (1975); Smookler v. Wheatfield Tp., 394 Mich. 574, 232 N.W.2d 616 (1975).

225. Sabo v. Monroe Tp., 232, N.W.2d at 536–37.

confusion still reigns in Michigan, as only three justices concurred in the majority opinion, one concurred in the result but wrote a separate opinion, one dissented, and two did not participate.

In the most significant federal case on point, the Fifth Circuit Court of Appeals first adopted the position that rezonings were "adjudicative," then, in a rehearing *en banc*, reaffirmed the legislative characterization.[226] Finally, two recent state cases involving text admendments to a zoning ordinance illustrate the definitional problems raised by the rezoning issue.[227] In one, an amendment permitted halfway houses in certain areas throughout the District of Columbia, in the other, PUD's were authorized for a town in Colorado. Both concluded that the text amendments were the product of legislative action. Future decisions will need to further define the limits of the quasi-judicial approach in terms of the size of the parcel involved, scope of text amendments, and so forth.

While a growing number of jurisdictions are adopting the *Fasano* approach, the rule in most states is still based on the traditional presumption of legislative validity. Likely to be of considerable influence in shaping future judicial decision-making is the American Law Institute's *Model Land Development Code*, which in its provision on special amendments specifically utilizes the *Fasano* standard[228] and treats such amendments as administrative actions.[229]

The Advisory Commission supports the administrative/quasi-judicial approach. By creating a definite standard to serve as a judicial reference point on review, coupled with basic standards of procedural due process, it represents a realistic view of rezoning as a flexible land-use control.

Procedural Safeguards for Discretionary Land-Use Decisions

The important substantive developments in the land-use field, discussed in this chapter and throughout the book have increased the need for procedural reforms. It may be, however, that too much energy has been devoted to developing new substantive land-use techniques, while too little effort has been spent developing procedural reforms that at least would make the system more credible.

226. South Gwinett Venture v. Pruitt, 482 F.2d 389 (5th Cir. 1973), *rev'd* 341 F. Supp. 703 (N.D. Ga. 1971), *rev'd on rehearing*, 491 F.2d 5 (5th Cir. 1974), *appeal dismissed* 94 S. Ct. 1625 (1974).

227. Sundance Hills Home Ass'n v. Board of City Comm'rs, 534 P.2d 1212 (1975); Dupont Circle Citizens Ass'n v. District of Columbia Zoning Comm'n, 343 A.2d 296 (D.C. App. 1975).

228. ALI Code, *supra* note 6, at § 2-312(2)(a).

229. *Id.* at § 2-312.

The fundamental questions of fairness, openness, and rationality must be addressed to encourage public confidence, in this as in any other system of law.

Notice. It is elementary that, prior to the adoption of a rule[230] or the undertaking of an adjudication,[231] some form of notice must be provided. The adequacy of notice is frequently the subject of litigation, and many cases stress that adequate notice is a jurisdictional requirement.[232] As a matter of procedural due process, notice must be of such content that interested parties are given actual notice.[233] The notice must neither be too vague for a person of reasonable abilities to comprehend nor so inaccessible that a reasonable person would be unable to be apprised of the proceedings.

An additional factor in this equation involves the open meeting or "sunshine" laws, which are gaining widespread popularity.[234] Such laws make notice and an open meeting, or both, conditions precedent for the administration of almost all public business, including land-use regulation. One zoning ordinance was invalidated because a portion of the proceedings prior to its enactment did not comply with charter provisions requiring open meetings.[235] Even in those states where failure to comply with such laws does not invalidate the proceeding,[236] it may be of considerable significance in judicial review.

Opportunity to Be Heard. Whether the setting is legislative or quasi-judicial, the right to be heard is a requirement of due process that must ordinarily be followed.[237] The opportunity must be "meaningful"—that is, there must be some assurance that the testimony given will be considered (although it does not necessarily mean that it must be acted upon). In a quasi-judicial setting, however, it is

230. *See* K. Davis, Administrative Law Text § 7.03 (1972).

231. *Id. See also* R. Anderson, American Law of Zoning §§ 4.14, 4.16 (1969) [hereinafter cited as Anderson].

232. *Id.* at § 16.21; Annot., 38 A.L.R.3d 167 (1971). The infinite variety of "open meeting laws" may influence the nature and contents of notice, as well.

233. This is the apparent "due process" requirement found in Mullane v. Central Hanover Trust Co., 339 U.S. 306 (1950).

234. *See, e.g.,* Or. Rev. Stat. §§ 192.610 to 192.690.

235. Skaggs v. City of Key West, 312 So. 2d 549 (Fla. App. 1975); Shaughnessy v. Metropolitan Dade County, 238 So. 2d 446 (Fla. App. 1970).

236. Oregon's open-meeting statute provides that no decision shall be voided solely because of a violation of its terms. Or. Rev. Stat. § 192.680. *See also,* Egge v. Lane County, 75 Or. Adv. Sh. 1874, 537 P.2d 744 (1975).

237. Note that the right is usually couched in terms in which the benefit of the information goes to the hearings body and not to other participants.

necessary to institute more formal rules for those who wish to participate. The courtroom may be looked to for guidance in limiting presentations.[238] Such guidelines become particularly important in the context of contested land-use cases, which often provoke considerable public interest and controversy.

Just as in a courtroom setting, irrelevant and immaterial testimony should be stricken, and full participation in a case with the rights attendant thereto should be limited to those with an interest in the outcome.[239] The American Law Institute's *Model Land Development Code* enumerates the following as those who should be accorded "party" status, with the right of full participation:

1. The applicant.
2. Those entitled to personal notice of the proceeding (e.g., those within, say, 500 feet of the subject property if that is the distance set by ordinance or other law).
3. Neighborhood organizations affected by the change.
4. Those who can demonstrate to the hearing officer or body that their rights are substantially affected by the outcome.
5. Those given standing by rule of the State Land Planning Agency.[240]

This list does not imply that others may not participate, particularly if the hearing body or officer permits others to participate. Yet it does encourage some distinctions to be exercised between those substantially affected and those whose interests are only peripheral.

The use of a quasi-judicial hearing process in more populated areas should mean the use of additional formal standards, including the use of rules of procedure,[241] so that all participants have some idea as to how the hearing will be conducted. The presiding officer, charged with carrying out the rules, should be given adequate power to conduct the hearing fairly and efficiently.

A Fair and Impartial Tribunal. The *Fasano* decision in Oregon created considerable controversy with its ruling that an "impartial tribunal" hear and decide a contested land-use case. The court defined that tribunal as one that has had "no pre-hearing or *ex parte* contacts."[242]

238. *See* suggested guidelines in R. Babcock, *supra* note 1, at 157.
239. Duddles v. West Linn, 75 Or. Adv. Sh. 1652, 535 P.2d 583 (Or. App. 1975).
240. ALI Code, *supra* note 6, at § 2-304(5).
241. The ALI Code, *id.*, § 2-302(2), encourages the use of such procedures. In Oregon the adoption of procedures is mandatory. Or. Rev. Stat. §§ 215.412, 227.170.
242. Fasano v. Board of County Comm'rs, 507 P.2d at 30.

The issue has been subsequently clouded by a later opinion[243] suggesting that the requirement is based not upon statutory law, but on constitutional law, probably emanating from due process considerations.[244] Nevertheless, while the availability of necessary conferences and negotiations between professional staff and the developer in the course of seeking development permission is sensibly left intact, the logic of the court's position with respect to appointed and elected public officials is unassailable. It is precisely the informal lobbying outside of required review sessions that casts a shadow on negotiated land-use decisions and weakens the extension of the "legislative" analogy.

A law review article upon which the *Fasano* court relied suggested a limitation on *ex parte* contacts by requiring all such contacts to be revealed on the record.[245] In the absence of constitutional authority for that proposition, it may be necessary to handle such contacts by amendments to land-use regulatory enabling legislation[246] rather than by judicial fiat.

Presentation and Rebuttal of Evidence. The characterization of a local legislature's response to individual requests for development permission as quasi-judicial actions can have its most beneficial effect in improving the quality of evidence presented to hearing bodies. Formerly, unfounded assertions were allowed to stand. Because such actions were viewed as legislative, the burden was on the opponent of the action to prove a negative—that is, that the action was contrary to public health, safety, and general welfare.[247]

A quasi-judicial characterization can assist hearing tribunals by intimating an administrative law standard to determine the quality of evidence in contested cases.[248] Professor Davis suggests three alternative administrative law standards: (1) replacing rules with discretion; (2) allowing in all evidence; and (3) utilizing the type of

---

243. West v. City of Astoria, 99 Or. Adv. Sh. 924, 938, 524 P.2d 1216 (1974) (Schwab, C.J., specially concurring). *But see* Tierney v. Duris, 536 P.2d 431 (Or. App. 1975).

244. 524 P.2d 1216.

245. Comment, *Zoning Amendments: The Product of Judicial or Quasi-Judicial Action*, 33 Ohio St. L.J. 130, 140 (1972).

246. *See* ALI Code, supra note 6, at § 2-304(9).

247. *See* note 138 *supra.*

248. In Oregon detailed evidentiary provisions for contested case hearings are set forth in Or. Rev. Stat. § 183.450. However, the Oregon Administrative Procedure Act, Or. Rev. Stat. ch. 183, applies only to *state agencies*, not to local land-use bodies. *See also* Dickenson v. Board of County Comm'rs, 75 Or. Adv. Sh. 1420, 533 P.2d 1395 (1975); SCAN v. Lindsey, 75 Or. Adv. Sh. 1978, 535 P.2d 1381 (1975).

evidence now ordinarily relied upon by reasonable persons in the conduct of their ordinary affairs.[249]

In the jurisdictions employing the *Fasano* rationale it is now necessary, as a practical matter, to assure the integrity of the record. For example, as in a judicial proceeding it should be clear which exhibit and portion of it is the subject of discussion. If evidence is contested, there should be some procedure, analogous to an offer of proof or rule in equity, wherein the evidence can be offered but does not necessarily have to be accepted, and whereby its admission can be tested.[250]

Another difficult problem is that presented by cross-examination, which frequently has been found to be a necessary element of contested land-use cases.[251] In this area the use of "party" status will relieve the possibilities of overly extended cross-examinations. Experimentation in Oregon has shown that cross-examination by the parties themselves, or through the chair, is possible.[252] The chair should also have the power to limit argumentative, irrelevant, and immaterial questions.

Findings. Basic to the notion of an adjudicative hearing is the requirement that findings be made so that the decision may be reviewed in an adequate manner.[253] There are a number of cases that have overturned land-use decisions on the basis of an absence of

249. K. Davis, Administrative Law Text §§ 14.01 to 14.06 (1972).

250. The Oregon Court of Appeals, in *Duddles 535* P.2d 583, and *Tierney*, 536 P.2d 431, approved a procedure whereby the reviewing court would consider, at a separate hearing, issues of standing and the effect of prehearing contacts.

251. Shelburne, Inc. v. Conner, 269 A.2d 409 (Del. Chapter 1970), *reviewed*, 281 A.2d 608 (Del. Sup. Ct. 1971); Dietrich v. District of Columbia Bd. of Zoning Appeals and Adjustment, 293 A.2d 470 (D.C. App. 1972).

252. Cf. the limitation placed on cross-examination in Chrobuck v. Snohomish County, 75 Wash. 2d 858, 480 P.2d 496 (1971).

253. *See, e.g.*, Robey v. Schwab, 307 F.2d 198 (D.C. Cir. 1962); Dietrich v. District of Columbia Bd. of Zoning and Adjustment, 293 A.2d 470 (D.C. App. 1972); Roseta v. County of Washington, 254 Or. 161, 458 P.2d 405 (1969); West v. City of Astoria, 524 P.2d 1216 (Or. App. 1974); McClellan v. Zoning Hearing Bd., 8 Pa. Commw. Ct. 537, 304 A.2d 520 (1973); Miernyk v. Board of Zoning Appeals, 181 S.E.2d 681 (W. Va. 1971); Schelley v. Zoning Bd. of Adjustment, 8 Pa. Commw. Ct. 169, 302 A.2d 526 (1973); B.J.M. Development Corp. v. Fayette County Zoning Hearing Bd., 1 Pa. Commw. Ct. 534, 275 A.2d 714 (1971); Melucci v. Zoning Bd. of Review, 226 A.2d 416 (R.I. 1967); Braun v. Zoning Board of Review 99 R.I. 105, 206 A.2d 96 (1965); Ruckland v. Board of County Comm'rs, 75 Or. Adv. Sh. 1992, 536 P.2d 444 (1975). In Northampton Corp. v. Prince George's County, 21 Md. 625, 321 A.2d 204 (1974), the court found that the adoption of a hearings officer's proposed findings was sufficient, and no new findings were required unless such a proposal was to be rejected or modified.

findings,[254] and future litigation may increasingly turn on the adequacy of such findings.[255] The standard of review against which such findings are measured can be the comprehensive plan.[256]

In some jurisdictions procedural requirements of the enabling legislation could provide the standard. Where the comprehensive plan is used as the standard, the confidence of the court in the findings made will be a function of the factual basis of the plan and the validity and reliability of methods used in its formulation. This aspect of procedural reform will place a heavy burden on the professional staff to provide an adequate basis for the findings of the hearing body. On the other hand, it should promote greater confidence in and reliance on staff work by public officials and thereby reduce the number of decisions taken for political or venal reasons.

The Record. Another result of the conceptual shift to a quasi-judicial model is the requirement that an accurate record of the hearing be made to enable the courts to determine the nature and quality of the evidence presented and to test the findings made at the hearing.[257] A pro forma record such as the official minutes of the meeting would appear insufficient; all records thereby would be left to the whim of the hearing secretary.[258] In such cases the court should enforce its mandate for a full transcript by remanding the case.[259]

In the case of a complete de novo review by the governing body, the need for a full record of the proceedings before the planning commission or other hearing officer or body is less important.[260] Nevertheless, the record of the proceeding upon which a final order is based must be accurate and complete. Some local jurisdictions meet or comply with this standard by the use of court reporters. It is usually required that those who appeal to another level of the administrative process pay for the transcript.

Judicial Review. The extent or scope of judicial review is as important as the procedural changes resulting from the re-characteriza-

254. Bennett v. Lincoln City, 12 Or. App. 72, 503 P.2d 724 (1972); Erickson v. Portland, 9 Or. App. 256, 496 P.2d 726 (1972).

255. Colton v. Board of Zoning Appeals, 252 Ind. 56, 245 N.E.2d 377 (1969); Barbone v. Zoning Bd. of Review, 107 R.I. 174, 264 A.2d 921 (197x).

256. Fasano v. Bd. of County Comm'rs 264 Or. 574, 507 P.2d 23 (1973). *See also* Baker v. Milwaukie, 75 Or. Adv. Sh. 1068, 271 Or. 500, 533 P.2d 772 (1975).

257. Fasano v. Bd. of County Comm'rs 507 P.2d 23 (1973).

258. Printzas v. Borough of Norristown, 10 Pa. Commw. Ct. 482 313 A.2d 781 (1973); Loveless v. Yantis, 82 Wis. 2d 754, 513 P.2d 1023 (1973).

259. However, only one public hearing needs to occur. West v. City of Astoria, 254 P.2d 1216 (Or. App. 1974).

260. *Id. See also* Tierney v. Duris, 536 P.2d 431 (Or. App. 1975).

tion of the decisions of the local legislature. Where land-use changes are viewed as legislative acts, some courts—reacting to a situation in which abuse is thought to be rampant—often find ways to circumvent the legislative label and proceed to review the merits of the case. The usual form of action for such review is a suit for declaratory or injunctive relief, or both.[261]

Once the action of the legislature is characterized as quasi-judicial, the entire body of adjudicative administrative law is relevant. The time-honored tradition in zoning law of "saving the evidence until trial" (in a Declaratory or Injunctive proceeding) is no longer appropriate if all of the above safeguards must be met.[262] Also inappropriate is the use of additional evidence not considered by the administrative hearing body, for it would effect a substitution of the judgment of the court for that of the administrative body.[263]

In the Advisory Commission's view, the correct approach, also adopted by the American Law Institute, is administrative law review or a variant of common law certiorari, in which the record would be

261. R. Anderson, American Law of Zoning. chs. 23–24 (1969).

262. A letter from Deputy City Attorney David A. Solomon, of Lakewood, Colorado, contained the following explanation of the Colorado Supreme Court's approach in Snyder v. City of Lakewood, 542 P.2d 371 (Colo. 1975):

> The Colorado Supreme Court, in addition to ruling that zoning is quasi-judicial, and citing *Fasano*, also ruled that rezoning can be reviewed only by means of a Writ in the nature of Certiorari (the State of Colorado has supposedly abolished all Common Law Writs and instead set forth what is known as a Rule 106 proceeding. Actually, each paragraph of Rule 106 is a Common Law Writ and paragraphs 4(a) and (b) are the paragraphs concerning certiorari) and limited Declaratory Judgments to those cases where the general zoning ordinance is attacked as unconstitutional.
>
> Moreover, the Supreme Court dismissed the case because the pleadings were not filed within the thirty day time limit set forth in Rule 106(b). It is important to note that the plaintiffs claimed to have a Declaratory Judgment Action, while the City argued that they had not perfected this Declaratory Judgment Action. The Supreme Court did not rule that the plaintiffs did or did not have a Declaratory Judgment Action; but by not doing so, they may have impliedly stated that Declaratory Judgment Actions must also be brought within the time period set by the rules governing Certiorari. If Certiorari is considered the direct attack on a rezoning action and the Declaratory Judgment as a collateral attack, *Snyder*, while allowing both means of attack, may have limited the time in which to bring a Declaratory Judgment action as well as a Certiorari action.
>
> What this really means is that land developers and owners and builders will have to utilize legal service at the level of the council and may be even below that at the level of the planning commission. Since this is where the record is made and there are only thirty days in which to file an appeal, the attorney who is brought into the matter after the council hearing, by the landowner or the neighbors, is at a great disadvantage and may not be able to do a single thing for his proposed clients.

263. *See* Sullivan, note 163 *supra.*

called up and examined for errors without the court substituting its judgment for that of the lower body.[264] The courts could remand the case to the administrative body for a new hearing, additional findings, or whatever was necessary to cure a defect. They would usually not grant or deny land-use changes but simply affirm or remand, in accordance with traditional judicial functions in administrative law.

The Hearing Examiner

The foregoing has attempted to provide a glimpse of some recent changes in land-use law which the Advisory Commission considers meritorious. The process is moving from one in which few procedural safeguards are available, and in which the "legislative" label either prohibited significant review or required courts to find dubious means to circumvent that label, to one that requires adherence to procedural rules associated with established norms of administrative law.

We may expect sophisticated development controls to proliferate, and the administration of the zoning ordinance to become more complex. Moreover, the increased use of flexible devices and the need for constant change and refinement of a community's zoning ordinance have already multiplied the administrative difficulties for local government bodies. These bodies—previously composed of lay people lacking expertise in planning matters and others subject to political pressures—spend considerable time hearing applications for variances, special-use permits, and rezonings. Huge backlogs of applications result because of slow and inefficient administration; and the number of court appeals from arbitrary, capricious, and sometimes politically motivated decisions continues to grow.

An increasing number of communities have sought—by use of the hearing examiner—to alleviate some of the problems that have plagued zoning administration. The procedural requirements placed on the staff and hearing bodies by a quasi-judicial approach to zoning amendments may further compel the use of the hearing examiner. The added administrative and planning sophistication thereby demanded could make it extremely difficult for a typical planning commission or city council to adequately handle a complicated and contested case. Indeed, the American Law Institute has recommended that state enabling legislation make the hearing examiner alternative available to local government.[265] It should be noted, however, that (in

264. *Id.; see* ALI Code, note 6 *supra,* at § 9-109.
265. *Id.* at § 2-301.

the absence of state or federal planning moneys) the hearing examiner may be a realistic alternative only for major municipalities or populous counties because of the financial investment required to establish the system and the need to have sufficient zoning activity to justify such an expenditure.

Concern over the problems of zoning administration has been continuous over the years since the standard enabling acts. A precursor of the hearing examiner, the zoning administrator, was instituted by some localities to introduce a degree of efficiency and fairness to the process. A 1967 study of zoning administrators[266] found that some had authority to grant variances and certain special exceptions. Most zoning administrators are charged with enforcement of ordinance provisions by the grant or denial of permits and by initiating and carrying through legal proceedings against violators. In many cases the title is the only distinction between a zoning hearing examiner and a zoning administrator.

In some jurisdictions the zoning hearing examiner is known simply as the hearings officer; in others as the zoning and subdivision examiner. As we shall see, hearing examiners, unlike zoning administrators, are not assigned enforcement responsibilities.[267] The first zoning hearing examiner positions in this country were established in two Maryland counties near the District of Columbia: Anne Arundel in 1965 and Montgomery in 1967. Citizens and officials in those suburban areas were familiar with the widespread use of hearing examiners by the federal government in various administrative proceedings,[268] and considered that experience as a useful model for zoning administration.[269]

264. *Id.; see* ALI Code, note 6 *supra*, at § 9-109.

265. *Id.* at § 2-301. *See also* the discussion of scope of review in Chapter 6 *infra*.

266. P. Faraci, The Authority of the Zoning Administrator (ASPO-PAS No. 226, 1967).

267. *See* D. Lauber, The Hearing Examiner in Zoning Administration (PAS No. 312, 1975), based on a report prepared for this Advisory Commission and used as a basis for the hearing examiner material in this chapter.

268. For a detailed history of the development of the administrative process in the United States and the development of the hearing examiner function as part of that process, see Final Report of the Attorney General's Committee on Administrative Procedure 7–24 (1941); Musolf, Federal Examiners and the Conflict of Law and Administration 23–80 (1952); E. Kintner *et al.*, Appointment and Status of Federal Hearing Officers 1–45. (1954).

269. In 1961 the federal government employed 402 hearing examiners: 111 were employed by the Interstate Commerce Commission, which had pioneered the concept about ten years before. Selective Certification Method of Appointing Hearing Examiners 49 (Hearings Before a Subcommittee of the Committee on Government Operations, House of Representatives, 86th Cong., 2d. Sess., Aug. 25 & 26, 1960.

The federal administrative process has been built upon the theory that Congress may rely upon administrative agencies to apply Congress's declared policies in the public interest. This process is designed to ensure proper formulation and application of an established system of legal principles or regulations. The hearing examiner has become the legal instrument for:

1. Holding fair hearings with responsibility for preparing intelligible records that will enable the agency to make the ultimate and necessary determinations of fact in light of the evidence produced by concerned parties.
2. Making initial findings of fact based upon this evidence.
3. Ensuring the orderly and clear development of the case both during the hearing and in the initial or recommended decision, in accord with the legal principles and policies established by his agency.
4. Drawing and applying conclusions of law to the facts as he finds them, and recommending appropriate disposition of the case.[270]

In the federal scheme, the agency rather than the hearing examiner bears the ultimate responsibility for determining the relevant facts. The agency is the maker of policy and final interpreter of the law, and its decisions are binding upon the examiner. Accordingly, the federal agency possesses the power to affirm or reverse its hearing examiners' rulings, findings, and conclusions, and to accept or reject their recommendations.[271]

The zoning hearing examiner concept is based upon these same precepts. Citizens and officials in Anne Arundel and Montgomery counties saw the application of the hearing examiner process to the determination of variances, special uses, and single-parcel rezonings as a means to correct some of the administrative problems generated by these devices. Spurred by their success, other jurisdictions throughout the country have adopted similar systems.

Even before the *Fasano* line of cases discussed earlier, judicial opinion in Maryland had influenced the adoption of hearing examiner systems in that state. In *Hyson v. Montgomery County Council* the court observed:

[T]here can be little doubt that administrative officials, in the conduct of their proceedings, should conduct such proceedings with impartiality and proper decorum, and they should . . . base their conclusions upon evidence as distinguished from opinions of individual members.[272]

270. W. Lester *et al.*, Appointment and Status of Federal Hearing Officers 5 (1954).
271. *Id.* at 7–8.
272. 242 Md. 55, 71, 217 A.2d 578 (1966). The court also held that a reasonable right of cross-examination must be granted to the parties in a zoning hearing. *Id.* at 67.

Traditional zoning administration procedures rarely meet the standards established by the courts in Oregon, Washington, and Maryland. However, application of the hearing examiner procedure to zoning administration and decision-making is well suited for meeting these judicially imposed standards.

Operation of the Zoning Hearing Examiner: A Brief Summary. Many of the responsibilities of a local legislative body, board of appeals, or planning commission can be delegated to the office of the zoning hearing examiner, although state enabling legislation may have to be amended. Zoning hearing examiners are empowered to hold quasi-judicial public hearings on applications for at least one of the three most common flexible zoning devices: variances, special use permits, or single parcel rezonings. Some jursidictions also require the hearing examiner to hold hearings on applications for planned unit developments, subdivision plats, variances from sign-ordinance provisions, waivers of parking requirements, or historic districts. Others also assigned to the hearing examiner are appeals of building inspector decisions or administrative rulings on short plats. The duties and powers of various zoning hearing examiners are shown in Table 4-1.

In the typical hearing examiner process, the examiner must hold a public hearing on an application for a special-use permit. This hearing replaces the separate hearings formerly held by the planning commission, the board of appeals, or the governing body under the traditional administrative and legislative process. Applications are submitted to the local planning department, reviewed by the department, and forwarded to the zoning hearing examiner. The examiner then sets a date for a public hearing. Within a specified period before the hearing is held, the examiner is required to provide notice of the hearing to the applicant, to all owners of property, to residents living within a defined radius of the applicant's property, and to persons or organizations who have filed a request with the hearing examiner to be notified of public hearings affecting property within a specific area.[273] A copy of the application is made available for public inspection during normal business hours.

The public hearing is conducted according to procedural rules usually proposed by the hearing examiner and approved by the local legislative body. The hearing itself is a quasi-judicial proceeding, and as such conforms to at least minimal due process requirements.[274]

273. *See* ALI Code, *supra* note 6, at § 2-304, and commentary to that section.
274. For a discussion of the term quasi-judicial, *see* text following note 134 *supra*.

Table 4–1. Duties and Powers of Selected Zoning Hearing Examiners

Jurisdiction and Method of Appointment	Variances	Special Use Permits (Conditional Uses)	Parcel Rezonings	Additional Responsibilities	Appeal of Examiner's Ruling Directed To:
Anne Arundel County, Md. Zoning Hearing Officer appointed by County Executive: established 1965	Conducts mandatory public hearings; enters written findings; decides all variances	Conducts mandatory public hearings; enters written findings; decides all special exceptions	Conducts mandatory public hearings; enters written findings; decides all rezonings		County Board of Appeals
Montgomery County, Md. Hearing Examiner appointed by District Council; established 1967			Conducts mandatory public hearings; enters written findings; makes recommendation to District Council		County Council
Prince George's County, Md. Zoning Hearing Examiner appointed by District Council; established 1971	Conducts mandatory public hearings; enters written findings; makes recommendation to District Council	Conducts mandatory public hearings; enters written findings; makes recommendation to District Council	Conducts mandatory public hearings; enters written findings; makes recommendation to District Council	Conducts mandatory public hearings; enters findings; makes recommendation to District Council on applications for variances under the sign ordinance, validation of permits issued in error, parking waivers	District Council
Harford County, Md. Zoning Hearing Examiners ap-	Conducts mandatory public hearings; enters written findings;	Conducts mandatory public hearings; enters written findings;	Conducts mandatory public hearings; enters written findings;	Conducts mandatory public hearing; enters written findings; makes recommenda-	Final decisions of County Council can be appealed directly to circuit

(continued)

Table 4-1 continued

Jurisdiction and Method of Appointment	Variances	Special Use Permits (Conditional Uses)	Parcel Rezonings	Additional Responsibilities	Appeal of Examiner's Ruling Directed To:
pointed by County Council; established 1973	decides all variances	makes recommendation to County Council	makes recommendation to County Council	tion to County Council on all other appeals of zoning decisions	court
Xenia, Ohio Hearing Examiner appointed by City Manager; established 1974	Conducts mandatory public hearings; enters written findings; decides all variances	Conducts mandatory public hearings; enters written findings; decides all conditional uses in traditional zones and special overlay zone	Hearings conducted by City Planning Commission; decision voted by City Commission (council)	Conducts public hearings; enters written findings; makes recommendation to Planning Commission on applications for planned unit developments	Review commission or board with appellate power
Tucson, Ariz. Zoning and Subdivision Examiner appointed by City Manager; established 1975	Done by Board of Adjustment	Done by Board of Adjustment	Conducts mandatory public hearings; enters written findings; makes recommendation to Mayor and City Council	Conducts mandatory public hearings; enters written findings; makes recommendation to Mayor and City Council on applications for creation of historic districts, tentative subdivision plat approval	City Council
King County, Wash. Zoning and Subdivision Examiner appointed by County Council; established 1970	—a	—a	Conducts mandatory public hearings; enters written findings; makes recommendation to County Council	Conducts mandatory public hearings; enters written findings; makes recommendation to County Council on applications for planned	Variances and special use permits; Board of Appeals Parcel rezonings: County Council

Jurisdiction				
Seattle, Wash. Hearing Examiner appointed by City Council; established 1974	Conducts mandatory public hearings; enters written findings; decides area and sign variances, petitions to revoke sign variances, applications for extension of nonconforming signs	Conducts mandatory public hearings; enters written findings; decides special exceptions and conditional uses	Conducts mandatory public hearings; enters written findings; makes recommendation to City Council on unit development, preliminary plat approval. Hears and decides appeals from decisions of administrative officer on short plats	**Board of Adjustment**: May authorize revocable permit for temporary uses; use of property in any zone for excavation of stone, sand, gravel, clay, or other natural deposits; platted lots separated by alley
Tacoma, Wash. Hearing Examiner appointed by City Manager; established 1975	Conducts mandatory public hearings; enters written findings; decides variances	Conducts mandatory public hearings; enters written findings; decides special and temporary uses and conditional uses	Conducts mandatory public hearings; enters written findings; makes recommendation to City Council	**City Council**: Conducts mandatory public hearings; enters written findings; makes recommendation to City Council on preliminary plat approval; decides applications for service station permits, shoreline management permits, waivers of zoning standards, site approvals, and appeals from building inspector's interpretations of city's land-use regulatory codes

(continued)

Table 4-1 continued

Jurisdiction and Method of Appointment	Variances	Special Use Permits (Conditional Uses)	Parcel Rezonings	Additional Responsibilities	Appeal of Examiner's Ruling Directed To:
Portland, Oreg. Hearings Officer appointed by City Commissioner with jurisdiction over land-use planning functions; ordinance adopted 1974[c]	Conducts mandatory public hearings; enters written findings; decides all variances	Conducts mandatory public hearings; enters written findings; decides all conditional uses	Conducts mandatory public hearings; enters written findings; makes recommendation to City Council	Conducts mandatory public hearings; enters written findings; makes recommendation to City Council on applications for revocable permits	Two-tiered: first appeal is to City Planning Commission, which has discretion to accept or reject appeal; second appeal is to City Council[b]
Eugene, Oreg. Hearings Official appointed by City Council; draft ordinance 1975[d]	Conducts mandatory public hearings; enters written findings; decides all variance applications filed in conjunction with application for conditional use	Conducts mandatory public hearings; enters written findings; decides all conditional uses	Conducts mandatory public hearings; enters written findings; decides rezonings	Conducts mandatory public hearings; enters written findings; decides sign district boundary changes	City Council

[a] The Zoning Adjustor conducts mandatory hearings, enters written findings, and decides variances and conditional uses. The Zoning and Subdivision Examiner can be, and has been, appointed Zoning Adjustor.

[b] The Planning Commission's decision may be appealed to the City Council. When the Planning Commission declines to accept an appeal, appeal may be made directly to the City Council.

[c] No appointment has been made.

[d] An ordinance is being considered.

Source: D. Tauber, The Hearing Examiner in Zoning Administration 6-7 (ASPO 1975). Copyright © 1975 by American Society of Planning Officials. Used by permission.

Within a specified time period following the hearing, which typically varies from five to fourteen days, the examiner is required to render a written decision or submit a written recommendation to the legislative or administrative body that grants or denies the application. This recommendation or decision includes findings of fact based on the record established at the public hearing, the actual recommendation or decision for approval or denial of the application, and conclusions and reasons for the decision.

If the hearing examiner submits a recommendation to the local legislative body (as opposed to a final decision on an application), the examiner's hearing supplements that of the legislature. The council may, at its discretion, request additional information from the applicant and examiner, but its decisions may be based only on the information and the record established at the examiner's hearing. Under most systems the council does not hold de novo hearings. Appeal of the council's decision is to the courts.

If the hearing examiner acts finally and issues special-use permits or variances, or decides rezonings, the council generally acts as the first appellate body (see Table 4-1), and it must base its decision solely on the examiner's record. In some instances the legislative body may accept additional testimony and evidence, remand to the hearing examiner for further testimony, or conduct de novo hearings. Appeal of the council's ruling is to the courts. Specific aspects of this process are discussed below.[275]

Notice. Notice of the hearing is essential to due process. Generally the ordinance that establishes the position of hearing examiner provides for notice by mail to persons directly involved in the proceedings, such as the applicant. Most ordinances require that notice by mail also be given to property owners within a specific radius of the land in question and to neighborhood organizations. Notice to the general public is conveyed by publication in a newspaper and by posting placards in conspicuous public places on or near the property.

Parties to the Hearing. The ordinance that creates the zoning hearing examiner position should also state who may participate in the hearings. Persons who wish to be parties to the hearing should make an appearance of record that may be either an oral statement that identifies the person, made at the hearing, or a signed written statement filed with the examiner or presented at the hearing. The

275. *See also* D. Lauber, *supra* note 267.

ordinance should specify that parties to the hearing are entitled—either themselves or through a representative to the public hearing—to appeal the examiner's decision to the governing body, to the board of appeals, or to the courts, as the case may be in the particular jurisdiction.

The owners and residents of property adjacent to the subject property should be allowed to participate as parties of record. Neighborhood organizations that meet requirements specified in the ordinance should also be allowed to participate as parties as of right.[276]

The ordinance should specify that more than one organization can represent a neighborhood and that the designation of neighborhood organizations for hearing participation as of right should expire every several years unless renewed by registration with the appropriate public official.[277] Use of this approach will result in the regular involvement of neighborhood associations in land-use decisions. As a party of record, an association is entitled to rights it would not possess if it participated only at the discretion of the examiner or, in the case of appeals, of the court. These rights include full participation in the examiner's hearing and the right to initiate administrative or judicial appeal of the examiner's decision.

Representation of Hearing Participants. It is not necessary for an individual or association to be represented by an attorney;[278] an organization may select a spokesperson to present its case. If an organization's members cannot agree among themselves to a proper spokesperson the hearing examiner may exercise discretion in designating someone to represent the organization during the hearing.

Presentation of Arguments. The planning department's report and recommendations should be heard first. The applicants should then present their case. Witnesses, in the order established by the hearing examiner's published rules, may testify and be questioned by appropriate parties. Remaining time would be allotted to neighbors or other individuals not formally recognized as parties. It is suggested that those who support the application speak first and be followed by those opposed, with an opportunity for rebuttal by the applicant.

The hearing examiner generally has the discretion to set time limits for the presentation of each case and to exclude or limit cumulative,

276. *See* ALI Code, *supra* note 6, at § 2-307, and commentary to that section.
277. *Id.*
278. 36 Ops. Ore. Atty. Gen. No. 7062, at 992.

repetitious, or irrelevant material.[279] In some jurisdictions the examiner may rule on procedural matters and generally regulate the course of the hearing. The examiner may have authority to cross-examine witnesses, call witnesses, and introduce documentary evidence. Cross-examination and rebuttal by involved parties should be permitted. While cross-examination is an essential part of due process, it should be limited to the legitimate purpose of testing the credibility of factual assertions of a witness; it should not be allowed to deteriorate into an exchange of the differing philosophies of the witness and questioner.

Evidence. Because this is a quasi-judicial hearing and not a common law court, strict rules of evidence are not appropriate. The Maryland Court of Appeals, in *Bonnie View Club v. Glass,* held that the conduct of zoning hearings is "not bound by the strict rules of evidence of a trial at law, but are permitted a reasonable discretion in admitting or excluding evidence."[280] The hearing examiner may rule upon the admissibility of evidence.

The zoning hearing examiner should have the power to compel the attendance of witnesses or to require the production of relevant books, papers, documents, or other evidence. Nearly every zoning hearing examiner has been granted such subpoena power, but where strict rules of admissibility of evidence are not imposed the subpoena power should be carefully defined.

Decision or Recommendation? Most hearing examiners are authorized to grant or deny applications for variances, and about half possess this power for special-use permits. Others merely submit a recommendation to the governing body, which may grant, deny, or approve the application with conditions (see Table 4-1). The survey conducted for this report suggests that the governing body nearly always follows the advice of the hearing examiner.

Only one existing zoning examiner has been identified that could grant an individual rezoning: the draft ordinance for Eugene, Oregon delegates this authority to the "hearing officials" (see Table 4-1). The others submit a recommendation to the local governing body that traditionally makes this decision. In Maryland, as a result of the

279. "There can be little doubt that the zoning authorities, in conducting their hearings . . . must be recognized as having the discretion to regulate, reasonably, the length of the time afforded to parties to present their evidence." Hyson v. Montgomery County Council, 242 Md. at 70–71.

280. 242 Md. 46, 54 (1966). *See also* Hyson v. Montgomery County Council, 242 Md. 55 (1966).

appeals court decision in *Baltimore County v. Missouri Realty, Inc.*,[281] the power to reclassify particular parcels of property may be validly delegated to the county board of appeals and the zoning commissioner (administrator) of Baltimore County.

As discussed earlier the rezoning of a single parcel of land should involve the appropriate interpretation of planning policy as previously established by the political process and incorporated in a comprehensive plan. If it is an administrative or quasi-judicial act, logic may suggest that it be decided by a hearing examiner; however, such a total delegation of power is neither realistic nor desirable. Rather, it is preferrable to retain the traditional division of functions in the zoning process.

Those decisions traditionally handled by administrative boards, such as variances, subdivision plats, and special permits, could be delegated to the hearing examiner with a right of administrative appeal to the governing body. Matters traditionally decided by the governing body, such as individual requests for development permission or rezonings, would be heard initially by the examiner, who would make a recommendation to the governing body. A hearing examiner may also play a particularly useful role in replacing certain functions of special boards, such as Historic Area or Architectural Review boards, which might more properly operate as advocates before a hearing examiner.

The zoning hearing examiner may be assigned responsibility for the conduct of hearings and the preparation of a written decision or recommendation on a variety of other applications, such as PUDs or sign ordinance variances. The delegation of such additional responsibilities should be made only if the hearing examiner's office is adequately staffed to handle the additional volume of work these tasks entail.

Findings and Record. Like his or her counterpart under the Federal Administrative Procedure Act,[282] the zoning hearing examiner must prepare a written decision that becomes part of the record. This decision must be written whether the hearing examiner makes a recommendation to another body for disposition of the application or makes this final determination independently. Typically this document includes a description of the proposed action, findings of fact, conclusions, the reasoning upon which the examiner's decision is

281. 219 Md. 155, 148 A.2d 424 (1959).
282. Administrative Procedure Act § 8(b), 60 Stat. 237 (1946), 5 U.S.C. § 1001 (1952).

based, the examiner's decision or recommendation, and a notice of right of appeal.

If quasi-judicial decisions are to be subject to meaningful review, the findings must be adequate. Findings should be presented so that reviewers will have adequate information to determine whether proper procedures were followed at the hearing and whether the findings have a sound basis in the evidence. Findings of fact should include such information as a description of the subject site and surrounding area, the existing zoning for the subject site and surrounding area, applicable comprehensive-plan policies or maps for the area, and probable social, environmental, fiscal, and physical impacts of the proposed action on the area.

The conclusion should set forth the reasoning upon which the decision of the zoning hearing examiner is based. This reasoning must be based on the evidence and testimony submitted at the public hearing and on accepted standards used to guide the zoning hearing examiner in making the decision. Prior decisions that involve similar situations should be noted and their relevance evaluated. Nearly every hearing examiner reports that the comprehensive plan plays at least a strongly advisory role in decision-making. The beginning of a trend toward mandatory planning and consistency between land-use decisions and the plan is an important development in the operation of the hearing examiner system.

The King County, Washington Zoning and Subdivision Examiner reports that "the hearing examiner system requires that planning policy be clearly articulated so that it can be identified and used as the criteria against which individual applications are evaluated."[283] When the Portland, Oregon hearings officer finds that the case before him raises a substantial question involving the application of policy, he can make a written request to the city planning commission for its interpretation of the policy.[284]

Comprehensive planning provides a policy basis for the zoning process and can help assure consistency in the administration of zoning. Lack of a comprehensive planning policy to guide zoning administration can lead to arbitrary and capricious decisions. Moreover, most of the hearing examiners conclude that a comprehensive plan drawn as a policy plan provides better guidance than does a mapped comprehensive plan. Mapped plans usually show only general rela-

283. King County's Office of Zoning and Subdivision Examiner 6 (Seattle, Washington, 1973, mimeo., on file with ASPO) [hereinafter cited as King County Examiner].

284. Portland, Ore., Ord. No. 139417, § 33.114.060(g).

tionships between land uses; a policy plan can provide specific guidelines upon which the zoning hearing examiner can base decisions.[285]

Appeal. In most jurisdictions the zoning hearing examiner's decision may be appealed to the local governing body. Several communities, though, assign the appeal function to the zoning board of
adjustment or appeals, while others provide for an initial "reconsideration" by the examiner who made the recommendations. The
Tucson, Arizona ordinance provides for any party of record who believes that the examiner's recommendation is based on errors of procedure or fact to make a written request for review by the examiner
within fourteen days of the conclusion of the hearing (the examiner's
recommendation must be made within five days of the conclusion
of the hearing). The request should specify the alleged errors. After a
review of the record, the examiner is empowered, at his or her discretion, to take further action such as conducting an additional hearing and rendering any revised recommendation.

When the hearing examiner recommends rather than makes a final
decision on an application, the hearing by the examiner should constitute the hearing by the local governing body. An aggrieved party
of record, though, usually can submit a written appeal to the council
that requests additional consideration.[286] Where the hearing examiner
makes a final decision, the local council or board of appeals hears
appeals of the decision. A number of jurisdictions grant the appellate body the option of conducting a de novo hearing—a new hearing
of the application.[287]

285. Planners in Great Britain have also found that most development plans,
prepared under the 1947 Town and Country Planning Act, have been far too detailed to be of any use in making development decisions. Although they should
be used as guides, they have become little more than land-use maps. The Ministry
of Housing and Local Government of Great Britain has recommended that
instead of preparing detailed mapped plans, comprehensive plans should consist
primarily of "statements of policy illustrated where necessary with sketch maps
and diagrams and accompanied by a diagrammatic or 'structure' map. . . ."
Great Britain, Ministry of Housing and Local Government, The Future of Development Plans (1965).

286. *See* King County, Washington, Ord. No. 00263 (1969), at 22-23.

287. In Anne Arundel County, Maryland, little evidence is presented at the
examiner's hearing because the appellate body, the County Board of Appeals,
is required by ordinance to conduct a de novo hearing on the appeal, and judicial review is based on this record rather than on that established before the
hearing examiner. Parties to controversial applications assume that someone
will appeal the examiner's decision; consequently they frequently fail to present a complete case to the hearing examiner and save their major efforts for the
County Board of Appeals. The purpose of the hearing examiner is defeated when
parties to a hearing fail to present a full case. It is reasonable to give appellate
bodies the option of holding a de novo hearing, but it certainly should not be
required.

The appellate body may also have the option of admitting additional testimony and evidence without holding a de novo hearing if it is satisfied that the testimony on evidence is newly discovered or could not have been presented at the examiner's hearing. In determining the admissibility of such testimony or evidence, an appellate body should consider possible prejudice to parties, the convenience of locating the evidence at the time of the examiner's hearing, surprise to opposing parties, and the competence, relevancy, and materiality of the proposed testimony or evidence. These same provisions are common to appeal procedures in jurisdictions where the local council makes the final decision on an application.

When the appellate body denies an application, nearly every jurisdiction that employs a zoning hearing examiner prohibits resubmission of substantially the same application for 12 or 24 months following final disposition of the application. If the aggrieved party chooses to appeal to the courts, judicial review is based on the record established before the hearing examiner.

An Evaluation. One of the major frustrations in the zoning process is the excessive amount of time taken up by requests for zoning changes. In every jurisdiction that has adopted the examiner process, the council's workload has been reduced. In King County, Washington, for example, the examiner system has relieved the county council of the need to sit through lengthy hearings on applications under the zoning and subdivision codes. The reduction in time spent by the council in what amounts to administrative hearings, and the way in which the examiner's report focuses on the important issues involved in each application, allow an informed decision with a much smaller investment of time than in the past.[288] As a result the local governing bodies have more time to devote to major policy matters.

Although the council avoids the burden of public hearings in these zoning matters, in jurisdictions where the examiner's decision is only a recommendation, the council still retains its power and responsibility to make the final decision. Where the examiner's decision is final, the governing body still retains the power to reverse, because it usually hears appeals from the zoning examiner's decisions. Only in Anne Arundel County, Maryland, where the examiner hears and decides parcel rezonings, is the entire zoning change process removed from the purview of the governing body.

Hearing examiners have also relieved planning commissions of the inordinate amount of time spent on land-use administration, often

288. King County Examiner, *supra* note 283, at 7.

at the expense of planning. Two jurisdictions that established a hearing examiner went on to reorganize the bodies that determine planning policy. With the creation of the hearing examiner position, King County replaced its planning commission with the Environmental Development Commission, a citizens' group comparable to the former planning commission but responsible only for recommending planning policy to the examiner.[289] Similarly, Tucson, Arizona, replaced its planning commission with the zoning hearing examiner and the Citizen Advisory Planning Committee. The latter considers planning policy and does not make recommendations on zoning applications.[290]

In most jurisdictions the local legislative body has followed the hearing examiner's recommendations. In Montgomery County, Maryland, only 2.5 percent of the examiner's 1,500 recommendations have been reversed by the county council. The Seattle City Council reversed only one of the hearing examiner's first 183 actions. In Prince George's County, Maryland, the examiner has been upheld in 95 percent of the cases where the council has declined to hear additional testimony, and has decided the case solely on the basis of the examiner's record. Where the council has heard additional oral testimony, it has reversed the examiner's recommendation in 40 percent of the cases. Moreover, appeals to the courts appear to diminish under the hearing examiner system.[291]

In every jurisdiction investigated for this report, the zoning hearing examiner also appears to comply with the customary standards of conduct, both in hearings and in written opinions. The examiner system probably provides a more equitable hearing, with more time available for testimony in hearings than was previously available before a lay administrative board or a legislative body.[292]

The perceived fairness of the hearing examiner process has also contributed to a general reduction in the number of applications

289. *Id.* at 6.
290. Mayor and Council Memorandum, Subject: Analysis of a Proposed Amendment to the Tucson Zoning Code Establishing: (1) the Position of Zoning and Subdivisions Examiner, and (2) the Citizens' Advisory Planning Committee 1-2, 8-9 (Oct. 31, 1974, on file with ASPO).
291. Before Montgomery County implemented the hearing examiner system in 1967, 25 to 30 percent of the county council's zoning decisions were appealed to the courts. Between 1971 and June 1974, only five cases were appealed to the courts. In Prince George's County the annual number of appeals of zoning decisions had fallen from twenty to thirty before the examiner system was initiated, to five to ten under the examiner system.
292. *See* King County Examiner, *supra* note 283, at 7; Trustian & Elston, *Zoning Hearing Examiner Process: In Use in Montgomery County, Md. for Four Years*, 1 Planners Notebk. 3 (1971); *Mayor and Council Memorandum, supra* note 290, at 9-10; Portland Planning Commission, The Hearing Officer Process 2, 4-5 (1974).

filed for zoning changes. Because potential applicants and their attorneys now know the basis upon which applications are judged by the hearing examiner, fewer frivolous applications are filed. Political influence has also been reduced by the employment of the examiner system in which *ex parte* contacts with examiners and legislators are prohibited or required to be made part of the record. The potential of reducing corruption in the zoning process through the use of the examiner system is a welcome benefit.[293]

Applicants are also aware that the examiner will explicitly consider the comprehensive plan in making decisions because most hearing examiners are required, by ordinance, to do so. This use of a full-time professional to administer the increasingly complex land-use control ordinances has helped to reduce the number of applications for variances, special-use permits, and rezonings. Although the examiner process has not eliminated the backlog of pending zoning applications, in most jurisdictions it has helped to reduce the backlog or at least to retard its growth. In some jurisdictions the processing time of applications for single-parcel rezoning has been reduced because the ordinance that creates the zoning hearing examiner sets a time limit on the decision-making process.

It would be a mistake to view the hearing examiner as a cure-all for the ills of zoning administration. However, as more expertise is required to develop and evaluate the modern comprehensive plan, so, too, is professional competence needed to interpret its policies and its implementing regulations.

Decentralization of Land-Use Decisions

Public concern over environmental and land-use issues has produced a situation in which forces—at first, apparently contradictory—are moving both to centralize and, at the same time, decentralize public involvement in these matters. While new legislation tends toward an extraordinarily complex overlay of regional, state, and federal regulation, other efforts at the local level, perhaps emerging from the citizen-participation movement of the 1960s, propose to place greater control over some environmental and land-use matters in the hands of neighborhood residents.[294]

The typical structure of local land-use decision-making reflects an early concern with public participation in the process. The appointed boards included within the two model enabling acts were intended to provide the general public with access to the system.

293. Lauber, *supra* note 267 at n. 85.
294. *See generally* E. Gill, Neighborhood Zoning: Practices and Prospects (ASPO–PAS No. 311, 1975).

Both the planning commission and the zoning board of appeals were to consist of lay persons who would assist elected officials by making recommendations (the planning commission) or serve as a check against governmental rigidity by granting variances (the board of appeals). Many of these local boards have gradually become dominated by individuals having special interests in the matters they are required to regulate. A real dilemma exists over whether a planning commission or board of appeals member needs special expertise to function effectively, or whether the members should represent a broad spectrum of average citizens.

Another difficulty has arisen from the reliance on areawide hearings in which difficult issues must be debated and decided. As evidenced by the urban renewal experience, such hearings have severe limitations as citizen participation devices:

1. The hearing, not being an on-going process, and taking place on one occasion only, might not be convenient for some, and will rarely be convenient for the old, the ill or disabled.
2. The hearing by itself is unlikely to attract those who are not interested or involved in neighborhood affairs or improvement. . . .
3. [The hearings are often characterized by] . . . an attitude which might range from outright hostility towards, or distrust of, government to at least a feeling of lack of personal efficacy to change the course of events set by governmental authorities.[295]

Depending upon one's perspective, examples of land-use decisions that may adversely affect neighborhood interests abound. While the matter of neighborhood decay and abandonment is obviously complicated, even well-conceived zoning policies and actions, done in accordance with a plan, may have some detrimental effect on general neighborhood vitality. Examples include overzoning for commercial uses; rigid adherence to exclusive, "Euclidean" zoning that hastens the disappearance of neighborhood shopping and other nonresidential uses; or overloading an aging neighborhood with special institutional uses such as hospitals, churches, or halfway houses.

A greater emphasis on preserving neighborhood values and existing housing may lead to the conclusion that there are some decisions that, in our larger cities, can best be made at the neighborhood level rather than at city hall. Some of these decisions might be so minor as to require no further review (such as a request to permit an addition to a home that will reduce a required side yard), while others may

295. Jowell, *Limits of the Public Hearing as a Tool of Urban Planning*, 21 Ad. L. Rev. 123, 137–39 (1970). *See also* Plager, *Participatory Democracy and the Public Hearing: A Functional Approach*, 21 Ad. L. Rev. 153 (1970).

still require additional hearings before a commission or hearing examiner and adoption by a city council (zoning changes, for example), as well as review for conformance with a comprehensive plan.

A more precise definition of those matters that should and can be dealt with at the neighborhood level is required. Allowing some decisions to be made at the neighborhood level is not necessarily inconsistent with other efforts to place certain powers of review in the hands of regional or state bodies.[296] Nevertheless, the danger of uncoordinated neighborhood, regional, state, and federal reviews of various development proposals indicates that the problem must be approached in a comprehensive manner.

The bitter legacy of many federally mandated citizen-participation programs may make suspect subsequent offers of neighborhood control over land-use matters. Neighborhood control also requires a difficult balance between preservation of both the physical and social fabric of the neighborhood and arbitrary exclusion from the neighborhood of land uses and residents. This requires great care in the identification of matters delegated to neighborhood organizations.

Approaches to Decentralization. Neighborhood participation in land-use matters ranges from authorized appearance by representatives at public hearings, to official, structured involvement in subdivision and zoning review, or more specific matters such as historic preservation[297] and central business district development.[298] The more structured form of neighborhood participation in review, which to this point has been exclusively advisory, is usually based on the

---

296. It is significant that precisely such an exercise in the re-allocation of power is now going on in the metropolitan areas outside the central city. The suburbs, large and small, long accustomed to wielding all the powers of government, are faced with demands that they divest themselves of control in those areas of power where the facts of our untidy environment require a wider consensus of decision making. In the case of the metropolitan area the transference of power is upward to state and regional agencies, impelled by the inability of the suburbs to deal individually with the exploding problems of transportation, the pollution of our air and water, our shriveling open spaces, and overwhelming densities. In the case of the central city, however, a similar and consistent re-appraisal requires the transfer of some power downward to the individual neighborhood. In each case, the hard job is to make a reasonable allocation of power that will recognize the legitimate interests of the neighborhood (or suburb) on the one hand, and the city (or region) on the other.

Babcock & Bosselman, Citizen Participation: A Suburban Suggestion for the Central City, 32 Law & Contemp. Probs. 220, 222 (1967).

297. *See* J. Costonis, Space Adrift 19-20 (1974).

298. A discussion of Detroit's efforts to involve the CBD in revitalization can be found in Babcock & Banta, New Zoning Techniques for Inner-City Areas 12 (ASPO PAS No. 297, 1973).

delineation of urban neighborhoods and recognition of qualified neighborhood organizations.[299]

Again, neither of these approaches grants actual decision-making authority to neighborhood organizations; instead they institutionalize an advisory role that many such organizations have traditionally played. Neighborhood organizations, however, particularly those with some exposure to earlier forms of citizen participation, may be reluctant to function in an advisory capacity. Moreover, the time and resources required to deal competently with complex land-use issues, without any real authority or professional staff assistance, are likely to be in excess of that to be expected from the most committed volunteers. On the other hand it should be noted that with adequate resources, even advisory boards can exercise considerable power merely by virtue of marshalling facts and political influence in the same manner as other parties in the land-use control process.

The central issue—aside from technical questions of limitation by state enabling legislation or improper delegation of the police power —is the willingness of government officials to divest themselves of some degree of power and authority. The lack of such willingness is usually attributed to limited confidence in the ability of neighborhood residents to sustain the effort or to exercise the skill necessary to handle various decisions. At the same time it could be asserted that this position has been a self-fulfilling prophecy: past gestures toward citizen participation have rarely granted any real authority, and those invited to participate have usually been unable to make significant contributions to the process. Even attempts to provide professional expertise to neighborhood groups in the form of advocate planners stops short of resolving the problem:

> As effective as advocacy planning might be in shifting some planning power to low-income neighborhoods and even occasionally stopping some governmental action such as a highway, these communities still have to operate within constraints set by those living outside their borders and whose interests are quite different from their own.[300]

As to the limits of decentralization, two general, nondelegable categories have been suggested:

1. Matters of indivisible city policy such as gross residential densities, large-scale commercial development, necessary public facilities, etc.
2. Regulations and underlying policies that are essential to public health and safety such as fire protection, sanitation, etc.[301]

299. *See generally* Gil, *supra* note 294; ALI Code, *supra* note 6, at § 2-307.
300. R. Goodman, After the Planners 23–24 (1971).
301. Babcock & Bosselman, *supra* note 296, at 225.

Examples of delegable authority could include: (1) specific parcel densities within general city policies; (2) amount and location of open space on individual parcels; and (3) permission for "home occupations."[302]

The full extent of delegable decisions will vary among municipalities, but the development of such a system could itself provide a significant opportunity for participation by all segments of the community in the detailed self-examination that should be required. At the same time, the community would be initiating the process of comprehensive policy planning that will form the basis for a system of decentralized control that is both fair and rational.

Greater neighborhood participation in the land-use control process must be evaluated in the context of other land-use reforms. Additional procedural requirements for zoning changes (such as adequate notice and opportunity to be heard), the use of hearing examiners, consistency between zoning and planning decisions, increased use of "flexible" controls, and the need to coordinate administrative review at many levels, are all factors that may both facilitate neighborhood participation or complicate its implementation. In other words, the rationalization of other aspects of the local process, with the addition of procedural safeguards, will in fact reduce the discretionary power now vested in local officials so that they will have less power to give away. However, greater emphasis on the role of the comprehensive planning process, procedural requirements, and more sophisticated control mechanisms will place a heavy operational burden on neighborhood boards and citywide agencies as well.

The comprehensive planning process itself, with its increased focus on social, environmental, and economic areas (and the need to consider regional demands), may be more effectively implemented by an organized network of neighborhood planning and zoning bodies. Most localities have already been struggling with citizen participation in their comprehensive planning, and the usefulness of that participation could be increased by some degree of neighborhood control over plan implementation. Furthermore, the trend toward comprehensive policy planning, with a de-emphasis on the physical elements of planning, lends itself to extensive neighborhood involvement.

Another issue (addressed *infra*) is neighborhood preservation, in the broad sense of preserving, rehabilitating, or preventing the deterioration of the existing housing stock. Although the financing of this effort is a major problem, certainly the identification of potential properties, the consideration of neighborhood dynamics that are essential to successful preservation, and the administration of land-

302. *Id.* at 224–25.

use controls that will reduce further deterioration in an area are all matters to which neighborhood participation is applicable.

Finally, to achieve a balance between neighborhood control and unacceptable exclusionary practices by neighborhoods, two factors should be considered. First, as in the relationship between municipal action and regional or state review, it may be necessary to provide a check on neighborhood control of some issues, the impact of which extends beyond neighborhood boundaries (low- and moderate-income housing and public facilities such as schools, and hospitals, for example). Second, every effort should be made to ensure that neighborhood decisions or recommendations are made under appropriate procedural and substantive requirements, and are followed. The confidence of a neighborhood in its ability to predict the outcome of the process is as essential to its stability as are its political and social foundations. These two factors—higher level review and neighborhood confidence—need not be mutually exclusive if the comprehensive planning process has been sufficient to put an area on notice that some matters of community-wide concern must be accommodated in neighborhood decisions.

Regional and State Review

The previous discussion has emphasized the need to make the increasingly complex land-use control system more fair and rational, both in fact and in appearance. The task has been complicated by a proliferating array of regional, state, and federal programs that frequently overlap in impact and sometimes conflict in their own planning and administrative review functions. The administration of these supra-local programs would benefit from the local administrative and procedural reforms that have been discussed in this chapter, and from the application of coordination mechanisms at the regional and state levels.

Regional Agencies. The development of regional agencies as mechanisms for dealing with various government problems that extend beyond local jurisdictional boundaries has been occurring for most of this century. These regional bodies range from single purpose agencies to state-created multi-county agencies with powers of taxation and eminent domain, and from county planning agencies to regional planning commissions and regional councils of governments. These supra- or multimunicipal bodies have resulted from state and federal encouragement and local recognition that some problems require extra-municipal evaluation.

A recent survey identified some 649 such agencies performing regional functions throughout the country.[303] They have at least four factors in common:

1. Their structure is usually based on some form of state enabling legislation that authorizes participation by units of local government, generally describes the administrative make-up of the agency, and grants limited powers and functions.
2. Proliferation of the agencies is tied to the expansion of organized metropolitan areas or designation as Standard Metropolitan Statistical Areas.
3. Agency functions are closely tied to some form of comprehensive planning.
4. Expansion of agency programs and functions are often related to a series of federal grant programs that require local planning review and areawide coordination.[304]

Another general characteristic of regional agencies is the voluntary nature of local government participation and the consequent limitations on the regional agency's power to implement plans and policies.[305]

Regional reviews of specific development proposals have usually been required in connection with federally assisted programs, and performed in the context of a regionally formulated comprehensive plan (often merely a composite of local plans). The agencies, designated as clearinghouses under the Office of Management and Budget's (OMB) A-95 review process,[306] are responsible for coordinating the comments of affected local governmental bodies on the impact of a federally assisted project. The OMB regulations require notification to the clearinghouse agency when a federally supported project is in its early stages. The regional agency is then expected to notify appropriate local jurisdictions, citizen groups, civil rights organizations, and other interested parties, soliciting comments on the proposed project.

The executive committee or board of the clearinghouse agency coordinates these comments into a recommendation to the federal agency responsible for funding the specific project. Some A-95 re-

303. Directory of the National Association of Regional Councils (Washington 1974).

304. Advisory Commission on Intergovernmental Relations, 1 Substate Regionalism and the Federal System 169–215 (1973). [hereinafter cited as ACIR-I.]

305. *See* Babcock, *Let's Stop Romancing Regionalism*, 2 Planning 120 (1972).

306. U.S. Executive Office of the President, Office of Management and Budget, OMB Circular No. A-95 (rev. 1971, 1972, 1973); *see also* ACIR-I, *supra* note 304, at 139–65.

views may produce negative recommendations, although local interest tends more toward facilitating the flow of federal assistance to the region. The federal funding agency is not bound by the comments generated in the review of the general findings of the A-95 agency, although a generally negative report might at least cause delay.

Other forms of regional involvement in the local development and planning process has generally occurred in connection with the siting of public facilities. For instance, the existence of certified regional plans for transportation or water and sewer facilities relates to state and federal aproval of assistance to locate and construct such facilities. While direct regional review of both private and public development has to date been infrequent, it is likely to increase as state legislation and federal land-use proposals move in this direction.

State Involvement in Land-Use Decision-Making. The involvement of state governments in land-use controls has been a major result of increased environmental consciousness, and the realization that a municipality cannot provide rational treatment for ecological problems that transcend local boundaries. It is curious that this development is viewed by some as a usurpation of local control. Municipal land-use controls are valid only because they are a delegation to localities of the police power of the state. Nevertheless, from special-purpose programs that regulate unique natural areas[307] or land uses with regional impacts (such as power plants)[308] to environmental legislation,[309] virtually every state is now involved in some form of legislation affecting land-use decisions.[310] The diversity of this state involvement is represented by legislation such as that in the following states:

1. *California:* Recent amendments to the zoning and planning enabling laws require local land-use decisions to be consistent with comprehensive plans[311] and prescribe essential elements of those

307. *E.g.,* Hackensack Meadowlands Reclamation and Development Act, ch. 404 Laws of 1968, N.J. Stat. ch. 13, § 17-1, *et seq.*

308. *E.g.,* N.Y. Public Service Law §§ 140–149 (McKinney 1974).

309. *E.g.,* Environmental Land and Water Management Act of 1972, Fla. Stat. Ann. §§ 380.012–10 (Supp. 1973).

310. Recent state land use legislation is summarized in Environmental Quality: Seventh Annual Report of the Council on Environmental Quality 66–76 (1976); N. Rosenbaum, Land Use and the Legislatures: The Politics of State Innovation (1976); R. Healy, Land Use and the States (1976).

311. Cal. Gov. Code § 65860 (West Supp. 1974).

plans.[312] The California Environmental Quality Act[313] requires an environmental impact report for various government actions determined to have significant environmental effect; the California Coastal Zone Conservation Act[314] requires regional permits for public and private development within the coastal zone.

2. *Florida:* The Environmental Land and Water Management Act regulates areas of critical state concern and developments of regional impact. The Local Government Comprehensive Planning Act of 1975 requires localities to adopt a comprehensive plan.[315]

3. *Hawaii:* A state land-use commission is empowered to divide the state into major land-use categories and regulate land use therein.[316]

4. *Maine:* The Site Location Law requires a state permit for commercial and industrial developments and subdivisions in excess of 20 acres.[317]

5. *Oregon:* SB 100 (1973) requires local consistency with statewide planning goals, and provides for legislative designation of activities of critical state concern;[318] SB 10 (1969) provides for assumption of local planning and zoning by the State Land Conservation and Development Commission when there is no local planning and zoning.[319]

6. *Vermont:* Act 250 requires a state permit for development of 10 acres or more.[320]

7. *Massachusetts:* Zoning Appeals Law[321] provides for override of local regulations prohibiting the development of low- and moderate-income housing.

The ALI *Model Land Development Code* has had an impact in this area of state-municipal relationships, and already has influenced various state and federal legislative proposals. Under Article 7 a state land planning agency,[322] after holding a legislative hearing on the matter,[323] may designate as an "area of critical state concern":

312. *Id.* at § 65303.
313. Cal. Pub. Res. Code §§ 21000-74 (West Supp. 1975), *amending* §§ 21000-21151 (West 1970).
314. *Id.* § 27000-650 (West Supp. 1975).
315. Fla. Stat. Ann. §§ 380.012-10 (Supp. 1973); Fla. Laws ch. 75-257 (1975).
316. Haw. Rev. Stats. ch. 205, *as amended by* 1970 Hawaii Sess. Laws, act 136.
317. Me. Rev. Stat. Ann., Tit. 38, § 481–488 (Supp. 1972).
318. Or. Rev. Stat. § 215.055.
319. Id. at § 215.505.
320. Vt. Stat. Ann., Tit. 10, §§ 6001-6091 (1972).
321. Mass. Gen. Laws Ann., ch.40B, §§ 20–23 (1971).
322. ALI Code, *supra* note 6, at § 8-101.
323. *Id.* at § 2-305.

(a) an area significantly affected by, or having a significant effect upon, an existing or proposed major public facility or other area of major public investment;

(b) an area containing or having a significant impact upon historical, natural or environmental resources of regional or statewide importance;

(c) a proposed site of a new community designated in a State Land Development Plan, together with a reasonable amount of surrounding land; or

(d) land within the jurisdiction of a local government that, at any time more than [3 years] after effective date of th[e] Code, has no development ordinance in effect.[324]

In addition to setting forth the basis of its designation, the state agency must suggest general principles for guiding the development of the area[325] and administer a development-permit system pending adoption of municipal development regulations for the critical area. These local development regulations must conform to the conditions of the critical area designation; failure to adopt local regulations allows the state agency to assume that role.[326] The ALI Code provides for notice to the state agency of development applications in critical areas so that state interests may be protected.[327]

The Code's treatment of developments of regional impact (DRI) is directed toward projects whose effect on the neighboring environment presents issues of state or regional significance. When it designates DRIs, the state land planning agency is required to consider such criteria as:

(a) the extent to which the development would create or alleviate environmental problems such as air or water pollution or noise;

(b) the amount of pedestrian or vehicular traffic likely to be generated;

(c) the number of persons likely to be residents, employees, or otherwise present;

(d) the size of the site to be occupied;

(e) the likelihood that additional or subsidiary development will be generated; and

(f) the unique qualities of particular areas of the state.[328]

Moreover, upon notice to the state by the developer, other projects—by virtue of the benefits they may provide beyond the boundaries of a single local government—are referred to as developments of regional

324. *Id.* at § 7-201(3).
325. *Id.* at § 7-201(1).
326. *Id.* at §§ 7-203, 7-204.
327. *Id.* at § 7-208.
328. *Id.* at § 7-301(2).

benefit, and will be processed as DRIs.[329] These include developments by other government agencies, developments for charitable purposes, public-utility projects, and development of housing for persons of low and moderate income.[330]

Again, the local land-development agency is encouraged to perform the basic regulatory and permit functions for DRIs. The Code also provides a rather detailed set of procedures[331] and standards[332] for the DRI permit process, including a method of evaluating net benefits and detriments for the locality and region.[333] The extent to which the official draft of the *Model Land Development Code* will be followed throughout the country remains to be seen. Some of the states listed above have already begun to pick and choose appropriate sections. Indeed, such severability is encouraged by the drafters of the Code.[334]

The probability of greater state participation in land-use decision-making underscores the need for greater coordination of the various levels of review.[335] The uncoordinated nature of many state and regional planning and review mechanisms is illustrated by the multiplicity of state and regional reviews required in California. Regional approvals can be required by flood-control districts; air-pollution control districts; water-quality control boards; airport land-use commissions; local agency formation commissions (if annexation or incorporation are needed); and special regional entities having permit approval powers, including regional coastal conservation commissions (with appeal to the California Coastal Conservation Commission), the San Francisco Bay Conservation and Development Commission, and the Lake Tahoe Regional Planning Agency.

State approvals may also be necessitated under a wide variety of enactments ranging from the Subdivided Lands Law to the energy siting approval Law.[336] In addition, California's legislative and judicial developments have given widespread application to the use of a state environmental-impact report process modeled after the

---

329. *Id.* at § 7-301(4).
330. *Id.*
331. *Id.* at § 7-7-303.
332. *Id.* at §§ 7-304, 7-305.
333. *Id.* at §§ 7-401, 7-402.
334. *Id.* at X.
335. F. Bosselman, The Permit Explosion: Coordination of the Proliferation (1977).
336. Outline prepared by R. Volpert, Esq. for ALI/ABA conference, New Orleans, Feb. 6–8, 1975. *See also* Winter, *Environmentally Sensitive Land Use Regulation in California*, 10 San Diego L. Rev. 693 (1973).

National Environmental Policy Act.[337] As other states continue to adopt similar legislation, the need for at least minimal coordination and the importance of fair and efficient procedural requirements becomes obvious, both for reducing delays and development costs and for accomplishing the substantive objectives of comprehensive planning requirements.

The Federal Impact. The subject of federal involvement in the land-use control process has grown in importance as the complex of federal legislation and regulations that affect land-use decisions becomes more apparent. The issue, again, is the problem of administrative inefficiency and lack of coordination in various regulatory programs as they affect housing costs, rather than the environmental goals at which the regulations are directed.

Congress has responded to the need for regional planning and has increasingly required comprehensive planning at the regional level in a variety of land-development and capital-facility programs. It has thereby created the need for an adequate state response that can provide an appropriate state-level legislative framework for the federal regional planning programs required.

Extensive regional planning is mandated by such diverse federal legislation as the Federal Air Highway Act and the air and water quality control legislation. Regional transportation planning under the federal highway act, which has now been extended to include planning for public transit,[338] provides the planning basis for state highway projects, and for federal acceptance of state projects in the federal-aid system. This regional planning program, which has been required since 1965, must be carried out in all metropolitan areas of 50,000 or more.

National air- and water-quality legislation has increasingly called for strengthened regional planning to implement national pollution-abatement goals. A regional waste treatment planning process is mandated by the Federal Water Pollution Control Act of 1972 for those metropolitan areas having serious water-quality problems.[339] This planning process is partly intended to provide a basis for the award of federal grants for waste treatment plants, but the metropolitan water-quality planning program also requires the preparation of a regional land-use policy as it relates to water quality. This pro-

337. Cal Pub. Res. Code §§ 21000-174 (West Supp. 1975), *amending id.* §§ 21000-21151 (West 1970); Friends of Mammoth v. Board of Supervisors, 8 Cal. 3d 247, 502 P.2d 1049, 104 Cal. Rptr. 701 (1972).

338. 23 U.S.C. § 134 (1970). *See also* 23 U.S.C. § 142 (1970), *as amended by* 23 U.S.C. § 142 (Supp. 1972).

339. 33 U.S.C. § 1288 (Supp. 1972).

gram includes a requirement for limited regulatory powers to be exercised by a regional agency, which must prevent the location of any new facilities in the region that would violate the plan.[340]

No explicit planning process in the conventional sense is mandated by the Clean Air Act of 1970.[341] The state implementation plans that are required by this legislation are really a specification of state strategies for the attainment and maintenance of national ambient air quality standards through the application of a variety of enforcement techniques, loosely characterized by the Environmental Protection Agency (EPA) as a "control strategy."[342] Nevertheless, the Clean Air Act has been interpreted by the EPA to include a planning component. One of the most important of these planning processes is the extensive regional planning that EPA now requires for the maintenance of air quality once the national air quality standards have been achieved.[343] Extensive land-use planning to implement air-quality maintenance objectives is included in the planning effort, which also contemplates land-use control and other regulatory measures to achieve the planning objectives of air-quality maintenance.[344]

Other federal legislation that effectively mandates a regional planning program is the National Coastal Zone Management Act of 1972.[345] Coastal states and territories receiving federal financial assistance under this legislation must prepare and adopt a coastal zone management program, and this program includes all the elements of a comprehensive planning process, though limited to coastal areas.[346] While the impact of this legislation in any state may be modest if the coastal zone is narrowly drawn, the state coastal zone program will have regional dimensions if the coastal zone is broadly defined to include more than just the narrow shoreline area.

This growing array of planning requirements at the federal level has led to demands that these various federal planning programs be

340. *Id.* § 1288(b)(2)(C)(ii) (Supp. 1972).

341. *See* Mandelker & Rothschild, *The Role of Land-Use Controls in Combatting Air Pollution Under the Clean Air Act of 1970*, 3 Ecology L.Q. 235 (1973).

342. 40 C.F.R. § 51.1(n) (1975). State implementation plans may contain land-use and transportation controls "as may be necessary" to attain and maintain national air quality standards, but there is no planning basis for these controls other than the state implementation plan which is required by the federal law. *See* 42 U.S.C. § 1857c-5(a)(2)(B) (1970).

343. 40 C.F.R. § 51.18 (1971).

344. U.S. Environmental Protection Agency, 3 Guidelines for Air Quality Maintenance Planning and Analysis: Control Strategies (1974).

345. 16 U.S.C. §§ 1451–1464 (Supp. 1972). *See* Mandelker & Sherry, *The National Coastal Zone Management Act of 1972*, 7 Urb. L. Ann. 119 (1974).

346. 16 U.S.C. § 1454 (Supp. 1972).

better coordinated. The need for coordination becomes particularly important because the land-use planning required in the environmental programs emphasizes more limited air and water quality and other environmental goals at the expense of more comprehensive planning objectives. Some rationalization of federal planning requirements may be afforded through the 701 planning assistance program administered by the Department of Housing and Urban Development (HUD), which is available on a voluntary basis to state, regional, and local planning agencies.

Under the Housing and Community Development Act of 1974, recipients of 701 funds are now required to establish an ongoing planning process that will provide for citizen participation and a comprehensive plan that at a minimum includes housing and land-use elements.[347] There exists no other authority in the federal statutes for the integration of planning assistance programs, either under the auspices of HUD or any other federal agency, although the growing use by federal agencies of inter-agency agreements to coordinate related federal planning requirements may provide a voluntary method for achieving better integration of federally required planning programs.[348]

The growing emphasis in federal legislation on mandatory state and regional planning creates serious problems of compliance at the state level. Attention needs to be given to the coordination of federally mandated planning within the states and regions, because many regional areas will often be subject to more than one federal planning requirement. A coastal zone subject to coastal zone planning, for example, also may be subject to the air-quality maintenance planning program of the Clean Air Act.

State and regional planning will occur notwithstanding mandatory state planning legislation, simply because federal law mandates it. But a coordinated network of mandatory state and regional plans may help give coherence to potentially overlapping federal requirements. Problems may also arise in regions that are not subject to any of the federal planning requirements, but whose planning needs to

347. 40 U.S.C. § 461 (b) (Supp. 1974).
348. An example of an agreement of this type is the agreement between HUD and EPA that coordinates water-quality planning with planning done by regional agencies with HUD financial assistance. *See* 40 Fed. Reg. 22302 (1975). The agreement provides, generally, that funds available under the HUD planning assistance program shall be used to provide the basic land-use planning element for both planning programs. *Id.* pt. III. *See also* 24 C.F.R. § 600.72(a), 40 Fed. Reg. 36856, 3682 (1975). This regulation authorizes government agencies receiving HUD comprehensive planning assistance to "develop the land use element [of their plans] in the form which will allow them to meet the requirements of other Federal programs requiring comparable land use elements. . . ."

be coordinated with both regional and federal planning programs elsewhere in the state if a coherent state plan is to be produced. A mandatory network of state and regional plans will also be useful in providing coordination in these situations.

Coordinated Regional and State Action. The existence of a disjointed, multilevel collection of land-use regulations necessitates some form of legislative coordination. The ALI *Model Land Development Code* suggests a joint hearing process for developments requiring multiple permits (which include Development of Regional Impact).[349] To briefly summarize these sections:

1. A state land-planning agency is required to prepare a register of all government permits required prior to development, and to categorize the permits as construction permits, specialized permits, or initial development permits.[350]
2. A developer, if the project requires multiple permits, may seek a joint hearing on all the permits. The hearing officers are designated by the state land-planning agency, and operate in accordance with the procedures required for an administrative hearing.[351]
3. The hearing officers are required to issue a proposed decision, containing findings of fact and conclusions of law subject to corrections by the parties, within two months, to be followed in six weeks by a recommended decision. The decision of the hearing officers is not binding on the various permit agencies, but the agencies must decide on the permits within three months of the recommended decision, allowing the applicant to take corrective action in the case of a denial. Appeals of agency decisions to an appropriate court,[352] or appeal of a land-development agency decision to the state land adjudicatory board is also provided.[353]

It is possible that the attempted expedition of the administrative process could itself be administered in such a way as merely to add another bureaucratic layer. Strict adherence to specified time schedules and good faith on all sides would appear to reduce the likelihood of such a result.

The obvious merits of systematic coordination would suggest that even in states and localities that do not adopt the ALI Code in its

349. ALI Code, *supra* note 6, art. 2, pt. 4.
350. *Id.* at § 2-401.
351. *Id.* at § 2-402, *pursuant* to art. 9.
352. *Id.* at § 7-502.
353. *Id.* at § 2-403.

entirety[354] and may still be left with the traditional local cast of characters, or that stop short of a state land-planning agency, serious efforts should be made to implement some form of coordination. It is conceivable that a similar joint-hearing process could be effected through existing regional agencies that have developed some experience in this area through the A-95 system.

Two states have attempted coordination and expedition of development applications, one along the lines of the ALI Code and the other geared specially to facilitating construction of low- and moderate-income housing. The Washington Environmental Coordination Procedures Act (ECPA)[355] was enacted in 1973 to simplify the process of obtaining state permits. The act operates at the option of the developer, who files a form at the designated county agency. After certification by local government that the project complies with local regulations, the application is sent on to the state's Department of Ecology. For ECPA to apply, a project must require at least one of the types of permits issued by the Department of Ecology, as well as at least one issued by another state agency.

Other agencies notified of the application by the Department of Ecology must indicate their interest in the project within fifteen days or lose their permit authority over the applicant. A consolidated hearing is eventually held in the county where development is to occur. The public is notified, afforded an opportunity to examine the applications, and allowed to participate in the hearing. Each agency participates in the hearing and renders a decision that is submitted to the hearing chairperson. These permit decisions are then forwarded to the applicant, unmodified by the Department of Ecology. Administrative (on the record) and judicial review are available to any person aggrieved by a final decision.[356] The impact of ECPA has yet to be measured due to its brief existence,[357] but the fact that it was adopted at all indicates a legislative recognition of the growing problem.[358]

Another attempt to expedite the development review process is that embodied in the Massachusetts Zoning Appeals Law,[359] a statute

354. *E.g.*, Florida enacted a variant of the ALI model code involving review of developments of regional impacts (Environmental and Water Management Act of 1972, Fla. Stat. Ann. § 380:012-10 [Supp. 1973]), but has not enacted a coordinated review mechanism for developments requiring multiple permits.

355. Wash. Rev. Code, ch. 90.62 (1974 Supp.)

356. *Id.* at § 90.62.070.

357. *See* Corker & Elliott, *The Environmental Coordination Procedures Act of 1973, or ECPA! ECPA! Rah, Rah, Rah!!*, 49 Wash. L. Rev. 463 (1974).

358. Oregon has also recently passed a coordinated permit statute, ch. 677, Or. Laws (1975).

359. Mass. Gen. Laws Ann., ch. 40B, §§ 20-23 (1971).

that has received more attention for its efforts to break down local barriers to low-income housing than for its procedural innovations.[360] Briefly, the act permits a qualified applicant (public agencies as well as nonprofit and limited dividend organizations intending to develop subsidized low- or moderate-income housing) to apply for a comprehensive permit with the local board of zoning appeals. This expedites the process by avoiding the usual separate permits from the building department, health department, planning commission, and so forth. If the permit is denied or is granted with conditions that make the project uneconomic, the applicant may appeal directly to the Massachusetts Housing Appeals Committee.[361]

The appeals committee holds a de novo hearing within 20 days of the receipt of the appeal and is to render a decision within 30 days after the hearing, with continuances by mutual agreement. The criteria for review of the local decision are reasonableness and consistency with local needs, and the committee's decision is subject to judicial review. The constitutionality of the act was upheld by the Supreme Judicial Court of Massachusetts in 1973 in a ruling that held that local home rule is not violated, spot zoning does not occur, and the standards for review are not impermissibly vague.[362]

CONCLUSION

It is, of course, impossible to delineate with precision the optimal amount of administrative discretion necessary for achieving a more effective and rational land-use control process. Flexibility in the administrative process is essential for responding to the rapidity and complexity of societal change. At the same time, a degree of administrative specificity is necessary to prevent abuse. Finally, the proper balance of flexibility and restraint will come only from an open planning process, supported by informed legislative action that offers policy guidance and criteria for fair administrative decision-making.

POLICY STATEMENTS

1. A primary concern in facilitating rational and equitable urban growth is the extent to which the traditional system of land-use con-

360. *See* Chapter 7 *infra*.

361. If the permit is granted, an "aggrieved person" may appeal to the appropriate court.

362. Board of Appeals of Hanover v. Housing Appeals Committee, and Board of Appeals of Concord v. Housing Appeals Committee, 294 N.E.2d 393 (Mass. 1973), discussed in Chapter 7 *infra*.

trols has evolved into a highly discretionary process. While this development has its salutary aspects, particularly in permitting local government to respond to the increased complexities of land-use decisionmaking, it has also strained the fairness and rationality of the regulatory system.

Because of the issues involved in reconciling discretionary action with procedural fairness, Chapter 4 in part concerns the legal distinction between "legislative" and "administrative" or "quasi-judicial" actions. The discussion of these labels, however, should not be emphasized to the point of distraction from the underlying concepts. The issue is one of procedural fairness and predictability that is adaptable to local conditions and capabilities. The use of terms such as cross-examination, fair and impartial tribunal, and the like, need not be interpreted in the same sense as they might be in an attempt to reform the judicial process.

2. A government body, in granting or denying development permission for a specific parcel of land at the request of a particular party, is engaged in an adjudicatory process. As such, the essentials of procedural due process normally expected of administrative bodies—adequate notice, an opportunity to be heard, a fair and impartial tribunal, and findings based on an adequate record—must be met. Furthermore, such local actions, when reviewed by the courts, need not be accorded the traditional presumption of legislative validity.

Traditionally, courts have viewed all amendments to a zoning ordinance as legislative acts, because they are granted by the local legislature. Consequently, such actions have been accorded a presumption of legislative validity. Under this presumption, challenges to the validity of a local action have been required to demonstrate that the decision is arbitrary, capricious, and unreasonable, and that it has no relation to the public health, safety, and welfare—an extremely onerous burden. The Advisory Commission recognizes that the local legislature, in enacting or amending a zoning ordinance applicable to all or a substantial part of a political jurisdiction, is acting in a different role from the one it assumes when making a decision on requests by parties or individuals for particular changes from the general scheme. The latter role is more akin to that of settling disputes, and therefore, to promote greater fairness and avoid the risk of arbitrariness, should be afforded greater due process standards. This approach does not affect text amendments applying to classes of land use or a collection of parcels within an area, comprehensive or planning area rezonings, and adoption of the comprehensive plan (in whole or by area); such actions should retain their "legislative" characterization and be subject to the traditional standards of judicial review. The legislative characterization may continue to be appropriate for individual requests for development permission that have a substantial or disproportionate impact on the community, regardless of the size of the parcel or parcels at issue.

3. State zoning enabling legislation should be amended so as to specify the requirements for administrative review of individual requests for zoning changes or development permission. Such legislation should be responsive to the varying financial capabilities and development activity existing in political jurisdictions of differing sizes, which would affect their ability to implement a sophisticated administrative process. (Small communities, for example, may lack the financial resources or a sufficient level of development activity to justify the changes necessary for such an approach.)

While the shift in attitude toward local land-use actions affecting specific parcels has been initiated largely by the judiciary, more flexible reform in this area could be brought about through legislative change. (*See, e.g.*, the *ALI Model Land Development Code.*)

4. To assure a fair and impartial tribunal for "quasi-judicial" actions, enabling legislation and local rules should be amended to limit pre-hearing or ex parte contacts between the parties to the action and the public officials involved, or to require that such contacts (excepting routine informational discussions with professional staff members) be on the record. This approach reduces the amount of lobbying or informal advocacy that often precedes the formal hearing and casts a shadow over the fairness of the entire proceeding.

5. Judicial review of the grant or denial of individual requests for development permission should proceed on the record established in the hearing below in accordance with general principles of administrative law or as prescribed by statute, unless determined otherwise by the court. This approach seeks to avoid de novo review in such cases. Accordingly, the record established at the hearing would be called up and examined for errors without the court substituting its judgment for that of the lower body. The court could remand the case to the administrative body for a new hearing, additional findings, or other actions in accordance with traditional judicial functions in administrative law. The efforts of the courts would thereby be focused on the record and findings made below, and the importance of fair and rational local government action would be emphasized.

6. The implementation of the procedural changes suggested in this chapter may impose additional administrative burdens on the plan commission, board of appeals, and legislative body. To lessen these administrative burdens, while at the same time assuring a more efficient and professional process, local governments should consider the creation of a hearing examiner system. The hearing examiner would hear and decide cases, subject to appeal to the local governing body, in conventional discretionary matters such as requests for variances, special permits, and subdivision plats. With regard to individual requests for rezonings of specific parcels, they too should be heard by the hearing examiner, with a complete record made of the proceedings. The hearing examiner's recommendations would then be submitted to the governing body, which would make the final decision on the basis of the record established before the examiner.

The hearing examiner provides a mechanism for diverting administrative burdens and leaving the public official with time for the more important tasks of planning, policy formulation, and making final decisions on the record made before the hearing examiner. It must be recognized that instituting a hearing examiner system will involve public costs and probably would be best justified in areas undergoing substantial development activity.

7. State enabling legislation should be amended to assure that "flexible" land-use controls such as planned unit developments, special permits, overlay zoning, incentive zoning, TDRs, etc., are applied by local governments in such a manner as to be consistent with comprehensive planning to encourage housing opportunity for all income groups and to accommodate the procedural safeguards essential to fair administration.

8. Local governments should encourage qualified neighborhood organizations to participate in the decisionmaking process for land-use actions that substantially affect their interests. While actual delegation of decisionmaking authority to neighborhood organizations remains fraught with problems, a systematic means of bringing neighborhoods into the land-use control process is essential. Methods already exist for establishing the boundaries of neighborhoods and the credentials of representative organizations. Further efforts should be made to determine matters that are appropriate for neighborhood review, as well as the extent to which the outcome of that review should affect a final decision.

9. Where multiple administrative reviews of land development applications are required at the local, regional, or state level, a con-

solidated administrative process should be substituted for separate agency reviews, provided consolidation neither diminishes the opportunity of the governing body to give adequate consideration to the matters at hand nor unnecessarily hampers the applicant in obtaining a fair and expeditious hearing.

The existence of a complex array of administrative hurdles for development proposals and the difficulty of coordinating intergovernmental actions creates additional problems in assuring a fair and rational process. In consolidating or expediting multiple administrative reviews, the addition of yet another layer of hurdles or potential delay should be carefully avoided, as should any change that further shields a project from effective public scrutiny.

✳ *Chapter 5*

The Role of the Local Comprehensive Plan in Land-Use Regulation

INTRODUCTION

Since the turn of the century, American municipalities have been actively engaged in the preparation of comprehensive or master plans to guide their growth and development.[1] However, fluctuating demographic patterns, changing economic conditions, shifting views of governmental responsibility, the development of more sophisticated planning theory, and the emergence of new problems peculiar to maturing cities and regions have all contributed to the continuous redefinition of comprehensive planning.[2]

Beginning with the City Beautiful movement of the late nineteenth century, comprehensive planning was perceived as a critical policy-making process that would assist American communities in providing the pleasant, livable, and well-ordered urban environment that was regarded as one of their major responsibilities. But early planning practice did not fully meet this challenge. It dealt with a limited range of policy issues, concentrating on planning for the provision of

1. For a history of American city planning, *see generally* J. Reps, The Making of Urban America: A History of City Planning in the United States (1965).
2. For a thorough review of the evolution of the planning profession in the United States, *see* M. Scott, American City Planning (1969). General theoretical works have been published that attempt to explicate the linkages between societal change and the evolution of planning practice. *See esp.* D. Schon, Beyond the Stable State (1971); J. Friedmann, Retracking America (1973); Michaels, Learning to Plan—Planning to Learn (1974); D. Godschalk (ed.), Planning for America: Learning from Turbulence (1974).

public facilities and the arrangement of land uses in relation to these facilities. This narrow perspective was reflected in early state legislation that provided a limited framework for the planning process, and in generally conservative court opinions that did not immediately concede a significant role in land-use control administration to the policies of comprehensive plans.

Changing social priorities have now introduced an urgency in local comprehensive planning programs not evident in this early period. Growing public concern with the provision of lower income housing, environmental protection, and growth management have provided new dimensions to comprehensive planning. These concerns are increasingly reflected in federal legislation mandating comprehensive planning in federal grant-in-aid and environmental programs, in state legislation mandating comprehensive planning at the local government level, and in a tendency on the part of the courts to assign a more important role to the comprehensive plan.

This chapter deals with the emerging role of the comprehensive plan in the local land-use control process. Traditional judicial and theoretical views of the role of the comprehensive plan as a guide to zoning administration are examined first. The limitations of these viewpoints are then assessed, as are changes in land-use control techniques and the state of the art in comprehensive planning that necessitate a mandatory planning process. Changes in judicial attitude toward the role of the comprehensive plan in land-use control administration are examined next, along with enacted and proposed state and federal legislation that mandates comprehensive planning.

This emerging role of the comprehensive plan as a policy guide to land-development controls is then evaluated, both as a substantive policy guide for local housing, environmental, and growth management decisions, and for courts asked to pass on the validity of local zoning regulations and changes. Also explored are issues about the impact of mandatory planning on local land-use controls, including the questions of what planning elements are essential to the mandatory planning process, how they should be expressed in statutory form, how the mandatory planning requirement should be legally enforced, and what level of state review of local comprehensive plans is appropriate. The reader is referred to the Appendix at the end of this chapter, which surveys the existing state of the art in comprehensive planning with a view toward identifying the capability of local governments to undertake mandatory planning and some of the difficulties inherent in that process.

THE TRADITIONAL VIEW OF THE COMPREHENSIVE PLAN AS A GUIDE TO LOCAL ZONING CONTROLS

Early Developments in Planning and Zoning

In his bibliographic essay supplementing T. J. Kent's classic work on comprehensive planning, *The Urban General Plan,* Holway Jones suggests that "to appreciate the significance of the general plan concept one must first become acquainted with the broad sweep of town and city development in the United States."[3] He offers an extensive review of city planning "progress" in the 1800s that culminates with the publication of the *Plan for Chicago* prepared by Daniel Burnham and Edward Bennett in 1909.[4] Jones points out that while Burnham's plan was an advanced view for the time, it was not in any sense a comprehensive plan by modern standards.[5] It was not until three or four years later that Frederick Law Olmsted, Jr., one of the foremost landscape architects of the twentieth century, articulated a more modern concept of the comprehensive plan:

> The city plan is a document intended to assist in making possible the intelligent control and guidance of the entire physical growth and alteration of cities. It should embrace all the problems of relieving and avoiding congestion as well as providing a forecast of the probable future requirements of land for collective uses and, finally, it is a device or piece of administrative machinery for preparing and keeping constantly up-to-date a unified forecast and definition of all the important changes, additions, and extensions of the physical equipment and arrangement of the city which a sound judgment holds likely to become desirable and practicable in the course of time.[6]

Two other men, Edward Bassett and Alfred Bettman, through their writings and their involvement in civic affairs in New York

3. Jones, *A Bibliographic Essay on the Urban General Plan (originally A Bibliographic Essay on the Evolution of an Idea),* Part III, The General Plan in the Urban Planning Process 22–40 (Exchange Bibliography No. 21; Oakland: Council of Planning Libraries, July 1962). Page numbers refer to the version printed in T.J. Kent, Jr., The Urban General Plan (1964).

4. Burnham & Bennett, Plan of Chicago Proposed During the Years MCMVI, MCMVII and MCMVIII (Charles Moore ed. 1909), *cited in* Jones, *supra* note 3, at 177.

5. Jones, *supra* note 3, at 197.

6. Olmsted, Jr., *Reply in Behalf of the City Planning Conference,* in Proceedings of the Third National Conference on City Planning (Philadelphia, May 15-17, 1911). *See also A City Planning Program,* in Proceedings of the Fifth National Conference on City Planning 1-16 (Chicago, May 5-7, 1913).

and Cincinnati, helped to shape the early concept of comprehensive planning.[7] Along with Olmsted, they were appointed in the early 1920s by Secretary of Commerce Herbert Hoover to the nine-man Advisory Committee on City Planning and Zoning. This advisory committee to the Department of Commerce promulgated in 1922 the Standard State Zoning Enabling Act (SZEA),[8] and then, in 1928, the Standard City Planning Enabling Act (SPEA).[9] These model statutes were widely adopted, and even today provide the statutory basis for local planning and zoning in a large majority of states.

When appraising the influences of these model laws, especially on the judicial interpretation of the role of comprehensive planning, it is important to realize that the SZEA was proposed first. The SZEA addressed planning only in terms of an enigmatic statement that "zoning shall be in accordance with a comprehensive plan."[10] It is this language that has provided the legal pivot for judicial interpretation of the comprehensive plan requirement in zoning administration.

While the "in accordance" language, literally applied, might be construed as imposing a requirement that zoning ordinances be consistent with a comprehensive plan that is independently prepared and adopted in addition to the zoning ordinance, notes appended to the SZEA and other legislative history (including, of course, the untidy historical facts that the SZEA was published several years prior to its statutory planning counterpart, and even then planning was only made optional) weigh against this interpretation. As the notes state, "This [the 'in accordance' requirement] will prevent haphazard and piecemeal zoning. No zoning should be done without such a comprehensive study."[11] As will be noted more fully later, most courts have

7. Bassett, *Recent New York Legislation for the Planning of Unbuilt Areas, Comprising the Text of the City and Village Planning Laws of the State of New York, a Description of Their Origin and Purposes, and Suggestions as to How They Should Be Administered*, in Regional Plan of New York and Its Environs (Bull. No. 11 1926); Bettman, *The Relationship of the Functions and Powers of the City Planning Commission to the Legislative, Executive and Administrative Departments of City Governments*, in Planning Problems of Town, City, and Region: Papers and Discussions at the Twentieth National Conference on City Planning 142–59 (Dallas and Fort Worth, Texas, May 7–10, 1929). *See also City Planning Legislation*, in City Planning: A Series of Papers Presenting the Essential Elements of a City Plan 431–71 (J. Nolen ed. 1929).

8. U.S. Department of Commerce, A Standard State Zoning Enabling Act (revised ed. 1926), *reprinted in* H. Rathkopf, The Law of Planning and Zoning 100–101 (1956) [hereinafter cited as SZEA].

9. U.S. Department of Commerce, A Standard City Planning Enabling Act (rev. ed. 1928), *reprinted in* E. Roberts, Land Use Planning 3–15 (1971) [hereinafter cited as SPEA].

10. SZEA, *supra* note 8, § 3.

11. *Id.* at n.22.

accepted the "comprehensive study" as an alternative to a true comprehensive plan in satisfaction of the statutory requirement.

Language in the model planning act that defines the content and role of the comprehensive plan throws further light on the legal effect of the plan. The SPEA defined the purpose of the master plan as

> [g]uiding and accomplishing a coordinated, adjusted, and harmonious development of the municipality and its environs which will, in accordance with present and future needs, best promote health, safety, order, morals, convenience, prosperity, and general welfare as well as efficiency and economy in the process of development, including, among other things, adequate provision for traffic, the provision of safety from fire and other dangers, adequate provision for light and air, the promotion of good civic design, wise and efficient expenditure of public funds, and the adequate provision of public utilities and other public requirements.[12]

The model law must be evaluated in the light of the progress that the planning movement had made at the time the law was drafted.

Careful historical research has verified the early concentration of city planning on local capital improvement programs. This influence, which can be explained in part by the important role that the civil engineering profession then exerted in the planning profession, is reflected in the model law's provisions governing the content of the plan.[13] These provisions can usefully be divided into two parts. The first part required the plan to include recommendations for the "development" of the "territory" covered by the plan, and, while not meant to be exclusive, the elements to be included to satisfy this requirement relate exclusively to recommendations for public capital facilities, streets, and open spaces.

A second provision required a "zoning plan," which is not defined, except that it is clear that the zoning plan is to cover land uses. Explanatory notes to the act contain contradictory statements about the form of the zoning plan, and do not clarify the confusion over the relationship of the zoning plan to the general comprehensive plan,

---

12. SPEA, *supra* note 9, at § 7.

13. *See id.* at § 6. These provisions were offered even though the draftsmen of the SPEA also state in a footnote to the act that no definition of the plan was thought necessary. Kent, *supra* note 3, at 44. However, the draftsmen were apparently divided on this point. *Id.* at 45. Note also that the section of the SPEA expressing the purposes of the plan does not limit these purposes to planning for public facilities. SPEA, *supra* at § 7. Kent does not make the distinction made in the text between public facilities and land-use planning, but this differentiation is clear from the provisions of the act.

which the law also authorizes.[14] There is a distinct impression, however, that the zoning plan is a document separate and apart from the comprehensive plan covering public facilities.

The commentary suggests that if an independently prepared plan was required by the statutory "in accordance" language, it was fulfilled by the SPEA's provision for a zoning plan and not by the plan that was defined to cover public facilities. Again, it should be noted that the model law did not make the comprehensive plan mandatory. Preparation and adoption of a comprehensive plan was optional with local governments, a preference carried forward in the state legislation that adopted the model law, and one that still prevails (with few exceptions) today.

Other features of the SPEA also suggest that a reference to the comprehensive plan as then understood was not intended by the "in accordance" language. Consistent with the act's apparent distinction between a zoning plan and a plan covering public facilities, the comprehensive plan is given legal effect only as it relates to the construction of these facilities. Its status is advisory. As the SPEA provides,[15] no public facility construction may be carried out until it is first reviewed by the planning commission, and even then planning commission disapproval can be overridden by a two-thirds vote of the entire membership of the governing body.

One exception to the advisory status of the comprehensive plan appears in the subdivision-control enabling legislation, which is in the SPEA and not the SZEA. This legislation requires the adoption of a "major street plan" as a condition to the adoption of local subdivision-control regulations.[16] While a major street plan is thus made a mandatory element of the subdivision regulation process, the street plan that is contemplated is clearly an element of the comprehensive plan covering public facilities, and not part of the zoning plan that was also contemplated by the SPEA.[17]

14. *Compare* SPEA, *supra* note 9, at n.38, *with id.* at n.41. Moreover, *see* Kent, *supra* note 3, at 38:

> In the first footnote the authors state flatly that the zoning plan is to be included as an integral part of the general plan; and in the second, third, and fourth footnotes, they contradict themselves and state that the general plan must remain general . . . and that zoning is simply one method of carrying out the general policies dealing with private property.

15. SPEA, *supra* note 9, at § 9.

16. *Id.* at § 13.

17. State legislation has not always followed the SPEA on this point. *See generally* R. Yearwood, Land Subdivision Regulation: Policy and Legal Considerations for Urban Planning (1971); Nelson, *The Master Plan and Subdivision Control,* 16 Me. L. Rev. 107 (1964).

Evolution of the Comprehensive Plan Concept

Following the promulgation of the SZEA and SPEA by the U.S. Department of Commerce, the model acts were widely enacted. They provided the basic framework for zoning and planning for the next fifty years. Theoretical debate continued, however, over the purposes of the master plan and its contents,[18] and also over the role of city planning boards in municipal government.[19] This debate was forced to yield for a time by the serious redevelopment problems faced by communities after World War II. The need to confront the panoply of ills caused by urban slums resulted in the enactment of the National Housing Act of 1949, which provided substantial federal subsidies for land acquisition and slum clearance.[20] The urban renewal program created by that act, and subsequently modified by the Housing Act of 1954, required that slum clearance projects conform to a plan, and that the project plan itself "conform to a general plan for the development of the locality as a whole."[21]

The conceptual problem of defining the plan continued, now influenced to a considerable extent by the federal requirements. Moreover, the question of whether a plan should be a fluid process or a static, end-state document now became an issue. The regulations for implementing the urban renewal program tended to stress a more fluid process. By allowing a community to defer "completion of the general plan until the submission of the final project plan, the federal agency allowed the content of the general plan to be influenced by ad hoc redevelopment decisions."[22]

At about this same time, two important articles by Professor Charles Haar viewed the statutory comprehensive plan as "an impermanent constitution"[23] and therefore as a separate document for purposes of zoning "in accordance with a comprehensive plan."[24] In light of the lack of specific authority in the SZEA, Haar recognized that his posi-

18. E. Bassett, The Master Plan: With a Discussion of the Theory of Community Land Planning Legislation (1938).

19. R. Walker, The Planning Function in Urban Government (1949). In response, *see* Tugwell & Fanfield, *The Planning Function Reappraised*, 17 J.A.I.P. 46–49 (1951); Howard, *In Defense of Planning Commissions*, 17 J.A.I.P. 87–94 (1951).

20. *See* Housing Act of 1949, 63 Stat. 414 (1949), *as amended by* Housing Act of 1954, 68 Stat. 662 (1954); 42 U.S.C. §§ 1451–60 (1958).

21. 42 U.S.C. § 1455(a)(iii), *cited in* Mandelker, *The Comprehensive Planning Requirement in Urban Renewal*, 116 U. Pa. L. Rev. 25–26 (1967).

22. Mandelker, *supra* note 21, at 43.

23. Haar, *The Master Plan: An Impermanent Constitution*, 20 Law & Contemp. Probs. 353, 356–61 (1955).

24. Haar, *In Accordance with a Comprehensive Plan*, 68 Harv. L. Rev. 1154 (1955).

tion was in the minority.[25] But today there is a demonstrable shift toward his point of view. The extent of this shift in the courts is the subject of an extensive discussion later in this chapter. It is ironic that while Haar's writing was widely quoted, and relied upon in a number of land-use decisions, he was frequently cited to support the "unitary" view of the statutory requirement (that is, the zoning ordinance itself suffices as the comprehensive plan), a position he attacked in his own writing.[26]

Two central questions characterized subsequent scholarly discussion of the plan concept: (1) Should planning be centered primarily on physical development? (2) Should planning be concerned primarily with desired long-term end-states or with shorter term programs of governmental intervention?[27] The traditional planning process seeks to predict physical needs and maximize economic efficiency, maximize relationships between land uses and physical structures, allocate land resources, and provide a pleasing urban design.[28] This traditional approach to planning has frequently been criticized, often on grounds that comprehensive plans sometimes carry planners' biases about physical developments that are not shared by the general public.[29] Moreover, the view of cities as physical structures rather than total systems may be overly simplistic in ignoring the influences of powerful forces outside the direct control of local government, such as market forces, national economic policy, and so forth.[30]

As criticism of comprehensive planning continued, the practitioners held on to the physical approach to planning, encouraged by increased support from the federal government for urban renewal and funds made available through the section 701 comprehensive planning program.[31] A basic four-step approach to planning held fast:

25. *Id.* at 1157.

26. Sullivan & Kressel, *Twenty Years After—Renewed Significance of the Comprehensive Plan Requirement,* 9 Urb. L. Ann. 33, 40 (1975); and Haar, *supra* note 24, at 1157.

27. Portions of the following discussion of the plan concept have been drawn from the commentary to Article 3 of the American Law Institute's Model Land Development Code (adopted May 21, 1975) (1976). Specific sections of the code are discussed at several points later in this chapter. [Hereinafter cited as ALI Code.]

28. *See* Mocine, *Urban Physical Planning and the New Planning,* 32 J.A.I.P. 234 (1966).

29. *See* Wheaton, *Operations Research for Metropolitan Planning,* 29 J.A.I.P. 250 (1963).

30. *See* Webber, *The Roles of Intelligence Systems in Urban-Systems Planning,* 31 J.A.I.P. 289 (1965).

31. Section 701, Housing Act of 1954, P.L. 560, 68 Stat. 590, 640, 40 U.S.C. § 461, *as amended by* § 601, Housing and Urban Development Act of 1968, P.L. 90-488, 82 Stat. 476, 43 U.S.C. § 1441, *and* § 401, Housing and Community Development Act of 1974, P.L. 93-383, 88 Stat. 686, 42 U.S.C. § 5301.

1. *Survey and analysis:* The collection of basic data required for the analysis of physical, social, and economic conditions.
2. *Goal formulation:* The identification of and agreement on social and economic objectives.
3. *Plan making:* The determination of suitable uses and densities for specific areas and for the circulation system and public facilities.
4. *Plan implementation:* The legal and administrative activities and tools required to carry out the plan and coordinate decisions.[32]

T.J. Kent's formulation of the general plan process and the official plan-document reinforced this general approach.[33] Regarding the relationship of the plan to governmental procedures, Kent suggested that plans should be in a form suitable for public debate, should be available and understandable to the public, should be identified as the city council's, should be designed to capitalize on their educational potential, and should be amendable. Kent further suggested that the subject matter of the general plan should focus on physical development; that the plan should be long-range, comprehensive, and general; and that it should clearly relate major physical-design proposals to the basic policies of the plan.

Another commentator defined these terms as follows:

Comprehensiveness means that the plan encompasses all geographical parts of the community and all functional elements which bear on physical development. General means that the plan summarizes policies and proposals and does not indicate specific locations or detailed regulations. Long-range means that the plan looks beyond the foreground of pressing current issues in the perspective of problems and possibilities 20 to 30 years in the future.[34]

The concept of comprehensiveness, however, was itself a matter of controversy, as expressed in the following statement of Professor Alan Altshuler:

Comprehensive planning requires of planners that they understand the overall goals of their communities. Truly comprehensive goals tend, however, to be too general to provide a basis for evaluating concrete alternatives. Consequently, it is difficult to build political interest in them, and politicians are rarely willing to let general and long-range goal statements guide their considerations of the lower-level alternatives. Many planners have themselves abandoned the comprehensive planning ideal in favor of the ideal of middle-range planning. Middle-range planners pursue opera-

32. W. Goodman & J. Kaufman, City Planning in the Sixties, *cited in* C. Haar, Land Use Planning 65 (1971).
33. T.J. Kent, Jr., The Urban General Plan 90–181 (1964).
34. Black, *The Comprehensive Plan*, Principles and Practice of Urban Planning 349 (W. Goodman & E. Freund eds. 1968).

tional though still relatively general goals. The middle-range planning ideal has much to recommend it. It provides no basis, however, for planners to claim to understand overall community goals.[35]

In response to Altshuler, John Friedmann argued that the notion of comprehensiveness did not necessarily refer "primarily to a special knowledge of the public interest." Friedmann suggested that "comprehensiveness in city planning refers primarily to an awareness that the city is a system of inter-related socio and economic variables extending over space." He continued:

> To uphold the principle of comprehensiveness, therefore, it is sufficient to say first, that functional programs must be consonant with the city-wide system of relationships; second, that the costs and benefits of these programs must be calculated on the broadest possible basis; and third, that all "relevant" variables must be considered in the design of individual programs. It follows that comprehensiveness is not a special feature of the planner's mind, a mind trained to a holistic view, but must be achieved by a process that will maximize the specialized contributions of the technical experts to the solution of urban problems.[36]

The concept of comprehensiveness brings up the second major issue in the planning debate—the question of a long-term plan, one that forecasts a picture of the community as it will look twenty to thirty years in the future, versus a short-term plan. The principal questions raised about such end-state plans involve several factors:

1. Difficulty in foreseeing changes in technology, economic conditions, social movements, and the like.
2. Failure to account for the social and economic impact of the physical design.
3. Inability to deal effectively with the implementation of plan objectives.
4. Difficulty in proceeding from the general to the particular, and of stating significant general objectives in the first place.[37]

These factors led some planning theorists toward the middle-range approach referred to above.[38] This form of planning focuses on con-

35. Altshuler, *The Goals of Comprehensive Planning*, 31 J.A.I.P. 186 (1965).
36. Friedman, *A Response to Altshuler: Comprehensive Planning as a Process*, 31 J.A.I.P. 195 (1965).
37. ALI Code, *supra* note 27, at 88–89.
38. *See, e.g.*, Meyerson, *Building the Middle-Range Bridge for Comprehensive Planning*, 22 J.A.I.P. 58 (1956); Webber, *Prospects for Policies Planning*, in The Urban Condition 319 (L. Duhl ed. 1963); Robinson, *Beyond the Middle-Range Planning Bridge*, 31 J.A.I.P. 304 (1964); Mitchell, *The New Frontier in Metropolitan Planning*, 27 J.A.I.P. 169 (1961).

tinuous shorter term programming, market analysis, and middle-range action programs. These more specific plans concentrate on a particular area or a functional element, such as transportation.[39]

Regardless of the labels attached to various planning theories, the significance of the planning debate for this discussion is in the movement away from purely physical, end-state documents, usually a map on which planned uses are matched with zoned uses. The increased emphasis on social and economic factors in urban development and the recognition that specific policies may be more important to legal validity than designations on a map was a major development. Its significance, as we shall see, will increase as states begin to require local comprehensive planning, and as local land-use decisions are required to be consistent with comprehensive plans.[40]

Planning Innovation

As the planning profession moved into its sixth decade, a growing number of professional planners, many of whom were actively involved in the political turmoil of the 1960s, voiced the opinion that the focus of planning should be changed.[41] Concern about the form of plans shifted to concern about the process by which plans were produced. Citizen involvement, an outgrowth of the Community Action Program, Model Cities, and other spinoffs of the Great Society programs, took on special significance. Discontent with the impact of urban renewal, expressway construction, and other physical expressions of planning caused many planners to veer sharply toward "social planning."[42]

The theoretical and practical struggles involved in this effort to redefine the role of planners and planning have led to several innovative approaches. Modification of classic planning theory has taken such diverse forms as: (1) client-oriented or advocacy planning; (2) experimental or learning-oriented planning; (3) capacity-building; (4) critical areas or conservation-oriented planning; (5) nongrowth planning; and (6) policy planning. Each represents an effort to respond to the criticism leveled against planning in the sixties, and perhaps more significantly, each represents a partial accommodation of the shifting institutional and political environment within which planning occurs in the United States. Each will be dealt with in more detail here.

1. *Client-oriented or advocacy planning* assumes that there are different client groups with unique perspectives on the objectives of

39. *See* Webber, *supra* note 30.
40. *See* discussion in text following note 99 *infra*.
41. *See* R. Goodman, After the Planners (1970); and H. Gans, People and Plans (1969).
42. Frieden, *Toward Equality of Urban Opportunity*, 31 J.A.I.P. (1965).

municipal planning. Paul Davidoff, Lisa Peattie, and others[43] suggested that the public interest is not something that can be determined by "rational-technical means." They argued that in a pluralistic society, "decision-making is a political activity" and that any group that wants its interests served has to fight to be heard. They suggested that powerless and inarticulate segments of society therefore needed "their own planners" to help them generate "alternative plans." On the assumption that the typical city planning department or commission was primarily responsive to powerful vested interests, and not accountable to the wishes of the poor and minorities, the advocate planners offered their services to minority and low-income groups in inner-city communities.

This advocacy planning concept grows out of the perpetual tension within the profession between personal convictions and the supposedly value-free objectivity of professional practice. Davidoff concluded that they can never be separated, and that very few (if any) public issues are wholly free of value choices, to be settled on objective technical grounds alone. It was also argued that while alternative plans have frequently been prepared, they have been overly technical and have never really offered valid alternatives to client groups with markedly different value orientations.[44]

One of the practical difficulties with advocacy planning is that the client groups are often unable to finance the service. Where local government, with its own or federal funds, has paid for advocate planners and assigned them to neighborhood groups, the planners have sometimes found themselves in situations of conflicting loyalty. It has been suggested that the advocate planner could become merely another illusion of power and participation, while the ultimate power still resides outside the neighborhood. Yet it is fair to say that the advocacy approach did focus attention on the shortcomings of a centralized planning system, and may well have been the germ for the frequently heard suggestion that planning commissions and their staffs function primarily as advocates before the local governing body, just as do neighborhood groups, developers, and other parties in the land-use control process.

2. *Experimental or learning-oriented planning* is perhaps a somewhat loose term to describe relatively new strands of planning theory. These focus on small-scale social experiments aimed at enhancing our

43. Davidoff, *Advocacy and Pluralism in Planning*, 31 J.A.I.P. (1965); Lisa Peattie, *Reflections on Advocacy Planning*, 34 J.A.I.P. 80 (1969).

44. Bolan, *Emerging Views of Planning*, 33 J.A.I.P. 234 (1967); E. Blecher, Advocacy Planning for Urban Development (1971); *see also* Davidoff, *supra* note 43.

ability to understand how the complex systems that make up a city actually operate.[45] Small-scale demonstrations or experiments will eventually lead, it is assumed, to a better understanding of the process of organizational learning, and thus increase the planners' ability to make better means-ends judgments. Coupled with this effort is an attempt to become more self-conscious about the theories of practice that planners use.[46]

3. *Capacity-building* is a citizen participation oriented approach to planning.[47] It is a culmination of efforts to find more effective ways of legitimizing the planning process through widespread public involvement in setting community goals. Capacity-building involves citizen-based planning built around sophisticated samplings of public opinion, media-oriented public educational efforts, and extensive training activities designed to create citizen planning organizations that can institutionalize public involvement in municipal policy reformulation and plan-making on a community-wide basis.

4. *Critical areas or conservation-oriented planning* is a spin-off of current interest in environmental control. Inner-city planners have adopted neighborhood stabilization as an overriding objective, with a concomitant focus on housing rehabilitation and conservation in declining neighborhoods. Instead of massive downtown renewal schemes, we see a new focus on neighborhood-oriented efforts to save and improve the existing housing stock.[48] Its suburban counterpart places a special emphasis on the protection of critically sensitive ecological resources, such as inland wetlands, coastal wetlands, water resources, and fragile wildlife preserves. Whether this approach represents a lasting redefinition of planning remains to be seen.

5. *Nongrowth planning* was also triggered by the advent of the environmental movement and general concern about growth. The assumption has always been that planning must accommodate unlimited future development. Nongrowth and slow-growth strategies have recently found their way, however, into the jargon of the planning profession:

> There is a basic feeling among some planners that almost any amount of growth can be handled, given the proper planning influence and controls. . . .

45. J. Friedmann, Retracking America (1973); Michaels, Planning to Learn—Learning to Plan (1974); C. Argyris & D. Schon, Theory in Practice: Increasing Professional Effectiveness (1975).

46. C. Argyris & D. Schon, Theory in Practice (1975).

47. J. Wollenberg et al., Capacity Building: A New Approach to Citizen Participation (1975).

48. Agelasto & Phillips, *Housing and Central Cities: The Conservation Approach*, 4 Ecology L.Q. 797 (1975).

But given the theoretical ability of planning to couple with growth, even the most objective observers would be hard pressed to explain some of the major environmental and social problems which have developed in some communities, such as those in California, which had professional planners on hand during most if not all of their history.[49]

The growth management movement and the concomitant interest in new land-use control techniques and environmental impact analysis may be a passing fancy if current economic conditions do not improve; or it may represent an important, permanent shift in planning thought with profound implications for municipal planning practice.

6. *Policy planning* is another innovation, which combines both process and substance.[50] While the concept evades precise definition (since selected policies and their format will vary from community to community), it seems to reflect a growing effort to respond to the complexity of the urban environment and to a recognition of the limits of physical determinism. Instead of emphasizing the physical, mappable elements of a comprehensive plan, an attempt is made to turn goals and objectives into specific policies that reflect the collective planning judgment of the community. Policy planning can then be a continuous, responsive process.

In regard to the primary concerns of this chapter—mandatory local planning and consistency between plans and local land-use actions—policy planning makes it possible for local governments to adapt planning requirements to local needs. The consistency required between local land-use decisions and policy plans, furthermore, can be more flexibly interpreted by local governments or the courts than a zoning classification and designated use in a mapped land-use plan. This approach recognizes the reality of the shift to flexible, discretionary land-use controls, but also places a greater emphasis on fairness and rationality in the process.

These innovations have had varying impacts on the practice of comprehensive planning. While theoretical disputes may flare in the journals and universities, the practice of planning changes very slowly. In fact, the definitions contained in federal regulations and programmatic guidelines may have more impact on the nature of planning practice than anything the academics or theorists might have to say. (These considerations underlie the survey of current planning under-

49. Finkler, *Non-Growth as a Planning Alternative: A preliminary Examination of an Emerging Issue,* in 1 Management and Control of Growth 118 (Urban Land Institute 1975).
50. Webber, *supra* note 38.

taken for this report, the results of which appear in Appendix B at the end of this book.)

TRENDS IN JUDICIAL ATTITUDES TOWARD THE COMPREHENSIVE PLAN

The Nature and Importance of Planning Practice to Judicial Acceptance of Planning

As both the theory and practice of planning continue to evolve, often at different rates and with varying degrees of congruence, it is apparent that the courts will play a significant role in interpreting these developments. At the same time that courts are asked to apply plans to specific projects through zoning decisions, they may also be required to interpret certain aspects of the plans themselves (such as housing elements) that involve the complex interweaving of social, economic, and political concerns of the community. The first section of this chapter attempted to provide some theoretical background for the planning process; the following sections explore some of the ways in which courts have approached the planning problem.

As the courts and legislatures give increasing recognition to the role of the comprehensive plan in the administration of land-use controls, they must also be sensitive to changes that have occurred in planning practice. As discussed above, comprehensive plans historically have included land-use maps that projected a rigid, end-state plan to which the community is to conform by the end of the planning period. These mapped, end-state plans have been criticized as an overly rigid and limited technique for the statement of community planning goals. In many communities they have been replaced by more flexible policy plans that de-emphasize mapping in favor of policy statements that textually stipulate the community's planning policies.

Policy planning, in addition to dropping the conventional emphasis on mapping land-development alternatives, has also moved to a closer relationship with the political process. In doing so the plan's function of projecting optimal land-development strategies has been diminished, and has been restricted to interpreting the planning consequences of alternative strategies for policy-makers, such as local governing bodies, which can then choose among these alternatives on the basis of the analysis presented.[51]

51. An example of this coordinated form of policy planning can be found in the General Plan Revision Program of Honolulu. City and County of Honolulu, Planning for Oahu: An Evaluation of Alternative Residential Policies (1974). The plan discusses four alternative growth strategies for the island of Oahu, on

The degree of precision that plans introduce in the land-use control process has been reduced, just as the substantial expansion of the range of planning policies covered by the plan has complicated the making of choices in the planning process. To some extent the precision with which the plan can describe future planning alternatives (whether textually stated or provided in mapped form) will depend on the nature and size of the jurisdiction that prepares the plan. In local governments of limited size, the alternatives available may also be limited, and any plan that is produced will need to make fairly precise choices no matter what form it takes in practice.

As the size of the jurisdiction increases, available alternatives may often expand at the same time the ability to predict future alternatives diminishes, due to an increase in the number of available options and the chance that future developments and trends will alter the original projections. For this reason, plans produced at regional and state levels are less able to definitively structure developmental alternatives, at the same time that firm planning guidance is required from the regional state planning perspective so that potentially restrictive and exclusionary local policies can be prevented.

Specificity will have to be achieved in policy planning by more flexible use of the mapping process, especially when policy plans cover large jurisdictional areas. These more flexible procedures contemplate the use of more specific mapped plans to indicate planning policies for planning sub-areas, such as intensive commercial areas, or designated residential sub-areas in an urbanizing county.[52] More detailed plans are adapted sequentially whenever they are needed to meet the demand for more detailed planning throughout the local

which the city-county is located. While it favors one of these as the preferred strategy, it is devoted primarily to an analysis of the government programs that would be needed to make each alternative effective. The plan also explores the impact that each strategy will have on such variables as housing, the protection of agricultural and environmental resources, and transportation systems.

52. A mapping system of this type has been adopted in Montgomery County, which is adjacent to the northern border of Washington, D.C. Montgomery County Planning Board, Planning, Zoning, and Subdivision in Montgomery County, Maryland 4–11 (1973). This mapping system is explained as follows:

> The General Plan indicates in broad terms those areas suitable for residential purposes, business or industry, agriculture, open space, transportation, recreation and community facilities. More detailed and specific land use recommendations are contained in local Area Master Plans, which deal with smaller portions of the County. Even more detailed guidelines may be put forth in Sector Plans, which cover particular localities such as Central Business Districts or areas in the immediate vicinity of a rapid transit station. An adopted Area Master Plan or Sector Plan is incorporated as an amendment to the General Plan.

Id. at 5.

jurisdiction. In this situation courts can rely on the more detailed sub-area plans in the consideration of land-use controls adopted to implement the planning process.

These changes in the nature of the planning process affect its role in the judicial review of specific land-use control actions, as well as legislative decisions on what kind of plan and planning process to require. While legislation can quite properly provide a series of planning options, leaving the decision on the form and purpose of the plan to the planning agency, courts will have to be sensitive to the changing function of plans as they depart from their traditional mapped form. Policy plans are not entirely without weight in the land-use controls process, but the weight given to these plans will have to vary with the specificity they can achieve. Most court decisions that have considered the role of the plan in land-use controls have nevertheless dealt with plans that make at least generalized indications of future land-use patterns; in some instances the plans have been sufficiently site-specific so that they controlled the land-use control decision before the court for adjudication.

Early Judicial Attitudes toward the Comprehensive Plan

While scholarly debate attempted to define the comprehensive plan as a concept, the courts were regularly faced with its definition in relation to zoning actions. Two sets of issues face courts that must resolve the statutory meaning of the language contained in the SZEA which requires zoning to be "in accordance" with a comprehensive plan, or, more broadly, determine the relationship between the plan and zoning.

First, the comprehensive plan will distribute development opportunities throughout the community, with the result that some landowners are restricted in the development of their land and some are not, for reasons that relate principally to the policies contained in the plan. Restricted landowners may then attempt to raise due process "taking" objections when the plan's policies are implemented through zoning restrictions that allegedly leave no "reasonable" alternative for the use of their land.

Second, landowners restricted by the plan may also claim that they have been unfairly treated compared to landowners accorded favorable zoning actions that also implement the policies of the plan. This claim attempts to raise equal protection issues, and usually arises in so-called spot zoning cases in which the zoning ordinance has been amended to allow a more intensive use to one landowner while others are not so favored. These landowners may be restricted to less intensive uses at sites not markedly distinguishable from sites at which the spot zoning has been allowed.

These due process and equal protection issues are presented in different litigation settings.[53] A landowner restricted in the use of a parcel of land may raise these issues through declaratory judgment and injunction proceedings in which the validity of the ordinance as applied to the land is considered directly. Since the landowner's suit directly attacks the restrictions that are placed on the site, the court may concentrate on the due process taking issue and ignore the larger community planning policies that underlie the zoning restriction. Spot zoning amendments given to landowners may be attacked by other landowners similarly situated, but standing problems may impede a lawsuit in this instance.[54]

Judicial attacks on spot zones are more frequently brought by neighboring landowners, usually residents of single-family dwellings who object to the intrusion of a more intensive use in their area. In these cases the court focuses on the reasons for the zoning amendment, since the zoning amendment must be justified by policy considerations applicable to the entire community. If equal protection problems are to be overcome, the court is more likely in these cases to rely on the comprehensive plan, if any, as the basis for approving the spot zone. This difference in the judicial approach to lawsuits raising the comprehensive plan as a defense to zoning actions must be kept in mind in the discussion of judicial doctrine affecting the role of the comprehensive plan in the zoning process.

Courts willing to follow comprehensive planning policies in deciding spot zoning disputes have to be convinced that the collective planning judgment adopted prior to the rezoning request can justify the favorable treatment to the landowner who has received the zoning change. On the other hand, the issue may not arise in the same way when the zoning ordinance is under attack from a landowner complaining of overly restrictive regulation of his or her property. In this instance, if the plan is to be given a binding effect, the question is whether the zoning ordinance and the restrictions it contains are a faithful reflection of the plan's policies, and if so, whether the policies of the plan should be respected.

Almost uniformly, the courts at first avoided an approach that would require them to make these judgments, accepting a "unitary" view of the SZEA's "in accordance" language that allowed them to

---

53. *See* D. Mandelker, The Zoning Dilemma 77–84 (1971) [hereinafter cited as Zoning Dilemma].

54. Standing problems in zoning litigation are analyzed in Douglaston Civic Ass'n v. Galvin, 36 N.Y.2d 1, 324 N.E.2d 317, 364 N.Y.S.2d 830 (1974).

find the required comprehensive plan within the text of the zoning ordinance.[55] Perhaps the leading case expressing this unitary view is *Kozesnik v. Montgomery Township,*[56] a New Jersey Supreme Court

55. This history is discussed in Sullivan & Kressel, *Twenty Years After—Renewed Significance of the Comprehensive Plan Requirement,* 9 Urb. L. Ann. 33 (1975). There is a growing literature on the role of the comprehensive plan in land-use controls. An early and widely cited article is Haar, *In Accordance with a Comprehensive Plan,* 68 Harv. L. Rev. 1154 (1955). For additional analysis *see* Haar, *The Master Plan: An Impermanent Constitution,* 20 Law & Contemp. Probs. 353 (1955); Bernard, *The Comprehensive Plan as a Basis for Legal Reform,* 44 J. Urb. L. 611 (1967); Heyman, *Innovative Land Regulation and Comprehensive Planning,* 13 Santa Clara Law. 183 (1972); Player, *The Planning/Land-Use Control Relationship,* 3 Land Use Controls 26 (1969); Tarlock, *Consistency with Adopted Land Use Plans as a Standard of Judicial Review: The Case Against,* 9 Urb. L. Ann. 69 (1975); Note, *Comprehensive Land Use Plans and the Consistency Requirement,* 2 Fla. St. U. L. Rev. 766 (1974); Comment, *Zoning Shall Be Consistent with the General Plan—A Help or a Hindrance to Planning?* 10 San Diego L. Rev. 901 (1973); Note, *Comprehensive Plan Requirement in Zoning,* 12 Syr. L. Rev. 342 (1961). For additional commentary by a land-use planner, *see* Raymond, *How Effective the Master Plan?* 2 J. Environ. Sys. 225 (1972). A general review of policy-making through the planning process is presented in Berry, *The Question of Policy Alternatives,* in The Good Earth of America 155 (C. Harris ed. 1974).

Professor Tarlock's article, *supra,* presents a carefully reasoned case against mandatory planning or the adoption of the requirements that land-use controls be consistent with an adopted plan. His argument has its origins in theories of property rights and property regulation, which prefer privately negotiated means for resolving land-use conflicts. These theories in turn are based on cost-free assumptions about the bargaining and negotiation process—assumptions that many urban economists view as tautological, if not unreal. Interview with Charles L. Leven, Director, Washington University Institute of Urban and Regional Studies, June 15, 1975. On the other hand, equally tautological assumptions—*e.g.,* that public decision-makers possess all needed data and can be expected to make optimal public policy decisions—could be constructed to "support" virtually unrestricted public planning and land-use regulation. Professor Tarlock has also published a fascinating account of an attempt to implement a comprehensive planning policy for shopping center development. Tarlock, *Not in Accordance with a Comprehensive Plan: A Case Study of Regional Shopping Center Conflicts in Lexington, Ky.,* 1970 Urb. L. Ann. 133.

For additional criticisms of the marketplace approach to land development, *see* Costonis, *"Fair" Compensation and the Accommodation Power: Antidotes for the Taking Impasse in Land Use Controversies,* 75 Colum. L. Rev. 1021, 1026-32 (1975); Oxley, *Economic Theory and Urban Planning,* 7 Environ. & Plan. 497 (1975).

56. 24 N.J. 154, 131 A.2d 1 (1957). Other leading cases adopting this view are Furtney v. Zoning Comm'rs, 159 Conn. 585, 271 A.2d 319 (1970); Nottingham Village, Inc. v. Baltimore County, 266 Md. 339, 292 A.2d 680 (1972); Udell v. Haas, 21 N.Y.2d 463, 235 N.E.2d 897, (1968); Ward v. Montgomery Tp. 28 N.J. 529, 147 A.2d 248 (1959); Allred v. City of Raleigh, 7 N.C. App. 602, 173 S.E.2d 533 (1970); Cleaver v. Board of Adjustment, 414 Pa. 367, 200 A.2d 408 (1964); Hadley v. Harold Realty Co., 97 R.I. 403, 198 A.2d 149 (1964); *See* 1 N. Williams, American Land Planning Law 435-38 (1974) [hereinafter cited as Williams].

In Shelton v. City of Bellevue, 73 Wash. 2d 28, 35, 435 P.2d 949 953 (1968) the court stated that a comprehensive zoning regulation may evidence and con-

case. The New Jersey zoning act had adopted the "in accordance" language of the SZEA,[57] and the court in *Kozesnik* dealt with a contention by plaintiffs challenging a zoning amendment that this language required the adoption of a comprehensive plan external to the zoning ordinance. No comprehensive plan had been prepared or adopted by the township. Plaintiffs' contention was rejected by the court.

A central feature of the court's holding was its conclusion, based on the history of planning and zoning legislation in that state, that no comprehensive plan external to the zoning ordinance was required by the "in accordance" language. New Jersey had followed the course of the SZEA legislation and had adopted its zoning act prior to its planning act. This fact of history led the court to conclude that the zoning act did not require a comprehensive plan "in some physical form" outside the zoning ordinance.[58] Relying on early zoning cases, the court also found that the intent of the plan was to prevent a "capricious exercise" of the zoning power, reading into the statute the fairness and reasonableness test imposed on zoning reclassifications by the equal protection requirement.

Without supplying an exact definition of the "in accordance" phrase, the court then noted that "'plan' connotes an integrated product of a rational process and 'comprehensive' requires some-

stitute a comprehensive zoning plan. However, "since [the comprehensive plan] usually proposes rather than disposes, it does not ordinarily, without further regulatory implementation in and by itself, impose any immediate restriction . . . but forms a blueprint for the various regulatory measures it suggests." Later cases have picked up on the "blueprint" theory of *Shelton*, that a comprehensive plan may be relied upon to support regulatory measures adopted in the zoning process. *See* State *ex rel.* Standard Mining & Dev. Corp. v. City of Auburn, 82 Wash. 2d 321, 510 P.2d 647 (1973); Buell v. City of Bremerton, 80 Wash. 2d 518, 495 P.2d 1358 (1972); Gerla v. City of Tacoma, 533 P.2d 416 (1975); Sharninghouse v. City of Bellingham, 4 Wash. App. 198, 480 P.2d 233 (1971); *see also* County Comm'rs v. Edmonds, 240 Md. 680, 215 A.2d 209 (1965) (master plan recommending uses different from those permitted in existing zoning ordinance does not give rise to presumption of change in conditions or mistake sufficient to overcome presumption of correctness accorded original zoning).

Cases taking the traditional unitary view may nonetheless rly on the policies of an adopted comprehensive plan in support of their decision. *See, e.g.,* First Hartford Realty Corp. v. Plan & Zoning Comm'n, 338 A.2d 490 (1973).

57. N.Y. Stat. Ann. § 40:55-32 (1967).

58. However, recently passed New Jersey legislation appears to alter the interpretation of *Kozesnik* by referring to a land-use plan element of a master plan and stating that "all of the provisions of such zoning ordinance or any amendment or revision thereto shall either be substantially consistent with the land use plan element of the master plan or designed to effectuate such plan element." N.J. Pub. Laws 1975, ch. 291, § 49 (1976). This statement is tempered by a following provision, which allows the governing body to disregard the consistency requirement if acting by majority vote and with the reasons stated in the record.

thing beyond a piecemeal approach, both to be revealed by the ordinance considered in relation to the physical facts and the [statutory] purposes."[59] This reading of the "in accordance" language to equate the plan with the zoning ordinance, and the concurrent reading of that language to impose a rational process requirement on the zoning function, was the usual approach courts took toward the statute in this early period.[60]

While not reading the "in accordance" language to require the preparation of a comprehensive plan independent of the zoning ordinance, *Kozesnik* does read the statute to impose a statutorily required "rational process" test if there is to be a successful defense against claims of improperly selective treatment in the zoning amendment process. The court may have been reflecting a concern over the possibly capricious nature of separately approved zoning amendments. Its scaled-down interpretation of the "in accordance" requirement gives it some leverage against the possibility that zoning amendments might be made arbitrarily. Nevertheless, the unitary view can be faulted for having effectively read the comprehensive planning requirement totally out of the SZEA.

Shortly after *Kozesnik* the Pennsylvania Supreme Court took a more deferential, though confusing, approach to the "in accordance" requirement. In *Eves v. Zoning Board of Adjustment of Lower Gwynedd Township*,[61] a text amendment authorizing a floating zone was adopted concurrently with a map change. The township had not adopted a comprehensive plan prior to the enactment of the floating-zone ordinance although it had engaged in some planning studies.[62] In an opinion whose rationale is not clear, the court invali-

---

59. 24 N.J. at 166, 131 A.2d at 7.

60. However, the *Kozesnik* opinion recently has been followed in Oklahoma. Tulas Rock Co. v. Board of County Comm'rs, 531 P.2d 351 (Okla. 1974). It has also been reaffirmed in New Jersey. Bow & Arrow Manor, Inc. v. Town of West Orange, 63 N.J. 335, 307 A.2d 563 (1973).

Crucial to the holding of the *Kozesnik* case was the judicial setting in which it arose. Since the zoning action challenged was an amendment to an existing zoning ordinance, the comprehensive plan requirement was invoked as a necessary prerequisite to zoning action that favored one landowner over others: thus the equal protection setting of the case. While the court read the statute to eliminate an external plan as a condition necessary to the exercise of the zoning power, its formulation of the "in accordance" test did not reach those zoning cases that raise a due process rather than an equal protection issue. Most of the cases following the New Jersey court's reading of the "in accordance" requirement have also arisen in spot zoning cases raising equal protection problems.

61. 401 Pa. 211, 104 A.2d 7 (1960). *Cf.* Sheridan v. Planning Bd., 159 Conn. 1, 19, 266 A.2d 396, 405 (1969).

62. This point is not clear from the opinion, but it is explained in Haar & Hering, *The Lower Gwynedd Township Case: Too Flexible Zoning or an Inflexible Judiciary?* 74 Harv. L. Rev. 1552, 1554–56 (1961).

dated the ordinance as a violation of the "in accordance" requirement, but did not clarify whether the adoption of a separate comprehensive plan was required. Yet elsewhere in the opinion the court also faults the township planning process, which is viewed as rudimentary.[63]

The township was found to have confused "comprehensive planning with a comprehensive plan." The court seemed to suggest that the planning requirement could be met only if the township extensively documented the planning policies that applied to individual developments, in a comprehensive plan that was external to the zoning ordinance. Subsequent decisions[64] by the Pennsylvania courts have eroded the authority of *Eves*, while new Pennsylvania legislation[65] clarifies the relationship between planning and zoning. Nevertheless, *Eves* still indicates how courts might construe the "in accordance" requirement when troubled by zoning techniques, such as floating zones, that arguably permit the exercise of administrative discretion which can lead to arbitrary decisions in individual cases.[66]

Eves also suggests that the *Kozesnik* interpretation of the "in accordance" requirement, which finds the required plan in a rationally considered zoning ordinance, is simply not possible when the district concept is abandoned and heavily discretionary techniques are substituted. Courts may be forced to reexamine the continuing vitality of the *Kozesnik* holding as local zoning practice moves increasingly in the direction of administrative techniques such as floating zones and planned-unit developments (see Chapter 4). An alternative approach is to disapprove the floating zone and similar administrative zoning techniques as unauthorized by the SZEA. While the case law is not fully developed in this area, a growing body of legislation specifically authorizes planned-unit development and similar ad-

63. 401 Pa. at 219, 104 A.2d at 11.

64. Russell v. Penn Tp. Plan. Comm'n, 348 A.2d 499 (1975); Rawm v. Board of Supervisors, 342 A.2d 450 (1975); Marino v. Zoning Hearing Bd., 1 Pa. Commw. Ct. 116, 274 A.2d 221 (1971). *But cf.* Appeal of Key Realty Co., 408 Pa. 98, 182 A.2d 187 (1962). *See also* J. Krasnowiecki, *Part I, The Legal Aspects*, in Legal Aspects of Planned Unit Residential Development II (Urban Law Institute Tech. Bull. No. 52, 1965); Krasnowiecki, *Planned Unit Development: A Challenge to Established Theory and Practice of Land Use Control*, 114 U. Pa. L. Rev. 47, 67–71 (1965).

65. Pa. Stat. Ann. tit. 53, §§ 10101–202, 10606 (1972). *See also* Krasnowiecki, *Zoning Litigation and the New Pennsylvania Procedures*, 120 U. Pa. L. Rev. 1029 (1972).

66. The case of 801 Ave. C, Inc. v. City of Bayonne, 127 N.J. Super. 128, 316 A.2d 694 (App. Div. 1974) invalidated an ordinance that set height and dwelling unit limitations on apartment buildings and then contemplated a variance and planning site approval procedure. The court found this procedure impermissible as allowing ad hoc approvals not based on a comprehensive plan or other permissible and objective zoning criteria.

ministrative controls, and the American Law Institute's *Model Land Development Code* authorizes a wide variety of administrative zoning procedures at the local level.[67]

An important effect of the prevailing adoption of the unitary interpretation of the "in accordance" requirement has been the severe demotion of the comprehensive plan as a guide to local zoning controls. Nevertheless, since the SZEA made the comprehensive plan optional with local governments, this judicial adoption of the unitary view was probably correct insofar as it recognized that many localities did not plan at all. This point was explicitly made with reference to New Jersey municipalities in the *Kozesnik* case. Judicial adoption of the unitary view meant that those municipalities that did plan faced no more restrictions on the exercise of their zoning powers than those municipalities that did not, because an independently adopted plan was not made a necessary legal condition to the local adoption and administration of zoning controls.

Judicial Acceptance of Comprehensive Planning Policies

This section will analyze those cases that have departed from the unitary approach[68] to the "in accordance" requirement, and that have given some weight to the comprehensive plan in land-use litigation. These cases have arisen primarily in zoning litigation, and usually in cases in which the courts have been asked to evaluate map amendments to zoning ordinances for consistency with the comprehensive plan. This type of case has received the closest judicial attention, but the comprehensive plan also functions in other meaningful ways in the land-use control context, and these must not be forgotten. Land-use allocations made through discretionary zoning techniques such as floating zones should be consistent with the policies of the comprehensive plan so that arbitrary decision-making is avoided.

Phased growth under growth management programs should also be ordered by the comprehensive plan so that development opportunities are distributed fairly throughout the growth management area. Land-use controls not dependent on the zoning process can be expected to raise questions about consistency with the plan, and many of these controls will be based on permit-approval systems that implement the plan directly rather than through the mapping of land-use districts in zoning ordinances. Subdivision controls are

67. *See* ALI Code, *supra* note 27, at art. 2.
68. The "unitary approach" equates the plan with the zoning ordinance and map. See discussion in text following note 56 *supra*.

included in this category, as the subdivision control ordinance is applied directly through an approval process.

Permit control systems that are adopted in environmental protec-tion programs may also be related to a plan. For example, the permit system established by the Washington State Shoreline Management Act[69] is explicitly related to the master programs prepared for local shoreline areas that contain stipulated elements of a plan. While de-cisions considering the application of planning policies through per-mit and similar direct approval systems are not yet numerous,[70] it can be expected that the consistency of permit and other direct approvals, with their controlling planning policies, will soon become a significant legal issue.[71]

The underlying issue in all these cases is the presumptive weight to be given to the comprehensive plan in land-use litigation. A com-prehensive plan reflects a collective planning judgment about de-velopmental opportunities throughout the community, and is made prior to a zoning change or lawsuit attacking a zoning restriction.[72] The issue is whether this prior collective judgment should be accorded presumptive weight as it affects land-development proposals allowed by a zoning amendment or that are subjected to litigation in a court challenge to a zoning restriction.

As the following cases will indicate, the courts have resolved this issue in different ways. The Advisory Commission concludes that the effective implementation of mandatory planning requires the courts to give presumptive weight to the policies of the comprehensive plan as they are applied in land-use control administration, unless circum-stances exist that indicate the plan is no longer entitled to this pref-erence. What these circumstances might be will be discussed in the following sections.

Planning as a Defense to Attacks on Land-Use Control Systems. In several cases, the municipality has adopted a comprehensive im-plementation program for planning and land-use controls that in some way restricts landowners in the current or prospective use of their land. These landowners have then sued to overturn the land-use controls of the plan as unconstitutionally restrictive. As a defense

69. *See, e.g.,* Washington Shoreline Management Act, Wash. Rev. Code §§ 90.58.010 (West Supp. 1974); Crooks, *The Washington Shoreline Manage-ment Act of 1971,* 49 Wash. L. Rev. 423 (1974).

70. *Cf. In re* Spring Valley Development, 300 A.2d 736 (Me. 1973).

71. *See, e.g.,* ALI Code, *supra* note 27, at § 2-111. This provision authorizes the adoption of land-use controls at the local level that may directly imple-ment local plans when they are adopted; however, planning remains optional.

72. *See* Tarlock, *supra* note 55, at 83–84.

against these attacks, municipalities—with varying success—have advanced the policies of the comprehensive plan as a justification for the land-use restrictions so challenged. These cases present an opportunity for the courts to deal broadly with the role of the comprehensive plan as a substantive, prior justification for the community's land-use control effort, as the lawsuit brought by the protesting landowner may challenge the fundamental premises of the community's land-use control policies.

One group of cases in this category has considered the role of the comprehensive plan as a justification for large-lot zoning restrictions that are aimed at implementing a community growth strategy. Large-lot zoning controls have been used for a variety of purposes, and have in recent years been under attack as an exclusionary zoning device intended to restrict urbanizing areas from new development.[73] Nevertheless, large-lot zoning can be a useful zoning device when it is used in connection with other zoning and related measures to implement planning policies calling for the control of community growth. When a local growth control plan is based on a regional policy of growth control, the exclusionary argument is less persuasive and courts may be inclined to uphold the planning policies on which the growth controls are based, along with the large-lot zoning that implements these policies.

An important case considering a large-lot zoning strategy in the context of a regional growth control plan is *Norbeck Village Joint Venture v. Montgomery County Council.*[74] The regional planning agency for the Washington, D.C. metropolitan area adopted a plan calling for controlled growth in radial corridors, separated by green

---

73. Southern Burlington County NAACP v. Township of Mount Laurel, 67 N.J. 151, 336 A.2d 713, *appeal dismissed and cert. denied*, 423 U.S. 808 (1975); Township of Willistown v. Chesterdale Farms, Inc., 462 Pa. 455, 341 A.2d 466 (1975) (follows *Mount Laurel*); Appeal of Kit-Mar Builders, Inc., 439 Pa. 466, 268 A.2d 765 (1970); Nat'l Land & Inv. Co. v. Kohn, 419 Pa. 215 A.2d 597 (1965). These and other leading anti-exclusionary zoning cases are discussed in Chapters 2 and 3 *supra*.

74. 254 Md. 59, 254 A.2d 700 (1969). *See also* discussion in 1 Williams, *supra* note 56 at 500–504. Montgomery County Council v. Luizman, 268 Md. 621, 303 A.2d 37 (1973) relied on the *Norbeck* case in upholding a comprehensive rezoning designed to create a buffer zone based on a master plan for the area. A lame-duck council had rezoned appellees' land from rural residential to commercial; appellees had been granted a building permit in the interim between the rezoning to C-1 and a subsequent rezoning to Residential-Town House (R-T), but had failed to begin construction. The court found that the R-T rezoning based on a desire to "build and preserve in concert with the natural environment," was valid.

See also County Council v. District Land Corp., 337 A.2d 712 (Md. 1975). *Cf.* Barnard v. Zoning Bd. of Appeals, 313 A.2d 741 (Me. 1974).

wedges of open space.[75] The principle of wedges and corridors was carried forward at the county level, and within Montgomery county was further implemented by the local plans, one of which was at issue in *Norbeck*.[76]

The local plan under review in *Norbeck* applied the concept of wedges and corridors to the town of Olney and its surrounding area. Specifically at issue in the case was a substantial (20 square miles) down-zoning that changed the minimum lot requirement from a half acre to two acres. The court relied heavily on the policies of the plan to sustain the large scale down-zoning. It questioned neither the substance of the policies nor the factual and numerical projections, and did not undertake an independent examination of its impact on development in the area. The fact that the local plan was based on regional planning concepts helped lead the court to give the plan a "good-faith" presumption.

These issues surfaced in an earlier and very similar case decided in Michigan, *Christine Building Co. v. City of Troy*,[77] which likewise reviewed the validity of a planning policy as a support for large-lot zoning. *Christine* involved a comprehensive community plan adopted by a new and fast growing suburb in the Detroit metropolitan area. The plan contemplated a sevenfold increase in the population of the city, and a tenfold increase in the sewer district area under review in this case. Population was limited by the sewer capacity expected to be available to this area under a multi-community contract providing for sewage to be handled for all these communities by the city of Detroit. In order to implement the plan for this target population, the city zoned plaintiff's lots at a density of a half acre. The density limitation was under attack in this case.

The majority opinion in *Christine* found for the plaintiff, noting that other lots near plaintiff's property were zoned at smaller lot sizes and were allowed to use septic tanks, and that the sewage disposal contract could be altered to allow for a larger capacity. The court also had doubts about the validity of a zoning and planning program that was oriented toward development in the future rather than conditions as they presently existed. There was a strong dissent, which was concerned that the favorable holding for the plaintiff would provide a "point of attack" for the gradual erosion of the community plan. Unlike the majority, the dissent was willing to

75. National Capital Planning Commission, National Capital Regional Planning Council, A Policies Plan for the Year 2000: The Nation's Capital (1961).

76. *See* Montgomery, *supra* note 52, at 4–5. A map of the planning areas is in *id.* at 6.

77. 307 Mich. 508, 116 N.W.2d 816 (1962).

credit the policies of the plan, noting that the sewer agreement had been executed on a cooperative basis in which several communities were involved.

The *Christine* case takes an unfavorable view of the role of the plan in guiding zoning designations, and since the court was unwilling to accept the population target adopted by the plan as a premise for the large-lot zoning, the decision was influenced by the fact that the plan had been adopted by only one municipality in a growing region. To this extent it can be distinguished from *Norbeck*. Nevertheless, the Michigan Supreme Court has since had second thoughts. In *Padover v. Farmington Township*, the court upheld zoning for half-acre lots.[78] While the court was split, a comment in one of the concurring opinions provides an important judicial rationale for acceptance of the comprehensive plan as a justification for zoning policies:

> If this Court is to remain dogmatic in its insistence upon proofs of validity having an absolute relevance to existing conditions then all planning and zoning based upon projections for future needs could logically be thwarted. Zoning in a new community where land uses have not already been determined is always prospective in nature. There is the need to plan for [expected] population densities so that community needs may be based thereupon. . . . The presumption is that if the plan is sound then the structure will also be sound. It takes time, however, for things to take shape. Community planners like homebuilders require this initial indulgence. If plans and projections fail to develop then validity may be challenged.[79]

Subsequent decisions by the Michigan Supreme Court, however, cast further doubt on the acceptability of planning policies as a basis for zoning restrictions,[80] and the *Padover* case touches—but leaves

78. 374 Mich. 622, 132 N.W.2d 687 (1965).

79. *Id.* at 642–43, 132 N.W.2d at 697 (concurring opinion).

80. Biske v. City of Troy, 6 Mich. App. 546, 149 N.W.2d 899 (1967), *rev'd*, 381 Mich. 611, 166 N.W.2d 453 (1969).

In Bristow v. City of Woodhaven, 35 Mich. App. 205, 192 N.W.2d 322 (1971), the court of appeals held that land uses that advance the general public interest must be recognized as preferred uses. (The uses here involved mobile-home and apartment developments.) When a preferred use has been established by the challenger, the municipality assumes the burden of going forward to justify its prohibition of the use. A minority of the court of appeals have also held that the burden of proof shifts as well. *Bristow* set out five allowable justifications for restriction of a preferred use, including adherence to an existing and flexible master plan.

In Cohen v. Canton Tp., 38 Mich. App. 680, 197 N.W.2d 101 (1972), the court of appeals upheld an agricultural classification of plaintiff's land under an ordinance that prohibited the use of the property for a mobile trailer park. The contested ordinance did not totally exclude trailer parks from the township; the evidence presented by defendants, when coupled with the recom-

unresolved—the question of whether zoning ordinances may constitutionally defer development for substantial periods of time if based on plans that contain explicit or implicit population limits for urbanizing areas.[81]

Unless it is conclusively shown that a local plan is based on exclusionary purposes, a court would be wise to credit the policies of the plan as a justification for the restrictions contained in the ordinance, since otherwise the "point of attack" described by the dissenting judge in *Christine* will provide an opportunity for the gradual erosion of the planning policy. The difficulty is that the courts may be unwilling to examine the policies of a local plan to determine whether they are acceptable from a state or regional perspective, since to review and modify these policies would involve them in matters beyond their competence and jurisdiction.[82]

This limitation on judicial review may explain why the opinions are characterized by a willingness either to accept or reject the plan with little examination of the policy on which it was formulated.

mendations in the master plan, was sufficient to meet the burden of proof established in *Bristow*.

The preferred-use doctrine has been altered somewhat by Kropf v. City of Sterling Heights, 391 Mich. 139, 215 N.W.2d 179 (1974), which expressly overruled the minority interpretation of the *Bristow* doctrine in the court of appeals, which would have shifted the burden of proof in zoning exclusion cases. Under *Kropf*, even a total exclusion of a legitimate use from a municipality may be valid if a reasonable governmental interest is advanced by the zoning classification and there is a rational purpose in excluding the use from the area in question. Nevertheless, under this standard the court in Tocco v. Atlas Tp., 55 Mich. App. 160, 222 N.W.2d 264 (1974) found unreasonable a de facto exclusion of trailer parks from the community. The role of the master plan in establishing the reasonableness of the exclusionary classification is not clarified by *Kropf*. See 8 Urb. L. Ann. 207 (1974) for an analysis of the *Bristow* line of cases and the impact of *Kropf*.

81. Camboni's, Inc. v. County of DuPage, 26 Ill.2d 427, 187 N.E.2d 212 (1963); Averne Bay Constr. Co. v. Thatcher, 278 N.Y. 222, 15 N.E.2d 587 (1938). These were cases in which undeveloped land was rezoned to considerably limit permitted uses. *Camboni's* sustained the ordinance over plaintiff's argument that although a comprehensive plan could validly designate his property for industrial use and exclude mobile homes, the zoning here was invalid as premature and in advance of the development of capital facilities. The court found the measure reasonable in light of anticipated growth in the area. In *Averne Bay*, however, the court held unconstitutional a downzoning from an unrestricted to a residential classification primarily because of the uncertainty of future development.

82. *But see* Southern Burlington County NAACP v. Township of Mount Laurel, 67 N.J. 151, 336 A.2d 713, *appeal dismissed and cert. denied*, 423 U.S. 808 (1975).

See also Florida Local Government Comprehensive Planning Act of 1975, ch. 75-257, § 12(3)(a) (1975). A court in reviewing local government action or development regulations may consider the "reasonableness" of the comprehensive plan.

Troy's plan in the *Christine* case, for example, was rejected because the sewage-capacity assumption on which it was based appeared easy to modify. The above cases underline the need for some administrative and politically acceptable method of plan review that includes the authority to modify as well as to accept or reject the local planning policy. The possibilities for such an approach are discussed below. Alternatively, explicit legislative authority may be needed that will at least allow courts to retain jurisdiction of a case until the plan can be amended to satisfy the court's objections.[83]

Other cases in this group have reviewed local timing and managed growth programs that have been based on comprehensive planning policies. Perhaps the best known of these is *Ramapo*, decided by the highest New York court.[84] In this case an urbanizing township in the outer reaches of the New York City metropolitan area amended its zoning ordinance to require a permit system for all new residential development. Permits could be granted only if the development was adequately served by public facilities, with adequacy determined by a point system based on the proximity of the development to each of these services. The opinion considered several issues raised by the application of the timing ordinance, including the authority of the township to enact the ordinance under the applicable New York zon-

83. Questions about the permissible scope of judicial relief in land-use control litigation have usually arisen in zoning cases. Most courts have refused on separation-of-power grounds to issue an order decreeing a revision in a local zoning ordinance held unconstitutional, although some courts have held to the contrary. *See* Note, *Beyond Invalidation: The Judicial Power to Zone*, 9 Urb. L. Ann. 159 (1975). In addition, some state legislation has sought to deal with this problem. *See* Pa. Stat. Ann. tit. 53, §§ 10609.1, 11004, 11011 (1972). Under the last section a court invalidating a zoning ordinance may approve a development or use for which plans have been submitted to the local zoning agency, or may approve the development in part and refer any unapproved elements to the local agency for further proceedings. The court may retain jurisdiction of the appeal during such further proceedings and may issue such supplementary orders as are necessary to protect the landowner's rights. This section was construed in Ellick v. Board of Supervisors, 333 A.2d 239 (1975). For discussion of the Pennsylvania zoning procedures *see* Krasnowiecki, *Zoning Litigation and the New Pennsylvania Procedures*, 120 U. Pa. L. Rev. 1029 (1972). For a similar proposal authorizing a judicial stay order until the municipality has amended its land-use regulations in accordance with the order of the court, *see* ALI Code, *supra* note 27, at § 9-112(2).

84. Golden v. Planning Bd., 30 N.Y.2d 359, 285 N.E.2d 291 (1972), 334 N.Y.S.2d 138, *appeal dismissed*, 409 U.S. 1003 (1973). Commentary on the *Ramapo* case is extensive. Much of it is adverse and emphasizes the exclusionary impact or potential of the growth-control program. H. Franklin, Controlling Urban Growth—But for Whom? (1973); Bosselman, *Can the Town of Ramapo Pass a Law to Bind the Whole World?* 1 Fla. St. U. L. Rev. 234 (1973); Scott, *Comments on Ramapo*, 24 Zoning Dig. 75 (1972). *But see* Note, *Phased Zoning: Regulation of the Tempo and Sequence of Land Development*, 26 Stan. L. Rev. 585 (1974).

ing legislation, which generally followed the outlines of the Standard Zoning Enabling Act. Authority to enact the ordinance was found, and in a complex opinion that relied in part on the fact that the ordinance implemented a well-considered plan for the community, the court upheld the timing control. This plan included a capital improvements program on which the public facility point system was based. "The restrictions conform to the community's considered land-use policies as expressed in its comprehensive plan and represent a bonafide effort to maximize population density consistent with orderly growth."[85]

Due process "taking" issues were raised by the fact that the timing control ordinance deferred development in some sections of the community by as much as eighteen years, but the court accepted this restriction as a necessary component of the timing ordinance. The court's handling of this due process issue must be understood in the context of the plan's objectives. No part of the jurisdiction was to be excluded from development, as the timing plan contemplated the development of the entire township by the end of the eighteen-year period, though at very low densities. Since development would be allowed eventually in the whole township, the timing control plan operated more as an interim control on development than as a permanent restriction.

While the potential eighteen-year delay in development contemplated by the plan might seem too long, the court may have considered the due process taking issue resolved by the township's apparent commitment to allow the private development of all of its land area within the prescribed period. More explicit interim zoning ordinances, aimed at achieving a holding pattern in land development pending the adoption of a plan or zoning ordinance, have also been judicially favored elsewhere.[86]

More troublesome in the *Ramapo* case is the potential for exclusion. The township was zoned at relatively low densities through large-lot zoning. As the court noted,[87] these densities were not challenged, although the court on first impression could find no reason for their justification. Consequently the application of timing controls in the context of the large-lot zoning pattern simply reinforced the low-density restriction, since even development that met the requirements of the point system could only occur at the low zoning densities. The court did consider the exclusionary argument

85. 30 N.Y.2d at 378, 285 N.E.2d at 302.
86. *E.g.,* State v. Snohomish County, 79 Wash. 2d 619, 488 P.2d 511 (1971); Collura v. Town of Arlington, 329 N.E.2d 733 (Mass. 1975).
87. 30 N.Y.2d at 367, 28 N.E.2d at 295, 334 N.Y.S.2d at 143 n.2.

in *Ramapo*, but became convinced that locally adopted timing programs deserve judicial sanction, in the absence of supervisory state and regional land-use controls that, at least in New York State, did not appear imminent.

In addition, the court was impressed by the timing and growth objectives of the ordinance. It put aside any objection that the timing controls, together with the low-density zoning that accompanied them, amounted to an unacceptable exclusion.[88] In part the court's decision on this point can be explained by the failure of the parties in the case to develop an adequate factual foundation on which the exclusionary argument could be based. Comprehensive planning programs including large-lot restrictions have fallen into judicial disfavor in other jurisdictions in cases in which the exclusionary argument has been pressed.[89] *Ramapo* may also be explained by the fact that down-zoning had not occurred prior to the adoption of the timing control ordinance, so that the legality of a down-zoning in conjunction with a timing program was not at issue.

More recently the New York Court of Appeals addressed the exclusionary problem in a case involving a total prohibition of multi-family dwellings.[90] The court noted its comments in *Ramapo* that cautioned against "community efforts at immunization or exclusion," and went on to state a two-branch test of the validity of a zoning ordinance:

1. Has the town provided a properly balanced and well-ordered plan for the community?[91]
2. Has the town, in excluding new multifamily housing, considered the needs of the region for such housing?[92]

While the facts in the case had yet to be tried, the court appears to suggest additional qualifications that might be applied to *Ramapo* types of situations in the future, particularly its apparent under-cutting of the low-density base in the *Ramapo* plan.

Neither did the *Ramapo* case consider the validity of the timing plan as applied to a specific development that had been disapproved and thus deferred under the point system. This issue arose in Michi-

88. Franklin, *supra* note 84, at 13–15.
89. *See, e.g.,* Southern Burlington County NAACP v. Township of Mount Laurel, 67 N.J. 151, 336 A.2d 713, *appeal dismissed and cert. denied,* 423 U.S. 808 (1975); and other cases discussed in Chapters 2 and 3 *supra.*
90. Berenson v. Town of New Castle, 38 N.Y.2d 102, 341 N.E.2d 236 (1975).
91. 341 N.E.2d at 242.
92. *Id.*

gan in *Biske v. City of Troy*.[93] The city had prepared a comprehensive plan that showed the site in question as part of a projected civic center and commercial complex. At the time of the case this area was almost totally undeveloped except for some municipal buildings. There was no explicit phased program for the development of the area in accordance with the plan's objectives. The plaintiff's property was at the corner of an intersection of two secondary highways, where he proposed to develop a gasoline filling station. Although filling stations occupied two of the other corners of the intersection, his request for a zoning change was refused because it was inconsistent with the plan's proposals. He brought an action alleging that the refusal to change the ordinance to allow construction of his filling station was unconstitutional.

The Michigan intermediate appellate court affirmed the city, in an opinion that followed the *Padover*[94] rationale, and was willing to justify the reasonableness of the zoning restriction by relying on the community's planning policy. But the state supreme court reversed and held for the landowner. In part the state supreme court's opinion was based on the fact that the city's plan had not yet been adopted legislatively, but it added an ambiguous comment that appeared to limit the *Padover* holding. By relying "too much" on the plan the city had adopted a "speculative" standard and had not sufficiently considered the effect of the plan on the landowner's use of his property. The property owner had to keep his property vacant, though subject to local taxes, while all the time hoping that the development proposed by the plan would materialize.

Biske once more was a timing case. The community did not object to commercial development on the property; its only objection was that the development proposed by the plaintiff was not intensive enough and did not fit the policies contained in the comprehensive plan. What makes the *Biske* plan speculative, as compared with the timing plan upheld in *Ramapo*, is that development was assured throughout the municipality in *Ramapo*, while in *Biske* there was no such guarantee.

Few municipalities will be able to give the guarantees that *Ramapo* was able to provide, and in these municipalities the "speculative" objection of the Michigan Supreme Court in *Biske* must be overcome. Perhaps the comment in the concurring opinion quoted above from *Padover* is relevant. Initial acceptance of the plan's proposals

93. 6 Mich. App. 546, 149 N.W.2d 899 (1967), *rev'd*, 381 Mich. 611, 166 N.W.2d 453 (1969). However, the plan was not officially adopted. *See* Zoning Dilemma, *supra* note 53, at 53–54.

94. Padover v. Farmington Tp., 374 Mich. 622, 132 N.W.2d 687 (1965).

appears warranted in order to provide reinforcement for the plan's policies. If the plan in fact appears speculative after a time because the development proposed by the plan does not materialize, or if development patterns do not follow the plan,[95] appropriate judicial relief can be provided. From this perspective, to enforce the plan in its initial years is to do no more than to support any restrictive zoning accompanying the plan on an interim basis. Interim zoning of this kind has respectable precedent.[96] Moreover, judicial relief is also appropriate if the municipality itself departs from the plan's policy recommendations.[97] If the courts are willing to take a flexible approach to plans imposing restrictions in order to achieve planning objectives, then the objections raised to the comprehensive plan in the *Biske* case can be resolved through prudent judicial supervision.

Planning policies may also be implemented through land-use control techniques other than large-lot zoning and timing controls. An example, closely related to the *Biske* situation, is the plan and accompanying zoning ordinance that contain locational policies for commercial and industrial uses, and that implement this policy through exclusive industrial and commercial zones in which residential uses are prohibited. Developers seeking to develop residentially in exclusive nonresidential zones, as well as developers seeking to develop for nonresidential purposes outside these zones, will be in a position to raise due process taking objections. These issues have

95. Town of Bedford v. Village of Mount Kisco, 33 N.Y.2d 178, 306 N.E.2d 155, 351 N.Y.S.2d 129 (1973). *Cf.* Bissell v. County Comm'rs, 12 Ore. App. 174, 506 P.2d 499 (1973), in which the court upheld the county's denial of commercial zoning at an arterial intersection which the plan had designated for commercial uses. There was evidence that the intersection had not developed for commercial uses as the plan had contemplated.

96. Freilich, *Interim Development Controls: Essential Tools for Implementing Flexible Planning and Zoning*, 49 J. Urb. L. 65 (1971). The court in *Ramapo* pointed out that although the developer could depend on nothing more than the town's good faith in adhering to its scheduled program of capital improvements, the landowner could bring an action to have the ordinance declared unconstitutional as applied to his property should the town default on its obligations.

97. Board of Supervisors v. Allman, 211 S.E.2d 48 (1975), in which a suburban county adjacent to Washington, D.C. had adopted but had not consistently followed a development policy favoring the location of new growth in a suburban new town. The court relied on this inconsistency in holding unconstitutional the low-density residential zoning that was applicable to the property in this case. This property was not within the area that had been planned for the growth of the new town. *See also* Board of Supervisors v. Williams, 216 S.E.2d 33 (1975).

98. Grubel v. McLaughlin, 286 F. Supp. 24 (D.V.I. 1968). *Cf.* Bosse v. City of Portsmouth, 523, 226 A.2d 99 (1967). *See* Note, *Industrial Zoning to Exclude Higher Uses*, 32 N.Y.U.L. Rev. 1261 (1957). *But cf.* City of Tempe v. Rasor, 536 P.2d 239 (1975). *See also* Southern Burlington County NAACP v. Township of Mount Laurel, 67 N.J. 151, 336 A.2d 713, *appeal dismissed and cert. denied*, 423 U.S. 808 (1975), in which exclusive industrial zoning was invalidated.

been litigated in cases not involving comprehensive planning policies, in which the courts have to a large extent accepted exclusive nonresidential zoning provided it represents an expected market demand.[98] Exclusive nonresidential zoning should likewise be entitled to judicial respect when it implements the policies of a plan for the proper location of nonresidential uses.

The Role of the Comprehensive Plan in the Zoning Amendment Process. The cases to be discussed in this section do not consider the constitutionality of community-wide or major zoning strategies that are justified by a comprehensive plan. They focus instead on zoning changes that amend the zoning ordinance to permit landowners to make more intensive use of their land.[99] These cases raise questions about the role of the comprehensive plan in zoning because the change in the zoning ordinance may have the appearance of a special favor if the rezoning is out of place with land uses in the surrounding area.

In recent years some courts have given the comprehensive plan greater weight in deciding whether or not to validate a rezoning to a more intensive use. These cases usually come from states that are in a position to review a rezoning on the basis of a change in community policy as well as a change in the area surrounding the rezoned parcel. To some extent these cases have also reversed the presumption of validity that usually accompanies rezoning actions (see Chapter 4). By reversing the presumption so that it works against rather than in support of the rezoning action, the court is in a position to demand justification from the municipality as to the basis for its rezoning action.

This judicial reliance on a shift in the presumption of validity to achieve better judicial leverage on the planning and zoning process is not unexpected. As noted above, courts may well avoid making decisions in which they are required to review and evaluate the policies of a comprehensive plan as the basis for their opinions. Indeed, the *Ramapo* case specifically noted the increasing sophistication of land-use controls as a reason for giving deference to the timing-control ordinance that was affirmed in that case.[100] By reversing the presumption of validity, the courts can place on the locality the burden

99. These cases also include some in which the developers proposed a use on their land not presently permitted by the zoning ordinance. When the use change was refused, these developers brought suit to have the zoning ordinance set aside as unconstitutional, and the courts relied to some extent on the policies of the plan when passing on the constitutionality of the zoning ordinance as applied.

100. 30 N.Y.2d at 376–77, 285 N.E.2d at 301, 334 N.Y.S.2d at 150.

of coming forward with supporting evidence to justify the zoning change. The policies of the comprehensive plan are one obvious source of support for municipal actions that rezone individual parcels to more intensive uses.

This approach is evident in a recent case decided by an Illinois intermediate appellate court. The court did not fully shift the presumption of validity, but relied on the absence of a comprehensive plan as a basis for its finding that the "presumption of validity which otherwise would attach to a county zoning ordinance" had been weakened.[101] This case reviewed a rezoning to permit apartment development in a suburban area of Cook County. Not only was it admitted that the county did not have a comprehensive plan, but the zoning agency that heard the request for the rezoning did not consult any of the county agencies charged with the planning function. The rezoning would have introduced from 4,000 to 6,000 new residents in what had previously been a single-family residential community. Local facilities, including schools, were inadequate to support this new population, and the proposed apartment complex possibly would have depreciated the value of adjacent single-family residences and created flooding problems. For these reasons the court invalidated the rezoning,[102] a decision with support in other states.[103]

Other decisions have modified the traditional presumption of validity by treating the zoning amendment as a quasi-judicial rather than a legislative process. Foremost among these cases is *Fasano v. Board of County Commissioners of Washington County*.[104] This case first

101. Forestview Homeowners Ass'n v. County of Cook, 18 Ill. App. 3d 230, 243, 309 N.E.2d 763, 773 (1974).

102. The court noted that this was not a case in which the zoning classification achieved a relative gain to the public and a hardship to the property owners. *Id.* at 246–47, 309 N.E.2d at 775. Further, the rule that a zoning classification will not be changed except for the public good supported the property owners. Courts have occasionally stressed a somewhat contrary theory—that property owners have no vested right in the continuation of existing zoning.

103. *See* Raabe v. City of Walker, 383 Mich. 165, 174 N.W.2d 789 (1970), in which the court found that the creation of an industrial zone in the midst of a residential area was hampered by the lack of a general plan for the area and unsupported by a change in conditions, and therefore was not in the public interest.

104. 264 Or. 574, 507 P.2d 23 (1973). The court built on, but to some extent qualified, its earlier holding in Roseta v. County of Washington, 254 Or. 161, 458 P.2d 405 (1969).

For Oregon cases further elaborating the *Fasano* holding, *see* Tierney v. Duris, 536 P.2d 435 (1975) (considers sufficiency of city council fact-findings in support of a plan change and zoning amendment); Dickinson v. Board of County Comm'rs, 533 P.2d 1395 (1975) (property owner did not meet burden of proof that denial of rezoning was improper); Culver v. Dagg, 532 P.2d 1127 (1975) (rezoning of more than half of county pursuant to a newly adopted comprehensive plan held legislative).

changed the usual rule—that zoning amendments are legislative— and adopted the contrary position that the zoning amendment pro- cess is quasi-judicial, completely shifting the presumption of valid- ity applied to zoning amendments. *Fasano* also placed heavy weight on the comprehensive plan as a justification for zoning amendments, and in so doing established strong judicial support for the role of the plan in the zoning process.

Fasano considered the adoption by the county of a floating zone to allow a mobile home park in an area not previously zoned for this use. Legislation in effect in Oregon at the time of this case mandated planning by counties, and intended that the plan "should be the basis" of local zoning regulation. Accordingly the court held that a zoning amendment must be consistent with the plan, but then qualified its assertion with several conditions that make the role of the plan ambiguous. While the court's opinion is not entirely clear, it also required that there be proof of a "public need" for the change, and that this need would best be served by making the change at the proposed location.[105] Since the purpose of the plan, in the broad sense, is to indicate public "needs" for land use, the function of the additional need-showing is not clear.

The court also noted that "[t]he more drastic the change, the greater will be the burden of showing that it is in conformance with the comprehensive plan as implemented by the ordinance."[106] This burden apparently requires a showing that alternative sites designated by the plan are not available, a requirement that strengthens the force of the land-use allocations made by the plan.[107] The court also held that a mistake in the original plan or ordinance, or changes in the physical characteristics of an area affected by the zoning change, would be relevant though not determinative, thus adopting a quali-

---

For discussion of the *Fasano* case, *see* Chapter 4 *supra*, and Sullivan. *From Kroner to Fasano: An Analysis of Judicial Review of Land Use Regulation in Oregon*, 10 Will. L.J. 358 (1974). Sullivan was counsel to the county in the *Fasano* case.

105. 264 Or. at 584, 507 P.2d at 28. The need test was applied to hold in- valid a rezoning from residential to commercial in South Central Ass'n of Neigh- bors, Inc. v. Lindsey, 535 P.2d 1381 (1975).

106. *Id.* at 58, 507 P.2d at 29.

107. An important case applying the alternative-site test is Duddles v. City Council of West Linn, 535 P.2d 583 (1975). While admitting that a tract shown as commercial on the city's plan was not as suitable for commercial use, the court nevertheless applied the policy of the plan to invalidate a rezoning to commercial of a nearby tract at a point not shown for commercial use on the plan. The court noted that either the plan should be amended to allow com- mercial use on the tract or the commercial designation for the nearby tract should be eliminated.

fied version of the Maryland change-mistake rule.[108] This part of the decision qualifies the court's reliance on the comprehensive plan as the basis for a zoning change, since a reliance on supportive changes in the surrounding area to justify a zoning amendment qualifies the impact of the plan whenever the plan proposes more intensive uses in areas whose character is not yet fully determined. In this situation there would be no comparable changes in land use in the surrounding area to support the proposed zoning amendment. Finally, although the court spoke throughout as if it were dealing with a plan containing fairly precise mapped designations, a footnote to the opinion describes a type of plan containing textual policies rather than mapped intentions, and recognizes that as the precision of the plan declines, the burden of showing conformance is more easily met.

On balance, what is of note in the court's opinion is its insistence that the burden of proof to justify the zoning amendment should increase as the impact of a proposed zoning amendment on the surrounding area increases. This approach weakens the impact of the plan whenever the plan proposes intensive uses for low-intensity or undeveloped areas. Nevertheless, it is in just these areas that a reliance on the comprehensive plan as a justification for the zoning change appears most necessary. When the proposed land-use change approved by a zoning amendment is consistent with at least some of the surrounding development, it ordinarily is not intrusive, and courts might well be able to validate the change on the basis of standard concepts, such as a mistake in the original zoning or a change in conditions. It is only when the plan proposes a use in an undeveloped area that implements the policy proposals of the plan that conventional standards cannot be applied to support the change, and reliance on the plan becomes essential.

While the *Fasano* case thus marks an important step forward in judicial elaboration of the role of the plan in validating zoning changes, the doctrinal basis for judicial reception of the plan in Oregon requires additional refinement and elaboration.[109]

This elaboration came in *Baker v. City of Milwaukie*,[110] an Oregon Supreme Court case subsequent to *Fasano*, which on its face appears to take a more absolute stand on the relationship between the comprehensive plan and zoning. While confused by the city's

---

108. *See, e.g.,* McDonald v. Board of County Comm'rs, 238 Md. 549, 210 A.2d 325 (1965). The Maryland change-mistake rule is discussed in text accompanying notes 132–135 *infra.*

109. It should be noted that the *Fasano* rationale is applicable to a failure to grant the requested zoning change. (*See* Chapter 4 *supra.*)

110. 533 P.2d 772 (1975).

grant of a variance to allow the development in question, *Baker* essentially considered the validity of a zoning ordinance allowing a residential density more intensive than that permitted by a subsequently adopted comprehensive plan. By the time the *Baker* case came before the court, the legislature had mandated the adoption of comprehensive plans by cities as well as counties,[111] but no language in this law explicitly treats the problem of zoning's consistency with an adopted plan.

Nevertheless, relying heavily on the *Eves* case (discussed earlier), on a California case holding a comprehensive plan adoption to be a legislative act subject to referendum,[112] and on legal commentary, the Oregon Supreme Court in unequivocal language accorded the comprehensive plan a binding status in local zoning actions:

> In summary, we conclude that a comprehensive plan is the controlling land use planning instrument for a city. Upon passage of a comprehensive plan a city assumes a responsibility to effectuate that plan and conform prior conflicting zoning ordinances to it. We further hold that the zoning decisions of a city must be in accord with that plan and a zoning ordinance which allows a more intensive use than that prescribed by the plan must fail.[113]

The impact of *Baker* on the *Fasano* case is not entirely clear. While limited to cities, there is no warrant in Oregon law for not applying the *Baker* rationale to counties, especially since Oregon legislation mandating adoption of a plan applies to counties as well.

Another important question is whether *Baker* has overruled some of the qualifications that *Fasano* placed on the controlling weight to be given to the comprehensive plan in zoning, such as the public-need test. Since *Baker* considered a zoning ordinance directly in conflict with an adopted comprehensive plan, the court may not have intended the rationale of the case to apply to the zoning amend-

---

111. Or. Rev. Stat. § 197.175(2) (1973). *See also* the discussion in the text at note 185 *infra*. The city planning legislation in Oregon had initially been permissive, and a plan was authorized but not required. *Id.* § 227.090(2). County planning has been mandatory. *Id.* § 215.050. The *Fasano* doctrine has been applied to city zoning amendments. See notes 91 and 94 *supra*.

112. O'Loane v. O'Rourke, 42 Cal. Rptr. 283 (1965). This case contains strong dictum supporting the binding role of the plan in land-use controls administration.

113. Baker v. City of Milwaukie, 533 P.2d 772, 779 (1975). The *Baker* decision also relies, but does not appear to be dependent, on a provision in the Oregon city zoning enabling act that requires local zoning ordinances to be based on a "well considered plan." Or. Rev. Stat. § 277.240(1) (1973). This language is similar to the "in accordance" language contained in the SZEA.

On the requirement of internal consistency between the plan map and the plan text, see Tierney v. Duris, 536 P.2d 435 (1975).

ment process. The *Baker* court states, however, that the comprehensive plan is binding on zoning *decisions* as well as zoning ordinances. These confusions aside, *Baker* would appear to have adopted as strong a view of the role of the comprehensive plan as any court that has considered the problem. It stands as a polar opposite to the *Kozesnik* opinion.[114]

Apart from these Oregon cases, other courts have increasingly considered the weight to be given the comprehensive plan when passing on amendments to zoning ordinances.[115] The majority of these courts continue to treat the rezoning as legislative. The cases can be grouped according to whether the proposed use is or is not consistent with the plan, and whether the court did or did not follow the policies of the plan when passing on the zoning amendment.

A Zoning Amendment Inconsistent with the Comprehensive Plan Is Disapproved. Several courts, though without much discussion, have given weight to the policies of the comprehensive plan when disapproving a zoning amendment that is inconsistent with those policies.[116] *Fasano* and *Baker* are especially strong judicial expressions of this position, but an important judicial companion is *Udell v. Haas*,[117]

114. *See* the discussion in the text at notes 56–60, *supra.*

115. For a similar analysis, though not based explicitly on the zoning amendment process, *see* 1 Williams, *supra* note 56 at 439–557. Williams distinguishes primarily between those cases adhering to the unitary view and those cases where there is a willingness to give some weight to an independently adopted comprehensive plan.

116. Fontaine v. Board of County Comm'rs, 493 P.2d 670 (Colo. App. 1972); Green v. County Planning and Zoning Comm'rs, 340 A.2d 852 (1974); Board of County Comm'rs v. Farr, 242 Md. 315, 218 A.2d 923 (1966); Schilling v. Midland, 38 Mich. App. 568, 196 N.W.2d 846 (1972); Heram Holding Corp. v. City of Albany, 63 Misc. 2d 152, 34 N.Y.S.2d 198 (Sup. Ct. 1970). *Cf.* Sampson Bros. v. Board of County Comm'rs, 240 Md. 116, 213 A.2d 289 (1965).

For Maryland change-mistake cases in which a zoning change inconsistent with a comprehensive plan was disapproved, *see* Valenzia v. Zoning Bd., 270 Md. 478, 312 A.2d 277 (1973); County Council v. Pleasants, 266 Md. 462, 295 A.2d 216 (1972); Howard Research & Dev. Corp. v. Zoning Bd., 263 Md. 280, 283 A.2d 150 (1971); Park Constr. Corp. v. Board of County Comm'rs, 245 Md. 597, 227 A.2d 15 (1967).

In Dunk v. Township of Brighton, 52 Mich. App. 143, 216 N.W.2d 455 (1974), the township adopted a land-use plan that recommended retaining the existing 15,000-square-foot minimum for the area in question, but a 40,000-square-foot minimum was nevertheless imposed. Based on the plan and testimony from a health department official, the court held that the plaintiffs had presented a prima facie case that the ordinance was unreasonable as applied to their property.

117. 21 N.Y.2d 463, 235 N.E.2d 897, 288 N.Y.S.2d 888 (1968). Professor Williams's view of this case can be found in 1 Williams, *supra* note 56 at 480–484; he put *Udell* in the category of cases that equate the comprehensive plan with general zoning mapping policy and then apply that policy to determine the validity of individual zoning changes.

a 1968 case decided by the highest New York court. *Udell* considered a down-zoning rather than an up-zoning, and so may be distinguishable from the Oregon cases, but the principles applied by the New York court would appear to apply in both situations. In *Udell* a small village on Long Island had rezoned a parcel of land on its periphery and abutting a major highway from commercial to residential uses. The down-zoning was challenged and the court found it invalid, relying in part on the principle that the down-zoning had not been "in accordance with a comprehensive plan" as required by the New York State zoning enabling statute.

New York has never interpreted its statute (which follows the SZEA) to require the adoption of an independent comprehensive plan, but has been willing to find the land-use policies of a community in a comprehensive plan, if one exists, as well as in the zoning ordinance and zoning map.[118] In this case the village, at least from the mid-1930s, had consistently zoned the areas in which the landowner's parcel was located for commercial uses, and in 1968 had adopted a "developmental policy" as an amendment to its zoning ordinance, which appeared to confirm this zoning. This policy called for a suburban low-density community, though other uses were permitted if they related to residential use or contributed to the community's tax base.

Prior to the down-zoning amendment challenged in *Udell*, the village's zoning map had been consistent with this policy, the only exception being the down-zoning at issue in this case. The down-zoning had been accomplished very quickly, after it became apparent that the owner of the parcel intended to build commercially as permitted by the existing zoning classification on the parcel before it was changed. In addition, there was testimony that the down-zoning was accomplished in part to accommodate the "feeling of the Village" that no extensive commercial use should be permitted in that area.[119] As the court pointed out, zoning could easily degenerate into "all sorts of arbitrary infringements on the property rights of the landowner." The opinion continued:

> To assure that this does not happen, our courts must require local zoning authorities to pay more than mock obeisance to the statutory mandate that zoning be "in accordance with a comprehensive plan." There must be some showing that the change does not conflict with the community's basic scheme for land use.[120]

118. *Id.* at 471–72, 235 N.E.2d at 902, 288 N.Y.S.2d at 895.
119. *Id.* at 476, 235 N.E.2d at 905, 288 N.Y.S.2d at 899.
120. *Id.* at 470, 235 N.E.2d at 901, 288 N.Y.S.2d at 894. For a case that follows *Udell, see* Randolph v. Town of Brookhaven, 37 N.Y.2d 544, 337 N.E.2d 763 (1975).

The problem is no less serious when an up-zoning is given at the behest of a single landowner—a circumstance that led the Pennsylvania court to call for comprehensive planning as the basis for a zoning change in the *Eves* case.[121]

A Zoning Amendment Inconsistent with the Comprehensive Plan Is Approved. These cases usually come from states in which the plan is treated as advisory because the "in accordance" requirement is not interpreted to require a comprehensive plan external to the zoning ordinance.[122] In these states a modification of the plan through subsequent zoning is accepted. The courts may also emphasize the planning commission's participation in the zoning change that modifies the plan.[123]

These cases have also considered floating-zone and planned-unit development (PUD) procedures in which the court is convinced that the higher density residential use that is allowed through these procedures is consistent with the previous zoning.[124] As these cases often arise in rural or urbanizing areas, the courts also may be sensitive to the function of the plan—and the previously existing low-density residential zoning that supports it—as a holding policy subject to revision as the need for more intensive development arises. While the plan could provide guidance on rezonings to higher densities, the court may be convinced that the PUD or a similar flexible technique provides a development guidance policy that can allow a departure from the plan in the particular case under review.

Opportunities for site plan review under the PUD or similar ordinance also may be a factor that leads the courts to accept a departure from the plan, as the development can be reviewed to insure its consistency with other lower density development that may occur in the area. Review standards frequently contained in these ordinances re-

121. Eves v. Zoning Bd. of Adjustment, 401 Pa. 211, 104 A.2d 7 (1970).

122. *E.g.*, Lathrop v. Planning & Zoning Comm'n, 164 Conn. 215, 319 A.2d 376 (1973); Furtney v. Zoning Comm'n, 159 Conn. 585, 271 A.2d 319 (1970); Doran Investments v. Muhlenberg Tp., 10 Pa. Commw. 143, 309 A.2d 450 (1973); Saenger v. Planning Comm'n, 9 Pa. Commw. 499, 308 A.2d 175 (1973); Township Bd. of Supervisors v. George Calantoni & Sons 6 Pa. Commw. 521, 297 A.2d 164 (1972). *Cf.* Tomasek v. City of Des Plaines, 325 N.E.2d 345 (1975). Williams also puts the Connecticut cases in the general mapping policy category. 1 Williams, *supra* note 56 at 480–484.

123. *E.g.*, Cheney v. Village 2 at New Hope, Inc., 429 Pa. 626, 241 A.2d 81 (1968).

124. *E.g.*, Loh v. Town Plan & Zoning Comm'n, 161 Conn. 32, 282 A.2d 894 (1971); Chrinko v. Township Planning Bd., 77 N.J. Super. 594, 187 A.2d 221 (1963); Cheney v. Village 2 at New Hope, Inc., 429 Pa. 626, 241 A.2d 81 (1968); Doran Investments v. Muhlenberg Tp., 10 Pa. Commw. 499, 308 A.2d 175 (1973). The ordinance must of course provide sufficient standards and criteria under which the use can be allowed.

quire the development to be consistent with its surroundings, and may give both the municipality and the courts an opportunity to insist that the development not be intrusive on its surroundings. To the extent that these standards authorize a review of the development to assure conformity with its surroundings, they meet one of the concerns of the *Fasano* case, namely, the impact of intensive development proposals on adjacent, less developed areas.

A Zoning Amendment Consistent with the Plan Is Approved. Other courts have been willing to give some weight to the plan in support of a zoning amendment to a more intensive use.[125] As in *Fasano*, these courts have had to consider just how the policies of the plan are to be related to the zoning process, a problem of less significance in cases such as *Baker* in which the conflict between the plan and the ordinance is clear. This problem is not serious in jurisdictions in which the plan is mapped at fairly detailed levels. In these jurisdictions the courts can apply with some precision the mapped land-use designations of the plan to zoning decisions. How the courts might allow minor deviations from mapped planning policy is more problematic.[126]

125. City of Louisville v. Kavanaugh, 495 S.W.2d 502 (Ky. 1973) (refusal to rezone was arbitrary in light of land-use plan); Ward v. Knippenberg, 416 S.W.2d 746 (Ky. 1967) (plan serves as a guide, and actual location of shipping center in zoning ordinance need not follow plan exactly); Henze v. Building Inspector 269 N.E.2d 711 (Mass. Super. Ct. 1971); Sonneland v. City of Spokane, 4 Wash. App. 865, 484 P.2d 421 (1971). *Cf.* Montgomery County Council v. Leizman, 268 Md. 621, 303 A.2d 374 (1973) (comprehensive rezoning in accordance with master plan given strong presumption of validity and correctness). For Maryland cases in which a zoning amendment consistent with a comprehensive plan was approved when it was supported by a change in neighborhood conditions, *see* Aspen Hill Venture v. County Council, 265 Md. 303, 289 A.2d 202 (1972); Montgomery v. Board of County Comm'rs, 263 Md. 1, 280 A.2d 901 (1971).

126. *Compare* Ward v. Knippenberg, 416 S.W.2d 746 (Ky. 1967) (in which minor deviation from comprehensive plan in mapping of a commercial zone was not held fatal), *with* Duddle v. City Council of West Linn, 535 P.2d 583 (1975), (in which court set aside commercial rezone when commercial rezoning was indicated not for that tract but for adjacent parcel). *See also* F.H. Uelner Precision Tool & Die, Inc. v. City of Dubuque, 190 N.W.2d 465 (1971). Here the court invalidated a commercial upzoning when the area covered by the upzoning was larger than what the comprehensive plan had recommended. *Cf.* Fuller v. Prince George's County, 264 Md. 410, 286 A.2d 772 (1972). For a case in which the policy of the plan was applied to support the disapproval of a rezoning even though the rezoning was consistent with the land use designated by the plan, *see* Dustin v. Mayor and Council, 23 Md. App. 389, 328 A.2d 748 (1974). For a conceptual analysis in an Israeli context of criteria for determining the consistency of land-use control administration with a comprehensive plan, *see* R. Alterman, Implementation of Urban Plans ch. 2 (Technical Research and Development Foundation, 1975).

More difficult questions of plan implementation are presented when the plan is expressed as a policy, when the mapping it contains is highly generalized and is not further reduced to more detailed levels, or when the plan is fairly precise in its mapping designations but allows some freedom of choice to the zoning agency. An example of the last problem is found in the Pennsylvania Supreme Court case of *Cleaver v. Board of Adjustment of Tredyffrin Township*.[127] While the Pennsylvania court follows the unitary view by not requiring an independently adopted comprehensive plan in order to satisfy the "in accordance" requirement, the case is nevertheless instructive on the role of the plan as a justification for a zoning amendment.

In *Cleaver* the township rezoned an 11-acre tract near a suburban Philadelphia railway station and major highway from single-family residential to apartment use.[128] The tract was bounded in part by single-family residences and by a large research center. So far as indicated by the court, the plan adopted by the township consists of policy statements that were generally formulated and that related as well to specific areas of land in the township. Generally, apartments were recommended throughout the township as transitional uses between residential and nonresidential areas. Access to "good highway and rapid transit facilities" was also recommended, and the plan called explicitly for the rezoning of designated tracts near railway stations—including the parcel in question—to apartment or professional uses. Neighbors objecting to the rezoning did not challenge these apartment location policies as inappropriate, but complained that the density permitted and the setbacks required under the rezoning were too generous. No policies for density or setbacks were contained in the plan.

Relying in part on the policies of the plan, the court found the rezoning valid. It first noted that a "comprehensive plan does not contemplate or require a 'master-plan' which *rigidly* provides for or attempts to answer in minute detail every possible question regarding land utilization or restriction."[129] It then held:

It is clear that the Tredyffrin Land Use Plan (a) permits a defined range of choices in the zoning of appellant's property . . . , and (b) *does not command* particular requirements of population density or set-back or spacing

127. 414 Pa. 367, 200 A.2d 408 (1964), *followed in* Schuback v. Silver, 336 A.2d 328 (1975); Pollock v. Zoning Bd. of Adjustment, 342 A.2d 815 (1975).

128. A map of the environs of this case is in D. Mandelker, Managing Our Urban Environment 976 (2d ed. 1971).

129. 414 Pa. at 375, 200 A.2d at 413.

for apartments thereon, and (c) clearly envisages and permits a proper zoning of the property here in question for apartments.[130]

The *Cleaver* court is thus more willing than the *Fasano* court to credit the policies of the comprehensive plan without qualification, although its view of the plan as an advisory document leaves room for the court to reject the plan in an appropriate case.[131] The *Cleaver* court was also willing to accept the failure of the plan to deal with density and setback requirements as a reason for not considering these issues when passing on the rezoning.

Some would argue that the plan's failure to consider density was disabling, as the very purpose of a rezoning to apartments is to increase the density allowed on the rezoned tract. As an alternative, if a plan is incomplete or inadequate, a court could (and should) reject its policies as not providing an adequate basis for a rezoning amendment. In this situation the plan would not present the "defined range of choices" to which the *Cleaver* court refers, and should not be entitled to judicial respect. The same result should be reached when the plan is too vague.

Another point to make here is that *Cleaver* and similar cases are applying the plan to determine whether the rezoning amendment is internally consistent with the planning policy. If no significant regional issues are raised, such as needs or environmental protection, the courts should be willing to accept the policies of the plan as generally controlling in the limited circumstances that have been under discussion—that is, to determine whether a rezoning amendment that allows a more intensive use properly serves community purposes and is not an attempt to confer a windfall on a single landowner.

A Zoning Amendment Consistent with the Plan Is Disapproved. Maryland has adopted a rule that zoning amendments must be justified by a mistake in the original ordinance or by a change in conditions in the neighborhood surrounding the rezoned site. Cases decided under the Maryland change-mistake rule have set aside zoning amend-

130. *Id.* at 378, 200 A.2d at 415.
131. The *Cleaver* court addressed the spot-zoning objections to the rezoning independently, but found that the rezoning was consistent with other applicable zoning in the surrounding area and that the tract was adjacent to the heavily used railroad tracts. The rezoning in *Cleaver* could thus have been independently supported as consistent with uses in the surrounding area, apart from the policies adopted in the township plan. While the court's assumption that apartments are properly placed near busy railroad tracks may be open to question, there is at least enough evidence in the case to indicate that the rezoning would not introduce an intrusive use into the area.

ments consistent with a comprehensive plan when there have been no changes in land use in the surrounding neighborhood that justify the amendment. A leading case of this type is *Chapman v. Montgomery County Council*,[132] in which plaintiffs challenged a rezoning of a 5.8-acre tract from rural residential to commercial in a fast-growing area of the county. The purpose of the rezoning was to allow construction of a convenience shopping center to serve the area, and the council had indicated that approval of this shopping center was necessary in order to avoid expansion of a nearby shopping center, which the plan did not favor. Nevertheless, the court set aside the zoning amendment, saying: A 'Master Plan' is not to be confused as a substitute for a comprehensive zoning or rezoning map, nor may it be equated with it in legal significance."[133] Substantial growth in the population of the neighborhood was not to be treated as a sufficient change in condition in this case.

Chapman represents the prevailing view in Maryland concerning the role of the comprehensive plan in supporting rezoning amendments.[134] It also provides some guidance on the problem raised in *Fasano*, to the extent that the court considered the intrusiveness of the commercial use in the surrounding residential area as a factor counting against the rezoning. Moreover, the case illustrates the deficiencies of the change-mistake rule, which requires a neighborhood change commensurate with the proposed use to support the rezoning, and which discounts substantially the role of the plan in supporting zoning changes. If the plan cannot be used to support zoning changes that implement the urban pattern proposed for the community, the community will always have to zone reactively—that is, after the character of the neighborhood has changed sufficiently to support zoning amendments to more intensive uses.

Legislation in Maryland has now codified the change-mistake rule, and lists a series of factors to be considered in determining whether a change in conditions has occurred.[135] This legislation encourages the recognition of the policies of the plan in cases like *Chapman*, in which urban development has progressed substantially and the application of the plan's policies in the rezoning process helps implement a reasonable growth pattern. As the dissent in *Chapman* noted,[136]

132. 259 Md. 641, 271 A.2d 156 (1970).
133. *Id.* at 643, 271 A.2d at 157.
134. However, a rezoning consistent with a comprehensive plan has been approved when it was supported by a change in neighborhood conditions. *See* note 107 *supra; see also* Board of County Comm'rs v. Edmonds, 240 Md. 680, 215 A.2d 209 (1965).
135. Md. Ann. Code art. 66B, § 4.05(a) (1970).
136. 259 Md. at 656, 271 A.2d at 163-64.

comprehensive plan revisions and comprehensive rezonings are expensive, difficult, and time-consuming, while population continues to grow in the interim between these comprehensive reformulations. The comprehensive plan should provide a guide to the local legislative body in meeting public needs for development that must be accommodated in this interim period.

The Role of the Comprehensive Plan in Floating Zone and Other Administrative Zoning Techniques. The discussion in the previous section has considered primarily the role of the comprehensive plan as a justification for zoning amendments. Comprehensive planning policies may also provide a justification for zoning changes made through floating zones, which may or may not require a zoning amendment, and through conditional use and special exception procedures, which are explicitly authorized by the SZEA.[137] As the discussion has noted, some courts have been willing to accept floating zone approvals even when the approval of the floating zone is inconsistent with the policies of the plan. These cases should be examined more closely. There is no apparent reason why conditional use and floating-zone changes should be favored over zoning amendments when the policies of the plan are at stake.

Why some courts have excused floating zone and conditional use changes from conformity with comprehensive planning policies may be evident in another Oregon case, *Archdiocese of Portland v. County of Washington*.[138] This case, decided prior to both *Fasano* and *Baker*, considered a request for a conditional use permit to allow the construction of a church, school, and gymnasium in a residentially zoned

---

137. SZEA, *supra* note 8, at § 7. *See also* Chapter 4 *supra*.

138. 254 Ore. 77, 458 P.2d 682 (1969). In State *ex rel.* Standard Mining & Dev. Corp. v. City of Auburn, 82 Wash. 2d 321, 510 P.2d 647 (1975), the city's zoning ordinance provided for gravel mining operations in "any district" if authorized by a special permit issued by the city council. At issue was the reasonableness of the conditions imposed by the council in granting the special permit. The court held that standards to guide the council in imposing conditions on the permit could be found by looking to the purposes of zoning as set out in the comprehensive plan and need not be stated in the ordinance itself.

A number of cases have upheld floating zones even though not recommended by the plan. Loh v. Town Plan & Zoning Comm'n, 161 Conn. 32, 282 A.2d 221 (1963) (master plan is merely advisory and is not the comprehensive plan, which is to be found in the scheme of the zoning regulations); Sheridan v. Planning Bd., 159 Conn. 1, 266 A.2d 396 (1969) (the court followed the unitary theory, distinguishing the *Eves* case and noting that the plan was advisory only). *Cf.* Lutz v. City of Longview, 83 Wash. 2d 566, 520 P.2d 1374 (1974) (lack of specific guidelines for PUDs in comprehensive plan did not mean that approval of a PUD was invalid as spot zoning). *See also* Kristensen v. City of Eugene Planning Comm'n, 544 P.2d 591 (Or. App. 1976) (upholding a conditional use for a mobile home).

area. The conditional use had been denied by the county board of commissioners, and the denial was upheld by the Oregon Supreme Court. Upholding the denial, the court treated the comprehensive planning issue as follows:

> [T]he ordinance itself reveals the legislative plan forecasting the likelihood that certain specified uses will be needed to maximize the use of land in the zone for residential purposes. . . . Therefore, unlike the spot zoning cases, the granting of permits for conditional uses is not likely to cause . . . [an] erosive effect upon the comprehensive zoning plan.[139]

This language needs interpretation. Zoning ordinance provisions authorizing conditional uses and floating zones must contain sufficiently precise standards to guide the discretion of the zoning agency when approving a development submitted under these provisions. Perhaps the court meant to say that the inclusion of these criteria removes any need to rely on the policies of the comprehensive plan as a guide to conditional use and floating zone approvals. This position may be accepted in the case of conditional uses, which are not usually discordant with existing uses in the area in which they are allowed. The same claim cannot be made for floating zones, which may be structured to allow intensive new development in previously undeveloped areas in which they create a substantial change in the land-use pattern.

If the floating zone provisions require a review of the floating zone to determine its compatibility with the area in which it is to be located, the courts might be led to rely on the criteria governing approval of the floating zone as an alternative to the policies of the comprehensive plan, even when the approval of the floating zone is not consistent with the plan. Nevertheless, an approval of a floating zone that is inconsistent with the comprehensive plan may severely distort planning policies. In this situation there is no reason why the floating zone, any more than the zoning amendment, would be allowed to depart from the comprehensive plan's proposals.

Courts should be sensitive to floating zone approvals that depart substantially from comprehensive planning policies. This problem can be handled through zoning enabling legislation or local ordinances, which can require floating zone and similar approvals—as well as zoning amendments—to be consistent with the plan.[140] These

---

139. 254 Ore. at 84–85, 458 P.2d at 636.

140. Suess v. Vogelgesang, 281 N.E.2d 536 (1972) (variance); Tavares v. Zoning Bd. of Review, 103 R.I. 186, 235 A.2d 883 (1967) (exception). The variance statute in the *Suess* case, Ind. Ann. Stat. Code § 18-7-2-71 (Burns 1974), applies only to Indianapolis and Marion County. *But cf.* Board of Zoning Appeals v. Shell Oil Co., 329 N.E.2d 636 (1975).

cautions apply with equal force to PUDs and other administrative approvals authorized by the zoning ordinance.

Revision of the Comprehensive Plan to Provide Consistency with Zoning Changes. Assuming that a court will give credence to the policies of a comprehensive plan when passing on the validity of a rezoning or floating zone, a question arises over the steps that must be taken to achieve a proper revision of the comprehensive plan that will support the amendment or floating zone. Some courts have been willing to accept a revision of the comprehensive plan concurrently with the zoning amendment[141] —a process that conceivably can lead to an abuse of the planning process. If the plan can be amended piecemeal in order to support a zoning change, the role of the plan as a well-considered and comprehensive statement of community planning policies will be diluted, and the reasons for relying on the comprehensive plan as a basis for a rezoning will be seriously compromised.

Some jurisdictions have now prohibited piecemeal rezoning and plan revisions. They may require rezoning amendments to be grouped for consideration at a limited number of times during the year, or may provide that comprehensive rezoning be carried out on a cyclical schedule.[142] Likewise, amendments to the comprehensive plan can be limited to a certain number of times during any one year.[143] These limitations do not entirely remove the danger of ad hoc rezonings or piecemeal plan amendments, but by grouping a number of amendments or plan revisions for consideration at a particular point, they do reduce the problem.

Some courts may also be willing to disregard the policies of a comprehensive plan when a considerable period of time has elapsed since the plan's adoption, and when changes in the nature of the community have made the plan's policies obsolete as applied to

141. Wiegel v. Planning & Zoning Comm'n, 160 Conn. 239, 273 A.2d 766 (1971); Malafronte v. Planning & Zoning Bd., 155 Conn. 205, 230 A.2d 606 (1967); Westfield v. City of Chicago, 26 Ill. 2d 526, 187 N.E.2d 208 (1963); Cheney v. Village 2, 419 Pa. 626, 241 A.2d 81 (1968); Furniss v. Township of Lower Merion, 412 Pa. 404, 194 A.2d 926 (1963); Donahue v. Zoning Bd. of Adjustment, 412 Pa. 332, 194 A.2d 610 (1963). *Cf.* Tierney v. Duris, 536 P.2d 435 (1975).

142. Cappolino v. County Bd. of Appeals, 23 Md. App. 358, 328 A.2d 55 (1974). The Baltimore County Code provides for periodic consideration of zoning reclassification petitions; a different section requires the planning board to recommend to the council a complete, countywide zoning map every four years. The court approved the cyclical consideration of zoning amendments as consistent with good zoning practice.

143. Cal. Gov't Code § 65361 (Deering 1974). For a recommendation endorsing this procedure, *see* Krasnowiecki, *Model Land Use Development Code*, in Maryland Planning and Zoning Law Study Comm'n: Final Report 53, 109–10 (1969).

the litigation at hand.[144] This approach has its dangers, such as timing and growth management programs in which the plan is expected to provide a framework for the phasing of new development over a period of many years. Nevertheless, communities should not be able to escape their responsibilities of plan revision.

An alternative judicial approach in cases in which an outdated plan has not been revised would presume that the plan is no longer representative of community policy, and would put the burden on the community to prove the contrary.[145] Otherwise, if the community contemplates a revision of the plan to support the zoning change, an independent and fully considered amendment of the comprehensive plan is necessary in order to prevent a pro forma change in the plan concurrent with the change in the zoning ordinance.

The basis on which a revision in the plan can be made was considered in a case arising under the Stamford, Connecticut city charter, which makes the city plan mandatory and which prohibits any "use in any area which is contrary to the general land use established for such area by the master plan." An independent and prior change in the land-use map is apparently necessary before a change can be made in the zoning ordinance. In *Rosenberg v. Planning Bd. of the City of Stamford*,[146] the Connecticut Supreme Court considered a change in the city plan authorizing the construction of office and laboratory buildings on an unimproved 35-acre tract in the city. The court rejected the argument that the plan may be amended only to reflect changes in conditions occurring since the denial of a previous

---

144. Town of Bedford v. Village of Mount Kisco, 33 N.Y.2d 178, 306 N.E.2d 155, 351 N.Y.S.2d 129 (1973). A tract of land was rezoned by the village from single-family to multifamily residential. This rezoning was inconsistent with a preexisting comprehensive plan that had not been amended in ten years. Noting that the proper standard by which to measure the "in conformity" requirement was current comprehensive planning, the court held that the particulars of the plan (which could have been amended) could be disregarded since the amendment was in harmony with the general policy of providing convenient housing near places of employment. Comprehensive planning, not strict adherence to a particular plan, was the objective.

Several problems are raised by this decision. One is that a court taking this position will be at liberty to disregard an adopted plan under its own view of whether the plan is outdated. This decision will in turn require an analysis by the court of whether conditions have so changed in the community that the policies of the plan are no longer to be credited, an analysis that will project the court into a policy-making role. Once the court decides that the plan can be disregarded it will likewise be able to decide on the validity of a zoning change based on its own view of local development policy, which will not have been considered and evaluated through the local planning process.

145. This problem could also be handled by a statutory provision requiring the comprehensive revision of the plan at periodic intervals. See note 142 *supra*.

146. 155 Conn. 636, 236 A.2d 895 (1967).

amendment of the plan to allow the same use. Otherwise, "a prime function of the planning board, which is to anticipate and direct the future orderly development of the city of Stamford" would be thwarted.[147]

Rosenberg allows the court considerable flexibility in amending the plan to reflect changes in planning policy. But it does not consider the procedures that must be followed in making amendments to the comprehensive plan. This issue is critical in any jurisdiction that adopts mandatory planning and a requirement that zoning be consistent with that plan. This requirement will be undercut if the community may arbitrarily revise comprehensive planning policies without going through procedures that can guarantee that any such revision has been properly considered. This concern may underlie decisions in Oregon that have applied *Fasano* reasoning to the comprehensive plan amendment process, and that require amendments to a plan affecting an individual piece of property to go through quasi-judicial procedures.[148]

Short of requiring quasi-judicial procedures in the plan revision process, a court may secure some considered attention to plan revisions by enforcing provisions found in many community charters and enabling acts that impose strict review and referral procedures on comprehensive plan revisions. This position was taken in *Dalton v. City and County of Honolulu*,[149] in which the court considered a provision of the Honolulu charter that requires all zoning ordinances to conform to and implement the general plan of the county. The provisions of the charter define the plan as "the council's policy for the long-range, comprehensive physical development"[150] of the county, and require any addition to or change in the general plan to be referred to both the planning director and the planning commission. If the commission disapproves or modifies the proposed change, the council may adopt it nonetheless—but only by an affirmative vote of at least two-thirds of its membership.

In *Dalton* this procedure was not followed, and the council amended both the general plan and the zoning ordinance on the same day to allow medium-density residential development, without hav-

---

147. *Id.* at 639, 236 A.2d at 897-9. *Cf.* dictum in Tierney v. Duris, 536 P.2d 435, 437 (1975) ("changes would appear permissible when the original plan was in error, or there has been a change in the community, or there has been a change in policy, such as could be produced [*sic*] by city and county election results").

148. *E.g.*, Marggi v. Ruecker, 533 P.2d 1372 (1975).

149. 51 Haw. 400, 462 P.2d 199 (1969). This case is discussed in 1 Williams, *supra* note 56 at 527-534.

150. 51 Haw. 400, 462 P.2d at 205.

ing referred the plan amendment, as required by the charter, for the advice of the planning director and the planning commission. The plan amendment was invalidated by the court. It held that no plan amendment could be made unless the specific procedures required by the charter were followed, for "[t]hese sections of the charter allow less room for the exertion of pressure by powerful individuals and institutions."[151] Moreover, the court held specifically that alterations to the plan must be comprehensive and long-range, and that amendments to the plan must be accompanied by new studies that support a need for additional housing. These studies must show that the housing should be located at the site in question, and that the proposed site is the "best site" for additional housing—taking into account the possibility that some other site might be used to meet housing need, or that the site in question might be put to some other use to meet some other need that was under-estimated in the original plan.[152]

The Honolulu plan under review in the *Dalton* case was quite detailed, and the effect of that case has been to require detailed amendments based on a change in planning policy.[153] Piecemeal elaborate

151. *Id.* at 416, 462 P.2d at 209.

152. The authority of the *Dalton* case may have been weakened by a 1972 amendment to the city charter that dropped the word comprehensive from the definition of the general plan as well as the requirement for detailed studies. Revised Charter of the City of Honolulu § 5-408 (1973). However, *see* Hall v. City & County of Honolulu, 530 P.2d 737 (1975), holding that the hearing requirement imposed by the *Dalton* case as a condition to the adoption or amendment of the general plan is not satisfied by a hearing on one of the detailed plans that the charter authorizes to more precisely spell out the policies of the general plan. The Honolulu charter authorizes a network of county and subcounty plans which is similar to the planning program adopted in Montgomery County, Maryland, as described *supra* note 52. For discussion, *see* League of Women Voters of Honolulu, The Citizen and the Planning Process: Understanding the System 2-3 (1974).

See also Colorado Leisure Products, Inc. v. Johnson, 532 P.2d 742 (1975). The court invalidated a rezoning because the council had failed to comply with the statutory requirement that amendments to a zoning ordinance be submitted to the planning commission for approval, disapproval, or comment.

A number of cases have upheld the statutory requirement of planning commission input prior to council action on a zoning change. *See, e.g.,* Houser v. Board of Comm'rs, 252 Ind. 301, 247 N.E.2d 670 (1969); Louisville v. McDonald, 470 S.W.2d 173 (Ky. 1971); Frankland v. Lake Oswego, 8 Ore. App. 224, 493 P.2d 163 (1972). *Cf.* Chrobuck v. Snohomish County, 78 Wash.2d 858, 480 P.2d 489 (1971). *But cf.* Wilhelm v. Morgan 208 Va. 398, 157 S.E.2d 920 (1967). The Kentucky court also requires adjudicative fact-findings following a trial-type hearing if the legislative body marked a zoning change contrary to the planning commission's recommendation. Hays v. City of Winchester, 495 S.W.2d 768 (Ky. 1973). The hearing may be held either by the commission or the legislative body. *See* Tarlock, *supra* note 55, at 94–101.

153. *See* Note, *Comprehensive Land Use Plans and the Consistency Requirement,* 2 Fla. St. U. L. Rev. 766, 770 772–75 (1974). How the *Dalton* case will be applied to the newly proposed generalized policy plan that might take the place of the existing detailed plan is not clear. *Id.* at 781–83.

amendments to the plan are thus permitted at any time under the *Dalton* case, provided the procedural and substantive requirements of the case have been met. This piecemeal amendment process is subject to abuse in spite of the court's call for long-range and comprehensive revisions to the plan. This problem to some extent is anticipated in that part of the *Dalton* opinion which places substantive constraints on plan revisions, thus echoing the comparison of alternative site requirement imposed on zoning amendments by the *Fasano* case.

Other problems of application are created by the *Dalton* decision. When communities adopt general policy plans in satisfaction of the comprehensive planning requirement, they may be so general that to require their amendment as a condition to a zoning change may be futile. This problem can to some extent be alleviated if communities are also required to adopt more specific sub-area plans to further articulate their generalized planning policies. The type of amendment procedures required under *Dalton* could then be applied to these sub-area plans.

The *Dalton* case also may produce problems if zoning agencies resist zoning changes simply to avoid the time and expense of updating the plan. This problem can be handled in the planning program if the plan is kept continuously under study, and if the locality will take steps to update the plan constantly through plan amendments, even though it may be necessary to do so on a less than comprehensive geographic basis.

A MANDATORY PLANNING REQUIREMENT FOR LOCAL GOVERNMENTS

Reasons for Mandatory Planning

Along with the failure of the model planning law to call explicitly for a comprehensive plan in the administration of the zoning process, the other major weakness of the legislation that time has revealed is the decision taken by the draftsman to make the planning function optional with local governments. The reasons for this decision were not made clear in the notes to the model law. Whatever they may have been, it is now apparent that changes in land-use control techniques, the expanded scope of comprehensive planning, and an increasing emphasis in federal legislation on mandatory planning in federal aid programs all underscore the need for mandating a comprehensive planning process at the local government level.

Significant procedural changes have affected the manner in which land-use allocations are made, and require an augmented planning base. Under the SZEA the assumption had been that land uses within communities would be allocated to zoning districts by the zoning map in advance of development. Development would then occur as a matter of right whenever it was consistent with the permitted mapped uses.

This assumption has given way as communities have increasingly relied on the zoning amendment process or on discretionary zoning techniques to make community land-use policy. Under this system the zoning ordinance is structured so that most new development requires a change in the zoning map or administrative approval before it can proceed. In this scheme zoning policy is made as zoning map changes and administrative approvals are granted, and is not reflected in the initial text and map of the zoning ordinance. Under this approach it is difficult to take a unitary view of the "in accordance" language and argue that the initial zoning map and ordinance manifest the plan, since the mapped zoning ordinance districts are not the major legal determinants of land use within the community. These districts may not be intended to indicate future land-use patterns in the area, which are determined instead as zoning map amendments are presented for consideration and approval. In other instances, as with floating zones and PUDs, the ordinance merely contains the text of the zoning district, and these districts are once more approved for mapping on a case-by-case basis.

An understanding of how the newer zoning system operates may have led the Pennsylvania Supreme Court in *Eves*[154] to call for an independent and well considered comprehensive plan as a prerequisite for the floating-zone process that the township had adopted in that case. While the *Eves* case is tinged by the court's dislike of discretionary techniques in zoning, its perception that the zoning ordinance can no longer function as the plan when the ordinance is not the true basis for land-use allocation is eminently sound.

Changes in the scope of comprehensive land-use planning also argue for a mandatory planning requirement at the local level. As noted above, land-use planning historically had been confined to planning for the arrangement of land uses in relation to existing and projected capital facilities. New pressures on the land planning and land-use control system now make more challenging demands. Especially in environmental and growth control programs, local planning policies are often needed that, among other objectives, will direct and contain new development so that environmental damage can be avoided, and maximum use made of existing and planned public

154. Eves. v. Zoning Bd. of Adjustment, 401 Pa. 211, 104 A.2d 7 (1960).

service facilities. These policies may restrict growth in certain areas of the community, such as wetlands and flood plains, while encouraging new growth at locations where environmental damage is not likely to occur. Higher densities may also be proposed at locations where new development is allowed, in order to minimize the encroachment of that development on agricultural and environmental resource areas. Mandatory comprehensive planning is needed more than ever before to rationalize public decisions to restrict or intensify development, so that landowners affected by these decisions will be fairly treated.

Lower income housing needs also demand attention in local and regional planning programs (see Chapter 6). Linkages between land-use planning and planning for lower income housing were particularly undeveloped in the early phase of land-use planning programs,[155] an omission caused in part by the fact that public subsidies for lower income housing were quite limited. Until the passage of the Federal Housing Act of 1968,[156] the only publicly subsidized housing available was public housing, and during most of the postwar years this program was funded by the federal government at minimum support levels.

The provision of federal subsidies for privately built lower income housing in the 1968 Act created a new awareness of the linkages between planning programs and decisions about the location and availability of subsidized housing. While the subsequent elimination of the 1968 housing production subsidies has somewhat reduced the pressure on planning programs that might otherwise be sensitive to lower income housing needs, the continuation of federal subsidies for privately built housing in the leased public housing program of the Housing and Community Development Act of 1974[157] has once more attracted some limited attention to the role of planning in the lower income housing effort.[158]

The effect of these newer substantive concerns on planning programs is that planning now requires judgments about land development alternatives that have increased impact on the land market. Planning and land-use control programs that implement environmental and growth control policies will have substantial impact

---

155. Mandelker, *The Comprehensive Planning Requirement in Urban Renewal*, 116 U. Pa. L. Rev. 25, 28, 29–30, 33–34, 56, 66, 67 (1967).

156. Housing and Urban Development Act of 1968, Pub. L. No. 90-448, 82 Stat. 476.

157. 42 U.S.C. § 1437f (Supp. 1974).

158. *See, e.g.*, City of Hartford v. Hills, 408 F. Supp. 889 (D. Conn. 1976) (appeal en banc pending in 2d Cir.).

on where development will occur. The containment policies often included in growth control programs are one example.

Planning policies that attempt to improve housing opportunities at the same time they provide environmental protection may also be in conflict.[159] Growth controls that limit the availability of land for development due to local service inadequacies may unduly restrict the amount of land available for development, and the resulting land scarcities may in turn inflate land prices so that housing opportunities for lower and even higher groups either disappear or are substantially diminished.[160] Some local growth control programs have attempted to deal with this issue through housing quotas that include mandatory set-asides for lower income housing before housing proposals for upper income groups will be approved. It remains to be seen whether these programs can accomplish their purpose in an unregulated land market. The major point is that comprehensive planning increasingly has been forced to choose between mutually exclusive, competing uses for land.

To the extent that the planning process can make these choices successfully, due process taking objections to land-use restrictions adopted in aid of the plan may be forestalled. This potentiality is another reason for legislating a mandatory planning requirement. Due process objections arise because land-use strategies that make mutually exclusive land development choices will inflict losses on landowners whose development opportunities have been restricted by these strategies. If these restrictions are imposed suddenly, with little notice, and not in accordance with a comprehensive planning policy, the market will not have an adequate opportunity to adapt.[161]

The best example of this situation is the down-zoning case. A community may down-zone land from high to lower residential densities, usually in aid of a growth restriction policy that requires a downward revision of expected development levels. Although technically the

159. "Although zoning must include schemes designed to allow municipalities to more effectively contend with the increased demands of evolving and growing communities, under its guise, townships have been wont to try their hand at an array of exclusionary devices in the hope of avoiding the very burden which growth must inevitably bring. . . ." Golden v. Planning Bd., 30 N.Y.2d 359, 375, 285 N.E.2d 291, 300, 334 N.Y.S.2d 138, *appeal dismissed*, 409 U.S. 1003 (1972).

160. *See* E. Bergman, External Validity of Policy Related Research on Development Controls and Housing Costs 20–29 (Center for Urban and Regional Studies, University of North Carolina, 1974); *digest version reprinted in* 3 Management and Control of Growth 527–26 (Urban Land Institute 1975).

161. For an analysis of the role of the plan in dealing with uncertainties in the land-use control process, *see* C. Haar, *The Master Plan: An Inquiry in Dialogue Form*, in Land-Use Planning 745 (2nd ed.; C. Harr ed. 1971). Haar's position is criticized in Tarlock, *supra* note 55, at 86–87.

landowner has no vested constitutional right to an existing zoning classification as applied to a parcel of undeveloped land, the courts have become increasingly hostile to piecemeal down-zonings not carried out as part of a comprehensive rezoning process.[162]

The problems created for the land market when zoning changes occur erratically can be avoided to some extent. When community policies for new growth and development are made comprehensively, and in advance, the market can internalize whatever restrictions are imposed in the name of planning policy and adjust accordingly. Land purchases at premium prices in restricted areas can then be viewed as a form of speculation against the system, and the inflated value paid for this land can be discounted in any appraisal of the validity of the restriction on police power grounds.[163]

This argument is not meant to suggest that firmly executed comprehensive planning will avoid all due process problems in land-use regulation.[164] But planning conceivably may reduce the incentive to buy land at a price that reflects a premium over its value for its planned use. In this way, planning may foreclose the possibility that developers may buy themselves into situations in which they believe land-development restrictions unconstitutionally deprive them of the right to develop their land for uses and densities that are profitable.

Mandatory planning is also needed to orient local land-use policies to a regional perspective. Housing markets are regional in scope, and lower income fair-share housing plans have usually been executed on a regional scale. Growth, pollution, and environmental control programs must also be focused on the regional level. No community can reasonably plan for growth control without taking the development policies of other communities in the region into account, and air and water pollution are certainly regional phenomena requiring regional control solutions.

162. Board of Supervisors v. Snell Constr. Crop., 214 Va. 655, 202 S.E.2d 889 (1974); Bagne, *Up and Down the Zoning Scale* (pts. 1-2), 26 Land Use L. & Zoning Dig. No. 10, at 6; *id.*, No. 11, at 6 (1974).

163. Krause v. City of Royal Oak, 11 Mich. App. 183, 195, 160 N.W.2d 769, 774 (1968) (dissenting opinion). On the other hand, the landowner who bought in reliance on established planning policies may well claim constitutional protection when these policies are changed. These problems have surfaced to some extent in the downzoning cases. *See* T.J. Kent, *supra* note 33.

164. Neither is this argument intended as an ad hominem approach to constitutional issues in land-use regulation. No inference is intended that the constitutional position of the landowner is dependent on speculative intent, although the cases are not without such suggestions. *See* American Nat'l Bank & Trust Co. v. City of Highland Park, 331 N.E.2d 597 (1975); Kraus v. City of Royal Oak, 11 Mich. App. 183, 160 N.W.2d 769 (1968).

These observations suggest that the regional focus of many land-development policies will create problems of inter-community equity when planning is not made mandatory throughout the region. If some communities plan while others do not, then only selected communities will have based their land-use controls on the necessary comprehensive planning that the administration of these policies requires. In that event, some areas of the regional land market will be subject to comprehensive planning programs and some will not. If too many communities fail to engage in a planning process, the unstabilizing effects on the regional land market can be substantial.

Recognition of this problem is seen in a growing array of federal legislation that requires state and regional involvement in several significant land development and capital facility programs that receive federal funds. Regional planning required under the Federal Highway Act,[165] the Water Pollution Control Act of 1972,[166] the Clean Air Act of 1970,[167] and the National Coastal Zone Management Act of 1972[168] combine to effect a massive, if sometimes unwitting, federal involvement in regional and local development decisions. Moreover, this involvement, when added to the requirements for environmental impact analysis under the National Environmental Policy Act[169] creates a disjointed maze of uncoordinated and overlapping programs for dealing with basic land-use and environmental issues.

The need for coordination of federal, state, regional, and local activities affecting land-use matters is discussed later in this book.[170] It should be noted, however, that state legislation mandating local planning can help secure the necessary local planning programs that can in turn relate to national, state, and regional planning efforts, and that can avoid conflicts among planning policies adopted at different governmental levels within the state.

State Legislation for Mandatory Comprehensive Planning

Court decisions giving weight to the comprehensive plan in litigation challenging zoning regulations can provide a helpful decisional

165. 23 U.S.C. § 134 (1970). *See also* 23 U.S.C. § 142 (1970), *as amended by* 23 U.S.C. § 142 (Supp. 1973).

166. 33 U.S.C. § 1288 (Supp. 1972).

167. *See* Mandelker & Rothschild, *The Role of Land-Use Controls in Combatting Air Pollution Under the Clean Air Act of 1970,* 3 Ecology L.Q. 235 (1973).

168. 16 U.S.C. §§ 1451–64 (Supp. 1972). *See* Mandelker & Sherry, *The National Coastal Zone Management Act of 1972,* 7 Urb. L. Ann. 119 (1974).

169. P.L. 90–190, 83 Stat. 852, 42 U.S.C. § 321, *et seq.* (1970).

170. *See* Chapter 4 *supra.*

base for the legal recognition of the planning process. The complex series of issues presented by the implementation of a mandatory planning and consistency requirement in land-use control administration suggest, however, that this requirement will have a firmer legal base if its details are spelled out in state planning and zoning enabling legislation.

State legislators face several major issues in developing state legislation of this type: (1) whether to mandate local comprehensive planning; (2) the form and content of the planning process as it is mandated at different governmental levels within the state; (3) the extent to which local land-use controls should be required to be consistent with locally adopted comprehensive plans; and (4) the extent to which local planning programs should be subject to review and modification by other government units.

Traditionally, state planning legislation in this country does not contain substantive planning policies, rarely prescribes the contents of the plan, and seldom indicates the goals that plan should achieve. This legislation is equally open-ended in describing the form the plan should take, although most planning legislation does require mapped plans. Given the varied contexts in which planning occurs within any state, this legislative stance is partly correct. At least during this period of rapid change in perspective, technique, and concept, state legislation should not force planners to choose between competing planning techniques (such as mapped and policy planning), but should allow the adoption of planning techniques that fit local needs.[171]

A more urgent question is whether state planning legislation should attempt some substantive guidance for the planning process, either by specifying the necessary linkages among the statutory planning elements that are required to produce an acceptable plan, or by prescribing the substantive goals of the planning process in those areas of concern where substantive guidance appears to be needed. Any such change in the character of state planning legislation would mark a significant modification of the SPEA and the state legislation that follows it.

These laws, as noted, were content to prescribe a shopping list of acceptable plan elements without indicating what policies the plan was to adopt or how these elements were to be combined to produce a plan that satisfied the statutory mandate. Modifications along these

---

171. State legislatures concerned about the overly vague plans produced by a policy-planning process may wish to circumscribe that process in some way— perhaps by requiring detailed subarea plans that give greater specificity to the textually stated policies of a policy plan. *See* note 521 *supra.*

lines may now be needed as planning broadens in scope to include new objectives, such as environmental protection, growth control, and meeting low-income housing needs. As frequently noted in the text, the concurrent pursuit of all these objectives at any one time in any planning jurisdiction will likely produce conflicting planning policies. Legislative direction is required that will at least mandate the development of a local plan in which these policy conflicts have been considered and resolved.

There are two central aspects of the mandatory planning question: (1) legislatures must decide whether and to what extent the exercise of local land-use controls must be consistent with an adopted plan; and (2) if state level land-use control powers are provided, legislatures must decide whether mandatory state planning should be a condition to the exercise of these controls. If planning is made mandatory throughout the state, closer attention will also have to be paid to the hierarchical distribution of planning responsibility. For example, it might be argued that the internal distribution of residential densities is a problem for local determination, while the determination of density levels and rates of growth for individual communities is a regional or state responsibility. Likewise, local planning generally can be trusted to make decisions on residential patterns, but the location and density of lower income housing should be decided at state or regional levels. State planning legislation will have to indicate which types of planning issues should be assigned to different levels of government within the state.

This section reviews recent legislative developments and proposals that either give some presumptive weight to the comprehensive plan as a guide to the administration of land-use controls, or make the comprehensive plan a mandatory requirement in the exercise of these controls. The role of a state statute in providing legislative guidance for the comprehensive planning function is examined first, while recent state legislation enacting a requirement that land-use controls be consistent with an adopted comprehensive plan will be examined next.

Statutory Elements of the Comprehensive Plan. In the area of urban growth management, a legislative direction should mandate that local planning consider the growth problem and provide the proper linkages between capital facilities programming, land-use projections, and density requirements so that a proper growth control program emerges.[172] Whether state legislation can go any further

172. *Cf.* Florida Local Government Comprehensive Planning Act of 1975, ch. 75-157, § 7(6)(a)(1975): "The future land use plan shall include a state-

than providing a direction that growth be orderly and balanced, with proper attention paid to the availability of urban services to support new urban development, is arguable.[173] Any attempt to provide by statute for a growth control policy that provides more substantive direction would probably be open to the charge that it legislates too much rigidity into the planning process.

An effort in this direction has been attempted in the 1974 Colorado land-use legislation. It does not mandate a planning process at the local level, but does delegate a permit approval authority to local governments over new major public facilities and facility extensions. Detailed substantive statutory requirements are provided to guide local governments in approving these facilities and facility extensions.[174] These requirements relate primarily to the need to protect some facilities, such as airports and highways, from congestion, but there is a statutory requirement that new urban development be adequately served by public facilities.[175]

Environmental concerns also need consideration in planning enabling legislation. The Colorado legislation noted above provides detailed substantive statutory requirements to ensure that environmentally sensitive areas are adequately protected from potentially

---

ment of the standards to be followed in the control and distribution of population densities and building structure and intensity as recommended for the various portions of the area."

173. One problem in doing so at the present time is that legislators face serious uncertainties about the constitutional limits of an acceptable growth-control program. One example is the limits of growth-control programs imposed by the federal right-to-travel doctrine. *See* Comment, *The Right to Travel: Another Constitutional Standard for Local Land Use Regulations?* 39 U. Chi. L. Rev. 612 (1972); *see also* Construction Industry Ass'n. v. City of Petaluma, 522 F.2d 897 (9th Cir. 1975), *cert. denied,* 47 L. Ed. 2d 342 (1976) and description of the case in Chapters 2 and 3 *supra.*

174. With reference to the extension of water and sewer facilities, the statute provides, Colo. Rev. Stat. § 106-7-704(b) (Supp. 1975):

Major extensions of domestic water and sewage treatment systems shall be permitted in those areas in which the anticipated growth and development that may occur as a result of such extension can be accommodated within the financial and environmental capacity of the area to sustain such growth and development.

175. *See also* Colo. Rev. Stat. § 106-7-204(7) (Supp. 1975):

When applicable, or as may otherwise be provided by law, a new community design shall, at a minimum, provide for transportation, waste disposal, schools, and other governmental services in a manner that will not overload facilities of existing communities of the region. Priority shall be given to the development of total communities which provide for commercial and industrial activity, as well as residences, and for internal transportation and circulation patterns.

See Bermingham, *1974 Land Use Legislation in Colorado*, 51 Denver L.J. 467 (1974).

harmful development.[176] Elsewhere, environmental planning problems have largely been handled in state legislation directed to environmental protection, and the environmental planning function has been explicitly delegated to state planning and environmental agencies. Examples are the coastal wetlands statutes adopted along the East Coast, which provide for close state supervision over development in coastal areas, and which in some cases include a planning component as the basis for the review of new development. The North Carolina coastal zone statute is in this category,[177] as is comparable legislation in California and elsewhere.[178]

State level authority for the designation and regulation of areas of critical state concern, which is contained in the American Law Institute's *Model Land Development Code* and which has been adopted in several states;[179] is another example of environmentally protective legislation, in this case not limited to coastal areas. However, the ALI critical areas proposal does not contain a mandatory state planning component, an omission that should be remedied so that statewide environmental area controls, like some of the more specific coastal zone control legislation, will be based on appropriate state planning policies. The inclusion of authority to plan and regulate critical environmental areas in local planning and land-use control legislation should also be considered. Subject to state review and direction where necessary, the inclusion of this authority in local enabling legislation is a necessary corollary to the provision of comparable state designation and regulation, as authorized by the ALI Code.

Another environmentally related planning concern to be considered for inclusion in the state planning program is the preservation

176. Colo. Rev. Stat. § 106-7-202(3) (Supp. 1975):

Areas containing, or having a significant impact upon, historical, natural, or archaeological resources of statewide importance, as determined by the state historical society, the department of natural resources, and the appropriate local government, shall be administered by the appropriate state agency in conjunction with the appropriate local government in a manner that will allow man to function in harmony with, rather than be destructive to, these resources. Consideration is to be given to the protection of those areas essential for wildlife habitat. Development in areas containing historical, archaeological, or natural resources shall be conducted in a manner which will minimize damage to those resources for future use.

177. Coastal Area Management Act of 1974, N.C. Gen. Stat. §§ 113A-100 to -128 (1975).
178. Cal. Pub. Res. Code §§ 27000 to 27650 (Deering Supp. 1975); Shoreline Management Act of 1971, Wash. Rev. Code Ann. §§ 90.58.010 to -.930 (Supp. 1975). *See also* Comment, *Coastal Controls in California: Wave of the Future?* 11 Harv. J. Legis. 463 (1974).
179. Mandelker, *Critical Area Controls: A New Dimension in American Land Development Regulation*, 41 J.A.I.P. 21 (1975).

of agricultural areas from intrusive urban growth. The Hawaii Land Use Law pioneered in this field at the state level by providing a state program of direct land-use regulation aimed primarily at protecting agricultural land.[180] There have also been proposals that a planning element directed to the preservation of agricultural lands be included in state legislation mandating a local planning program.[181] A policy for the protection of agricultural land is only one component of a comprehensive local growth control program, but legislative concern for agricultural protection requires some attention to this problem in state comprehensive planning enabling legislation.

One difficulty with growth control and environmental protection programs is that localities, inadvertently or otherwise, may use these programs to exclude housing for lower income groups. Recent judicial authority has emphasized the need to provide for lower income housing as a necessary component of local zoning programs.[182] Attention to the lower income housing issue is an essential part of local planning efforts if comprehensive policies are to be provided to which local zoning actions sensitive to the lower income housing issue can respond. Local planning enabling legislation should include specific substantive provisions requiring a lower income housing element, and these provisions should require the provision of a balanced supply of housing for all income groups. There is some statutory precedent for this approach.[183]

Substantive policy direction for planning lower income housing programs appears warranted because of the danger that local governments will not be sensitive to this issue, and because of the relative consensus about the need for planning programs to respond to housing problems.[184] In fragmented metropolitan areas, the danger exists that a mandated local planning program for lower income housing will be difficult to apply because of the problem of requiring each

180. Hawaii Rev. Stat. ch. 205 (Supp. 1975). *See* Mark, *It All Began in Hawaii*, 46 State Gov't 188 (1973).

181. Washington State House Bill No. 168, § 16(2), 44th Reg. Sess., 1975. The bill died in committee.

182. Southern Burlington County NAACP v. Township of Mount Laurel, 67 N.J. 151, 336 A.2d 713; *appeal dismissed and cert. denied*, 423 U.S. 808 (1975). *See* discussion of other such cases in Chapter 2 *supra.*

183. *See* note 31 *supra. But cf.* Ybarra v. Town of Los Altos Hills, 503 F.2d 250 (9th Cir. 1974). A New York State study commission has likewise called for the preparation of a mandatory housing element in local plans to provide a broad range of housing alternatives. This mandatory housing element would in turn provide a basis for judicial review of local land use regulation. Report of the Temporary State Commission on the Powers of Local Government, Strengthening Local Government in New York State, Part 2: Services, Structure, and Finance 55–61 (1973).

184. *See generally* Chapter 6 *infra.*

local government in the area to provide for some portion of regional lower income housing need. The New Jersey Supreme Court has been sensitive to this issue, recognizing the practical problems at the regional or state level of articulating a fair-share distribution of lower income housing that takes regional needs into account.[185]

State planning enabling legislation is needed that can provide a statutory basis for state and regional planning for lower income housing, and that can take into account the varying capacities of local governments to provide for this housing. State legislation can also provide a basis for integrating the new and existing regional fair-share housing plans with the housing assistance plans (HAPs) that are now required as part of the federal community development block grant program.[186]

Other enacted and proposed legislation, such as the American Law Institute's *Model Land Development Code*, provides a separate statutory review process for dealing with the lower income housing problem that does not require the adoption of a comprehensive plan at either the state or local levels.[187] This approach can be of assistance in meeting lower income housing needs; but without a planning base for the siting and review of lower income housing developments, this model legislation provides an incomplete statutory response to the lower income housing issue.

Consistency Between the Comprehensive Plan and Land-Use Controls. Several states have now adopted legislation mandating planning by local governments within the state; some of this legislation also requires that local zoning be consistent with the comprehensive plan once it is adopted.[188] This legislation usually expands the list of

185. *See* Oakwood at Madison, Inc. v. Township of Madison, 117 N.J. Super. 11, 283 A.2d 353 (1971), aff'd —— N.J. ——, 371 A.2d 1192 (1977), expanding and modifying the *Mount Laurel* rule, and discussion of the *Madison Township* case in Chapters 2 and 3 *supra*.

186. *See* discussion of regional "fair-share" housing plans and housing assistance plans in Chapter 6 *infra*.

187. Lower income housing is classified as development of regional benefit. ALI Code, *supra* note 27, at § 7-301(4)(d). Any local land-development control decision affecting such development may be appealed to a state adjudicatory board, which in passing on the development is to consider as one factor the need for housing that is reasonably accessible to places of employment. *Id.* § 7-402(5). Another section of the code contains special review procedures that prohibit the approval of major employment facilities unless housing is available for employees that is reasonably accessible to the facilities. *Id.* § 7-305. *See* discussion of these provisions in Chapter 7 *infra*.

188. The California, Florida, Kentucky, and Nebraska legislation is discussed in the text *infra*. For additional legislation mandating a local plan, see Alaska Stat. §§ 29.33.070, 29.33.085, -.090 (Supp. 1975) (also requires zoning to be

planning elements and makes some of these elements mandatory, but otherwise does not modify the definition of the comprehensive plan in the SPEA. Statutory innovation has occurred primarily in provisions that for the first time require local zoning and other land-use regulations to be consistent with the local comprehensive plan once it is adopted.

California. California requires local governments to adopt a plan that includes both mandatory and optional elements, but the statute provides mandatory substantive planning policies only for the housing element. The zoning enabling legislation then requires zoning to be consistent with an adopted local plan, and defines the term consistent in the following way: "the various land uses authorized by the ordinance are compatible with the objectives, policies, general land uses and programs specified in such a plan."[189] This definition of

consistent with plan); Del. Code Ann. tit. 9, §§ 6807(a), 6904 (Sussex County, same as Alaska); D.C. Code §§ 1-1002(a)(4)(D), 5-414 (Supp. 1975) (same as Alaska); Hawaii Rev. Stat. § 225-21 (Supp. 1975) (also requires local plans to conform to state plan); Idaho Code Ann. §§ 67-6508, 67-6511 (Supp. 1975) (same as Alaska); Ind. Ann. Stat. Code § 18-7-2-31 (1974); Va. Code Ann. §§ 15.1-427-46 (Supp. 1975). *See also* the recent New Jersey legislation discussed in the text accompanying note 58, *supra.*

Local planning is not mandatory in Arizona and Maine, but once a plan has been adopted, local zoning regulations must be consistent with the plan. Ariz. Rev. Stat. Ann. § 9-462.01(E) (Supp. 1975); Me. Rev. Stat. Ann. tit. 30, § 4962 (1)(A) (Supp. 1973). *Cf.* Minn. Stat. Ann. § 462.357(2) (Supp. 1976) (planning agency to prepare zoning ordinance "at any time" after adoption of land-use plan). The planning agency is required to prepare a plan in Rhode Island and in Washington counties, but adoption by the governing body is optional. R.I. Gen. Laws § 45-24-3 (1956); Wash. Rev. Code Ann. § 36.70.320 (Supp. 1975). Nev. Rev. Stat. §§ 278.640-75 (Supp. 1975) authorizes the governor to prescribe, amend, and administer land-use plans and zoning regulations for any county lands not subject to comprehensive plans and zoning regulations as of 1975. The governor may enjoin any development that does not conform to an applicable plan. *See also* Md. Ann. Code art. 23A, § 9(c) (1970). This law specifies that for a period of five years following annexation, an annexing municipality may not rezone the annexed land to permit a land use substantially different from that allowed by the land-use plans to which the annexed land was subject prior to annexation. This provision was upheld in Maryland-National Capital Park & Planning Comm'n v. Mayor & Council, 272 Md. 550, 325 A.2d 748 (1974).

For a locally adopted mandatory county planning requirement, *see* Charter of Broward County, Florida, § 6.605(D)(G) (1974). The charter requires all zoning governing uses and densities to comply with the county land-use plan.

For a Canadian example, *see* Ottawa Regional Community Act, National Assembly of Quebec, c. 85, § 142 (1969), *as amended by* c. 85, § 1 (1974).

189. Cal. Gov't. Code § 65860 (Deering 1974). Cal. Bus. & Prof. Code §§ 11526(c), 11549.5 (Deering Cum. Supp. 1973) require subdivisions to be consistent with the "general or specific plans of the city or county." *Id.* § 11526.1 mandates enactment of a specific plan for the area in which the subdivision is to be included. Under *id.* § 65052(c), which requires that every general plan in California have a housing element, and *id.* § 65008, which states that federally financed housing is to be treated the same as conventionally financed housing, federally financed housing is also subject to the consistency requirement unless the city or county has a state-approved plan for federal housing.

consistency may be defective because it only requires the land uses "authorized" by the zoning ordinance to be related to the plan, and thus does not apply specifically to zoning amendments, unless a land use permitted by a zoning amendment is authorized by the zoning ordinance once the amendment is adopted. This interpretation appears consistent with the statute as it is written.

"Compatible" is the key term that provides the link between the comprehensive plan and the zoning ordinance under the California statute. As yet there have not been any appellate court cases interpreting this term,[190] but some interpretive help has been provided by guidelines issued at the state level for the preparation of local plans. These guidelines note that the comprehensive plan is generalized and long range, while the zoning ordinance has "immediate force and effect on each parcel of land."[191] They then state that "[t]he zoning ordinance should be considered consistent with the general plan when the allowable uses and standards contained in the text of the ordinance tend to further the policies of the general plan and do not inhibit or obstruct the attainment of those articulated policies."[192] The guidelines thus appear to state a "rule of reason" for relating the zoning ordinance to the comprehensive plan, which is similar to the position that courts have taken on the same issue without the benefit of a statutory requirement.[193]

Growth timing problems are not explicitly considered by the California legislation, although the guidelines suggest that zoning should gradually be revised to reflect the plan's projection of future growth patterns.[194] Similar problems are created by a provision in the statute that requires the zoning ordinance to be amended in a reasonable

190. There have been some attorney general opinions, *e.g.,* Op. Att'y Gen. No. CV 72-114(a) (Jan. 15, 1975). *See also* Coalition for Los Angeles County Planning in the Public Interest v. Board of Supervisors, No. 6-63218 (Cal. Super. Ct., Mar. 12, 1975), in which petitioners successfully challenged the adoption of a new general plan on numerous grounds, including the failure of the plan to be internally consistent in implementing the housing elements required by the California statute.

191. *See* California Council on Intergovernmental Relations, General Plan Guidelines II-11 (1973).

192. *Id.* at II-13.

193. *But cf.* Roseta v. County of Washington, 254 Ore. 161, 458 P.2d 405 (1969) (court suggested that a planning policy generally designating an area for residential use did not justify a zoning amendment shifting a lot in the area from a single-family to a multifamily classification).

194. The zoning ordinance, being current and precise, reflects the existing phase of land development, but should gradually follow the general plan into the future as appropriate in relation to timing and sequence of uses. Thus it would be inconsistent with the plan to zone a large area of existing low intensity use . . . [for high intensity] scattered uses [that] might . . . contravene a general plan policy calling for compact urban development.

Guidelines, *supra* note 191 at II-12.

time to conform with any amendments in the plan. An allowance for the gradual revision of the zoning ordinance to conform to a plan amendment would be helpful in this situation as well. Greater flexibility in meeting the zoning consistency provision also would be achieved if more detailed sub-area plans were prepared to implement general plan policies, such as long term growth policies, as they matured.[195] The statute could also specify that a community could meet the consistency requirement through the adoption of a floating zone, PUD or similar procedure, through which zoning changes to meet the policies of the plan could be made as needed.

Under the California statute, compliance with the statutory consistency requirement may be enforced through a court action brought by a resident or property owner in the municipality. This provision has been interpreted broadly by the attorney general, who has ruled that the cause of action authorized by the statute arises when the zoning ordinance is inconsistent with the plan, when there is no adopted plan, or when a plan does not include all the required statutory elements.[196] While this ruling raises questions about the competence of the court to grant all the relief the attorney general considers possible, he suggests that the court can retain jurisdiction to enforce compliance with the consistency requirement, and can enjoin the issuance of building permits or any other zoning actions until the consistency requirement has been met. A similar approach has now been taken by the Oregon Supreme Court in enforcing a plan consistency requirement that has been judicially imposed on cities in that state.[197]

The California attorney general also ruled that while a court cannot mandate the preparation of any specific planning policies, it can at least mandate the preparation of a plan containing such policies as the locality chooses to adopt.[198] Since the California planning enabling legislation contains a substantive requirement mandating the preparation of a housing element in local plans providing a reasonable balance of housing for all segments of the community, a court could also rule on the extent to which the locality has complied with this substantive mandate. In this event it could presumably inspect the housing element of the plan to determine whether or not the plan has been faithful to the statutory directive.

---

195. There is explicit statutory authority in California for this type of plan. Cal. Govt. Code §§ 65450–52 (Deering 1974).

196. Op. Att'y Gen. No. CV 72-114(a) (Jan. 15, 1975).

197. Baker v. City of Milwaukie, 533 P.2d 772 (1975). Without the benefit of a statutory provision, the court held that a mandamus action was available to a resident of the community to enforce zoning consistency with a master plan.

198. Op. Att'y Gen. No. CV 72-114(a) (Jan. 15, 1975).

Florida. A plan consistency provision that is both more focused and broader in scope has been adopted in Florida. Planning by counties, municipalities, and special districts is statutorily required in Florida. County plans are to govern within the limits of munici-palities and special districts if these governmental units do not pre-pare plans; and the state planning agency may prepare a plan for any county that does not prepare a plan by the statutory deadline.[199] Mandatory and optional elements are prescribed for all plans, includ-ing a mandatory housing element, which must provide for low- and moderate-income housing needs. Some direction for the preparation of growth control programs is also provided. The statute lists the coordination of the various planning elements as a major goal of the planning process.[200]

This statutory framework for comprehensive planning provides the basis for an extensive consistency provision, which is directed to development by government agencies as well as to local land-use regulations:

> After a comprehensive plan . . . has been adopted . . . all development un-dertaken by, and all actions taken in regard to development orders by, governmental agencies in regard to land covered by such plan . . . shall be consistent with such plan. . . . All land development regulations enacted or amended shall be consistent with the adopted plan.[201]

This provision is reinforced by another provision stating that it is the intent of the act that the adoption and enforcement of local land development regulations be related to and implement the compre-hensive plan.[202] Another section authorizes court review of the relationship between the comprehensive plan and government ac-tions, or land development regulations that implement the plan.[203] Land development regulations are defined to include zoning, sub-division controls, and all other regulations "controlling the de-velopment of land."[204]

Apart from its extension of the consistency requirement to land development regulations other than the zoning ordinance, and its

---

199. Florida Local Government Comprehensive Planning Act of 1975, ch. 75-257, §§ 4(4), 4(5) (1975). A county plan recommended by the state plan-ning agency must be adopted by the state administration commission, which consists of the goveror and cabinet.
200. *See id.* § 7.
201. *Id.* § 12(1).
202. *Id.* § 14.
203. *Id.* § 12(3)(a).
204. *Id.* § 12(2)(b).

explicit inclusion of amendments to these regulations, the major contribution of the Florida consistency provision is its direct application of the policies of the plan to development actions by governmental agencies. In this fashion it follows British planning legislation, which applies the policies of the plan directly through development control orders without the intervention of a locally adopted ordinance, such as a zoning ordinance.[205]

As applied to public agency development, the Florida law apparently makes the policies of an adopted comprehensive plan directly binding on land development policies, modifying the traditional view which has not always held development by government agencies to be subject to zoning regulations.[206] If applied to private development, a similar provision would mark a substantial change in land development control administration, as private development would be tested directly by the policies of the plan and not indirectly by zoning or other land development regulations that implement the policies of the plan.

There is some warrant for interpreting the Florida law to apply to private development, as it requires all "actions taken in regard to development orders" by government agencies to be consistent with planning policies. A development order is defined in turn as "any order granting, denying, or granting with conditions an application for a development permit."[207] In short, government actions authorizing private land development by order apparently must be consistent with the policies of the plan, whether or not they directly implement the provisions of a zoning or other land development regulation.

Kentucky. A more limited plan consistency provision is contained in the Kentucky planning act. This act permits the adoption of a zoning ordinance once the objectives of the comprehensive plan have been adopted.[208] Preparation of the plan in full is not required.

205. *See* Hagman, *Articles 1 and 2 of A Model Land Development Code: The English Are Coming*, 1971 Land Use Controls Ann. 3.

206. *See generally* Comment, *The Applicability of Zoning Ordinances to Governmental Land Use*, 39 Tex. L. Rev. 316 (1961). Under the Florida law, government agencies are defined to include federal, state, local, and special-district agencies. The applicability of the consistency provision to development by federal agencies is questionable in view of federal sovereign immunity. *See* Comment, *Preemption of Local Zoning by Federal Lessee*, 1971 Urb. L. Ann. 200.

207. *Id.* § 3(5). This definition appears to be borrowed from a like definition contained in ALI Code, *supra* note 27, § 1-201(13). It should be noted that the code does not require the adoption of local zoning or similar ordinances in order to regulate development. *Id.* § 2-101.

208. Ky. Rev. Stat. Ann. § 100.201 (1974). Section 100.187 imposes four minimum requirements for the comprehensive plan: (1) a statement of goals,

Once the zoning ordinance has been adopted the statute provides the following plan consistency requirement for zoning amendments:

> Before any map amendment is granted, the planning commission or the legislative body or fiscal court must find that the map amendment is in agreement with the community's comprehensive plan, or, in the absence of such a finding shall be recorded in the minutes and records of the planning commission or the legislative body or fiscal court.
>
> (1) That the original zoning classification given to the property was inappropriate or improper.
>
> (2) That there have been major changes of an economic, physical or social nature within the area involved which were not anticipated in the community's comprehensive plan and which have substantially altered the basic character of such area.[209]

This provision imposes a plan consistency requirement as an alternative to the Maryland change-mistake rule.[210] It appears to qualify, for Kentucky, the holding of those Maryland cases (discussed above) that refuse to approve a zoning amendment consistent with the plan but located in areas where no change in conditions has occurred. However, the statute does not require judicial validation of a zoning amendment whenever the zoning amendment follows the plan but cannot be justified by a change in conditions. It merely requires the planning commission or legislative body to make a finding of plan consistency when there has been no such change.

The Kentucky statute has been given a close and literal reading by the state's highest court in a zoning amendment case in which the statutory requirements had not been met.[211] In this case the zoning

---

objectives, policies and standards to guide physical, economic, and social development; (2) a land-use plan projecting future uses; (3) a transportation plan; and (4) a community facilities plan, again projecting future needs. Section 100.191 requires the substantive elements of the plan to be based on a specified research process. To further ensure that the plan will not merely perpetuate existing land-use characteristics, § 100.193 requires the planning commission to adopt a statement of objectives and principles to guide an ongoing planning and implementation process. Section 100.197 imposes a public hearing requirement. *See* Tarlock, *Kentucky Planning and Land Use Control Enabling Legislation: An Analysis of the 1966 Revision of K.R.S. Chapter 100*, 56 Ky. L.J. 556, 581–82 (1968).

209. Ky. Rev. Stat. Ann. § 100.213 (1974). This section of the statute appears to codify Hodge v. Luckett, 357 S.W.2d 303 (Ky. 1962). *See* Fritts v. Ashland, 348 S.W.2d 712 (Ky. 1961); Tarlock, *supra* note 208, at 587–89, 594. Bellemeade Co. v. Priddle, 503 S.W.2d 734 (Ky. 1974) construed this legislation broadly and held that it authorized planned neighborhood development units (floating zones).

210. See text accompanying note 108 *supra*.

211. Hines v. Pinchback-Halloran Volkswagen, 513 S.W.2d 492 (Ky. 1974). *See also* Manley v. City of Maysville, 528 S.W.2d 726 (Ky. 1975).

amendment was inconsistent with the policies of the plan as initially adopted. Because the Kentucky statutes require a land-use element to be adopted as part of the comprehensive plan, the court first indicated that the adoption of that element is an essential prerequisite to the validity of a zoning amendment that is justified by the plan. The court then held that plans could only be amended by following the formal research and hearing requirements of the statute, a holding that echoes the *Dalton*[212] opinion. Since these procedures had not been followed, the zoning amendment was invalidated, as it was neither consistent with the plan as originally adopted nor justified by a change in conditions.

Nebraska. Another effort at providing a consistency requirement is contained in the Nebraska zoning enabling legislation. This legislation applies only to counties:

> Zoning regulations shall be adopted or amended by the county board only after the adoption of the county comprehensive development plan by the county board and the receipt of the planning commission's specific recommendations. Such zoning regulations shall be consistent with the comprehensive development plan and designed for the purpose of promoting [the health, safety and general welfare and specified zoning purposes].[213]

This provision sweeps further than the Kentucky law, in that it applies to zoning ordinance adoptions as well as amendments. It also contains by inference a requirement that zoning adoptions and amendments must be based on recommendations from the planning commission, presumably interpreting the policies of the plan as applied to the adoption or amendment of the zoning ordinance in question. This statute has been interpreted by the Nebraska Supreme Court in a case that considered a rezoning in a county that had not

212. Dalton v. City and County of Honolulu, 51 Haw. 200, 462 P.2d 199 (1969).

213. Neb. Rev. Stat. § 23-114.03 (1970). In addition, in all villages and the larger cities a zoning ordinance may be adopted only after the legislative body has adopted a comprehensive plan. *Id.* § 19-901 (Supp. 1975). An amendment to this section in 1975 removed any inference from the statute that the comprehensive plan was intended to be advisory. Neb. L.B. 410, § 10 (1975). *See also* Neb. L.B. 317, § 2 (1975), requiring a county containing a city of the first class to have prepared a comprehensive plan by July 1, 1977. By the same date, any county in a Standard Metropolitan Statistical Area may "prepare, adopt, and enforce zoning and subdivision regulations that are based upon a comprehensive plan" for any municipality that has not adopted such regulations and has not organized and staffed to enforce them. *Id.* § 1, *as amended by* L.B. 410, § 31 (1975).

adopted a comprehensive plan.[214] The court held that the statute applied, immediately upon enactment, to all existing zoning ordinances, and that the lapse of almost four years without county adoption of a comprehensive plan was unreasonable. The rezoning was set aside.[215]

Minnesota. The Minnesota legislature recently enacted a mandatory planning statute for the Minneapolis–St. Paul metropolitan area.[216] Local governments are required to submit a comprehensive plan for review by the Metropolitan Council, including a land-use plan with a housing element, a public facilities plan, and an implementation program. The implementation program must ensure conformity between the local comprehensive plans and the metropolitan system plans. In addition, school districts are required to prepare a capital improvement program for review by the Metropolitan Council, as well as by local governments, for compatibility with proposed comprehensive plans.

Consistency between local implementation actions and the comprehensive plans is specifically required:

> A local governmental unit shall not adopt any official control or fiscal device which is in conflict with its comprehensive plan or which permits activity in conflict with metropolitan system plans.[217]

The statute further provides a procedure for administrative and judicial review and, more significantly, for some degree of technical assistance to local governments, including the establishment of a planning assistance fund for making grants and loans. It should be noted that this statute is not applicable to the entire state, but to a particular metropolitan area that already has a rather unique and sophisticated metropolitan agency. As experience is gained in Minnesota, however, other parts of the country may be led to consider similar efforts at requiring comprehensive planning.

---

214. Bagley v. County of Barry, 189 Neb. 393, 202 N.W.2d 841 (1972). *See* Deans v. West, 189 Neb. 518, 203 N.W.2d 504 (1973).

215. In dictum, the court did indicate that a county engaged in zoning ought to adopt a comprehensive plan within a reasonable time. It did not indicate whether an interim zoning ordinance could be adopted pending the adoption or revision of the plan. Bagley v. County of Barry, 189 Neb. 393, 202 N.W.2d 841 (1972).

216. Minn. Stat. H.F. 1530, ch. 127 (1976), *amending* Minn. Stat. § 462.355 (1974), and Minn. Stat. §§ 473.121 (1975 Supp.), sub. 1 and 473.175.

217. *Id.* at § 16, sub. 2.

Concluding Comments on the Consistency Issue. The consistency legislation reviewed thus far has delegated enforcement of the consistency requirement to the courts, and these statutes indicate some of the issues that legislatures must face when the courts are relied upon to assure compliance with the consistency requirement. Legislatures should provide as much direction as possible for judicial enforcement of the consistency requirement without placing overly restrictive limitations on local governments engaged in the planning and zoning process. Special attention should be paid to the statutory specification of the required and optional planning elements and their linkages, which the plan consistency provision reinforces.

This problem is partly addressed in the Kentucky legislation, which errs on the conservative side by requiring only the adoption of planning objectives as a condition to the adoption of a zoning ordinance. More broadly stated legislation, such as the California law, links the zoning power to the adoption of all of the required elements of the plan, and in this fashion gives the court a legal pivot that allows it to determine whether the plan has properly included all of the required elements.

More attention also needs to be addressed to the phase-in problem. This issue was handled in the California legislation by deferring the date on which the statute adopting the plan consistency requirement took effect, in order to provide time for the adoption of local plans. Kentucky specifically provides for the enactment of interim zoning ordinances pending adoption of the land-use plan's objectives,[218] and this approach provides another alternative. Legislative enactment of a time limit for the adoption of the plan can then place some limits on the length of time during which interim zoning ordinances can be allowed to be in effect while the plan is being prepared.

Definition of the consistency requirement presents more troublesome questions. Preferably, the consistency requirement should be broadly stated so that it applies to the entire land-use control process and not just to the map amendment procedure, as in Kentucky. As noted above, there is no reason why consistency with the plan should not also be required for such other administrative zoning techniques as floating zones, variances, and conditional uses.[219] All but the Cali-

218. Ky. Rev. Stat. Ann. § 100.334 (1974). This provision applies when the commission "is conducting" or "in good faith is preparing to conduct" the studies required for a comprehensive plan.

219. *See* note 124 *supra. See also* Cow Hollow Improv. Club v. DiBene, 245 Cal. App. 2d 160, 53 Cal. Rptr. 610 (1966) (variance); Carlton v. Board of Zoning Appeals, 252 Ind. 56, 245 N.E.2d 337 (1964) (variance); Crane v. Board of County Comm'rs, 175 Neb. 568, 122 N.W.2d 520 (1963) (conditional use); Jacobi v. Zoning Bd. of Adjustment, 413 Pa. 286, 196 A.2d 742 (1964) (conditional use); 40 A.L.R.3rd 372 (1971).

fornia and Florida laws simply require, but do not define, consistency. A definition should be provided, and it should contain both a spatial and a timing dimension. Zoning actions must be consistent with spatial policies contained in the plan, whether specified on a map or by a textual statement. The statute should consider the timing problem as well, for in many cases the plan will call for land-use changes at some time in the future, when development in the community has further progressed and intensified.

Problems arise when disgruntled landowners, on whose land development has been deferred subject to the plan, object to zoning ordinances that restrict development in the interim period consistent with local timing plans. The right to do so should be explicitly recognized in the legislative definition of consistency. Finally, consistency between land-use decisions and comprehensive plans should not be construed narrowly, as a rigid relationship between a mapped land use in the plan and a corollary designation on a zoning map. Rather, the stringency with which the plan is applied to local land-use decisions, as a standard for judicial review, should correlate with the court's perception of the appropriate standard for review in light of the character of the plan.

Because both the planning process and its products vary considerably—ranging from rigid, end-state documents to flexible policy plans—the implementation of a plan through land-use controls should not be required by the courts to be any more rigid than the plan itself. Moreover, where state enabling legislation (or, perhaps, state and federal constitutional law) provides a specific basis for consistency with the plan—such as consideration of regional housing needs or protection of critical environmental areas—the consistency requirement may be necessarily more rigid and demanding because of the complexity and controversy associated with such issues.

STATE AND REGIONAL REVIEW OF COMPREHENSIVE PLANS

Delegating the enforcement of the mandatory planning and plan consistency requirements to the courts places the burden of achieving compliance with the statute on local residents and property owners who are willing and able to seek court relief. It depends as well on the willingness of the courts to interpret liberally the planning and plan consistency provisions. Even courts willing to take a strong view of the statute may be limited in the relief they can provide, and, as in the Nebraska and Kentucky cases, they may be forced to issue a blanket injunction on local zoning actions in order to enforce the statutory mandate.

Judicial enforcement of the mandatory planning and consistency requirement thus has its limitations. As an alternative, the planning statute can provide for an administrative review for compliance with the consistency requirement, which can provide greater assurance that the requirements of the statute have been met. If this administrative process is located at the state or the regional level, the state or regional review agency can also assure that local planning is consistent with state and regional planning policies.

A limited statutory procedure for state level review of local plans has been adopted by the American Law Institute's *Model Land Development Code.*[220] The Code has taken the position that planning, both at state and local levels, should remain optional rather than mandatory. Nevertheless, some of the more sophisticated local land development control regulations, such as PUD ordinances, may not be adopted unless the locality has a comprehensive plan,[221] and these provisions are viewed as an incentive to localities to engage in land-use planning.

Additional incentives to local planning are attempted in the state planning and judicial review articles of the ALI Code.[222] These incentives combine the review of local plans by the state planning agency with legislative provisions strengthening the judicial presumption accorded local land development control regulations when they are consistent with an adopted state plan. As indicated, state planning is optional, but the state planning agency may review local comprehensive plans (but not local development control ordinances) once a state plan is adopted.

State planning agency disapproval of all or a part of a local plan has only a limited effect. If a local plan is disapproved, "no aspect of the local Plan . . . so specified shall be entitled to any weight in support of the validity of any action of the local government under this Code."[223] In the context of the local land development control process, what state disapproval of a local plan apparently means is that no local land development control power may be exercised that is dependent on a local plan once that plan has been disapproved by the state planning agency. Presumably, any presumptive weight that

220. D. Mandelker, Environmental and Land Control Legislation ch. 2 (1976).

221. ALI Code, *supra* note 27, at § 2-212.

222. *See id.,* art. 8 & 9.

223. *Id.* § 8-503(b). *See also* Florida Local Government Comprehensive Planning Act of 1975, ch. 75.257, § (7). The state planning agency may make recommendations for the modifications of local plans insofar as these plans affect state planning policies or the responsibility of state agencies, but these recommendations need not be accepted by the local government.

local planning policies may provide for the local land development control effort is also voided.

Additional weight is given to the state plan in the judicial review article of the ALI Code. It provides that in any judicial proceedings "concerning" the relationship of an order, rule, or ordinance to "the public health, safety, or welfare," the court shall give "due weight" to the "consistency of the challenged action" with an applicable state plan.[224] This section would apply to any local land development control ordinance, rule, or adjudicative order affecting land development, as well as to any state land development regulation that implements the policies of a state plan.

The ALI Code stops short of full administrative review at the state level of local plans and ordinances, but alters the judicial presumptions accorded land development control actions depending on whether or not they are consistent with a state plan. By relying on favorable judicial presumptions to encourage consistency with the state plan, the Code indirectly encourages compliance with state planning policies. As a method for enforcing the policies of comprehensive plans in land-use control administration, the American Law Institute's approach is at best a compromise, though consistent with its decision not to mandate a comprehensive planning process.

State administrative procedures to require local plans and land-use controls to be consistent with state plans have now been provided in legislation enacted in Oregon and Wyoming.[225] The Oregon law is the more comprehensive of the two. It mandates comprehensive planning by all cities and counties in the state, and the enactment of "zoning, subdivision and other ordinances or regulations" to implement comprehensive plans.[226] The comprehensive plan is then defined in conventional terms as a "land use map and policy statement" covering "all functional and natural systems and activities relating to the use of lands."[227] There is no further attempt to define precisely the elements to be contained in comprehensive plans.

Planning is also mandated at the state level. A state Land Conservation and Development Commission is established, and it is the duty

---

224. ALI Code, *supra* note 27, at § 9-110(3). This provision is further explained in notes to the code that indicate that courts are to pay "special attention" to the plan. *Id.* at 493. "No negative implication is intended by calling attention to these facts. The court may . . . give special attention to other facts and may . . . draw no adverse conclusion from the absence of a plan." *Id.* at 493–94.

225. For a history of the development and enactment of the Oregon law, *see* C. Little, The New Oregon Trail (Conservation Foundation, 1974).

226. Ore. Rev. Stat. § 197.175(2) (1973).

227. *Id.* § 197.015(4).

of this commission to "[e]stablish statewide planning goals consistent with regional, county and city concerns,"[228] and to "prepare statewide planning guidelines."[229] In developing its goals and guidelines, the commission is to "consider" the existing plans of state agencies and local governments, and in addition is to give "priority consideration" to areas and activities designated by the statute which are of more than local significance.[230] These activities include the siting of public facilities, which requires a permit from the commission; and designated areas include lands adjacent to freeway interchanges and environmental areas, such as wetlands, wilderness areas, flood plains, and agricultural lands.

The commission's attention to these key environmental areas will afford them the needed protection from potentially intrusive new development. These state goals and guidelines are not intended as mere interpretive commentary to assist localities in their conduct of the planning process. They function instead much like policy statements in policy plans, and provide generalized principles for the guidance of land development in the state.

Within one year after the state planning goals and guidelines have been adopted by the commission, it must review all state agency, city, county, and special district comprehensive plans and land-use controls to determine their consistency with the state goals.[231] The statute nowhere defines the state goals and guidelines, and local planning and land-use controls are to conform only with the commission's goals. The types of policies the goals are to include remains unclear. Legislative history accompanying the law indicates only that the goals are to have "the full force of authority of the state to achieve the purposes . . . of the Act," while the "Guidelines . . . are suggested directions that would aid local governments in activating the mandated goals."[232]

Administrative review, modification, and enforcement powers are given to the commission for its review of local plans and ordinances. On its own motion the commission may prescribe and if necessary "amend and administer" local comprehensive plans and land-use controls that do not comply with the state planning goals.[233] The com-

228. *Id.* § 197.040(2)(a).
229. *Id.* § 197.040(2)(d).
230. *Id.* § 197.230.
231. *Id.* § 197.250.
232. Oregon Land Conservation and Development Commission, Statewide Land Use Goals, Guidelines, and the Columbia River Gorge as a Critical Area 1 (1974).
233. Ore Rev. Stat. § 197.325(1) (1973). The statute also authorizes counties to review all comprehensive plans within the county and advise the govern-

mission may also enjoin any land use or building construction not conforming with a local comprehensive plan or land-use regulation, thus providing a method for enforcing the state planning goals on which commission review of local plans and ordinances is based.[234] On petition by a local government or state agency, the commission may also review any local plan, land-use regulation, or action that is inconsistent with statewide planning goals.[235] Orders entered by the commission in a review proceeding are enforceable in court.

A regional planning agency for the Portland, Oregon metropolitan area has been authorized by other legislation.[236] This agency is authorized to adopt "regional land use planning goals and objectives," prepare a plan for the region in conformity with these goals and objectives, and review comprehensive plans and land-use regulations within the region. Apparently the regional agency may only amend local plans, although it may review local land-use regulations and make recommendations.[237] Regional goals and objectives adopted by the regional commission presumably are subject to review for compliance with the state planning goals.[238]

Similar state and local planning and plan review legislation has been adopted by Wyoming:

> All local governments shall develop a land use plan within their jurisdiction. The plans shall be consistent with established state guidelines and be subject to review and approval by the [state land-use] commission.[239]

---

ment or agency preparing each plan whether it is consistent with statewide planning goals. *Id.* § 197.255. Counties are also responsible for coordinating all planning activities affecting land use within the county "to assure an integrated comprehensive plan for the entire area of the county." *Id.* § 197.190. The statute exempts Portland from this provision. This review and coordination function may also be assumed by a voluntarily formed regional planning agency or a council of governments. *Id.* § 197.190(3), (4). Counties and cities representing a majority of the population in the area may petition the State Land Conservation and Development Commission for an election to form a regional planning agency. If the commission "finds that the area described in the petition forms a reasonable planning unit," and the majority votes to create the agency, it shall be established. A voluntary association of local governments may perform the review if each county and a majority of cities ratify a resolution adopted by the association authorizing this function.

234. *Id.* §§ 215.510(3), 215.535, *as amended.*
235. *Id.* § 197.300(1). Under § 197.305, this review shall be based on the administrative record prepared for the plan or action being challenged. "In conflict" is the § 197.300(1) term for "inconsistent." A petition for review may also be filed by "a person or any group of persons whose interests are substantially affected." *Id.* § 197.300(1)(d).
236. Ore. Rev. Stat. §§ 197.190 to .795 (1973).
237. *Id.* § 197.755.
238. *Id.* § 197.300.
239. Wyo. Comp. Stat. Ann. § 9-856(a) (Supp. 1975).

The commission in turn is to adopt statewide "land use goals, policies and guidelines".[240] All these terms are defined by the act, though not in a manner that removes all doubts about their nature and function.[241] Local plans need only be consistent with the state guidelines, and a guideline is defined as a "checklist of methods through which a land use policy is established." Just what a "checklist of methods" should contain is not made clear. Neither does the Wyoming statute contain the specific local plan modification and administration powers that are contained in the Oregon law.

Both the Oregon and Wyoming laws are notable for the innovative manner in which they provide the substantive basis for the review of local planning and (in Oregon) land-use controls within the state. Implicitly in Oregon and explicitly in Wyoming, the state goals and guidelines that are to be prepared at the state level are not a substitute for a state plan, and in Wyoming a state land-use plan is to be developed by the state land-use commission following the adoption of the state goals, guidelines, and policies.[242] Presumably, local planning and land-use controls continue to be reviewed for conformity to the state planning goals and guidelines in each state, even after the state land-use plan has been prepared.

This approach to state policy making for local land-use planning and state review of local planning and land-use controls thus avoids the problems of delay in implementation that would arise were state review of local planning and land-use controls deferred until a state plan could be prepared. State plans require substantial time and expenditure, and state review of local planning and land-use controls would be delayed for long periods if it had to await the preparation and adoption of a state plan. Reliance on state goals and guidelines avoids this problem. At least as conceived in Oregon, the goals and guidelines are intended to contain generalized policies for land-use regulation throughout the state. They do not, however, constitute a fully articulated set of proposals for the physical development of the state, as would be found in a state land-use plan.

Whether state planning goals and guidelines adopted under statutes such as these can be made sufficiently precise and substantive so that they provide an adequate basis for the exercise of state review powers remains to be seen. Assuming that sufficient precision and substance can be achieved, the Oregon and Wyoming statutes provide an innovative link between the policy planning that increasingly is favored as a replacement for the more conventional mapped plan, and the need

240. *Id.* § 9-853(a)(vi) (Supp. 1975).
241. *Id.* § 9-850(f), (g), (q).
242. *Id.* § 9-853(a)(vii).

to create a viable legal process in which the adequacy of local planning and plan implementation can be reviewed and evaluated.

A combination of methods will have to be used to enforce the requirements of mandatory planning legislation that local land-use controls be consistent with the policies of an adopted plan. Judicial review is one method of enforcing this requirement, but state and regional administrative review procedures of the type adopted in Oregon and Washington have an advantage over judicial enforcement techniques. Administrative review can be used to secure a comprehensive evaluation of local land-use regulations that does not rely on the willingness and ability of private litigants to bring lawsuits challenging the consistency of these regulations with local plans. State and regional agency review will thereby assure the implementation of the consistency requirement, provided the statute makes the review of local land-use regulations mandatory and confers sufficient authority on the review agencies to conform local regulations to planning policies. As in the Oregon law, explicit authority to amend local land-use regulations may be necessary.

The Oregon and Washington legislation is directed primarily to state-local relationships, however, and is concerned primarily with the consistency of local plans and land-use regulations. The requirement that local regulations be consistent with local plans is implicit in the review procedures authorized by these laws. If administrative reviews are to be provided, however, the state or regional level appears to be the appropriate place to conduct such reviews if local planning policies are to be examined in the context of state and regional planning needs.

Reliance on a state or regional agency to adopt planning policies implementing the state's planning legislation will also avoid the rigidities that would occur if legislatures attempt to include substantive state planning policies in state planning legislation. However, lower income housing and some environmental issues may require legislative adoption of substantive planning policies. State and regional administrative review can then be used to make local planning conform to the statutory requirements of state planning legislation and to state planning policies, as well as to make local land development regulations conform to the policies of adopted comprehensive plans.

CONCLUSION: ADVANTAGES AND POTENTIAL LIMITATIONS IN MANDATORY PLANNING

While the importance of comprehensive planning to land-use control has been recognized for some time, it is only recently that courts and legislatures have accorded more than minimal recognition to the role of the comprehensive plan in land-use controls. Part of the problem was created by the equivocation with which the drafters of the early model planning and zoning enabling legislation approached the legal basis for the comprehensive planning requirement. Ambiguities in the model legislation, and judicial assumptions about the ability of the zoning process to provide a binding framework for local land-use control actions, led most courts to accept a unitary view of the statutory requirement that zoning be "in accordance" with a comprehensive plan. The unitary view allowed a comprehensive and legislatively developed zoning ordinance to substitute for an independently adopted comprehensive plan that would both be external to the ordinance and provide an independent policy basis for the examination of zoning regulations.

Recent years have seen a modification of this point of view. Some courts have conceded a greater role for the comprehensive plan in zoning administration, and state legislatures have more frequently mandated a comprehensive planning process for local governments and required local zoning and land-use regulations to be consistent with an adopted local plan. This chapter has argued that this trend in court decisions and in planning and zoning legislation is correct, that comprehensive planning should be mandatory at the local level, and that local land-use controls should be made consistent with the adopted local plan. The reasons for these recommendations may be summarized as follows.

At the local level, mandatory comprehensive planning provides a policy basis for the land-use control process, which can help assure internal consistency in zoning actions. In the absence of a comprehensive planning policy at the local level, zoning and rezoning actions by local governments may err on the side of the ad hoc and the arbitrary. More than any other reason, this concern has moved courts to accord a greater role to the comprehensive plan as a check on local zoning administration. The need for comprehensive planning as a check on local land-use control is especially acute in outer suburban areas that are undergoing urbanization. Because many communities in these areas adopt holding zone strategies for their undeveloped sections, and local zoning policy is articulated in the zoning amendment process, the need for recourse to a comprehensive plan as a check on arbitrary decisionmaking is especially urgent.

Mandatory comprehensive planning can do more than provide the necessary policy base essential to achieve internal consistency in the administration of local land-use control programs. We have consistently emphasized the duty of local planning and plan implementation efforts to be responsive to more than local demands, especially in the area of housing opportunity for all income groups. This report has also noted the increasing concern with environmental protection, the need to manage an orderly progression from a rural to an urban environment through growth control programs, and the conflicting pressures on the land-use planning and control process. These pressures need to be balanced and accommodated so that no special concern is emphasized to the exclusion of other equally pressing interests. The comprehensive plan, if properly executed and properly implemented, is the appropriate vehicle in which these often conflicting pressures on local growth policies can be accommodated and resolved.

Although the survey undertaken for this report (included in the Appendix) suggests that local comprehensive planning efforts have become substantially more meaningful and politically realistic, it also indicates that there are still potential limitations. In the long term these limitations include the complex problems involved in attempting to manage growth and development in what is basically a free-market system; the dubious attitude that many Americans still seem to have toward planning; the difficulty of sparking citizen interest in the planning process in the absence of crisis conditions; jealousies and conflicts between the various levels of government, each anxious to exercise additional prerogatives; and the value dilemmas involved in any effort to initiate social change.

These difficulties are not likely to disappear in the foreseeable future. Some, however, can be attacked directly by restructuring both the formal and informal planning mechanisms in city government and by paying closer attention to the antecedents of and commitments to comprehensive planning.

The movement toward state legislation that requires local planning, prescribes certain elements of those plans, and requires consistency between plans and implementing land-use decisions involves some difficulties. The California experience suggests that it is not easy to describe elements in ways that are uniformly applicable to communities throughout a state. Moreover, the mandatory inclusion of elements does not mean that they will be handled appropriately or have a bearing on local decisionmaking.

A recent independent study of the California planning consistency requirement, while recognizing the need to better define consistency and allow for more time to achieve it, concluded:

> While the findings of this early survey suggest that the eventual impact of the consistency requirement will be the upgrading rather than atrophy

of the planning process, they should also lead to introspection among planners. Perhaps the most disturbing finding is that many professional planners, politicians and community leaders were unconvinced that existing plans were sound enough to justify the force of law added by the consistency requirement.[243]

In addition, it appears that zoning decisions are becoming less important than other middle range implementation techniques, particularly in more developed cities with established land-use patterns. In requiring consistency between local actions and plans, it may be more appropriate to require all local budgets (especially capital budgets) to be reviewed annually for consistency with the priorities spelled out in the general plan.

State mandated local planning necessitates the corollary of state supported local planning. It would be well for state governments to compensate localities for the planning work already generated by existing regulations before adding further requirements. However, even with adequate funding, plans are not likely to carry much weight in local decisionmaking unless there is public involvement in the planning process. A state mandate cannot counteract public apathy or local resistance to planning. Nor can a state mandate ensure that municipalities will make the financial investments and administrative commitments needed to initiate a worthwhile planning effort.

Enforced compliance with mandatory planning through state and regional review of local plans could also be counterproductive, by emphasizing existing conflicts between local and areawide planning bodies and thereby undermining the effectiveness of such planning efforts. There are good arguments, on the other hand, for regional or perhaps state authorities to supersede local land-use planning and growth management decisions when larger regional interests are threatened. In the case of the distribution of subsidized housing for low-income families throughout a region, for example, it may be appropriate for state government to override local exclusionary actions. But this ought to be handled through a state appeals process created by state law. When issues of statewide significance or unwanted regional facilities are at stake, the state government should be in a position to countermand local decisions.

As important as these considerations are, they should be tempered by the need to avoid unnecessary administrative delays. State or regional override of local planning decisions should be limited to in-

243. Catalano & DiMento, *Heresy in the Land of T.J. Kent: Planning Is Zoning Is Planning,* 1975 Nat. Res. Law. 4515.

stances in which issues of more than local concern are obviously at stake, and should come only after the fact; that is, local plans should not be reviewed regularly in an effort to anticipate decisions that might be inappropriate. Only after it has become apparent that a local decision has an adverse effect within the region—and only after the offending locality is given an opportunity to correct or compensate those affected by past decisions—should regional or state agencies be empowered to countermand or override local priorities and decisions.

Recognizing the basic need to strengthen local planning capabilities, and given the difficulties inherent in elevating land-use decisions to higher levels of decisionmaking, the following factors might be considered. First, all local planning activities currently required by state and federal statute should be supported by grants-in-aid commensurate with the obligations they create. Second, municipalities might consider altering their charters, as Atlanta has done (see Appendix B) to establish neighborhood oriented planning reviews linked to the annual budget cycle. Third, in amending state enabling legislation for comprehensive planning, certain important steps in the planning process should also be mandated.

Examples of a mandated local planning process might include: (1) a required hearing process, and publication of an annual planning progress report indicating the extent to which the objectives of the plan have either been fulfilled or modified; (2) a requirement that dissenting points of view (disagreements with the plan) filed by a substantial minority of residents be published regularly along with the plan; and (3) a requirement that a written statement be prepared and published annually by the municipalities indicating the ways in which municipal budget priorities (both operating and capital) are designed to help fulfill the objectives contained in the comprehensive plan. Where appropriate, state and federal funds should be allocated in accordance with these priorities.

In every city and town studied for this report (and discussed in Appendix B), the federal 701 program was either the primary source of financial support for ongoing planning or a critical element in the preparation of the original comprehensive plan. In this new era of federalism, during which great importance has been attached to providing funds to state and local governments to do with as they may, it is perplexing to watch while repeated efforts are made to eliminate the only local capacity building program presently in operation. The requirement of the Housing and Community Development Act of 1974 that each community prepare a Comprehensive Community Development Plan has provided new impetus for comprehensive planning; unfortunately, that Act does not earmark funds for planning, and 701 funds, which might be used for this purpose, are being cut back.

Mandating comprehensive planning for local governments will not necessarily guarantee that local land-use controls will be internally consistent in their administration or faithful to regional and state policies, even if state and regional review of the local planning effort is provided. But the increasing and sometimes competing pressures for the better management of our land environment demand a comprehensive set of policies for the administration of our land-use control systems. These policies can be provided through an adequate comprehensive planning process at state, regional, and local levels. Whether we as a nation are up to the planning and land management challenge that the heightened awareness of a more responsible generation has forced upon us must be left for history to decide.

POLICY STATEMENTS

1. Historically, early model legislation and judicial interpretation thereof has been unclear about whether an independent, comprehensive plan is required beyond the zoning ordinance and zoning map. As greater emphasis is placed on the need for zoning actions to be in accordance with a plan, that plan should be an independent, comprehensive document expressing the collective planning judgment of the community.

2. As the substantive and procedural elements of land-use decisions increase in complexity and include new objectives such as environmental protection, lower income housing needs, and regional growth management, comprehensive planning is essential as a policy base to insure internal consistency, to provide predictability, and to reduce the tendency toward arbitrary local decisionmaking. State enabling legislation, traditionally permissive in its approach to local planning, should be amended to require local comprehensive planning and to require that the exercise of local land-use controls be consistent with local comprehensive plans.

3. Consistency with local comprehensive plans is not to be viewed in terms of a direct, rigid relationship between a mapped land use in the plan and a corollary designation on the zoning map. Rather, the consistency envisioned here should encompass three factors:

   a. The comprehensive plan and the requirement that it be consistent with local land-use controls is important as a standard for judicial review by which the court can evaluate the extent to which local actions are responsive to the collective planning judgment of the community; therefore, the stringency of the consistency requirement should correlate with the court's perception of the appropriate standard for review in light of the character of the plan.

b. Because both the planning process and its products vary considerably among communities and as perceived by planners themselves (*i.e.*, the movement away from rigid, end-state document toward flexible policy plans), the implementation of a plan through land-use controls should not be required by the courts to be any more rigid than the plan itself—a flexible policy plan allowing for flexible consistency that is appropriate to the circumstances.

c. Where state enabling legislation, or, perhaps, state and federal constitutional law, provide a specific basis for consistency with the plan—*e.g.*, consideration of regional housing needs or protection of critical environmental areas—the requirement for consistency between local land-use action and the plan may necessarily be more rigid and demanding due to the complexity and controversy associated with such issues.

4. Mandatory planning and the direct implementation of planning policies through land-use control administration requires the provision of greater financial assistance to local governments so that they can prepare and implement the necessary planning policies and land-use regulations. Continued and increasing federal and state financial support of local planning and plan implementation programs is an essential prerequisite for mandatory comprehensive planning.

5. The development of planning practice and theory has resulted in innovative departures from the classic paradigm of planning (*i.e.*, survey and analysis, goal formulation, plan and map-making, and implementation). These innovations, particularly as they emphasize the importance of citizen involvement, policies, and a planning process (rather than a mapped, static end-product), should be encouraged through state legislation and judicial recognition. However, state legislation should retain the local option to adopt such plans, within broad statutory standards, as the locality deems appropriate.

6. A comprehensive plan reflects a collective planning judgment about development opportunities throughout the community, a judgment made prior to a zoning change and prior to a lawsuit attacking a zoning restriction. The issue is whether this prior collective judgment should be accorded presumptive weight as it affects landdevelopment proposals allowed by a zoning amendment or that are subjected to litigation challenging a zoning restriction. It is concluded

in this Report that the effective implementation of mandatory local planning requires the courts to give presumptive weight to the policies of the comprehensive plan as they are applied in land-use control administration, unless circumstances exist that indicate the plan is no longer entitled to this preference.

7. Local planning that is required by state enabling legislation raises the question of whether state enabling legislation should contain guidance for the local planning process, either by specifying the necessary linkages among the statutory planning elements required to produce an acceptable plan, or by prescribing goals for the planning process (without prescribing the contents of the local plan). Legislative direction is required that at least will mandate the development of a local plan in which these policy issues will be considered and resolved.

8. The Advisory Commission views opportunities for decent living accommodations in decent environments, freedom from law-imposed discrimination based on income, and access to employment and educational opportunities as fundamental values. Planning enabling legislation should include specific provisions requiring a housing plan as part of the local comprehensive plan.

9. The primary responsibility for government regulation of the location, pace, volume, and design of urban growth ought to remain with local government so long as such regulation is consistent with regional needs. People in a neighborhood or city often believe that their interests conflict with regional needs, particularly with reference to the location and construction of low-income housing. To resolve controversies between those who would build and those who would deny or limit construction, it may be useful for state or regional agencies to become involved in the decisionmaking process. It is therefore desirable for states to articulate in advance the occasions when such involvement would be appropriate and to structure such involvement in administrative proceedings that relieve the burden on courts to resolve such conflicts.

10. In legislation requiring consistency between local comprehensive plans and local government actions, the coordination of comprehensive planning with capital improvement programming should be encouraged. This could be accomplished administratively by requiring a direct link between planning and budgeting agencies or by including capital improvement criteria in the land-use control process. Alternatively the statute could require regular public review of the extent to which government actions reflect the coordination of comprehensive planning with capital improvement programming.

Appendix to Chapter 5

The State of the Art in Local Planning

INTRODUCTION

With the backdrop of planning theory and practice provided in Chapter 5, and with the traditional legal context in mind, a survey of the state of the art of planning was undertaken for this Report. The obvious difficulties inherent in attempting to prescribe approaches to planning for municipalities with varying capabilities make it imperative to have a current picture of the activities that comprise local planning efforts.

A list of 27 communities (see Table 5-1 and Figure 5-1) was compiled through a series of contacts with people whose experience would allow them to recommend appropriate subjects for the study. Twelve consulting firms[1] with extensive experience in the preparation of municipal comprehensive plans were briefed on the objectives of this study, and asked to suggest three communities with especially interesting or effective master plans or comprehensive planning processes.

Staff members of the Department of Housing and Urban Development (HUD) in Washington and in each of ten HUD regional offices were briefed in a similar fashion.[2] Each was asked to suggest com-

1. The consulting firms contacted included: Medcalf and Eddy, Philip B. Herr & Assoc.; Alan Vorhees Assoc.; Kaplan, Gans & Kahn; Marcou, O'Leary and Assoc.; Livingston and Blaney; Crane Assoc.; Raymond Parish & Pine; LeLeuw Cather and Co.; Candeub, Fleisig & Co.; Justin Gray Assoc.; Hammer, Siler & George.
2. HUD Staff members contacted include: Washington—Lawrence Houston and Richard Alexander; Region I—Harold Kramer; Region II—Constantine

Table 5-1. Municipalities Included in the Sample (1970 population figures)

Over 400,000		100,000–400,000		Under 100,000	
Philadelphia, Pa.	1,949,996	Ft. Worth, Tex.	393,476	Wilmington, Del.	80,386
Dallas, Texas	844,401	Tulsa, Okla.	330,350	Boulder, Col.	66,870
Cleveland, Ohio	750,879	Birmingham, Ala.	300,910	Portland, Me.	65,116
Indianapolis, Ind.	746,302	Rochester, N.Y.	296,233	Oak Park, Ill.	62,511
San Francisco, Ca.	715,674	Akron, Ohio	275,435	Brookline, Mass.	58,689
San Diego, Ca.	697,000	Tucson, Arizona	262,933	Fayetteville, N.C.	53,510
Denver, Col.	514,678	Tacoma, Wash.	154,407	Petaluma, Ca.	24,870
Atlanta, Georgia	497,421	Lincoln, Neb.	149,518	Redmond, Wash.	11,020
Cincinnati, Ohio	451,455	Fremont, Ca.	101,969		
Minneapolis, Minn.	434,400				

munities that seemed to best illustrate the state of the art in comprehensive planning. Three professional organizations—the American Society of Planning Officials, the American Institute of Planners, and the Urban Land Institute—were also contacted, along with faculty members at selected university planning departments.[3] Only five cities were nominated unanimously by our contact groups (practitioners, HUD staff, professional societies, and academicians). These were Minneapolis, Cleveland, Philadelphia, San Francisco, and Atlanta. None of the other 23 communities ultimately selected received more than two nominations. In compiling this list we placed disproportionate weight on the opinions and recommendations of staff members in the HUD regional offices—especially the veteran administrators of the 701 program—who were invariably the most knowledgeable about recent comprehensive planning efforts.[4]

The selection of sample communities was based on geographical diversity as well as a range of population levels: communities with less than 100,000 inhabitants, those with 100,000 to 400,000 residents, and those with populations of more than 400,000. Every effort was made *not* to define what we meant by "especially interesting" or "effective" examples, so that a range of viewpoints would surface for subsequent analysis. In each of the 27 communities (including ten with over 400,000 inhabitants, nine in the 100,000 to 400,000 range, and eight with fewer than 100,000 residents) the planning department was contacted by phone and asked to forward copies of their latest master plan and any supporting documents

---

Vlatos, Leonard Schwartz; Region III—Arthur Foley, Bill Skwersky, Ted Stevenson, Bob Cummings; Region IV—Jim Bittings, Cleveland Talmadge, Tim Raines and Leo Zuber; Region V—Jack Peters, Dolores Koziel, Paul Stuhr, Richard Goodwin, Bob Duncan, Mark Lancaster, Tim Foley; Region VI—Dave Baker, Jim Legrote, Don King and Frank Seavey; Region VII—Ellsworth Duresky; Region VIII—Joe Lontim; Region IX—Rosemary Basey; Region X—Bob Gilliland.

3. University departments contacted include Berkeley, Wisconsin, University of North Carolina, Harvard, MIT, UCLA, and Cornell.

4. Cities that were mentioned by at least one person but were not selected: Tuscaloosa, Alabama (65,773); Albuquerque, N.M. (244,000); Bridgeport, Conn. (156,542); Montgomery, Ala. (133,386); San Jose, Ca. (446,537); Spokane, Washington (171,000); Baltimore, Md. (905,787); San Antonio, Tex. (654,000); Phoenix, Ariz. (582,000); Albertville, Ala. (9,963); Altoona, Pa. (62,898); Ann Arbor, Mich. (99,797); Cambridge, Md. (11,395); Hayward, Cal. (93,059); Passaic, N.J. (55,124); Fort Lee, N.J. (30,631); Peekskill, N.Y. (19,283); Silver Springs, Md. (77,411); Simi Valley, Cal. (59,832); Berkeley, Cal. (117,000); Portland, Oregon (379,967); Oklahoma City, Okla. (368,377); Barrington, Ill. (8,674); Duluth, Minn. (101,000). Our objective was to develop a list of ten communities in each of three size categories that were well distributed geographically. Three additional communities that were initially selected—Lexington, Ky. (108,137); Austin, Minn. (25,031); and Anondale, Va. (27,405)—were ultimately dropped when it became difficult to track down the necessary planning documents within our time deadline.

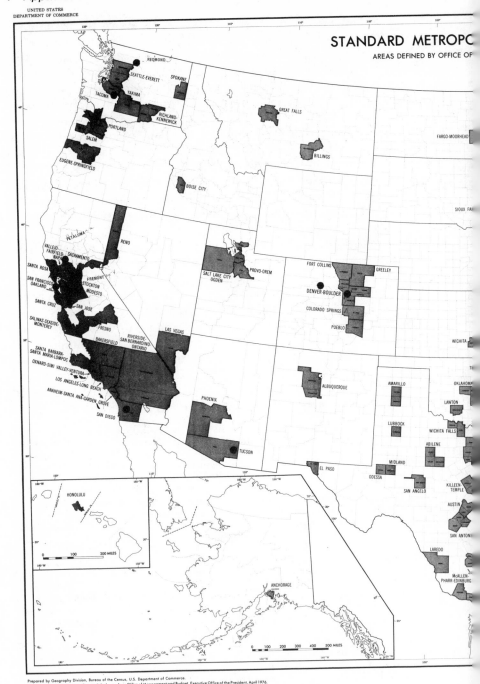

Prepared by Geography Division, Bureau of the Census, U.S. Department of Commerce.
Definitions of standard metropolitan statistical areas from Office of Management and Budget, Executive Office of the President, April 1976.

Figure 5-1. Communities Studied

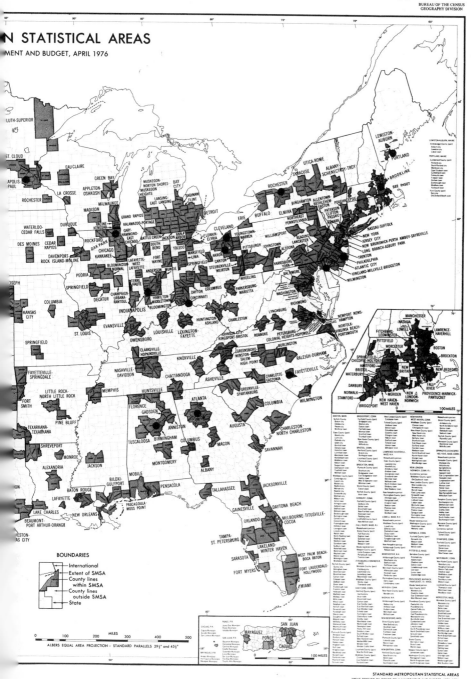

Source: U.S. Dept. of Commerce, Bureau of the Census.

describing the scope, methods, and purpose of their planning effort. The materials were summarized and keyed to eighteen items that provided a common description of planning activities in the communities.

The summary of planning documents was keyed to the following items:

1. Population of the community.
2. Title of plan.
3. Date of plan; date of most recent amendments; time horizon of the plan.
4. Consultant or staff planners involved.
5. Rationale for the plan (if stated).
6. Goals of the planning process (if stated).
7. Elements; scope of plan.
8. Process by which the plan and development policies were created.
9. Process of amending the plan.
10. Citizen participation process.
11. Locus of planning in the municipality.
12. Political structure of the city as it relates to planning.
13. Linkage of the plan to the regulatory process (including growth-management techniques).
14. Implementation mechanisms and strategies.
15. Linking of the planning department and planning process to decisionmaking in the municipality.
16. Relation of the city to regional/county planning.
17. State-mandated planning requirements (if any).
18. Level of 701 support.

A list of contact persons was prepared for each community, including the head of the planning department, the head of the planning commission or citizens advisory group, and the person in the chief elected official's office most knowledgeable about the comprehensive planning process. At least two phone interviews were then conducted to confirm or deny what the planning documents claimed or appeared to suggest.

Each interview covered a variety of items and included a set of a dozen questions:

1. How was the plan developed?
2. What is the rationale for comprehensive planning? Is it changing?
3. How were the goals for the plan derived?
4. How was the scope of the plan defined?

5. Are implementation strategies built into the plan? Does the planning agency have sufficient power to implement the plan? If so, what implementation techniques are used?
6. How do the plan and the planning agency link into the city's regulatory system?
7. What is the linkage between the planning agency's plan-making process and the rest of the municipality's decisionmaking structure? Both formal and informal?
8. What is the relationship between the city's planning operation and the regional or county planning bodies?
9. Is there state planning legislation that impacts on local comprehensive planning? If so, please describe.
10. Has local comprehensive planning been substantially affected by federal programs and funding?
11. Have comprehensive planning and the present plan had a significant impact on the city's development patterns? If not, why not? If so, why and how?
12. How could the plan and the planning process be made more effective?

Because the results are more akin to case studies than to survey research, the findings are in no way statistically significant. Moreover, a number of the plans were in process or only recently completed, making it difficult to assess their impact. This is a natural result of the selection process—plans viewed as especially interesting are likely also to be recent. If there is a bias, it is probably on the side of choosing better rather than worse examples. These caveats aside, the study does provide a glimpse of some of the more interesting and innovative attempts to develop municipal comprehensive plans.

The description of the findings that follows is organized under six headings: (1) the rationale for comprehensive planning; (2) the goals of comprehensive planning; (3) the form and elements of the plan; (4) the process of preparing and updating plans; (5) implementation mechanisms and strategies; and (6) approaches to citizen involvement. These are the dimensions of the planning process most sensitive to the shifts that have occurred in planning practice over the past few years.

1. The Rationale for Comprehensive Planning
In most instances municipal planning involves more than just a reluctant response to federal or state requirements. Land-poor inner cities that attempt to spark redevelopment, as well as rapidly bur-

geoning suburban areas that seek to direct or retard growth, continue to search for more effective means to coordinate public investment with private development decisions. Comprehensive planning is viewed in many (if not all) cities as a means of coordinating long-term and short-term actions, and integrating the independent decisions of private actors and public decisionmakers.

Most of the comprehensive plans prepared in recent years and covered by this survey fall into one of two categories: centrally conceived plans that seek to provide a broad, flexible framework within which to consider day-to-day decisions; or composite plans that attempt to spell out specific development priorities on a sector-by-sector or neighborhood-by-neighborhood basis. Both types of plans contain general goal statements and policy recommendations, and often rely on maps of one kind or another; but the centrally conceived plan assumes that it is the responsibility of the planning department, the operating agencies, and other elected and appointed officials to define appropriate short-range decisions within the context of a broad set of overarching community-wide goals. The plan that seeks to delineate specific development priorities assumes that a "bottom-up" approach, built on neighborhood or sectoral involvement, is necessary to predict community response and obviate subsequent conflict.

The level and rate of development account in part for the choice of a "top-down" as opposed to a bottom-up (or "neighborhood-up") approach to planning. Cities that are still growing are likely to opt for a centralized approach to coordinating land-use decisions and inventorying future land-use requirements. A top-down approach typically involves the preparation (by an outside consultant or by planning department staff) of a basic conceptual design or overall development plan. This plan is subject to review either through a hearing process, by organized citizen committees, or by a select citizens' advisory committee. Operating agencies are also given a chance to react and suggest modifications. A revised draft is finally forwarded to the planning commission and, ultimately, to the city council for review and approval.

Often the differences between a top-down and a bottom-up approach do not appear to be substantial. For example, in a centrally run comprehensive planning process, meetings may be held on a neighborhood basis to encourage residents to react to proposed development plans. The key difference, however, is in asking neighborhoods to react to existing plans as opposed to asking those neighborhoods to participate in the development of such plans. Examples of municipalities that have adopted the top-down approach include

Denver, Indianapolis, Tuscon, Tacoma, Boulder, Lincoln, Portland, Oak Park, Fayetteville, Petaluma, and Redmond.

The top-down approach assumes first that community goals and aspirations can be identified, and second, that the forces of urbanization can indeed be controlled through public action. The underlying rationale of the Boulder plan is typical of this approach:

> Either growth and redevelopment will be guided in a logical and planned manner, or it will likely develop in a haphazard fashion, ignoring the human scale of the community. Without consideration for circulation, varied types of housing, preservation of natural areas, and contiguous growth pattern, our community will needlessly be duplicating the mistakes of other communities throughout the country. . . . The Plan is intended to offer a general design for the patterns of future land use in the Boulder Valley predicated on the policy guidelines and community-wide objectives. It is meant to serve as a vision of the future and a catalyst in effectively responding to the challenges of building a quality community.

Cities involved in a neighborhood-up effort realize that they are sacrificing some degree of comprehensiveness. Yet in Fort Worth, for example, city officials feel that "what is lost in comprehensiveness is gained in achieving an implementable plan which truly reflects local priorities." The bottom-up approach, then, is a departure from the classic paradigm—it sacrifices generality, the long-range time horizon, and comprehensiveness (in the sense of interlocking area-wide politics). It trades these off for a more realistic and action-oriented program of development that must be continually reviewed. The neighborhood approach discards the one-shot, end-state document in favor of a continuous process arrived at by setting relatively short-range priorities. While a centralized process can do this, too, policies and programs initiated by neighborhoods are likely to be both more realistic and implementable.

Akron, Forth Worth, and Atlanta have used the bottom-up approach; Atlanta's is perhaps the most advanced. An amendment to the Atlanta City Charter requires the city government to prepare annual fifteen-, five-, and one-year comprehensive development plans dealing with the physical, social, and economic growth of the city. The fifteen-year plan provides goals, policies, and objectives for growth and defines the general locational character and extent of services, facilities, and improvements. The five-year plan offers guidance for capital improvements programming in a series of one-year plans. The one-year plan provides a framework for the year's capital budget and identifies specific programs, projects, and development for that year. The charter revision in Atlanta came about, in part, in response to the realization that many key development decisions were being made by outside private and public interests in an unpredictable and uncoordinated manner. A major controversy involving an interstate highway brought home this point quite clearly and spurred citizen groups to press for the charter revision.

Some cities—such as San Diego, Cincinnati, Tulsa, and Dallas—seem to be searching for something midway between top-down and neighborhood-up planning. They are attempting to update earlier master plans by relying on neighborhood planning groups (with technical support from the planning department) to develop local detailed plans that fit within the broad context of the longstanding master plan or a centrally conceived set of guidelines. This approach is not merely an effort to involve local groups in the ratification of a centrally conceived plan; neither is it a completely decentralized process. In San Diego the 25 to 30 community planning groups have a somewhat uneven record of developing local detailed land-use plans. The plans vary in scale and date targeted for completion. Neighborhood plans are to be adopted by the city council as amendments to the general plan.

There are other factors besides the level and rate of growth that seem to account for the particular orientation of the planning process in any given city. Past patterns of citizen involvement can carry over into the design of comprehensive planning efforts. If there are strong community or neighborhood boundaries, or substantial ethnic divisions within the city, a neighborhood approach is likely to find favor. When these conditions hold, even rapidly growing areas may opt for a neighborhood-up approach, as in the cases of Dallas and Tulsa.

Scale, too, can have a bearing on the selection of an approach to comprehensive planning. In the very largest cities it is extremely difficult to develop a set of community-wide objectives; in such cases, only vaguely termed objectives may be possible. It often seems as though development or redevelopment policies need to be broken up and framed in terms applicable to neighborhood-scale problems.

Plans, whether top-down or neighborhood-up, tend to be increasingly policy-oriented. As the Redmond plan states:

Future land uses are not precisely located with respect to individual properties as would be the case in a zoning map. This is necessary to allow latitude in making specific short term day to day decisions, which are necessary for Plan implementation. It is impossible to determine the location of all land uses in advance of need and development. Therefore, "development policies" are the basis of the Plan.

This is especially true in mature cities where land-use questions are not necessarily as important as other issues. The planning director in Cleveland, for example, has suggested that "the urban crisis has very little to do with land-use planning," and has chosen instead to focus on issues such as poverty and income distribution.

Another general problem is that the very concept of municipal planning is viewed with suspicion in certain parts of the country. Extensive public control over private investments and land-use decisions is seen as a threat to notions of basic liberties and free-market competition. Yet even in these areas the underlying rationale associated with top-down planning—coordination—is generally acceptable. This attitude also reflects, of course, the pattern of political power in many metropolitan areas. In rapidly growing areas, large landowners and real estate interests look to elected officials to pursue development opportunities in a manner consistent with the best interests of private groups. It is easier for those who seek to influence favorable decisions to do so in highly centralized situations. There appears to be some correlation between the organization of political power and the rationale for comprehensive planning that those in power tend to favor.

2. Comprehensive Planning Goals

Goal statements often have a rather bland, nonsubstantive quality. Sometimes there are fierce battles over the inclusion of innocuous goal statements that for one reason or another have taken on symbolic significance in a particular local setting. The goals contained in the Tacoma plan are typical:

> Tacoma is a residential and working environment. It is a growth center for the county, unenviably, but can keep growth orderly and desirable. Goals are to achieve and maintain a safe and healthy environment; to insure conservation of the shore line and guarantee balanced development; to see to it that every citizen has sound and healthy housing and locational choice; to provide convenient, well balanced compatible commercial development; to maintain, rehabilitate, and diversify industry for employment; to achieve a multi-model transportation system; to broaden the range of recreational facilities; to ensure an equitable distribution of facilities and services.

In some instances, as in Atlanta, efforts have been made to stratify goals. The Atlanta Planning Department talks about "umbrella goals" (protection of human, economic, and physical assets; enhancement of the attractiveness and enjoyment of the city; maximization of individual choice; and greater governmental responsiveness) as well as "special goals" (maintenance of a strong central business district; preservation of neighborhoods in close-in areas; provision of balanced housing; southside redevelopment; re-use of state acquired highway properties; and sensitivity to the natural environment). San Diego seems to have goals that are reasonably pegged to its unique situation: creation of a strong central core; advance acquisition of public sites; pollution prevention; nonconforming use abatement; attention to oceanic resources; coordination of local and metropolitan planning; and elimination of exclusive zoning. Goals typically relate to promoting or shaping development. There are, however, examples of comprehensive planning programs aimed at limiting development (and not just in undesirable areas). Petaluma, California is such a case. In an effort to bridge the gap between the very broad goals of a twenty-year general plan and the more immediate consideration involved in day-to-day administration of its zoning ordinance, the town has adopted a five-year environmental design plan based on an analysis of current fiscal, environmental, and social impacts of development options. The overriding goals of the Petaluma Environmental Design Plan are to "retain a small town character, to develop a permanent greenbelt, to actively encourage urban beautification, and to protect historical sites."

Most master plans, while giving passing mention to socioeconomic objectives, deal mainly with patterns of physical development. Cleveland is an exception; its plan refers explicitly to social welfare needs. The preface to the Cleveland comprehensive plan states that "in context of limited resources and pervasive inequalities, priority attention must be given to the task of promoting a wider range of choices for those who have few if any choices."

All in all, the goals of comprehensive planning are somewhat predictable and relatively uninspiring. More often than not they are general enough so that they apply uniformly to the entire community, and in most cases they assume that growth and development are desirable if channeled properly. The fact that most goal statements relate to physical development is not surprising since, for the most part, that is what planning commissions and planning departments are equipped and expected to deal with.

3. The Form and Elements of the Plan
The general plan may have a section setting out official goals and concepts, but this is not always the case. The traditional comprehensive plan usually does include, however, background material describing the present situation in social, economic and physical terms; and a series of functional plans for residence, industry, commerce, recrea-

tion and open space, public facilities, and transportation. Each section is accompanied by a map of the particular use, and the plan usually culminates in an overall map of the comprehensive plan.

The comprehensive plan for Philadelphia, completed in 1960, is an excellent example of such a plan, and has been used as a model by many other cities. However, as the Philadelphia Planning Commission remarks in its 1974 annual report, "even as one of the best plans of its type, the Plan has a structural weakness shared by all such 'end-state' plans: that of relative insensitivity to demographic and economic changes." Such a plan is static and therefore hard to keep up to date. Often, as in the case of Philadelphia, only the map is regularly updated and used; this makes it difficult to tie the plan into day-to-day decisions.

While cities have continued to search for more effective means to organize and present the results of their comprehensive planning efforts, no single alternative to the traditional form has yet emerged. But a number of formats for plan organization do exist: (1) single-document, citywide plans; (2) plans prepared neighborhood by neighborhood; and (3) plans prepared by compiling individual functional elements. Even cities with more traditional master plans (prepared in the 1960s) are now opting for the second and third formats in their updating activities.

Other cities have elected to develop their comprehensive plans element by element. A plan developed this way can either cover *all* elements, as in Akron, Rochester, and San Francisco; or focus on a few particularly critical topics within the context of a comprehensive goal, as in Cleveland. The Cleveland Commission explains its choice of a more selective set of elements:

> This first Policy Planning Report excludes topics such as education, crime, health, and recreation. While recognizing their importance, the Commission has devoted priority attention to analyses of income, housing, transportation and community development. In these areas, the Commission feels it has the best chance to affect decisions.

The plans of California's cities represent a separate class of element plans. The element-by-element format of these plans—sometimes grafted onto a single-document general plan, sometimes without an umbrella document as in San Francisco—results from the incremental requirement of specific elements by the state legislature.[5] This has resulted in an approach such as that outlined in a recent update of a 1945 general plan in San Francisco:

5. *See* discussion of California legislation in text accompanying notes 189–198 *supra.*

The work of revision has been separated into a series of elements, each representing a category of city concerns of facilities. These elements include residence, recreation, education, public safety, health care, social services, employment, industry, commerce, transportation, urban design and seismic safety. All of the elements are interrelated, and when combined in the comprehensive plan they will provide a strong basis for the setting of priorities for the whole community. Each element must be studied separately however, and each is a distinct area of concern and of policy. For each element, therefore, there will be a separate Plan for inclusion in the total comprehensive plan.

The original plan for San Diego included the following land-use elements: residential, commercial, parks and recreation, public facilities, public works, and transportation. Among the elements that have since been added are seismic safety, scenic highways, public safety, and conservation.

There remains disagreement about the inclusion and importance of a summary map in the comprehensive plan. Some planners are uneasy about perpetuating the traditional importance of the map, stressing that it must be secondary to the policies of the plan. This is explicitly stated, for example, in Fremont's plan:

The Summary Map functions as a key to the planning system. It summarizes the pieces of the General Plan into one document, gives an overall schematic illustration of the planned physical development for Fremont, . . . but may not be used without the rest of the General Plan. . . . [I]f there is conflict between the General Plan Text and the General Plan Map, the Text shall have higher authority.

Other cities, such as Philadelphia and Cincinnati, emphasize the importance of the map as a visual and coordinating tool. Thus in Philadelphia, the plan states:

The part of the 1960 Plan which has proved to have the greatest continuing usefulness is the Citywide Land Use Allocations Map, both as a synthesis of policy in the various program categories, and as a visual aid in deriving a sense of the interplay among the various policies for Philadelphia. Accordingly, the City expects to continue to use the land allocations map, revising and updating it systematically, as time and manpower permit.

Finally, a striking addition to the elements of recent plans is the inclusion of a separate section explaining the process by which the plan was produced and emphasizing procedures for implementation, particularly the process by which the comprehensive plan will be linked to the capital program and budget.

4. The Process for Initiating and Revising Plans

Comprehensive planning efforts have been initiated or revised in the past decade in response to a variety of stimuli that range from increased community pressure for more sensitive municipal policy and more efficient service delivery (Cincinnati, Atlanta) to increased awareness and fear of the impact of rapid growth (Redmond, Tacoma, Boulder, Tucson, Portland, Oak Park). In all 27 communities studied, the comprehensive planning process was in full swing— either starting for the first time or updating plans prepared in the early 1960s. Once a decision is made that a new or revised plan is needed, the process by which plans are developed varies, depending on the philosophical approach and political traditions in the city.

The preparation of a citywide plan—whether single-document or element-by-element—is quite well represented by the activities of Tacoma and San Francisco. Tacoma produced a single Land Use Management Plan in the following manner:

1. The staff developed an initial document through research, discussion of city ordinances and reports, interpretation of recent city decisions, and review of the activities of other cities (fall 1973 to spring 1974).
2. This document was then reviewed by the planning commission.
3. At the planning commission's request, the city council created the Citizens Land Use Policy Advisory Committee in September 1974 to review the goals and policies in the plan and make recommendations to the planning commission based on public meetings and other citizen input.
4. These recommendations were made, reviewed, and incorporated into the draft plan.
5. The draft plan was subjected to additional public hearings and amended accordingly.
6. On February 13, 1975 the plan was adopted by the planning commission.
7. The plan was adopted by the city council on February 22, 1975.

The process by which the elements of the plan are adopted in San Francisco is similar:

1. A background study and a staff draft of the element are prepared.
2. Both documents are distributed widely to neighborhood organizations.
3. After a one- to- three-month review, public hearings are held and testimony taken.

4. The draft is revised, based on comments.
5. Revisions are published and circulated for comment.
6. Additional comments are incorporated.
7. Final recommendations are forwarded to planning commission.
8. The element is adopted as part of the General Plan by planning commission.

This process of preparing or updating plans can be relatively straightforward, as described above, or extremely complex, as in Tucson, where development of the plan included extensive use of both print and electronic media, mass mailings, community meetings with slide shows, attitude surveys, extensive public consideration of alternative growth concepts, consultant studies of growth costs, and other activities over a period of several years. The process of preparing the five-year Environmental Design Plan for Petaluma suggests the range of steps that can be involved (see Table 5-2).

In 1969 the Fort Worth City Council decided tu revise its plan by means of "sector" planning. This approach entailed dividing the city into sections, or sectors, and assisting the citizens in each to form a council and work with the planning staff on a physical guide plan to serve their area over a 30-year period to the year 2000 (presuming frequent reviews). After the initial organization of the sector planning councils, committees immediately began to study existing problems within their neighborhoods. When these are completed the planning staff will present a group of conceptual design alternatives to the committees for their consideration. After selection of a concept plan the citizens develop goals and objectives for their neighborhood. Then, using this concept plan and its goals and objectives, the citizens prepare a final detailed plan with written policies for their sector. The sector planning council recommends the final report and plan to the city planning commission for adoption.

In addition to a process for amending the general plan, many communities have formally adopted an ongoing review process. Sometimes additional documents such as neighborhood plans are informally appended to the comprehensive plan without formal adoption. In many cities, as in Fremont, California, the planning commission is required to "render an annual report to the City Council on the status of the Plan and progress toward its implementation." In cities where the planning process is closely linked to capital budgeting, the budget cycle provides a regular annual review. The 1974 City Charter for the City of Atlanta requires an annual update of the plan, with one-, five-, and fifteen-year projections. This update process must include two public meetings held in each of the neigh-

Table 5-2. Steps Involved in Plan Preparation in Petaluma

1970	The planning director, city manager, and civil engineers assessed the impact of proposed subdivisions.
January 1971	The city council passed a moratorium on additional development until the general plan and the zoning ordinance were updated.
March 1971	A questionnaire was distributed to households with water bills and in the local newspaper. The responses were analyzed to determine growth preferences.
April 1971	A two-day development policy conference was held for all interested citizens.
May 1971	An official development policy conference was held by the city council building on the April conference.
May 1971– March 1972	One hundred citizens, the planning commission, the city council, and the planning staff developed an environmental design plan as a means of carrying out desired policies of growth control identified by the 1971 conferences.
August 1972	The city council adopted a residential development control system for allocating 500 units of new housing per year.
September 1972	The housing element of the general plan was adopted.
June 1973	In a citywide referendum, 82 percent of the population approved the growth-control strategy adopted by the city.

borhood planning units (also mandated by the charter), allowing input from neighborhood planning committees. Underlying all these approaches is a recognition that the process by which the plan is developed is at least as important as the plan itself and must be managed on an ongoing basis if the comprehensive plan is to be useful.

5. Implementation Mechanisms and Strategies

In the last decade increasing importance has been attached to the design of mechanisms and strategies for implementing comprehensive plans. The increased emphasis on implementation has resulted in a surprising shift in the locus of planning responsibility from the periphery to the center of local government. This shift has taken a number of forms, contingent in part on the relative complexity of the particular municipal government.

In smaller cities, such as Oak Park or Redmond, the planning staff performs planning, budget, and management functions for the city manager and provides staff support for many of the city's commissions and boards. The planners and the plan tend to be an integral part of the day-to-day decisionmaking process.

In larger cities the situation is somewhat different. In Philadelphia, due to the size and complexity of Philadelphia's governmental structure, the planning function is greatly dispersed. This dispersal makes it more difficult for the planning department, and especially for citizen's groups, to implement policies developed as part of the comprehensive plan. In response to this problem, some cities have revised their organizational structure in an effort to better coordinate planning and policy implementation. Examples of such cities include Atlanta, where planning has been included in a new Department of Budget and Planning, in which all budget, planning, and management functions have been centralized under a commissioner who is directly responsible to the mayor and has review power over the plans and budgets of line agencies; Indianapolis, where the metropolitan government (created in 1970) has developed a Unified Planning Program that merges the city's planning functions; San Diego, where over the last three years the mayor has gradually transferred related functions to the planning department (transportation, environmental issues, housing, and economic analysis); and Wilmington, where the planning staff is involved in analyzing annual program budgets submitted by each city department.

In large cities there are sometimes conflicts between the segment of the local government responsible for comprehensive planning and the unit responsible for community development (urban renewal). Here, too, the trend is toward merging the two departments—a policy, for example, presently being implemented in Birmingham. Efforts to further enhance the implementation of the comprehensive plan include restructuring the membership of local planning commissions, as is the case in Tacoma, to include the head of the public works and public facilities departments as well as the city's chief engineer. In Wilmington the planning commission now includes the assistant to the mayor and the director of public works.

The appropriate strategy for implementing a comprehensive plan depends in large measure on the relative stability of the political structure in the city and the relative capability of line agency staff. In some cities it is possible for the planning staff to make considerable headway because it is the only source of planning expertise and provides considerable technical assistance to line agencies. As one planning director suggests, "when you are the only people around with a defined plan and a clear agenda it is not difficult to remain one step ahead of the game." Formal restructuring of the relationships between the planning department and line agencies must be accompanied by a shift in informal relationships. In Atlanta the official reorganization has not yet taken hold. At present the mayor has not entirely shut off direct lines from line agencies to his office, leaving open the option of bypassing the planning department.

The effort to link comprehensive planning to ongoing municipal decision-making has resulted in repeated efforts to integrate long-range planning and five- to six-year capital-improvement programs which are reworked almost every year. This approach allows the planning department to exert leverage on the budget review process and provides an opportunity for a yearly reevaluation of priorities and overall development goals. Of course, this system requires the planning department to be able to adapt to the rapidly changing nature of community priorities and expectations, and to be prepared to depart from the mandates of the comprehensive plan when and if other opportunities present themselves.

When the planner's formal powers of implementation are limited, as they are in most instances, he or she must rely on the exercise of influence.[6] Action strategies must be chosen on the basis of prevailing interests and the level of credibility that can be sustained in the local political climate. This approach is most highly developed in Philadelphia and Cleveland. This has been recognized as a logical and potentially powerful approach to implementation, and other cities have or are adapting their planning strategies to allow for such linkages.

The second process innovation aimed at linking planning with development is the requirement that all development proposals be reviewed by the planning commission to ensure their consistency with the comprehensive plan. Many cities already impose this requirement (as included in the Standard City Planning Enabling Act), but it is not always taken seriously. Regardless of the planners' recommendations, the city council tends to act on its political preferences. Yet in some cities the enforcement of this kind of review process has been extremely effective. For example, in San Francisco, where many municipal activities are conducted by independent commissions, the planning department received little cooperation from the fire department in the development of a comprehensive facilities plan. Yet the commission, by law, had to approve any plans for new stations. These proposals were constantly refused on the grounds that they were not consistent with the overall plan for the city. The fire department finally accepted the planners' offer to work with them in developing a comprehensive plan.

This use of review powers must be supported by the mayor/manager and city council. If this support is forthcoming, the review process can be an effective means of conveying to the line agencies that the comprehensive plan must be taken seriously. But there is also a countervailing point of view. The director of long-range planning in

6. An excellent analysis of the political roles that planners play, including the technician, the broker, and the mobilizer, can be found in F. Rabinovitz, *City Politics and Planning* ch. 4 (1970).

San Diego suggests that the requirement that zoning be in compliance with the plan will continue to cause problems. Whereas before, each zoning variance or change was argued on its own merits after a more general comprehensive plan had been adopted, "now everyone with a specific objection will oppose the Comprehensive Plan. This may paralyze efforts to gain approval of the updated plan when it is finished in the near future." However, it may be that relocating the process of political compromise to the planning state is preferable to politicizing the increasingly complex land-use decisionmaking process.

Inevitably, as planning activity mushrooms at the local, regional, state, and national levels, intergovernmental tensions and conflicts erupt. There are some functional elements that can be planned most effectively at the regional level (such as transportation, housing, solid-waste disposal, air-pollution control). Personality conflicts and turf battles are bound to emerge within the region, however, although these are less important than conflicts in priorities between the principal city in a region and its surrounding municipalities. While some conflict is inevitable, a greater effort at the national and state levels to clearly identify and then allocate responsibility and funding among the levels of government might ease some of these tensions.

The most frequent disagreements involve projected and desired levels of growth and transportation. A municipality may develop a policy of growth management contrary to the policy, interests, or philosophy of the region. Denver, Tucson, and Petaluma are all experiencing this problem. Also, the construction of expressways through or immediately adjacent to a city has caused major controversies dividing central cities and their suburban neighbors. Of the cities surveyed, Atlanta, Cleveland and Minneapolis fall into this category.

Yet a number of cities are engaged in productive and cooperative working relationships with their surrounding counties and regional planning agencies. In some cases, including Lincoln/Lancaster County and Fayetteville/Cumberland County, one planning staff simultaneously serves both the city and county.

6. Approaches to Citizen Involvement

A high level of commitment to citizen involvement is expressed in practically every plan we reviewed and was underscored by almost all the interviews. This new surge of interest in citizen participation and the realization of the importance of citizen input springs from two sources—rising expectations generated by the former Office of

Economic Opportunity and Model Cities programs of the 1960s, and the environmental movement of the early 1970s. Cincinnati and Atlanta are examples of cities with highly sophisticated citizen organizations.

The public generally seems more knowledgeable about the workings of local government than it did ten years ago, and is better organized and able to demand more responsive services. The skepticism about government generated by Watergate and post-Watergate policies has also made responsive government an important political issue in many cities. Planners have come to realize that the only way to ensure plan acceptance and subsequent implementation is to create *a constituency for planning.* They are now prepared to go to the public and get as many people as possible involved and committed, so that policy-makers will have little choice but to adopt the plans produced.

The most prominent example of this recent commitment to citizen involvement is found in Atlanta, where the 1974 city charter explicitly states:

> It is hereby found and declared that in order to be truly comprehensive, city plans must be responsive to the needs and concerns of citizens; that a plan which allows for diversified and responsive citizen involvement must be developed within the scope and content of the Atlanta City Charter; and that it is in the public interest to adopt this proposed plan by incorporating it as a new Charter of the City Code.

The mayor is required by the charter to prepare an annual report describing the manner in which citizen involvement has been solicited in preparation of the comprehensive development plan.

Fort Worth is another city with an overt commitment to involving the public in the preparation of the comprehensive plan. The operational imperative in Fort Worth was a belief that there is a fundamental relationship between the size of an area and the degree of citizen participation. "Citizen apathy is inversely proportional to the proximity of a proposed project and to the direct benefits or disbenefits expected to accrue to the individual and his neighborhood." Citizens are naturally more knowledgeable and concerned about the specific areas in which they live, work, and shop.

Almost all cities surveyed that have updated their plans in the last five to ten years have developed some type of citizen participation mechanism beyond the standard planning board or commission. Oak Park, Lincoln, Tucson, Tulsa, Redmond, Portland, Tacoma, Brookline, and Fremont are only a sample of the cities that have had active citywide citizen groups participating in the planning process. Many of the participants have moved on from this activity to run for local office, frequently running on a platform calling for the implementation of the goals and plans developed by citizen groups. It should be noted, however, that successful citizen involvement is extremely costly, both in terms of staff time and the expense of printing, publicity, and project costs. Cities with serious fiscal problems, such as Rochester, cited the cost of citizen participation as a serious constraint. According to the mayor's deputy, it is "more useful to focus on problems of coordination within city government than to collect citizen priorities, using staff we can't afford to hire, when there isn't enough money to meet the newly collected priorities anyway."

Atlanta, Cincinnati, Cleveland, Wilmington, and Indianapolis, among others, cited the scarcity of funds for community planners as a serious impediment to any participatory effort. However, as the Oak Park plan concludes:

> The continued and expanded use of local talent in the planning process is a necessary factor in improving community spirit and providing fresh inputs into the decision-making process. Many of those who have served on the Citizens Action Committee, for example, have been appointed to various commissions and committees of the Village government. The continued involvement of more citizens is important for maintaining the planning momentum.

A recent report by the Urban Institute, *Citizen Involvement in Land Use Governance: Issues and Methods,*[7] provides an excellent summary of citizen involvement efforts throughout the country. Interestingly, the majority of innovative efforts cited in that report are in communities that are also included in the sample of 27 cities studied for this survey.

Another study of planning and management processes in 268 communities across the country revealed some important data about citizen participation. Local officials were asked to state whether they had used various means of increasing citizen participation in their government processes and to rate these various devices. The five mechanisms for increasing citizen participation most frequently mentioned were: (1) informal contact with citizens and citizen groups by staff and department personnel (96 percent of those returning the questionnaire); (2) advisory roles for citizen groups (93 percent); (3) staff assistance groups (86 percent); (4) newsletters, TV, etc., to pro-

7. N. Rosenbaum, Citizen Involvement in Land Use Governance: Issues and Methods (1974).

vide information to citizen and citizen groups (82 percent); and (5) direct involvement of citizen groups in planning, development, implementation, and management (80 percent).

In an attempt to locate and assess the major barriers to increased citizen participation, these same officials were asked to rate a number of possible problem areas. The five potential impediments to citizen participation mentioned most often were: (1) inadequate financial resources, (2) time required to complete planning involving citizen participation, (3) inadequate staff resources, (4) maintenance of adequate interest and involvement by citizens and citizen groups, and (5) citizen pressure to deliver results sooner than is realistic.

Finally, the officials were questioned about how they felt about involving citizens in various ways that would affect planning and management in their cities. A large majority of the respondents thought the following uses of citizen participation would strengthen the planning and management process by: (1) providing feedback about effects of programs and projects (93 percent); (2) serving as a sounding board for ideas and proposals (90 percent); (3) facilitating community acceptance of plans and programs (89 percent); (4) assisting in defining neighborhood needs and priorities (88 percent); (5) serving in an advisory capacity (70 percent); and (6) assisting in the development of programs and plans (68 percent).[8]

A great deal can be learned from these experiments. While refinements are undoubtedly in order, new approaches to citizen involvement have blossomed in the past few years and have had an important—indeed dramatic—impact on the nature of comprehensive planning activities in the United States.

CONCLUSION

Factors Accounting for the Relative Effectiveness of Comprehensive Planning

There appear to be certain antecedents of effective planning. The first involves the match between the rate of growth and the scope and style of a municipality's planning activities. Very rapid growth tends to underscore the need to see a pattern of what is happening and some way of controlling it. In Fremont, Tucson, Boulder, and Petaluma, where the rate of growth is an important issue, a centrally conceived planning effort keyed to growth control has aroused widespread popular support. In these situations, planning is perceived as

8. Thorwood, *The Planning and Management Process in City Government,* 1973 Municipal Y.B. 29-38.

an especially important activity of city government, and implementation mechanisms receive a great deal of attention. The success of the planning process is measured in terms of the city's ability to contain and direct growth.

The level of maturity of a city dictates, at least in part, the kind of planning effort likely to succeed. The issues facing cities which are almost entirely developed, such as Cleveland, Philadelphia, Cincinnati, Akron, Brookline, San Francisco, and Rochester, differ from those confronting communities such as Tucson, Lincoln, San Diego, Boulder, and Tacoma, which are faced with the prospect of having to expand facilities and services into newly populated areas. Mature cities require a planning process that focuses on the use of public dollars to preserve and enhance already developed areas, while rapidly growing communities are inclined to expect their comprehensive planning process to deal with the allocation of anticipated growth and methods of constraining private development decisions.

Another key factor in the success of any planning effort is the stability of the city's political structure. A stable political system that provides continuity of perspective regarding the city's future, and an ongoing commitment from the chief executive to a professional planning effort, can make an important contribution to the credibility of the planning effort and the prospects for institutionalizing the priorities contained in the plan. Oak Park and Portland are examples of communities where the stability of the political structure accounts in large measure for the success of the planning operation.

A great deal of time can be consumed in developing political alliances and finding a comfortable working relationship between the central planning staff and the heads of various line agencies and citizen groups. If these relationships are constantly in flux, there is very little time left to devote to the work that needs to be done.

A fourth antecedent is the presence of crisis or emergency conditions. In Tulsa, for example, severe flooding required the city to install storm sewers. In order to lay out such a system it was first necessary to make basic assumptions about the level and direction of growth in the years to come. This emergency helped to overcome a lingering resistance to planning. It may be that in some communities only an emergency or a crisis will topple the normal resistance to centrally planned change or extensive public control over land-development decisions.

A fifth antecendent of effective planning is the state of the local economy. Planners in several cities, including Wilmington, Tucson, and San Diego, have suggested that the depressed state of the economy has added to the population's unwillingness to accept the need for planning. This is particularly true in cities trying to implement growth-management schemes and to set standards by which proposed developments can be evaluated. In Wilmington, for example, practically any proposal that holds out the promise of new jobs has been deemed acceptable, regardless of the environmental consequences. Another impact of the recession is that financially pressed municipalities may look to their planning departments for careful analyses of the potential increases in costs to the city implied by additional development. Overall, though, economic hardship has weakened support for local planning. Anything that threatens jobs is opposed. Moreover, growth rates diminish when the economy slows down, removing some of the pressure for planning in rapidly growing areas.

The sixth and final antecedent of effective comprehensive planning is the prior level of citizen involvement. Cities with extremely active citizen groups, created during the heyday of the OEO and Model Cities programs, have not had to invest substantial amounts of money in organizing neighborhood participation efforts. Urban renewal project-area committees as well as more traditional block associations have become involved in comprehensive planning. Atlanta's particularly strong emphasis on citizen involvement can be traced to prior efforts to stop a proposed interstate highway project scheduled to slice through the city.

There are, of course, problems created when cities rely on existing organization networks. Certain neighborhoods that are already well organized may have disproportionate inputs, while heavier concentrations of staff effort need to be invested in unorganized areas. Previously organized groups are also more inclined to adopt a conflict-oriented approach to decisionmaking. They sometimes have difficulty accepting the need to set citywide priorities or to work within a citywide planning framework.

In addition to these six antecedents of effective comprehensive planning there are three kinds of commitment that are essential. The first is an ongoing commitment from the mayor or city manager to the planning process. In all cases surveyed, the plan remains an advisory document. The commitment of the city's chief executive to the plan and the planning process is crucial to successful policy implementation. This is particularly true in cities that require all development projects to conform to the plan. If this requirement is taken seriously and backed up administratively, it can be an extremely powerful implementation tool.

The second kind of commitment is obvious—financial support to underwrite the costs of staff activities. And the third commitment is no less important—a willingness to develop linkages between central planning and the operation of line agencies and departments. Preparation of the capital improvements program and the annual operating budget are important to the implementation process. These offer a direct means of affecting the contents of the long-range plan. Planning staffs responsible for the preparation of capital improvement programs must work with staff members in other line agencies, forcing both groups to confront the obvious gap between long-range plans and the day-to-day needs of city government. Atlanta's fifteen-, five-, and one-year plans seem to offer a means of minimizing the gap. Philadelphia's planning program focused on the linkages between long-range development plans and short-range capital improvement programs is a prime example of the kind of commitment needed to implement the comprehensive plan.

One interesting aside is about the tension that has developed in some cities between the planning department and the community development department over the allocation of community development block grants. Some community development departments have been inclined to make allocations without particular attention to comprehensive plan. This has been solved in several instances by forming coordinating committees. There is some question, however, about locating long-term planning in one department and short-term decisions in another—particularly if the long-term effort involves community-based efforts to determine citizen priorities, while the short-term operation runs a similar citizen-involvement campaign. Combining the two may endanger the longer-range perspective of the planning department, but it appears this may well be worth the risk since community development block grants can be another important tool for implementing development priorities.

Overriding Issues in Building Local Planning Capacity

Friction between local and areawide planning agencies appears to be inevitable. Rivalries have arisen between planning agencies at the city and metropolitan levels, as in Minneapolis; metropolitan government remains fragmented, as in Indianapolis where the three largest towns in the county besides Indianapolis refused to join the metro government; differences in espoused growth policies persist between cities such as Petaluma, which try to limit growth, and counties that continue to encourage growth. Basic philosophical differences erupt between local and county officials and their staffs (such as Tucson and Lincoln) resulting in departures from the county plan; bickering occurs over the definition of regional responsibility, especially about transportation policies, as in Atlanta and Cleveland.

Regional agencies have gained a substantial amount of power through federally mandated programs, many of which guarantee substantial financial assistance.[9] The cities are frustrated because federal assistance for local planning has not increased, while the regional agencies have more staff than they seem to need. A number of the elected officials said they are often called upon to mediate between "turf conscious" city and regional planners (Minneapolis, San Diego, and Atlanta). It is extremely difficult to build local planning capabilities when cities and areawide bodies are in competition, and when federal funds are being siphoned off by regional agencies while city planning departments remain understaffed.

A number of cities have not as yet developed an effective approach to citizen participation, and indeed there are numerous obstacles. Planning staffs in several cities bemoan the fact that they have been forced to train a second generation of local leaders because the initial group moved on to elected office. They also indicate that citizen participation drops off or ceases altogether during political campaigns because the most active people were also active in campaigns for public office. This dilemma was mentioned by respondents in Tulsa, Tucson, Fort Worth, Atlanta, San Diego, Minneapolis, Fremont, Petaluma, and Wilmington.

Although the importance of citizen participation is almost universally acknowledged, the cost of doing effective organizational work and neighborhood planning is a clear deterrent. Lack of funds to hire additional neighborhood planners has delayed implementation of neighborhood planning in Atlanta and Rochester. Such planning is being done a few neighborhoods at a time in many cities, because the staff is simply insufficient.

There is one other impediment to effective citizen participation, and that is a failure to recognize that input must come not only from good-government groups such as the League of Women Voters, but also from the Chamber of Commerce and local business leaders. Since business groups already have reasonably strong ties to city hall, they often fail to become involved in ad hoc or extracurricular planning activities. Yet, if they have not been involved in helping to articulate neighborhood plans, they often scuttle such operations as they near the final approval stage. Efforts to strengthen local planning capabilities must involve a broad range of groups from the outset.

9. Programs frequently mentioned that provide substantial funds to staff regional agencies were the A-95 clearinghouse function and the activities under § 208 of the Water Pollution Control Act.

A third issue in building local planning capacity involves the specification of performance standards. It is often difficult to measure whether general long-range planning is having the predicted effect. The time frame of most centrally conceived plans is often as much as twenty to twenty-five years. In the interim, while the planners search for ways of linking middle-range decisions, such as capital improvements and other public actions, to the over-arching intent of the plan, the public waits, unable to judge the results.

Growth management techniques which provide specific performance standards (such as site plan review criteria, development impact criteria, and environmental design standards) may help to strengthen planning activities in growing cities. Citizens need some way of holding both the elected and appointed officials accountable. Performance standards that provide a measure of the suitability of proposed development projects offer some hope in this regard. Even without additional powers of implementation, planning departments may be able substantially to enhance their ability to follow through on the comprehensive plan if they develop criteria or standards that permit the public to trace their effectiveness.

Especially in smaller cities, which usually rely on outside professional help, performance standards can serve as indicators of progress toward planning goals, thus putting local officials on the line and drawing them more closely into contact with the planning process. Such standards are not as difficult to set as might be expected. The success of Boulder and Petaluma bears this out. In more mature cities, which have adopted a neighborhood or district process and produced rather specific lists of priorities for investment and development, the problem of accountability is less severe since these priority lists serve as performance measures.

A fourth issue in building local capacity relates to the strategic link between planning and regulation. In the past it was assumed that zoning and subdivision controls ought to be the key mechanisms for implementing the intent of the master plan. As it turns out, zoning is not as strong a coordinating device as was originally conceived. Zoning deals mostly with private development decisions, which are shaped mainly by market forces, and has very little to do with the process of setting priorities for public investment in services and facilities. Moreover, market forces as well as the political clout of many private land interests tend to supersede the power of the zoning ordinance. Since planning is a political process, it may be necessary to broaden the linkage between planning and land-use decisions to include a component for public development activity.

A fifth issue involved in building local planning capabilities does involve a formal or structural modification. The experience in Atlanta suggests that a city charter provision requiring an annual planning review cycle can do more to stimulate concern for planning than even the most entrepreneurial planning department. It is important to distinguish regular updating efforts from the legally required amendment process. Most cities have already spelled out procedures for amending the general plan (or the zoning map, as the case may be). But few cities have formally established an annual review cycle through which neighborhood groups or an umbrella citizens advisory committee reviews the progress toward fulfilling the objectives of the general plan. To some extent the planning commission may be presumed to play this role. But in fact, with planning moving closer to the administrative center of city government, annual reviews by planning commissions do not have much impact. The way to underscore the importance of planning is to mandate, in rather detailed terms, how an annual review process should operate. Legislating process guidelines is less difficult than legislating the form, content, or strategies for enforcing the general plan.

A sixth issue in upgrading planning capabilities has to do with money. As localities find themselves increasingly burdened by federal- or state-mandated planning requirements, an enormous amount of time and energy is taken away from substantive planning activities. Not only should localities be provided with funds to undertake federal- and state-mandated planning activities, but higher levels of government ought to do more to provide technical assistance to communities that are either too small or too short of funds to gear up an ongoing planning process of their own.

Finally, there is a growing recognition that different neighborhoods have different needs and therefore require separate and specially tailored planning strategies. For example, Portland identifies three types of neighborhoods: stable areas, areas of development, and areas in need of transformation. Other cities suggest that one reason for planning from the neighborhood up is that there are different priorities in each area that cannot be determined by the central planning department. Rochester has hesitated to implement a citywide advisory council for fear of further polarizing the different factions in the city's neighborhoods. In Atlanta, although the city charter mandates the organization of a citywide body made up of representatives of the individual neighborhood planning committees, these same planning committees have opposed the formation of the central committee, fearing that it will dilute the stated preferences of their neighborhoods. They prefer to deal directly with the city government and city council fearing that an additional layer of administration might filter out neighborhood differences. It may well be necessary to decentralize comprehensive planning efforts in order to enhance local planning capacity.[10]

It was suggested at the outset of this chapter that the scope and style of comprehensive planning remained relatively unchanged throughout the 1950s and 1960s, unaffected by the criticism from within and without the profession. Slowly, however, the dominant approach to local comprehensive planning does appear to be changing. The rationale for comprehensive planning is shifting, partly in response to the realization that mature central cities are no longer growing, and partly in response to the urgings of the no-growth and slow-growth advocates.

The primary assumption used to be that a centrally conceived framework for planning was needed to provide effective coordination and to allow for the integration of short- and long-term public actions. Now there is an emerging feeling that a decentralized approach might be equally, if not more, appropriate; and that short-term and middle-range development proposals can and ought to be spelled out in detail within the context of an ongoing comprehensive planning process. Planners have finally relinquished their claims to comprehensiveness (in both Kent's and Altshuler's definition of the word). They have moved toward a policy-oriented approach that is much more practical and responsive.

The goal statements contained in the most recently updated master plans still have a hollow ring. But the inclusion of relatively specific recommendations and programmatic suggestions on a district or element-by-element basis seems to blunt the charge that comprehensive plans have little bearing on actual decisionmaking. Many cities have adopted a district- or neighborhood-up approach to policy formulation and priority setting. These processes tend to result in comprehensive plans that vary from traditional form and content. New elements have been added, although the fundamental stress on land use, circulation, and community facilities still remains.

The process of updating or producing new master plans has been altered. There is much more emphasis on broad-based public involvement, and independent planning commissions seem to play decreasing roles in the comprehensive planning process. An emphasis on implementation coincides with a shift in the locus of planning activity toward the center (executive branch) of city government. A 1971 survey of almost 1,000 municipalities by the International City Man-

10. *See* the discussion of decentralized land-use controls in Chapter 4 *supra.*

agers Association indicated, even then, "a trend toward planning agencies becoming integrated into the general government structure."[11] New linkages between planning and budgeting, and relatively successful experiments with new growth-control techniques, suggest that the thrust toward implementation and the effort to link the general plan with day-to-day decisionmaking may well succeed.

Whether the most recent comprehensive planning efforts will actually shape development or alter the quality of life for residents remains to be seen. The results of the survey suggest that older master plans were not inaccurate in the land-use patterns they predicted; indeed, the opposite would have been quite astounding, since the planning commissions who directed the preparation of the preceding wave of master plans were most responsive to the vested interests guiding private development and public investment decisions.

This is not to say that the past comprehensive plans conditioned the rate or pattern of development, only that they were likely to reflect the same set of values and operating assumptions internalized by those in power. The claim that master plans have had little direct effect on municipal development may be accurate to the extent that most plans contained such vague and general proposals that there was little chance that the plan itself would influence specific policy choices. The same, however, may not be true of the most recently prepared comprehensive plans.

Finally, the positive movement toward plans that are comprehensive in the sense of addressing the full range of social, economic, environmental, and political problems facing communities today is an important factor in the successful implementation of mandatory planning and plan-consistency requirements. That these plans are being developed by a process that is more flexible and open, at the same time that the courts are requiring land-use control administration to demonstrate basic fairness and rationality, augurs well for a successful juxtaposition of planning theory and legally defensible implementation mechanisms.

11. Harman, *City Planning Agencies: Organization, Staffing and Functions*, 1972 Municipal Y.B. 55-79.

Table 5-3.   Persons Interviewed

City	
Akron	Al Sulin. Department of Planning and Urban Renewal Sister Bridget, Chairman, Planning Commission
Atlanta	Israel Mac, Planner in Charge, Comprehensive Plans Section Walter Huntley, Assistant to the Mayor Panke Bradley, City Council member
Birmingham	Robert Thompson, Assistant Director, Planning & Zoning Department Robert Land, Director, Department of Community Development
Boulder	Edward Goff, Assistant Director, Planning Department Robert Westdyke, Assistant to the City Manager
Brookline	[a]Mark Eldridge, Assistant Planning Director
Cincinnati	Richard Alice, Senior Planner Duane Chapman, Office of the City Manager
Cleveland	Norman Krumholz, Director, City Planning Commission
Dallas	Douglas Waskom, City Planning Department Daniel Petty, Mayor's Assistant
Denver	Merlin Logan, City Planner, City and County of Denver
Fayetteville	[a]Clifford Strassenberg, Planning Director, Cumberland County Planning Board
Fort Worth	[a]Wayne Snyder, former Planner, City Planning Department, present Director, Stockyards Area Redevelopment
Fremont	Shelley Mark, City Planning Department Carolyn Tissal, City Planning Commission
Indianapolis	[a]Nicholas Shelley, Assistant Administrator for Planning and Zoning
Lincoln	Rurl Borg, Assistant Director, Lincoln City–Lancaster County Planning Staff
Minneapolis	Gordon Wagner, City Planning Department Marsha Townley, Mayor's delegate to the Planning Commission
Oak Park	William Merrill, Assistant Director of Planning & Development Karl Raney, Assistant to the Village Manager
Petaluma	[a]William Gray, former Director, Community Development, present Director, Office of Environmental Affairs
Philadelphia	Robert Lourcott, Director of Comprehensive Planning
Portland	Donald Megathlin, Planning Director George Flaherty, Assistant to the City Manager
Redmond	[a]Julian Sayers, Planning Director
Rochester	Fahsun Ku, Senior Planner, Bureau of City Planning Joanne Elferink, Assistant to the City Manager
San Diego	David Smith, Senior Planner Michael Madigan, Assistant to the Mayor

Table 5-3 continued

City	
San Francisco	George Williams Lou Blazej Department of City Planning
Tacoma	[a]Joseph Quilici, Principal Planner and Zoning Administrator
Tucson	James Hummer, Assistant Director of Planning William Ealy, Office of the City Manager
Tulsa	Stanley Williams, Planning Department, Assistant Director Denton Kent, Director, Department of Community Development
Wilmington	John Demsey, Senior Planner Mrs. Hoagland, Planning Commissioner

[a]Designates a planning staff member also recommended by the mayor or city manager's office as an authority in the city on planning.

Table 5-4. List of Planning Documents

Akron	Capital Investment Budget 1974-79 Vacant Industrial & Commercial Land: An Inventory Solid Waste Disposal in the Akron Area Akron Metropolitan Area Transportation Study Summit County Housing Development Plan
Atlanta	Ordinance of the Council of the City of Atlanta Relating to Citizen Involvement in the Planning Process 1975 Comprehensive Development Plan "How to Do Neighborhood Planning" description of the duties of the divisions of the Department of Budget and Planning (mimeo)
Birmingham	The Comprehensive Plan The City Planning Function (mimeo) The Scope of Operation and Procedure for Committees of the Birmingham Planning Commission (mimeo) Processing Guide—Planning and Zoning Department (mimeo)
Boulder	The Boulder Valley Comprehensive Plan Growth Management System—Proposed Policies for Public Review and Comment (mimeo)
Brookline	Working Draft—Preliminary Comprehensive Plan Revision 1960 Comprehensive Plan
Cincinnati	A Framework for Integrating City Programs to Provide a Comprehensive Response to Community and Budgetary Needs (mimeo) A Framework for Recommendation Proposals (mimeo)

Table 5-4 continued

Cleveland	Policy Planning Report, Volume I Cleveland's Population A Proposed Change in State Legislation to Assure City Recovery of Costs incurred in the Demolition of Condemned Private Property Impact of New Construction on the Market for Existing Downtown Office Space Cleveland's Abandonment Problem Transportation and Poverty—Guidelines for Cleveland Recommendations for an Alternative Route for I-290 A Housing Allowance Program for Cleveland Comparative Analysis of Housing Programs Evaluation of the Rent Supplement Program Evaluation of the 236 Program Evaluation of the Public Housing Program Staff Report on the Ten-Year Transit Development Program Urban Solid Waste Collection and Disposal Poverty and Substandard Housing Housing Abandonment in Cleveland Housing for Low and Moderate Income Families A Fair-Share Plan for Cuyahoga County for Low Rent Housing Toward Equitable Transportation Opportunities for Cleveland's Elderly and Poor The Proposed Federal Family Assistance Plan Jobs and Income Cleveland's Urban Renewal Experience Economic Feasibility Analysis
Dallas	A Systematic Approach to Land Use Planning Comprehensive Land Use Plan—Land Use Policies
Denver	Denver 1985: A Comprehensive Plan for Community Excellence
Fayetteville	Cumberland County Joint Planning Board 1974 Annual Report Commercial Areas Plan Land Use Plan The Economy of Cumberland County—Development Policies
Fort Worth	400,000 City Planners—A City Agency Moves Toward Advocacy Arlington Heights Sector General Plan
Fremont	General Plan—Fremont, California (summary) The Fremont General Plan
Indianapolis	Comprehensive General Land Use Plan Comprehensive Plan Definition Work Program—Short Range Update of the Comprehensive Plan—1975 Work Program—Long Range Update of the Comprehensive Plan for Indianapolis–Marion County Integrated Grant Application for the Unified Planning Program

Table 5-4 continued

Lincoln	Comprehensive Regional Plan for the Lincoln City—Lancaster County Metropolitan Area Lincoln City-Lancaster County Preliminary Preferred Land Use Plan (Memo) Lincoln City-Lancaster County Goals and Policies Review
Minneapolis	Goals, Objectives, and Principal Policies
Oak Park	The Comprehensive Plan
Petaluma	Environmental Design Plans A Unique Approach to Growth Control (mimeo) Rationale, Operation, and Evaluation of Residential Development Control in the City of Petaluma (mimeo)
Philadelphia	Comprehensive Plan for the City of Philadelphia Report on the Comprehensive Plan—1974 Application for Recertification of the Workable Program for Community Improvement (1974-75) Recommended 1976-1981 Capital Program and 1976 Capital Budget
Portland	Land Development Plan 1974
Redmond	Optimum Land use Plan
Rochester	Comprehensive Master Plan Master Plan Update Program—Preliminary Goals Statements Comprehensive Planning Program Proposal Fiscal 1975-76
San Diego	Progress Guide and General Plan for the City of San Diego Seismic Safety Element Scenic Highway Element Noise (Transportation) Element Safety Element Conservation Element Housing Element
San Francisco	Urban Design Plan Improvement Plan for Residence Transportation Element Recreation and Open Space Environmental Protection Community Facilities
Tacoma	Land Use Management Plan Ordinance No. 20266 Amending the City Planning Commission
Tucson	The Comprehensive Plan—A Draft for Community Review Cost/Revenue Analysis—Four Alternative Plans for Growth General Land Use Planning Housing Issues Community Issues

Table 5–4 continued

	Comprehensive Planning
	Community Response
	Introduction to the Comprehensive Plan
Tulsa	What's to Become of Tulsa? (pamphlet)
	Alternatives for Urban Growth
	Alternatives for Urban Growth and Form
	Phase Two: Development Guidelines
	Economic and Land Use Analysis
	Urban Form Selection, Implementation Policies, Development Guidelines
	Development Guidelines: Staff Recommendations for Implementation
	The District 18 Plan Report
	Citizens Handbook for Neighborhood Planning
Wilmington	Neighborhood Comprehensive Development Plan for the Delaware Avenue Area
	Program Budget: Department of Publis Works, Division of Motor Vehicles

✳ *Chapter 6*

Housing Planning

INTRODUCTION

As has been stated throughout this book, decent and afford-able housing is one of the most important elements in the life of every American. Housing is more than shelter, as it allows access to educational and employment opportunities, transportation, recreation, and other public and private services and facilities. As a result, hous-ing availability both effects and is affected by a wide variety of pub-lic and private actions, and must therefore be coordinated with all forms of planning and implementation activities. The Advisory Com-mission has concluded that the opportunity for decent living ac-commodations and freedom from law-imposed discrimination are fundamental values that will not be realized without both private and public intervention, the latter including judicial intervention where it is necessary.

In many respects the housing problem has become more pervasive in recent years, at least in part because greater numbers of Americans are affected by it. According to recent statistics the average selling price of a new house jumped from $22,900 in 1965 to $42,600 in 1975, an increase of 86 percent. Average interest rates during the same period rose from 5.8 percent to 9.2 percent.[1] Based on these statistics it has been estimated that one-half to two-thirds of Ameri-

1. U.S. League of Savings and Loan Associations, 1976 *Savings and Loan News* 36 (March).
2. *Id.* at 37.

can households are unable to buy a typical new house.[2] Of course, new housing accounts for only a portion of the housing market, but even as the total supply of decent housing increases, households are required to allocate a higher percentage of income to housing costs,[3] reducing the income available for other necessities, the costs of which are also increasing dramatically.

Generally, expenditures for housing are the most significant costs American families will face in the course of their lives. Moreover, while land is used for many different purposes, over 40 percent of developed land is used for residential construction. This is to say that the nature of the housing problem in America necessitates conscious planning and action at all levels of government. Housing planning should be coordinated at the federal, state, regional, and local levels so that the benefits to be achieved through planning are not diminished by inefficient and duplicative government efforts.

Most of what has been done in the name of housing planning has, however, been limited, focusing on new construction of low- and moderate-income housing, often in the form of regional allocation plans, and generally based on available housing subsidies. Housing planning should instead be viewed as much broader in scope, addressing all the components of the housing process. A comprehensive housing strategy (as described later in the chapter) may facilitate this approach and increase the likelihood of acceptance of housing goals by the various actors in the political process, who have not always viewed housing planning in a favorable light.

In this chapter, then, we attempt to outline a broad framework for housing planning, in part by providing information to state and local governments to assist them in undertaking housing planning. Criteria for the courts are suggested, as well, to be used in evaluating the sufficiency of state and local plans, growth-management systems, housing and community development programs, and other governmental actions relating to housing. Implicit throughout is a recognition of the complexity of the housing process and its relationship to such other vital community concerns as land use, environmental preservation, and fiscal stability. A primary concern is the Advisory Commission's view that housing must be treated in a regional context, and that housing planning should be mandated by the states.

2. *Id.* at 37. The outlook for the future is even more bleak. *See* text at note 8 in Chapter 1 *supra*.

3. In 1950, 30.8 percent of all American households paid more than 25 percent of their incomes for rent; by 1974, over 42 percent of the households were paying rent at that rate. 3 Hous. & Dev. Rep. 1230 (1976).

HOUSING: AN ESSENTIAL PART OF COMPREHENSIVE PLANNING

The Important Role of Housing Planning

Why engage in housing planning at all? Good planning may highlight problems, but it does not solve them, nor do housing plans build houses. Nevertheless, the existence of housing plans, in concert with other government planning and implementation efforts, can facilitate housing activity by creating public acceptance of the importance of the housing issue and can guide and coordinate public and private actions to maximize benefits and minimize costs.

The place of housing planning in the crossword puzzle of government plans and programs varies from city to city. In general, housing planning should be considered as a component of the comprehensive planning process. There should be a housing plan component of the comprehensive plan. Moreover, there should be a dynamic housing strategy *process*, which systematically focuses attention on what needs to be done and marshals resources to that end. The housing plan is a formal statement on the housing strategy process.

A related question is, What is included within the housing strategy and its more formal statement, the housing plan? Housing planning is not an attempt to divide the community into residential elements with labels; rather, it is a perspective from which all elements of the community may be viewed and interrelated. Housing planning is not a discrete plan element as much as it is a set of actions designed to. achieve specific goals and objectives related to housing-oriented needs and problems. As such, housing planning cuts across plan elements, programs, budgets, agencies, and constituencies.

The constituency issue is both pervasive and persuasive as it relates to housing planning in our central cities and suburbs. Elected officials, in particular, are highly sensitive to the views of those who put them in office—the people who are already in the community. It is therefore difficult for these officials to embrace housing planning that endeavors to accommodate "outsiders," including those with different characteristics and those of future generations. But housing planning is vital to realistic growth management and need not be incompatible with such efforts. The housing strategy, to be effective, must interrelate with the overall growth and development objectives of the community. At the outset it is necessary to recognize the growing importance of housing planning and how dramatically the pressures brought to bear on that planning have changed over the last ten years. In the late 1960s a series of major government studies thoroughly documented the problems of urban housing and growth. The National Commission on Urban Problems (the Douglas Commission) and the President's Committee on Urban Housing (the Kaiser Committee) astutely examined how federal programs, development controls, and other incentives could be altered and used to improve patterns of metropolitan development and more fairly expand housing opportunities for all citizens.[4] These studies resulted in the enactment of the Housing and Urban Development Act of 1968, which was responsible for our nation's most active period of development of both subsidized and conventional housing. Indeed, the amount of federally assisted housing for low- and moderate-income families produced between 1968 and 1973, largely under the Section 235 homeownership and Section 236 multifamily programs established by the 1968 Act,[5] almost exceeded the amount provided during the thirty years from 1942 to 1972.[6]

In the 1970s, fiscal stability has become a foremost concern for urban communities, increasing efforts are being made to control growth, environmental protection requirements strictly regulate development, and rising housing costs are affecting even middle-income households. In the preface to the Housing and Community Development Act of 1974, Congress found that:

> [T]he Nation's cities, towns, and smaller urban communities face critical social, economic, and environmental problems arising in significant measure from (1) the growth of population in metropolitan and other urban areas, and the concentration of persons of lower income in central cities; and (2) inadequate public and private investment and reinvestment in housing and other physical facilities, and related public and social services, resulting in the growth and persistence of urban slums and blight and the marked deterioration of the quality of the urban environment.[7]

These problems show no immediate sign of improvement and the planning required to cope with them is indeed quite complex.

There are at least three considerations that have mounted in importance for housing planning in the last decade: (1) public costs

4. The National Commission on Urban Problems, Building the American City (1968) [hereinafter cited as Building the American City]; The President's Committee on Urban Housing, A Decent Home (1968) [hereinafter cited as A Decent Home]. *See also* National Advisory Commission on Civil Disorders, The Kerner Commission Report (1968).

5. Housing and Urban Development Act of 1968, §§ 101(a), 201(a), *adding* § 235 and § 236 to the National Housing Act (now 12 U.S.C. §§ 1715z, 1715z-1).

6. Mageda, *Housing Report: Major Programs Reversed to Stress Community Control*, Nat. L. Rep. 1376 (1974).

7. Pub. L. No. 93-383, § 101(a), 42 U.S.C. § 5301(a) (1974).

and revenues and the fiscal impact of growth on communities; (2) the protection of environmental quality and the impact of development on that quality; and (3) the need to protect and expand housing opportunities for minority and lower income households. Housing planning, then, must attempt to balance these concerns in competing and difficult situations.

While housing planning is a necessary response to the complexities of housing, it is a response that up until this time has not been up to the task. As housing problems touch a greater proportion of this nation's population each year, the demand for effective housing planning becomes more apparent. Simultaneously, it becomes increasingly difficult to meet the needs of lower income households that have historically been directly or indirectly deprived of housing opportunities.

Planning for the Needs of Low- and Moderate-Income Households

The housing needs of many low- and moderate-income households remain unmet by the private market because these households cannot compete economically for housing units. As a result these households have been forced to accept substandard private housing stock and public or subsidized units made available to them through limited government programs. Low- and moderate-income households have been able to exercise little if any choice in the selection of their housing: either its type, its location, or the available services, facilities, and environmental amenities accompanying it. Middle- and upper-income households, however, have been assisted by a variety of government programs—such as FHA and VA insurance and tax incentives—which have permitted those households to attain considerably greater housing choice.[8]

While the private market has been unable to provide housing for low- and moderate-income households, government programs have not been vastly more successful. In spite of government intervention in housing markets, there still remain enormous unmet housing needs for low- and moderate-income households.[9]

This nation has not only failed to meet the housing needs of its low- and moderate-income citizens, but according to a recent report

8. *See* A. Solomon, Housing the Urban Poor—A Critical Evaluation of Federal Housing Policy (1974); and H.J. Aaron, Shelter and Subsidies—Who Benefits from Federal Housing Policies? (1973).

9. *See* Commission on Civil Rights, Twenty Years After Brown: Equal Opportunity in Housing (1975) [hereinafter cited as Twenty Years After Brown]; D. Falk & H. Franklin, Equal Housing Opportunity: The Unfinished Agenda (1976).

of the U.S. Commission on Civil Rights, there is still widespread discrimination against minorities and women in the provision of available housing. This discrimination is a basis for residential segregation in virtually all major metropolitan areas.[10] Table 6-1 shows how population growth is occurring outside central cities, but primarily for the white population. Thus we are faced not only with enormous unmet housing needs but also with the need to eliminate past discrimination and overcome continued discrimination.

There are three primary reasons to plan specifically for low- and moderate-income households: (1) the definition of need is changing, while altering economic and social conditions placing an increasing number of households in this category; (2) balancing the housing supply is essential to the long-run vitality of a metropolitan region; and (3) public opposition to the threatened influx of families with lower incomes is so intense that without specific planning, the goal of equal housing opportunity will not be achieved.

Changing Concept of Need. Economic need has always been the basis for housing assistance. Yet, as issues of inequality were raised by and for minorities and the disadvantaged, particularly since the mid-1960s, new dimensions have been added to the definition of need. In housing, the question of choice has become almost as much an ingredient of need as have the qualities of a standard dwelling unit. It has become necessary to measure not only the quantity and quality of housing for lower income households, but also to determine the locational characteristics of these units.

The President's Committee on Urban Housing (the Kaiser Committee) concluded that:

> The location of one's place of residence determines the accessibility and quality of many everyday advantages taken for granted by the mainstream of American society. Among these commonplace advantages are public educational facilities for a family's children, adequate police and fire protection, and a decent surrounding environment. In any case, a family should have the choice of living as close as economically possible to the breadwinner's place of employment.[11]

The locational opportunities for low- and moderate-income housing have become particularly important as increased emphasis has been given to claims that problems of low- and moderate-income housing are metropolitan in scope and require the application of the vast

10. Twenty Years After Brown, *supra* note 9, at 7.
11. A Decent Home, *supra* note 4, at 13.

Table 6-1. Population of Standard Metropolitan Areas, Inside and Outside Central Cities, by Race, 1950–1970 (thousands)

	1950		1960		1970	
	Number	Percent	Number	Percent	Number	Percent
Total SMSA Population	94,579	100.0%	119,595	100.0%	139,387	100.0%
In Central Cities	53,817	57.0	59,964	50.1	63,816	45.8
Outside Central Cities	40,762	43.0	59,631	49.9	75,570	54.2
White SMSA Population	85,099	100	105,180	100	120,424	100
In Central Cities	46,791	55.0	49,440	47.0	48,796	40.5
Outside Central Cities	38,308	45.0	55,741	53.0	71,628	59.5
Black SMSA Population	8,850	100	12,710	100	16,876	100
In Central Cities	6,608	74.7	9,950	78.3	13,097	78.0
Outside Central Cities	2,242	25.3	2,760	21.7	3,689	22.0

Source: U.S. Commission on Civil Rights, "Twenty Years After Brown: Equal Opportunity in Housing," p. 125.

resources available in suburban and outlying areas of these metropolitan regions.[12] Similarly, there is greater awareness of the nexus between residential location, school desegregation, and patterns of employment opportunities.

Meeting current housing need (as opposed to projected need) may require vastly different efforts. Given existing resources, even current needs in some areas will exceed local capabilities. However, identifying an existing, measurable problem is within the capacity of most local governments. It is the complexity of projecting future housing needs and producing a complementary housing strategy that is at the same time extremely difficult and important.

The difficulty lies in the task of forecasting social, economic, and political forces over which local governments have little control. Factors affecting a jurisdiction's housing need may be outside its own governmental boundaries. It is important, therefore, that local governments deal with impediments to housing opportunity that are within their respective spheres of influence (such as land-use controls, building codes, and so on) and then cooperate in a metropolitan or regional effort to assess and balance the needs of neighboring jurisdictions. This form of cooperative housing planning will at least allow local governments to respond realistically to the many forces that impinge upon the housing market from both private and public actions at the national and state levels, and can dramatically alter and expand the way in which a jurisdiction identifies its housing need.

In addition to this geographic extension of housing need identification, the time element has become particularly important as well, because concepts of "additional or expected" growth have expanded obligations for housing and have thus expanded the concept of housing need. If a community is to meet the housing needs resulting from growth pressures or expanding employment opportunities, the period within which these needs will occur is important in determining the total housing need, as is the regional context in which the housing needs exist.

The concept of need has also been altered in other ways. As the private market increasingly reaches a smaller proportion of the population, a greater number of households require assistance in obtaining suitable housing. Federal and state programs that were originally intended for the lower income categories of the population have been redesigned or effectively operate now to assist moderate- or middle-

12. *See* H. Franklin, D. Falk, & A. Levin, In-Zoning—A Guide for Policy-Makers on Inclusionary Land Use Programs 74–78 (1974), for a brief description of location as a housing concept. [Hereinafter cited as In-Zoning.]

income families. Legislation creating state housing finance agencies commonly defines low income to include families or individuals whose housing needs cannot be met through conventional private sources.[13] In practice, as implemented by agency regulation, this can mean assistance for families with incomes in the $18,000 to $20,000 a year range.[14]

The federal Section 235 homeownership subsidy program, recently revived after its abrupt and controversial suspension by the Nixon Administration in its housing moratorium of January 1973, is now aimed at lower-middle-income families—those with incomes of about $11,000 a year. Under the original 1968 program, Section 235 was designed to serve low- and moderate-income families with incomes between $5,000 to $7,000 a year.[15] Moreover, while maximum income levels for eligible homeowners under the 1968 program were set at 135 percent of public housing limits, they were raised to 80 percent of the area's median income under 1974 amendments, and further increased to 95 percent of the area's median income under a 1976 amendment.[16]

The Section 8 Leased Housing program,[17] established as the major federally assisted housing program under the Housing and Community Development Act of 1974, provides the most current definition of income levels. It defines the low-income family—one eleigible for housing assistance payments—as a family of four whose income does not exceed 80 percent of the median family income of that area. The act also established a new category of eligible families—those of very low incomes—whose incomes cannot exceed 50 percent of the area's median, adjusted for family size. The act requires that 30 percent of all families assisted on a national basis under the Section 8 program

13. The statute creating the Illinois Housing Development Authority, for example, defines low- and moderate-income households as those "families and persons who cannot afford to pay the amounts at which private enterprise, without assisted mortgage financing, is providing a substantial supply of decent, safe, and sanitary housing." Ill. Rev. Stat. ch. 67.1/2, § 302(g).

14. *See* discussion of state housing finance agencies in Chapter 7 *infra*.

15. Under the revised Section 235 program, HUD reduces the effective interest rate on the mortgage down to 5 percent, as opposed to 1 percent under the original program, and substantially increases the down payment requirements. For a comparison of the programs, *see* 3 Hous. & Dev. Rep. 470–71 (1975).

16. Housing Authorization Act of 1976, § 3(e), Pub. L. No. 94-375 (August 3, 1976).

17. The Housing and Community Development Act of 1974, Tit. II, § 201 (a)(8) established the Section 8 program as a revision of the U.S. Housing Act of 1937, 42 U.S.C. § 1401. Regulations implementing the Section 8 program are in 24 C.F.R. §§ 880 to 883. Section 8 is discussed in greater detail in Chapter 7 *infra*.

be such very-low-income households. While the income ranges under the program are adjusted for family size (to reflect the area's fair market rents, and so on) it has been estimated that over 40 percent of the nation's population technically could qualify for assistance under the Section 8 program. The resources actually available under the program, of course, are in no way commensurate with the numbers of families and persons who are eligible.

Throughout the convoluted history of federally assisted housing in America, income limits for federal subsidy programs have varied with the perception of need, but in general, subsidy programs have been geared to meet the needs of moderate-income households.[18] As will be further explored below, a number of commentators have noted that at least a portion of moderate-income households could have their housing needs met through the private market if excessive restrictions on the construction of residential units and on the development of residential land were removed.

The Desirability of a Balanced Housing Supply. The second reason to plan for low- and moderate-income housing is that there are significant benefits to be realized from balancing the housing supply, as housing opportunities are expanded for households living in substandard, overcrowded, or too expensive dwellings in inner cities. An increased housing supply in suburban areas will benefit the entire metropolitan area. In order for central cities to improve living conditions, regain stable populations, reinforce the tax base, and realize other benefits of a more desirable environment, existing central-city populations must have suitable alternative housing locations so that the central-city rebuilding and renovating process can occur. Opening suburban housing markets is essential to this process.

To the extent that job opportunities are expanding in areas outside central cities, providing housing there for lower income and minority households would facilitate access to those jobs. The relocation of employees has been more common for those who can afford homes in the suburban area where a firm is relocating than for those minorities or lower income persons who do not find housing so accessible. Moreover, the benefits to suburban areas of an expanded housing supply for low- and moderate-income households are in part related to greater opportunities for filling lower income jobs, even municipal jobs, within the community through a more balanced population. It is important also to note the need for low-income housing for those already living in the suburbs.

18. D. Mandelker, Housing Subsidies in the United States and England 47–52 (1973).

With the rapidly increasing fiscal problems of central cities, the nation cannot ignore the overwhelming disparities that exist between suburban areas and central cities. Attempts must be made on several fronts to achieve a greater balance in fiscal capability and fiscal responsibility in metropolitan areas throughout this nation. The generally declining resources available for services and facilities in central cities has resulted in the widening disparities between city and suburb. The quality of such services, particularly education, has been an important cause of migration to suburban areas. As a consequence, expanding low- and moderate-income housing supplies in outlying areas could increase educational benefits for these households, as well as decrease the pressure on central-city resources. Residentially based integration would have a practical impact on school integration and could, over the long term, substantially reduce the need for alternative desegregation systems.[19]

To whatever extent other services and facilities, such as open space and environmental quality, are more characteristic of suburban areas than central cities, then low- and moderate-income households would benefit from suburban locations. In addition, where an expanded housing supply results in a more balanced community population both racially and economically, the residents of that community could benefit from the heterogeneity provided. In *Trafficante v. Metropolitan Life Insurance Co.*, the U.S. Supreme Court has recognized that where minorities were excluded from a residential complex, present residents lose "important benefits from interracial associations."[20] The Court held that residents of an apartment complex could sue landlords for discriminatory practices under federal fair housing laws.

Anthony Downs, a leading real estate economist and proponent of the "open suburbs" movement, has summarized the benefits to be achieved from a balanced housing supply:

19. It is now generally agreed that schools and neighborhoods have a reciprocal effect upon one another. See Keyes v. School District No. 1, 413 U.S. 189, 93 S. Ct. 2686, 2697 (1973), in which Justice Powell, concurring, acknowledges that residential housing discrimination is the root cause of school segregation, citing Taeuber, *Negroes in Cities*, 1965 Scientific Am. 36 (August). *See also* comments of Chief Justice Burger in Swann v. Charlotte-Mecklenberg Bd. of Education, 402 U.S. 1, 20–21 (1971), discussing the interrelationship of segregated school facilities, metropolitan patterns of residential development, and "neighborhood zoning." Other federal cases have also recognized and discussed the substantial correlation existing between racial segregation in public housing and nearby schools. See, e.g., Morgan v. Hennigan, 379 F. Supp. 410, 469–71 (D. Mass. 1974), *aff'd, sub nom.* Morgan v. Kerrigan, 509 F.2d 580 (1st Cir. 1974), *cert. denied* 95 S. Ct. 1950 (1975).

20. Trafficante v. Metropolitan Life Insurance Co., 409 U.S. 205 (1971).

1. Better access to expanding suburban job opportunities for workers in low- and moderate-income households, especially the unemployed.
2. Greater opportunities for such households to upgrade themselves by moving into middle-income neighborhoods, thereby escaping from crisis ghetto conditions.
3. Higher quality public schooling for children from low-income households who could attend schools dominated by children from middle-income households.
4. Greater opportunity for the nation to reach its officially adopted goals for producing improved housing for low- and moderate-income households.
5. Fairer geographic distribution of the fiscal and social costs of dealing with metropolitan-area poverty.
6. Less possibility of major conflicts in the future caused by confrontations between two spatially separate and unequal societies in metropolitan areas.
7. Greater possibilities of improving adverse conditions in crisis ghetto areas without displacing urban decay to adjacent neighborhoods.[21]

Housing Planning and Public Opposition. The third reason for planning for low- and moderate-income housing relates to the need to enlighten the public and to foster positive actions in order to address both public apathy and opposition. Planning as a political process to determine community values and their relative priorities has a valuable role to play in compensating for and overcoming community and neighborhood resistance to low- and moderate-income housing. Effective housing planning must recognize that there are many reasons for such resistance.

Resistance to lower income housing is long standing and the product of many factors. Although restrictive land-use controls have been the focus of numerous civil rights challenges,[22] the phenomenon of exclusion contains many other components. Perhaps most basic are the underlying fears and myths associated with poor and minority persons, and with subsidized and public housing and their impact on a neighborhood. Efforts aimed at opening the suburbs consequently often elicit vociferous arguments in support of home rule, the right to control the destiny of a community, and protection of the character of a neighborhood. While sometimes overlooked as mere expressions of misguided prejudice, these views influence de-

21. A Downs, Opening Up the Suburbs 26 (1973). *Cf.* Glazer, *Opening Up the Suburbs,* 34 Pub. Interest, 89 (Fall 1974).
22. *See* discussion of these cases in Chapters 2 and 3 *supra.*

velopers who are unwilling to risk the abuse and gamble on the feasibility of a project that might meet delays and controversies generated by angry residents. Public officials, too, are swayed (or supported, as the case may be) by the protests of their constituents to take action against proposed developments and to direct future growth in a manner proper for preserving the character and fiscal base of the community.

Related to these concerns are the restrictions placed on future development through municipal capital programming. The availability of roads, traffic controls, recreational areas, schools, sewer and water facilities, flood controls, fire and police protection, and most other community services and facilities are essential to future residential development. Given the lack of proper improvements, where the developer either chooses to provide the necessary services and facilities or is required to do so, a project may well be unable to allow the inclusion of low- and moderate-income households because of excessive development costs.

The development of low- and moderate-income housing requires substantial initiative by an entire array of participants in the housing development process. Government or public officials, however, by virtue of their offices, bear unique responsibility. Local officials mirror their constituents and rarely risk stepping outside what is expected of them. Planning is a political process and will not progress into unpopular fronts without the support and encouragement of public leaders. Acting affirmatively to encourage low- and moderate-income housing by cooperating with willing developers, working through a housing authority, encouraging state assistance in the production of low- and moderate-income units, and other such activities is completely within the realm of proper activity of government officials in their community development responsibilities.

While fiscal political considerations continue to be important, environmental controls have more recently presented some of the most damaging and long-range consequences to efforts to expand housing opportunities. Not only have environmental arguments crept into virtually all litigation about housing and land use, but the long-range planning of waste water treatment facilities will virtually dictate the amount, type, and location of growth throughout entire regions of the nation. Thus far, environmental protection programs have sometimes ignored the social and economic consequences of their efforts.

Social equity and environmental protection are both necessary objectives for land-use planning. Yet the potential conflict between them has gone virtually unnoticed, and as the fiscal, environmental, and social consequences of suburban development were initially not apparent, so too might the worthwhile undertakings of environmental protection programs progress without full awareness of their social impact.[23]

The Need for Coordination of Housing and Comprehensive Planning

Housing planning is related to comprehensive planning in several important ways. First, it is essential that a housing plan has a similar relationship to land-use controls as does the comprehensive plan. (The relationship of land-use controls to comprehensive planning is discussed at length in Chapter 5. Since land-use controls are specified in the comprehensive plan, housing planning will affect the response of those land-use controls to the type, amount, and location of residential development. In fact, as closer relationships are drawn between comprehensive planning and land-use controls, the need to integrate housing planning into comprehensive planning becomes more critical.

Second, to whatever extent capital improvement programs relate to comprehensive planning, that relationship must include housing planning. The capital program controls the type, amount, location, timing, and distribution of public projects, from water and sewer facilities to streets, public buildings, and community services. The recent advent of growth-management ordinances that control the timing of improvements and development emphasize the fact that residential development is dependent upon supporting facilities and services. The availability of public services and facilities is important because they virtually determine the location, if not the feasibility, of future residential development. The degree to which the lack of these facilities or the failure of a local unit of government to provide such facilities is regarded as an acceptable deterrent to additional growth has been a highly debated and litigated issue.[24] The Supreme Court of the Commonwealth of Pennsylvania, for example, has "explicitly rejected the argument that sewerage problems could excuse exclusionary zoning."[25]

The availability of adequate services and facilities has been expressed as an element of the project selection criteria for federal sub-

---

23. *See* M. Brooks, Housing Equity and the Environment—The Needless Conflict (1976); Babcock & Callies, *Ecology and Housing: Virtues in Conflict*, in M. Clawson (ed.), Modernizing Urban Land Policy 205 (1973). *See also* T. Muller, State Mandated Impact Evaluation: A Preliminary Assessment (1976).

24. *See* H. Franklin, Controlling Urban Growth—But for Whom? (The Potomac Institute 1973); Bosselman, *Can the Town of Ramapo Pass a Law to Bind the Rights of the Whole World?* 1 Fla. St. U. L. Rev. 234 (1973).

25. *In re* Appeal of Kit-Mar Builders, 439 Pa. 466, 472, 268 A.2d 765 (1970).

sidized housing. These provisions state that the proposed project must be "accessible to social, recreational, education, commercial, and health facilities and services, and other municipal services that are equivalent to or better than those typically found in neighborhoods consisting largely of standard, unsubsidized housing of a similar market value" to receive a superior rating.[26] One of three locational criteria to be considered by applicants for block grants in preparing housing assistance plans (HAPs) under the Housing and Community Development Act of 1974 is the identification of a location "assuring the availability of public facilities and services adequate to serve" those projects.[27]

Recent efforts at preparing regional housing allocation plans have moreover, consistently included criteria for distributing proposed units according to a locality's ability to accommodate additional units. These criteria measure such factors as availability of water and sewer facilities and other community services and facilities, accessibility to transportation facilities, impact on present school system capacities, and per capita fiscal resources.[28]

A third reason for integrating housing planning into comprehensive planning is the potential benefit to residents of that housing. This is true for all housing, and it is particularly true for low- and moderate-income housing. Access to jobs, transportation, and to community services and facilities is important for all households. The notion that the benefits to be received from housing are in concert with benefits available from many other aspects of community development such as education, employment, recreation, and the environment is a long-standing one. In addition to these benefits, however, it is important that housing developments be free from adverse effects due to environmental conditions, isolation of the site, or incompatible land uses. While recent standards for development have improved, low- and moderate-income housing has historically been relegated to marginal areas believed unsuitable for other types of housing. A greater coordination between housing planning and comprehensive planning could avoid, to some degree, these detrimental impacts on low- and moderate-income housing developments.

The need to balance housing opportunities and employment opportunities should be a major consideration in housing planning for low- and moderate-income households. That a municipality should make possible the construction of housing suitable for all persons

26. 24 C.F.R. § 200.700 (1973).
27. Housing and Community Development Act of 1974, § 104(a)(4)(c) (iii).
28. M. Brooks, Lower Income Housing—The Planner's Response 20 (1972). *See also* D. Listokin, Fair Share Housing Allocations (1976).

who work within that community has been a basic theme in numerous court decisions, the American Law Institute's *Model Land Development Code*,[29] and the housing assistance plan (HAP) re-requirements of the Housing and Community Development Act of 1974.[30] The HAP provision requires a locality to assess the housing assistance needs of those persons "expected to reside" in the community as a result of employment and other demographic changes. The availability of jobs has been a criterion many regional planning agencies have included in allocating proposed low- and moderate-income housing units to communities, and in at least one instance a jobs/housing balance has been the basis for promoting a distribution of low- and moderate-income housing.[31]

Finally, a relationship between housing planning and comprehensive planning is important because the comprehensive plan embodies the goals, objectives, and official policy guide for future development of a community, region, or state. While the adoption of an official position is important for all development, it is particularly so for the inclusion of all income groups within a community. Rarely do housing policy statements exist outside of a particular housing plan. Nonetheless, the importance of such policy statements has been described and stated as follows:

> An inclusionary land use program is unlikely to be effective unless its governing policies have been formulated and formally adopted by the local legislative body. To maximize its impact and effect, legislative adoption should be preceded by dialogue with local community leaders, open public hearings, and broad publication. The formal, official adoption of the program by a popularly elected body would constitute a commitment by the community to low- and moderate-income housing, would serve to alert private entrepreneurs to the community's commitment, and would provide legal status for the inclusionary program in the courts.[32]

A housing policy statement should call for an increase in the supply of housing opportunities within the community for all persons regardless of racial or economic status. It should attempt to expand opportunities geographically by providing for development in proper environments and in an amount the community is capable of supporting. It should also outline reasonable steps to affirmatively

29. American Law Institute, A Model Land Development Code § 7-301(4) (d) (adopted May 21, 1975) (1976) [hereinafter cited as ALI Code].
30. 42 U.S.C. § 5304(a)(4).
31. *See* Tri-State Regional Planning Commission, Dwellings and Neighborhoods (1974).
32. *See* In-Zoning, *supra* note 12, at 102.

provide for the achievement of these goals and for the removal of obstacles and circumstances that prevent their attainment.

Recognizing that housing planning efforts must be tied to a more inclusive or comprehensive planning program is certainly not a new idea. In 1968, the National Commission on Urban Problems stated:

> The most serious shortcoming of present development standards and instruments is that neither the environment nor the dwelling is treated by communities in a comprehensive way, in terms of the "complete environment" and of the "complete dwelling."[33]

Also in 1968, the National Association for Housing and Redevelopment Officials (NAHRO) began a study of the fragmentation of housing programs in metropolitan areas.[34] At that time NAHRO could find "virtually nothing in current practice or research that went beyond housing market analysis." The study, released in 1973, found that four basic conditions frustrate the development of housing programs:

1. Lack of current data.
2. Failure to identify the specific and appropriate relationships of planning agencies to housing and community development agencies and others involved in housing matters.
3. Lack of citizen involvement.
4. The general failure to relate the housing function to a comprehensive guide covering goals, policies, and physical development functions.

The report concluded that the best current efforts "to develop a housing element in comprehensive planning . . . all move toward defining a housing function as part of a total policies and physical development plan."[35]

Government has a responsibility to engage in housing planning. It is the Advisory Commission's view that housing planning should be mandated by state statutes and relevant federal programs as an essential element of a community's total plan—its comprehensive plan—and its housing and community development programs. Housing planning should involve planning for all economic segments of a community, particularly low- and moderate-income households.

---

33. *See* Building the American City, *supra* note 2, at 308–09.
34. M. Nenno, Housing in Metropolitan Areas: Roles and Responsibilities of Five Key Actors (1973).
35. *Id.* at 53.

THE COMPONENTS OF THE HOUSING SYSTEM

The Housing Process

The production of housing is a complicated process, obviously more so than the construction of a single unit. Before housing can be built, there must be a community infrastructure of streets, sewers, water lines, and other utilities available to service the units. For the developer there is a preparation phase, in which plans are prepared, necessary permits are secured, and financing is arranged. Construction itself has two phases: site preparation and building construction. Finally, the units must be marketed through either sale or rental. A lack of infrastructure, or failure to obtain financing, or zoning, or subdivision approval can prevent new construction. Most new construction takes place in suburban areas where vacant land is available and generally less expensive.

Property ownership is widespread in this country. In 1970 about 63 percent of all households owned the unit they lived in. Ownership is the preferred form of tenure, and one traditionally encouraged by government policies, including FHA and VA mortgage insurance and preferential income tax treatment (deductions for mortgage interest and property taxes). Because housing is primarily provided by the private sector, the income of occupants is significant in determining access to housing.

Ours is a mobile society, with about one in five households moving each year. Most of these moves are made within the same region. The access to housing units, and the ability to move, is dependent upon the availability of vacant units. Most housing moves are made within the existing supply. Only about one in every seven moves is into new housing. "Filtering" is a process in which some households improve their housing conditions by moving into better units as they are vacated by households moving into newer units.[36] Reliance on the filtering or "trickle-down" process as the dominant strategy to solve our housing problems is based on two questionable assumptions: (1) aid to the middle class will help the poor and the entire society in a collective way; and (2) the poor at the end of the filter are integrated economically into the system and capable of receiving benefits.

If the economic status of the entire society remains stagnant, however, or if the poor remain outside the economic life of the soci-

36. See *Housing Market Dynamics: The Filtering Process*, Housing in America 225-27 (1973); H. Aaron, *supra* note 8, at 163; Downs, *Housing the Urban Poor: The Economics of Various Strategies*, 59 Am. Econ. Rev. 647-49 (1969).

ety, reliance on the trickle-down process will be misplaced.[37] The point, of course, is that while filtering does occur at the upper- and middle-income levels, other factors may prevent it from functioning effectively for lower income households. Moreover, some families may choose not to participate in a filtering process that, because of economic segregation, requires a move to an entirely different neighborhood.

The availability of mortgage money and the level of interest rates are major determinants of whether households can purchase homes and whether investors will purchase rental properties. The demand for money for housing must compete with other demands; therefore, the interest rate is determined by factors largely external to housing itself. The lending practices of commercial banks, savings and loan institutions, insurance funds, and other financial institutions play a large role in housing, as does government regulation of these institutions. The Kaiser Committee concluded in its 1968 study that one of the most important steps public officials could take for housing was to avoid fiscal and monetary policies that severely restrict funds available to housing.[38]

In the formulation of their own lending practices, lending institutions determine who will get mortgage money and what areas will be eligible for loans. It is well documented that mortgage moneys have often been denied to older and declining, or transitional neighborhoods. These discriminatory lending practices have been termed "redlining." (See discussion of redlining in Chapter 7). Few people without a mortgage can purchase a home or afford to renovate one. Similarly, few investors can purchase a rental property without borrowing. The growing demand for money nationwide—and even internationally—has led to rising interest rates, and has severely affected the costs of housing.

The Housing Market Area or Region

The housing market area is a key factor in housing planning. Housing is a unique product in that it is intrinsically related to its location. Thus, housing must exist where it is needed and where people wish to live; units of housing must be available where people have established living and working patterns. The housing market area is the cohesive economic, geographic, and social area where theoretically all

37. For analyses of drawbacks to the "trickle-down" strategy, *see* Aaron, *supra* note 8, at 165-67; Phillips & Agelasto, *Housing and Central Cities: The Conservation Approach*, 4 Ecology L.Q. 797, 805-07 (1975); Lowry, *Filtering and Housing Standards*, 160 Land Econ. 362 (November).

38. A Decent Home, *supra* note 4, at 129.

units of housing are in competition with one another for the users of housing:

> A housing market area is the physical area within which all dwelling units are linked together in a chain of substitution. . . . In a broad sense, every dwelling unit within a local housing market may be considered a substitute for every other unit. Hence, all dwelling units may be said to form a single market, characterized by interactions of occupancy, prices and rents.[39]

Housing is related to jobs, transportation, community facilities and services, educational and health institutions, and the great variety of activities that relate to people's lives.

The component parts of a regional housing market are interdependent, and as a whole comprise a social and economic entity. A region is geographically contiguous. While boundaries of any region or housing market area are not precise, they are defined by a number of criteria. These can include a shared economic base, shared labor market, common institutions, wholesale and retail trade areas, communication networks, and other relationships of mutual interdependence. The major factor in defining a housing market area is an interdependent economic and employment structure, particularly in urban, non-agricultural areas. Major employment centers and their commuting network help define such areas. Frequently, topography, geography, and other natural features define such areas. They may be responsible for determining the economic base of an area, its transportation patterns, and basic social and economic focal points. They may determine agricultural areas, mining regions, recreational areas, major trading locations, transportation centers, and manufacturing locations.

In reality there are many submarkets for housing within a single housing market area.[40] These differ as to the specific location, type, size, quality, cost, and tenure of housing units, and depend upon the demands of varying households within any market area. There is a demand from single-person households and large households, from families with and without children, from those dependent upon public transit and those with cars, from those with low incomes and those with high incomes. The types of housing vary accordingly, including single- and multifamily units, owner-occupied and renter-occupied units, multibedroom units and efficiency units, and so on.

39. C. Rapkin, L. Winnick, & D. Blank, Housing Market Analysis 9–10 (1953). *See also* U.S. Department of Housing and Urban Development, Urban Housing Market Analysis 5–6 (1966); U.S. Department of Housing and Urban Development, FHA Techniques of Housing Market Analysis 11–16 (1970).

40. *See* W. Grigsby, Housing Markets and Public Policy 30–83 (1963).

The submarkets are quite numerous but are parts of the same market area, and are generally distributed throughout any region.

Housing market areas may overlap and seldom include a single political jurisdiction. Invariably they are large enough to incorporate the services, institutions, and jobs upon which day-to-day living depends, and are small enough to accommodate most daily travel.

The precision of defining a housing market area is less important than the various considerations used. Whether the base unit is a county, a multicounty area, a Standard Metropolitan Statistical Area, an Urbanized Area, or a Housing Market Area as defined by HUD, the definition of the region must recognize an interrelationship of population and supporting institutions and services.[41] In *Hills v. Gautreaux* the U.S. Supreme Court discussed the problem of a regional remedy in terms of the Housing Market Area:

> The relevant geographic area for purposes of the respondents' housing options is the Chicago housing market, not the Chicago city limits. That HUD recognizes this reality is evident in its administration of federal housing assistance programs through "housing market areas" encompassing "the geographic area 'within which all dwelling units. . . .' are in competition with one another as alternatives for the users of housing." . . . . The housing market area "usually extends beyond the city limits" and in the larger markets "may extend into several adjoining counties." . . . . An order against HUD and CHA regulating their conduct in the greater metropolitan area will do no more than take into account HUD's expert determination of the area relevant to the respondents' housing opportunities and will thus be wholly commensurate with the nature and extent of the constitutional violation.[42]

As such an area is interdependent, then its population and the housing of that population is an interdependent responsibility. When considering a local government's "regional" housing needs, that region can and should be the housing market area in which the jurisdiction is located.

Housing Supply and Demand

The demand for housing is the ability and willingness of households to pay for housing units at some given time. There is a demand for existing housing, and a demand for new housing. There is a de-

41. For a discussion of various ways in which a region can be defined, *see* Rubinowitz, *Exclusionary Zoning: A Wrong in Search of a Remedy*, 6 U. Mich. J.L. Ref. 625, 652 (1973).

42. Hills v. Gautreaux, 96 S. Ct. 1538, 1546–47 (1976), quoting from HFA Techniques of Housing Market Analysis 8, 11 (1970).

43. New stock is not net addition to supply. Much is replacement for units

mand for rental units and owner-occupied units. Coupled with the demand concept is the supply of housing, which is all the units existing at some given time. This includes units that are occupied or vacant, and can be classified in any number of ways—by tenure, cost, condition, type of structure, availability, and so on. The United States does not have an absolute deficit of supply, since almost everyone has some form of housing. We may have deficiencies in the supply, however, based on concepts of need. In a private housing market such as ours, the demand and supply of housing is balanced through market choices.

Housing supply consists of the existing stock and new additions (through production or construction). Much housing planning and particularly allocation planning has concentrated on new housing. However, new housing comprises a very small part of the total housing supply—rarely more than 3 percent of the existing stock. The largest year for homebuilding ever in the United States was 1972, when almost 2.4 million units were started. This still constituted only 3.3 percent of existing housing, which was estimated then at about 71 million units[43] (see Table 6-2).

Table 6-2.   New Housing Units Started, United States, 1960–1973 (thousands)

| Year | Total | Private | Private Starts Only | | | | Mobile Home Shipments |
| | | | Single-Family | | Multifamily | | |
			Number	Percent	Number	Percent	
1960	1296.0	1252.1	994.7	79.4%	257.4	20.6%	
1961	1365.0	1313.0	974.4	74.2	338.6	25.8	
1962	1492.4	1462.7	991.3	67.8	471.4	32.2	
1963	1642.0	1610.3	1020.7	63.4	589.6	36.6	150.8
1964	1561.0	1528.8	970.5	63.5	558.3	36.5	191.3
1965	1509.6	1472.9	963.8	65.4	509.1	34.6	216.5
1966	1195.9	1165.0	778.5	66.8	386.5	33.2	217.3
1967	1321.9	1291.6	843.9	65.3	447.7	34.7	240.4
1968	1545.5	1507.7	899.5	59.7	608.2	40.3	318.0
1969	1499.6	1466.8	810.6	55.3	656.2	44.7	421.7
1970	1469.0	1433.6	812.9	56.7	620.7	43.3	401.2
1971	2084.5	2052.2	1151.0	56.1	901.2	43.9	496.6
1972	2378.5	2356.6	1309.2	55.6	1047.3	44.4	575.9
1973	2057.5	2045.3	1132.0	55.3	913.3	44.7	566.9

Source: U.S. Bureau of the Census, *Construction Reports*, Series C-20. Data includes farm housing.

43. New stock is not net addition to supply. Much is replacement for units removed. From 1960 to 1970, about 14.4 million units were started in the United States, for a net addition to the total stock of about 10.4 million units.

Housing in this country is almost completely supplied by private industry. Other than some military housing, the federal government directly provides no housing. Locally created housing authorities, with federal assistance, have provided a relatively small amount of public housing for the lowest income families. However, many recent government housing subsidy programs, while generally underfunded, rely primarily upon private industry to actually provide the units. The provision of housing is largely dependent on its economic feasibility for the private sector.

One of the most significant influences on housing has been the rapid rise in costs in recent years. The cost of housing has risen faster than the consumer price index, a result of increased interest rates, rising land costs, and increased labor, materials, and energy prices. Since 1955 the average cost of a new home has gone up 191 percent, while the total cost of operating the home has increased 303 percent. At the same time, average take-home pay has increased only 193 percent.[44]

Rising land and infrastructure costs have been responsible for increasing the density of residential development. In 1960 about 21 percent of new units were multifamily; the total rose to 45 percent in 1973. Increasingly, single-family units are also built on smaller lots. About 20 to 25 percent of new single-family housing starts are

Table 6-3. Housing Units and Housing Starts, United States, 1960-1973 (thousands)

Year	Housing Units (rounded)	Housing[c] Starts	Starts as Percent of Housing Units
1960	58,330[a]	14,428.9 (from '60-'69)	N.A.
1970	68,680[a]	1,469.0	2.1%
1971	69,710[b]	2,084.5	3.0
1972	71,170[b]	2,378.5	3.3
1973	72,840[b]	2,057.5	2.8

[a]U.S. Bureau of the Census, *Census of Housing*, 1960 and 1970.
[b]Estimated by author.
[c]U.S. Bureau of the Census, *Construction Reports*, exclusive of mobile homes.

44. Business Week, Jan. 12, 1976, at 21.

townhouses. The availability of land zoned for more dense residential use is vital for reducing land costs per unit and overall housing costs. The increases in housing costs have also contributed to the increase in mobile home production. Mobile homes now represent a major source of new housing for an ever-larger segment of the population.[45]

Housing Need

The term housing need is often used interchangably with housing demand. It is necessary, however, to clarify the difference: need is a social concept based on assumptions about adequate housing standards; demand is an economic term. Housing need represents the housing that would be required to provide adequate housing for every household. Adequacy is determined by establishing standards as to condition, cost, or some other criteria. While there is considerable disagreement about such standards, households without adequate housing, as defined by existing standards, are in need. To the extent that the private market cannot provide such housing, then government housing assistance is necessary.

Standards. Standards of adequacy vary in different societies according to values, standards of living, and social goals. The standards that are traditionally used to evaluate housing need in our society deal with condition of units, location, access to utilities and community facilities, cost, crowding, and choice.

Households may be living in units that are in *poor condition*, in an inadequate neighborhood, without adequate plumbing or access to services, that cost too much relative to available income, have too many people in too little space, or are in locations where the households do not wish to live. Often these conditions overlap. People with inadequate income have the fewest housing choices and are more likely to end up in physically defective units, usually described as substandard, deteriorating, or dilapidated. Units may be structurally unsound, without plumbing, with dangerous wiring or heating, have other fire hazards, or be unsanitary, with rats, insects, or debris abounding.

Location also may be poor if the environment is unhealthy, as measured by air and noise pollution, traffic hazards, high incidence of street crime, proximity to physical barriers such as expressways or rail yards, and other threats to human safety and health.

Access to utilities such as sewer, water, and energy sources is critical. Also important is access to community facilities and services

45. *See* M. Drury, Mobile Homes: The Unrecognized Revolution in American Housing (1972).

such as health care, social services, police and fire protection, commercial facilities, transportation, recreation, and education programs.

Housing cost is a consideration that is relative to income. Households may be inadequately housed if they are paying an excessive proportion of their incomes for housing, usually at the sacrifice of other needs like food, clothing, and health care. It is generally assumed that a low- or moderate-income family should be spending no more than 20 to 25 percent of its income for housing.[46]

Crowding is a measure of inadequacy based on the number of people living in a given unit, usually a matter of people per room. Crowding is considered a threat to physical and mental health. The usual standard in this country is a maximum of one person per room.

Choice is also considered a housing standard. An adequate vacancy rate, usually measured as between 4 and 7 percent, is necessary to provide a degree of choice. A rate lower than 4 percent indicates a tight market; one higher than 7 percent indicates some economic distress in the market–overbuilding–or a recession. It should be noted that these rates vary between rental and individually owned housing. Discrimination, which excludes some people from access to housing, is another restriction on choice.

When it has been measured, by whatever criteria, housing need in our society has usually been overwhelming relative to our total supply of housing. A large percentage of our households are inadequately housed, whether measured by physical conditions or income conditions. We add to our housing stock very slowly and our public commitment to housing has never matched the scale of the need. In the aggregate, we are in no danger of oversupplying adequate housing to all income groups in our society (although some areas are overbuilt).

It is not necessary that we measure need with the latest and most reliable data in order to justify public action. The magnitude of housing need is so great that we could safely work with data several years old and still be dealing with unmet need. It is absurd to feel stymied because we do not know the exact dimensions of the problem; we have not come close to dealing with the problems that we do know about. For example, we do know that the low- and moderate-income households are the most disadvantaged; even without specific housing surveys we could rely on income information as an indication and measure of housing need.

46. The so-called Brooke Amendment limits rents in public housing to 25 percent of a family's income. Housing and Urban Development Act of 1969, § 213(b), Pub. L. No. 91–152 (December 24, 1969), *amending* § 2(1) of the U.S. Housing Act of 1937, 42 U.S.C. § 1437(a)(1).

Estimates prepared for the Kaiser Committee in 1968 indicated that 13.4 million households were unable to afford decent housing. Surveys also indicated that 6.7 million housing units were in substandard condition, with others deteriorating and moving toward substandard.[47] There is overlap between these categories, but taking either one gives a measure of the magnitude of housing need. Following the 1968 Kaiser Committee study, the nation quantified its housing goals for the first and only time. In the Housing Act of 1968, Congress called for 26 million new and rehabilitated housing units by 1978. Six million of these were to be for low- and moderate-income households.[48] After a promising start between 1968 and 1972, however, when 655,923 units were produced under the Section 235 and 236 programs,[49] progress was halted by the combined effects of inflation and the imposition by President Nixon of a moratorium on subsidized housing in January of 1973.[50] Table 6-4 illustrates the halting progress in the move toward achieving the 1968 goal.

A more recent study by the MIT-Harvard Joint Center for Urban Studies has quantified total construction needs through the seventies and made estimates of the number of households inadequately housed in 1970.[51] An estimated 23.3 million new units were projected for

Table 6-4. Housing Starts, 1968-1974 (thousands)

Year	Total Units[a]	Federally Subsidized Units[b]
1968	1,899.5	198.6
1969	1,944.3	232.0
1970	1,910.9	470.5
1971	2,622.0	471.0
1972	3,005.2	389.6
1973	2,657.6	280.8
1974	1,732.9	270.5

[a]Includes mobile home shipments.
[b]Includes federally subsidized rehabilitation.
Source: U.S. Department of Housing and Urban Development, *Housing in the Seventies*, table 2, chap. 4, p. 86, and subsequent HUD data.

47. A Decent Home, *supra* note 4, at 41-44.
48. Housing and Urban Development Act of 1968, Pub. L. No. 90-488, 83 Stat. 476, 42 U.S.C. § 1441(a).
49. Twenty Years After Brown, *supra* note 9, at 57.
50. *Id.* at 58.
51. Joint Center for Urban Studies of the Massachusetts Institute of Technology and Harvard University, America's Housing Needs: 1970 to 1980 (1973).

the period 1970 to 1980. As of 1970 a total of 13.1 million "housing-poor" households existed. Of these, 6.9 million suffered from physical inadequacy of their units; another 6.2 million were suffering from excessive cost or inadequate size of their units. These estimates of construction needs and housing needs are not necessarily related, as there is no assurance that new construction will alleviate housing problems. Whether available housing resources are directed at the problem is the critical question, and one that must be addressed in housing planning. The M.I.T.-Harvard study found that housing problems were shifting from the physical condition of the units to the problem of cost relative to the ability of a household to pay,[52] an acute problem for low- and moderate-income households.

THE FEDERAL GOVERNMENT AND HOUSING PLANNING

The federal government plays a variety of roles that substantially influence housing and housing planning. For one, it has been the primary source of direct financial support for housing for low- and moderate-income families. Far more significant, both in scope and expenditure, are the following policies that indirectly subsidize, but directly affect, the availability housing for middle-America:

1. Income tax provisions giving deductions to homeowners and incentives to owners of rental properties.
2. Provision of mortgage insurance through the Federal Housing Administration and the Veterans Administration.
3. Participation in the secondary mortgage market through the Government National Mortgage Association and the Federal National Mortgage Association.
4. Regulation of the flow of credit which is critically important to the housing industry through the Federal Reserve System and Federal Home Loan Bank.

In addition, housing planning at the local and regional levels has in large measure been stimulated by federal grants and requirements. These federal programs place emphasis on linking housing planning to a broader and more comprehensive planning and community development effort. While recognizing the importance of the federal government in housing activities in the larger sense, this section will focus on the impact of the federal government on hous-

52. *Id.* at 1–6.

ing planning. The programs that have had the most influence on housing planning are the Comprehensive Planning Assistance (701) Program,[53] and the A-95 Review Process.[54] The impact of these programs is analyzed below.

Federal Planning Requirements

701 Program. The housing element requirements of the Comprehensive Planning Assistance Program have probably produced more housing planning than any other federal program to date. States, cities, urban counties, and areawide organizations (including councils of government) are eligible for 701 funds. The Comprehensive Planning Assistance Program was enacted in 1954 and has been amended three times since, in 1959, 1968, and 1974. The 1959 amendment essentially provided a framework for comprehensive planning, to be carried out and coordinated at a regional level. In 1968 a "housing element" requirement was added to influence localities to consider regional housing needs as part of local planning.

The 701 program was further revised by the Housing and Community Development Act of 1974 which required the preparation of a land-use element as an essential component of a comprehensive planning effort. This addition was designed "to integrate all existing land use policies and functional planning activities impacting land use" and to serve as a guide for decisionmaking on all matters related to the use of land, including housing. After August 22, 1977, HUD is directed to withhold comprehensive planning funds from local agencies that are not engaged in comprehensive planning, including the requisite land-use and housing elements.[55]

The preparation of the housing element is to take into account all available evidence of the assumptions and statistical bases upon which the projection of zoning, community facilities, and population growth is based, so that the housing needs of both the region and the local communities studied in the planning will be adequately covered in terms of existing and prospective population growth. The housing element, as well as the land-use element, is to specify: (1) broad goals and annual objectives; (2) programs designed to accomplish these objectives, and (3) procedures, including criteria set forth in advance,

---

53. Housing Act of 1954, § 701, Pub. L. No. 560, 68 Stat. 590, 640, 40 U.S.C. § 461; *as amended by* § 601, Housing and Urban Development Act of 1968, Pub. L. No. 90-448, 82 Stat. 476, 42 U.S.C. § 1441; and Housing and Community Development Act of 1974, § 401, Pub. L. No. 93-383, 88 Stat. 686.

54. U.S. Executive Office of the President, Office of Management and Budget, *OMB Circular No. A-95* (rev. January 2, 1976).

55. Housing and Community Development Act of 1974, § 401(b).

for evaluating programs and activities to determine whether they are meeting objectives. The housing element and the land use element are to be consistent with one another and with national growth policy.[56]

The 701 program has fostered the preparation of numerous housing plans by agencies for whom Comprehensive Planning Assistance grants are often the principal source of funds. In the past, most of these housing plans have consisted of the collection and analysis of substantial amounts of housing data. The implementation record of these plans has been limited.[57] Fortunately, the 1974 amendments placed greater emphasis on allocating responsibilities for meeting housing needs throughout an area.

In the last five years HUD has viewed favorably those 701 housing plans that seek to disperse housing opportunities throughout a region. While numerous examples of 701 sponsored regional housing allocation plans exist, their actual impact on expanding housing opportunities has been minimal. Only those plans that were developed at the height of activity with the Federal housing subsidy programs—such as those undertaken in the Miami Valley, Twin Cities, or by the Washington Council of Governments—were able to achieve a significant degree of implementation. Whether the 1974 amendments to the 701 program will substantially influence local housing and land use policy will depend in large part on federal administration of the new legislation, and to a lesser degree on the extent to which courts use the resulting plans as standards in determining whether actions are violative of the general welfare.[58]

A-95 Review Process. Regional planning received its greatest impetus through the so-called A-95 Review Process, which requires among other things areawide review of applications for federal assistance by regional planning agencies. The A-95 Review Process is set forth in an instructional memorandum, Circular No. A-95, issued by the Federal Office of Management and Budget.[59] The cir-

56. Housing and Community Development Act of 1974, § 401(c). On February 1, 1977, HUD released additional regulations for the housing and land-use elements of the Comprehensive Planning Assistance Program in order to clarify the appropriate contents of the elements and to assist applicants in obtaining HUD approval as required by § 401(5) of the act. Accompanying the regulations are guidelines that provide examples of the activities that applicants may undertake in satisfaction of these requirements. 42 Fed. Reg. 6094 to 6103 (1977).

57. *See* Senate Select Committee on Housing and Urban Affairs, Department of Housing and Community Development v. Housing Needs of the People's of the State of California (1974).

58. *See* In-Zoning, *supra* note 12, at 174.

59. *Circular A-95* is an outgrowth of Section 204 of the Demonstration Cities and Metropolitan Development Act of 1966, and the Intergovernmental Cooperation Act of 1968. For a report on the role of A-95 agencies in the community development process, see 4 Hous. & Dev. Rep. 699-70 (1977).

cular establishes a Project Notification and Review System (PNRS) as a vehicle for advance review of applications for federal financial assistance. The review process permits state, regional, and local agencies that might be affected by a project submitted to the federal government for funding to comment on the potential effect of that project. The procedure is intended to coordinate state, regional, and local planning and development; to assure the consistency of proposed programs with federal, state, and local requirements; and to assure that federal funds are expended in a manner beneficial to the community as a whole.

Areawide planning organizations, nonmetropolitan areawide agencies, and state agencies are designated as clearinghouses for the review procedures. Comprehensive planning, housing, and community development grant applications are required to pass through the A-95 clearinghouse review. An applicant must notify the clearinghouse of its intent to apply for federal funds. The clearinghouse reviews the application, and submits to the federal funding agency findings about the application's consistency with areawide plans.

Few agencies have used the A-95 review process to insure or encourage compliance with regional plans. In part this is because not many areawide agencies have adopted comprehensive plans, and because those that do only review applications of their own constituents and have little power of enforcement. Where the clearinghouse recommends disapproval of an application, the funding agency, while not bound by the negative comment, must take the comment into consideration in making its decision on funding. As applied to housing proposals, the process has been used primarily to encourage negotiation and cooperation with a regional housing allocation plan.

The A-95 process is applicable to both the Section 8 housing subsidy program and to the community development block grants established by the Housing and Community Development Act of 1974. The marriage of these two programs, through the housing assistance plan requirement of the act, discussed below, offers a significant opportunity to utilize the A-95 process in a more effective manner than was possible under the prior housing subsidy and community development programs.

Housing and Community Development Act of 1974

With the passage of the Housing and Community Development Act of 1974,[60] the housing assistance plan (HAP) has become the focal

60. 42 U.S.C. § 5301 *et seq.*

point of federal housing assistance in the United States. Under Title I (Community Development) of the act, a HAP is required of all applicants for community development block grants. The local HAP must:

1. Survey the condition of the community's housing stock and assess the housing assistance needs of "lower-income persons (including elderly and handicapped persons, large families, and persons displaced or to be displaced) residing in or expected to reside in the community."
2. Specify a realistic annual goal for the number of dwelling units for persons to be assisted, including: (a) the relative proportion of new, rehabilitated, and existing dwelling units; and (b) the size and types of housing projects and assistance best suited to the needs of lower income persons in the community.
3. Indicate the general locations of proposed housing for lower income persons with the objective of (a) furthering the revitalization of the community; (b) promoting greater choice of housing opportunities and avoiding concentrations of assisted persons in areas containing a high proportion of low-income persons; and (c) assuring the availability of public facilities and services adequate to serve such housing.[61]

The HAP requirement, together with provisions of Title II (Assisted Housing) of the act, represents a major innovation in federal housing and community development policy. Under Title II every application for housing assistance under HUD programs must be submitted to the local government for its certification as to the application's consistency with its HAP.[62] In addition, the allocation of housing assistance funds to communities is to be based in part on the housing needs specified in these plans.[63] This decisionmaking about the types (such as new, rehabilitated, and existing) and num-

---

61. 42 U.S.C. § 5304(a)(4).

62. 42 U.S.C. § 1439(a). This requirement does not apply to (1) applications for federal housing assistance involving twelve or fewer housing units; (2) housing in federally assisted new community developments; (3) housing financed by loans or loan guarantees of a state or agency thereof, except where a unit of general local government objects in its housing assistance plan to this exemption for state-financed housing. 42 U.S.C. § 1439(b).

63. 42 U.S.C. § 1439(d)(1). The act directs the secretary of HUD to "consider the relative needs of different areas and communities as reflected in data as to population, poverty, housing overcrowding, housing vacancies, amount of substandard housing, or other objectively measurable conditions, subject to such adjustments as may be necessary to assist in carrying out activities designed to meet lower income housing needs as described in approved housing assistance plans submitted by units of general local government. . . ." *Id.*

bers of units to be assisted, the general location of the housing, and the persons to be served has been largely shifted away from private developers and HUD into the hands of local governments. Consequently, communities are now in a position to plan unified community development and housing programs. As the Congressional report on these provisions of the act commented:

> For the first time, after nearly three decades of Federal aid for housing and community development, communities will be able to coordinate the location of new housing units with existing or planned public facilities and services, such as schools, transportation, police and fire protection, recreational facilities, and job opportunities. The committee bill will put an end to a system of support for community development and housing activities which recognized their close relationship but fails to provide the mechanisms necessary to permit them to be undertaken on a unified basis.[64]

The preparation of HAPs by communities receiving housing and community development funds has been the subject of sharp criticism. It has been charged that some of the principal objectives of the act (including "the spatial deconcentration of housing opportunities for persons of lower income") have been frustrated in large measure because of HUD's alleged failure to thoroughly monitor the HAP submissions.[65] In the case of *City of Hartford v. Hills*,[66] Hartford, Connecticut sued seven of its surrounding suburban communities and HUD, seeking to enjoin the approval of block grant community development funds to those communities which, the city claimed, refused to accept their responsibility in meeting the needs for housing low- and moderate-income households in the region. The Federal District Court for the District of Connecticut held that HUD, in approving the local applications, had improperly administered the Housing and Community Development Act of 1974 and its own regulations, by failing to require the surrounding municipalities to evaluate the housing needs of those "expected to reside in the community" as part of their HAPs. HUD, along with four of the

---

64. 42 U.S.C. § 5301(c)(6).

65. *Cf.* The Potomac Institute, The Housing Assistance Plan: A Non-Working Program for Community Improvement (1975), *with* U.S. Department of Housing and Urban Development, First Annual Report, Community Development Block Grant Program (1975). *See also* Comptroller General of the United States, Meeting Application and Review Requirements for Block Grants under Title I of the Housing and Community Development Act of 1974 (1976); Hearings on the Community Development Block Grant Program Before the Senate Committee on Banking, Housing and Urban Affairs, 94th Cong., 2d Sess. (1976).

66. 408 F. Supp. 889 (D. Conn 1976), *rev'd sub. nom.* City of Hartford v. Twns. of Glastonbury, ——F.2d—— (2d. Cir. Aug. 15, 1977) (*en banc*).

neighboring suburbs originally named as defendants, accepted the lower court ruling and decided not to appeal. The towns of Glastonbury, West Hartford, and East Hartford have appealed.[67]

The near-automatic approval of local HAPs that serve as guides for the location of subsidized housing may have a seriously deleterious effect on the goals of expanding housing opportunities for low- and moderate-income households.[68] The failure to check or require conformance of local HAPs with regional housing planning efforts works to frustrate if not render ineffective such regional plans. Restrictions on the mobility of assisted families can only ensure that housing planning efforts will be undermined. (In addition, HUD's difficulty in making the housing assistance program operative seriously undercuts a major means by which housing planning efforts can be implemented and supported.)[69] Finally, the degree to which the Housing and Community Development Act of 1974 is able to actually benefit low- and moderate-income households will be the test of whether communities, historically reluctant to respond to these housing needs, are any more responsive under a program requiring housing assistance policies and programs as a condition to receiving community development funds.[70]

Many of the problems with the first year's performance under the 1974 act were addressed during the second year. Requirements for the second year of Housing and Community Development applications were refined, and indications are that HUD has been more strict in its review and approval of these applications. Efforts are underway, moreover, to assist applicants in obtaining necessary information to prepare adequate HAPs. Reviews of the second-year applications, furthermore, have had the benefit of a required performance report on the first year's program.

---

67. *Id.* While the book was at press, the Court of Appeals, sitting *en banc*, reversed, finding that plaintiffs lacked standing.

68. See The Potomac Institute, *supra* note 65.

69. As of January 31, 1976, some 18 months after the Housing and Community Development Act of 1974 was signed into law, only 7,672 units of Section 8 housing had been occupied. 3 Hous. & Dev. Rep. 950 (1976). Fortunately, HUD's performance has since substantially improved. *See* 4 Hous. & Dev. Rep. 874 (February 21, 1977).

70. At least one community, in response to a lawsuit by open-housing advocates, has decided that it would do without federal community development money if required to accept new low-cost housing. Brookhaven, in Suffolk County, N.Y., is expected to lose some $2 million in community development block grants next year because of its opposition to such housing. However, some 24 other Suffolk County communities are not so indifferent to this aid—which may total $11 million countywide—and have agreed, in the same case, to give low-income housing their best efforts. Leebaw & Haberman, *Low-Income Housing on L.I.*, N.Y. Times, February 6, 1977, at E5.

Nonetheless, while improvements are evident, substantial complaints are still being lodged against HUD for failing to adequately meet the intent and requirements of the 1974 Act. Testimony before the Senate Committee on Banking, Housing and Urban Affairs on the Community Development Block Grant Program during the summer of 1976 provided evidence that abuse was still present. Several groups that had been monitoring applications for housing and community development funds found that performance during the second year mirrored many of the violations found during the first year.[71]

LOCAL HOUSING PLANNING

Responsibility to Plan

Local governments clearly have the primary responsibility to deal with their housing problems. They provide the infrastructure for housing and the bulk of services for residents. Their land-use controls, codes, and subdivision regulations determine what housing is allowed in their jurisdictions. To the extent that they have provided for low- and moderate-income housing, it has usually been in conjunction with federal programs, participation in which is a discretionary local activity.

Housing planning at the local level occurs in a wide variety of communities. The variations between central-city and suburban areas, between developing and already-developed communities, between industrial and bedroom communities, between metropolitan and nonmetropolitan communities, highlight the difficulty in discussing housing planning as if it were one phenomenon for all local units of government. In fact the components of local housing planning efforts vary enormously. The objectives in housing planning nonetheless remain the same, and each community has its own part to play in attaining them. The competing pressure on localities to undertake housing planning and alternative pressure to attend to other problems place enormous burdens on the local unit of government. Yet a community engaged in housing planning has little in the way of guidance in these efforts.

71. *See* Senate Hearings, *supra* note 65. However, recently revised regulations concerning the local housing assistance plan limit HUD's discretion in approving a grant application. The secretary of HUD is now required to review each year's performance report (which must document the community's progress in meeting prior year's housing and community development objectives) before approving the next grant. 42 Fed. Reg. 5099 (1977).

Affirmative Action at the Local Level

The Advisory Commission takes the position that local governments, at a minimum, have an affirmative legal duty: (1) to plan for present and prospective housing in a regional context; (2) to eliminate those local regulatory barriers that do not make it realistically possible to provide housing for persons of low- and moderate-income; and (3) to offer incentives to the private sector in this regard. A discussion of the doctrinal basis for these conclusions occurs in Chapters 2 and 3.

Judicial guidelines in this area are only now beginning to evolve.[72] Federal constitutional principles, which have long been held to prohibit discrimination in housing,[73] are general in concept and provide the courts with little guidance in formulating affirmative relief in complex housing and land-use litigation. Federal civil rights statutes are often not a great deal more explicit. For example, Title VIII of the Civil Rights Act of 1968,[74] commonly called the Fair Housing Act, mandates that federal agencies administer their programs and activities relating to housing and urban development in a manner that affirmatively furthers the purpose of fair housing. The concept of affirmative action, which originates with this law, was never fully defined by Congress. The legislative history of Title VIII indicates a congressional intent to correct the effects of past discrimination, which the federal government itself had long acquiesced in and actively supported.[75] A number of federal court decisions are gradually defining the appropriate federal response necessary to erase the effects of this history of discrimination, and to promote, encourage, and pursue equal housing opportunities.[76]

72. Chapters 2 & 3 *supra* contain an in-depth treatment of this subject.

73. Sixty years ago, in Buchanan v. Warley, 245 U.S. 60 (1917), the U.S. Supreme Court unanimously held that a local ordinance prohibiting "non-Caucasians" from residing on any block in which a majority of homes were occupied by Caucasians violated the Equal Protection Clause of the Constitution. In 1948 the Court held that racially restrictive covenants were prohibited by the Fourteenth Amendment. Shelley v. Kraemer, 334 U.S. 1 (1948). And in 1976, in Hills v. Gautreaux, 96 S. Ct. 1538 (1976), the Court found that HUD had violated the Constitution in acquiescing to Chicago's discriminatory selection of sites for public housing (*see* full discussion of the case in Chapter 3 *supra*).

74. Pub. L. No. 90-284 (April 11, 1968), 42 U.S.C. §§ 3601–19.

75. A discussion of the federal government's role in promoting patterns of racial discrimination in housing can be found in Chapter 1 *supra.*

76. *See, e.g.,* Laufman v. Oakley Building and Loan Co., 408 F. Supp. 489 (D. Ohio, 1976) (mortgage underwriting decisions in racially integrated neighborhoods held to have discriminatory impact, which is discussed in the Section "Redlining" in Chapter 7 *infra*); Clark v. Universal Builders, Inc., 501 F.2d 324 (7th Cir. 1974), *cert. denied,* 419 U.S. 1070 (1974) (exploitation of dual

Recent decisions in several state supreme courts, relying on equal protection and due process provisions of state constitutions—rather than on counterpart provisions of the federal Constitution or on federal civil rights statutes—are substantially broadening the affirmative responsibilities of local governments in correcting past abuses and promoting housing opportunities. In the landmark case of *Southern Burlington NAACP v. Township of Mount Laurel*,[77] the New Jersey Supreme Court ordered broad affirmative relief after invalidating the local zoning ordinance on state constitutional grounds. The Court's discussion of affirmative relief is particularly instructive, and has already proved extremely influential in other states.[78] The following affirmative standard was articulated for Mount Laurel and all "developing municipalities.":

> [T]he presumptive obligation arises for each such municipality affirmatively to plan and provide, by its land use regulations, the reasonable opportunity for an appropriate variety and choice of housing, including, of course, low and moderate cost housing, to meet the needs, desires and resources of all categories of people who may desire to live within its boundaries.[79] To this end, the *Mount Laurel* court concluded: It must permit multifamily, without bedroom or similar restrictions, as well as small dwellings on very small lots, low cost housing of other types and, in general, high density zoning, without artificial and unjustifiable minimum requirements as to lot size, building size and the like to meet the full panoply of these needs.[80]

The *Mount Laurel* standard was affirmed and further refined by the New Jersey Supreme Court in *Oakwood at Madison, Inc. v. Township of Madison*.[81] In invalidating Madison Township's ordinance as exclusionary under the *Mount Laurel* standard (for failing "to provide the opportunity to meet a fair share of the regional burden for low- and moderate-income housing needs"), the court found that it was nonetheless not incumbent upon the courts to establish specific quotas for low-income housing needs. Agreeing with *Mount Laurel* that "[c]ourts do not build housing,"[82] the court

---

market housing situation by charging higher prices in black areas found to perpetuate discrimination, though the builder was not racially motivated). Other such cases are discussed in Falk & Franklin, *supra* note 9.

77. 67 N.J. 151, 336 A.2d 713 (1975), *appeal dismissed*, 423 U.S. 808 (1975).

78. *Mount Laurel* and other leading state anti-exclusionary cases are discussed in detail in Chapters 2 & 3 *supra*.

79. 336 A.2d at 728.

80. *Id.* at 732.

81. —N.J.—, 371 A.2d 1192 (1977). Since the oral argument in the case, the name of the municipality has been changed from Madison to Old Bridge.

82. 336 A.2d at 734.

in *Madison* ruled that the "provision by zoning for density bonuses keyed to quantitative or bulk concessions by the builder (*e.g.*, added bedrooms) is both valid and mandatory where necessary to achieve sufficient suitable least-cost housing. . . ."[83] As did *Mount Laurel* before it, the *Madison* court placed great emphasis on the need for housing planning in order to achieve an effective remedy.

Municipal Role and Policies in Housing Planning

In spite of all the criticisms that have been directed at localities for their failure to respond to housing problems, as well as for their emphasis on fiscal over human concerns, these same local governments have been given increasingly important responsibilities for housing.

Under the former public housing programs, the responsibility to create a local housing authority rested with the local unit of government, pursuant to state enabling law. Some earlier federal subsidy programs required specific local approval of proposed projects. Not until the 1968 Housing Act, which established the Section 235 and Section 236 interest-reduction housing subsidy programs, could federally supported housing be constructed without the express approval or initiative of the local unit of government.

More recently the Housing and Community Development Act of 1974 provides for a local disapproval option for all subsidized housing programs.[84] HUD must notify the local unit of government within ten days of the receipt of an application for housing assistance. The local government has 30 days to disapprove the project. Disapproval must rest on the fact that the proposed project is not consistent with the HAP of the community. HUD then has 30 days to agree or disagree with the local action and may overrule local disapproval if the project is found to be consistent with local plans.

As has been indicated in earlier sections of this chapter and throughout this book, localities certainly have other techniques at their disposal to control the construction of housing. Thus, with subsidized housing in particular, but with all forms of residential construction, the local unit of government, through zoning and subdivision controls, may determine what housing will be constructed, where it will be located, and when it will be built.

---

83. 371 A.2d at 1255. The court went on to enumerate a minimum of seven ways in which the municipality could modify its zoning ordinance to facilitate the provision of least-cost housing. *Id.* at 1228. *See* note 92 *infra*.

84. 42 U.S.C. § 1439(a).

It is important to explore possible local initiatives for a housing program so that courts, federal officiels, citizens, and local officials can better understand the options available to a local unit of government in pursuing housing objectives and goals. Too frequently, in criticizing the lack of local initiative, there have been few recommendations made to improve a community's housing program. Too often, changes in the zoning ordinance and the creation of a housing authority have represented the total substance and form of recommendations for a local action.

Locally approved housing policies agreed upon by all members of the local governing body can serve as a means for achieving housing objectives. The formal adoption of a housing program, however, may have no meaning for a locality intending only to appease potential opposition, to comply minimally with court orders, or to narrowly meet federal requirements. A meaningful housing policy statement should set forth a community's intent to:

1. Provide adequate housing for all households at a price they can afford by increasing the supply of good-quality housing units especially for low- and moderate-income households.
2. Conserve that portion of the housing inventory that is sound and repair or rehabilitate deteriorating housing stock.
3. Provide a quality living environment for all households by providing adequate public services and facilities and by maintaining sound, viable neighborhoods, and revitalizing those which have suffered disrepair and neglect.
4. Expand the range of housing opportunity for everyone geographically, and ensure a balanced distribution of housing and employment opportunities.
5. Encourage the development and utilization of all appropriate human services, particularly those affecting the quality of life for low- and moderate-income households.
6. Encourage housing development designed to facilitate constructive social interaction between low- and moderate-income households and their neighbors in the larger community.
7. Improve housing planning, policy-making, and implementation processes.

The Local Housing Strategy

Leaving out the national and military references, Webster's defines strategy as the science and art of employing the political, economic, psychological . . . forces . . . to afford the maximum support to adopted policies. Clearly a strategy entails careful planning—a plan and a set of actions to achieve specific goals and objectives. A housing strategy should be comprehensive and inclusive in order to overcome fragmented and nonrational attempts to deal with housing problems. The strategy needs to involve public officials and agencies, private businesses, and citizens. Further, there should be political consensus about what the problems are, how they should be solved, and who is to do what. Such a strategy is a continuing process of evaluation, planning, commitment, and action.

Housing strategies as described herein have been attempted in Cincinnati and other cities with some positive results. A brief description of the major elements that should be a part of any comprehensive housing strategy follows, including research, participants, goals, actions, and implementation.

Research on Problems, Needs, Resources, Opportunities. *Analysis of the local housing industry*, including: (1) data on construction trends and characteristics of new housing; (2) identification of local builders and contractors and consideration of their motivations, plans, problems, and suggestions; (3) analysis of the housing price structure, key competition in the area, sales and rental absorption rates, and vacancies; (4) review of the land-development and building regulatory process; (5) evaluation of subsidized housing projects in the community; (6) forecasts of supply and demand by type of housing, price, and general location.

Description of the administrative organization of the community, including departments, boards and commissions; describing for each: (1) housing-related functions; (2) other development functions; (3) formal relationships with other agencies; (4) types of contacts with citizen groups, builders, property owners, and other governments; (5) any apparent problems or deficiencies that might affect housing production, maintenance, preservation, or renewal.

Analysis of the existing housing stock, including: (1) physical characteristics such as types of buildings and numbers of bedrooms; (2) physical condition of both structures and neighborhoods by subareas of the community; (3) occupancy (owner-renter) information by subarea; (4) housing value levels and trends by subarea; (5) sales-transaction trends over five years by subarea.

Evaluation of urban renewal and neighborhood preservation programs, both public and private, including: (1) nature of programs; (2) key participants and their roles; (3) "before" characteristics of project area: (4) accomplishments; (5) major problems or difficulties; (6) determinants of success and failure; (7) expectations for the project.

Analysis of household characteristics by subareas, including cross-related data on: (1) household size; (2) household income; (3) number of wage-earners; (4) occupations; (5) general locations of employment; (6) age of household head; (7) number of school-age children; (8) years in present residence; (9) percent of income spent on housing (including utilities); (10) minorities; (11) handicapped.

Forecasts of population by subareas, including: (1) natural increase; (2) migration prospects; (3) households by size and incomes; (4) population by general age ranges.

Determination of housing needs by subareas, including: (1) comparison of projections of housing and households to determine potential supplemental needs by type and price; (2) assessment of needs for housing rehabilitation; (3) determination of the need for clearance and redevelopment.

Evaluation of the general conditions and adequacy of neighborhood facilities and services by subareas, including: (1) schools, (2) parks and recreation facilities; (3) utilities; (4) streets and sidewalks; (5) storm drainage; (6) trash collection; (7) police and fire protection; (8) health services; (9) family services; (10) housing counselling.

Review of financing for housing, including: (1) availability and cost of construction financing, mortgage financing (new and existing housing), and home improvement loans; (2) potential redlining practices by subarea; (3) savings practices of residents by subarea and potential leakage of local savings to other areas; (4) potential public funds for capital improvements in neighborhoods and housing subsidies.

Analysis of the local economy including: (1) role of the community's economy in the region (in- and out-commuting of workers, regional or multicommunity functions located in the community, major centers of employment for working residents, general residential pattern of those working in the community by general type of employer and income level; and (2) characteristics and general location of jobs in the community in industry, commerce, institutions, and government, by wage level.

Participants, Organization, Roles, Commitments. Key to the successful implementation of the housing strategy is to involve all the major participants from the outset. Both elected and appointed officials should actively participate, with adequate technical assistance. In addition, private-sector representatives must have influential roles to play—particularly bankers, builders, insurance executives, labor leaders, and civic leaders. Neighborhood and other citizen groups should participate as well—perhaps through subarea organizations. With such a diverse group of participants, it is apparent that decision-making is best achieved by understanding and consensus. Accordingly, the housing strategy process is necessarily long and involved.

While a dual-level organizational structure probably is essential for adequate representation and effective operation, the specifics of the organization structure and roles can vary considerably. It is very important that roles and tasks be meaningful and well defined. Realistic target dates should be fixed and met. One of the main reasons for involving a relatively large number of key participants is to get them individually committed to the housing strategy as it is being formulated. These commitments should become increasingly formal and binding as the effort progresses.

Goals, Objectives, and Policies. As the housing strategy participants are getting organized, the technical research should be well underway. Research and issue papers should be presented for review and consensus. Concurrently, statements of housing goals, objectives, and policies should be prepared and discussed. The goals may be relatively ambitious and long term. The objective should relate to the goals and be more specific and short term. Policies are guidelines to follow in implementing action which, in turn, are intended to attain the goals and objectives.

It is probable that statements of community goals, objectives, and policies already exist. Those that pertain to housing can serve as a basis for preparing housing goals. Since the focus is on housing and not overall community development, the existing goal statements may well need to be translated, refined, and detailed to specifically apply to housing planning. Other possible goals, objectives, and policies should emerge from consideration of the findings of the ongoing housing research. These tentative goal statments should be considered and refined by the key participants. Before adoption, however, there should be adequate public hearings on the proposed statements of housing goals, objectives, and policies.

While it is appropriate that the substance of these goal statements will vary greatly from community to community, they all should address: potential community growth and change; new construction; neighborhood facilities and services; housing regulations (including land development); the impact of existing laws (land use, environment, tax assessment practices, codes) on housing price and location; housing maintenance; neighborhood preservation; housing finance; subsidies; redevelopment; housing abandonment; household housing capabilities; counselling services; population changes; and citizen involvement. Other considerations, such as transportation, environment, and energy use, would also be appropriate as expressed from a housing perspective.

Actions and Priorities. Having ascertained housing conditions, needs, and resources, and the goals and objectives to seek as well as the policies to follow, the housing strategy participants are ready to identify, evaluate, and select actions to take. This part of the strategy formulation is most difficult because the agreed-upon needs will seemingly be far beyond the resource-constrained capabilities of both government and the private sector. This real dilemma is managed by carefully establishing priorities and providing for monitoring of cost-effectiveness during implementation.

Possible actions should be listed and discussed. Those with the greatest promise should be refined and combined into alternative sets of consistent and mutually supportive actions. Each action set should be related to either a different assumption on resource availability or it should focus on a housing emphasis, such as rehabilitation rather than new construction. After due consideration, one specific set of actions should be selected as part of the housing strategy. Timing and budgeting priorities must then be determined for each of the action programs in the selected set.

Implementation.   Analysis and goal-setting must be combined with action. In the past this has often been limited to addressing only the needs that could be met by federal subsidy programs, when the plan should address the ways in which government (at whatever level) acts to facilitate, regulate, or supplement the private market. Contrary to common perception, there are a variety of activities a locality can undertake to expand the supply of housing and housing opportunities, both in conjunction with federal and state programs and, to some extent, independent of them. In general, they fall into seven categories:

1. Increasing the receptivity to federal and state funds by the creation of local agencies to administer such monies, donation of surplus land, property tax abatement, small-scale rent supplement programs, or the assumption of some site development costs.
2. Ensuring housing maintenance and the rehabilitation of existing housing stock by the creation of rehabilitation loan funds, code enforcement, institution of homesteading programs, or various tax incentives such as the elimination or suspension of new taxes on improvements.

3. Expediting the construction of new housing by actively soliciting development and suitable sites, encouraging the inclusion of low- and moderate-income units in large-scale planned unit developments, or expediting the administrative process for projects that respond to housing needs.
4. Balancing housing and employment opportunities by relating the location of public and private employment centers, such as new government agencies or major industrial or commercial facilities, to the availability of decent housing, even to the extent of developing a site-selection process and standards based on this principle.
5. Coordinating housing planning with capital improvement programming by relating the provision of public facilities such as water, sewer, roads, and schools to the availability of lower income housing.
6. Providing services and facilities to lower income households as well as to the housing units by making available counselling, management training, housing referal and placement services, and other programs that foster both economic and social stability in new residential areas.
7. Revising both the substance and procedure of local land-use and housing regulations so as to facilitate new construction of lower income housing and to make it possible to renovate the existing housing stock for the use of lower income households.

A variety of these techniques are discussed in some detail in the following chapter. Subsequent sections of this chapter focus on the role of local regulatory devices and on the importance of relating local efforts to housing planning at the regional and state levels.

Housing-Related Activities: The Impact of Regulatory Devices

Land-use controls within any given unit of government are comprised of a panoply of ordinances: the zoning ordinance; subdivision regulations; housing, building, and plumbing codes; other engineering or sanitation codes; and so forth. Land-use controls for the most part regulate new development. The rehabilitation of existing housing is generally subject to fewer controls. The zoning ordinance has remained the single most influential land-use control affecting the variety of housing within communities. As a consequence, zoning ordinances have been the focus of numerous court challenges to remove regulatory barriers to the development of housing.

A primary relationship between land-use controls and housing is one of cost. By establishing minimum lot sizes, minimum bedroom requirements, and the like, land-use controls can affect the development of housing by increasing or reducing the cost of dwelling units.[85] A second relationship centers on opportunity. Land-use controls can affect the development of housing by providing an opportunity to build lower cost housing. A developer must be given the opportunity to develop, and the capability to do so at a reasonable profit, or housing will not be built at any price.

Land-use controls can reduce the cost of housing by assuring that sufficient land is available in proper locations and allowing higher density development with adequate facilities and services. The cost of housing can be further reduced by permitting units to be constructed at or within realistic standards necessary to create a safe and sanitary dwelling unit. Finally, cost can be reduced through savings in time resulting from streamlined administrative procedures governing zoning changes and necessary building permits designed to facilitate or encourage developments that are intended to expand the range of housing available to lower income households.[86] There are, of course, limitations on what modifications of land-use controls can realistically be expected to achieve. Surely, in the absence of favorable economic conditions and governmental leadership, modified land-use controls cannot by themselves assure expanded housing opportunity.

There is reason to believe, however, that no changes of land-use controls *per se*, will reduce costs sufficiently to enable the construction of low-cost housing. If housing is to be made available for low-income families, government subsidies for either the unit or the household are essential.[87] This realization has led the New Jersey Supreme Court, in its important *Oakwood at Madison* decision, to

85. Professor Norman Williams discusses some of the effects of zoning restrictions on housing costs in 3 N. Williams American Land Planning Law 119–140 (1974) [hereinafter cited as Williams]. He also discusses some of the empirical research, including L. Sagalyn & G. Sternlieb, Zoning and Housing Costs: The Impact of Land Use Controls on Housing Prices (1973). *See also* E. Bergman, Development Controls and Housing Costs: A Policy Guide to Research (1975).

86. *See* discussion of administrative reforms in Chapter 4 *supra* and Chapter 7 *infra*, especially the analysis of the Massachusetts Zoning Appeals Law and the A.L.I. Model Land Development Code.

87. This subsidy has most often been a production subsidy, usually geared to the construction of multifamily developments (*e.g.*, public housing and housing under the Section 221(d)(3) and Section 236 programs). Increasingly, however, federal policy seems to be moving toward direct subsidy of the consumer through housing allowance experiments, housing payments to welfare recipients, or subsidy of individual units within a development (*e.g.*, the Section 8 leased housing program). These latter forms of subsidy tend to provide housing planners at the local level with more politically acceptable options.

speak in terms of "least cost housing."[88] The court noted that in light of the nation's current economic condition and the paucity of governmental subsidies, nothing less than zoning for "least cost housing," consistent with minimum standards of health and safety, could satisfy the mandate of its earlier *Mount Laurel* decision.[89] In the words of the *Madison* court:

> While compliance with that direction may not provide *newly constructed* housing for all in the lower income categories mentioned, it will nevertheless through the "filtering down" process . . . tend to augment the total supply of available housing in such manner as will indirectly provide additional and better housing for the insufficiently and inadequately housed of the region's lower income population.[90]

The court recognized that expanding the opportunity to construct lower cost housing would require the provision of density bonuses[91] and other cost-saving incentives to developers, as well as numerous revisions in the town's zoning ordinance.[92] Density bonuses have frequently been proposed as an economic incentive to induce private developers to provide a type, amount, or cost of housing suitable for lower income households.[93] Incentive zoning has usually referred to the provisions of density bonuses in central-city areas to encourage desired amenities in exchange for increased floor area. Generally, increased densities increase profit and enable the reduction in costs of individual units.

Little attention has been devoted to devising other incentives for developers. One such incentive would encourage a developer to make

88. Oakwood at Madison, Inc. v. Township of Madison, 371 A.2d at 1225. *See* text accompanying note 83 *supra*.
89. See text accompanying notes 77–80 *supra*.
90. 371 A.2d at 1208.
91. See text accompanying note 88 *supra*.
92. The court specified that the revisions, at a minimum, should: (a) allocate substantial areas for single-family dwellings on very small lots; (b) substantially enlarge the areas for dwellings on moderate-sized lots; (c) substantially enlarge existing multifamily zones or create other enlarged multifamily zones; (d) reduce the large acreage zones to the extent necessary; (e) modify the restrictions in the multifamily zones and PUD areas which discourage the construction of apartments of more than two bedrooms; (f) modify the PUD regulations to eliminate the undue cost-generating requirements indicated; and (g) generally eliminate and reduce undue cost-generating restrictions in the zones allocated to the chievement of lower income housing. 371 A.2d at 1228.
93. *See generally*, M. Brooks, *supra* note 28; E. Erber & J. Prior, Housing Allocation Planning: An Annotated Bibliography (Council of Planning Librarians Exchange Bibliography No. 547, 1974). *See also* discussion of incentive zoning in Chapter 4, *supra*.

use of internal financial arrangements, such as internal skewing of rents, to provide a proportion of lower cost housing units.[94] Bonuses could also be made available for including a certain number of units with three or more bedrooms where the need for large units is evident. Similarly, bonuses have been provided where units were made available to elderly households.

One recent and thorough analysis of inclusionary zoning techniques concludes:

> The foregoing analyses lead to the conclusion that developers can substantially reduce costs on the required units by building smaller, more modest units, but that in high land cost areas developers may lose money on the required units (or pass losses along to buyers, tenants, and landowners) without a density bonus or other cost savings devices.[95]

Further studies support these conclusions. In a study on the impact of land-use controls on housing prices, it was concluded that public land-use policies do affect housing prices. The provision of lower cost units necessitate, however, a willingness on the part of developers to reduce the size and amenities of the units in addition to the benefits available from reduced standards to generate more housing at lower cost.[96]

Another program often proposed to reduce the cost of housing is a land banking or advance acquisition program to be used in combination with other local programs (see Chapter 7). The objective is to make land available that is suitable or desirable for the construction of low- and moderate-income housing. A land banking program carried out in conjunction with capital improvement programs can provide ideal sites for the location of needed housing and can be carried out in conjunction with other land development programs. These programs could also be followed in conformance with housing allocation plans to encourage a distribution of housing opportunities within the community. Land acquisition programs have been carried out extensively in conjunction with transportation and other public facilities, but only to a limited extent with housing.

94. The statute creating the Massachusetts Housing Finance Agency expressly provides for rent skewing. *See* discussion of state housing finance agencies in Chapter 7 *infra.*
95. Kleven, *Inclusionary Ordinances—Policy and Legal Issues in Requiring Private Developers to Build Low Cost Housing,* 21 U.C.L.A. L. Rev. 1432, 1490 (1974). *See also* discussion of mandatory inclusionary ordinances in Chapter 7 *infra.*
96. These guidelines and other parts of this section are drawn from Suburban Action Institute, A Study of Exclusion (1973).

Identification of "Exclusionary" Activities

As part of a local housing plan and implementation program local agencies should evaluate their own regulations and actions to determine whether they have an exclusionary effect. While it is unrealistic to label a community either exclusionary or inclusionary, an indication of excessive restrictions, actions that could be taken to remove those restrictions, and the steps that could be taken to increase opportunities for the construction of low- and moderate-income housing is the ultimate aim of a study of exclusion.

Identifying whether land-use controls are restrictive is but a first step. Recognizing that local regulations may have a valid purpose but an unnecessarily restrictive effect, the following criteria may be useful as guidelines in determining whether exclusionary practices, in fact, exist:

1. Few lower income families currently live there, or few housing units are available to lower income ranges of the region's population.
2. Development and zoning of vacant land has been programmed without regard to providing for a variety of housing types.
3. Land-use controls are generally more restrictive on multifamily dwelling units and mobile homes than on single-family dwellings by prohibiting the former or requiring more extensive or detailed procedural approvals, or requiring more excessive design and improvement requirements.
4. Land-use controls are consistently in excess of those necessary to protect the health and safety of residents through restrictive yard and bulk requirements, lot sizes, densities, minimum building sizes, and so on, and in effect increase the cost of dwelling units.[97]

The basic analysis of exclusion raises two major questions:

1. Are there land-use restrictions imposed by the community which preclude the availability of low- and moderate-income housing and which are in excess of those regulations necessary to protect the health, safety, morals, and welfare of its residents?
2. Is there housing within the community at a cost which is available to low- and moderate-income households throughout the region?

A municipality must always be compared to the region within which it lies to assess whether the community is responsive to housing

97. *See* L. Sagalyn & G. Sternlieb, Zoning and Housing Costs: The Impact of Land Use Controls on Housing Prices 69 (1973).

needs of poorer households. An analysis of a community in isolation is not a sufficient test of exclusion when those very persons in need of housing are forced to live or work elsewhere in the region.

In identifying the restrictiveness of land-use controls, three major aspects must be reviewed: (1) requirements and regulations governing the development of residential units; (2) the manner in which zoning districts have been mapped and acted upon by the community; and (3) the administrative and procedural requirements applicable to residential development.

Zoning Requirements. In reviewing the first of these considerations—the requirements and regulations governing the development of residential units—five areas may be explored:

1. The type of dwelling units that are allowed to be developed within the community.
2. The densities permitted for each type of dwelling unit allowed. Minimum lot sizes and other density regulations must be reviewed.
3. The yard requirements applied to each type of dwelling unit allowed. Minimum yard requirements and maximum building coverages must be reviewed.
4. The regulations applied to the size or bulk of each type of dwelling unit allowed. Minimum floor-area requirements, limitations on the number of bedrooms, and height regulations must be reviewed.
5. The structural requirements applied to residential units related to the design and improvement of that unit. Architectural requirements, required amenities such as covered garages, landscaping, walls or fences, and the like must be reviewed.

A variety of dwelling units should be allowed within each community. If there are areas within the municipality that are not suitable for high densities and should be limited to low-density development for topographic or environmental reasons, these areas can be indicated in the development plan for the community or on the zoning map.

The types of zoning restrictions listed above should be analyzed both in terms of specific requirements in the ordinance and the way in which they are applied by local agencies. Rather than suggest a meaningless arbitrary standard for yards, building height, and so forth, local regulations should be evaluated for excessiveness, recognizing that the specific requirements will vary—for example, unique environmental or historic areas in one community that require what would be excessive restrictions in another community. In addition, the regulations should be measured against the four guidelines mentioned earlier to determine if such effects are produced by the regulations in question.

Mapping Zoning Districts. In analyzing the mapping practices of the community, it is possible to assess how much developed and how much vacant land is zoned in such a way as to permit the construction of residences that would be available to low- and moderate-income families, usually multifamily, mobile homes, planned developments, and so forth. A relative balance of mapped districts outlined in the zoning ordinance is desirable so that a sufficient amount of vacant and developable land is zoned to permit residential development of any type.

An important concern here relates to the hazards of premapping, particularly for multifamily dwellings. Mapping for multifamily use changes the response of the private land market to that property and, all other variables being equal, the land price will rise. Moreover, premapping for multifamily dwellings in a community generally unwilling to accept such housing may result in inferior locations and highly unsuitable or restricted sites. As a result, proposals have been made that more effective alternatives would be: (1) to permit multifamily housing on any land within the community zoned for residential uses and suitable for multifamily development; or (2) to permit subsidized housing, low- and moderate-income housing, or multifamily housing meeting specified requirements to be permitted as a special exception in all parts of the municipality suitable for residential development.

Administrative Procedures. The purpose of analyzing the administrative practices is to ascertain what review procedures are required of residential uses suitable for low- and moderate-income housing that might not be required of other residential uses. Excessive procedural or administrative requirements are an additional and costly barrier to the construction of such units. Administrative procedures need to be streamlined. Suggestions have been made that either all residential units be permitted as of right where suitable if they meet requirements set forth in the land-use controls, or to approve through a special-permit procedure the requirements necessary to have subsidized, low- and moderate-income or multifamily developments.[98] The intent is to set forth clearly the criteria for deciding whether an application for residential development should be granted and thereby prevent the use of an arbitrary system.

Large-scale developments may require more complex administra-

98. *See* note 86 *supra.*

tive procedures. Even these procedures, however, might reasonably be limited by such guidelines as:

1. No more than one public hearing at a preliminary stage is needed.
2. No more than a three-step process is necessary, including initial conference, preliminary application, and final approval.
3. Time limits should be established for all stages.
4. One application process should suffice for all land-use controls in force (zoning ordinance, subdivision ordinance, planned-unit development ordinance, and so on), and the same application data should be sufficient for all reviewing bodies. (Administrative reforms are discussed in Chapter 4.)

Evaluation and Use of Housing Plans

Housing planning might ideally be viewed by community officials to be as germane and important as public works planning and annual budgeting, but this usually is not the case. Few communities have prepared and implemented housing plans purely of their own volition. For those communities which only prepare housing plans under compulsion, therefore, it may be necessary to have some basis for determining the adequacy of such plans. And once a housing plan exists it may be necessary to have some basis for determining the adequacy of such plans.

The housing plan ought to be supported by the appropriate analyses and certifications so it can be reasonably evaluated by the information included in the plan document. An evaluation of the housing plan and supporting documentation should allow the following sixteen determinations:

1. Have housing conditions and trends been thoroughly and realistically analyzed?
2. Have the characteristics of households—particularly their housing circumstances and capabilities—been carefully investigated?
3. Has sufficient consideration been given to housing people who work in the community but live elsewhere?
4. Have spatial patterns of housing, educational and recreational facilities and services, employment opportunities, and transportation been adequately taken into account?
5. Have restrictive regulations and controls been evaluated and proposals made for revising them, so as to overcome patterns of discrimination and segregation?
6. Do the forecasts of population, employment, and housing provision appear reasonable in light of past trends and regional projections?

7. Has the role of the community in terms of housing, education, employment, tax base, population composition, and growth prospects been adequately assessed?
8. Have all the above factors been analytically interrelated in order to arrive at clear, concise, and objective determinations of housing problems and needs?
9. Have comprehensive and well-considered sets of goals and objectives been formulated and adopted that clearly and substantially relate to the problems and needs identified?
10. Have community resources been analyzed to determine both the public and private financial and management commitments that could be made to implementing the housing plan?
11. Has the potential availability of federal and state housing assistance been considered and established?
12. Has a wide range of action options been identified and systematically considered for adoption?
13. Have subarea differences in needs and opportunities been adequately reflected in consideration of actions?
14. Do the adopted plans and specific actions adequately reflect housing needs, goals, and objectives, and have sources of funding for them been clearly and realistically set forth?
15. Have monitoring, review, and updating programs been spelled out?
16. Have at least tentative comments of key participants been obtained and have certifications been made?

The above questions provide guidelines for reviewing the housing plan or strategy. Given satisfactory answers to these questions, the bases have been established for evaluating the actual implementation of the plan. In effect, the major elements of the housing plan become the criteria to use in evaluating its implementation (assuming the housing plan is as explicit and complete as suggested herein).

STATE AND REGIONAL HOUSING PLANNING

In this chapter we have seen that traditionally, most housing planning has occurred as a result of a combination of federal and local initiatives. In recent years, however, state and regional governments and agencies have assumed increasingly important roles in housing planning. (Other state activities in housing production, finance, and the like are discussed in Chapter 7).

State-Imposed Housing Planning

One method for assuring the consideration of housing opportunity in local growth-management programs is through a new planning framework within which local governments must plan for the housing needs of their residents and revise their land-use controls accordingly. This method has the advantage of allowing localities to participate in developing their own strategies for resolving their housing needs in a broader community context. As such, it may be less fiscally onerous and may avoid potential local controversy. A local housing planning requirement, moreover, is supportive of requirements for a local HAP necessitated by the Housing and Community Development Act of 1974.

There is statutory precedent for such mandatory local housing planning in California and Florida. California planning law requires every city and county to adopt a comprehensive general plan that must contain certain mandatory elements, including housing, land-use, circulation, conservation, open-space, seismic safety, noise, and scenic highway elements.[99] The law further requires that local zoning ordinances be made consistent with a community's general plan, including the mandatory elements. The housing element is to consist of "standards and plans for the improvement of housing and for provisions of adequate sites for housing," and "shall make adequate provision for the housing needs of all economic segments of the community."[100]

The law explicitly authorizes any resident or property owner within a city or county to bring an action in the state superior court to enforce the requirement that city and county zoning ordinances be consistent with the general plan.[101] The section only provides specific remedies in conjunction with open-space elements, however. Unless the permit, map, or ordinance is consistent with the local open-space plan, the issuance of building permits, approval of subdivision maps, and adoption of open-space ordinances are prohibited.

The lack of statutory remedies in housing element cases has been a hindrance to securing meaningful action through a lawsuit, since many judges are unwilling to fashion extraordinary remedies themselves. There would appear, however, to be legislative leeway for a court to order all or part of a housing element to be submitted or approved by a special master, citizens groups, regional planning bodies, or other interested parties such as the attorney general or councils of government.

99. Cal. Gov't Code § 65860(a).
100. *Id.* § 65302.
101. *Id.* § 65860(b).

While a majority of California cities and counties have adopted housing elements, a large minority have not. Even those cities and counties that have adopted housing elements have not, in many cases, met the statutory requirements. A potentially powerful tool for increasing housing opportunity, the mandatory housing element requirement has been plagued by legislative ambiguities and inconsistences. Complicating the problem was the passage of a tax reform bill, known as SB 90, which in effect requires that the state must bear any costs to local governments of conforming with the planning and zoning law. Since no money was appropriated to pay the SB 90 costs, there was considerable laxity in requiring adoption of local housing elements and ensuring compliance with local land-use laws.[102]

Some of the ambiguities in the California statute were clarified and its intent reaffirmed by legislation passed in 1975, the Housing and Home Finance Act.[103] This act permanently established the California Department of Housing and Community Development and charged it with preparing a statewide housing plan. The plan is to be an affirmative step toward low-income housing and its distribution throughout the state; it must consider housing conditions for all economic segments of the population; and have a regional context. The plan must establish housing development and assistance goals for each year from 1975 to 1980.[104] If adopted legislatively, the state plan will elevate housing to a functional state concern.

The state of Florida has also enacted legislation which mandates local housing planning. The Local Government Comprehensive Planning Act of 1975 requires counties and local governments to prepare and adopt comprehensive plans for future development.[105] The law defines the required and optional elements of such plans, and gives them the legal status to control all future development. Local governments have until 1979 to prepare plans, and if they fail to do so, the state is authorized to prepare the local plan. The plan must contain a housing element, which is defined in the law: to include standards, plans, and principles to be followed in the provision of housing for the existing population and for anticipated growth; to provide for the elimination of substandard dwelling conditions; to improve existing housing; to provide adequate sites for future housing, including housing for low- and moderate-income families and mobile homes,

102. For a discussion of the problems in implementing the California housing element, *see* Senate Select Committee on Housing and Urban Affairs, *supra* note 57.

103. Cal. Act A.B. 1-X, § 41125 *et seq.*

104. *Id. See generally* Rehm & Pearlman, *Housing and Community Development: The California Approach*, 9 Clearinghouse Rev. 613, 617 (1976).

105. Fla. Laws ch. 75-257 (July 1975).

with supporting infrastructure and community facilities; to provide relocation housing; to identify housing for conservation, rehabilitation, and replacement; and to formulate housing implementation programs.[106]

In New Jersey, since 1970, a number of studies have documented the needs and the nature and extent of exclusionary land-use practices.[107] During the same years, several lower courts in New Jersey had handed down significant anti-exclusionary decisions. In response to the studies and litigation, former Governor Cahill had, on several occasions, called upon the legislature to consider strategies to increase housing opportunities, including the need to consider regional housing needs in the exercise of local land-use powers.[108] As a result of this executive initiative, a number of bills were submitted in the legislature, though not enacted, which sought to increase the number of sites available for low- and moderate-income housing through mandatory land-use and housing planning. One bill, called the Comprehensive and Balanced Housing Act,[109] required the Department of Community Affairs to ascertain the state's fifteen-year housing needs, establish five-year guidelines for each county, and consider regional housing needs. The counties would be required to survey housing needs, and allocate these to municipalities. In turn the municipalities would prepare a housing development program for meeting their housing share. If either the counties or municipalities should fail to act appropriately the state would be authorized to act and adopt appropriate goals. The Balanced Housing bill languished in the legislature.

Following the landmark decision by the New Jersey Supreme Court in the *Mount Laurel* case—which moved the issue of fair-share housing planning from the problem-defining stage to the remedial-action stage by redefining the relationship between housing opportunity and municipal land-use powers—the legislature remained intransigent. The lower courts in the meanwhile were attempting to work within the general guidelines of *Mount Laurel* with some lack

---

106. *Id.* at § 7(5)(f).
107. N.J. Dep't. of Community Affairs, The Housing Crisis in New Jersey (1970); N.J. Dep't. of Community Affairs, Land Use Regulation: The Residential Land Supply (1972); N.J. County & Municipal Government Study Commission, Multi-family Housing and Suburban Municipalities—Fiscal and Social Impact (1973); N.J. Department of Community Affairs, An Analysis of Low and Moderate Income Housing Need in New Jersey (1975).
108. W. Cahill, A Blueprint for Housing in New Jersey (1970); N.J. Dep't. of Community Affairs, New Horizons in Housing (1972).
109. This bill, S.B. 3100, was introduced in the New Jersey legislature in 1975.

of uniformity in results.[110] (The *Mount Laurel* court, anticipating the need for a statewide resolution of the problems that would likely ensure, had wisely, but unavailingly, called upon the legislature to respond.[111]) Consequently, in April of 1976, Governor Byrne issued an executive order directing that:

1. The Director of the Division of State and Regional Planning . . . shall prepare State housing goals to guide municipalities in adjusting their municipal land-use regulations in order to provide a reasonable opportunity for the development of an appropriate variety and choice of housing to meet the needs of the residents of New Jersey.
2. The Director shall allocate housing goals pursuant to this Order, as expeditiously as feasible, but no later than 10 months from the date of this Order and no later than 2 years after each future decennial census. . . .
3. State officials administering state and federal programs providing grant and loan aid and technical assistance to municipalities and counties for open space preservation, sewerage improvements, community development, local program managment and comprehensive planning, housing development and demonstration projects, housing finance, interlocal services; and the construction, repair, and maintenance of municipal and county roads and bridges; local street lighting projects, and programs supporting public transportation shall, in accordance with existing law and for purposes of providing incentive aid consistent with the objectives of this Executive Order, give priority where appropriate to municipalities which are meeting or are in the process of meeting a fair share of low- and moderate- income housing needs. . . .[112]

---

110. *See* Rose & Levin, *What is a "Developing Municipality" Within the Meaning of the Mount Laurel Decision?*, 4 Real Est. L.J. 359 (1976); Ackerman, *The Mount Laurel Decision: Expanding the Boundaries of Zoning Reform*, 1976 U. Ill. L.F. 1.

111. 336 A.3d at 732–33 n.22.

112. State of New Jersey Executive Order No. 35 §§ 1, 2, 12 (April 2, 1976). Section 12 continues:

State officials participating in regional planning activities and regional clearinghouse review and comment decisions on municipal and county applications for federal funding shall take into account whether a municipality or group of municipalities is meeting or in the process of meeting a fair share of low- and moderate-income housing. Any municipality in which a disproportionately large share of low- and moderate-income households resides and which is making an effort to improve housing conditions shall not be assigned a lower priority under the provisions of this section.

Id. A lawsuit has since been filed by seventeen Republican assembly members challenging the governor's authority to impose restrictions on state aid to communities that refuse to accept lower income housing, pursuant to the executive order. The Potomac Institute, Metropolitan Housing Program Memorandum 77-2 at 9 (February 11, 1977).

In November 1976 the New Jersey Division of State and Regional Planning released a draft report in compliance with the executive order, outlining housing allocations for each community in New Jersey.[113] The following month the governor issued a new executive order calling for further study of the recently released housing allocation goals "to assure that they take into account current programs designed to revitalize the cities of New Jersey, including such programs as neighborhood preservation and urban economic development programs; redevelopment possibilities for the more developed municipalities of New Jersey. . . ."[114] The governor contended that the plan had placed too much emphasis on new construction rather than on rehabilitation, and in some instances had overburdened communities with insufficient vacant land.[115] December 1977 was set as the deadline for the revised plan.[116] The New Jersey situation is illustrative of the problem of implementing local housing requirements mandated by higher authorities.

In fragmented metropolitan areas there is a danger that mandatory local housing elements will not respond adequately to regional housing needs. This problem can be remedied through a statutory declaration of state and regional housing needs that would take into account the varying capacities of local governments to provide for housing. Sophisticated formulas for determining such capacity have already been developed by numerous regional planning bodies in their fair-share housing allocation plans. State legislation might provide a basis for integrating the regional fair-share housing plans already developed by areawide agencies. It has been suggested further that the California experience demonstrates that some local jurisdictions have engaged in housing planning only because they have been required by law to do so; but their capacity to plan in general has been strengthened as a result.[117]

The matter of implementation and enforcement of state housing planning requirements presents additional problems. Local governments still have the major control over housing; this local control should be retained where it does not adversely affect overall state goals and regional responsibility. There are three basic ways of en-

113. A Statewide Housing Allocation Plan for New Jersey (Preliminary Draft for Public Discussion, November 1976).
114. State of New Jersey Executive Order No. 46 (December 8, 1976).
115. Press Release, Office of the Governor, December 8, 1976.
116. It has been noted that the December 1977 deadline set by the executive order is one month after the November 1977 New Jersey gubernatorial election. 4 Hous. & Dev. Rep. 666 (1976).
117. Conversation between the commission staff and commission member Pete Wilson, Mayor of San Diego, California, August 1976.

couraging local governments to undertake compliance with state plans or to prepare their own: (1) by giving bonuses or incentives for compliance; (2) by providing penalties for failure to comply; and (3) by direct intervention by the state.

With respect to bonuses, the state distributes various monies to local governments for transportation purposes, schools, public utilities, and a variety of other specified purposes. Sometimes monies are for unspecified or only generally defined purposes. The state could set aside bonus amounts to be distributed only to those local governments that comply with state housing legislation. As residential development for families does place burdens on local governments, state grant formulas could take this factor into account, and attempt to minimize or eliminate any burdens to local governments incurred through complying with state requirements. There are also state discretionary funds available under federal block grant programs that could be used for this purpose.

Leveling of penalties would be politically difficult. However, the state could withhold certain state-grant or state-shared revenues from municipalities that failed to comply. It could rule out any open-space grants, or refuse to undertake certain public works or other programs in areas not meeting housing requirements, as New Jersey has done by executive order.[118] The state could also act as a developer or allocator of rent subsidies in such areas, or take direct zoning action in areas that did not act to adequately meet housing goals, as is done in Massachusetts.

Under the Massachusetts Zoning Appeals Law,[119] enacted in 1969, specified housing sponsors (limited-dividend, nonprofit, or public agencies) of low- or moderate-income housing can apply to the local zoning board for a comprehensive development permit. If the permit is denied or unreasonably constrained, the developer may appeal to a state board—the Housing Appeals Committee of the Department of Community Affairs. If the local government does not grant a permit, and has not met its defined quota of such housing, the state board can override the local board. The quota or share of need is satisfied by a local government if 10 percent of the units are already low- and moderate-income; or if 1.5 percent of the land zoned for residential, commercial, or industrial use is occupied by low- and moderate-income housing; or if, in one calendar year, 0.3 percent of such zoned land is proposed for development of low- and moderate-income housing.

118. *See* text accompanying note 112 *supra.* Other such strategies are discussed in L. Rubinowitz, Low-Income Housing: Suburban Strategies (1974).
119. Mass. Gen. Laws. Ann. ch. 40B, § 30-23.

To date, the Zoning Appeals Law has not resulted in the production of substantial amounts of housing.[120] In large measure this is a result of initial administrative hesitancy pending a test of the law's constitutionality (the act was finally upheld in 1973).[121] Even then, since the appeals procedure is subject to court review, a steady stream of dilatory litigation at virtually every instance of administrative override has impeded progress under the act. Moreover, another barrier was created by the subsequent passage of state environmental laws creating new requirements not covered in the comprehensive permit.[122]

Another example of potential state involvement in the implementation of local housing plans is contained in provisions of the American Law Institute's *Model Land Development Code*. The many innovative features of this document are discussed in detail throughout this book, but of particular interest is the section dealing with "Developments of Regional Benefit."[123] Just as a State Land Planning Agency may, under the Code, designate Developments of Regional Impact[124] and establish standards with which local decisions affecting those developments must comply, the same applies to Developments of Regional Benefit. The latter concern types of development that typically provide benefits to an area beyond the boundaries of a single local government, and that may cause some problems within a local community. Housing for persons of low- and moderate-income is designated as such a development.[125]

Housing Planning at the Regional Level

Two types of regional agencies are involved in housing planning: (1) councils of government, which are voluntary organizations of public officials and local governments created by interlocal agreement or state enabling legislation; and (2) regional planning commissions, which are multijurisdictional agencies created by state legislatures to carry out comprehensive areawide planning. Much attention has been given to the need for planning that crosses municipal boundaries, including federal support through the 701 program. However, few metropolitan units of government have a sufficient legal-political base to implement these efforts.

120. The latest published figures are provided in the lengthier discussion of the Massachusetts program, in Chapter 7 *infra*.

121. Board of Appeals of Hanover v. Housing Appeals Committee, 294 N.E.2d 393 (Mass. 1973).

122. Other defects of the Massachusetts statute are discussed in Chapter 7 *infra*.

123. ALI Code, *supra* note 39, at § 7-301.

124. *Id.*

125. *Id.* at § 7-301(4)(d).

The A-95 review process, for example, is (or could be) a significant planning tool for regional agencies,[126] yet due to their cooperative base and sensitive political dependence, most regional agencies have reduced this review authority to a paper-shuffling process. Consequently, although federal requirements encourage housing planning on a regional basis, these agencies are generally too weak to pursue housing policies that threaten the constituent communities.

The housing planning effort most commonly associated with regional agencies is the fair-share, or allocation, plan. Housing allocation plans have played a key role in defining housing planning not only for planning agencies but for counties and states as well. The housing allocation plan has been described as:

> an attempt to distribute future housing units throughout a jurisdiction in such a way as to balance overconcentration of such units in some areas with available resources in other areas for receiving them. The plan is generally applied to low- and moderate-income units and/or publicly subsidized units to be distributed in a manner that promotes equal opportunities for low- and moderate-income households in making locational choices.[127]

Surveys of housing need, housing market analyses, studies of housing location or site-selection standards, and even studies of jobs/housing balance, are important components of a housing allocation plan.

The first housing allocation model was developed by the Miami Valley Regional Planning Commission (Ohio) as a part of its housing element. It was accepted and promoted by HUD as a means of satisfying the housing element requirement of the 701 program. It is important to realize that the allocation plan was only a part of a much more comprehensive planning effort on the part of Miami Valley. In its housing plan summary the Miami Valley Regional Planning Commission states well its broader planning aims:

> It is important to understand . . . that expanding the lower-income housing supply is just one part of the comprehensive Regional Housing Program. The provision of physical shelter alone is recognized as an incomplete approach to solving housing problems, a fact that has been demonstrated many times in recent decades. For this reason, it is the responsibility of the MVRPC and its staff to carry out a comprehensive effort that addresses the many concerns related to housing itself. During the four and one half years of the program, a substantial number of components have been incorporated that broaden and strengthen it.[128]

126. *See* text accompanying note 54 *supra*.
127. In-Zoning, *supra* note 12, at 153–54.
128. Miami Valley Regional Plan Commission, Housing for the Miami Valley Region: A Regional Plan and Program—A Summary 1 (1974).

Because of its special treatment by HUD in the allotment housing subsidies, the Miami Valley plan met some measure of success. Subsequent efforts by other regional agencies have fallen short, some because of the lack of housing subsidies, others due to the inherent weaknesses of the agencies themselves. This has not been the case for the Twin Cities Metropolitan Council in Minnesota which, as a legislative-created agency with actual power and a tax base, produced a regional housing plan that resulted in the allocation of low- and moderate-income units. Yet its efforts, too, were impeded by the moratorium on federal subsidies.

Had there not been a moratorium on federal subsidies in January 1973, it is possible that many of the regional allocation plans would have produced more significant results. One study has analyzed three allocation plans adopted before the 1973 moratorium.[129] It found that suburban participation in low- and moderate-income housing development had begun to increase, that more such housing was being produced, and that it was distributed on a wider geographical basis than before. When viewed against the total supply of low- and moderate-income housing, the impact was negligible: most public and subsidized housing was still concentrated in central cities. Nevertheless, the plans are generally regarded as the singular most successful effort to date to increase housing opportunities for lower income households throughout a metropolitan region.

The need for housing allocation planning developed from the exclusionary actions of many communities toward low- and moderate-income housing. For many years suburban communities have refused to build public housing or to accommodate the private developers who might want to undertake subsidy programs. Under the programs developed in the 1968 Housing Act, federal subsidies became more plentiful, and the programs were attractive to more developers. The restrictive nature of some government actions became more apparent as these projects were proposed. While most central cities did have public housing and subsidy programs, some confined such housing to areas already concentrated with low- and moderate-income households. With plentiful subsidies, however, the possibility of wider distribution was possible.

Allocation plans have concentrated on distributing either shares of available federal subsidies or portions of the regional housing need. Very often the need has been defined as a portion of new housing construction possible within a designated time period. The plans to date have concentrated on housing for low- and moderate-income groups. It is possible, however, to develop an allocation for any

129. In-Zoning, *supra* note 12, at 163–69.

portion of housing need. It requires only the quantification of some housing goals and the distribution of that number throughout a housing market area or region.

Nevertheless, given the limitations of the plans, they have achieved prominence in housing planning. HUD, still short of mandating them, will consider them, where they exist, as a guide for distributing Section 8 contract authority,[130] and as a component of the required HAP. The courts have often looked to regional fair-share plans as a means of evaluating a locality's zoning patterns. The effectiveness of these plans is limited to the vigor of implementation efforts, to acceptance within the region, to cooperation from funding sources, and to the actions of builders.

The Housing Opportunity Plan (HOP) concept, recently developed by HUD, is the closest the Department has come to endorsing allocation plans. HUD has developed a program whereby bonus Section 8 housing funds, and in some cases additional Comprehensive Planning Assistance (701) funds, are available to communities within a region where a Housing Opportunity Plan has been approved by HUD. In order for the plan to be acceptable it must be a "system for allocating housing assistance which provides for greater housing opportunities for lower income households outside areas of undue concentrations of low income households." A majority of jurisdictions within the area must agree to the plan. The plan must assess housing needs on an areawide basis, and for each jurisdiction it must establish numerical goals for the distribution of lower income housing. The plan must be used in the A-95 review of applications.[131]

The first set of awards went to seven regional planning agencies: Joint Planning Commission of Lehigh and Northampton counties, Pennsylvania; Metropolitan Council of the Twin Cities area, Minnesota; Metropolitan Washington Council of Governments; Regional Planning Commission of Miami Valley, Ohio; Puget Sound, Washington Council of Governments; Southern California Association of Governments; and Southern Iowa Council of Governments.

FORMULATING A HOUSING ALLOCATION PLAN

The Underlying Concept

The purpose of an allocation plan is to expand housing choices and opportunities throughout a geographic region. It is a conscious effort to quantify housing goals and distribute them in a region or

130. *See* note 131 *infra*, and accompanying text.
131. 41 Fed. Reg. 25982 (June 23, 1976).

housing market. The assumption underlying an allocation plan is that every jurisdiction within a region has a responsibility to assume a fair share of housing required to meet the needs of the region. It is an attempt to equalize (or to move toward equalizing) the provision of housing throughout a region. The distribution considers the capacity and the responsibility of political subdivisions within a region to absorb housing.

Without quantification of goals, it is unlikely that governments will work to accomplish housing objectives. Without the cooperation of all units of government in a metropolitan area, the likelihood of satisfying housing needs is seriously curtailed. In essence these plans seek three objectives: (1) to expand available housing supply; (2) to increase geographical dispersal of housing opportunities; and (3) to promote cooperation in meeting these needs by local units of government.

Housing allocation plans do not produce housing, they do not identify specific sites for housing, and they provide no assurance that funds will be forthcoming. So they are not self-implementing. Since the adoption of the first of these plans in 1970, many have been produced, and shelved, with little effort and perhaps no intent to use them even as guidelines for future low- and moderate-income housing. Political commitment, involvement and cooperation is absolutely essential for allocation plans to be implemented.

Housing plans are important, but they are not enough. It is also necessary to have housing strategies that complement the plans with strong implementation commitments. Such housing strategies should include not only planning and programming but also ongoing monitoring, evaluation, and revision to ensure that the plans are kept current and are effectively implemented. Although most allocation plans have been undertaken by regional agencies, they can be formulated for any level of government. The process is much the same, whether done by a state, region, or locality. A state would probably have several housing market areas within its boundaries; a regional plan would probably define itself as the market area; and a local government would define an area beyond its own boundary limitations as the market area.

The steps in an allocation model are not always explicit, but there are generally eight steps involved:

1. Defining the structure of government in the area.
2. Defining the housing market area (or areas) to be considered.
3. Defining needs and goals.
4. Establishing the distribution process.

5. Establishing the criteria for distribution.
6. Finding adequate measures of the criteria.
7. Deriving the formula for utilizing the criteria and measures.
8. Implementing the allocation developed.

Example of an Allocation

It is easier to understand the process of housing allocation when illustrated by an example. It also becomes apparent that there are infinite combinations of criteria, measures, and applications that can be utilized. The example here is a simple one: it assumes that the allocation is done by a regional agency, either independently or as part of an overall state approach.

The region given as an example is comprised of four counties, each of which contains several municipalities. The region contains a total of 500,000 households. The four-county region defines itself as the housing market area. After surveying housing needs, the regional agency sets a goal of attaining 10,000 units of low- and moderate-income housing within the next four years. This would be an annual addition for low- and moderate-income households of 0.5 percent per year—relatively modest, but considerable in view of the current housing situation. It determined that such housing can be provided by Section 8 contracts, shares of community development block grants, and mobile homes, depending upon the desires of the individual communities.

The agency establishes a two step distribution process, first to counties, and then within counties to the municipalities or unincorporated areas. The first allocation to the counties is done with the assumption that every county should have an amount of low- and moderate-income housing in proportion to its share of the regtional or housing market area households. Table 6–5 illustrates this distribution. Each county is given a share of the 10,000 unit goal in proportion to its share of households. County *A* contains 40 percent of the housing market area households, and is therefore given 40 percent of the housing goal—or 4,000 units—as its fair share for the four-year period.

From the county to the governmental subdivisions within the county, the agency selects a more complex allocation procedure (although it could reasonably repeat the same process). Within each county it further allocates units to the political subdivisions on the basis of four measures: (1) the number of poverty households; (2) the fiscal capacity of the units of government; (3) the households in each area; and (4) the areas' current amount of assisted housing. These reflect the criteria outlined previously, with the first measuring

Table 6-5. Example of an Allocation Process: Distributing Regional Goals to Counties

Counties in Region or Housing Market Area	Households (Number)[a]	Households (Percent)[c]	Proportion of Housing Goal[d]
County A	200,000	40.0%	4,000
County B	150,000	30.0	3,000
County C	50,000	10.0	1,000
County D	100,000	20.0	2,000
Total region	500,000[b]	100.0	10,000 units[e]

[a] Number of households in each county.
[b] Total households in region or housing market.
[c] a ÷ b.
[d] c × e.
[e] Goal established for region.

need; the second, capacity; the third, size of community; and the fourth, previous housing effort. Other criteria could easily be substituted for those illustrated here. By adding more complex variables and components, the allocation formula can become more sophisticated. Alternatively, fewer criteria could be used, resulting in a more simplified, but nonetheless adequate, system.

Poverty Households. The degree of local need can be measured by any number of criteria; and the measure can be used directly or inversely. Here, because other measures are used to equalize the distribution, the measure works toward providing housing assistance in the areas where it is needed. Often this is necessary to gain political acceptance for an allocation formula. The example proceeds with allocation within County A. It contains three incorporated areas, and the balance of the county, which is unincorporated. The three municipalities and balance of the county each receive a share of the county's 4,000 unit allocation based on this measure. (*See* Table 6-6).

Fiscal Capacity. Fiscal capacity is one measure of the suitability or capability of an area to absorb additional housing. Other measures, such as school capacity or service ability, could also be used. The use of property assessment, particularly if it is computed at a true rather than assessed value, is usually a good measure. Total assessed value can be used, as can a per capita tax-base computation. Tax rates per se are not adequate indicators, as they can mean either a

Table 6-6. Poverty Households

Example	Number of Poverty Households[a]	Percent of County[c]	Share of County A[d]
Municipality # 1	15,000	50.0%	2,000 units
" # 2	4,000	13.3	532
" # 3	6,000	20.0	800
Balance of county	5,000	16.7	668
Total County *A*	30,000[b]	100.0	4,000 units[e]

[a] Census data.
[b] Total for county.
[c] a ÷ b.
[d] c × e.
[e] County assigned goal.

high level of service or an inadequate tax base. Here the measure used is the true property valuation in various parts of the county, and units are allocated in proportion to their share of the county base (see Table 6-7).

Households in Area. The number of households in an area is an indicator of demand. The underlying assumption of equalizing the share is that every area should have an equal proportion of housing units for low- and moderate-income households. In this example the goal is allocated to each area in proportion to the total number of households (see Table 6-8).

Previous Housing Effort. This is a measure which takes into account the previous efforts of the communities in providing housing for low- and moderate-income groups. The application of the measure assumes that each jurisdiction should have a share of assisted housing proportional to its total households, as the example in Table 6-8. In this application, the newly assigned goal is added to the current existing total, and these are distributed in proportion to the households. The difference between what a community has and what it should have becomes the basis for this allocation. Any number of criteria can be incorporated into an allocation model. Any number of measures can be utilized to apply the criteria, and this includes the manner in which the measure is used to produce an allocation. (See Table 6-9.)

Table 6-7. Fiscal Capacity

Example	True Property Valuation (in millions)[a]	Record of County Property[c] (percent)	Share of County Allocation[d]
Municipality #1	$1,600	26.7%	1,068
" #2	500	8.3	332
" #3	600	10.0	400
Balance of county	3,300	55.0	2,200
Total County *A*	$6,000[b]	100.0	4,000[e]

[a] Property valuation of areas.
[b] Total for county.
[c] a ÷ b.
[d] e × c.
[e] County assigned goal.

Table 6-8. Households in Area

Example	Households: (Number)[a]	Households: (Percent)[b]	Share of Allocation[d]
Municipality #1	80,000	40.0%	1,600 units
" #2	20,000	10.0	400
" #3	25,000	12.5	500
Balance of county	75,000	37.5	1,500
Total County *A*	200,000[b]	100.0	4,000 units[e]

[a] Census data or some other estimate.
[b] County total.
[c] a ÷ b.
[d] c × e.
[e] County assigned goal.

The usual way of considering all the measures or criteria together to produce a final allocation is to average them, either with or without assigning weights to them. This is illustrated below, where each of the four measures is assigned a weight, according to its importance in the consideration of those doing the allocation: "poverty households" is given a weight of 1; "fiscal capacity" is given a weight of 2; "households" is given a weight of 3; and "previous housing effort" is given a weight of 1. Each allocation developed earlier is multiplied by its weight, all of the totals are added together and then divided by 7, which is the total of the weights given the allocations. The final num-

Table 6-9. Previous Housing Effort

Example	Existing Number of Assisted Units[a]	Percent of County Households[c]	Total Equalized Share[d]	Difference of Share[f]
Municipality #1	3,500	40.0%	3,600	100
" #2	500	10.0	900	400
" #3	400	12.5	1,125	725
Balance of county	600	37.5	3,375	2,775
Total County A	5,000[b]	100.0	9,000[e]	4,000[g]

[a] Existing assisted housing for low and moderate income groups.
[b] Total for county.
[c] Percent of households.
[d] c × c.
[e] b + g.
[f] d – a.
[g] Assigned county goal.

ber then represents the allocation for the portion of the county for the four-year time period. (Allocation plans can be developed utilizing more sophisticated statistical procedures for determining the allocation.)

In this instance, the way in which the area meets its allocation is determined by the unit of government itself. As pointed out earlier these can be met by Section 8 housing, a share of block grants, or accommodations for mobile homes. A community might develop some other strategy for meeting its goal, as long as it resulted in additional housing for low- and moderate-income households. (See Table 6-10.)

CONCLUSION

This chapter has covered several aspects of the housing problem, with a specific focus on the essential elements of housing planning. If there is any overriding point to be made, it is that housing planning is not to be viewed as merely another bureaucratic mandate, but rather as an activity that is vital to the health of local governments and the regions in which they exist. The plans, of course, will not build houses; nor can they have meaning in the absence of a wide array of public and private commitments to equal housing opportunity. Nevertheless, given the enormous complexity of the housing process and the web of social, economic, and political factors related to

Table 6-10. Example of an Allocation Process: Distribution from County to Areas Within

Area	Allocations based on Criteria and Measures					
	Poverty Households $\times 1^a$	*Fiscal Capacity* $\times 2^b$	*Households* $\times 3^c$	*Previous Housing* $\times 1^d$	*Sum of Allocations^e*	*Final Allocations*
Municipality # 1	2,000	2,136	4,800	100	9,036	1,291
" # 2	532	664	1,200	400	2,796	400
" # 3	800	800	1,500	725	3,825	546
Balance of county	668	4,400	4,500	2,775	12,343	1,763
Total County *A*	4,000	8,000	12,000	4,000	28,000	4,000^g

^{a} Poverty household allocation $\times$ 1.
^{b} Fiscal capacity allocation $\times$ 2.
^{c} Household allocation $\times$ 1.
^{d} Previous housing allocation $\times$ 1.
^{e} (a + b) $\div$ (c + d).
^{f} e $\div$ 7 (sum of weights for allocations).
^{g} Assigned county goal.

housing, it is essential that local governments assess their own needs as well as cooperate in a regional effort to balance the housing supply.

Other chapters in this book have pointed out developments in the law that will increase the importance of active housing planning. As local governments are required to conduct their land-use procedures with greater fairness and rationality and to base their decisions on a plan that is a valid expression of the condition, goals, and capabilities of the community, then housing plans, as part of a process of comprehensive planning, will play an important role in justifying local actions. The evolving concept of the "regional general welfare" will, moreover, necessitate local and regional plans that provide a solid basis for the application of such a legal doctrine.

Finally, as other significant national issues such as energy conservation, environmental protection, and fiscal stability become more a part of the decisionmaking process at the local level, it will be essential for local governments and their constituents to be able to continually balance these larger concerns with the fundamentally human issue of adequate housing for all.

POLICY STATEMENTS

1. Decent and affordable housing is one of the most important elements in the lives of American citizens. The realization of such housing will not occur without both private and public intervention. To this end, governments at all levels should engage in and coordinate housing planning and implementation efforts.

2. Housing planning should be mandated by state statutes as an essential element of a community's comprehensive plan. It involves planning for all economic segments of a community, particularly low- and moderate-income households.

3. In exercising their police powers, local governments, at a minimum, have an affirmative legal duty to: (a) plan for present and prospective housing in a regional context; (b) eliminate those local regulatory barriers that do not make it realistically possible to provide housing for persons of low-and moderate-income; and (c) offer incentives to the private sector in this regard.

4. In developing their housing plans, governments should consider regional housing circumstances and needs, and should formulate affirmative goals and action programs that are responsive to regional housing considerations. A municipality's housing plan must be assessed in the context of the region within which it is situated, to determine whether the community is responsive to housing needs of poorer households.

5. State statutes, in mandating housing plans, should specify process and procedural considerations as well as goals to be achieved and obligations to be attained (*e.g.*, quantified regional and local housing needs). In fragmented metropolitan areas there is a danger that mandatory local housing elements will be deficient in responding to regional housing needs. This problem can be remedied through a statutory declaration of state and regional housing needs, which would take into account the varying capacities of local governments to provide for housing.

6. Housing plans at the local, regional, state, and federal levels should be coordinated to effectively achieve a hierarchy of established goals and objectives. However, local governments should retain the major control over housing as long as local control is not abusive of overall state goals and regional responsibilities.

7. Housing plans should include specific implementation actions that are clearly related to the assessment of needs, opportunities,

resources, likely achievements, and other human and community development objectives. Moreover, housing plans should be formulated as comprehensive housing strategies that involve citizen groups, business and labor leaders, and public officials interacting as part of an explicit, systematic, and on-going process of education, consensus, monitoring, goal-setting, programming, action, and evaluation.

8. It is important that local governments deal with impediments to housing opportunity that are within their respective spheres of influence (*e.g.*, land-use controls, building codes, etc.), and then cooperate in a metropolitan or regional effort to assess and balance the needs of neighboring jurisdictions. Adequate implementation of such housing planning requires government and private sector cooperation at all levels, sufficient funding, and other technical assistance.

9. For purposes of judicial review, courts should examine the housing plans of municipalities and regional agencies. Where such plans are deemed adequate and fairly designed, they should be given great weight in determining both the housing obligations of the community as well as in aiding the defense against challenges of exclusionary land use.

10. Housing planning should specifically address the needs of low- and moderate-income households because:

a. Changing economic and social conditions have increased the number of households in this category.
b. A balanced housing supply is essential to the future vitality of metropolitan areas.
c. Suburban opposition to low- and moderate-income housing is so intense that without specific planning this goal will not be achieved.

Chapter 7

State and Local Roles in Housing and Community Development

INTRODUCTION

Preceding chapters have focused principally on reforming legal doctrines, administrative procedures, and planning practices relating to traditional land-use controls. While such reforms can be counted on to promote greater rationality and equity in the growth management process, they cannot in and of themselves provide adequate housing for those in need. If we are to meet our housing goals and needs, much more active effort and cooperation on the part of state and local governments and the private sector is essential. Such actions, and their legal underpinnings, are the basic concern of this chapter.

At the outset it must be noted that many of the most fundamental issues concerning housing are beyond the control of state and local governments. Only the federal government has the resources and authority to affect capital formation, interest rates, the availability of mortgage capital, and to influence the distribution of incomes. Moreover, federal policies designed to slow inflation, lower unemployment, and encourage increased rates of economic growth all profoundly influence levels of housing production. In short, the federal government has the primary resources for strengthening and facilitating the private sector's efforts in providing housing to those able to afford it and providing assistance for those forced to spend too much for housing. To date, however, housing—and particularly lower income housing—has not ranked high among national priorities. The United States does not now have and has never had a coherent housing policy.[1]

The Advisory Commission believes that the federal government must give housing a much higher priority than it has in the past. The Commission agrees with both the Council of State Governments and the National League of Cities that a national housing policy should be established to coordinate economic policies and other federal actions to bring about a greater volume and continuity of production, both in the private market and under public programs.[2] Further, efficient housing assistance programs for lower income families should be funded at higher levels to encourage new construction, rehabilitation, and maintenance, in both the suburbs and the cities.

At the same time the federal government must continue its responsibility for ensuring that federal dollars be used to further the goals and national objectives that Congress has developed in over thirty years of housing and community development legislation. It is beyond the scope of this book to make specific recommendations about federal fiscal and monetary policies, the form of federal housing assistance, or the manner of federal control over local expenditures of federal funds. Rather, the emphasis of this chapter is placed on strengthening the capacities of state and local governments to carry out federal programs and to undertake their own programs to meet regional and local needs.

The states have a variety of powers at their disposal for increasing the availability of decent and affordable housing. As the New York

1. The history of the federal government's role in housing from the enactment of the original National Housing Act of 1934 to the present is intricate and tangled. The nation's housing laws today are a complex maze of accumulated authorizations for over 60 programs, embodied in hundreds of pages of statutes, and replete with inconsistencies, obsolete provisions, conflicting objectives, and a total lack of a coordinated structure or overall design. The following studies trace the history of federal housing programs and provide analyses of their strengths and weaknesses from a variety of perspectives: National Commission on Urban Problems, Building the American City (G.P.O. 1968) [hereinafter cited as Building the American City]; Department of Housing and Urban Development, Housing in the Seventies: A Report of the National Housing Policy Review (G.P.O. 1974) [hereinafter cited as Housing in the Seventies]; Subcommittee on Housing and Community Development, House Committee on Banking, Currency and Housing, Evaluation of the Role of the Federal Government in Housing and Community Development (G.P.O. 1975); U.S. Commission on Civil Rights, Twenty Years After Brown: Equal Opportunity in Housing (G.P.O. 1975). More scholarly treatments of selected federal housing programs and policies can be found in H. Aaron, Housing and Subsidies: Who Benefits from Federal Housing Policies? (1972); A. Solomon, Housing the Urban Poor: A Critical Evaluation of Federal Housing Policy (1974).

2. See Council of State Governments, State Growth Management 57-58 (Lexington, Ky. 1976); National League of Cities, National Municipal Policy 1976, at 40-41 (Washington, D.C., December 1975).

State Court of Appeals explained in 1936, in upholding the nation's first public housing program:

> The fundamental purpose of government is to protect the health, safety, and general welfare of the public. . . . Its power plant for the purpose consists of *the power of taxation, the police power,* and *the power of eminent domain.* Whenever there arises, in the state, a condition of affairs holding a substantial menace to the public health, safety, general welfare, it becomes the duty of the government to apply whatever power is necessary and appropriate to check it. . . . [I]t seems to be constitutionally immaterial whether one or another of the sovereign powers is employed. [Emphasis added.][3]

In the past, however, beyond passing enabling legislation that allowed local governments to establish housing authorities or urban renewal agencies, or that delegated state police powers over zoning, building, and housing codes to the cities, most states have played a minor and passive role in housing their people. Only recently have the states, making use of their superior taxing power, fiscal stability, and greater access to the national bond markets, acted to stimulate housing through a variety of financing and taxation programs. Recently, too, the states have begun to act to assure that localities do not abuse their state delegated regulatory powers or that the private sector does not deny, through antiquated landlord-tenant laws or discriminatory lending practices, equal opportunities and choice for decent housing.

In spite of the significant expansion of activity in housing and community development, progress among the states has been very uneven. Since local governments possess no powers other than those expressly authorized by the states,[4] most of the reforms treated in

3. New York City Housing Authority v. Muller, 270 N.Y. 33, 34, 41 N.E.2d 153, 155 (1936).

4. In discussing local government's role in promoting housing opportunity, it is important to recognize that the powers and authority of local government in different states vary considerably. In all 50 states the relationship of local government to that of the state is defined by the state constitution and statutes; and in all the states, local governments have only the powers granted them by the states—they have no inherent power. Direct constitutional or statutory limitations on a local government's ability to act are expressed in terms of the permissible structure and organization of local government, on the range of powers, and on the scope of their fiscal power (*e.g.,* through limiting type and amount of taxes that may be levied and the amount of debt that may be incurred). *See* F. Michelman & T. Sandalow, Materials on Government in Urban Areas ch. 2 (1970) for a thorough selection of cases and materials dealing with the distribution of power between state and local government units.

It is generally agreed that state constitutional and statutory limitations on local governments have inhibited the solution of urban problems in most states. *See* Grad, *Urban Needs and State Response: Local Government Reorganization,* in The States and Urban Crisis 27 (A. Campbell ed. 1970); Committee

this chapter involve state legislative action. Moreover, in view of the serious economic condition of cities throughout the nation,[5] we will focus on ways in which they can more creatively and effectively make use of available federal and state resources. The methods by which localities can promote housing opportunity through local land-use controls such as planned unit developments, special permits, transfer of development rights, density bonuses, and so on, and through more affirmative housing planning, are dealt with in Chapters 4 and 6.

While this chapter cannot recapitulate all possible housing and community development strategies, it does attempt to examine a number of actions which, if properly employed, can be effective in promoting decent housing. The chapter is organized into two parts. The first deals with facilitating housing (by increasing the stock of decent housing or lowering its costs) through financing, taxation, and eminent domain. The second part is concerned with selected government regulatory actions which can either remove impediments to housing development and opportunity, or require the inclusion of lower income housing to meet regional housing needs.

PART I
FACILITATING HOUSING AND COMMUNITY DEVELOPMENT THROUGH FINANCING, TAXATION, AND EMINENT DOMAIN

HOUSING AS A PUBLIC PURPOSE: THE THRESHOLD TEST

Although the difficulties of providing adequate housing cannot be decided purely in financial terms, there is no doubt that the housing

on Government Operations, Unshackling Local Government: A Survey of Proposals by the Advisory Commission on Intergovernmental Relations, 90th Cong., 2d Sess. (1968).

Moreover, constitutional or statutory provisions on home rule powers—encompassing the range of permissible activities of local government and the range of allotted municipal powers—differ significantly from state to state in the manner in which such powers are granted and defined. *See* Sandalow, *The Limits of Municipal Powers Under Home Rule: A Role for the Courts*, 48 Minn. L. Rev. 643 (1969).

5. A recent survey of cities with 30,000 population or more, undertaken by the U.S. Conference of Mayors, revealed "a new economic crisis facing America's cities . . . [which] is national in scope. It includes small and large cities as well as central, suburban and sunbelt region cities." Reflected in increasingly widening local revenue-expenditure gaps, the fiscal crisis confronting city governments was attributed primarily to inflation, unemployment, and an inadequate rate of economic growth—conditions largely outside local government control. U.S.

of the country's growing population cannot be accomplished without substantial infusions of public capital. This is true at the state as well as the federal level. To supplement and leverage federal moneys that are available, and to undertake new programs of their own, state and local governments must raise revenues, incur indebtedness, and make expenditures. Any such fiscal involvement in housing development is predicated on satisfying the threshold constitutional test that public funds be expended for only a valid public purpose. This limitation is either expressed[6] or implied[7] in all state constitutions.[8]

Although courts have often attempted to define and elucidate the term public purpose, its meaning eludes precise definition. Rather, public purpose is an expanding concept that changes with the social, political, and economic needs of the polity.[9] Appropriately, courts have given considerable latitude to the findings and declarations of the legislature,[10] but in testing the expenditure of public funds as a public purpose, courts have evolved certain general principles. All agree that the activity must: (1) benefit the community as a whole; (2) be directly related to the functions of government; and (3) not

Conference of Mayors, The 1976 Economic Report of American Cities: A Study of the Fiscal Problems of Cities in the United States (Prepared for the 44th Annual Meeting of the U.S. Conference of Mayors, June 26, 1976).

6. An example of an explicit public purpose clause is Alaska's: "No tax shall be levied, or appropriation of public money made, nor, public property transferred, nor shall the public credit be used, except for a public purpose." Alaska Const. art. IX, § 6.

7. Numerous state courts have construed specific constitutional gift and loan or credit restriction as simply codifications of the public purpose requirement. Thus, for example, the New Jersey Supreme Court in Roe v. Kervick, 42 N.J. 191, 199 A.2d 636 (1964), read a public purpose requirement into the following clause: "No donation of land or appropriation of money shall be made by the State or any county or municipal corporation to or for the use of any society, association or corporation whatever." N.J. Const. art. VII, § 3, para. 3.

8. The Fourteenth Amendment to the U.S. Constitution sets an outer limit to the uses that a state or its subdivisions may make of public funds or property. It is a violation of the due process clause for a state to use the power of taxation or eminent domain for private purposes. Carmichael v. Southern Coal and Coke Co., 301 U.S. 495, 514-18 (1937); Jones v. City of Portland, 254 U.S. 217 (1917). However, this federal test imposes no significant restriction on state action; it prevents only the "plain case of departure from every public purpose which [can] reasonably be conceived." Carmichael v. Southern Coal & Coke Co., 301 U.S. at 515. Thus no state decision on public purpose has ever been overruled by the Supreme Court.

9. "As the needs change, the area of permissible governmental activity must change to meet those needs." Roe v. Kervick, 42 N.J. 191, 208, 199 A.2d 834 (1964).

10. As the Supreme Court stated in the landmark case of Berman v. Barker, 348 U.S. 26, 32 (1954): "[S]ubject to specific constitutional limitations, when the legislature has spoken, the public purpose has been declared in terms well-nigh conclusive."

have as its primary objective the promotion of private ends (though private interests may derive an incidental benefit from the activity).[11]

The early court decisions addressing the issue of housing as a public purpose arose in the context of challenges to state enabling legislation authorizing the creation of public housing authorities. These local authorities developed, owned, and managed low-rent public housing for families "in the lowest income group."[12] For the most part they were financed under the United States Housing Act of 1937, which made federal assistance conditional on local cash contributions or tax exemptions. The act also required that new housing units built be matched by the removal of a "substantially equal number" of unsafe or unsanitary units by "demolition, condemnation, and effective closing," or rehabilitated by "compulsory repair or improvement."[13] This latter requirement, known as "equivalent elimination," firmly linked public housing with slum clearance, and was intended to avoid public housing competition with the private housing industry.

In uniformly upholding the public character of local housing projects, the courts relied heavily on the legislative findings that slum clearance and the provision of sanitary low-rent housing reduced crime and juvenile delinquency, improved general health conditions, reduced the cost to the public of police, fire, and health services, and prevented the spread of slums to other areas.[14] Decisions often stressed slum clearance rather than the housing purposes of such programs.[15] As the Supreme Judicial Court of Massachusetts stated in the 1939 case of *Allydonn Realty Corporation v. Holyoke Housing Authority*,[16] upholding the constitutionality of the state's Housing Authorities Law:

> The real purpose of the statute is therefore the elimination of slums and unsafe and unsanitary dwellings, and the provision by public funds of low-rent housing is only a means by which the main object is to be accomplished. The statute as a whole is designed to serve a public need, and the money expended for low-rent housing, as well as that expended for slum clearance, is for a public use.[17]

11. *See* City of Pipestone v. Madsen, 827 Minn. 357, 178 N.W.2d 594; O. Oldman & F. Schoettle, State & Local Taxes & Finance 789–92 (1974).

12. For a thorough description of the Housing Act of 1937 and subsequent public housing programs, *see* Building the American City, *supra* note 1, at 109–51.

13. *Id.*

14. *See* McDougal & Mueller, *Public Purpose in Public Housing: An Anachronism Reburied*, 52 Yale L.J. 42, 47–48 (1942).

15. *See* cases collected in Riesenfeld & Eastland, *Public Aid to Housing and Land Development*, 34 Min. L. Rev. 610, 635 (1950).

16. 23 N.E.2d 665 (1939).

17. *Id.* at 669.

Once slums were judicially recognized as a menace to the public health, safety, and welfare, government had wide discretion in seeking their eradication. The police power, eminent domain power, and the power to tax were all available.[18]

From the late 1930s through the 1950s, low-rent housing and slum clearance were upheld in nearly every state undertaking such programs.[19] And in the process, public housing enabling legislation was held not to contravene the variously phrased prohibitions against lending state credit for private activities, municipal debt limitations, home rule provisions, and the rule against delegation of legislative powers.[20] In the 1960s and 1970s, as housing problems intensified and affected larger segments of the population, state legislation and judicial review have focused less on slum clearance and more on direct assistance to those in need of adequate housing. While the slum clearance rationale has not been entirely abandoned by the courts, the public interest in assisting those unable to afford housing on the private market has become the dominant theme. Concomitantly, the doctrine of public purpose has been expanded to accommodate the burgeoning housing need and to facilitate more sophisticated public-private involvement.

Recent cases have often involved the provision of mortgage financing by state housing finance agencies, a subject discussed below. Like the local public housing authority, but with state-wide jurisdiction, the housing finance agency (HFA) is a public corporation that finances housing through the issuance of its own tax-exempt obligations. Unlike the public housing authority, the state HFA does not develop, own, or manage the housing it finances; nor does it acquire land or engage in slum clearance or redevelopment. Rather, with the proceeds of its bonds, the HFA makes below-market interest rate loans to qualified sponsors (or to lending institutions that in turn issue loans to qualified sponsors). The sponsors then construct, own, and operate their own housing, which is subject to agency regulation. The nature of HFA bond financing is such that without additional federal or state subsidies or guarantees, the agencies cannot serve the low-income families traditionally assisted by public housing. Consequently the HFAs have aimed at persons and families of moderate and middle incomes.

The creation of state HFAs has been based upon legislative findings, frequently supported by state housing surveys, declaring a critical shortage of housing "within the financial means of families and persons of low or moderate income." Persons of low- and moderate-

18. New York City Housing Authority v. Muller, 1 N.E.2d 153, 155 (1936). *See* quotation in text accompanying note 3 *supra.*
19. *See* cases collected in Riesenfeld & Eastland, *supra* note 15.
20. *Id.* at 635-37.

income are commonly defined as those "families and persons who cannot afford to pay the amounts at which private enterprise, without assisted mortgage financing, is providing a substantial supply of decent, safe, and sanitary housing."[21] The provision of such housing is determined essential to promote health, safety, and general welfare, to prevent the recurrence of slum conditions, to encourage the investment of private capital, to stimulate residential construction and employment, and to promote sound urban growth.

In addition, the statutes invariably include the finding that "private enterprise and investment, without the assistance contemplated . . . is not disposed to nor can it economically achieve the needed construction of decent, safe, and sanitary housing at rentals which persons and families of low and moderate income can afford. . . ."[22] This form of state aid represents a markedly different form of public involvement in housing. For one thing, state aid is not directed at the segment of the population that has traditionally been the recipient of public largesse. For another, in providing this assistance the state has entered into a financial venture that was once in the exclusive domain of the private sector. At the same time there is an increased reliance on the private sector to develop, own, and manage the assisted housing.

In uniformly upholding HFA legislation, the courts have addressed the public character of this evolving state intervention. Thus the Supreme Court of Pennsylvania in its 1973 decision in *Johnson v. Pennsylvania Housing Finance Agency* expressly rejected the contention that the Pennsylvania agency does not perform a public use because it embarks on a finance venture that was traditionally within the sphere of private enterprise.[23] The court said:

> It is no constitutional objection to the statute, nor does it derogate from the public character of its objective . . . that the Authority [Agency] will to some extent conduct what heretofore have been regarded as a private enterprise; to hold otherwise would mean that the State would be powerless, within constitutional limitation, to act in order to preserve the health and safety of its people even though such action were imperative and vital for the purpose.[24]

When the government wishes to enter a traditionally private sphere of enterprise, it does not always do so directly. The far more typical situation has been for the government to finance or otherwise aid

---

21. Ill. Rev. Stat. ch 67½, § 302(g).
22. *Id.* at § 303.
23. 309 A.2d 528, 534 n.4 (1973).
24. *Id.*

private instrumentalities in achieving a desired goal. This has been true since the first half of the nineteenth century when private companies were assisted by states and localities in building canals, bridges, and turnpikes. While the propriety of certain types of public-private involvement has had a somewhat tortuous legal history,[25] the issue is a continually recurring one.

While we live in a country where most people have a relatively restrained idea of what functions government should perform, these same people have nevertheless had strong opinions about the "public good" and how to promote it. The result has been a growing number of government programs in aid of our rather imprecise goal of the public good[26] —most of them promoted wholly or partially by private persons or concerns. These interests naturally hope to make money from their involvement, and usually do so, even if the public policy is of limited success or fails to meet rigorous cost-benefit scrutiny. It is this private profit that accrues as a result of a policy that is "public" that often leads to legal challenge.

In the field of housing finance, for example, private lenders and mortgagees are beneficiaries of federal and state housing programs. Not surprisingly, plaintiffs opposed to the programs have sought to make this fact serve as a basis of attack; and also not surprisingly they have been unsuccessful. The New Jersey Supreme Court in 1970 responded to the argument in the same fashion that American courts have responded to it for the better part of two centuries:

> Thus, the participating private lenders are more than mere borrowers; they become agencies which are required to implement the public purpose of the law, i.e., to issue new residential mortgages. Finally, any private gain by the mortgagees are merely incidental to the achievement of that purpose. Such incidental private benefit is permissible under our cases.[27]

The great majority of jurisdictions considering HFA statutes have had little difficulty in finding a public purpose in the financing of

25. Indeed, the public purpose requirement, commonplace in state constitutions and exemplified by the provisions in notes 6 and 7 *supra*, as well as state and local constitutional debt limitations, originated in the nineteenth century as a reaction to the failure of publicly financed railroads and canals. *See* Note, *Incentive to Industrial Relocation: The Municipal Industrial Bond Plans* 86 Harv. L. Rev. 898, 900–01 (1953); Pinsky, *State Constitutional Limitations on Public and Industrial Financing: An Historical and Economic Approach*, 111 U. Pa. L. Rev. 265 (1963).

26. *See generally* cases and materials relating to "The Relationship Between Public and Private Decision" collected in Michelman & Sandalow, *supra* note 4, at 33–110.

27. New Jersey Mortgage Assistance Agency v. McCrane, 267 A.2d 24, 29 (1970).

housing for moderate-income as well as low-income families otherwise unable to afford adequate housing. Times change, and doctrine evolves to keep pace. The need to provide housing assistance to other than low-income persons, said the Minnesota Supreme Court in 1973, is more a product of the changing conditions than of a change in the public nature of the activity:

> [W]hen . . . the cost of housing has risen so that even moderate-income families find themselves priced out of the housing market, it would seem that the instant case falls fully within the public purpose. . . .[28]

Numerous other courts have taken similar positions. The Vermont Supreme Court, for instance, simply said that "if the measures adopted by the General Assembly succeed in their objective to provide safe, adequate and sufficient housing, the general welfare of the State will be served."[29]

Those few jurisdictions that have not expressly held the provision of housing for moderate- and middle-income families per se to be a valid public purpose, have achieved the same results by relying on the older slum clearance and low-rent housing rationale. In *Massachusetts Housing Finance Agency v. New England Merchants National Bank of Boston,* the Supreme Judicial Court of Massachusetts held that providing mortgage financing at favorable interest rates for projects in which three-quarters of the tenants were of moderate or middle income was "only incidental to the primary objective, although contributing to its achievement."[30] That objective was the provision of housing for low-income families (the other one-quarter of the tenants in a project), and the prevention of slums.

The court reasoned that below-market interest rentals for moderate-income families would provide an inducement for such families to live in projects or neighborhoods with people of substantially lower income. An upward adjustment (or skewing) of rentals on these moderate-income units, moreover, would permit reduced rentals for the low-income units through an internal subsidy. The resultant "mixing of families of varied economic means," said the court, will "accomplish slum clearance more effectively and more permanently than in earlier subsidized public housing by avoiding undue concentration of low-income tenants and by achieving for

28. Minnesota Housing Finance Agency v. Hatfield, 210 N.W.2d 298, 306 (1973).
29. Vermont Home Mortgage Credit Agency v. Montpelier Nat'l Bank, 263 A.2d 445, 449 (1970).
30. 249 N.E.2d 599, 606 (1969).

such tenants 'exposure to and close contact in as many areas as possible with more successful members of society.'"[31]

The result of the case was that the Massachusetts court, despite its tenacious reliance on traditional slum clearance and prevention objectives, substantially broadened the scope of housing finance tools available to achieve those ends. The court upheld "rent skewing" and thereby sanctioned the agency's internal performance of an economic reallocation function conventionally in the domain of the legislature (and outside the traditional interests of the private sector).

The California Court of Appeals, an intermediate court, also relied on the slum clearance rationale in upholding a program under which *all* persons, not just persons of low and moderate incomes, are eligible for rehabilitation loans, provided that the residence is located within a specifically designated code enforcement area.[32] The court relied on several state and local legislative findings: (1) neighborhood deterioration and its attendant social and economic consequences cannot be arrested by presently existing means; (2) a joint private-public effort is essential to generate sufficient resources for effective rehabilitation; and (3) the more costly and socially disruptive remedy of slum clearance and redevelopment will ultimately be required if the designated areas continue to decline and decay.

The California court accordingly held that any benefit to private parties receiving loans is merely incidental to the primary public purpose of rehabilitation, and hence that the loans do not violate the constitutional prohibition against the giving or lending of public moneys or extending credit to private parties. It also rejected the contention that the loans would be a financial bonanza for absentee landlords who are capable of financing their own code compliance, saying that without the challenged program, the "redlining" of certain San Francisco neighborhoods would mean that alternative funds would either be unavailable or else available only on impractical terms.

Not all such cases have turned on the slum clearance rationale, however. The New Jersey Supreme Court, for example, upheld that state's plan to finance mortgages without regard to the mortgagor's income, and it did so on the basis of the general housing need.[33]

31. *Id.* at 605–06.

32. Board of Supervisors v. Dolan, 119 Cal. Rptr. 347 (1975), upholding the California Residential Rehabilitation Act, Cal. Health & Safety Code §§37910 *et seq.* (West 1973). The case involved a variation of HFA lending whereby cities and counties and their redevelopment agencies and housing authorities are empowered to issue tax-exempt revenue bonds and to lend the proceeds, in the form of long-term low-interest loans, to private parties to finance the rehabilitation of residential properties.

33. New Jersey Mortgage Finance Agency v. McCrane, 267 A.2d 24 (1970).

The New Jersey Mortgage Finance Agency Law provides for the direct channelling of the proceeds of the agency's revenue bonds into the private mortgage market by making loans to private lenders. The private lenders must in turn make loans "for new residential mortgages." The law is not limited to low- or moderate-income housing— in fact, it makes no recommendations as to its ultimate beneficiaries and places no dollar limit on any one loan.

In upholding the statute, the court concurred with the legislature's finding of a housing crisis, "a major cause of [which] is the lack of funds available to finance housing by the private mortgage lending institutions of the State."[34] This finding was supported by a report prepared by the state's Department of Community Affairs indicating that:

> the present housing production rate of about 47,500 new dwelling units per year must be more than doubled if the State's housing needs are to be met. The statewide vacancy rate has dropped to an estimated 1.1% with some northern cities well below the 1% mark even with sub-standard housing included in the estimates. The minimum acceptable rate is said to be 3% with a range of 4% to 6% "healthy." Housing choice is virtually nonexistent at rates below 2%.[35]

In these circumstances, the court concluded, "a program designed to increase housing production clearly satisfies the constitutional requirement of fostering a valid public purpose."[36]

The New Jersey decision and those from other states upholding the public purpose of state HFA laws, in exhibiting a more sophisticated understanding of today's housing problems, have paved the way for more innovative state and local housing programs that cannot be economically and socially accomplished by the private sector alone.

THE STATE ROLE IN HOUSING FINANCE AND DEVELOPMENT

The Advent of State Housing Finance and Development

The emergence of the states as a force in housing finance and development is a relatively recent phenomenon. While there have been a

34. *Id.* at 27.
35. *Id.* at 28.
36. *Id.* One commentator on the *McCrane* case has cautioned that as the definition of the public purpose is expanded to encompass ever larger portions of the populace, those most in need of government largesse are likely to lose out in the political process—and not be the principal beneficiaries of the state-assisted housing program. *See* 84 Harv. L. Rev. 1921 (1971).

few significant state housing initiatives dating back to the early 1920s—notably the veterans home loan program in California[37] and the limited dividend housing law in New York[38] —the basic pattern of public-sector involvement in housing finance has been largely defined by the federal government. Since the Great Depression of the 1930s, Congress, through a variety of federal housing programs, has channeled resources to various private and public beneficiaries. Aid to private beneficiaries has come either through direct subsidies or through indirect mortgage loan guarantees and preferential tax treatment. Aid to local public housing authorities has come in the form of annual contributions that service and secure the principal and interest on tax-exempt bonds issued by the authorities to finance the construction of publicly owned and managed low-income housing.[39]

The pattern of state housing involvement began to change in 1960, when New York established the nation's first state HFA. The New York State Housing Finance Agency was created to finance moderate- and middle-income housing primarily in urban areas so as to stem the rapid out-migration of the middle class to the suburbs—a trend that was attributed in large part to the Federal Housing Administration's favored treatment of single-family suburban homes.[40] The New York State HFA was structured as a statewide public corporation that could raise capital in the tax-exempt bond market and lend the proceeds, at below-market interest rates and at favorable loan-to-value ratios and mortgage terms, for privately owned and constructed housing. Similar agencies were created in Illinois, Massa-

37. The Cal-Vet Home Loan Program is the nation's oldest and largest state housing finance program. Established in 1921, the program has provided direct loans on below-market terms—through the proceeds of the sale of California's tax-exempt general obligation bonds—to over 270,000 veterans for the purchase of either newly constructed or rehabilitated housing. The Cal-Vet Program differs from the HFA programs described above in that in the former, loans are made directly to individuals for the purchase of housing, while in the latter loans are made to developers who produce the housing or to lending institutions who in turn originate loans to developers or individuals. *See* N. Betnun, State Housing Finance Agencies and Public Purpose Housing 412 (Ph.D. dissertation, Massachusetts Institute of Technology, 1975).

38. *See generally* Morris, *The Development of New Middle Income Housing in New York*, 10 N.Y.L.F. 492, 508 (1964).

39. The complex and multifaceted role of the federal government in housing had its origin basically in the collapse of the housing economy during the Great Depression of the 1930s. The National Housing Act of 1934 created the Federal Housing Administration to stimulate the revival of the residential construction industry through the issuance of loans made by private lending institutions for new construction and modernization of existing residential properties. The United States Housing Act of 1937 established the basic pattern of federal assistance for low-income housing, which has continued essentially unchanged until only recently. For a history of the federal government's role in housing, *see* sources collected in note 1 *supra*.

40. *See* O. Nelson, Report of the Governor's Task Force on Middle Income Housing (1959); and Morris, *supra* note 38, at 510.

chusetts, Michigan, and New Jersey in 1967 and 1968; today some 44 states have authorized the creation of HFAs.[41]

The recent proliferation of state HFAs is attributable to a number of factors:

1. The Housing and Urban Development Act of 1968, which established the Section 235 and 236 subsidy programs, encouraged the creation of state HFAs by authorizing scarce subsidy funds to states capable of leveraging those funds by providing assistance through mortgage financing, insurance, or tax abatement.[42]
2. The Tax Reform Acts of 1969 and 1976 created and continued tax incentives for developers of subsidized housing while curtailing certain other tax preferences.
3. Rising housing costs and interest rates (accentuated by the credit crunches of 1969–1970 and 1973–1974), which placed increasingly large segments of the population out of the private housing market, made the beneficial financing available from state HFAs politically attractive. Simultaneously, the doctrine of "public purpose" was judicially and legislatively expanded to accommodate increased public intervention.
4. The Housing and Community Development Act of 1974 encouraged the states to play a major role in implementing the new Section 8 leased housing program.
5. State interest has grown in tailoring programs to better meet particular local and regional housing needs.

State HFAs have the capacity to play a significant role in national housing efforts. This is demonstrated by the performance of the eleven agencies that were active between 1968 and 1974. Through their direct lending programs they were responsible for developing more than 200,000 housing units (including 20 percent of all the units developed nationally under the federal Section 236 interest reduction subsidy program), representing an investment of over $6 billion.[43] Through their mortgage purchase and loans-to-lenders programs, state HFAs have indirectly financed over 60,000 housing units—an

41. A complete listing of housing finance agencies, their enabling legislation, principal programs, and pertinent statistical information can be found in Hous. & Dev. Rep., ref. file 2 § 50:0001 *et seq.*

42. Housing and Urban Development Act of 1968, § 236(b), *as amended by* Housing and Urban Development Act of 1970, Pub. L. No. 91-609, 84 Stat. 1770, 1772.

43. All HFA statistics used in this chapter, unless otherwise attributed, are taken from Council of State Housing Agencies, State Housing Agencies Roles and Accomplishments (1976); and Hous. & Dev. Rep. *supra* note 41.

investment of over $1.2 billion. In establishing this impressive record, state HFAs have relied heavily on the availability of federal subsidies.

The termination of these subsidy programs by the Nixon Administration's 1973 moratorium on federally assisted housing had a severe impact on the HFAs. Subsequently, the dramatic change in the national housing market, which resulted from the government's inability to control escalating prices in a time of decreased production, and HUD's inability to implement expeditiously and effectively its new Section 8 leased housing program, also adversely affected HFAs. Further difficulties were experienced by the housing agencies following the financial emergencies of New York City and various New York State financing agencies, when the national municipal credit markets temporarily closed to several HFAs and caused across-the-board increases in HFA borrowing costs.

Collectively, these events cast a shadow over the future ability of HFAs to fulfill their public purposes. Yet by going into temporary holding patterns, broadening the range of their activities, and developing mechanisms to at least soften these serious setbacks, HFAs have demonstrated remarkable resiliency and thus continue to show considerable promise for the future.

Mortgage Financing Role

State HFAs are generally constituted as public-benefit corporations independent of state executive departments.[44] Their primary function is to borrow capital in the tax-exempt bond market and to lend the proceeds in the form of below-market rate construction and permanent mortgage loans for the private development of low-, moderate-, and middle-income housing. These loans are made directly to qualified housing sponsors or indirectly to them through loans to private lending institutions; both in turn are partially regulated by the agencies. Legislation creating the state HFAs typically requires a finding that loans such as the agency would make are otherwise unavailable in sufficient volume from private lending sources.

Source of Mortgage Capital—The Tax-Exempt Bond Market.[45]

Mortgage capital is raised by HFAs through the issuance of negoti-

44. For operational accounts of HFAs, *see* P. Morris, State Housing Finance Agencies (1974); Stegman, *Housing Finance Agencies: Are They Critical Instruments of State Government?* 40 J. A. I. P. 307 (1974); Betnun, *supra* note 37; Hous. & Dev. Rep., *supra* note 41. For a discussion of public corporations in general, *see* Shestack, *The Public Authority*, 105 U. Pa. L. Rev. 553 (1957).

45. While the subject is well beyond the scope of this book, it should be noted that the federal tax exemption as a method of assisting ("subsidizing") state and local governments has long been severely criticized on both equity and

able bonds and notes in amounts usually limited by statute. It is well established that as independent public corporations—political instrumentalities of their states—HFAs may issue their own tax-exempt revenue obligations[46] without affecting the credit of the state or running afoul of state constitutional debt limitations.[47] The bonds of those agencies which in the past were most active have been secured by a pledge of project mortgages and revenues, reserve funds, federal subsidies (when available), and commonly the non-binding moral obligation of the state to make up any deficiencies in debt service payments.[48] Those agencies which have been authorized to issue revenue bonds but which lack either a moral obligation or debt service makeup provision (such as Colorado, Idaho, Missouri, and South Carolina) have been able to market their bonds largely by restricting their lending operations to federal, state, or privately insured mortgages, and have thus been more limited in their lending volume and flexibility.

HFA bonds—with or without a state's moral obligation pledge—

---

efficiency grounds. Annually, bills are submitted in Congress aimed at altering the current system. Any change, however, would raise serious legal questions stemming from the doctrine of "reciprocal tax immunity." For a discussion of the arguments that have been propounded for and against tax-exempt municipal bonds, *see* J. Peterson, Changing Conditions in the Market for State and Local Government Debt 55–60 (Prepared for the Joint Economic Committee of Congress, G.P.O. 1976); R. Heufner, Taxable Alternatives to Municipal Bonds (Federal Reserve Bank of Boston 1972).

46. *See* I.R.C. § 103.

47. *See, e.g.,* Johnson v. Pa. Housing Finance Agency, 309 A.2d 528, 535 (1973); *In re* Advisory Op. on Const. of Act No. 246, 158 N.W.3d 416, 421 (1968); and other HFA cases cited at notes 27–30 *supra. See contra,* State, *ex rel.* Brown v. Beard (Ohio Sup. Ct., Dec. 22, 1976), reported in 4 Hous. & Dev. Rep. 708 (Jan. 10, 1977), holding that the Ohio HFA statute violates the state constitutional prohibition on lending of credit.

48. The "moral obligation" is, in effect, the expression of one legislature's intent, but not a binding obligation (since one legislature cannot legally bind a subsequent legislature), that a future legislature will appropriate from general revenues money to make up, or supply any deficiencies in the agency's debt service reserve fund. This reserve fund is required to be maintained at a level that will cover the principal and interest coming due on an agency's outstanding bonds in any succeeding year. If the reserve fund, for any reason, were to be reduced below this minimum statutory level, the agency is prohibited from issuing any further bonds, and the governor is required then to request a legislative appropriation to replenish the fund. The courts have consistently held that a legislature may legally make such an appropriation as it would constitute a valid public purpose; and further that such an appropriation, being purely permissive on the part of the legislature, would not constitute creation of state debt in violation of state constitutional debt restrictions. Mass. H.F.A. v. N.E. Merchants Nat'l Bank, 249 N.E.2d 599 (1969); Johnson v. Pa. H.F.A., 209 A.2d 528 (1973); N.J. Mort. Fin. Ag. v. McCrane, 267 A.2d 699 (1971). *But see* Gibson v. Smith, 531 P.2d 724 (Or. Ap. 1975); Rich v. State (Ga. Sup. Ct., decided July 9, 1976). *See generally* Griffith, *Moral Obligations Bonds: Illusion or Security?* 8 Urb. Law . 54 (1976).

are designed to be completely self-liquidating from pledged project revenues. As a result HFA bonds have generally received high investment grade ratings and the agencies have thus obtained favorable yields, often only slightly lower than those on the state's general obligation bonds, which are supported by the full faith and credit of the state's taxing power. More recently, however, the market reaction to the financial difficulties of New York State agencies—which have borrowed extensively in the national moral obligation bond market— has created a credibility gap that has adversely affected the marketability of all moral obligation bonds, including those of the most highly respected and financially solvent HFAs. Consequently, as discussed below, these agencies are looking increasingly toward other forms of bond security.

Direct Financing for Multifamily Housing. The proceeds of HFA securities are used primarily to make direct construction loans (through the sale of short-term notes) and permanent mortgage loans to qualified housing sponsors—principally to limited dividend, non-profit, and cooperative entities, and to individuals—who own, build, and finance the housing.[49] About 98 percent of the units financed by direct loans from HFAs have been in multifamily residential developments.

The HFAs have low borrowing costs because the interest on their obligations is exempt from federal and many state taxes. These lower costs are in turn reflected in interest rates to borrowers that have averaged 1.5 to 2 percent below private market rates, and in more favorable loan-to-value ratios and mortgage terms than are available from private lenders (90 percent vs. 75–80 percent, and 40 years vs. 25–30 years). The saving is passed along to the developer and reflected in moderate reductions in the monthly cost of housing for the consumer. In exchange for these favorable financial considerations, the agencies retain the power to limit the developer's rental and other charges, its profits and fees, and to control the sponsor's disposition of the property.

In addition the agencies charge a one-time fee from developers on each project to meet their processing costs, and they receive annual fees in the form of a markup on the interest rate that they charge borrowers to meet their mortgage servicing costs and to provide for reserves. In this way, and often only after a small initial start-up loan or grant to provide funds for administration, the agencies eventually become self-sufficient. The Virginia Housing Development Au-

49. The various direct financing schemes and the roles of the developer/ sponsors are discussed in Morris, *supra* note 44.

thority, for example, returned its $300,000 start-up appropriation within the first two years of operation.

While the private sector constructs, owns, and manages HFA financed housing, the agencies actively participate in site selection and design review, and in the determination of size and number of units in a given project. Standards for equal employment opportunity and marketing for the housing are also established by the agencies.

Linkage with Federal and State Subsidy Programs to Meet Low- and Moderate-Income Housing Needs. Since FHA tax-exempt bond financing provides at best only a shallow capital subsidy, additional federal or state assistance is essential for state HFAs to effectively serve families and individuals in the low- and moderate-income range; that is, those earning less than $9–11,000 a year.[50] In the seven year period from 1968 to 1974, well over half the more than 200,000 units completed have received federal interest-reduction subsidies under the Section 236 (multifamily) and Section 235 (home owner-ship) programs, and have thus been available for moderate-income families. More than 25,000 units were additionally made available to low-income families through assistance from the federal rent sup-plement and leased public housing programs.

The Nixon Administration suspended both the Section 236 and the Section 235 programs. Section 235 has now been revived in a restricted form (smaller mortgages are available at higher interest rates than under the former program, and targeted at higher income groups);[51] but Section 236 is still not operative. In making use of the federal subsidy programs, HFAs were exempted from the often rigid FHA regulations and requirements. Their projects were typically processed and open for occupancy in from twelve to sixteen months, compared to an average of 34 months for projects processed by HUD.[52] Project amenities and architectural design in HFA housing have also been considered to be of consistently higher quality.

Several HFAs have been particularly successful in serving a full range of housing needs. Others, however, have been validly criticized for their failure to either pursue available subsidies aggressively and otherwise provide for a significant portion of low-income residents,[53]

50. *See* Pearlman, *State Housing Finance Agencies and the Myth of Low-Income Housing*, 7 Clearinghouse Rev. 640 (March 1974).

51. *See* description of the revised Section 235 program in Hous. & Dev. Rep. ref. file 1, sec. 10:1224.

52. Housing in the Seventies, *supra* note 1, at 145–46.

53. *See* Pearlman, *supra* note 50. Several projects financed by the Pennsyl-vania Housing Finance Agency, and discussed in note 55 *infra*, well illustrate agency laxity in this regard.

or channel their resources into areas with the most critical housing needs.[54] Possibly the failure to make the more "difficult" loans may be justified as a start-up strategy for newly created agencies; it allows them to develop their processing procedures, underwriting expertise, and investor confidence, and to establish reserves that will help support the agencies in their early stages. Such a policy cannot, however, be sanctioned for more established agencies with clearly delineated statutory objectives for meeting low-, moderate-, and middle-income housing needs.[55]

Several HFAs have income mix requirements for their projects. The experience of the Massachusetts Housing Finance Agency (MHFA) demonstrates that such requirements, in developments with superior design, construction, and management, can achieve an economically and socially successful integration of low- and middle-income households within each project. MHFA requires a minimum of 25 percent of the residences in each of its developments to be made available to low-income families or persons (generally with incomes of less than $6,000 a year) at rents not in excess of 25 percent of their adjusted incomes.[56] By aggressively pursuing federal subsidies and by utilizing a variety of state subsidies, MHFA, as of 1973, had actually surpassed

54. Surveys indicate that over 80 percent of all state-sponsored housing units have been new construction in the suburbs—and that 90 percent of the buyers or renters have had incomes in the moderate- to middle-income range. (Only Massachusetts, New York, and Michigan have made any credible record in rehabilitation and central-city development.) While building in suburban areas is essential to promoting economic and racial integration and housing opportunity, these objectives can be achieved only as part of a well-conceived and comprehensive open-house strategy. There is no indication that HFAs have intentionally pursued such strategies in connection with their lending practices. *See* R. Alexander, New Directions for State Housing Finance Agencies (1974); Silverman, *The States Emerge as Primary Clients for Subsidized Housing*, 63 J. Am. Inst. Arch. 24 (Feb. 1975).

55. Not infrequently, HFA enacting legislation has failed to define the terms "low-" and "moderate-income" housing, leaving the definition to internal administrative regulation. Some agencies have taken advantage of this legislative leniency. The Pennsylvania Housing Finance Agency, for example, financed a "moderate-income" project, which had the following income characteristics: median family income in project area, $14,417; lowest resident family income, $10,000; highest resident family income, $35,000; median resident family income, $18,400. In an official audit of the agency, the Pennsylvania auditor general concluded: "In our opinion, these incomes cannot be construed as being 'moderate.'" The auditor recommended that the state legislature amend the definition of low- and moderate-income persons and families by clearly defining income ranges for each classification. It suggested that the Massachusetts HFA's definition of income levels be used as a model: low income means less than $6,000 a year; moderate income, between $6,000 and $12,000; with the ranges varying from one municipality to another. Pennsylvania Housing Finance Agency, Audit Report for the Six-Month Period Ending December 31, 1974, at 43–44 (1975).

56. Mass. Gen. Laws Ann. ch. 23A, §§ 1–6(b).

the statutory minimum by providing 34.8 percent of its housing units (approximately 7,000 units) to low-income occupants.[57]

Several other state HFAs, including those in Michigan, Illinois, New York, Colorado, and West Virginia, have income mix requirements. One important value of maintaining an economic mix is the ability to funnel part of the rental proceeds of the middle-income tenants (usually by charging a rent slightly higher than their pro rata housing costs require) to reduce the rents of the low-income tenants in the same project. This internal subsidy is called rent skewing.

Another advantage of maintaining an economic mix is the special treatment thereby accorded HFAs in the allocation of federal subsidies under the new Section 8 leased housing program (discussed below). The amount of Section 8 contract authority allocated to HFAs is determined by several criteria, including "the Agency's ability and willingness to limit the number of units leased by assisted families to 20 percent or less of the units in projects of more than 50 units and not designed for use primarily by the elderly and the handicapped."[58] Agencies that meet this criteria will receive from HUD a bonus set-aside: for every four units subject to the 20 percent priority, HUD will award one additional set-aside unit in the allotment for the next fiscal year.[59] The California legislature is requiring its recently created HFA to avail itself of Section 8 set-asides by mandating that in all housing developments containing twelve or more units, at least 20 percent of the units must be for those with very low incomes.[60]

A number of states have their own housing subsidy programs, which often channel assistance directly through state HFAs. These programs are generally tied to state appropriations; however, due to the financial squeeze confronting many states, total funding is quite limited. Massachusetts has an interest subsidy program[61] and a leased public housing program,[62] both modeled after the federal programs. New York State has developed a low-rent capital grant program[63] that

57. Pearlman, *supra* note 50. A recent study of the agency has disclosed what appears to be a gradual subordination of the goal of mixed housing to the maintenance of the financial viability of the projects. This trend has been attributed to two factors: (1) high capital costs have made later projects expensive to rent relative to existing competition; and (2) increased operation and maintenance charges require deeper subsidies and subsidizing additional units. Report of the Massachusetts Housing Finance Agency Study Commission 14–15 (June 1976).

58. 24 C.F.R. § 883.104(d)(6).

59. *Id.* at § 882.104(e).

60. Housing and Home Finance Act of 1975 (A.B. 1-x), Cal. Gov't Code § 41496. *See generally* Rehm & Pearlman, *Housing and Community Development: The California Approach*, 8 Clearinghouse Rev. (1976).

61. Mass. Gen. Laws Ann. ch. 23A, § 13a.

62. Mass. Gen. Laws, ch. 121B, §§ 42–44.

provides rental assistance to low-income families to help them afford units financed through its state agencies. Several states have loan or grant programs to reduce the size of down payments on the purchase of certain types of housing, and some others have adopted state-financed public housing programs to provide assistance in areas where local housing authorities do not operate.[64] Utah, for example, has allocated $3 million of the state's general revenue-sharing funds to local, county, and regional bodies primarily to be used for rehabilitation of low-income housing. And in a November 1976 referendum, the voters of New Jersey approved a $25 million general obligation bond issue designed to help subsidize projects of its HFA.[65]

Property tax abatement is another means to reduce the cost of housing for low-income persons. In Michigan, tax abatement has resulted in rental reductions of up to $30 per month on a $20,000 unit financed by the HFA.[66] While municipalities in all states abate taxes on public housing projects and charge a payment in lieu of taxes of no more than 10 percent of shelter rent, several states (Alaska, Colorado, Connecticut, Massachusetts, Minnesota, New York, and Vermont) extend tax abatement to privately owned federal- and state-assisted housing.[67] Connecticut, moreover, reimburses municipalities for a negotiated percentage of the property tax revenues foregone through tax abatement on subsidized housing; its localities are thus not penalized for accepting low- and moderate-income families.[68] Property tax abatement for the elderly has become an increasingly popular form of assistance, and is authorized in some form or another in almost every state. Some of the legal and political issues of tax abatement are discussed later in this chapter.

The Section 8 Leased Housing Program.   The housing subsidy programs that were utilized by the state HFAs prior to the housing moratorium of 1973 have been replaced by the Section 8 leased housing program, the major housing assistance program of the Housing and Community Development Act of 1974. Under Section 8 the Department of Housing and Urban Development (HUD) makes housing

63. N.Y. Real Prop. Law ch. 41, § 44A (McKinney 1973).
64. *See* note 41 *supra.*
65. However, referenda in Florida and California did not fare as well. 4 Hous. & Dev. Rep. 538–39 (Nov. 15, 1976).
66. Comments of Isaac Green, Chief Deputy Executive Director, Michigan State Housing Development Authority, Workshop on Alternative Housing Programs for HFAs, 3d Ann. Conference of State Housing Agencies, Minneapolis, Minn., Feb. 11, 1974.
67. R. Schafer, N. Betnun & A. Solomon, A Place to Live: Housing Policy in the States 30–31 (Council of State Governments 1974).
68. Conn. Gen. Stat. Ann. § 8-216(a) (West 1971).

assistance payments on behalf of eligible lower income families to cover the difference between the rent charged by the landlord and 15 to 25 percent of the eligible families' adjusted income.[69] HUD is required to use the lower percentage in the case of a "large very low-income family" or a "very large lower-income family" or for a family with "exceptional medical or other expenses."[70] Eligible lower income families are those with adjusted incomes not in excess of 80 percent of the median for the area in which the project is located.[71] To assure that very low-income families will also be assisted, the act requires that at least 30 percent of the families assisted on a national basis[72] must have adjusted incomes not in excess of 50 percent of the area median income.[73]

In enacting the 1974 Act Congress anticipated that HFAs would play a major role in the implementation of Section 8. The Act permits Section 8 assistance payments to run for 40 years in projects financed by HFAs (as opposed to a maximum of 20 years for privately financed projects),[74] and allows the HFAs, pursuant to annual contributions contracts with HUD, to serve as conduits for the allocation of the payments, Moreover, HUD has issued special regulations for state HFAs. They give greater program responsibility in areas such as site and developer selection, and design and contract control to those HFAs that provide mortgage financing to projects assisted under Section 8 but lacking federal mortgage insurance.[75] Of the 45,000 unit reservations for Section 8 new construction and substantial rehabilitation housing authorized by HUD for fiscal year 1975, 41,000 were allocated to HFAs.[76]

The Section 8 program potentially offers HFAs a significant advantage over the supplanted Section 236 program. Under the latter program the federal interest-reduction subsidy was set at a fixed amount and could not be adjusted to reflect increases in operation and maintenance costs brought about by inflation. Section 8, by contrast, provides a subsidy coverage that can adjust to changes in circumstances, such as increases in operating costs resulting from higher real property taxes, utility rates, and so forth.[77] However, Section 8 as originally written into law contained a major defect insofar as state HFAs are concerned: federal housing assis-

69. 42 U.S.C. § 1437f(c)(3).
70. *Id.*
71. *Id.* at § 1437f(f)(1).
72. *Id.* at § 1437f(c)(7).
73. *Id.* at § 1437f(f)(2).
74. *Id.* at § 1437f(e)(1).
75. 24 C.F.R. § 883 *et seq.* (1975).
76. 3 Hous. & Dev. Rep. 493–94 (Oct. 20, 1975).
77. 42 U.S.C. § 1437f(c)(2)(B).

tance payments were only to continue for up to 60 days for units that were unoccupied during initial rent-up or became vacant thereafter.

This lack of an assured income stream for units unoccupied after the 60-day period created a basic security problem for bond financing of Section 8 projects, which was exacerbated by the pervasive uncertainty in the municipal bond market that followed in the wake of the financial emergencies of New York City and the New York State Urban Development Corporation (discussed below). The ability of HFAs to provide substantial tax-exempt financing for Section 8 projects was consequently severely limited, and in turn the Section 8 program showed little progress or promise as a viable means of providing new or rehabilitated housing for the nation's housing poor.[78] The Housing Authorization Act of 1976, however, should have remedied some of the problems, at least insofar as HFA-financed Section 8 projects are concerned. HUD is now authorized to continue making payments for unoccupied new or substantially rehabilitated Section 8 units for up to one additional year (beyond the initial 60 days) in an amount equal to the debt service attributable to the unit, if a good faith effort is being made to fill the housing unit.[79]

Indirect Financing—Mortgage Purchase and Loans-to-Lenders Programs. A large number of HFAs are using their tax-exempt borrowing power to carry out indirect financing programs in the secondary mortgage market. Designed to increase the amount of capital available for credit, the two major programs in use—mortgage purchase and loans-to-lenders—are in large part a direct outgrowth of the national credit crunches experienced in the 1970s and the lack of significant federal subsidy funds subsequent to the 1973 housing moratorium. Virtually all HFAs established in this period have been authorized to undertake these indirect lending activities.

While there are numerous variations of the two basic programs,[80] they are all primarily geared to serve the moderate- and middle-income home purchaser (with incomes of $12,000 a year and up), rather than the low-income purchaser. Since these programs generally involve mortgages that are underwritten with FHA, VA, state or pri-

78. E. Holsendolph, *1974 Housing Act Helping Few of the Nation's Poor,* N.Y. Times, November 2, 1975, at 1. *See also* 3 Hous. & Dev. Rep. 453 (Oct. 6, 1975).

79. Housing Authorization Act of 1976, Pub. L. No. 94-377, § 2(d). For the reactions of officials of the bond-rating agencies to the program revisions, *see* 4 Hous. & Dev. Rep. 650 (Dec. 27, 1976).

80. For more detailed descriptions of the various indirect financing programs, *see* Hous. & Dev. Rep., *supra* note 41; Morris, *supra* note 44.

vate mortgage insurance, the bonds of agencies undertaking them are generally viewed as better secured than those issued for direct financing of multi-family programs, which are uninsured and tend to serve lower income groups. It is therefore likely that these indirect financing programs will further proliferate during periods in which HFAs experience difficulty in gaining access to the capital markets with their somewhat riskier direct lending programs.

Under the mortgage purchase program, active in at least fourteen states,[81] HFA bond proceeds are used to purchase mortgages from local portfolios or from newly originated sources so as to free funds in the local mortgage market and enable banks to make new residential mortgages, often to moderate-income borrowers. Under the loans-to-lenders program (primarily a home ownership program) tax-exempt bond proceeds are used to make loans to private mortgage lenders, who are required in turn to make new mortgage loans. About eight states have active loans-to-lenders programs.[82]

In both programs, HFAs generally set the interest rates for the financed housing, and establish qualifications for the recipients of the loans. To minimize operating costs or to handle a large volume of business with a small staff, HFAs generally permit the originating private lending institution to service the mortgage for a fee. Since the mortgage purchase and loans-to-lenders programs can be implemented in a short time, they are especially advantageous for new HFAs. At the same time, servicing fees and other charges paid to intermediaries increase the costs to the consumer.

While not oriented to the lower income home purchaser, several of the indirect lending programs are designed to assist in meeting particularly serious housing needs. The New Jersey Mortgage Finance Agency, which established the prototype loans-to-lenders programs, provides incentives to lending institutions, in the form of higher permissible interest charges, for loans made in high need areas of the state as designated by the agency, particularly in high-risk inner-city neighborhoods. Massachusetts, like New Jersey, has established a separate state agency—the Massachusetts Home Mortgage Finance Agency—to operate a loans-to-lenders program aimed at

81. Alaska, California, Connecticut, Georgia, Kentucky, Maine, Minnesota, Missouri, New York, Tennessee, Virginia, Vermont, Wisconsin (New York State has its own Mortgage Finance Agency distinct from its Housing Finance Agency). At least 23 other HFAs have authorization for mortgage purchase programs. *See* Council of State Governments, State Growth Management 30–33 (May 1976).

82. Colorado, Illinois, Maine, New Jersey, Rhode Island, Vermont, Virginia, West Virginia, Wisconsin (New Jersey has its own Mortgage Finance Agency that is distinct from its Housing Finance Agency). At least 19 other HFAs have authorization for loans-to-lenders programs. *Id.*

making mortgage credit available in older neighborhoods. The Illinois Housing Development Authority has established a loans-to-lenders program aimed at combating mortgage redlining of older communities in Chicago. The program makes funds available to community banks and savings and loans institutions at tax-exempt rates, provided that these are matched in equal amount by mortgage loans by the local lending institutions within their communities.[83]

State Insurance Programs. Another indirect method of housing finance likely to be used increasingly by the states in the future is the provision of mortgage insurance. These programs, generally funded with legislative appropriations from general funds or through the issuance of the state's general obligation bonds, permit housing to be financed under riskier circumstances for inner-city neighborhoods, for older homes, or for purchasers who are considered credit risks by private conventional lenders.

Among the most innovative and successful state mortgage insurance programs is the one operated by the Maryland Housing Fund, a division of the Maryland Department of Economic and Community Development. Funded with a $20 million insurance reserve from the state's general obligation borrowing, the Housing Fund is authorized: (1) to insure the top 20–25 percent of the loan amount of conventional single family first mortgage loans on 80–100 percent of the loan-to-value ratio; (2) to provide 100 percent single family mortgage insurance coverage on 80–100 percent of the loan-to-value ratio in high risk inner-city areas of Baltimore in which conventional lenders are not active; and (3) to provide construction loans and permanent mortgage insurance for multifamily projects financed by approved public and private lenders. The fund is capable of leveraging its $20 million insurance reserve to insure mortgages at a total face value amount of $190 million.[84]

Mortgage insurance programs are also operating in Connecticut and Missouri. Numerous other HFAs have mortgage insurance powers but have not implemented them.

Combining Financing and Development Powers: The New York State Urban Development Corporation. Somewhat of a hybrid on the state HFA theme is the New York State Urban Development Corporation (UDC).[85] Like the typical HFA, the UDC, which was

83. Illinois Housing Development Authority Annual Report (1974).

84. Maryland Department of Economic and Community Development, Community Development Administration: Functional Statements 4 (1975). *See also* Goldberg & Elenowitz, *Maryland Housing Insurance Programs: Forerunner of Future State Activity,* 5 Urb. Law 524 (1973).

85. *See generally* E. Brilliant, The Urban Development Corporation (1975),

created in 1968, was structured as a public corporation and empowered to finance low- and moderate-income housing through the issuance of its own tax-exempt bonds. Unlike other HFAs, the UDC was designed to operate in an active and direct development capacity. It was authorized to plan, initiate, finance, build, and operate a project, and, at any point, to sell it to, or to sell and lease it back from private entities or a government unit. In order to deal comprehensively with the urban environment, the UDC was authorized to develop industrial and commercial facilities in areas of high unemployment and to provide for complementary educational, recreational, and civic facilities (and indeed entire new communities), as well as for housing.

To achieve these objectives the UDC was created with a panoply of unique powers including:

1. The power to acquire sites by purchase, lease, or condemnation.[86]
2. The power to create subsidiary corporations to undertake UDC's activities and to make loans to these subsidiary corporations.[87]
3. Full or partial exemption of the projects of UDC and its subsidiaries from real property and other state and local taxes.[88]
4. The power to develop projects without complying with local zoning ordinances, building codes, or other local laws or regulations when such compliance is not feasible or practical, and when approved by a two-thirds vote of the UDC's board of directors.[89] (Following a major controversy in Westchester County, the state legislature in 1973 partially revoked UDC's authority to use this override power in conjunction with its residential projects in towns and villages.)[90]

Reilly & Schulman, *The State Urban Development Corporation: New York's Innovation* 1 Urb. Law. 129 (1969); Amdursky, *The New York State Urban Development Corporation* N.Y.S. Bar J. 100 (1969); Restoring Credit and Confidence: A Report to the Governor by the New York State Moreland Act Commission on the Urban Development Corporation and Other State Financing Agencies (March 31, 1976) [hereinafter cited as Moreland Act Commission Report].

86. N.Y. Unconsol. Laws § 6255(7).

87. *Id.* at §§ 6255(8), 6262.

88. *Id.* at § 6272.

89. *Id.* at § 6266(3). This power was upheld by the New York Court of Appeals in Thomas Floyd v. New York State Urban Development Corp. 70 Misc. 2d 187, 333 N.Y.S.2d 123 (1972).

90. 1975 N.Y. Laws ch. 446, § 3. For a discussion of the controversy leading to the legislative amendments, *see* Brilliant, *supra* note 85, at 90; Hirshorn, *Homerule vs. Override: The New York State Urban Development Corporation's Suburban Housing Program* (Paper presented at Annual Conference of American Institute of Planners, Oct. 1975).

By using its override power, usually at the request of local communities,[91] UDC was able to facilitate its development schemes, substantially speed up the development process, and open up new areas for development. By employing the so-called fast-track system of processing and development, by which several facets of development (site acquisition, preparation of architectural plans, obtaining federal subsidies, negotiation of construction, ownership and management arrangements) proceed simultaneously, UDC was able to cut substantially through red tape and shorten the period of time between project conception and project construction. (Under the traditional "sequential" approach, one decision is taken at a time and every other decision must wait its turn.)

With its unique powers and highly innovative development methods, UDC was able to establish a remarkable record. In its first six years of existence, UDC started over 30,000 housing units (about half in New York City, the rest in urban areas throughout the state, often in high risk areas), three major new communities, a hotel, a convention center, and a department store, and sold over $1 billion worth of bonds. In some respects many of the factors that contributed to UDC's success also led to its near total collapse in 1975, when it defaulted on $100 million of bond anticipation notes (the default was ultimately cured through legislative appropriations). According to a special state commission established to investigate the financial difficulties of the UDC and other New York State financing agencies,[92] the default of the UDC was a consequence of several factors: (1) its rapid accumulation of construction commitments, which led to heavy and increasing short-term borrowing without commensurate cash flow from project revenues (since new projects were commenced before earlier projects were completed and occupied); (2) lack of adequate scrutiny ("tension") stemming from the fact that UDC served as both developer and lender; (3) the high risk nature of many of its projects located in marginal areas for families who could not afford to pay market rents; and (4) "inadequate financial controls and an unwarranted assumption that the agency could continue to borrow for its needs almost indefinitely."[93]

Other factors, external to the UDC's operations, also contributed to its financial difficulties: the unexpected suspension of federal subsidies in 1973; concern in the financial community that the state might be unwilling to support the moral obligation backing the

91. From 1968 through 1973, UDC utilized its override powers approximately sixty times; only about 17 percent of these actions involved local political opposition; 83 percent were technical in nature, to facilitate development. Hirshorn, *supra* note 90, at 2.

92. Moreland Act Commission Report, *supra* note 85.

93. *Id.* at 11.

UDC's bonds; and a general skepticism in the financial community over any real estate investment following the widespread national failure of real estate investment trusts. Moreover, no provision was made by the UDC or the state for any of these developments or for the event that adequate funds could not be borrowed.[94] Notwithstanding its financial difficulties, UDC demonstrated its potential as a powerful tool for social change and achieved many of its intended objectives.[95]

Opportunities for HFAs in Local Community Development Programs

The Housing and Community Development Act of 1974 created important new opportunities for cooperation between state HFAs and local governments. By consolidating the older, more narrowly conceived categorical grant programs for community development into a single block grant, the 1974 law gives localities much greater freedom in spending federal community development funds and coordinating existing or planned public facilities, services and job opportunities with assisted housing.[96] One of the major purposes of the legislation is to encourage and enable local communities to plan unified housing and community development programs.

To qualify for community development funds, local governments must prepare comprehensive community development programs and housing assistance plans (HAPs). The HAP must survey the condition of the community's housing stock, assess lower income housing needs, specify realistic goals for meeting those needs, and indicate the general location of housing for lower income persons, with three objectives: (1) furthering the revitalization of the community; (2) promoting greater choice of housing opportunities and avoiding concentrations of assisted persons in areas containing a high proportion of low-income persons; and (3) assuring the viability of public facilities for such housing.[97] Development of the local HAP requires localities to formulate a more sophisticated set of housing goals and programs than they have been responsible for in the past. It is extremely important that communities satisfy these new planning responsibilities since entitlement to funds in later years will depend on federal review of local performance.

94. *Id.*

95. *Statement of Vice President Nelson A. Rockefeller*, before the N.Y.S. Moreland Act Comm'n on the Urban Development Corporation and other State Financing Agencies, Dec. 3, 1975.

96. *See generally* Fishman, *Title I of the Housing and Community Development Act of 1974: New Federal and Local Dynamics in Community Development*, 7 Urb. Law. 189 (1975).

97. 42 U.S.C. § 5304(a)(4).

State HFAs, with their reserves of technical expertise and advantageous financing capabilities, are uniquely equipped to assist localities in applying for and obtaining federal assistance as well as in making feasible the goals and objectives of local community development programs and HAPs. The greater degree of program responsibility accorded HFAs for review, evaluation, and processing of proposals under Section 8 of the Act includes a more liberalized and expedited processing procedure. As experience is gained with the Section 8 program, fast-track processing should result in sizable savings to local developers in terms of reduced processing costs and time, as well as greater flexibility in design and quality control.

It is also possible to reduce housing costs by using HFA loans in tandem with local government subsidies available under the Housing and Community Development Act of 1974. While the 1974 Act prohibits the use of community development funds for new residential construction,[98] it does permit the financing of site acquisition and clearance, as well as such on- and off-site improvements as landscaping, recreational and neighborhood facilities, solid waste disposal facilities, street lighting, and security systems, in connection with a local community development plan.[99]

The 1974 Act also allows local governments to use their funds to finance the acquisition and resale of buildings for HFA financed rehabilitation. Since HFAs commonly include such acquisitions and improvements in the mortgage amount financed—at costs often amounting to as much as 8 to 10 percent of the total cost per unit— the combination of HFA financing and community development block grant funds can be useful in lowering costs and creating feasible projects. Alternatively, sites might be leased on a 99 year basis at nominal consideration so that the total mortgage is reduced.

Finally, state HFAs, with their panoply of housing powers, are in a position to assist those cities and counties entitled to community development block grants but which are inhibited by state constitutional and statutory limitations from performing activities otherwise authorized under the 1974 Act. Surveys undertaken by the National League of Cities and the National Association of Counties indicate that a number of city and county recipients of block grants throughout the nation do not currently possess the legal authority to perform certain housing and community development functions.[100]

98. 39 Fed. Reg. No. 220, § 570.201(e), at 40143 (November 13, 1974).
99. 42 U.S.C. § 530(a)(2).
100. National Association of Counties, Community Development Capabilities Study: An Urban County Report (August 1975); National League of Cities, *Community Development Block Grants: The First Year*, 1975 Nation's Cities 21 (July).

Numerous counties, for example, are not legally authorized to directly undertake programs or even homeownership counseling. In most instances, however, such jurisdictions do have the authority to enter into agreements with other public agencies (such as local public housing authorities) for the provision of services and the performance of specific activities. In geographic areas in which local housing authorities do not exist or do not function efficiently, state HFAs—with their ability to allocate, finance, and administer Section 8 units throughout a state according to actual needs and priorities—can obviously play an important role.

The Future of HFAs—Regaining Easy Access to the Bond Markets

Because of several major events having widespread influence in the national bond markets during 1975 and 1976, many HFAs found it exceedingly difficult to borrow at the favorable rates they could obtain in the past.[101] Among the developments that adversely affected the marketability of HFA bonds and notes were the financial difficulties of the New York State UDC and of other New York State finance agencies. These agencies relied heavily on moral-obligation bond financing and their troubles caused a reassessment of this method of financing.[102] Other factors which have had an impact on HFA borrowing include the fiscal crises in New York City and State; increasing investor wariness of long-term real estate investment in the aftermath of widespread failures of real estate investment trusts; and declining institutional interest in tax-exempt bond investment.

The problem as it affected HFAs outside of New York was in many respects due more to investor psychology and risk perception (often based on misinformation and confusion) than to any inherent defects in the underlying HFA security or credit. For example, the financing role and activities of HFAs as well as their bond issuing mechanisms are markedly different from those of the New York State UDC. The problems of the UDC stemmed in part from the fact that the agency assumed the roles of both mortgage lender and developer, and was consequently forced to absorb risks normally taken by private developers.[103] (Ironically, UDC's difficulties involved a default on certain short term notes that did not enjoy a moral obligation pledge and the default was ultimately

101. *See New Yorkitis Infects the Municipals Markets*, Business Week, October 13, 1975 at 80–82; other reports in 3 Hous. & Dev. Rep. 453 (Oct. 6, 1975); *id.* at 499 (Oct. 20, 1975); *id.* at 860 (Feb. 10, 1976); *id.* at 963 (March 8, 1976).

102. *See* notes 107 and 108 *infra*.

103. *See* Moreland Act Commission Report, *supra* note 85, at 11–12; and text accompanying notes 92–94 *supra*.

cured through affirmative action of the New York State legislature. The pledge behind the bonds of the UDC was never really tested.)

HFAs, on the other hand, are not developers. Unlike the UDC, they do not spend bond proceeds to acquire housing sites, develop plans, engage in other front-end development, or undertake actual design or construction (the costs of which may not be recoverable under the ultimate mortgage). Rather, HFAs use their bond proceeds only for specific loans, payments of notes issued for specific mortgages, funding their reserves, and paying expenses specifically related to issuance of the bonds. HFA bonds, moreover, are secured by mortgage loans on specific housing projects; the underlying security—the specific piece of real estate—is thereby more visible to the investor than that behind the UDC's general purpose urban development bonds (a security unique to municipal finance), which are secured by the general revenues from all development activities, even those that do not result in a revenue producing project.

The experience and operations of the New York State HFA, which has also recently suffered financial difficulties as a result of its inability to roll-over its notes,[104] are also substantially different from the nation's other HFAs (even though that agency served as the prototype for subsequent HFAs). The technique of the New York State HFA of financing middle-income housing through moral obligation bonds was initially so successful that a decision was made in the early 1960s to use the HFA to finance the construction of educational and hospital projects. These projects generated an income stream that supported HFA bonds of a different and perhaps lesser quality than rental or other housing occupancy charges.[105]

The New York State HFA debt grew from $52 million in 1961, to almost $1.25 billion in 1967, to over $5 billion at the end of 1975.[106] Over half this debt is for financing construction activities other than housing. The agency's $5 billion in total outstanding moral obligation bonds represents well over twice the bonds issued by all other HFAs in the nation combined, and exceeds even the amount of full-faith and credit debt issued by the State of New York. While the agency has always (at least through mid-1975) been viewed by the financial community as a model of fiscal prudence and safe policies, the magnitude of its borrowing eventually glutted the national market. Taken in combination with the financial problems besetting New York City, New York State, and the UDC, the difficulty of the

104. *See* note 101 *supra.*

105. Hershman, *Opening Statement to the New York State Moreland Act Commission on the Urban Development Corporation and Other State Financing Agencies* 6 (New York, October 14, 1975).

106. Elsen, *id.* at 3.

New York State HFA in marketing its bonds is easily explained. New York relied too heavily on the moral obligation bond[107] and thereby caused the financial community to reassess its view of all such bonds.[108]

While the New York State legislature ultimately came to the rescue of its distressed financing agencies,[109] the crisis of uncertainty that ensued in the national market had a damaging effect on HFAs elsewhere. HFA borrowing costs rose rapidly, reducing the margin between the agencies' cost of capital and the rates they could charge for loans or add to rents (a 1 percentage point increase in borrowing costs is estimated to add $25 to monthly rentals in HFA projects.)[110] At the end of 1975 the yields on long-term HFA bonds had risen from the normal 60 to 70 percent to more than 80 percent of the rates on insured mortgages.[111] HFAs succeeded in several states (but only with considerable difficulty) in rolling over short-term notes into long-term bonds.[112] But construction delays resulted in additional project costs.

Ultimately, however, HFAs managed to weather the storm—some

107. Moody's Investor Service had earlier stated about these bonds; "As the amounts for which a state becomes 'morally obligated' increase, its future ability or willingness to meet such commitments may become impaired."

108. In June 1975 statement of policy, Moody's revised its position on moral obligation bonds:

> Because of the high degree of uncertainty surrounding the deficiency make-up or moral obligation type pledge we feel it provides very little in the way of security to the bondholder. . . . In our opinion, the . . . "moral obligation" feature deserves no consideration as a part of a bond's security. . . . Bonds can be rated only on revenues pledged to their support and the quality of those revenues.

Moody's Bond Survey 1093-94 (June 30, 1975). Following this statement, Moody's downgraded the credit rating of several moral obligation agencies.

109. The UDC was resuscitated, and construction on its many projects permitted to continue essentially uninterrupted, by a complicated plan involving almost $200 million of direct state appropriations and the establishment of a new state agency, the Project Finance Agency, that channeled bank loans into the corporation. *See* Moreland Act Commission Report, *supra* note 85.

Subsequently the New York State legislature amended the legislation creating the UDC and HFA to prevent the future issuance of moral obligation bonds beyond those needed to meet current commitments. 1976 N.Y. Laws ch. 38, §§ 8670 and 8709 (March 11, 1976).

110. *See* statement of W. White, *Debt Financing Problems of State and Local Governments: The New York City Case*, in Hearings Before the House Committee on Banking, Currency and Housing, October 22, 1975, at 1361-68.

111. Remarks by R. Forbes, *State Aid to Local Government*, Panel 3, National Governors' Conference, Washington, D.C., February 24, 1976. *See also* note 101 *supra*.

112. For reports on the difficulties of the Massachusetts, Pennsylvania, Illinois, and New York HFAs, *see* 3 Hous. & Dev. Rep. 568 (Nov. 3, 1975); *id.* at 616, 618 (Nov. 17, 1975); *id.* at 872 (Feb. 9, 1976); 4 *id.* at 156 (July 26, 1976).

treaded water waiting for the bond markets to reopen, others under-took less risky projects which met with less resistance in the financial markets (and also tended to be less oriented toward achieving their statutorily defined public purposes). The tax-exempt bond market eventually did reopen to HFAs, as life insurance companies and other institutional investors who had not purchased tax-exempt securities for over a year began to reenter the market, and as tax-exempt mutual bond funds, which came into existence after the Tax Reform Act of 1976, began to expand the market for HFA securities by attracting new buyers. Equally important, the HFAs were able to demonstrate to the financial community the strength of their securi-ties by going to the market only with projects that were soundly conceived, economically viable, well managed, and in all respects attractive investments. As a result the yields on HFA bonds began regaining their once favorable levels.[113]

The difficulties experienced by HFAs over the past two years illus-trate well both their vulnerability to exogenous forces and their durability (and commitment to survive) as efficient mechanisms for housing delivery. During the darkest periods in the financial crunch, pressure was brought to bear on the federal government to imple-ment several programs authorized by the Housing and Community Development Act of 1974 which could have greatly helped the HFAs to more easily and quickly regain access to the bond markets. The federal response was excruciatingly slow; by the time the programs were made operational by HUD they were either no longer imme-diately needed by the HFAs or were deemed to be so overburdened with federal red tape and restrictions as to seriously limit the HFAs' highly valued flexibility.[114]

Future HFA financial crises might be largely avoided—and their deleterious impact on national housing efforts substantially miti-gated—if the following federal programs were effectively imple-mented and were available to provide standby support:

1. Section 802 of the Housing and Community Development Act of 1974 authorizes HUD to guarantee *taxable* HFA bonds issued to finance "housing and related facilities through land acquisition, con-

---

113. *See* 4 Hous. & Dev. Rep. 398–400 (October 4, 1976); *id.* at 444 (Oct. 18, 1976); *id.* at 539–40 (Nov. 15, 1976); *id.* at 626 (Dec. 13, 1976). For an ex-amination of the long-term quality of HFA securities, *see* R. Fishman, *Are State Housing Finance Agencies Self-Supporting?* Paper prepared for the ABA Bar Activation Program in Housing Law, Washington, D.C., November 1975.

114. The generally negative reactions of HFAs to the programs discussed in the text accompanying notes 115-118 *infra*, are reported in 4 Hous. & Dev. Rep. 259 (Aug. 22, 1976); *id.* at 446 (Oct. 18, 1976); *id.* at 753-54 (Jan. 24, 1977).

struction, or rehabilitation, for persons of low, moderate, and middle income . . . in connection with the revitalization of slums or blighted areas. . . .[115] The guarantee of the full faith and credit of the United States would assure the marketability of such bonds. In addition, HUD is authorized to combine the guarantee with an interest-differential grant of up to one-third of the interest payable on these obligations. This grant is designed to make up the difference between the interest cost on such taxable obligations and the lower interest that would have to be paid on similar tax-exempt obligations normally issued by HFAs.

2. Section 802 also authorizes HUD to make interest-differential grants of up to one-third of the interest payable on *taxable* HFA bonds without the federal guarantee and not issued to finance the revitalization of slums and blighted areas.[116] This authority would enable HFAs to raise capital in a wider market than the tax-exempt bond market by attracting investors such as pension funds and insurance companies. Congress has appropriated $15 million for the interest subsidy approach, which it has been estimated could subsidize approximately $400 million of HFA bonds issued at an 11 percent interest rate.[117]

3. Under the Section 244 coinsurance program of the Housing and Community Development Act of 1974, the federal government and the state HFAs could agree to share the risk on any mortgage financed by an HFA, provided the state assumes not less than 10 percent of the risk of loss.[118] The states would be required to establish a reserve of cash or liquid assets to demonstrate to the investment community that they can meet their share of the risks. The higher the portion of the risk that HUD would be willing to assume, the easier it would be for the HFAs to establish the requisite reserve, and also, probably, the greater the likelihood that the states would get favorable credit ratings and therefore pay lower interest rates at the same time. To the extent that HUD's portion of the risk were lowered, the federal agency's coinsurance volume would probably be greater, and the coinsurance program would almost certainly enhance the bond market acceptance of Section 8 housing.

The problem with Section 244, however, is that under present regulations FHA insurance involves excessive red tape, so that

115. Housing and Community Development Act of 1974 § 802(a) and (c)(1); 42 U.S.C.A. § 1440.
116. *Id.* at § 802(c)(2).
117. 3 Hous. & Dev. Rep. 453 (Oct. 6, 1975).
118. Housing and Community Development Act of 1974 § 307, *amending* Title II of the National Housing Act, 12 U.S.C. § 17152-9, *by adding* § 244(a). *See generally* Hance & DuVall, *Coinsurance: The Key to the Future of State Housing Finance Agencies*, 8 Urb. Law. 720 (1976).

participation by the federal agency would limit the flexibility now enjoyed by HFAs. This should not be the case. Where risks are shared, federal red tape should be eliminated or at least substantially minimized.

In the absence of effective federal support, the state HFAs will have to rely on their own resources to assure the continued marketability of their bonds. Among the measures that HFAs have either successfully utilized or might consider using in the future are:

1. The creation of separate state insurance or reserve funds through state general obligation issuances,[119] legislative appropriations,[120] or through the pledge of revenues from other sources.[121] These funds could be leveraged according to standard actuarial practices to underwrite loans in substantial face value amounts.
2. The use of private mortgage insurance.[122]
3. The establishment of an escrow account to assure operations success and to fund increased operating costs by withholding a portion of the developer's syndication profits over a number of years.[123]
4. The experimentation with new forms of real estate and municipal finance, such as variable-rate mortgages, altering the length of terms on bonds and mortgages, selling smaller issues more frequently and with shorter maturity schedules, and concentrating on the retail market.

State HFAs have demonstrated the capacity to be efficient instruments for the delivery of housing assistance. To allow their experience and expertise to be dissipated by forces beyond their control would be imprudent and shortsighted.

---

119. An example is the Maryland Housing Fund, discussed in text accompanying note 84 *supra*.

120. The California legislature has established a Supplementary Bond Security Account for its HFA, with an appropriation of $10 million. Cal. Gov't Code § 41801 (1975). The Minnesota legislature appropriated $34.2 million for its HFA, a substantial portion of which is to be used for a variety of reserve funds. 3 Hous. & Dev. Rep. 1167 (May 3, 1976).

121. The Wyoming Community Development Authority has established a special reserve fund equal to one year's debt service on outstanding bonds, which is financed through proceeds from a state excise tax on mineral extraction. *See* Hous. & Dev. Rep. ref. file no. 2, § 50:0017 (1975).

122. The Tennessee Housing Finance Agency has become the first state HFA to have projects insured by private mortgage insurance. Up to $30 million has been committed by the Mortgage Guarantee Insurance Corporation to insure two Section 8 projects, an elderly and multifamily project. 4 Hous. & Dev. Rep. 627 (Dec. 13, 1976).

123. The Michigan State Housing Development Authority requires a 5 percent escrow account during the first six years of a project's operation. Hous. & Dev. Rep. ref. file no. 2, § 50:0017 (1975).

HOUSING REHABILITATION

A great deal of reinvestment in the older housing stock occurs in neighborhoods that are considered sound, older, well-established areas. It is in neighborhoods just beginning to experience decline that publicly financed or stimulated housing rehabilitation efforts might have great promise. In these areas public programs can help to arrest some decay, can turn pessimism among homeowners and lenders into optimism, and can induce the myriad private decisions that ultimately decide whether an area will be upgraded over time.

Although a great deal of housing capable of rehabilitation is likely to be located in such areas, it is not possible to determine this from national figures. A discussion of the quality of existing housing is often clouded by a lack of clear definitions for "standard" and "substandard," by insufficient data, and by a change in measurement procedures over the years. The 1970 census contained no measurement of the degree of substandardness because the Census Bureau determined that the information gathered by enumerators in the 1960 survey had provided inaccurate data. However, a recent study undertaken by the Harvard-MIT Joint Center for Urban Studies provides a projection of housing conditions for 1980.[124] By aggregating census data for individual market areas to make a national projection and using a consistent definition, the study estimates that about 6 percent of the 1980 housing stock will be substandard.[125] The study further reports that stock will continue to improve, but at a slower pace than during the previous decade.

It is important to distinguish between total or "gut" rehabilitation on the one hand, and modest rehabilitation on the other. The distinction is important because it is not clear that both kinds of projects are equally feasible, or even equally worthwhile. For example, the Rand Institute's 1970 study of *Rental Housing in New York City*, after noting that about $3 billion would be required to bring the city's dilapidated and deteriorated housing stock up to current standards of livability, concluded that much of it was not worth

124. Joint Center for Urban Studies of MIT and Harvard, Housing Needs: 1970 to 1980 (1973).

125. *Id.* at B-8. The study's definition of substandard included dilapidated units with all plumbing; units with inadequate plumbing but in sound condition; and dilapidated units lacking some or all plumbing facilities. The study found a pattern of increasing deteriorations and diminishing renovations: "The number of substandard units with inadequate plumbing (the easiest type of substandard units to renovate) is becoming a much smaller proportion of the total substantial stock. Furthermore, the number of dilapidated units with all plumbing (the most difficult type of substandard unit to renovate) is becoming an increasingly larger component of the substandard stock." *Id.* at B-3.

saving. At an average cost of $10,000 per unit, gut rehabilitation of most older tenements was too expensive. By contrast, "minor and moderate rehabilitation of deteriorating but not dilapidated housing presents a much more promising focus for city efforts," and could be done for an average of $1,000 per unit.[126] Studies in Baltimore and Oakland produced similar findings. In Oakland it appears that modest rehabilitation (about 20 percent of the value of the dwelling) is all that is necessary for preserving much of the housing stock.[127] Other experts also agree that the most cost-effective effort is modest rehabilitation in transitional neighborhoods.[128]

If it is discouraging to realize that much of the country's urban housing is not only badly deteriorated but also may not be worth saving, some encouragement may nevertheless be derived from the fact that a large portion of the declining units classified as substandard are only marginally substandard. This means that a policy of modest rehabilitation may be widely useful as well as feasible. It was found in Baltimore, for example, that 45 percent of inner-city privately owned dwellings needed ordinary maintenance and that 32 percent needed merely painting and fix-up. Of the remainder, 13 percent required minor rehabilitation (at $2,000 each), 3 percent required intermediate rehabilitation (at $4,500 each), and only 1 percent required extensive rehabilitation (at $7,000 each). Six percent of the dwellings needed to be totally gutted or replaced by new construction.[129]

In addition to possessing a stock of substandard or deteriorating units, cities are experiencing a related phenomenon of abandonment of residential units, sometimes culminating in the abandonment of entire neighborhoods. The causes of this breakdown in the market, as previously noted, are complex. Older cities of the Northeast face the severest abandonment problem—New York City with 180,000 units; Philadelphia with 35,000 units; Cleveland with 5,000 units— but cities in the Southwest and West are also experiencing this problem.[130] During the initial phases of abandonment, many of the

126. Rand Institute, Rental Housing in New York City 28 (1970).
127. *1966 Household Survey, reprinted in* City of Oakland Housing Assistance Plan (1975).
128. G. Sternlieb & D. Listokin, Rehabilitation Versus Redevelopment—Cost-Benefit Analyses 4 (Nat'l Tech. Info. Service Doc. PB-232-932, 1973).
129. W. Grigsby, Housing and Poverty at table IX-2 (1971).
130. The figures in the text and more detailed discussions of abandonment appear in Cleveland City Planning Commission, *Housing Abandonment in Cleveland,* Cleveland Housing Papers (1974); F. Kristoff, *Housing and People in New York City,* 10 City Almanac (Feb. 1976); Comment, *Philadelphia's Urban Homesteading Ordinance,* 23 Buffalo L. Rev. 735 (1974); Phillips & Agelasto, *Housing and Central Cities: The Conservation Approach,* 4 Ecology L.Q. 808 (1975).

units can be reclaimed through modest rehabilitation; but the longer they sit the more deteriorated they become through arson, vandalism, and neglect, until they are eventually beyond repair.

The effects of abandonment go beyond the fiscal considerations of lost municipal tax revenue or failure to capture a potential resource. The social effect on the neighborhood and those unable to escape is disastrous. The spectacle of acres of abandoned property in the core of great American cities undermines any citizen's civic pride and confidence in the future. It becomes mute but eloquent testimony to the "failure of the system" to permit continued private ownership and maintenance of the housing stock in large areas of our cities. Given the large quantity of marginally substandard units and the prospects of further residential abandonment, rehabilitation may be the most cost-effective means of preventing residential abandonment—if begun in time.

Past Efforts at Rehabilitation

Much has been written about publicly stimulated or financed housing rehabilitation but with little concrete result. The federal government has never made a full-scale commitment to housing rehabilitation.[131] Rehabilitation programs have always remained in the shadow of programs designed for the production of new units. During the period from 1934–1973, less than 1 percent of all loans insured under FHA programs were for rehabilitation.[132] In almost forty years of operation, FHA has insured over 11.7 million privately owned housing units and 2.1 million units of rental multifamily housing. Rehabilitated units number under 250,000.[133]

HUD's involvement in rehabilitation has also been relatively modest. In April 1968 the department initially estimated that 2 million substandard units would be rehabilitated as part of the ten-year production goal of the 1968 Housing Act. But in its *Second Annual Report on National Housing Goals*, released in April of 1970, HUD revised the subsidized "rehab" production goal downward to 1 million.[134] This 50 percent decrease was explained as resulting

131. *See* Agelasto, Neighborhood Conservation Through Housing Preservation (Congressional Research Service, Oct. 1975); *see also* U.S. Cong., Senate Committee on Banking and Currency, Subcommittee on Housing and Urban Affairs, Rehabilitation Programs (1967).

132. U.S. Department of Housing and Urban Development, 1973 Statistical Yearbook 140 (1975).

133. *Id.* at 141. The FHA statistics in the accompanying text are drawn from *id.* at 140–45.

134. President of the United States, Second Annual Report on National Housing Goals, H.R. Doc. 91-292, 91st Cong., 2d Sess. 26 (1970).

from "the high cost of rehabilitation of older structures brought on by the general rise in construction costs." In addition, "as it turns out there are relatively few cities which have a concentration of large blocks of units for which rehabilitation is feasible.[135] The Nixon Administration's 1973 moratorium on existing housing programs effectively suspended HUD rehabilitation activity, and its analysis of the effectiveness of HUD programs that followed the suspension paid little attention to rehabilitation.[136]

Currently, the most important sources of money for residential rehabilitation are those available under the Section 8 and community development block grant programs established by the Housing and Community Development Act of 1974. In filing an application for community development funds, each community, as part of its required HAP, is required to assess its housing needs and specify a realistic annual goal for the number of dwelling units or persons to be assisted (including the relative proportion of new, rehabilitated, and existing dwelling units). Section 8 is the only sizable production program available, and it has been expected to absorb much of the new construction and substantial rehabilitation activity that was formerly financed under the suspended Section 236 interest-reduction subsidy and traditional public housing programs.

HUD's review of local HAPs for the first year of the program showed that communities planned on using 30 percent of Section 8 funds for rehabilitated housing.[137] In early 1977, however, after two years of the program, HUD had allocated only 5 percent of the Section 8 production funds for rehabilitated housing.[138] This discrepancy may be a manifestation of a further federal de-emphasis on rehabilitation,[139] combined with a perceived local overemphasis on rehabilitation in conjunction with local community development plans.

---

135. *Id.* at 25.

136. *See* Housing in the Seventies, *supra* note 1.

137. U.S. Department of Housing and Urban Development, Community Development Block Grant Program: First Annual Report 48 (Dec. 1975). The report also indicated that low- and moderate-income families and neighborhoods were to be the primary beneficiaries of rehabilitation and neighborhood conservation activities. *Id.* at 11. Several subsequent studies have questioned HUD's initial findings. *See, e.g.,* U.S. Government Accounting Office, Meeting Application and Review Requirements for Block Grants Under Title I of the Housing and Community Development Act of 1974 (June 23, 1976); R. Deleon and R. LeGates, Redistribution Effects of Special Revenue Sharing for Community Development (Prepared for the Institute of Government Studies, University of California at Berkeley, July 1976).

Under the 1974 Act, communities may use community development block grants for housing rehabilitation loans and grants. In its first annual report to Congress on the community development program, HUD found that communities appeared to be emphasizing improvements to existing neighborhood infrastructures and the use of rehabilitated housing in their local community development programs. In its second annual report, HUD found that communities had been able to attract approximately $2.40 in private funds for each $1 in block grants spent on rehabilitation, by utilizing six basic techniques to leverage the community development funds:[140]

1. Interest Subsidy. Block grant funds are used to pay part of the interest charges on rehab loans made by private financial institutions (with subsidized interest rates often lowered to around 5 percent).

138. 4 Hous. & Dev. Rep. 874 (Feb. 21, 1977). As of the end of calendar 1976, of the 227,920 Section 8 units under annual contributions or housing assistance payment contracts, 21,222 were designated for new construction, 1,188 for substantial rehabilitation, and 205,510 for existing units. *Id.*

HUD has more recently attempted to show a greater commitment to rehabilitation; it has initiated, with Section 8 contract authority, a special demonstration housing rehabilitation program in which unions agree to work at reduced wage scales (roughly 75 percent of prevailing wage rates). After considerable delays, involving conflicts between HUD, the Department of Labor, and local and national unions, some 22 cities have been selected to participate in the $50-million program. Before the programs become operational, HUD must approve the cities' labor-management agreements concerning work rules, reduced wage rates, etc. *See* 4 Hous. & Dev. Rep. 517 (Nov. 15, 1976); *id.* at 693 (Jan. 10, 1977); *id.* at 738 (Jan. 24, 1977); *id* at 873 (Feb. 21, 1977).

139. The lack of major federal commitment is not surprising in view of the Nixon Administration's earlier halving of the national housing rehabilitation goal, and suspension of federal subsidy programs (see text accompanying notes 134-36 *supra*) and the Ford Administration's conclusory declaration, in the President's 1976 Report on National Growth and Development, that "reliance on rehabilitation and remodeling as a major method of upgrading the nation's housing stock has not proved to be realistic." Changing Issues for National Growth 113 (G.P.O. 1976). Officials from the nation's cities obviously do not share this view. At its annual meeting in December 1975, the National League of Cities adopted the following statement as part of its National Municipal Policy—1976: "Conservation and better use of the existing stock of urban housing should be a top priority. Federal programs should emphasize major commitment to rehabilitation, which is vigorously promoted, is adequately funded, and provides appropriate funding to lower income families who need it." *Id.* at 41.

140. U.S. Department of Housing and Urban Development, Community Development Block Program, Housing and Community Development Act of 1974: Second Annual Report 125-30 (G.P.O. Dec. 1976). The leverage ratio varied significantly with each technique. In turn, the speed of the program seemed to depend on the leverage ratio; with the most quickly implemented rehab programs being directly correlated with the lowest leveraged program. *Id.*

2. Loan Guarantee. Block grant funds are used to set up an escrow account which guarantees the loans made by private lending institutions to city-approved applicants regardless of their credit risk.
3. Revolving Loan Fund. Block grant funds are placed on deposit with private lending institutions agreeing to make rehab loans in specified areas. Depending on the type of community account established (interest bearing, interest free, and so on), the rehab loans are made at lower interest rates, in reduced principal amounts (subsidized by community development funds), or with other favorable terms (such as no service charge).
4. Tax-Exempt Municipal Loans. Block grant funds are used to provide additional security for tax-free housing bonds issued by public agencies, or to supplement the revenues required by the agencies to service their debt. The proceeds of the bonds are in turn used to make rehab loans—either indirectly through private lending institutions or directly by the agencies to the property owner.
5. Rehabilitation Grant or Loan. Block grant funds are paid or loaned directly to cover a portion of the cost of private rehabilitation (often between 50 to 80 percent of the cost)—the owner pays the remainder from personal savings or private loans (this is clearly the least effective leveraging method).
6. Grant Rebate. Block grants are used to reimburse a property-owner for a portion of the cost, usually 10 to 30 percent of rehabilitating a dwelling. The owner must obtain the initial financing.

In addition to leveraging their block grant funds in the above ways, a number of communities, according to the HUD report, were piggybacking the funds to facilitate or make usable other programs; that is, block grant funds were used to supplement rehabilitation costs not covered fully by federal Section 312 rehabilitation loans or by locally financed rehabilitation or homesteading programs.

The Housing and Community Development Act of 1974 established the federal Urban Homesteading program, whereby HUD can dispose of HUD acquired properties at no cost to the transferee.[141] In view of the fact that HUD is the country's largest owner of inner-city housing, the program might offer the hope of greater promise. The number of units actually involved under the program, however, is *de minimus* in relation to HUD's total holdings, and the federal

141. Housing and Community Development Act of 1974 § 810, *Urban Homesteading Demonstration Program*, 40 Fed. Reg. 26053 (June 20, 1975).

assistance available for financing the rehabilitation of the relatively few available units is woefully inadequate. In addition, the federal program suffers from many of the same basic problems that locally operated programs have experienced.

A growing number of cities have attempted housing rehabilitation and neighborhood conservation through locally initiated homesteading programs. Properties which the cities acquired through abandonment, tax delinquency foreclosures, or dedication, are conveyed to eligible families at nominal cost. The families must then commit themselves to major repairs and to live in the dwelling for a specified number of years.[142] The programs are rarely targeted for the poor or even the lower-middle class; such families cannot afford to obtain financing for the substantial rehabilitation costs often necessitated (particularly in the absence of a pool of high-risk mortgage funds that might be made available under one of the community development strategies mentioned above). Moreover, the programs are generally of such limited scale—with the houses involved often physically situated so far apart—that they can scarcely be expected to save entire neighborhoods.[143]

Other kinds of rehabilitation or neighborhood conservation programs are now being undertaken or planned in hundreds of municipalities, given impetus by the community development block grant program and various public-private joint ventures.[144] While most of the local programs still operate on a relatively small scale, there are strong indications that cities are learning from one another's

142. For operational accounts of some of the prototypical homesteading programs, *see* Note, *Homesteading 1974: Reclaiming Abandoned Houses on the Urban Frontier,* 10 Colum. J.L. & Soc. Probs. 416 (1974); Note, *From Plows to Pliers—Urban Homesteading in America,* 2 Fordham Urb. L.J. 273 (1974); *Philadelphia's Urban Homesteading Ordinance, supra* note 130.

143. The "promises" made in conjunction with urban homesteading programs often exceed the actual accomplishments (in terms of income groups that can be served and the ability of the programs to stem the tide of neighborhood blight). *See generally* Robinson & Weinstein, *Urban Homesteading: Hope . . . or Hoax?* 8 J. Housing 395 (1973); Note, *Urban Homesteading Programs,* 4 Law Proj. Bull. 10 (March 15, 1974). *See also* articles cited in note 142 *supra.*

144. Useful summaries of a wide variety of these programs can be found in U.S. Department of H.U.D., Neighborhood Preservation: A Catalog of Local Programs (G.P.O. 1975); H.U.D., Examples of Local and State Financing of Property Rehabilitation (G.P.O. 1974). An in-depth case study of the Neighborhood Housing Services (NHS) program—an outgrowth of the Federal Urban Reinvestment Task Force and a joint effort of several federal financial regulatory agencies and HUD to stimulate the development of local partnerships of neighborhood residents, private lenders and local government—is contained in R. Ahlbrandt & P. Brophy, Neighborhood Revitalization: Theory and Practice (1975). The study discusses the Pittsburg NHS program, the nation's first, and the prototype for subsequent programs.

experiences, and as a result the various programs are becoming increasingly sophisticated. As the states begin to develop anti-red-lining measures[145] and as their HFAs devote greater attention and financial resources to inner-city housing, a more comprehensive (and ultimately fruitful) approach to the highly complex problems associated with rehabilitation and neighborhood conservation is likely to evolve.

THE PROPERTY TAX

Few other factors affecting housing and patterns of urban growth have generated as much attention and controversy as has the role of the property tax. An *ad valorem* tax—so called because it is an annual tax levied as a percentage of the market value of property—the property tax has a long history as the major revenue source for local governments in America. According to the conventional wisdom on the subject, the property tax tends to debilitate private attempts to rehabilitate and improve existing housing, and thus leads to neighborhood decline; it places a disproportionate burden on lower income households; and it encourages fiscal zoning and intra-metropolitan fiscal competition that distorts equitable and rational regional growth.[146]

This section will examine various legislative efforts that have been undertaken to ameliorate some of these perceived negative implications commonly associated with the property tax, and identify the legal issues frequently raised in conjunction with these reforms. (We will also point out, where appropriate, some of the more current, revisionist thinking on the property tax, but will leave to further economic study the resolution of the conflicting views and cost-benefit analyses of the various reforms discussed herein.)

145. See the discussion of the redlining problem that appears subsequently in this chapter.

146. The classical view on the deficiencies of the property tax and the need for reform is that expressed in D. Netzer, Economics of the Property Tax (Brookings Institution 1966). *See also* D. Netzer, Impact of the Property Tax: Its Economic Implications for Urban Problems (Prepared for the National Commission on Urban Problems 1968); J. Heilbran, Real Estate Taxes and Urban Housing (1966); Heilbran, *Reforming the Real Estate Tax to Encourage Housing Maintenance and Rehabilitation*, in Land and Building Taxes (Becker ed. 1969). Many of the traditional assumptions about the effects of the property tax are questioned in the following works: G. Peterson, ed., Property Tax Reform (Urban Institute 1973); H. Aaron, Who Pays the Property Tax? (Brookings Institution 1975); Ladd, *The Role of the Property Tax: A Reassessment*, in Broad-Based Taxes: New Options and Sources (R. Musgrave ed. 1973).

Tax Abatement and Housing Rehabilitation

One of the major criticisms leveled against the property tax is that it discourages housing rehabilitation.[147] Whenever a landowner rehabilitates a piece of property, an increase in assessment resulting from the newly appreciated value, and a corresponding increase in property taxes, must be accepted; this is a clear disincentive to rehabilitation.[148] Consequently, before a landowner will make a capital expenditure on rehabilitation, the net return must be calculated to reflect both the actual cost of rehabilitation and the increased taxes. If the landowner requires an 8 percent rate of return on invested capital, for instance, the imposition of an additional 4 percent effective tax will discourage all improvements that would yield a pretax rate of return of between 8 and 12 percent. The public sector, however, can influence this economic calculus by reducing rehabilitation costs and expected property taxes.

A number of states authorize tax abatement for private rehabilitation efforts; and a few even mandate tax abatement.[149] Generally the state programs provide tax abatement by following one of two approaches. Under the first approach, the rehabilitated property is completely exempt from the property tax (that is, the tax increment that would be caused by the added value of the structure), and participating municipalities are allowed to collect a service charge in lieu of taxes.[150] This service charge is usually set to reflect preexisting taxes and is collected as a proportion of the gross rent. Under the second tax exemption approach, the property tax is maintained, but reassessments resulting from rehabilitation are

147. *See* Netzer, Impact of the Property Tax, note 146 *supra.*

148. Recent studies have shown that as a practical matter in inner-city areas, reassessment and increased property taxes often lag far behind rehabilitative efforts if, in fact, they occur at all. *See, e.g.,* Arthur D. Little, Inc., A Study of Property Taxes and Urban Blight (Prepared for the U.S. Department of Housing and Urban Development 1973). Such findings have contributed to the current view that the inefficient administration of the property tax makes the tax's influence on housing investment and abandonment much less significant than it was commonly thought to be. *See* Peterson, *The Property Tax and Low-Income Housing Markets,* in Peterson, *supra* note 146, at 107–24. (The Arthur D. Little study, *supra,* did, however, indicate that unequal tax assessments, as among neighborhoods of the same city, may contribute significantly to blight.)

149. For a discussion of various tax-abatement statutes, *see* Alpert, *Property Tax Abatement: An Incentive for Low Income Housing,* 11 Harv. J. Leg. 1 (1973) [hereinafter cited as Alpert]. An example of a mandatory abatement statute is Ind. Code Ann. § 6-1-10. 1-1 (Burns 1972).

150. *See, e.g.,* Mass. Gen. Laws Ann. ch. 121A, § 10 (1969); Ohio Rev. Code Ann. § 1728.11.

deferred.[151] The duration of deferral varies from state to state: the minimum is five years,[152] the maximum is fifty.[153]

In practice, tax abatement only minimally encourages private rehabilitation because the subsidy it provides for landowners is very small. Consequently, unless a landowner can increase rents to offset rehabilitation expenditures, investment will not occur.[154] Tax abatements are therefore usually made part of a broader government assistance program. Of the states that provide some type of tax exemption for profit seeking landowners, eight give exemptions to redevelopment companies as part of urban renewal programs, and only six states currently authorize tax exemptions in the absence of any other government subsidy program.[155] Several states, recognizing the need for further financial assistance, indirectly reimburse landowners for their investments by increasing the amount of subsidy to include abatement of existing taxes.[156] In New York, for example, existing property taxes can be abated for an equivalent of 8.33 percent of the cost of the rehabilitation for up to twelve years.[157]

Tax Increment Financing

A variation on the theme of tax abatement is tax increment financing (sometimes called tax allocation financing). A "bootstrap" method of financing urban redevelopment, tax increment financing has been described as a "process whereby moneys are borrowed and used to undertake urban renewal activities, with the increase in real property taxes resulting from the urban renewal activities first being directed to the repayment of the moneys borrowed."[158] The process

151. *See generally* N.Y. Priv. Hous. Fin. Laws § 93; Pa. Stat. Ann. tit. 72, § 4711-16 (Supp. 1973).

152. Ohio Rev. Code Ann. § 3735.67.

153. *See* N.Y. Priv. Hous. Fin. Law § 93(5).

154. *See* Alpert, *supra* note 149, at 6.

155. The eight states with tax exemptions for redevelopment companies are: Hawaii, Massachusetts, Michigan, Minnesota, Missouri, New Jersey, New York, and Ohio, *Id.* at 13. The six states that provide tax exemptions for nongovernment assisted rehabilitation efforts are: Connecticut, Indiana, New York, Ohio, Pennsylvania and Vermont. *Id.* at 22.

156. *Id.* at 26.

157. N.Y. Real Prop. Tax Law § 489(2). For a discussion of several of New York City's tax-abatement programs and a description of an economic model for analyzing the fiscal cost-benefit elements of tax subsidy programs in housing investment, *see* G. Sternlieb, E. Roistacher & J. Hughes, Tax Subsidies and Housing Investment: A Fiscal Cost-Benefit Analysis (1976).

158. *See* Hegg, *Tax Increment Financing of Urban Renewal—Redevelopment Incentive Without Federal Assistance*, 2 Real Estate L.J. 575 (Fall 1973).

is premised on the fact that property values—and hence real estate taxes—invariably rise as the result of a successful urban redevelopment project. Simply stated, the following steps are involved in tax financing:

1. A project area is specifically designated in an urban redevelopment plan.
2. The value of the properties within the project area are determined at a fixed date prior to any project activities.
3. The level of tax receipts in that area, as indicated on the tax digest, is frozen.
4. Tax increments created by the new development are pledged to reduce the indebtedness on the bonds issued by a redevelopment authority or district to finance the project.
5. Once the bonds are retired, all tax receipts (increments plus base) are added to the city's tax digest.[159]

Eleven states presently have some form of tax increment financing.[160] Of these eleven, both California and Oregon have constitutional enabling provisions, while the other states do not.[161] Alaska, Iowa, Minnesota, Nevada, Oregon, Utah, and Wyoming have legislation identical or similar to that of California.[162]

Tax increment financing can be used as a supplemental method of financing, as an alternative mode of financing, and to some extent as a means of subsidizing certain commercial and industrial uses. But,

159. One commentator has noted that the political acceptability of tax increment financing is perhaps more of an obstacle than economic feasibility.

There is generally controversy over even the smallest modifications of the tax system, especially property tax. Freezing assessed valuation in a project area limits increase in tax revenues until the bonds are fully retired. Loss of tax revenue increases during the bond term may result in increased levies elsewhere in the taxing jurisdiction. To make the deal more attractive project sponsors often make gifts of land and offer lease-back arrangements. This tension may be alleviated as less reliance on property tax as a tool for local self-financing occurs in the future.

Morris *supra* note 44, at 109-12.
160. Alaska Stat. §§ 18.55.695 to .697, .945 (1974); Cal. Health & Safety Code §§ 33670 to 74 (West 1973); Colo. Rev. Stat. § 31-25-1112(5) (1974); Iowa Code Ann. § 403.19 (Supp. 1974/75); Minn. Stat. Ann. 462.585 *et seq.* (Supp. 1975); Nev. Rev. Stat. §§ 279.674 to .680 (1973); Ohio Rev. Code Ann. § 725.04 (Page Supp. 1975); Or. Rev. Stat. §§ 457.410 to .450 (Rpl. Pt. 1971); Utah Code Ann. §§ 11-15-149 to -150, (Rpl. Vol. 1973); Wash. Rev. Code Ann. § 35.81.100(5) (Supp. 1975); Wyo. Stat. Ann. §§ 15.1-512 to -513 (Rpl. Vol. 1965).
161. Cal. Const. art. XVI, § 16 (formerly Cal. Const. art. XIII, § 19); Or. Const. art. IX, § 1(c).
162. *See* note 160 supra.

of course, property values after redevelopment must be sufficiently higher than the property values before redevelopment; otherwise the tax increments will be insufficient to pay off the redevelopment agency's net cost plus interest over the period required to service its debt, which is usually twenty to thirty years. Application of the tax increment method to finance or subsidize low- and moderate-income housing alone is therefore problematic. However, the provision of such housing may be facilitated to some extent in projects that pair low- and moderate-income housing with intensive and highly leveraged economic redevelopment, such as office and commercial buildings.[163]

A study by the National Council for Urban Economic Development surveyed a number of advantages and disadvantages in the use of tax increment financing as a tool for community development.[164] Among the advantages noted are the following:

1. The ability to provide substantial capital for economically feasible development projects.
2. Tax revenues that were collected prior to the development project continue to be collected; thus the community does not lose tax revenues.
3. Once a project is completed and the bonds have been retired, the increased tax revenues become available to the city and other jurisdictions.
4. Since tax allocation bonds are not part of the city's debt limitation, a public referendum is usually not required.
5. Since the success of the financing scheme is dependent on attracting private investors in the bond market, the projects must be well conceived and economically sound.

The disadvantages identified in the study include:

1. The system does not provide any increase in tax revenues until the bonds are retired (which may be a period of several decades). In the interim, the new development produces service demands without generating revenues to meet these new demands. As a result, taxpayers outside the project area indirectly subsidize any increased service needs (police and fire protection, education services, and so forth) during this period.
2. Tax allocation bonds are generally more expensive (that is, have

163. *See* Morris, *supra* note 44, at 112.
164. D. Harbit, Tax Increment Financing 6 (National Council for Urban Economic Development Information Service No. 1, Sept. 1975).

higher interest rates) than general obligation bonds backed by the full faith and credit of the city.

3. The system has been abused when agencies have designated large areas of the city in order to capture tax increments that may not be attributable to the public investment financed by the tax increment scheme.

4. If the increment does not materialize, other sources of funds must be obtained to prevent default.

5. Since the bonds are issued by independent redevelopment authorities, citizens have little control over decisions that may significantly affect the amount of tax revenues available to the city.

Weighing these various costs and benefits, the study concluded that at least some of the potential problems associated with tax increment financing "can be solved through judicious use of the tool by economic development professionals who have carefully analyzed [its] potential impact . . . on the local budget."[165]

Restraints on Tax Abatement Programs

A major restraint on tax abatement programs, which may help explain their limited use in conjunction with housing rehabilitation and urban redevelopment, is the importance of the property tax in local financing. Notwithstanding the fact that federal and state aid to local governments has expanded dramatically over the past decade,[166] the property tax is still the primary source of revenue for most local governments: in 1971 the local property tax constituted 84.6 percent of all local tax revenues and 39.9 percent of all local general revenues.[167] Consequently, unless additional funds are made available by federal and state governments, or the reliance on the property tax as a means of local funding of basic services is otherwise altered by broadening the local tax base, local tax abatement programs will likely remain a very limited policy tool for stimulating housing rehabilitation, particularly in communities that are hard pressed financially.[168]

165. *Id.*

166. Federal aid to state and local governments expanded dramatically in the sixties and early seventies—from $8.8 billion in 1963 to over $43 billion in 1973. Yet this increased aid has not been sufficiently concentrated in the central cities to enable them to deal effectively with their fiscal problems. *See* C. Schultze, E. Fried, A Rivlin & N. Teeters, Setting National Priorities: The 1973 Budget 291-305 (1972); *see also* Tax Foundation, Inc., The Financial Outlook for State-Local Government to 1980 (1973).

167. U.S. Department of Commerce, Bureau of the Census, *Government Finances: 1970-1971* (Series GF-71, No. 5), *reprinted in* O. Oldman & F. Schoettle, State and Local Taxes and Finance: Text, Problems and Cases 137 (1974).

168. Upon objective analysis, many communities might find, however, that

Connecticut is one state which has recognized this problem. In order to promote low- and moderate-income housing, it provides compensatory financial assistance to municipalities that agree to offer tax abatements. Connecticut law provides:

> The state, acting by and in the discretion of the commissioner [of community affairs], may enter into a contract with a municipality for state financial assistance for housing solely for low or moderate income persons or families in the form of reimbursement for tax abatements. . . . Such contract shall provide for state financial assistance in the form of a state grant-in-aid to the municipality equal to the amount of taxes abated by the municipality. . . . [169]

This reimbursement—up to $450 per dwelling unit per year—may continue for up to 40 years.[170] Thus, Connecticut makes it both financially possible and politically more palatable for its municipalities to grant significant tax incentives by reimbursing the cities for revenue lost by abatement.

Another important limitation on tax abatements is the common state constitutional provision that prohibits or restricts differential assessments. Twenty-one states allow tax exemptions other than those specifically permitted by their constitutions.[171] In these states a tax exemption is generally upheld if the exemption, as a policy tool, is rationally related to a permissible governmental purpose.[172] This "rationally related" test of the Equal Protection Clause allows states and localities to exercise broad discretion. Five states allow exemptions beyond those specified in their constitutions, but the test is more rigorous than that of mere rationality.[173] One of the five,

the benefits accruing from a tax abatement program (the multiplier effects of new construction, increased employment, etc.) could well exceed the immediate costs of foregone tax revenues. *See* Sternlieb, *supra* note 157.

169. Conn. Gen. Stat. Ann. §§ 8-215, 216, *as amended* (1975).

170. *See* Connecticut Department of Community Affairs, Statutory Tax Computation for State Reimbursement of Tax Abatement (Sept. 30, 1975). Connecticut's approach to providing reimbursement for local tax abatements was originally recommended by Advisory Commission on Intergovernmental Relations, The Role of the States in Strengthening the Property Tax 12 (1963).

171. The states that permit property tax exemption beyond those specified in their constitutions are: Alabama, Alaska, Connecticut, Delaware, Hawaii, Iowa, Maine, Michigan Maryland, Mississippi, New Jersey, New York, North Dakota, Oregon, Pennsylvania, Rhode Island, South Dakota, Vermont, Washington, Wisconsin, and Wyoming. Oldman, Cobb & Oosterbuis, *Problems Under State Law of Federal Residential Property Tax Relief Proposals*, in Financing Schools and Property Tax Relief—A State Responsibility 220 (Advisory Commission on Intergovernmental Relations 1973).

172. *E.g.*, Lehnhansen v. Lake Shore Auto Parts Co., 410 U.S. 356 (1973).

173. The states that apply a rigorous test for exemptions are: Idaho, Kansas, Massachusetts, Minnesota, and New Hampshire. *See* J. Hellerstein, State and Local Taxation: Cases and Materials 220 (1969).

Massachusetts, allows tax abatements absent a constitutional amendment when the tax-exempt entity is a redevelopment corporation.[174] The remaining twenty-four states forbid the exemption of any property from taxation, regardless of the Equal Protection Clause, except for certain types of property specificially exempted by their constitutions.[175] In these states, state constitutional amendments authorizing the abatements would have to be enacted.[176]

Circuit Breakers

A second criticism leveled against the property tax is that it is regressive.[177] This view holds that because property taxes are generally levied in proportion to the value of real property rather than in relation to household income, households with lower incomes often pay a greater percentage of their income for property tax. A family owning and occupying its own house and having a yearly income of less than $2,000, for instance, pays over 16 percent of its income for real property tax; but the effective property tax rate for all incomes is only 4.9 percent.[178] Another segment of the society that pays a disproportionate amount of its income in real property taxes is the elderly. Over six million aged homeowners pay on an average 8.1 percent of their household income as real property tax, whereas the average tax rate for all nonelderly homeowners is 4.1 percent.[179]

To make the property tax more equitable and to eliminate its

174. Opinion of Justices, 334 Mass. 760, 135 N.E.2d 665 (1956).

175. The states that do not allow property tax exemptions except for purposes enumerated in their constitutions are: Arizona, Arkansas, California, Colorado, Florida, Georgia, Illinois, Indiana, Kentucky, Louisiana, Missouri, Montana, Nebraska, Nevada, New Mexico, North Carolina, Ohio, Oklahoma, South Carolina, Tennessee, Texas, Utah, Virginia, and West Virginia. *See* Hellerstein, *supra* note 173, at 219.

176. *Id. See, e.g.,* Land Clearance for Redevelopment Authority v. City of St. Louis 270 S.W.2d 58, 64-65 (Mo. 1954).

177. For the view that the property tax is severely regressive, *see* Netzer, *supra* note 146; *see also* Shannon, *The Property Tax: Reform or Relief?* in Peterson, *supra* note 146, at 25-52. For a newer (and increasingly more prevalent) view that holds that once permanent income is properly defined, property taxes are approximately neutral with respect to income, and probably even somewhat progressive on the average (although the view acknowledges that lower income families are generally exposed to heavier burdens), *see* Aaron, *supra* note 146; and Peterson, *supra* note 146, at 4-7. A less common assertion—that the property tax, when applied at a uniform rate, is definitely progressive—is made by Gaffney, *An Agenda for Strengthening the Property Tax,* in Peterson *supra* note 146 at 65-84.

178. Shannon, *The Property Tax: Reform or Relief?* in Peterson, *supra* note 146, at 27.

179. Advisory Commission on Intergovernmental Relations, Property Tax Circuit Breakers: Current Status and Policy Issues 15 (1975) [hereinafter cited as Circuit Breakers].

harsh consequences, all fifty states have enacted property tax relief programs.[180] The most rapidly growing form of relief is the "circuit breaker."[181] Generally, circuit breakers are designed to protect household income from tax "overload"; thus, when the property tax bill (or, in some states, when the tax equivalent for renters[182]) exceeds some established maximum, the circuit breaker becomes operative and relief is granted from the tax overload.[183] The type of relief granted under the circuit breakers varies from state to state,[184] but there are three broad approaches:

1. The taxpayer receives an amount that is equal to the tax overload as a state income tax credit.
2. The taxpayer receives a cash rebate equivalent to the tax overload.
3. The taxpayer deducts the tax overload directly from a property tax bill.

180. *Id.* at 1. In the economics community, the case for property tax relief programs of the homestead exemption variety is extremely weak. Such exemptions, introduced in the 1930s and given to all homeowners regardless of income, are criticized for, among other things, substantially reducing the local tax base, furnishing a hidden subsidy, and adding to the administrative burden of the property tax. *See* Ladd, *supra* note 146.

181. In 1964 Wisconsin was the only state with a circuit breaker; by 1973, twelve jurisdictions had a circuit breaker program; and as of February 1975, twenty-five jurisdictions had such programs. Circuit Breakers, *supra* note 179, at 1. The circuit breaker generally receives much higher grades than the homestead exemption, Peterson, *supra* note 146, because, in addition to reasons mentioned in the preceding note, it attempts to deal directly with the low-income problem by establishing an upper-income limit and by including low-income renters as well as homeowners.

182. The jurisdictions that permit circuit breaker tax relief for renters are: Arizona, Colorado, Connecticut, District of Columbia, Illinois, Indiana, Iowa, Maine, Minnesota, Missouri, Nevada, Pennsylvania and West Virginia. Circuit Breakers, *supra* note 179, at 4. The tax equivalent for renters is computed as some percentage of the gross rent, ranging from 25 percent in Arizona, Illinois, and Maine, to 12 percent in West Virginia. *Id.* at 20–25.

183. To determine when the property tax is excessive, two basic approaches are followed: "threshold" and "sliding scale." Under the threshold approach, an acceptable tax burden is defined as some fixed percentage of household income (usually different percentages are set for different income levels), and any tax that exceeds this threshold is excessive. Under the sliding scale approach, a fixed income percentage of the property tax is rebated for each eligible taxpayer within a given income class; the rebate percentage declines as income rises. The sliding scale approach is used in eight jurisdictions: Arizona, California, Idaho, Indiana, Iowa, Minnesota, Ohio, and Pennsylvania; whereas the threshold approach is used in thirteen jurisdictions: Arkansas, Connecticut, District of Columbia, Illinois, Kansas, Maryland, Michigan, Missouri, Nevada, North Dakota, Oklahoma, Vermont, and West Virginia. Unique formulas are used in Colorado, Maine, Oregon, and Wisconsin. *Id.* at 3–4.

184. For a comprehensive discussion of the various types of property tax relief enacted by the states, *see Real Property Tax Relief for the Elderly*, 7 Mich. J.L. Ref. 388 (1974).

The coverage provided by the circuit breaker also varies among the states. All state programs provide coverage to elderly homeowners (variously defined); and in most states, elderly renters are also eligible for tax relief.[185] In addition, some states provide relief regardless of age and occupancy status to all households with incomes below a certain level.[186] Naturally, when the coverage is expanded, the cost of the program is increased, but inequities and potential legal challenges are diminished.

In sum, circuit breakers offer two major features as a tax relief measure. Since they are financed by the states (and higher levels of government are generally accepted as being more suitable for accomplishing redistribution of income), they do not reduce the local tax base or otherwise impair the financial capabilities of localities. Properly enacted and administered, they can be targeted at those segments of the population most in need of aid.

Challenges to circuit breakers are usually founded on equal protection grounds and on the typical state constitutional provision mandating uniform property taxation.[187] In *State ex rel. Garvey v. Morgan*[188] a taxpayer brought a lawsuit challenging the constitutionality of the Wisconsin circuit breaker program—and specifically the denial of tax relief to persons under age 65. The taxpayer argued that since persons under age 65 may have a greater economic need for relief than some persons 65 or over, the law was arbitrary and unrelated to traditional welfare concepts based on need.[189] The Wisconsin Supreme Court analyzed this argument under both the equal protection doctrine and the uniformity doctrine, and concluded that the circuit breaker was valid. The court reasoned that since 65 is commonly regarded as the retirement age and the point when other governmental benefits begin to be provided, the age limitation was reasonable and rationally related to the purpose of the law.[190] There was therefore no violation of equal protection guarantees.[191]

The second issue analyzed by the court involved the application of the state's constitutional uniformity provision.[192] Recognizing the

185. *See supra* note 179, at 20-25; *Detailed Features of Principal State Property Tax Relief Programs for Homeowners and Renters*, in Peterson, *supra* note 146, at 42-52, table 7; Circuit Breakers, *supra* note 179.

186. Maryland, Michigan, Oregon, Vermont, and Wisconsin provide general tax relief to all needy persons. *See* sources in note 185 *supra*.

187. E.g., Minn. Const. art. 9, § 1 states: ". . . Taxes shall be uniform upon the same class of subjects, and shall be levied and collected for public purposes. . ."

188. 30 Wis. 2d 1, 139 N.W.2d 585, 591 (1966).

189. *Id.* at 585.

190. *Id.* at 588.

191. *Id.; accord*, Opinion of Justices, 110 N.J. 206, 266 A.2d 111 (1970).

192. Wis. Const. art 8, § 1.

broader social aims of the circuit breaker, the Wisconsin court held that the program did not affect the property tax itself and was therefore not subject to the rule of uniformity.[193] Instead the court characterized the program as another welfare program for the aged needy and thereby avoided the uniformity question entirely. Among the specific factors used by the Wisconsin Supreme Court to characterize the circuit breaker as a welfare program and not an unlawful property tax were the following:

1. Not all eligible claimants were actually required to pay property taxes; renters as well as owners were eligible for relief.
2. Landlords were required to pay all property taxes regardless of whether any of their tenants were eligible for relief.
3. When relief was granted, payment was made either as a credit against state income taxes or from state general appropriations, neither of which are related to the property tax.
4. Given the nature of the relief, local property tax receipts and disbursements remained unaffected by the circuit breaker.[194]

The case may be said to have turned on the difference between a legal and an economic view of the incidence of a tax. The court was unwilling to look beyond the legal liability for the property tax; it was interested only in knowing that owners and not renters pay the property tax in the first instance. It is obvious, however, that landlords pass the tax along to tenants in the form of higher rents, and that owners pass it along to buyers in the form of higher prices. By declining to engage in this kind of analysis, and by scrutinizing only the legal arrangements for payment of the tax, the Wisconsin court was able to avoid an anachronistic and unpopular constitutional provision. But *Garvey* applies only to Wisconsin law, and whether its reasoning will or can be adopted elsewhere remains to be seen.

The Property Tax and Fiscal Zoning: Implications for Reform Posed by the Exclusionary Zoning and School Finance Cases

The structure of the property tax is an important source of local resistance to the construction of new lower income housing. The fiscal pressures on local jurisdictions are usually so great that the

193. State *ex rel.* Garvey v. Morgan, 139 N.W.2d at 591 (1966).
194. *Id.*

use of land controls to increase the local tax base and limit the costs perceived to be associated with lower income housing is often irresistible. The most common exclusionary devices are zoning regulations that favor: (1) single family houses on large lots; (2) apartments that are too small for families with many school-aged children; and (3) industry and commerce. Generally, the aim is to keep out as many school children as possible, or at least to insure that families with children have substantial houses for tax assessments, and to attract high tax ratables. Fiscal zoning is the term that has been used to describe the zoning and housing regulations designed to discourage the migration of families whose local tax contributions are not expected to cover the cost of supplying them with public services at the current levels in that community.[195] Although fiscal zoning acts primarily to restrict low-income families to central cities and rural areas, it can also be used to exclude middle-income groups from wealthier communities.

The use of governmental power to keep the poor and lower-middle class out of a jurisdiction is commonly justified by reference to the desirability of local self-determination, and in some circumstances this rationale has credibility. More often, however, the community that defends its exclusionary policies in terms of self-determination and homogeneity is not noticeably homogeneous, and its primary concern is nearly always to avoid new tax burdens. "Local leaders justify 'home rule' in planning and zoning on the basis that local people should have the right to determine the kind of community they want," says a recent report of the New Jersey Tax Policy Committee. "But debate on most plans or zoning ordinances in New Jersey focuses almost entirely on taxes, not the pattern of community that will result. . . . [A] lmost all communities on the fringe of urbanization are zoned with the intention of keeping school taxes in check."[196] New Jersey is typical in this respect.

Fiscal zoning represents the use of the government's police powers for ends that often have no apparent relationship to the general

195. There is a discussion of fiscal zoning in Chapter 1 *supra*. *See generally* Building the American City, *supra* note 1, at 330; R. Babcock & F. Bosselman, Exclusionary Zoning: Land Use Regulations and Housing in the 1970s (1973). For an economist's view on the subject, *see* Hamilton, *Property Taxation's Incentive to Fiscal Zoning*, in Peterson, *supra* note 146, at 125–39. Hamilton shows that in jurisdictions with a high reliance on locally raised revenues to pay for public schools, there seems to be a markedly higher degree of income segregation among communities than elsewhere. He also finds evidence that fiscally motivated zoning has resulted in a reduction in the total amount of land available for low-income housing. *Id.*

196. Report of the New Jersey Tax Policy Committee: The Property Tax 19 (1972).

welfare. Its aim is to limit the redistributive effects of government. Accordingly, fiscal zoning has come under increased attack as a misuse of the police power. The New Jersey Supreme Court, for example, in *Southern Burlington County NAACP v. Township of Mount Laurel*, reaffirmed the New Jersey doctrine that it was appropriate for a municipality to seek out and encourage "good" tax ratables (such as industrial parks) to create a better economic balance for the community, *provided* that such was "done reasonably as part of and in furtherance of a legitimate comprehensive plan for the zoning of the entire municipality."[197] The court went further in explicitly ruling out fiscal considerations as a justifiable basis for excluding "bad" ratables, such as low- and moderate-income housing.[198]

Exclusionary zoning litigation does not generally attack the property tax system per se, nor is it likely that such a strategy would be successful or meaningful in reforming non-land use inequities.[199] However as anti-exclusionary zoning doctrine becomes accepted in a greater number of jurisdictions (as municipal power to exclude large numbers of people becomes increasingly unacceptable), the the underlying rationale that is expounded is likely to have a salutary effect in expanding awareness about the infirmities of the property tax system. The fact is that the zoning and property tax systems are analogous in a fundamental way: the major problems that are commonly associated with each system are, in large part, a function of their parochial administration and the desire for local autonomy, not of inherent defects with the mechanisms themselves.[200]

A more direct approach to reducing the deleterious effects of fiscal zoning may be to alter the structure of the property tax itself. This may be the ultimate result of the school financing cases being litigated throughout the country and the reform legislation that they are generating.[201]

197. 66 N.J. 151, 336 A.2d 713, 731 (1975), *appeal dismissed*, 423 U.S. 808 (1975), *citing* Gruber v. Mayor & Township Committee, 39 N.J. 1, 9–11, 186 A.2d 489, 493 (1972).

198. Justice Hall, speaking for the majority, stated, "In other words, such municipalities must zone primarily for the living welfare of the people and not for the benefit of the local tax rate." 336 A.2d at 732.

199. *See* Hamilton, *supra* note 195, at 139. And Professor Norman Williams concludes that "in bringing about the end of fiscal-exclusionary zoning, probably the most important move—and a not inconceivable one—would be for the state government to take over the financing of both educational and welfare services," 5 N. Williams, American Land Planning Law 481–483 (1975) [hereinafter cited as Williams].

200. This observation about the property tax is made by Ladd, *supra* note 146.

201. *See generally* Long, *The Property Tax and the Courts: School Finance*

In 1972, in *Serrano v. Priest*,[202] the California Supreme Court held that plaintiffs had stated a claim upon which relief could be granted in alleging that the California scheme for financing public education, with its heavy reliance on the property tax, constituted a denial of equal protection of the laws under the federal and California constitutions, in discriminating on the basis of wealth in the provision of public education. The *Serrano* case led to the filing of similar suits in virtually every state, with decisions shortly thereafter in federal courts in Minnesota[203] and Texas,[204] and state courts in New Jersey,[205] Wyoming,[206] and Arizona,[207] holding that educational financing schemes were unconstitutional. However, the reform movement suffered a setback in 1973 when the U.S. Supreme Court in *San Antonio Independent School District v. Rodriguez*[208] reversed the lower federal court decision invalidating the school finance system in Texas on federal constitutional grounds. The *Rodriguez* decision undercut the utility of the equal protection clause of the Fourteenth Amendment as grounds for striking down public education financing systems based primarily on *ad valorem* taxation, although Justices Potter and Stewart, while voting with the slim 5-to-4 majority, did declare their support for legislative reform.

Following the decision in *Rodriguez*, the Supreme Court of New Jersey, in *Robinson v. Cahill*,[209] avoiding any federal constitutional basis, invalidated the state's funding scheme for its public schools under provisions of the New Jersey Constitution pertaining to the

---

After Rodriguez, in Peterson, *supra* note 146, at 85-105. The most recent developments in the school finance area are in Lawyers' Committee for Civil Rights Under Law, Summary of State-Wide School Finance Cases Since 1973 (Washington, D.C., Feb. 1977) [hereinafter cited as Lawyers' Committee. A more journalistic commentary is in Fiske, *Dilemma Growing Over Inequities in Financing School Systems Through Property Taxes*, Times, Feb. 17, 1977, at 16.

202. 5 Cal. 3d 584, 487 P.2d 1241, 96 Cal. Rptr. 601 (1971) [Serrano I], subsequent opinion [Serrano II], 135 Cal. Rptr. 345, 557 P.2d 929 (1976). See text accompanying notes 211-12 *infra*.

203. Van Dusartz v. Hatfield, 334 F. Supp. 870 (D. Minn. 1971).

204. Rodriguez v. San Antonio Independent School District, 337 F. Supp. 280 (W.D. Tex. 1971), *rev'd*, 411 U.S. 1, 93 S. Ct. 1278 (1973).

205. Robinson v. Cahill, 118 N.J. Super. 223, 287 A.2d 187 (1972), *aff'd*, 62 N.J. 473, 303 A.2d 273 (1973) [Robinson I]. *See* subsequent decisions [Robinson II], 67 N.J. 333 (1975); 69 N.J. 449, 355 A.2d 159; 96 N.J. 155, 358 A.2d 457 (1976), *summarized in* Lawyers' Committee, *supra* note 201.

206. Sweetwater County Planning Comm'n v. Hinkle, 491 P.2d 1234 (Wyo. 1971).

207. Hollins v. Shofstall, No. 253652 (Ariz. Super., June 1, 1972), *rev'd*, 110 Ariz. 49, 515 P.2d 590 (1973).

208. 411 U.S. 1, 93 S. Ct. 1278 (1973).

209. Robinson I, 62 N.J. 473, 303 A.2d 273 (1973).

state's responsibility for the establishment and administration of a "thorough and efficient system of free public schools," and uniformity requirements for purposes of taxation. In contrasting its decision with that of the U.S. Supreme Court in *Rodriguez*, the New Jersey court stated:

> Conceivably a State Constitution could be more demanding [than the U.S. Constitution]; for one thing there is absent the principle of federalism which cautions against too expansive a view of a federal constitutional limitation upon the power and opportunity of the several States to cope with their own programs in light of their own circumstances.[210]

In December 1976 the *Serrano* case, having been remanded to the trial court in 1971 for further proceedings, received a final ruling. In *Serrano II*[211] the California Supreme Court ruled that the state's school finance system was unconstitutional—notwithstanding intervening legislation that significantly increased state aid to localities—on the ground that it violated the equal protection provision of state constitution. In language not dissimilar to that used by the New Jersey Supreme Court, the California court stated:

> [O]ur state equal protection provisions, while "substantially the equivalent of" the guarantees contained in the Fourteenth Amendment to the United States Constitution, are possessed of an independent vitality which, in a given case, may demand an analysis different from that which would obtain if only the federal standard were applicable. . . . [D]ecisions of the United States Supreme Court defining fundamental rights are persuasive authority to be afforded respectful consideration, but are to be followed by California courts only when they provide no less individual protection than is guaranteed by California law [citations omitted].[212]

Because the constitution of each state has its own bill of rights and also special provisions for public education, the question of whether or not financing education through local property taxes is unconstitutional is open for decision by the courts of each state.[213]

210. *Id.* at 282.
211. Serrano v. Priest 135 Cal. Rptr. 345, 557 P.2d 929 (1976).
212. *Id.* at 950.
213. These state constitutional provisions are listed in Manley, *Legal Aspects of Financing Education*, 6 Urb. Law. 337, 344 (1974). The state cases vary widely in concept and scope depending on the constitutional language involved, the mechanics of the school finance statute, and the factual setting. *See* Lawyers' Committee, *supra* note 201, for a summary of the various litigation approaches.

The Connecticut Supreme Court recently held the state's school financing scheme to be unconstitutional,[214] and numerous suits of this nature are pending in state courts from New York[215] to Georgia[216] to Washington.[217]

While the extension of *Serrano II* or *Robinson II* (or the enactment of remedial legislation in other states) is uncertain, such actions should increase the financing of public primary and secondary education from the state level, which would have important implications on exclusionary land regulation. Shifting the drain on local property taxes to the state level could deprive the municipality of a primary motivation for exclusionary policies—that is, the burden imposed on local funds and services by larger, lower-income families.

Regional Tax Allocation Programs

Competition among localities for high tax ratables distorts the location of industrial and commercial firms, and encourages exclusionary land-use practices.[218] This consequence of the property tax is generally acknowledged; yet only a few remedial taxing programs have been enacted to attempt to cope with the phenomenon. A significant one is the Minnesota Metropolitan Revenue Distribution Act,[219] commonly referred to as the Minneapolis Plan or the Metropolitan Fiscal Disparities Act. Its purpose is "to increase the likelihood of orderly urban development by reducing the impact of fiscal

214. Horton v. Meskill, 31 Conn. Sup. 377, 332 A.2d 813 (Hartford County Super. Ct. 1974), *aff'd.* —Conn.— April 19, 1977).

215. Board of Education v. Nyquist, Index No. 8208-74 (Nassau County, N.Y. Sup. Ct.) (trial completed in Jan. 1977; parties had until June 1977 to complete post-trial briefs).

216. Thomas v. Stewart, Docket No. 8275 (Polk County, Ga. Super. Ct.) (complaint filed in Dec. 1974; preparation for trial is underway).

217. Seattle School Dist. No. 1 v. State (Order No. 53750, Thurston County Super. Ct., Jan. 14, 1977) (holding Washington school finance system unconstitutional and retaining jurisdiction pending appropriate legislative relief by July 1979). *See* other cases cited in Lawyers' Committee, *supra* note 201.

218. *See* notes 195 and 198 *supra*, and accompanying text.

219. Minn. Stat. Ann. ch. 472F (Supp. 1974). The other major intermunicipal tax base sharing scheme is that established by the Hackensack Meadowlands Development Commission and Reclamation Act, N.J. Stat. Ann. §§ 13-17 *et. seq.*, Pub. L. No. 1968 ch. 404, as a way of compensating localities whose land is withdrawn from industrial development for environmental purposes. *See* Hackensack Meadowlands Development Commission, Intermunicipal Tax Sharing: Theory and Operation (Oct. 1972). The tax-sharing scheme was upheld in Meadowlands Regional Redevelopment Agency v. State, 63 N.J. 35, 304 A.2d 545 (1973).

For a general analysis of tax base sharing plans and their potential effects on location decisions, the local fiscal cycle, and land-use planning decisions (using a statewide base sharing scheme proposed in Maryland for illustrative purposes), *see* Lyall, *Tax Base-Sharing: A Fiscal Aid Towards More Rational Land Use Planning,* 1975 J.A.I.P. 90 (March).

considerations on the location of business and residential growth, and of highways, transit facilities and airports."[220] Its aim is to promote regionalism in the seven-county Minneapolis-St. Paul area—encompassing over 300 independent taxing districts—by reallocating new growth among the various local governments.[221]

To accomplish its objective the Act allocates 40 percent of the increase in assessment valuation throughout the metropolitan area for all commercial-industrial valuation subsequent to January 2, 1971. Each government unit is required to impose two separate tax levies: (1) a local levy on 60 percent of the increment in the number of *units* of commercial-industrial valuation, plus all other taxable property within the jurisdiction; and (2) a separate areawide levy on the metropolitan *pool* representing the 40 percent increment in commercial-industrial valuation.[222] A particular government unit, however, is only entitled to receive from the areawide levy an amount directly proportional to the local levy, and is thus prevented from raiding the areawide tax base.[223]

Once the areawide tax is collected, it is channeled through the county to the state treasurer, and allocated to local units of government on the basis of their fiscal capacities.[224] The allocation is based on an areawide tax base distributional formula.[225] The effect of the legislation is to reallocate the areawide tax base thus pooled to all municipalities in direct relation to need and inverse relation to fiscal capacity.[226]

The act was challenged and upheld by the Minnesota Supreme Court in *Village of Burnsville v. Onischuk.*[227] The principal issue in the case was whether the benefits of the allocations were sufficiently related to the tax burden borne by each jurisdiction to meet the constitutional requirements of uniformity.[228] The trial court had found the tax unacceptable because jurisdictions with higher fiscal capacities

220. Minn. Stat. Ann. § 472F.01 (Supp. 1974).

221. The Minneapolis plan is discussed in Freilich, *Resolving Regional Fiscal Disparities,* 6 Urb. Law. vii (1974). *See* Windhorst, *The Minnesota Fiscal Disparities Law,* 1973 Land Use L. & Zoning Dig. 7.

222. Village of Burnsville v. Onischuck, 222 N.W.2d 523, 525, *appeal dismissed,* 95 S. Ct. 1109, 43 L. Ed. 2d 388 (1975)

223. Freilich, *supra* note 221, at viii–ix.

224. Fiscal capacity is defined as "its [a municipality's] valuation, determined as of January 2 of any year, divided by its population, determined as of a date in the same year." Minn. Stat. Ann. § 473 F.02 (14).

225. The distributional formula is: Population of the locality equals average fiscal capacity for all municipalities divided by the fiscal capacity of the locality.

226. Village of Burnsville v. Onischuk, 222 N.W.2d 523, 525-26 (1974).

227. *Id.*

228. Minn. Const. art. 9, §1, states ". . . Taxes shall be uniform upon the same class of subjects, and shall be levied and collected for public purposes. . . ."

received a smaller allocation of the tax proceeds. Some jurisdictions were taxed for the benefit of others, and this was found to plainly violate the uniformity requirements.

The Minnesota Supreme Court reversed the decision. It found that the benefits of the scheme were not entirely monetary. The court reasoned that substantial, nonmonetary, intangible benefits accrue to commercial-industrial areas from metropolitanwide open spaces, lakes, parks, golf courses, zoos, churches, schools, and hospitals. Accordingly, the court concluded that the indirect regional benefits received by jurisdictions with high commercial-industrial capacities offset their higher tax burden under the Act and thereby justified the taxing scheme.

As presently enacted, the Fiscal Disparities Act is only concerned with locational and fiscal inequalities caused by commercial-industrial development. The Act does not consider fiscal disparities caused by residential development, and it therefore is inadequate in itself for resolving tax related exclusionary zoning concerns.[229] Nonetheless, Minnesota's Fiscal Disparities Act has made some gains in removing fiscal competition, and in combination with the planning and development framework of the Minneapolis-St. Paul Metropolitan Council does appear to represent an innovative and promising long-range approach for more rational metropolitan growth.[230]

LAND BANKING

The price of raw land in major metropolitan areas of the United States roughly doubled between 1950 and 1965.[231] The cost of raw land is the fastest rising element of all major housing costs,[232] and

229. Since the tax-base disadvantage from which central cities suffer stems primarily from an imbalance in residential property values rather than from an unequal distribution of nonresidential property, the Minneapolis tax-base sharing plan, according to one commentator, is unlikely to achieve much in terms of enhancing the central cities' revenue-raising capacity (even in cities less prosperous than the Twin Cities). Peterson, *Finance,* in The Urban Predicament 81 (W. Gorham & N. Glazer eds. 1976).

230. Only the earliest data are available from which even tentative conclusions about the success of the tax-base sharing program can be drawn. *See* Windhorst, *supra* note 221. For an examination of the tax-base sharing scheme in the broader context of the area's regional comprehensive planning strategy, *see* Freilich & Ragsdale, *Timing and Sequential Controls—The Essential Basis for Effective Regional Planning: An Analysis of New Directions in Land Use Control in the Minneapolis–St. Paul Region,* 58 Minn. L. Rev. 1009 (1974).

231. President's Committee on Urban Housing, A Decent Home (1968) [hereinafter cited as A Decent Home].

232. *Id.* at 26, 110. Although data are limited, available information suggests that in a number of major SMSAs urban land prices rose between 1970 and 1974 at a faster pace than in any previous period: an average of from 20 to 30 percent annually compared to an 8 to 10 percent increase over the previous two decades.

its soaring value has crippled governments' ability to provide urgently needed low-income housing and supporting facilities. Moreover, as documented in a 1974 report by the Council on Environmental Quality, the supply of vacant land for development is dwindling.[233] At the same time, the population has been increasing, bringing with it rising development pressures both inside and outside of cities. There is now a widespread tendency to regard land as a public resource that must be employed in well-planned, efficient, and equitable ways.[234] In short, there is increasing pressure to plan land development, and one result of that pressure has been a series of proposals for land banks.

Although the term land banking is not always used uniformly, it may be broadly defined as a scheme by which a government takes and holds land for future rather than immediate development. Ordinarily a government uses its eminent domain powers only for specific public purposes as occasions arise. By contrast, a government that operates a land bank is empowered to take land for its anticipated but unspecified needs. In an inflationary real estate market, a government with a land bank might save large sums of money simply by anticipating what land it will need for public purposes and taking it in advance. (However, it has also been argued that the act of withholding land from the market, at least initially, will increase land prices.[235]) Not only would such a scheme allow a government to obtain desirable development sites for housing and other purposes, but it would also preempt certain private development that would otherwise take place, with adverse public consequences. To a limited extent government would thus become an active intervenor in the real estate market and would play a more direct role in allocating a limited public resource.

Much analysis remains to be done regarding the technique of managing land banks. For example, it has been suggested that addi-

---

President's 1976 Report on National Growth and Development: The Changing Issues for National Growth 3-4 (1976).

233. From 1960 to 1970, a period of relatively slow growth, over 2,000 acres of land a day shifted from rural to urban use. Council on Environmental Quality, Environmental Quality: Fifth Annual Report (G.P.O. (1974) [hereinafter cited as Environmental Quality].

234. *See* W. Reilly, ed., The Use of Land: A Citizens' Policy Guide to Urban Growth (1973).

235. S. Kamm, Land Banking: Public Policy Alternatives and Dilemmas 11-12 (Urban Institute 1970). The Council on Environmental Quality responds that "[t]he initial inflationary effect can be avoided by purchasing land sufficiently distant from the urban fringe that it is not yet effectively a part of the urban land market and thus is much less expensive. However, such an approach would prevent land banking from having any significant short-range impact on the urban growth process." Environmental Quality, *supra* note 233, at 60.

tional objectives might be achieved by land banks, including: (1) the provision of leverage on market prices; (2) the recapture of private values generated by government-sponsored developments (such as the increased land value in the neighborhood of a new subway station); and (3) the encouragement of orderly urban growth.[236] In order to achieve these goals, however, more must be learned about the optimum scale and timing of public intervention in the land market as well as about the differential between public and private holding costs and the impact of such differentials on initial land bank objectives. Moreover, it is important to develop an equitable accounting system able to define and quantify the values resulting from government actions. It is problematic whether these technical problems are currently easily solvable.[237]

Land banking proposals have found support among diverse influential groups. The President's Committee on Urban Housing, for example, recommended direct federal acquisitions of land for subsidized housing and grants to local governments to finance similar acquisitions.[238] The American Law Institute, in its *Model Land Development Code*, recommended that the states establish a "land reserve agency" with broad powers to acquire, hold, and dispose of land.[239] Another major proposal for the public acquisition of land for housing was made by the National Commission on Urban Problems (the Douglas Commission). Citing the polarization of rich and poor and the need to assure greater choice in the location of housing, the Douglas Commission recommended that state governments enact legislation authorizing state, regional, and local agencies to acquire land for present and future housing needs.[240]

Similar proposals have also been made by other prominent public commissions and private organizations.[241] Such programs have ob-

236. Most proposals to use land banking as a means of promoting orderly growth draw from the European, Canadian, or Puerto Rican experiences. For a criticism of the transferability of the foreign experience to the American social, political, and economic context, *see* Kamm, *supra* note 235, at 15-17.

237. Many of the most salient problems and questions about land banking are cogently raised in *id. See also* Kamm, *The Realities of Large Scale Public Land Banking*, in 3 Management and Control of Growth 86 (Urban Land Institute 1975); H. Franklin, D. Falk, & A. Levin, In-Zoning: A Guide for Policy Makers on Inclusionary Land Use Programs 177-197 (Potomac Institute 1968) [hereinafter cited as In-Zoning].

238. A Decent Home, *supra* note 231, at 26, 146.

239. American Law Institute, A Model Land Development Code (adopted May 21, 1975) (1976), art. 6 [hereinafter cited as ALI Code].

240. Building the American City, *supra* note 1, at 243, 246.

241. *See, e.g.*, President's Council on Recreation and Natural Beauty, From Sea to Shining Sea 115-16 (1968); President's Task Force on Suburban Problems, Final Report 76-81 (1968); Advisory Commission on Intergovernmental Relations, Urban and Rural America 152-61 (1968); Puerto Rico Planning

vious inclusionary potential since the housing mix could be determined without interfering with private developers' rights. But in spite of the growing support for land banking, numerous questions remain about whether and how land banks would work,[242] and not all of these questions are economic or administrative. The first question is whether they would be legal.[243]

Legal Constraints

All fifty state constitutions either expressly or through judicial interpretations require that public monies be expended only for valid public purposes.[244] This requirement not only limits appropriations of public monies, it also restricts the use of public credit and the transfer of public property, and it is intended to prevent the public largesse from being used for private purposes. In this context the manner in which the land bank controls the use and disposition of its land ultimately determines whether private interests are being enriched, and whether the bank's operations are thus legally invalid; or whether the lands are primarily retained for the public welfare, in which case the scheme is valid.

The courts have analyzed three general categories of land disposition cases: (1) where land is obtained and held by government or government created agencies; (2) where land is obtained by government created agencies and is leased to private interests; and (3) where land is obtained by government or government created agencies and is sold to private interests. The issues of private enrichment are etched most sharply in the third category.

The easiest method to insulate land banking from charges of private enrichment is for the public to acquire, develop, and hold the land for itself, as in the case of schools and public housing. Continued public ownership, even after development, is used by Montgomery

---

Board, Urban Land Policy for the Commonwealth of Puerto Rico 95-106 (1961); New York State Office of Planning Coordination, New Communities for New York 64-66 (1970). *See also* American Institute of Planners, Policy Statement on New Communities (1968); National Committee on Urban Growth Policy, The New City 169-174 (1969); National Urban Coalition, Counter-Budget: A Blueprint for Changing National Priorities, 1971-1976, at 132-46 (1971); American Institute of Architects, The First Report of the National Policy Task Force (1972); Citizens Advisory Committee on Environmental Quality, The Use of Land 257-61 (1973).

242. See note 237 *supra*.

243. For legal analyses of land banking, *see generally* F. Bosselman, Alternatives to Urban Sprawl: Legal Guidelines for Governmental Action 41-68 (National Commission on Urban Problems Research Report No. 15, G.P.O. 1968); Note, *Public Land Banking: A New Praxis for Urban Growth*, 23 Case W. Res. L. Rev. 897, 948-62 (1972) [hereinafter cited as *Public Land Banking*]; ALI Code, *supra* note 239, at 264-66.

244. *See* discussion in text accompanying notes 231-39 *supra*.

County, Maryland and California in their limited land banking programs. The courts have frequently reviewed this form of land program,[245] and for the most part have allowed municipalities to acquire land for "not only the present demands of the public but even those which may be reasonably anticipated in the future. . . ."[246]

Even when the land is retained by the public, a court may still label the acquisition arbitrary if there is no evidence, such as a comprehensive plan, to indicate a definite need for the land.[247] A land bank can obviate this judicial concern by adopting a comprehensive plan to forecast future housing and community needs. The Puerto Rican land banking program, for instance, which was upheld in *Commonwealth of Puerto Rico v. Rosso*,[248] was tied to a prior study by the Puerto Rican Planning Board that investigated and estimated the supply and demand of land for the next fifteen years in Puerto Rico's urban areas.[249]

The second category of land disposition is leasing. Many European land banks, especially in Sweden, lease developed properties to the public for as long as seventy years.[250] In the United States leasing programs have been undertaken as part of urban renewal projects and industrial revenue bond programs, and have been advocated by the President's Committee on Urban Housing.[251]

State judicial support for land bank leasing may be inferred by analogy. In at least twenty-two jurisdictions the highest appellate courts have, without constitutional amendment, upheld legislation authorizing governmental industrial revenue bond programs.[252] In all

---

245. *See, e.g.*, City of Waukegan v. Stan Czak, 6 Ill. 2d 594, 129 N.E.2d 751 (1955) (school land); Dade County v. Paxsom, 270 So. 2d 455 (Fla. App. 1972) (sewer and water system).

246. Rindge Co. v. County of Los Angeles, 262 U.S. 700, 707 (1923).

247. *See, e.g.*, Board of Education v. Baczewski, 340 Mich. 265, 54 N.W.2d 810 (1954).

248. 95 P.R.R. 488 (1967); *appeal dismissed*, 393 U.S. 14 (1968).

249. Puerto Rico Land Administration Act of May 16, 1962, No. 13, *Statement of Motives* (a). For a discussion of the Puerto Rican legislation and the context in which it was enacted, *see* Public Land Banking, *supra* note 243, at 916-23.

250. G. Edwards, Land, People and Policy 47-76 (1969). *See also* Passow, *Land Reserves and Teamwork in Planning Stockholm*, 36 J.A.I.P. 179 (1970). A novel and well-reasoned proposal for reducing some of the inequities in urban development—drawn largely from the European experience—suggests removing entirely from private ownership the right to develop or not to develop. *See* Lefcoe, 56 Ore. L. Rev. 31 (1977).

251. A Decent Home, *supra* note 231, at 26.

252. The states are cited in Mitchell v. North Carolina Indust. Dev. Fin. Authority, 273 N.C. 137, 159 S.E.2d 745 (1968), *excerpted in* O. Oldman and P. Schoettle, State and Local Taxes and Finance: Text, Problems and Cases 781 (1974).

these cases courts rejected arguments that industrial revenue bond programs and their favorable lease arrangements enriched private interests. Instead they found that the net public benefits derived from these programs outweighed the private gains, and held that these programs constituted a valid public purpose. In thirteen additional states, state constitutions were amended to permit industrial revenue bonds.[253] The supreme courts in only four states (North Carolina, Massachusetts, Florida, and Idaho) still maintain that such programs do not involve a public purpose.[254] Therefore, the vast majority of states, either through judicial opinion or constitutional amendment, now authorize public acquisition, development, and leasing of industrial sites.

The third category of land disposition is for a land bank to sell its land directly to private builders. However, the potential for abuse and private enrichment under this mode of land disposition is great, unless care is taken. If the land bank only minimally restricts the future use of its land, for example, private interests will simply use the lower priced land for more profitable uses. Even if the land is exclusively devoted to low- and moderate-income housing, developers can later resell it and obtain windfall profits to the extent that their original purchase was below market value. To some extent, however, a land bank can control the future use of its land after disposition through the use of deed restrictions, covenants, and land-use regulations.[255]

The direct resale of publicly acquired land to private developers has frequently been tested in the urban renewal field and, with the lone exception of South Carolina,[256] the courts have allowed direct sale dispositions to private developers.[257] In reaching their decisions the courts rejected arguments that public acquisition of land and its later resale to private developers constituted an invalid public purpose. Instead the courts have recognized that "if upon completion of the [urban renewal] project the public good is enhanced, it does not matter that private interests may be benefited."[258]

The applicability of these urban renewal cases to land banking

253. *Id.* at 782–83.

254. *Id.*

255. North Carolina Office of State Planning, Department of Administration, Growth Management Through Development Timing 140 (May 1975). For an examination of potential restrictions on land bank dispositions, *see* Note, *Judicial Review of Land Bank Dispositions*, 41 U. Chi. L. Rev. 373 (1974).

256. Edens v. Columbia, 228 S.C. 562, 91 S.E.2d 280 (1956).

257. Cases collected in 44 A.L.R. 2d 1406 (1954)

258. Murray v. LaGuardia, 291 N.Y. 320, 329–20, 52 N.E.2d 884, 888, *cert. denied*, 321 U.S. 771 (1943).

may be somewhat limited because they involved the removal of slum and blighted areas; however, a smaller number of cases have dealt with predominantly open areas that were "destined" to become blighted.[259] Nevertheless, the urban renewal decisions emphasized the prior publicly approved plan in upholding governmental power, not unlike the decision in *Commonwealth of Puerto Rico v. Rosso.* Accordingly, it is prudent to say that while many state courts are expanding their definitions of "public purpose," and while there is reason to be optimistic that land banking programs would be upheld in many state courts, the outcome of such future litigation is not entirely free from doubt.

Organization of Land Banks

Conceptually, land banking may be roughly divided into two kinds.[260] The first has been described as general purpose land banking, which is aimed at acquiring large areas of urban land without regard to specific future use. Such land banking would be intended to have a major impact on the urban land market. A second kind has been described as special purpose land banking. Such land acquisitions may vary enormously in scope from modest programs to ensure adequate land for schools and fire houses, to more ambitious acquisitions for future housing construction.

Whatever the scope of its jurisdiction, the land banking entity must be legally authorized to acquire land, to hold it, and to either dispose of it or use it. If future housing supply is to be one of its concerns, it must also have the financial capacity to acquire a sufficient number of housing sites, and it must be able to assess and plan for regional housing needs. Given these prerequisites, selecting the appropriate agency to administer the program is crucial to the eventual disposition of the acquired land. The literature discusses three basic structural forms through which a land bank entity might operate (short of establishing general purpose metropolitan governments), namely: municipalities, state agencies, and state created public purpose corporations operating at either state or regional levels.

The state-created public-purpose corporation has received the most attention, and, as mentioned above, the ALI Code advocates

259. *See, e.g.,* People *ex rel.* Gutknecht v. Chicago, 3 Ill. 2d 539, 121 N.W.2d 791 (1954); Foeller v. Housing Authority 198 Or. 205, 256 P.2d 752 (1952).

260. For more detailed operational and financial accounts of land banking, *see generally* Kamm, *supra* note 235; W. Letwin, Municipal Land Banks: Land Reserve Policy for Urban Development (1969); *Public Land Banking, supra* note 243 (drawing certain financial and operational analyses from an unpublished and unattributed draft of Kamm, *supra* note 235); In-Zoning, *supra* note 237; Fitch & Mack, *Land Banking,* in The Good Earth of America 141 (C. Harris ed. 1974).

this approach. The major problem with it is that public corporations usually must adhere to local development controls. If, for example, the corporation is unable to use the land for multiple-family housing because of exclusionary regulations, it will fail to achieve its housing objectives. Some power to override local controls would therefore be essential to the success of such a land bank.[261]

Another possibility is to permit municipalities themselves to engage in land banking. But even if municipalities with undeveloped land were willing to provide low-income housing, the financial resources available to muncipal governments are limited. Furthermore, since most urban growth typically occurs beyond the jurisdiction of a built-up city, a land bank must be able to acquire and dispose of land lying outside municipal boundaries if it is to integrate housing and employment opportunities.

The last suggested location for a land bank entity is the state government—as a state agency. Until recently, state governments generally remained indifferent to urban problems. In recent years, however, state governments are becoming more involved in local planning and development. In some cases their concern has included the financing of land acquisition for low-income housing, as in Hawaii. In many ways the states are the most sensible level at which to operate a land bank: they have greater financial resources than do lesser units of government; they are more politically accountable; and they generally encompass total metropolitan areas. The states are better equippped than municipalities to engage in land banking, and reliance on them would avoid a further, undesirable proliferation of special purpose government units. Finally, it is worth pointing out that nothing prevents both a state and its municipalities from concurrently undertaking land banking programs.

Financing Land Banks

The acquisition of vacant land in metropolitan areas would be expensive regardless of how it came about. (The purchase and transfer of development rights, discussed in Chapter 4, may well be a less expensive method.) In 1973 the national average cost of a single-family FHA housing site was $1.32 per square foot,[262] and this figure was probably higher in metropolitan areas. In Montgomery County,

261. The New York State Urban Development Corporation possessed such essential override powers and utilized them effectively until they were repealed by the state legislature—following substantial political controversy in the suburbs. *See* notes 89–91 *supra*, and accompanying text.

262. Department of Housing and Urban Development, Statistical Yearbook 1973: FHA Trends of Home Mortgage Characteristics (1973).

Maryland, the purchase of land associated with its early housing site acquisition program exceeded $1,800 per unit.[263]

There are two basic ways for a land bank to finance its land acquisitions. The first is to use normal government appropriations or federal grants. There is, however, a major difficulty with financing a land bank primarily through normal government appropriations, because the bank would lack power to commit unappropriated funds and would therefore be unable to enter into installment purchase or option agreements.

Federal general revenue sharing funds and the Community Development Act of 1974 can also be used to finance land banks. Under federal law, however, general revenue-sharing monies cannot be used to fulfill local matching contribution requirements for federally assisted programs. Therefore, if the expenditure of local funds for the purchase of land were required as a local matching contribution, the use of revenue-sharing funds would be prohibited.[264]

By contrast, the Community Development Act of 1974 greatly increases the flexibility with which a locality may use federal funds. Most important, the Act allows federal assistance for payment of the nonfederal share required under federal grant-in-aid programs where they are undertaken as part of a locality's community development program.[265] Section 105(a) of the legislation specifically allows a locality to obtain and use its federal grant for the acquisition of undeveloped real property. Moreover, the 1974 Act eliminates the former federal requirement that land acquired with federal funds must be disposed of at fair value. It also specifically authorizes land disposition through sale, lease, or donation for public purposes.[266] This makes it possible to use community development funds for low-income housing sites.[267]

A second method for financing land bank programs is debt financing. But if a land bank program merely acquired land without developing it, it is unlikely that there would be a sufficient cash flow to pay borrowing costs, especially if acquired lands were sold at discount

---

263. Interview with Gary Cuddeback, Office of Housing, Montgomery County, Maryland, May 20, 1975. *See also* note 267 *infra;* D. Shoup, Advanced Land Acquisition by Local Governments: Benefit-Cost Analysis as an Aid to Policy 70 (1968).

264. Office of Research and Statistics, Land Banking Program for Fairfax County, at app. B (Fairfax, Va. 1973).

265. 42 U.S.C.A. § 5305(a)(9).

266. 42 U.S.C.A. § 5305(a)(7).

267. Montgomery County, Maryland has indicated that it intends to use $315,000 of its community development grant to acquire vacant land for 100–120 modest-income housing units annually. *See* Community Dev. Dig., February 25, 1975, at 10.

prices. Debt financing thus remains an unlikely method of funding a land bank unless HUD activates provisions of the Housing and Community Development Act of 1974 which guarantee federal loans for property acquisition.[268]

PART II
REGULATORY ACTIONS TO INCREASE
HOUSING OPPORTUNITY

BUILDING CODES

Building codes make the construction of decent housing more difficult and expensive. Together with housing codes they can add from 2 to 250 percent to the cost of a house.[269] The issue is not whether to abolish building codes, however. Few persons advocate such an extreme step, which would undoubtedly result in the erection of many shoddy and unsafe dwellings. Rather, the issue is whether the standards established by many building codes are really related to health and safety, or whether they merely add unnecessary costs to residential construction. All too often these standards seem difficult to justify.

The codes are innocent enough in their origin. They are the means by which local governments, through the exercise of the state's police power, regulate the construction of new buildings and the rehabilitation of old ones. Their proper purpose is to promote the public safety by establishing minimum standards of durability and sanitation. They also protect against fire, dilapidation, and collapse. Since low construction standards have never been an insurmountable problem for those who can afford expensive housing, the point of the codes was to insure that cheap housing was built to an adequate minimum standard.

The primary effect of these regulatory schemes on lower cost housing has been to make it uneconomic to construct. This issue

---

268. 42 U.S.C.A. § 5308.

269. R. Babcock and F. Bosselman, Exclusionary Zoning: Land Use Regulation and Housing in the 1970s, at 13-14 (1973). The National Commission on Urban Problems estimated in 1968 that code requirements unnecessarily add $1,838 to the cost of a $12,000, 100-square-foot family unit without an improved lot. Building the American City, *supra* note 1, at 262.

More recently, New Jersey's commissioner of community affairs estimated that statewide adoption of the model code promulgated by the Building Officials and Code Administrators International (BOCA) could reduce the average price of a home in New Jersey by $2,000. 4 Hous. & Dev. Rep. 754 (Jan. 24, 1977).

has been widely recognized. The National Commission on Urban Problems conducted an extensive national survey on building codes and practices and made the following findings, among others:[270]

1. Archaic and superfluous code provisions increase housing cost by creating delays and increasing the cost of materials; they prevent the use of new materials, innovative design, and modern construction techniques.
2. Diverse code provisions within single metropolitan areas and states increase costs and curtail production by preventing the standardization of plans, materials, and building operations.
3. Codes are often administered arbitrarily by incompetent and sometimes corrupt local officials; this problem is complicated by the absence of effective appeal procedures.

At best, building codes are a benignly created hodgepodge of inefficient regulation. At worst they produce a system of corrupt mismanagement and misuse of the police power for exclusionary purposes. It must be emphasized that corruption and misuse are not to be found everywhere; but neither are they isolated aberrations in a well-oiled system. The fact is, higher building standards mean higher home prices and therefore higher income residents, and this is no secret to local administrators and legislators.[271]

Intuitively many would think that the poor must be made better off by the enforcement of tougher construction standards. But no one is made better off by the enforcement of standards that are arbitrary, difficult to meet and tenuously related to health and safety; and poor people are not made better off by regulations that make low-cost housing too expensive to build or buy.

Beyond the problem of arbitrary standards that are unrelated to health and safety, the effect of the codes on the construction industry is worsened by a lack of uniformity. There are four major national model codes in the United States, each drafted by a different organization.[272] (These codes, however, are often modified extensively by the cities and towns that adopt them.) The varia-

270. Building the American City, supra note 1, at 264–73.

271. See C. Field and S. Rivkin, The Building Code Burden 98 (1974); C. Hartman, Housing and Social Policy 40 (1975).

272. Building Officials and Code Administrators, International, Inc., The Basic Building Code; International Conference of Building Officials, Uniform Building Code; American Insurance Association, The National Building Code; Southern Building Code Conference, The Southern Standard Building Code. The National Commission on Urban Problems viewed these codes as being reasonably progressive and up-to-date. Building the American City, supra note 1, at 265.

tions among model codes are to some extent regional: heating and insulation standards, snow-load factors, and antitremor standards must of course vary in an area as large as the United States. For the most part, however, discrepancies among building codes cannot be explained so rationally, because discrepancies within regions cannot be accounted for by objective variations among regions.

In response to this situation, statewide building codes should be adopted, the provisions of which must be related to health and safety (and not to middle class notions of comfort and convenience), and must not unnecessarily increase the cost of housing. An effective statewide code must do the following:

1. Preempt local codes, at least where the local code does not meet specified standards.
2. Establish statewide standards for the licensing and training of building code officials.
3. Establish a fair and efficient appeals procedure.
4. Deal with special problems of manufactured housing components and mobile homes.
5. Establish minimum standards applicable to areas within the state not already covered by a local code.

Statewide building codes are now the trend, as many states begin to recover some of the authority that has traditionally been delegated to municipalities. According to a 1974 HUD survey, approximately fifteen states have state building codes, twenty-eight have preemptive laws governing factory-built housing components, and thirty-eight have preemptive mobile home construction regulations.[273]

Problems nevertheless remain that cannot be solved by statewide codes. In many parts of the country, the construction trade is an interstate industry. Indeed, several metropolitan areas, such as New York City, Philadelphia, and Washington, D.C., are themselves interstate markets, and the plethora of jurisdictional rules in such places disrupts the efficiency of such markets with no objective gain in public safety or health. In some cases it may be possible that states will move toward regional solutions to these problems as they have done with certain transportation authorities.

Alternatively, the federal government may begin to assume a role in building regulations. First steps in this direction can be seen in the

273. Housing in the Seventies, *supra* note 1, at 151. Recent reports indicate that six more states are considering adopting or have recently adopted one of the statewide model codes. New York and North Carolina have adopted their own codes. 4 Hous. & Dev. Rep. 754 (Jan. 24, 1974).

Housing and Community Development Act of 1974, which created the National Institute of Building Sciences (NIBS)[274] and includes a Mobile Home Construction and Safety Standards Act (Title VI).[275] However, delays in appointing members and a failure to receive appropriations has prevented NIBS from becoming established as an effective national clearinghouse on building science and technology information. But the policy goals already formulated by NIBS indicate that once made operational the institute may well play an important role in improving the state of the building sciences. Among its goals are the following:

1. To devise a system that permits the formulation, promulgation and monitoring of nationally recognized building performance criteria and standards.
2. To create a national system for the evaluation and prequalification of existing and new building technologies.
3. To develop demonstration programs for a coordinated and unified building regulatory process.
4. To develop and promote scientific and technological innovations and performance criteria and standards to advocate to local, state and federal regulatory officials.[276]

The trend is clearly toward uniformity, but whether the uniformity will come through federal intervention or through the adoption by individual states of a uniform code remains to be seen. In summary, what building codes really do is to make inexpensive housing illegal to build. Given the fact that the nation does not (and will not) ensure that all persons are housed in middle-class accommodations, and given the fact that building codes often make it illegal to build anything else, these code standards ought to be drastically revised. Their function should be to prevent direct threats to health and safety, and that is all. At present these codes, along with such regulations as those for minimum lot size, help to make housing too expensive for a growing number of our people. The states, having delegated these regulatory powers to local governments, have the responsibility to supervise their use. Alternatively, they should reassert their

274. 12 U.S.C. § 1701j-2. The creation of the National Institute of Building Sciences (as a constituent body of the National Academy of Sciences–National Academy of Engineering) was first recommended by the National Commission on Urban Problems in 1968. Building the American City, *supra* note 1, at 266.
275. 42 U.S.C. §§ 5401 *et seq.*
276. *See* 4 Hous. & Dev. Rep. 565 (Nov. 29, 1976); *id.* at 739–40 (Jan. 24, 1977).

authority and promulgate statewide codes that will preempt unsatisfactory local codes.[277]

HOUSING CODES

Housing codes are like building codes in that they apply to structures; they have no direct effect on new construction, however, because they apply only to existing dwellings. Whereas building codes regulate the minimum conditions for development, housing codes regulate the minimum conditions for occupancy. They are applied retroactively to remove substandard nonconformities created by changes in minimum housing requirements. They establish minimum standards for such things as sanitation, light, ventilation, space heating, and cooking equipment. They also regulate maintenance and safety; fix the responsibilities of owners, operators, and occupants of all buildings; and provide for administration, enforcement, and penalties.

While the four model codes[278] currently in use contain similar statements of purpose, the place of such codes in a larger housing policy is a matter of controversy. The National Commission on Urban Problems has observed that at "almost all levels of government there are conflicting policies as to what housing codes are and confusion as to what they should do, how they can be enforced, and what role if any, they should play in helping to provide an abundance of decent housing for American people."[279] To most nineteenth-century reformers, improved housing was essential to any program that could hope to wipe out the pattern of social evils represented by slum life. The proponents of the New York Tenement House Law of 1867, which many regard as the first housing code,[280] blamed the slumlord

277. The immediate impact that such state action can have is illustrated in New Jersey. The mandatory building code adopted in January 1977—based on the BOCA model—automatically supersedes regulations adopted over the years by 567 of New Jersey's municipalities. *Id.* at 754.

278. The four widely used model codes are: (1) American Insurance Association, The National Code of the American Insurance Association; (2) American Public Health Association and Public Health Service, Recommended Housing Maintenance and Occupancy Ordinance; (3) National Institute of Municipal Law Officers, Minimum Housing Standards Ordinance; and (4) Building Officials and Code Administrators International, Inc., Basic Housing, Proper Maintenance Code.

279. Building the American City, *supra* note 1, at 273.

280. Law of May 14, 1867, ch. 908, §§ 1-19, N.Y. Laws 90 Sess. 2265. Others argue that the first modern version of a housing code was enacted in Baltimore in 1941. For a general discussion of the history of housing codes and of other slum reform programs, *see* Freidman, Government and Slum Housing: A Century of Frustration (1968).

not only for the appalling physical conditions in which urban slum dwellers had to live, but also for the social pathology typical of slum life. For the reform movement, the purpose of housing codes was to eliminate the social pathology of poverty.

Most people today are skeptical of single-factor explanations for eliminating poverty. Social scientists prefer to speak more modestly about "correlations among various factors" than about "causes" of such things as poverty. This tendency is salutary insofar as it deflates overblown expectations about the likely results of public policies. Yet in spite of what may be a growing sophistication about poverty, many still assert that the housing code is an important tool that can improve neighborhoods or prevent their decline. Is this true? What role should these codes have in an equitable housing policy?

How Housing Codes Work

Housing codes, like building and zoning codes, are exercises of the state police power. Most of them are enacted and enforced by municipalities, although a few counties have also done so.[281] Most codes are applicable only within the municipal limits, but in a few cases they have limited extraterritorial effect.[282] While the four model codes previously referred to serve as the basis for many local codes, most localities add their own embellishments. At the same time, while the model codes have had widespread acceptance among the smaller cities, most major cities have chosen to draft their own. Among the exceptions are Detroit, Memphis, New York, Philadelphia, and St. Louis.[283]

The first step in code enforcement is a visit by an inspector from the municipal department charged with the supervision of existing housing. Such an inspection may be part of a regular system, or it may come in response to a particular complaint. In either case, if the housing code provides for criminal penalties the inspector must have either the consent of the occupant or a search warrant in order to enter.[284] The occupant, owner, or other appropriate party is then informed of any violations that may exist, and requested or ordered to remove the violations and "bring the dwelling up to code." The

281. Spencer Perratt, Housing Code Administration and Enforcement 2 (U.S. Public Health Service Publication No. 1999, 1970).

282. In Michigan, for example, state law permits cities to enact and enforce housing laws within one mile of city limits. Mich. Housing Law art. I, § 125.401.

283. Landman, *Flexible Housing Code—Mystique of the Single Standard: A Critical Analysis and Comparison of Model and Selected Housing Codes Leading to the Development of a Proposed Model Flexible Housing Code*, 18 Howard L.J. 251, 258 (1975).

284. Camara v. Municipal Court, 378 U.S. 523 (1967); See v. City of Seattle, 387 U.S. 541 (1967).

responsible party who fails to comply is subject to coercive administrative, judicial, and private remedies.

In New York, for example, the Commissioner of Real Estate can be appointed by the court as a receiver to collect rents and use the money to make repairs.[285] And where a New York tenant's rent is paid by welfare agencies, payment may be withheld as long as the unit remains in noncompliance with the housing code.[286] In some jurisdictions any tenant has a right to withhold rent for code violations.[287] Most municipalities are authorized to prosecute violations of housing codes and other ordinances as misdemeanors. Jail terms are often authorized, and civil penalties may be available.[288] For the most part, however, criminal sanctions tend to be used only after administrative persuasion has failed to produce voluntary compliance.[289] In a limited number of localities, occupants may institute their own actions, but more typically only the municipality may start the proceeding.[290]

Routine inspections are rare in most slums, and violations are handled only after a private complaint has been received.[291] Even then, code enforcement is insisted on only for conditions that pose immediate threats to health or safety. Not only is it usual for the level of enforcement to be lowest in the worst parts of town, but the applicable standards may also vary (at least in practice) with the neighborhood.[292] In effect, therefore, there is often no uniform standard. The recent trend has fortunately been to consolidate code enforcement in a single agency, though it it still typical for related standards to be enforced by different local agencies or departments. In New York during the 1960s, for example, six separate agencies shared administrative responsibilities for the housing code.[293] The recent rationalization is partly a result of the federal Housing Act of 1964, which authorized federal assistance for some types of local

285. N.Y. Mult. Dwell. Law, § 309(5)(c)(1) (McKinney).

286. N.Y. Soc. Ser. Law § 143-B (McKinney).

287. *See* discussion of landlord and tenant law that follows in this chapter; *see also* Abbott, *Housing Policy, Housing Codes and Tenant Remedies: An Integration*, 56 B.U. L. Rev. 1 (1976).

288. For example, the St. Louis Code, § 393.110 (1970), provides for fines of up to $500 and imprisonment for up to 90 days for violations of the housing code.

289. Salsich, *Housing and the States*, 2 Urb. Law. 40 (1970).

290. *See* Garrity, *Redesigning Landlord-Tenant Concepts for an Urban Society*, 46 J. Urb. L. 695 (1969); Indritz, *Tenants' Rights Movement*, 1 N.M. L. Rev. 1 (1971).

291. Lieberman, Local Administration and Enforcement of Housing Codes: A Survey of 39 Cities 23 (1969).

292. *Id.* at 24.

293. J. Slavet & M. Levin, New Approaches to Housing Code Administration 92 (National Commission on Urban Problems Research Report No. 17, 1969).

code enforcement activities.[294] Under the Act, only those municipalities with coordinated enforcement could qualify for funds, and this requirement in many instances led to consolidation of code-enforcement responsibilities in a single agency.[295] Both the 1964 Act and the Housing and Urban Development Act of 1965 required a local code-enforcement program as a condition for receiving federal funds, and these enactments resulted in the adoption of housing codes by almost 5,000 municipalities.[296]

Housing codes across the nation have been adopted on the premise that housing could be improved, neighborhoods maintained, and adequate housing provided by requiring that owners of dwellings maintain them to a minimum standard. Now that housing codes have become widely adopted, it is apparent that they are not achieving these goals.[297] The question is, why not? There is almost always an administrative explanation for the failure of a policy such as the cost and difficulty of training an adequate staff to perform inspections, difficulties in gaining entrance to dwellings, and so on. And almost always there are deeper explanations, too. To begin with, housing codes primarily affect the dwellings of persons with lower incomes, who generally live in rental housing. Their effect on more expensive housing (owner-occupied or rental) is rarely as severe. Code violations are a particular problem for tenants who do not have sufficient resources to make repairs, and it is these people whom housing codes are intended primarily to benefit.

Economics has more bearing on modern housing maintenance and improvement than does the law. A landlord thinking about modernizing a kitchen, for example, will calculate whether an increase in rent will exceed the cost of the work over the life of the improvement. If it does, an economically rational landlord will modernize the kitchen, and will make every other improvement whose cost is less than the increase in rent the improvement will generate. When an improvement would support a rental increment that is less than the cost of improvement, the landlord will stop making improvements. In economic terms, the marginal rate of return on investment at this point is zero, and any further investment will actually diminish the return. Unfortunately, the point at which the marginal rate of return

294. Housing Act of 1964, Pub. L. No. 88-560, § 301(b).

295. *See generally* Slavet & Levin, *supra* note 293, at 115; Note, *Housing Codes and the Prevention of Urban Blight—Administrative and Enforcement Problems and Proposals*, 17 Vill. L. Rev. 490 (1972).

296. Building the American City, *supra* note 1, at 275.

297. Comptroller General's Report, Enforcement of Housing Codes: How We Can Help to Achieve the Nation's Housing Goals, B-118754 (1972). See sources collected in Abbott, *supra* note 287.

is zero (or even worse) is reached sooner rather than later as a housing unit becomes less desirable and the people who live in it have less money to spend on rent. Some landlords may decide to increase their return by deferring maintenance. Even for the conscientious landlord whose tenants are poor, or whose tenants are not respectful of the property, the cost of maintenance and improvements can become uneconomic.

Part of what housing codes attempt to do is to change this situation by fiat; that is, they compel landlords to improve and maintain certain properties at a costlier level than some landlords think they are worth. Such codes typically do not distinguish between the landlord who is milking a property and a landlord who is conscientious but faced with economic losses. The point may come where the landlord's rate of return is less than just comparable to what could be realized if the money were invested elsewhere or simply put in a bank.

Strict housing code enforcement can thus persuade a landlord to go out of business, and if some other and more efficient landlord does not take over that share of the market, the housing code will have counterproductive, at least in this case, for instead of improving the quality of rental housing, it will have reduced the supply. The fact that a few marginal landlords of low-quality housing are driven off the market, however, may not in itself be significant. Indeed, this may be a desirable result if the general tendency of the code is to improve low-income housing without having much effect on supply. Therefore, in order to decide whether a housing code is a desirable policy tool, one has to know a great deal about the landlords who supply poor people's housing in a given metropolitan area. The effects of a code's standard will vary from place to place and from time to time.

Because of these variations, the authorities in Yonkers, New York are experimenting with flexible code enforcement. In Yonkers, enforcement agents conduct a study of the income, operating costs, condition, ownership, and tenancies in each building where code violations may be a problem. They are then supposed to suggest what types of improvements can be made without resulting in rents that are too high for the tenants or too low for the landlord.[298] Before any changes are ordered, a meeting is held between the property owner or manager and the tenants, with a city official present. In many cases a voluntary agreement emerges: the tenants agree to

298. Further information can be obtained from S. Tuminaro, Housing Manager, Yonkers Housing Department, Yonkers, New York.

some rent increase, the landlord agrees to some improvement in services or maintenance. City officials hope that the program will reduce the level of abandonment of rental housing. Reportedly the Yonkers program has resulted in the upgrading of many properties without the dislocation of tenants.

Another suggestion for flexible enforcement of housing codes comes from a group of authors who advocate tenants' participation in the code enforcement process.[299] They propose that tenants act as inspectors of their own units. Self-inspection allows tenants to make meaningful choices between strict enforcement and rent increases on the one hand, and looser enforcement and rent stability on the other. This technique is being attempted in Chicago by the Metropolitan Area Housing Alliance, a private organization that attempts to arrange meetings between tenant groups and landlords before formal court action is taken about housing code violations. Reportedly the organization has had some success in obtaining agreements between landlords and tenants that result in properties being upgraded without substantial rent increases. What may emerge from such experiments is a greater understanding that legal fiat must accommodate itself to market realities, without being arbitrary, if long term public welfare objectives are to be attained in the maintenance of our existing housing stock.

While these flexible techniques may prove valuable in assisting to improve and upgrade the present housing inventory, it must be recognized that housing code enforcement alone cannot assure that all residents will live in housing which meets a minimum standard of health and safety. To reach this goal, as the National Commission on Urban Problems recognized in 1968, a number of additional steps must be taken in conjunction with improving code enforcement:

1. An adequate supply of temporary or relocation housing must be available so that the occupants of below-minimum housing do not have to be put out in the street or moved into worse conditions of deterioration or overcrowding when the code is enforced.
2. The total amount of housing built for low-income groups and for society in general must be substantially increased. In the long run,

---

299. Hartman, Kessler, & LeGates, *Municipal Housing Code Enforcement and Low-Income Tenants,* J.A.I.P. (March). Flexibility can also be provided in the more formal setting of a courtroom. In the Housing Court of the City of Boston, a housing specialist will assist the parties in working out a relatively inexpensive manner of repair (including the utilization of government grants, if available) if the responsible party has insufficient funds to correct a violation. *See* Garrity, *Housing Courts: An Appropriate Response to Complex Issues* 6 Special Issue 9, 19 (A.B.A. Dep't of State and Local Bar Services, Feb. 1976).

effective housing code programs will depend on the existence of an abundance of new housing, the demolition of dilapidated and deteriorated housing, and the natural working of the filter-down process.

3. Adequate loans, grants, and other incentives and aids to low-income home-owners, landlords, and tenants must be provided to promote repair to code standards, in order that the enforcement of housing codes does not merely increase housing costs and thus make standard housing economically inaccessible. Since the provision of at least a part of new and rehabilitated housing for the poor by society is a long acknowledged responsibility . . . the provision of adequate aid for housing code administration nationwide is clearly within this recognized duty of society.[300]

MOBILE HOMES

The Growth of Mobile Homes in the Housing Market

The National Mobile Home Construction and Safety Standard Act of 1974 defines a mobile home as

"a structure, transportable in one or more sections, which is eight body feet or more in width and is thirty-two feet in length, and which is built on a permanent chassis and designed to be used as a dwelling with or without a permanent foundation when connected to the required utilities, and includes the plumbing, heating, air conditioning, and electrical systems contained therein."[301]

As the average price for a single-family conventional home continues to climb beyond the reach of a large portion of the population, the mobile home has become one of the few available alternatives for those people who wish to own rather than rent. By 1967, mobile homes accounted for 23 percent of the single-family, nonfarm housing starts;[302] by 1974, mobile homes constituted 40 percent of the total.[303] The average unit (14 feet by 65 feet) then sold for $8,640, and the average so-called double-wide unit for $14,320.[304] By contrast, the average price for a new conventional house in 1975 was $42,600.[305]

300. Building the American City, *supra* note 1, at 275.
301. Housing and Community Development Act of 1974, tit. VI, Mobile Home Construction and Safety Standards § 603(b), 42 U.S.C. § 5402(b).
302. Building the American City, *supra* note 1, at 438.
303. Manufactured Housing Institute, Quick-Facts 7 (1974).
304. *Id.* at 4.
305. 1976 Savings & Loan News 36 (March).

The design and construction techniques employed are distinct from the traditional "stick-built" house and are responsible for the much lower base cost of the mobile unit. Mobile homes are constructed on an assembly line and are transported to the site ready for occupancy and utility connection. Once on site they are infrequently moved.[306] The price of the mobile home generally includes a fully furnished unit. Once regarded as mere trailers, these units are now larger and less mobile than ever before—and more practical as reasonably permanent homes. The mobile home has grown from a unit averaging 8 feet by 30 feet (a recreational vehicle by today's standards), to one at least 12 feet wide and sometimes over 80 feet long.[307]

Whether the mobile home represents a real low cost alternative to conventional housing is nevertheless a matter of dispute.[308] A mobile home is normally financed and regulated as a vehicle rather than as real property. This means that while its base cost is cheaper, its financing terms are not really favorable. Most loans must be repaid within seven years (some as long as ten). This short term, plus the need to pay site rental, means that monthly costs are not significantly cheaper than for conventional housing.[309] Insurance is also

306. Building the American City, *supra* note 1, at 439.

307. Mobile Home Manufacturer's Association, 1974 Mobile Home Data Book 11 (1974).

308. An Australian commentator made the following observations about mobile homes in America:

> . . . In the business of providing new bad, cramped half-sized and substandard housing for their poor, the Americans are as busy and creative today as they've ever been. . . . [A] fifth of all the new accommodations they produce each year comes in the form of "mobile" housing. Hardly any of it ever moves. It's not really meant to move. It's meant to avoid legal definition as "housing" so that it can evade the laws that require houses to meet minimum standards of size and quality. . . . Some of those [who live in mobile-home caravan camps] are free spirits who like to live that way; for many of them caravans on the ground are better than flats; and some caravan communities have a friendlier spirit than some conventional suburbs do. But most of the people in the camps are only there because they can't do better. Their caravans and trailer-houses tend to be about half the size of a basic house, and worse equipped. . . . There's less personal privacy and less common living space inside them, and not always any private space outside. Plenty of people own their caravans, but caravans rot faster than houses, and they have to be bought on hire purchase instead of on mortgage, so their owners pay double interest rates, to get an asset whose value then deteriorates instead of increasing as the values of many houses do. They can thus be sold shelter without getting any share in the rising value of land under it; and there's more profit in making vans than in making small houses, both for the builders and for the money-lenders.

H. Stretton, Housing and Government 11 (Boyer Lectures, Griffith Press, Australia, 1974).

309. Building the American City, *supra* note 1, at 439.

costlier. Critics also say that there are substantial maintenance problems, difficulties over depreciation and resale, excessive fees for mobile home park entry and exit, and other less tangible problems, which are discussed below. These costs and difficulties, they say, make mobile homes a questionable choice for lower income families. Yet for some, particularly in moderate climates, a mobile home may represent reasonably durable and comfortable shelter for $8,000.

That mobile homes have come to play such a large role in the housing market is in itself remarkable. The mobile home and its residents exist in a hostile cultural and legal atmosphere, and mobile homes have still not overcome their early image as trailers existing in dense and unsightly courts or parks populated by transients commonly thought to be undesirable additions to a community. The persistence of this image, in spite of the changing character of mobile home parks and their residents, is reflected in an extraordinary legal framework.[310] There are also many other problems, such as vulnerability to fire and to wind damage, highway transportation risks, and unsightliness that are beyond the scope of this section.[311] The following pages focus on the regulation of mobile homes and of related factory-built housing.

Mobile Home Regulation: Necessary Reforms

Most mobile home regulation falls into five categories: (1) financing; (2) taxation and licensing; (3) zoning; (4) landlord-tenant law; and (5) construction standards.

Financing. A mobile home is really a hybrid kind of property. On the one hand it is mobile, suggesting that personal property laws apply to it; and on the other hand it is a home, implying that real property laws govern. In fact, the situation is a confusing mixture of applicable law that varies from one jurisdiction to another. Financing is one area that is governed by personal property law. The result of this classification is that Article 9 of the Uniform Commercial Code applies to mobile homes and also to the foreclosure of mobile home

---

310. *See generally* F. Bair, The Regulation of Modular Housing with Special Emphasis on Mobile Homes (American Society of Planning Officials 1971); Center for Auto Safety, Mobile Homes: The Low-Cost Housing Hoax (1975); M. Drury, Mobile Homes: The Unrecognized Revolution in American Housing (1972); B. Hodes & G. Roberson, The Law of Mobile Homes (1974); R. Newcomb, Mobile Home Parks, Part I: An Analysis of Characteristics (1971); M. Wehrly, Mobile Home Parks, Part II: An Analysis of Communities (1972).

311. For discussion of these problems, *see* Mobile Homes: The Low-Cost Housing Hoax, *supra* note 310.

loans.[312] Repossession is possible for late payment (ten to twenty days), and a purchaser of a defective unit is probably courting repossession if he or she attempts to delay payment in order to induce the dealer to repair.

California has amended its Automobile Sales Finance Act[313] to provide some protections. It bans deficiency judgments except where the owner has substantially damaged the unit, and it gives the owner the same defenses against the assignee (buyer of the sales contract) as against the original dealer.[314] Nevertheless, in most states the quick depreciation of mobile homes means that the proceeds from the disposition of the collateral upon foreclosure are often insufficient to satisfy the remaining debt. Consequently, foreclosure of a mobile home loan may be more disastrous for its owner than foreclosure of a conventional home mortgage.[315]

Section 309 of the Housing and Community Development Act of 1974[316] authorizes a new federal program of FHA insurance which may help transform mobile home loan financing from consumer to real estate loans. Previously, FHA insurance was available only for loans on individual mobile homes or for mortgages on mobile home parks financed by developers. The current program provides FHA insurance of a loan to purchase a developed or undeveloped lot on which the owner may place a mobile home already owned, or a lot-home combination loan covering a single-wide or double-wide home built in accordance with the National Mobile Home Construction and Safety Standards Act of 1974.[317] Moreover, the program facilitates long-term loans (twenty years, thirty-two days for a double-wide home and lot at a $27,500 amount), and more favorable interest rates, enabling a greater number of families to qualify for higher quality mobile homes.

Taxation and Licensing. Laws in this area are varied and sometimes the subject of confusion about who bears the tax burden. California, for example, exacts three separate payments from mobile home purchasers: a vehicle registration fee, a sales or use tax, and a

312. U.C.C. § 9-102(1)(a).

313. Cal. Civ. Code § 2983.8 (West Supp. 1974).

314. Vernon, *Mobile Homes: Present Regulation and Needed Reform*, 27 Stan. L. Rev. 164 n. 24 (1974).

315. Moreover, the Uniform Commercial Code § 9-502 permits deficiency judgments unless the parties otherwise agree.

316. Amending Title I of the National Housing Act, 12 U.S.C. § 1703. HUD regulations implementing the program are contained in 24 C.F.R. 201(D) (Jan. 1977).

317. Pub. L. No. 93-383, 42 U.S.C. §§ 5-401 *et seq. See* discussion of this act in text accompanying notes 373-78 *infra.*

vehicle license fee. The sales tax is applied to the entire purchase price of the unit. A conventional house, by contrast, is taxed only on materials used in its construction. As personal property, mobile homes are not directly subject to the real property taxes used by localities to provide public facilities and services.[318]

During transportation the mobile home is a vehicle and is therefore subject to licensing and registration fees for the privilege of using state highways. As a fixed residence, the mobile home becomes part of a community and enjoys that community's benefits and protections. States have justifiably been concerned that mobile home owners might not bear their fair share of the cost of providing such services.[319] In some states, such as New York, Pennsylvania, and Delaware, mobile homes are taxed as real estate or by excise tax.[320] In a majority of states, however, mobile homes are taxed as personalty, or by other more direct means. Moreover, the usual rule is that:

> the tax rate is the same for realty and personalty, so that in most states the owner of the mobile home fully discharges his obligation to share in the tax burden. Controversies arise in those states where realty and personalty are not equally taxed. The outcome has been either the enactment of special levies on mobile homes or the treatment of parked mobile homes as real estate assessable and taxable to the owner of the park.[321]

In addition, the mobile home owner contributes to community revenue indirectly, since the incidence of real estate taxes is shifted forward by the park owner as a part of the rental fee.[322]

Zoning. A majority of mobile homes are located in licensed parks, to which mobile home use is restricted in many states.[323] Restrictions are generally upheld as valid exercises of the police power,[324] commonly on the basis that better public facilities can be provided

---

318. B. Hodes & G. Roberson, *supra* note 310, at 155. By making his more or less permanent home in a trailer, an individual could derive the benefit of all the services provided by the local government while leaving the burden of paying them on his neighbors who lived in more conventional type dwellings. New York Mobile Homes Ass'n v. Steckel, 9 N.Y.2d 533, 536, 215 N.Y.S.2d 487, 488, 175 N.E.2d 151, 152 (1961), *appeal dismissed*, 369 U.S. 150 (1962).
319. Hodes & Roberson, *supra* note 310 at 157.
320. *Id.*
321. *Id.* at 155.
322. *Id.*
323. *Id.*
324. *See, e.g.*, Napierkowski v. Township of Gloucester, 29 N.J. 481, 150 A.2d 481 (1959).

and supervision can be enhanced when mobile homes are confined to certain limited areas.[325] Some early cases upheld the total exclusion of mobile homes from municipalities.[326] The far better view, however, is that such prohibitions are arbitrary and are not a reasonable and justifiable exercise of the police power.[327] Most recent cases have therefore invalidated such zoning schemes.[328]

In many areas special "trailer districts" have been established, usually in combination with exclusion of mobile homes from other districts.[329] A trailer district of the floating type was held unconstitutional, however, when its creation was shown to be arbitrary.[330] Where mobile homes are permitted in some districts within the municipality, most courts have upheld exclusion from low-density districts.[331] Exclusion from rural areas is a more questionable practice, especially since it can have the effect of total exclusion from the municipality.[332] Moreover, in the open rural situation, the argument about depreciating property values is much less convincing,[333] and such restrictions have generally been struck down.[334]

Some communities allow mobile home use only by special permit.[335] The denial of such permits has generally been upheld,[336] and

325. *See, e.g.*, Town of Granby v. Landry, 341 Mass. 443, 170 N.E. 2d 364 (1960). *See* cases collected in 2 Williams, *supra* note 199, at 506–508.

326. Davis v. McPherson, 132 N.E.2d 626 (Ohio App. 1955), *appeal dismissed*, 164 Ohio St. 375, 130 N.E. 2d 794 (1955); Vickers v. Township Committee, 37 N.J. 232, 181 A.2d 129 (1962), *appeal dismissed*, 371 U.S. 233 (1963).

327. Hodes & Roberson, *supra* note 310, at 219; 2 Williams, *supra* note 199, at 506–508.

328. *See, e.g.*, Anderson v. Township of Highland, 21 Mich. App. 64, 174 N.W. 2d 909 (1962); Gust v. Township of Canton, 342 Mich. 436, 70 N.W.2d 772 (1955). *Cf.* Southern Burlington County NAACP v. Township of Mount Laurel, 336 A.2d 713 (N.J. 1975), *cert. denied*, 423 U.S. 808 (1975).

329. 2 Williams, *supra* note 199, at 472–473.

330. Summerell v. Phillips, 238 So. 2d 786 (La. App. 1970). *See also* Anderson v. Township of Highland, 20 Mich. App. 64, 174 N.W.2d 909 (1962).

331. *See* 2 Williams, *supra* note 199, at 473–479; Connor v. West Bloomfield Tp., 207 F.2d 482 (6th Cir. 1953).

332. 2 Williams, *supra* note 199, at 484–491.

333. Conner v. West Bloomfield Tp., 207 F.2d at 484.

334. *E.g.*, Smith v. Plymouth Tp. Inspector, 346 Mich. 57, 77 N.W.2d 332 (1956); Lakeland Bluff, Inc. v. County of Will, 114 Ill. App. 2d 267, 252 N.E.2d 765 (1962). *But see* Napierkowski v. Township of Gloucester, 29 N.J. 481, 150 A.2d 481 (1959).

335. 2 Williams, *supra* note 199, at 497–502.

336. Crane v. Board of County Comm'rs, 175 Neb. 568, 122 N.W.2d 520 (1963); Crowther, Inc. v. Johnson, 225 Md. 379, 170 A.2d 768 (1969).

the issuance of special permits has likewise been sustained against attack by complaining neighbors.[337] Similarly, the denial of variances for mobile home use has commonly been upheld,[338] and their issuance sustained as well.[339]

Although many zoning regulations for mobile homes have been unreasonable, there may in fact be practical reasons for restricting mobile homes to parks. Mobile homes not only look anomalous among conventional houses, and tend to have a less stable occupancy, but they do not last nearly as long. To allow them in conventional residential neighborhoods might conceivably have deleterious effects on the neighborhood environment and decrease surrounding property values. Yet the net effect of restricting mobile homes to parks is often to restrict severely the availability of sites—sometimes leading to the creation of a monopoly. And monopolization of sites is a major contributing factor to the frequent abuses of the rights of mobile home residents.

The restrictive zoning of mobile home parks has lately come under increasing judicial attack. In *Bristow v. City of Woodhaven*,[340] the Michigan Court of Appeals—employing the so-called preferred use doctrine—struck down a zoning ordinance that effectively excluded trailer parks from the municipality. The doctrine created a presumption in favor of certain "favored" uses.[341] Plaintiff must establish that the given land use advances substantially the regional public interest and is an appropriate use for the site in issue. Once these basic facts are established, the presumption arises, and the burden of persuasion is shifted to the municipality, which must then justify the exclusion of the use.[342] Thus, the preferred use doctrine served to modify the traditional presumption of validity that applies to most zoning provisions.

In *Kropf v. City of Sterling Heights*,[343] however, the Michigan

---

337. *See, e.g.*, Colt v. Bernhard, 279 S.W.2d 527 (Mo. App. 1955).

338. Hebb. v. Zoning Bd. of Appeals, 150 Conn. 539, 192 A.2d 206 (1963).

339. Allen v. Humboldt County Bd. of Supervisors, 241 Cal. App. 2d 158, 50 Cal. Rptr. 444 (1966).

340. 35 Mich. App. 205, 192 N.W.2d 322 (1971).

341. Note, *The Michigan Preferred Use Doctrine as a Strategy for Regional Low-Income Housing Development: A Progress Report*, 8 Urb. L. Ann. 207, 210–11 (1974) [hereinafter cited as *Michigan Preferred Use Doctrine*].

342. *Id.* at 211. *See* discussion of the preferred use doctrine in Chapter 5, note 79, *supra*.

343. 391 Mich. 139, 215 N.W.2d 179 (1974).

Supreme Court retreated somewhat from the liberal application of the preferred use doctrine.[344] Under the *Kropf* decision the plaintiff must establish the unreasonableness of the ordinance by a showing that no reasonable governmental interest would be achieved by the exclusion, or that the zoning classification irrationally excludes other legitimate uses from the area in issue. Upon a showing that a zoning provision totally excludes the legitimate use, a presumption of unlawful discrimination arises.[345]

A recent decision that is likely to be of significance in other jurisdictions is that by the influential New Jersey Supreme Court in *Taxpayers Association of Weymouth Township, Inc. v. Weymouth Township*,[346] upholding an ordinance creating a mobile home park district for the exclusive use of the elderly. Noting a marked demographic shift upward in the population of the elderly and a resulting critical shortage of housing to meet their needs and desires, the court found the ordinance at hand particularly well suited for meeting those needs. Mobile home developments, according to the court, can provide a relatively inexpensive form of housing, can afford the elderly an important age-homogeneous environment, and can provide housing of an ideal size for older persons who have both physical and financial limitations. The ordinance, the court concluded, clearly promotes the general welfare and is within the purview of the zoning enabling act.

Landlord and Tenant. Here again the characterization of mobile homes as vehicles and personalty presents problems, because landlord-tenant law does not typically pertain to mobile home dwellers. The most serious issue is eviction. Rental agreements, rather than leases, have historically been used by mobile home parks (although leases affording minimal protection to both parties are now being used more frequently). The common form of mobile home park tenancy is tenancy-at-will, which becomes in effect a month-to-month tenancy, terminable by either party without cause.[347] The rental agreement is usually accompanied by a set of park regulations that prescribe tenants' behavior, sometimes to an unusual degree.[348] Tenants are

344. *Michigan Preferred Use Doctrine, supra* note 341, at 217–18.
345. *Id.*
346. 71 N.J. 249, 364 A.2d 1016 (1976).
347. Nyberg, *The Community and the Park Owner Versus the Mobile Home Residents: Reforming the Landlord-Tenant Relationship,* 52 B.U. L. Rev. 810 (1972).
348. *Mobile Homes: The Low-Cost Housing Hoax, supra* note 310, at 61–66.

required to sign their names to some rules that could only be described as oppressive, but nevertheless could become grounds for summary eviction. For example: "The management reserves the right to evict anyone who persistently and deliberately speaks in a derogatory manner of the park. . . ."[349]

The unusual burden that eviction places upon the park tenant is a result of his "unique position of owning his home while renting the land on which it is placed,"[350] and of the dominant position of the park landlord. Since the tenant does own a movable home, eviction forces the homeowner either to move it or to abandon it. Locating a new homesite poses special difficulties when vacancies are as limited as they are in the mobile home context:[351]

> Also, even if a mobile home owner can find another park, relocating another home is expensive. "In most instances, it costs at least $200 to move a mobile home from one side of town to another, and the charge on hauls of 1,000 miles or more can be up to $1,600."[352]

The evicted tenant must forfeit any entrance fees (which may exceed $2,000) as well as the value of any improvement he or she may have made to the parksite.[353] Of course, the tenant will be forced to tender another entrance fee and to make additional improvements at the new site in most instances, assuming that a new site is available.

A few states have responded legislatively to these problems.[354] California, for example, requires a showing of cause for eviction.[355] Acceptable causes are limited to those set forth in the statute, and the landlord must state with specificity the bases for eviction.[356] Furthermore, any attempt to obviate these provisions by contractual

---

349. Wehrly, *supra* note 310, at 126.

350. Nyberg, *supra* note 347, at 813.

351. *See id.* at 811-13; Note, *Mobile Home Park Practices: The Legal Relationship Between Mobile Home Park Owners and Tenants Who Own Mobile Homes,* 3 Fla. St. U.L. Rev. 103, 110-11 (1975) [hereinafter cited as *Mobile Home Park Practices*].

352. *Id.* at 120.

353. *Id.* at 111.

354. *See* Mass. Gen. Laws Ann. ch. 140, § 32J (1974); Minn. Stat. Ann. § 327.44 (Supp. 1974); 1974 N.Y. Laws ch. 973, § 1 (§ 233(b)); Cal. Civ. Code § 789.5(d)(1)-(5) (West Supp. 1975).

355. Cal. Civ. Code § 789.5(d)(1)-(5) (West Supp. 1975).

356. *Id.* at § 789.5(f) ("Neither reference to subdivision and paragraph numbers, nor recital of the language of this section, nor both, shall be compliance with this subdivision.").

waiver is "contrary to public policy" and therefore void.[357] Other one-sided practices by park landlords are prohibited in California, as well. Tenancies cannot be terminated "for the purpose of making the tenant's space in the park available for a person who purchased a mobile home from the owner of the mobile home park or his agents."[358] Fees in excess of rent, utilities, "or incidental reasonable service charges" are prohibited.[359] Entry fees and transfer or selling fees are explicitly proscribed.[360] And with limited exceptions, a tenant cannot be prohibited from remaining in the park in the event of its sale by the owner to a third party.[361]

The primary weakness of these provisions lies in the ease with which a park owner can evict a tenant for violation of park rules. No requirement of reasonableness is made, although the rules must have been established "in the rental agreement at the inception of the tenancy or as amended subsequently with the consent of the tenant, or without his consent upon six months written notice."[362] Obviously the owner of the park may legitimize eviction by promulgating many unreasonable rules, the violation of even the most trivial of which would come within the authorized cause.

Florida has recently enacted more progressive legislation. The Florida law, which seems to meet the chief shortcoming of the California act in that park rules upon which eviction may be predicated must be reasonable,[363] was upheld against constitutional attack in *Palm Beach Mobile Homes, Inc. v. Strong*,[364] and *Stewart v. Green*.[365]

357. *Id.* at § 789.5(a).
358. *Id.* at § 789.6.
359. *Id.* at § 789.7.
360. *Id.* at § 789.8.
361. *Id.* at § 789.10.
362. *Id.* at § 789.5(d)(3).
363. Fla. Stat. § 383.69 (1973) (bracketed words supplied by statutory revision):

1. A mobile home park owner or operator may not evict a mobile home or mobile-home dweller other than for the following reasons:
   (a) Nonpayment of rent.
   (b) Conviction of a violation of some federal or state law or local ordinance, which [violation] may be deemed detrimental to the health, safety and [or] welfare of other dwellers in the mobile home park.
   (c) Violation of any reasonable rule or regulation established by the park owner or operator, provided the mobile home dweller received written notice of the grounds upon which he is to be evicted at least thirty days prior to the date he is required to vacate. . . . A mobile home park rule or regulation shall be presumed to be reasonable if it is similar to rules and regulations customarily established in other mobile home parks located in this state or if the rule or regulation is not immoderate or excessive.

In both cases the park owners alleged that the act restricted their freedom to contract and infringed upon valuable property rights. Noting the special nature of the mobile home landlord-tenant relationship,[366] the court ruled that the legislature had the authority "to impose reasonable regulations upon mobile home parks . . . under its broad police power in view of the fact that this enterprise peculiarly affects the public interest and bears a substantial relation to the public health, safety, morals, and general welfare."[367] These decisions manifest the court's concern with the unequal bargaining power of the park owner[368] and willingness to permit rental agreements and park rules to be subject to scrutiny.[369]

An encouraging judicial response to the eviction problem is the First Circuit's case of *Lavoie v. Bigwood*,[370] where a park resident brought an action under federal civil rights statutes alleging retaliatory eviction. In deciding for the plaintiff the court found "state action" in the local zoning scheme that gave the defendant park owner an effective monopoly over mobile home sites. But while *Lavoie* may be an encouraging approach in some respects, it is hedged with difficulties. The court was careful to limit its holding to cases where the local zoning's monopolistic effect is clear. Thus where alternative sites or other types of housing are available, state action may not be

---

(d) Change in use of land comprising the mobile home park or a portion thereof . . . provided all tenants affected are given at least ninety (90) days' notice, or longer if provided for in a valid lease, or the projected change of use and of their need to secure other accommodations.

2. Cumulative eviction proceedings may be established in a written lease agreement between the park owner or operator and a mobile home dweller in addition to those established by law.

3. This section shall not preclude summary eviction proceedings, and if the park operator does not have one of the above grounds available the park tenant may raise the same by affirmative defense.

364. 300 So. 2d 881 (Fla. 1974).
365. 300 So. 2d 889 (Fla. 1974).
366. *Id.* at 892.

The legislature finally recognized by Section 83.69 that a hybrid type of property relationship exists between the mobile home owner and the park owner and that the relationship is not simply one of landowner and tenant. Each has basic property rights which must reciprocally accommodate and harmonize. Separate and distinct mobile home laws are necessary to define the relationships and protect the interests of the persons involved.

367. Palm Beach Mobile Homes, Inc. v. Strong, 300 So. 2d 881, 884.
368. *See* Stewart v. Green, 300 So. 2d 889, 892.
369. *Id.* at 894. *See* Palm Beach Mobile Homes, Inc. v. Strong, 300 So. 2d at 884.
370. 457 F.2d 7, 14-15 (1972).

found. From a practical standpoint, the mobile home park tenant has little protection if he or she is relegated to establishing the un-constitutionality of an eviction.[371] Constitutional litigation can be protracted and expensive—much more so than most state summary eviction proceedings.[372]

Construction Standards. The National Mobile Home Construc-tion and Safety Standards Act of 1974,[373] created by Title VI of the Housing and Community Development Act of 1974, au-thorizes federal mobile home construction and safety standards and preempts all state and local standards that are not identical with the federal ones.[374] It also provides for civil and criminal penalties for violation,[375] inspection and investigation procedures (which may be delegated by contract to state, local, or private agencies),[376] a procedure for notifying purchasers of defects,[377] and authorization for states to initiate regulation of matters not covered by Title VI and to assume enforcement responsibilities pur-suant to a plan approved by HUD.[378] If adequately implemented, the new federal law promises to substantially advance the quality and liv-ability of mobile homes.

Conclusion
As has been established by their rapidly rising position in the over-all housing market, mobile homes represent a low-cost alternative to conventional housing. Their base price is continuing to drop further behind that of the average conventional house. Whether mobile homes can become a housing alternative in which the general public can have confidence, and whether their regulation can assure the pro-tection of legitimate local concerns about land use while at the same time protecting the purchaser, are matters of great importance. To these ends the following recommendations are presented:

371. Nyberg, *supra* note 347, at 818.
372. *Id.*
373. 42 U.S.C.A. §§ 5401 *et seq.*
374. *Id.* at § 5403(d).
375. *Id.* at § 5410.
376. *Id.* at § 5413.
377. *Id.* at § 5414.
378. *Id.* at § 5422.
379. *See* F. Bosselman & D. Callies, The Quiet Revolution in Land Use Con-trols (Prepared for the Council on Environmental Quality, G.P.O. 1971); R. Healy, Land Use and the States (Resources for the Future 1976); Domestic Council, 1976 Report on National Growth and Development: The Changing Issues for National Growth 130–39 (G.P.O. 1976). For a summary of the various state land-use programs, *see* Council on Environmental Quality, Environmental Quality: Seventh Annual Report of the Council on Environmental Quality 66–75 (G.P.O. Sept. 1976).

1. Localities should adopt comprehensive land-use plans which, in their housing element, recognize mobile home parks as a desirable land use under defined circumstances. These circumstances include attractive site design, landscaping, and screening, and the efficient provision of public facilities on the same basis as they are provided in conventional subdivisions. The public does have an interest in ensuring that mobile home development does not create blight and that mobile homes are not eyesores. But intelligent planning can avoid these undesirable effects. And the public has no interest whatever in forms of regulation that make the provision and servicing of low-cost housing more onerous and expensive.

2. With the provisions just outlined, mobile home subdivisions should be regulated like other subdivisions.

3. Serious consideration should be given to reclassification of mobile homes as real property; or, if this is impractical, to the codification of mobile home law in order to avoid results that follow from their classification as personalty. The taxation and licensing of mobile home parks should be among the areas of law that are reformed.

STATE REVIEW OF LOCAL LAND-USE DECISIONS AFFECTING LOW-INCOME HOUSING

The past few years have witnessed the steady accretion by the legislatures and courts in numerous states of the hitherto unquestioned prerogative of local governments to regulate land use and development within their boundaries. The authority to regulate the use of land through the exercise of the police power has always resided in the states and has merely been delegated to local government by enabling legislation based on the Standard State Zoning and Planning Acts of the 1920s. That power is now being reasserted, but to date principally in the area of environmental management.[379]

The Massachusetts Zoning Appeals Law

Only Massachusetts thus far has enacted legislation specifically providing for state review of local actions that adversely affect the development of low- and moderate-income housing. The Massachusetts Zoning Appeals Law[380] is designed both to provide a means for over-

380. Mass. Gen. Laws Ann. ch. 40B, §§ 20-23 (Supp. 1973). The law is known colloquially as the "anti-snob" zoning law, and more formally as Chapter 774, An Act Providing for the Construction of Low- or Moderate-Income Housing: Cities and Towns in which Local Restrictions Hamper Such Construction.

riding local regulations that would otherwise prohibit construction of such housing, and to simplify the process for obtaining permits to build low- and moderate-income housing.

By the late 1960s it had become clear that widespread patterns of suburban zoning—characterized by prohibitions on multifamily housing, height restrictions, large-lot zoning, and minimum floor-space requirements—had excluded low- and moderate-income families, thereby aggravating the housing shortage, socioeconomic problems, and racial disparities in metropolitan areas of Massachusetts.[381] At about the same time, the National Commission on Urban Problems made similar national findings about zoning in metropolitan areas, and, quite independently, recommended state legislation strikingly similar to that ultimately adopted in Massachusetts.[382]

The Massachusetts zoning appeals law was enacted in 1969 after much compromise, and over substantial opposition. Most observers agree that it would not have been passed at all if conservative urban representatives, still smarting from the fight over the school racial imbalance bill, had not wanted to even the score with the suburbs.[383] As a result of the numerous amendments and modifications adopted in the various stages of enactment, the legislation contains language that was ambiguous even to the bill's supporters, and that consequently has impeded the law's expeditious and effective implementation.

The statute establishes a one-step procedure by which limited-dividend corporations, nonprofit corporations, or public agencies may secure permission to construct publicly assisted low- and moderate-income housing by applying to the local zoning board of appeals for a comprehensive permit.[384] The application for a comprehensive permit is made in lieu of filing separate applications with numerous other boards responsible for administering zoning, subdivision control, building, housing, plumbing, electrical, health, and fire-prevention ordinances. The local board must grant the comprehensive permit, notwithstanding any restrictive local requirements and regulations that would otherwise prevent the construction of the housing, if the application is reasonable and "consistent with local needs."[385]

381. See Commonwealth of Massachusetts, Senate, Legislative Research Council, Restricting the Zoning Power to City and County Government (Rpt. 1133, 1968). For an excellent legislative history of the law, see K. Schneider, Innovation in State Legislation: The Massachusetts Suburban Zoning Act (unpublished honors thesis at Radcliffe College, 1970).

382. Building the American City, supra note 1, at 239–40.

383. See Schneider, supra note 381, at 5.

384. Mass. Gen. Laws Ann. ch. 40B, § 21.

385. Id. at § 20.

The law defines "consistent with local needs" in terms of the *regional* need for low- and moderate-income housing. A local community has satisfied the Act's requirements in meeting the regional need when (1) low- or moderate-income housing constitutes 10 percent of a locality's total dwelling units; (2) such housing occupies 1.5 percent or more of the total land area zoned for residential, commercial, or industrial uses; or (3) the aggregate area of housing sites proposed for development of low- and moderate-income housing during any one calendar year exceeds 0.3 percent of the land area zoned for residential, commercial, or industrial uses, or ten acres, whichever is larger.[386]

If a locality has not met its quota, it may still be entitled to deny an application under its own regulations, but it can do so only if it determines that the regional need for low- and moderate-income housing is outweighed by valid planning considerations. Such considerations include "the need to protect the health or safety of the occupants of the proposed housing or of the residents of the city or town, to promote better site and building design in relation to the surroundings or to preserve open spaces. . . ."[387] However, as the Supreme Judicial Court of Massachusetts subsequently made clear when it upheld the Act's constitutionality in 1973, a municipality's failure to meet its minimum housing obligations, as defined in the statute, "will provide compelling evidence that the regional need for housing does in fact outweigh the objections to the proposal. . . ."[388] In that event the board must override any restrictions, local requirements, and regulations that impede the construction of the housing, and must grant the comprehensive permit.

An applicant who is denied a comprehensive permit, or whose application is approved with conditions which make the development uneconomic, or a party who is aggrieved if the permit is granted, may appeal to the state Housing Appeals Committee (HAC),[389] situated within the State Department of Community Affairs. The Housing Appeals Committee is empowered to hold de novo hearings on the matter, but its review is limited to the issue of whether the local decision was "reasonable and consistent with local needs." If the HAC finds that the denial of the permit or conditions attached are invalid, it can override the local board and order it to grant the necessary permit without unreasonable conditions. An adverse

386. *Id.*
387. *Id.*
388. Board of Appeals v. Housing Appeals Committee, 294 N.E.2d 393, 413 (Mass. 1973).
389. Mass. Gen. Laws Ann. ch. 40B, §22.

decision by the HAC does not preclude additional review by the courts. Rather, the statute provides for an appeal to the state court for any party who is aggrieved by the issuance of a comprehensive permit.[390] The law's administrative appeals process thereby adds a level of decision-making between the local zoning board and the state judiciary. In addition, the HAC and the housing sponsor are authorized to enforce the orders of the committee in state court.

In the four years immediately following the statute's enactment, the appeals process functioned under a legal cloud.[391] The version of the statute that was enacted into law did not specifically state (as had earlier versions) that the local board had the power to grant permits for uses that violated local zoning ordinances. This led the legislation's opponents to argue that this provision had been deliberately deleted, and that the legislation was intended only to speed up the permit process—not to override local zoning laws. Local communities as well as the HAC were reluctant to act based on the law, and the Department of Community Affairs did not allocate a sufficient budget for HAC's staff and administrative expenses.

Little progress was made under the Act before March 1973, when its constitutionality was upheld in *Board of Appeals of Hanover v. Housing Appeals Committee.*[392] The court decided cases from two towns. Both local zoning boards, relying on traditional zoning grounds such as impact on traffic congestion, drainage, and water supply, had denied applications under the statute for comprehensive permits to build low- and moderate-income housing, and had been reversed by the HAC. In a long opinion, concerned primarily with special questions of Massachusetts law, the court held that the zoning appeals law "represents the Legislature's attempt to satisfy the regional need for housing without stripping municipalities of their power to zone."

> By creating a "consistent with local needs" criterion which expands the scope of relevant local needs considered by the local boards to include the regional need for low- and moderate-income housing, the Legislature has given the boards the power to override the local exclusionary zoning practices in order to encourage the construction of such housing in the suburbs. By fixing a ceiling on the extent to which a board must override

390. *Id.* at § 21.
391. For discussions of the zoning appeals process in its earlier years, *see* M. Barr, *The Massachusetts Zoning Appeals Law: Lessons of the First Three Years*, (Submitted for presentation at the American Society of Planning Officials Conference, Aug. 1972); N. Taylor, *Reconsidering the Massachusetts Suburban Housing and Zoning Reform Law: The Need for Change*, (submitted for presentation at the A.S.P.O. conference, Aug. 1972).
392. 294 N.E.2d 393 (Mass. 1973).

local zoning regulations, the Legislature has clearly delineated that point where local interests must yield to the general public need for housing. This ceiling establishes the minimum share of responsibility that each community must shoulder in order to alleviate the housing crisis that confronts the Commonwealth.[393]

In September 1974 the court issued a decision on a second case under the zoning appeals law. The court held, in *Mahoney v. Board of Appeals of Winchester*,[394] that the legislation permitted a zoning board of appeals to override the state's subdivision control law when granting a comprehensive permit.

The Massachusetts zoning appeals law is essentially a passive instrument: it is neither an initiator of housing proposals nor a direct development tool. Similarly, it does not affect the availability of sites, the high cost of land, or the scarcity of housing subsidies. What it does offer is an alternative approach to attaining local approval for lower income housing when proposals for such housing have been rejected on grounds that are viewed (by the developer) as unreasonable or discriminatory. The relative passivity of the law is largely responsible for its durability. Following the creation of the New York State UDC in 1968,[395] there was considerable support in Massachusetts for the establishment of a similar public corporation with substantial powers to condemn property, to override local zoning and other regulations, and to directly undertake large-scale development.[396] But both the housing interests and the legislature were divided over the creation of such a super-agency. There was concern that once established the agency might develop its own agenda and not be held accountable.[397]

While the UDC proved to be extremely successful in constructing low- and moderate-income housing, it eventually lost its power to override suburban communities when the New York legislature, following a major political controversy in Westchester County, authorized towns and villages to veto UDC projects.[398]

The Massachusetts' housing appeals procedure has been most suc-

393. *Id.* at 399.

394. 316 N.E.2d 606 (Mass. 1974).

395. *See* discussion of the New York State Urban Development Corporation in the section on Housing Finance Agencies, in text accompanying notes 85-93 *supra*.

396. J. Breagy, Overriding the Suburbs: State Intervention for Housing Through the Massachusetts Appeals Process 7-8 (Citizens Housing & Planning Association of Metropolitan Boston, May 1976).

397. *Id.*

398. *See* note 358 *supra*.

cessful in producing housing at the level of the local zoning board of appeals (ZBA). As of November 1975, local ZBAs had issued 27 permits comprising a total of 2,281 units.[399] Of these, 734 units in eight developments had been completed and occupied. Another 1,547 units were in the planning stage in twelve developments. To date, the state HAC has received forty-nine appeals of local decisions. In twenty-eight instances the committee has overruled local decisions and granted comprehensive permits for projects involving well over 3,000 units; in two instances local decisions were upheld. Of the HAC decisions, twenty have been further appealed to the courts, of which nine have been sustained in the Superior Courts and two in the Massachusetts Supreme Judicial Court. All other HAC decisions that have been appealed to the courts are still pending disposition. Every HAC decision on which the courts have acted on appeal has been sustained by the courts.[400]

The ability to tie up housing development in the courts is a grave problem with the law's procedures. Several projects have in fact been withdrawn as a result of problems involved in raising the necessary capital to fight lengthy legal battles. On the one hand, due process requirements may make access to the courts constitutionally necessary, at least on some issues;[401] on the other hand, access to the courts allows opponents of low- and moderate-income housing to make such housing uneconomic through the filing of dilatory suits. A developer's front-end costs are high to begin with. If construction loan commitment must be carried at high interest rates through a long court fight, during which time the developer cannot begin construction, the feasibility of the project is bound to be threatened. This largely explains why no units were built under the Act for several years, and why, when the first units were built, it was only because the Catholic Archdiocese of Boston, as developer, had committed its vast resources and determination to the project.[402]

Numerous other ambiguities or defects still remain to impede the Act's effectiveness. For example, there are inadequate planning standards for site location (access to community services and facilities, jobs, shopping, public transportation, and so on). The Act also fails

399. The figures in the accompanying text are taken from J. Breagy, *supra* note 396.

400. *Id.* at 31.

401. Constitutionality may always be litigated, but other issues as to the applicability and interpretation of a statute may be left to the final determination of administrative body. Crowell v. Benson, 285 U.S. 22 (1933).

402. Austin, Yoshida & O'Conner, *Subsidized Housing and the Anti-Snob Zoning Act*, in The Land Use Controversy in Massachusetts: Case Studies and Policy Options 111-23 (L. Susskind ed. 1975).

to distinguish between housing for the elderly and for low- and moderate-income families, and as a result the limited success the law has had among local ZBAs has been predominantly with housing for the elderly.[403]

The subsequent enactment of state environmental laws[404] has created additional problems by imposing requirements not fulfilled in a comprehensive permit. This has caused the permit to lose its comprehensiveness and has provided another level of delay for foes of low-income housing. Developers have actually fought lengthy appeals for comprehensive permits all the way to the state's highest court, only to have to repeat the process over environmental impact statements. This has happened in Concord (the site of the 1973 constitutional court test), where the proposed housing was never built because of conditions required of the developer by the local Conservation Commission under the state's wetlands law.[405] Struggles like this turn housing advocates into foes of environmental legislation and even of zoning reforms. Many of these problems, however, are capable of being remedied by legislation that might be considered in other states.[406]

403. Breagy, *supra* note 396, at 26. The statutory quotas do not distinguish between elderly housing and accommodations for families. It is thus possible for a community to meet its local obligation by granting rezonings only for subsidized housing for the elderly and legitimize the total exclusion for low- and moderate-income families. Indeed, the statutory formula bears no relationship to actual regional housing needs; rather, it was based upon political reality—the most generous formula that could obtain the necessary votes for passage. Thus even if the formula were satisfied, it would not come close to meeting actual regional needs.

404. *E.g.*, the Massachusetts Environmental Policy Act, Mass. Ann. Laws ch. 30, §§ 61, 62 (1973) (providing for the filing of environmental impact statements for specified actions); "Hatch Act," Mass. Ann. Laws ch. 131, § 40, *as amended* by 1974 Mass. Acts ch. 818 (wetlands protection).

405. Breagy, *supra* note 396, at 55. Thus a developer can fight a lengthy appeals battle for a comprehensive permit all the way to the state's highest court, only to have to repeat this struggle over an environmental impact statement. *See* Austin *et al.*, *supra* note 402, at 123.

406. A proposed Connecticut version, for example, defines regional housing needs using criteria similar to those used by regional planning agencies in their housing allocation plans, including: (1) the amount of substandard housing in the region; (2) the availability of jobs for low- and moderate-income people; (3) regional population projections; and (4) projected available financing for subsidized housing. Further, in recognition of the political realities of such a scheme, the Connecticut bill contains incentives for localities to cooperate, including state grants-in-aid to communities for educational purposes, based on the number of students residing in low- and moderate-income housing built under the statute, and state matching funds for the provision of municipal sewerage and water facilities necessitated by the construction of low- and moderate-income housing. A critique of the Massachusetts law and other similar laws proposed in other states is in L. Rubinowitz, Low-Income Housing: Suburban Strategies 94–99 (1974).

The ALI Model Land Development Code
and Housing

The ALI Code[407] establishes, as part of its comprehensive revision of the statutory law of zoning, planning, and subdivision control, a statewide regulatory procedure for granting consolidated development permits and for reviewing specifically defined local land-use and development decisions. The permits and review are granted only for developments that are of state or regional significance, including low- and moderate-income housing. Further, in recognizing the vital links between development, employment, and housing, the Code seems to obviate certain housing distribution problems that might occur without state intervention. The drafters of the Code, moreover, have benefited from their observations of the problems with the Massachusetts zoning appeals law.[408]

The ALI Code combined zoning and subdivision control into a single "development ordinance"[409] to be administered by a local "land development agency."[410] A developer seeking to undertake certain types of development requiring multiple permits—including low- and moderate-income housing—is authorized by the ALI Code to apply for a joint hearing on some or all of the permits.[411] This procedure does not change any of the substantive standards under which the permits are to be issued, but merely authorizes a coordination procedure to simplify and speed up the administrative process.[412]

While the ALI Code places primary responsibility for regulation of land use and development on local government, it nonetheless recognizes the need for expanding state participation in the vast majority of decisions that have regional or statewide significance. Accordingly, Article VII of the Code authorizes a state land-development agency to define certain categories of development which—because of their size, nature, or effect on surrounding land—constitute "developments of regional impact."[413] It also authorizes the agency to establish standards and special development procedures with which local decisions affecting these developments must comply. Other types of development may qualify as developments of regional

407. ALI Code, *supra* note 239.
408. Barr, *supra* note 391 at 4.
409. ALI Code, *supra* note 239, at § 2-101.
410. *Id*. at §§ 2-301 *et seq*.
411. *Id*. at § 2-402.
412. *Id*. at n., § 2-402.
413. *Id*. at § 7-301. For a thorough discussion of these provisions, *see* D. Mandelker, Environmental and Land Use Control Legislation ch. 3 (1977).

impact even though they are not among the categories identified by the state agency. This section of the Code has already influenced land-use legislation in other states.[414]

Another type of development is designated as a "development of regional benefit."[415] These typically provide benefits to an area beyond the boundaries of a single local government, but apparently might cause some problems within a local community. The development of housing for persons of low and moderate income is one of the categories of development so designated.[416] The reason for including housing in this classification is explained in the drafters' note to this provision:

> Local governments often believe that the heavily subsidized programs have an unfavorable cost-revenue impact, and there may be social and racial prejudice against the anticipated occupants. Thus it has been difficult to find sites for housing of this type that will be approved by local governments.[417]

As a development of regional benefit, a proposed low- and moderate-income housing development that is allowed under the local development ordinance may be denied a permit only if the local land-development agency finds that "the probable net detriment from the development exceeds the probable net benefit."[418] If the development would not otherwise be entitled to a permit under a local ordinance, the permit is nevertheless to be granted by the local agency if three standards are met: (1) the probable net benefit from the development exceeds the probable net detriment; (2) the development does not substantially or unreasonably interfere with the ability to achieve the objectives of an approved local or state land development plan; and (3) the development departs from the ordinance no more than is reasonably necessary to enable a substantial segment of the population of the state to obtain reasonable access to housing, employment, educational, and recreational opportunities.[419] The

414. *See* discussion of ALI Code in Chapters 4 & 5 *supra*.

415. ALI Code, *supra* note 239, at § 7–301(4), and accompanying notes.

416. *Id.* at (d). Other "developments of regional benefit" include developments by other government agencies, developments of religious, charitable, educational, or public utility purposes, which will serve a substantial number of nonresidents of the community in which they are located. *Id.* at § 7–301(4)(a)-(c).

417. *Id.* at § 7–301 n.4(d).

418. *Id.* at § 7–304(1).

419. *Id.* at § 7–304(2). The last requirement serves two purposes. First, it requires the proponents of the development to establish the existence of a public need or public purpose on a DRI to justify overriding local controls. Second, it enables the local agency to impose appropriate conditions upon the development so as to minimize adverse effects. Fox, *A Tentative Guide to the American Law Institute's Proposed Model Land Development Code*, 6 Urb. Law. 928, 945 (1974).

ALI Code requires the local agency not to restrict its consideration to benefit and detriment within the local jurisdiction, but to consider all material impact on surrounding areas.[420]

The ALI Code then makes a brave leap into a difficult area: "Detriments or benefits shall not be denied consideration on the grounds that they are indirect, intangible or not readily quantifiable."[421] The problem that the Code's drafters were trying to deal with here is that certain costs (especially environmental ones) are typically not paid for by the activity that creates them. In a so-called perfect market, all the costs of an item—whether it is land or something else—will be reflected in its price. A buyer who pays this price will therefore have to take the costs into account when purchasing in the market, because the costs will have affected the price. Often, however, all of the costs (or all of the benefits) of a purchase or of engaging in an activity are not reflected by the market, and the market is thus called imperfect. The benefits and costs that fail to show up in a price are called externalities.

When a private owner decides to build a new factory or housing subdivision, for example, costs are imposed on the public in the form of sewer, electricity, and other services that must be provided, and in the form of new roads that may have to be built. These costs are not typically reflected in the price of the goods that the factory makes or in the price of the houses. They are borne by the taxpayers of the local jurisdiction. Sometimes, in fact, the costs cannot be confined to a single jurisdiction. Suppose the factory produces smoke that pollutes the air of a surrounding area, for instance; or suppose the rush-hour traffic from the factory creates traffic jams in a neighboring town. This complicates the externality problem even more, because the problem is external to the jurisdiction as well as the industry, and the adversely affected town has no power to regulate the offending activity. And while some adverse effects such as new sewers have easily quantifiable costs, many do not. How much does the public

420. ALI Code, *supra* note 239, at § 7-402. The note to the section also makes clear that the consideration should not be limited only to those factors that can be easily translated into dollar figures, and gives the following as an illustration:

When people are unable to find housing that is reasonably accessible to their job, it increases their cost of transportation and the burden on the taxpayers for providing transportation facilities and causes hardship for employers as well. The extent to which any development application will improve the geographic relationship between housing and jobs is an important factor to be considered.

Id.

421. *Id.* at § 7-402.

lose when the air is fouled or a park ruined? This is the specific problem addressed by the language, "intangible or not readily quantifiable."

Here, then, are two of the knotty problems that the ALI Code attempts to solve. One is the problem of regional impact of those activities that produce effects beyond a single jurisdiction, and the Code, as we have seen, establishes a mechanism to deal with that. The other is the balancing of detriments and benefits that cannot be easily or plausibly quantified—or, arguably, that cannot be quantified at all—against detriments and benefits whose costs are readily ascertainable. In this case, the ALI Code has merely indicated the problem to be grappled with, rather than solve that problem, and since economic theorists do not know how to solve the problem either, this could hardly be otherwise.[422]

For the present we are left in an unsatisfactory quandary. Not to deal with factors whose costs and benefits are difficult to quantify would be to turn a blind eye to the most challenging problem of environmental law and economics, and the ALI Code's drafters properly refused to do that. But having decided to face the issue, the Code stops short of articulating substantive standards for making decisions. The Code instead has proposed a method for shifting the decisionmaking process to a higher level of government in certain circumstances.

Other problems, such as the relationship between homes and jobs, are treated more substantively. The ALI Code requires close scrutiny of those developments of regional impact that will "substantially increase employment opportunities" within a municipality in order to assure that adequate housing is built in areas of expanding job opportunities.[423] Even though otherwise qualified, a local land-development agency is prohibited from granting a permit for a development of regional impact that will create more than 100 new full-time employees within the local jurisdiction, unless the agency also finds that:

1. Adequate and reasonably accessible housing for prospective employees is available within or without the jurisdiction of the local government.
2. The local government has adopted a land development plan designed to make available adequate and reasonably accessible housing within a reasonable time.

422. The examples in the note to § 7-402 *id.* purport to elucidate the process by which this balancing is to be done, but they plainly do not. The note states two problems and two conclusions but gives no clue to how the conclusions were reached.

423. *Id.* at § 7-305.

3. A State Land Development Plan shows that the proposed location is a desirable location for the proposed employment source.[424]

The rationale given by the drafters for this provision is that "[t]he local government that seeks to attract industry to improve its tax base but refuses to provide the housing that is a necessary concomitant to the new jobs is throwing an unreasonable burden on the neighboring communities that should not be permitted lightly.[425]

In any proceeding that requires a balance of detriments and benefits, the ALI Code allows a state land-planning agency to intervene and submit a report on its views on the question of regional impact.[426] And the Code *requires* such a report to be submitted (by the state planning agency or a delegated regional planning division) when it is requested by a local agency.[427] Thus a state agency that has a well-prepared analysis of statewide housing needs or of regional housing allocation plans could exert great influence over local determinations simply by having the best information.

In passing on permit applications, a local land-development agency is required to hold what amounts to a full-scale administrative hearing. It must then set forth written findings showing that its decision is supported by substantial evidence. A developer whose permit application is denied by a local agency is given an unqualified option, after notifying the agency,[428] to appeal the decision to the state Land Adjudicatory Board.[429] This board is given all powers that a local land-development agency has in issuing the initial decision, including the power to attach conditions and restrictions.[430]

But unlike the Massachusetts zoning appeals procedure, the ALI Code does not intend a de novo review at the state level; if additional evidence is needed, the proceeding is to be remanded to the local agency with directions to hear such evidence. In this way the state Land Adjudicatory Board remains merely an appellate body and need not set up the complex and expensive administrative machinery necessary to hold hearings and take evidence. Moreover,

424. *Id.*

425. Note to *id.* at § 7-305. While the Code does not explicitly discuss the provisions of low- and moderate-income housing in conjunction with employment and housing opportunities, it does point out in its explanatory note that the housing be available at a cost or rental within the means of the employees and that the determination of "reasonable accessibility" would vary with ability of the worker to afford the type of transportation facilities available. *Id.*

426. *Id.* at § 7-403.

427. *Id.*

428. *Id.* at § 7-502(3).

429. *Id.* at § 7-501.

430. *Id.* at § 7-503.

opponents of a project would be on notice that if they did not build an adequate record at the local hearing, they might never again have the opportunity.

Finally, the Code sets up an appropriately narrow standard of judicial review. In order to reverse the board's decision a court must find *inter alia,* that the state agency's action was arbitrary and capricious, or otherwise not in accordance with law.[431] In noting the expertise and sophistication that will be developed by the state Land Adjudicatory Board in the process of balancing benefits and detriments, furthermore, the Code directs the court to give special weight to the decisions of the board in reviewing local orders about developments of regional impact.[432] These provisions streamline the entire review procedure.

While the ALI Code's statutory review process for dealing with lower income housing needs cures many defects of the Massachusetts approach, its major deficiency is its lack of a planning base for the siting and review of low-income housing. The drafters of the ALI Code decided after long debates not to require local government to adopt a land development plan as a prerequisite to the power to regulate development. The drafters sought to avoid the wrath of smaller and less urban communities that likely would consider the planning process contemplated in Article 3 of the Code to be too complicated and expensive, particularly if the community desired only a simple and general development ordinance and a few special-permission provisions. Moreover, in view of the substantial authority given to state government under Articles 7 and 8 of the Code to plan and regulate areas of the state that present potential problems, it was not viewed necessary to coerce cooperation from unwilling local governments.[433]

While these reasons are not persuasive to the Advisory Commission (in light of its endorsement of mandatory planning set forth in Chapters 5 and 6), their adverse implications are offset to a degree by the ALI Code's offer of incentives to those municipalities which choose to engage in planning. Only these municipalities are permitted (among other activities) to adopt special procedures for planned unit developments; to engage in certain development activities, such as reserving land by future acquisition in "special planned areas"; to adopt special preservation districts; and to exercise broader powers to discontinue existing land uses.[434]

431. *Id.* at § 9-110.
432. Note to *id.* at § 9-110(2).
433. *See* discussion in notes following *id.* at §§ 2-301, 3-101.
434. The powers that are conditioned on the adoption of a plan are summarized in *id.* at § 3-101 n. 3.

MANDATORY INCLUSIONARY TECHNIQUES

Not all communities have sought to exclude low- and moderate-income housing. A few have done just the opposite. Two suburban counties adjacent to Washington, D.C. (Fairfax County, Virginia, and Montgomery County, Maryland) and the City of Los Angeles have enacted ordinances that *require* most new housing developments to include a minimum number of units for sale or rent to low- and moderate-income families.[435] Cherry Hill, New Jersey, and Lewisboro, New York, have adopted similar ordinances.[436]

The first three have attracted the most attention. Although they vary in details,[437] they share important similarities. The first is that each of them applies only to multifamily developments of a certain size. The Los Angeles ordinance does not apply to projects of fewer than five units, and the suburban ordinances exempt developments of fewer than fifty-one units. The Fairfax County ordinance (which, as discussed below, was subsequently invalidated by the Virginia Supreme Court) was also drawn to exempt apartment buildings of six or more stories.

The second common feature of these ordinances is the allocation scheme. The Fairfax and Los Angeles ordinances set aside 6 percent of the units for "low-income families" and an additional 9 percent for "moderate-income families"—these income levels are geared to statutory definitions used in federal housing programs (the former Section 236 and public housing programs). The Montgomery County ordinance is different in these respects. It contains its own income definitions and it does not distinguish between low-income and moderate-income families.

Mandatory inclusionary land-use programs are to be achieved

435. County of Fairfax, Va. Code ch. 30 (1961), Amendment 156 (June 30, 1971); Montgomery County, Md. Code ch. 25A; Amendment F-803, Montgomery County, Md. Code ch. 59 (1973); Los Angeles, Cal. Municipal Code §§ 12.03, 12.39, 13.04, *as amended by* Ordinance No. 145, 927 (April 30, 1974).

436. *See generally* Erber & Prior, *The Trend in Housing Density Bonuses,* 26 Land Use L. & Zoning Dig. 6, 7 (1974).

437. Only the Los Angeles ordinance, for example, requires that low- and moderate-income units be dispersed throughout the development and contain the same average mixture of bedrooms as the market-rate units. The Fairfax ordinance authorized developers to meet their obligation by building the low- and moderate-income housing on a separate site. There are also other differences regarding the applicability of other zoning requirements, resale or increased rentals of units, etc. For further discussion of the three prototype ordinances, *see* Klevin, *Inclusionary Ordinances—Policy and Legal Issues in Requiring Private Developers to Build Low Cost Housing,* 21 U.C.L.A. L. Rev. 1432 (1974) [hereinafter cited as Klevin].

through one of two methods: density bonuses or federal subsidies. The density bonus approach was that contemplated chiefly by the Montgomery and Fairfax County ordinances. The bonuses (up to a 20 percent increase) allow additional market-rent units for every one or two low- and moderate-income units included. Increased density allows a developer to decrease the cost of land per unit and thus to make the project more feasible. The Los Angeles ordinance offers no density bonuses. By requiring all units to be rented at fair market value, it assures that low- and moderate-income families will either have to pay the full rent or else obtain a public subsidy.

Tying those ordinances to public subsidies means that they are subject to the vagaries of federal housing law and administration. The Los Angeles and Fairfax ordinances, nevertheless, were designed to excuse compliance if federal subsidies were unavailable—provided in Los Angeles that the local housing authority has the option to lease or require the leasing of up to 15 percent of the units (presumably when federal subsidies later become available); and in Fairfax, that the unavailability of federal subsidies could not be attributed to the proposed high development costs of the project (that is, lack of project feasibility).

But federal subsidies present problems aside from their obvious unreliability, stemming either from inadequate congressional appropriations or unsatisfactory HUD administration. One of these problems, for example, is that the former federal Section 236 program did not facilitate differential rentals in similar apartments, making it difficult to avoid the physical segregation of subsidized tenants. Fortunately, the new federal Section 8 leased housing programs is more flexible in this respect. In fact, the mixing of subsidized and unsubsidized units within the same building is the preferred arrangement under the more recent federal program.[438]

Problems nevertheless remain with a mandatory inclusionary ordinance that relies exclusively on federal subsidies. For example, HUD establishes the maximum rents that owners can receive for subsidized units. These may be too low to permit an attractive economic return on the project. Also, HUD may determine that the supply of housing available for subsidized occupancy is adequate, in which case it will decline to release any subsidy funds for new construction in a given housing market area.[439] Indeed, recent federal deemphasis on new construction programs raises serious questions for inclusionary zoning policies in high-growth areas.

438. 42 U.S.C. § 1437f(c)(5).
439. C.F.R. § 1273.103(a)2.

Mandatory inclusionary ordinances are designed to increase the supply and the dispersal of low- and moderate-income housing in areas that presently have little. It is difficult to know whether they will work. From the start it was clear that such ordinances would require years of operation to create a great reduction of existing concentrations of lower income families. But in even more limited terms, their effectiveness has been difficult to evaluate. The Fairfax ordinance, for example, was invalidated by the Supreme Court of Virginia[440] before the ordinance had an opportunity to be effectively tested.

A question is often raised as to whether broad income-mixing within single projects can work. While the small amount of available empirical evidence is not conclusive, it does allow a rather modest optimism. One of the most favorable studies was done on developments financed by the Massachusetts Housing Finance Agency (MHFA).[441] This study suggested that the design and management of the development has more to do with tenant satisfaction than the mix of tenants. Other sociological studies suggest that wide cultural and income discrepancies are not readily accepted at the neighborhood or block level.[442] The problem is that too little study has been made of successful subsidized housing developments in middle-income areas to determine whether fears of neighbors have been validated by experience.

In addition to the sociological issues raised by mandatory inclusionary ordinances there are also relevant economic ones. Can a development with a 15 percent low- and moderate-income housing requirement be profitable?[443] The answer seems to depend on the following factors: (1) the granting of adequate density bonuses under the ordinance; (2) the developer's ability to cut construction costs by reducing the size and amenities of the low- and moderate-income units; (3) the sale and rent levels for these units; and (4) whether rent reductions on these units can be recouped through an internal subsidy generated by the higher rates on the remaining units or from the landowner through a reduced price for the development site. According to these criteria, the most promising ordinance is Montgomery

440. Board of County Supervisors v. DeGroff Enterprises, 214 Va. 235, 198 S.E.2d 600 (1973). *See* discussion of this case in text accompanying notes 444–49 *infra.*

441. W. Ryan, A. Sloan, M. Seferi & E. Werby, All in Together: An Evaluation of Mixed-Income Multi-Family Housing (Massachusetts Housing Finance Agency 1974).

442. See Klevin, *supra* note 437, at 1462–66, and particularly n. 98.

443. *See id.* at 1476–90. *See also* In-Zoning, *supra* note 237, at 131–41.

County's, which not only grants generous density bonuses but also sets sales-price limits and rental maximums at levels above those established under the various federal programs yet still adequate to assist a fairly broad range of lower income families.

The mandatory ordinances raise other very practical and straight-forward economic issues. For one, a developer may simply be unwilling to accept what he perceives to be unnecessary risks and decide to build elsewhere. (Logically, then, mandatory ordinances really ought to exist throughout a housing market area.) The existence of an active state HFA may, to an extent, obviate this problem by allaying some of the developer's fears about project risk. These agencies are specifically created to assist financing of low- and moderate-income housing. To achieve this objective they provide mortgage money at below-market interest rates and favorable loan-to-value ratios to residential developers of low- and moderate-income housing (see previous discussion of state HFAs).

When state-assisted financing is not available, the amount of reserved low- and moderate-income housing units established by the ordinance may affect the project's ability to obtain conventional financing. Mandatory inclusionary housing ordinances may cause lenders to doubt the ability of residential developers to repay construction loans. Lenders may consequently withhold mortgage moneys from such developments. Even if financing is available, investment might be deterred by lenders insisting that developers pay higher interest rates and put more equity into their projects.

A proper number of reserved units can, however, be established to obviate this concern. In all mortgage feasibility studies, lenders automatically consider a vacancy factor. Generally, as with the mandatory inclusionary ordinances, this factor is established as some percentage of the anticipated housing units. Because these units are considered vacant, they have no cash flow and are inconsequential for determining interest rates and equity requirements. Therefore, by correlating the reserved housing quota of an inclusionary ordinance with local banking practices, potential financing difficulties might be minimized.

Another potential problem with mandatory inclusionary ordinances not generally discussed in the literature is the need to relate the housing thereby mandated to broader planning considerations. Under the existing ordinances, low- and moderate-income housing is to be built wherever new construction is located, regardless of the availability of community facilities for low-income households. It is thus possible to provide low-income housing in areas that are inadequately served by public transportation, schools, health-care centers, an other needed facilities. Moreover, any community can be subjected to low-income housing—assuming a willing multifamily developer—regardless of that community's relative fiscal capacity to absorb such housing and provide the requisite services. These problems can, however, be resolved by integrating the mandatory inclusionary ordinance into an overall comprehensive housing and planning program (as discussed in Chapter 6).

These social, planning, and economic issues are inextricably related to the numerous legal questions raised by mandatory inclusionary ordinances. In the only direct test of a mandatory inclusionary ordinance for low-income housing to date, the Fairfax County ordinance was invalidated by the Virginia Supreme Court in *Board of Supervisors of Fairfax County v. De Groff Enterprises, Inc.,*[444] an opinion that left much to be desired in terms of elucidating the salient legal issues involved. The decision rested primarily on two grounds. The court found that the mandatory ordinance was *ultra vires* the municipality's authority under the state zoning enabling act because it was motivated by considerations of the users of the land, not its physical characteristics. The court referred to an earlier decision[445] where it had invalidated large-lot zoning in half of an urbanizing county because its intent was to concentrate the county's housing development, particularly for low- and middle-income households, in the other half of the county:

> The effect of this decision is to prohibit socio-economic zoning. We conclude that the legislative intent was to permit localities to enact only traditional zoning ordinances directed to physical characteristics and having the purpose neither to include nor exclude any particular socio-economic group.[446]

While it is to the court's credit that it recognized the deleterious characteristics of exclusionary zoning, the court's opinion can be viewed as somewhat curious in light of the generally accepted fact that zoning affects (and is usually intended to affect) broader aspects of the social and economic characteristics of a community.[447]

444. 214 Va 235, 198 S.E.2d 600 (1973).
445. Board of Supervisors v. Carper, 200 Va. 653, 107 S.E.2d 390 (1959).
446. 198 S.E.2d at 602.
447. *See* New York and New Jersey inclusionary cases discussed in the text accompanying notes 454-60 *infra; see also* cases collected in note 461 *infra.*

One possible explanation of the *DeGroff* decision is that Virginia traditionally construes narrowly the delegations of authority from the state legislature to the municipal governments and agencies, thus being one of the few remaining states to continue adherence to *Dillon*'s rule. *See* Board of Supervisors v. Horne, 216 Va. 113, 215 S.E.2d 453 (1975). However, because of the *DeGroff* decision,

The second reason adduced by the court for invalidating the ordinance was that the requirement of selling or renting 15 percent of the units to low- and moderate-income persons at prices not fixed by the free market constituted confiscation without just compensation. This conclusion seems out of line with established principles defining when public regulation constitutes a public taking, since the owners are not deprived of the reasonable use of their property. The issue is somewhat analogous to that raised by rent-control cases, where courts have generally sustained the limiting of private profits in jurisdictions with an inadequate supply of housing, when the property-owner receives a net return that is at least comparable to investments of a similar nature and risk.[448] Applying these cases to mandatory inclusionary housing ordinances has led one commentator to conclude that an "ordinance which allows an average moderately efficient developer in the housing market to earn a reasonable return should pass muster."[449]

However, the *De Groff* holding may also be explained as the court's way of protesting the singling out of the private multifamily developer to bear the costs of solving a regionwide problem of inadequate

---

both Montgomery County and Los Angeles have based the authority of their mandatory ordinances on the municipal police powers granted them under their home-rule charters, instead of on their municipal zoning powers. *See* In-Zoning, *supra* note 237, at 138–39.

448. *See, e.g.*, Kress, Dunlap & Lane Ltd. v. Downing, 193 F. Supp. 874 (6th Cir. 1961); Inganomort v. Borough of Fort Lee, 62 N.J. 521, 303 A.2d 298 (1973). *See generally* Baar & Keating, *The Last Stand of Economic Substantive Due Process—The Housing Emergency Requirement for Rent Control*, 7 Urb. Law. 447 (1975). However, when the courts find the net return is inadequate, the rent-control regulation will likely be held "confiscatory" and invalid. F.H. Smith Co. v. Verzi, 53 D.C. App. 363, 290 F.2d 338 (1923).

The analogy between rent-control laws and mandatory exclusionary housing ordinances may not be suitable. When rent-control laws are enacted, the jurisdiction is generally concerned that landlords will exploit the shortage in the housing market to make windfall profits. Block v. Hirsh, 256 U.S. 135, 157 (1920). Consequently, even though landlords' potential profits are reduced, the rent-control ordinance is fairly applied to landlords who in the absence of such regulations would exploit low- and moderate-income households. *Id.* But mandatory inclusionary housing ordinances are enacted when developers fail to participate in the low- and moderate-income housing market.

Another important limitation on the rent-control analogy is the judicially imposed requirement of an emergency. Levy Leasing Co. v. Siegal, 258 U.S. 242, 245 (1922). Rent-control laws can only be enacted when there is an emergency, *Id.*, and when the emergency ceases such laws are invalid. Peck v. Fink, 55 D.C. App. 110, 2 F.2d 912 (1924), *cert. denied*, 266 U.S. 631 (1924).

Nevertheless, the rent-control cases illustrate that developers' profits can be reasonably limited without being labeled an unlawful taking. *See* Baar & Keating, note 448 *supra*.

449. *See* Klevin, *supra* note 437, at 1523; and text accompanying note 452 *infra*.

housing for low- and moderate-income families, a problem that the developer did not create. A similar issue arises in other contexts. For example, courts typically uphold subdivision regulations requiring a developer to pay for the streets, utilities, and even the land for schools that will serve primarily the subdivision's population.[450] Since the subdivision created the demand for the additional public services, courts have not found it unfair to require the subdivision to bear their additional costs. On the other hand, where the subdivision regulations require the developer to bear the cost of public facilities that will not be used primarily by the subdivision residents, the courts may strike them down.[451] Similarly, zoning districts are justified on the basis that the odors, noise, and congestion from industrial and commercial uses would be unhealthy and would destroy the economic value of residential property mixed in with it. These uses are therefore thought incompatible and may be separated to prevent the harmful external side-effects of one type of use from impinging on the others.

But mandatory inclusionary zoning has a different rationale. It has broad social objectives that are not directly related to any individual project, and yet the project owner or developer is singled out to bear their burden. In other words, these ordinances involve an individual rather than a social form of wealth transfer. As mentioned above, however, adequate compensatory features built into the ordinance—such as increased densities—which "equalize" the profit potential of the development (that is, eliminates the burden), may cure this objection.[452]

Two later decisions in New York and New Jersey that deal with inclusionary ordinances of a somewhat different type nonetheless indicate that other state judiciaries may be more receptive to the concept than was the Virginia court.[453] In 1975 the creation of a

450. *See, e.g.,* Associated Home Builders v. City of Walnut Creek, 4 Cal. 3d 633, 484 P.2d 606, 94 Cal. Rptr. 630 (1971). *See* cases collected in R. Freilich & P. Levi, Model Subdivision Regulations: Text and Commentary (American Society of Planning Officials 1975).

451. *See, e.g.,* Pioneer Trust & Savings v. Village of Mount Prospect, 176 N.E.2d 79 (Ill. 1961); *see also* Freilich & Levi, *supra* note 450.

452. *See* Klevin, *supra* note 437, at 1523. Another approach lies in tying the inclusionary ordinance into an overall comprehensive housing program. Such a program should be designed to have a regional perspective, with each municipality supplying its fair share of the expected regional housing need. This strategy would rely on a number of different housing programs and would be aimed at attacking a range of housing problems.

453. Indeed, in light of its posture in *DeGroff,* the Virginia Supreme Court would likely have difficulty with the "milder" inclusionary ordinances upheld in New York & New Jersey and discussed in the text below. *See also* note 447 *supra.*

special inclusionary zoning district for the elderly was challenged by neighboring homeowners. The majority of the New York Court of Appeals, in *Maldini v. Ambro*,[454] responded to the dissenting position that the town ordinance impowers a town board to regulate the *use*, not to specify the users,[455] by stating:

> That the "users" of the retirement community district have been considered in creating the zoning classification does not necessarily render the amendment suspect, nor does it clash with traditional "use" concepts of zoning. Including the needs of potential "users" cannot be disassociated from sensible community planning based upon the "use" to which property is to be put. The line between legitimate and illegitimate exercise of the zoning power cannot be drawn by resort to formula, but as in other areas of the law, will vary with surrounding circumstances and conditions.[456]

In the final analysis the court was unwilling to invalidate the special elderly district because of the court's view of the strong public interest being served:

> Certainly, when a community is impelled, consistent with such criteria, to move to correct social and historical patterns of housing deprivation, it is acting well within its delegated "general welfare" power.[457]

The same issues were subsequently raised in New Jersey where that state's supreme court reviewed local zoning ordinances creating a special district for mobile home parks for the elderly (defined as persons over 52 years of age). The court, in *Taxpayers Ass'n of Weymouth Township, Inc. v. Weymouth Township*,[458] indicated that the ordinance would be valid only if there was a genuine relationship between the effect of the ordinance and the regulation of land uses:

> Furthermore, zoning ordinances which bear too tenuous a relationship to land use will be stricken as exceeding the powers delegated to municipalities by the enabling act.[459]

But the court concluded that the special mobile home ordinances "bear a real and substantial relationship to land use."[460]

454. 36 N.Y.2d 481, 330 N.E.2d 403 (1975).
455. *Id.* at 408.
456. *Id.* at 407–08.
457. *Id.* at 406.
458. 71 N.J. 249, 364 A.2d 1016 (1976).
459. 364 A.2d at 1031.
460. *Id. See* Shepard v. Woodland Committee and Planning Bd., 71 N.J. 230, 364 A.2d 1005 (1976) (upholding ordinance providing for senior citizen communities as special-use exception in residential-agricultural district).

In sum, the future treatment of mandatory inclusionary zoning ordinances in the courts is not at all clear. The legal picture does, however, offer some reason for optimism. Rent controls and subdivision exactions also involve a similar kind of private- rather than public-wealth transfer, and they have survived legal attack. Moreover, an ordinance that provides density bonuses and other benefits under the zoning and building codes, or is contingent upon the availability of federal subsidies, stands a better chance of success in the courts than one that does not. These benefits are in the nature of a quid pro quo for the low- and moderate-income housing requirements, and they operate to eliminate losses that might otherwise result from compliance with the ordinance. Finally, several prominent state courts have recognized the broader social and economic ends that can properly be achieved through zoning.[461]

LANDLORD AND TENANT: LAW REFORM

Existing landlord-tenant law in the United States, except as modified by statute or judicial interpretation, is a product of English common law developed within an agricultural society in the late Middle Ages, when doctrines of promissory contract were unrecognized.[462] Thus, the lease was viewed solely as the creation of a minor estate in the land. The tenant sought and expected nothing more than a right to possess and work the land; the landlord sought the collection of rent and minimum regulation of the occupancy of the property, short only of waste. The covenants of the parties were independently enforceable.

Today, both landlord and tenant expect a great deal more of one another. The medieval legal doctrines are inappropriate to modern urban conditions and are not responsive to the vital interests of the parties and the public. During the past ten years, the law of landlord and tenant has been undergoing tremendous change. The concept of landlord-tenant law as involving a mere grant of an interest in prop-

461. Other cases upholding local inclusionary provisions in municipal land-use regulations include: DeSimone v. Greater Englewood Housing Corp. No. 1, 56 N.J. 428, 267 A.2d 31 (1970) (upheld special-use variance for federally subsidized lower income housing development); Brunetti v. Township of Madison, 113 N.J. Super. 164, 325 A.2d 851 (1974) (upheld special-use variance for privately financed moderate-income housing); Cameron v. Zoning Agent, 357 Mass. 757, 260 N.E.2d 143 (1970) (upheld special building code requirements for low-rent public housing).

462. See 3 Holdsworth, A History of English Law 122-23 (5th ed. 1966); see also Javins v. First National Realty Co., 428 F.2d 1071, 1074-75 (D.C. Cir. 1970), cert. denied, 400 U.S. 195 (1970); Green v. Superior Court, 10 Cal. 3d 616, 622, 517 P.2d 1168 (1974).

erty governed by the rules of real property is rapidly being abandoned in favor of a new interpretation that views the relationship as an agreement between the parties for the provision of essential services.[463] This consumer-oriented view emphasizes principles of contract law and diminishes reliance upon real property law—and in so doing broadens considerably the field of tenants' rights and remedies.

Reform of antiquated landlord-tenant laws will not guarantee decent housing for every American renter. Basic changes in the law, however, which penalize neglect and give tenants the bargaining tools they need to insure that a landlord meets all responsibilities to maintain rental units, can assist in preventing the deterioration of some of the 22 million units of rental housing in the United States. In addition, reform can help prevent marginal housing from becoming uninhabitable housing and then, inevitably, abandoned housing. At the same time, legislative reform, such as that embodied in the Uniform Residential Landlord and Tenant Act (discussed below) offers protection to landlords to encourage investment of their capital in rental housing.

Decent Housing: Basic Legal Reforms

The transformation of the laws governing the landlord and tenant relationship in the United States that has occurred in the last decade has progressed along two separate lines—one dealing with the quality of housing put on the rental market, particularly for moderate- and low-income tenants, and the other attempting to assure fair treatment for all tenants.

---

463. This theory was well expressed by Judge J. Skelly Wright in his opinion in Javins v. First National Realty Corp., 428 F.2d at 1074:

> The assumption of landlord-tenant law, derived from feudal property law, that a lease primarily conveyed to the tenant an interest in land may have been reasonable in a rural, agrarian society; it may continue to be reasonable in some leases involving farming or commercial land. In these cases, the value of the lease to the tenant is the land itself. But in the case of the modern apartment dweller, the value of the lease is that it gives him a place to live. The city dweller who seeks to lease an apartment on the third floor of a tenement has little interest in the land 30 or 40 feet below, or even in the bare right to possession within the four walls of his apartment. When American city dwellers, both rich and poor, seek "shelter" today, they seek a well-known package of goods and services—a package which includes not merely walls and ceilings, but also adequate heat, light and ventilation, serviceable plumbing facilities, secure windows and doors, proper sanitation and proper maintenance. . . . In our judgment the trend toward leases as contracts is wise and well considered. Our holding in this case reflects a belief that leases of urban dwelling units should be interpreted and construed like any other contract.

Warranty of Habitability. When a potential tenant walks into a rental office and comes to terms with the landlord, they both emerge with some kind of agreement; even if they write nothing down, an agreement will be implied. The agreement may be that the landlord will make certain rooms available to the tenant, along with heat, gas, and electricity, and that the tenant in return will pay rent. What happens when the landlord fails to provide heat in the dead of winter? Under the traditional common law doctrine—still in effect in twenty-one states—the tenant can sue the landlord for damages and that is all. This is so because for centuries leases have been governed by the law of property. Accordingly, agreements within a lease constitute independent covenants (unless the parties agree otherwise); meaning that each party must continue to perform his part of the bargain regardless of whether the other party continues to perform his. Given the trouble and expense of going to court, the long dockets, and the short terms of many leases, the remedy of suing the landlord for damages is often no remedy at all.

Twenty-nine states and the District of Columbia[464] have recognized the emptiness of this remedy and have by case law or statute

464. Alaska: Alaska Stat. §§ 34.03.100, 34.03.160, 34.03.180 (1974); Arizona: Ariz. Rev. Stat. Ann. §§ 1324, 1361 (1974); California: Cal. Civ. Code § 1941 (West 1974); and Green v. Superior Ct., 10 Cal. 3d 616, 111 Cal. Rptr. 704, 517 P.2d 1168 (1974); Connecticut: Conn. Gen. Stat. Ann. §§ 27–24 *et seq.*; and Todd v. May, 6 Conn. Cir. Ct. 731, 316 A.2d 793 (1973); Delaware: Del. Code Ann. tit. 25 § 5303 (1972); District of Columbia: Javins v. First Nat'l Realty Corp., 428 F.2d 1071, 1082, *cert. denied,* 400 U.S. 925 (1970); Florida: Fla. Stat. Ann. §§ 83.51, 83.56 (1973); Georgia: Ga. Code Ann. § 61-111 (1974); and Stack v. Harris, 111 Ga. 149 (1900); Hawaii: Haw. Rev. Stat. § 521-42 (1974); Illinois: Jack Spring, Inc. v. Little, 50 Ill. 2d 351, 280 N.E.2d 208 (1972); Indiana: Old Town Dev. Co. v. Langford, Ind. Ct. App. 2d, (June 17, 1976); Iowa: Mease v. Fox, 200 N.W.2d 791 (1972); Kansas: Steele v. Latimer, 214 Kan. 329, 521 P.2d 304 (1974); Kentucky: Ky. Rev. Stat. Ann. §§ 383-595, 383-625; Maine: Me. Rev. Stat. Ann. tit. 14, § 6021 (1974) (allows cancellation of lease); Maryland: Baltimore City Pub. Local Laws §§ 9-9, 9-10, 9-14.1; and Montgomery County Code, Fair Landlord-Tenant Relations ch. 93A; Massachusetts: Mass. Gen. Laws Ann. ch. 239, § 8A (1974); and Boston Housing Authority v. Hemingway, 293 N.E.2d 831 (1973); Michigan: Mich. Comp. Laws Ann. § 554.139 (1974); and Rome v. Walker, 38 Mich. App. 458, 196 N.W.2d 850 (1972); Minnesota: Minn. Stat. Ann. § 504.18 (1974); and Fritz v. Warthen, 298 Minn. 54, 213 N.W.2d 339 (1973); Missouri: King v. Moorehead, 495 S.W.2d 248 (1971); New Jersey: Marini v. Ireland, 56 N.J. 130, 765 A.2d 526 (1970); New York: New York City, Real Prop. Actions § 755 (1963); Ohio: Ohio Rev. Code Ann. §§ 5321.07 (1974); Oregon: Or. Rev. Stat. §§ 91.770, 91.800 to .815 (1974); Pennsylvania: Commonwealth v. Monumental Properties, Inc., 329 A.2d 819 (1975); Virginia: Va. Code Ann. §§ 55-248.2, .13, .25; Washington: Wash. Rev. Code Ann. § 59.18.060 (1974); and Foisy v. Wyman, 83 Wash. 2d 22, 515 P.2d 160 (1973); Wisconsin: Pines v. Perssion, 14 Wis. 2d 590, 111 N.W.2d 409 (1961). (*But see* Posnanski v. Hood, 46 Wis. 2d 172, 174 N.W.2d 528 (1970).

adopted the implied warranty of habitability, which obligates the landlord to comply substantially with housing codes or with other minimum standards of health and safety.[465] An implied warranty changes the substantive bargain between the parties by providing that when a landlord rents a place to live, a place that is livable must be provided. It also changes the tenant's remedies. A warranty, unlike a covenant, is a matter of contract law rather than of property law, and therein lies all the difference: in contract law each party is bound by his part of a bargain only so long as the other party performs his.[466] Accordingly, the tenant does not have to go on paying for "essential services" that are never received. As before, the tenant can sue for damages, but he or she can also withhold rent without becoming subject to eviction. This change gives tenants enormously increased bargaining power.

When a tenant chooses to sue for damages upon breach of the warranty of habitability, there are several competing formulas for their computation. One is the difference between the market value of the premises in habitable condition, less their market value in deteriorated condition.[467] Another is a percentage diminution of rent based upon loss of use of the premises.[468] A third (as yet untried) formula is the tort-related theory of damages based on inconvenience and suffering.[469] Regardless of the theory of damages applied, the implied warranty of habitability places an economic sanction on the landlord and therefore should induce repair and maintenance. During the period of time that repairs are underway or in the event that a landlord declines to comply, tenants enjoy the benefit of reduced rent.[470]

465. Only Oregon enumerates the defects that amount to breach of warranty in the statute. 1973 Or. Laws ch. 559, §14. This was done because much of rural Oregon does not have housing codes.

466. *See* Javins v. First National Realty Co., 428 F.2d at 1082–83; *see also Landlord-Tenant Law—Dependency of Lease Covenants: Covenant to Pay Rent is Dependent upon Landlord's Warranty of Habitability*, 2 Ford. U.L. Rev. 433 (1974).

467. This is currently the most prevalent method for valuation of damages. *See* Mease v. Fox, 200 N.W.2d at 797; Boston Housing Authority v. Hemingway, 293 N.E.2d at 785; Green v. Superior Ct., 10 Cal. 3d at 638. The problem with this method is that some trial court judges require expert testimony to ascertain the market value of the premises in question.

468. This method is probably the easiest to apply for courts and tenants, since it does not require expert testimony and can be proved by the tenant's own testimony. *See* Academy Spires, Inc. v. Brown, 111 N.J. Super. 477, 268 A.2d 556, 561–62 (1970), cited with approval in *Green*.

469. This method of damages appears to present no substantial proof problems. At present, however, it has not been adopted by any statute or published decision. *See* Moskovitz, *The Implied Warranty of Habitability—A New Doctrine Raising New Issues*, 62 Cal. L. Rev. 1444 (1974).

470. *See* Green v. Superior Ct., 10 Cal. 3d at 635–36; Marini v. Ireland, 56 N.J. at 140.

The major limitations of the warranty of habitability lie in its inherent failure to mandate repair of the premises by the landlord, to provide enough money damages for tenants to make substantial repairs to deteriorated housing, and to be self-enforcing. A tenant may have to return to court month after month to obtain a rent abatement from a recalcitrant landlord. Because the economic sanction of the warranty of habitability is limited, moreover, tenants will often find that landlords would rather accept the abatement than make the repairs, thus leaving the tenant with a lower monthly rent but unimproved living conditions. Whether the rent reduction will be sufficient to allow the tenant to make the repairs personally will depend on the individual case. Nevertheless, whatever its shortcomings may be in some instances, the warranty of habitability represents the most important conceptual change in the residential lease relationship in hundreds of years, and the Advisory Commission believes that it should be adopted in every state.

Utility Shut-Off. Any cessation of utilities by the landlord, even if inadvertent, creates a direct threat to habitability, and where arbitrary or vindictive it is a prime example of unfair treatment of tenants. In response to this problem a growing number of states have, by statute[471] or public utility regulation,[472] moved to protect tenants. This protection takes the form of criminal sanctions,[473] civil remedies with stated damages,[474] or injunctive relief against offending landlords. In addition to these protections against landlord termination of utilities, public utilities may be obligated to provide tenants with notice and a hearing before services can be terminated.[475] Privately owned utilities do not have a constitutional obligation, to hold hearings.[476]

Repair and Deduct. Repairing the premises and deducting the cost from the rent is a companion remedy to rent abatement. It is

471. *See, e.g.*, Ariz. Rev. Stat. ch. 10, §§ 33-1364 *et seq.*; Cal. Civ. Code § 789.3; Conn. Gen. Stat. § 19-65: Mass. Gen. Laws ch. 164, §§ 124, 186, § 14; N.Y. Real Prop. Law § 235; 1973 Or. Laws ch. 559, § 22; R.I. Gen. Laws § 34-18-17; Tex. Civ. Stat. Ann. § 52-36.

472. *See, e.g.*, Maine Public Utility Commission, Reg. Gen. Order No. 36.

473. *See, e.g.*, Conn. Gen. Stat. § 19-65; N.Y. Real Prop. Law § 235.

474. *See, e.g.*, Cal. Civ. Code § 789.3 ($100 per day); Mass. Gen. Laws ch. 186, § 14 (three months' rent or actual damages); 1973 Or. Laws ch. 559, § 22 (two months' rent or double damages); Tex. Civ. Code Ann. § 52-36 (one months' rent or $100 per day).

475. *See* Davis v. Weir, 328 F. Supp. 317, 321 (1971) (tenant entitled to notice of termination under Fourteenth Amendment due process clause when landlord failed to pay utility bill), *citing* Goldberg v. Kelly, 397 U.S. 254 (1970), *and* Bell v. Burson, 402 U.S. 535 (1971).

476. Jackson v. Metropolitan Edison Co., 419 U.S. 345 (1974).

intended to accomplish repair of the premises, while rent abatement yields only monetary damages to the tenant. "Repair and deduct" allows a tenant to remedy a serious defect in habitability after notice to the landlord and the landlord's failure to repair within a reasonable time. The tenant exercises this right by initiating repairs, either personally or through a contractor, and deducts the cost from the next month's rent.[477] Repair and deduct has been adopted by case decision or statute in twenty states and the District of Columbia.[478] At least one state supreme court has adopted this remedy on the unique theory of partial constructive eviction based on failure to maintain vital facilities.[479] In states that have adopted the warranty of habitability by case or statute, but have not recognized repair and deduct, if may perhaps be argued that the implied warranty of habitability has the effect of placing, into every residential lease, a covenant to repair on the part of the landlord. The exercise by the tenant of repair and deduct might then be viewed as a mitigation of future damages that would otherwise be incurred by the landlord pursuant to rent abatement.[480]

Repair and deduct as it exists in statutory form is a limited remedy, since the size of deductions and the frequency of use[481] is re-

477. The tenant runs a calculated risk in exercising repair-and-deduct. The landlord may sue for the portion of rent deducted, and the tenant will have to justify the deduction. Academy Spires, Inc. v. Brown, 268 A.2d at 559, has a discussion of "vital facilities" versus "amenities." California lists by statute those defects which trigger the repair-and-deduct remedy. Cal. Civ. Code §§ 1941 *et seq.*

478. Alaska: Alaska Stat. § 34.03.180 (1974); Arizona: Ariz. Rev. Stat. Ann. § 33–1363 (1974); California: Cal. Civ. Code § 1942 (West 1954); Delaware: Del. Code Ann. tit. 25, § 5306 (1972); Georgia: Ga. Code Ann. *as interpreted in* Dougherty v. Taylor and Norton Co., 5 Ga. App. 773, 63 S.E. 928 (1909); Hawaii: Haw. Rev. Stat. § 521–64 (Supp. 1974); Illinois: Jack Spring, Inc. v. Little, 50 Ill. 2d 351, 280 N.E.2d 208 (1972); Kentucky: Ky. Rev. Stat. Ann. arts. 2693–94 (West 1975); Massachusetts: Mass. Gen. Laws Ann. ch. 111, § 1276 (1974) Nebraska: Neb. Rev. Stat. § 76–1427 (Supp. 1974); New Jersey: Marini v. Ireland, 56 N.J. 130, 765 A.2d 526, 535 (1970) (remedy adopted on the theory of partial constructive eviction based on failure to maintain vital facilities); North Dakota: N.D. Cent. Code § 47–16–13 (1973); Ohio: Ohio Rev. Code Ann. § 1923; Oklahoma: Okla. Stat. Ann. tit. 41, § 31 (1974); Oregon: Or. Rev. Stat. § 91.805 (1974) (limited to repair of utilities or essential services only); Rhode Island: McCardell v. Williams, 19 R.I. 701 (1897), 36 A. 719 (1897); South Dakota: S.D. Compiled Laws Ann. § 43–32–9 (1967); Virginia: Va. Code § 32–64–66 (1969) (toilet facilities only); and Va. Code, ch. 13.2, § 55–248.23 (for essential services only).

479. *See* Marini v. Ireland, 765 A.2d at 534–35.

480. *See* Masser v. London Operating Co., 106 Fla. 474, 145 So. 79, 84 (1932); Rosen v. Needleman, 83 So. 2d 113, 114 (1955); *see also* 5 Corbin on Contracts § 1039 (1964); Calamari & Perillo, Law of Contracts § 216 (1970); D. Dobbs, Remedies §§ 3.7, 12.6 (1973) (mitigation of damages).

481. *E.g.,* Ariz. Rev. Stat. ch. 10, § 33–1363 (limits deduction to half a month's rent or $150, whichever is greater); Cal. Civ. Code § 1942 (limit of one month's rent); Mass. Gen. Laws ch. 111, § 127L (limit of four months' rent).

stricted.[482] The effectiveness of this tool is greatly increased when it is used by tenants acting collectively.

Receivership. Receivership is a statutorily authorized system aimed at the preservation of existing housing, and is based upon the state or local police power to protect the health and safety of the public.[483] At least fourteen states have adopted receivership statutes.[484] The courts are called upon either by the local code enforcement agency or by tenants[485] to appoint a receiver for the purpose of collecting rents from severely dilapidated buildings in order to establish a fund to rehabilitate those buildings. After repairs are completed and all expenses have been paid, the building is restored to the landlord.

The receivership process has the additional purpose of bringing together all parties with an interest in the building, including tenants, owner, managers, mortgagees, lienors, and city government. Several interrelated problems exist, however, that significantly diminish the potential of receivership as a broad scale remedy for deteriorated housing. Buildings are rarely put into receivership until they have become severely dilapidated; there is usually no authority to subordinate existing mortgage liens; and the cost of repair of such buildings is often so high that it will exceed the income available from rents over a reasonable period of time.

But see Marini v. Ireland, 56 N.J. 130, 765 A.2d 526 (1970) (no limit on deductions under common law repair-and-deduct).

482. *E.g.*, Cal. Civ. Code § 1942 restricts use to one month's deduction in a twelve-month period. Similarly, Massachusetts restricts use to four months in a twelve-month period. Mass. Gen. Laws ch. 111, § 127L.

483. Receivership statutes have been upheld as a valid exercise of the police power. *In re* Dept. of Buildings, 14 N.Y.2d 291, 200 N.W.2d 432, 436 (1964); Community Renewal Foundations, Inc. v. Chicago Title & Trust Co., 44 Ill. 2d 284, 255 N.E.2d 909, 912 (1970). *See also* 63 Mich. L. Rev. 1304 (1965).

484. Connecticut: Conn. Gen. Stat. § 19–347B (Supp. 1965); Delaware: Del. Code tit. 25, ch. 63, *as amended* June 29, 1972; Illinois: Ill. Ann. Stat. ch. 24, § 11–31-2 (Supp. 1966); Indiana: Ind. Ann. Stat. § 48–2333(3), (4) (Supp. 1973); Massachusetts: Mass. Ann. Laws ch. 111, §§ 127H *et seq.* (Supp. 1966); Michigan: Mich. Comp. Laws Ann. § 125.530 (1968), § 5.2891(15) (1969); Minnesota: Minn. Stat. Ann. § 566.29 (1973); Missouri: Mo. Rev. Stat. ch. 441.570 (Supp. 1974); New Jersey: N.J. Stat. Ann. § 2A:42-85 *et seq.* (1973), and § 40:48-2.12(h) (Supp. 1965); New York: N.Y. Mult. Dwell. Law § 309(5) (McKinney Supp. 1974/75); Ohio: Ohio Rev. Code § 5321.01; Pennsylvania: Pa. Stat. Ann. tit. 35, § 1700–1 (Supp. 1973); Rhode Island: R.I. Gen. Laws § 45–24.2-10 (1971), and § 45-24.3-19 (Supp. 1973); Wisconsin: Wis. Stat. Ann. § 280 (Supp. 1974/75).

485. All states allow municipalities to move for the appointment of a receiver. Several states also allow tenants to do so. *See, e.g.*, N.J. Stat. Ann. § 2A:42-85; N.Y. Mult. Dwell. Law § 309.

Fair Treatment: Basic Legal Reforms

Retaliatory Action. Underlying all other reforms in the area of fair treatment is the protection against retaliatory action by landlords. Without this protection, tenants cannot safely exercise any other right or remedy leading to either fair treatment or decent housing. Tenants are now protected by case or statute against retaliatory actions by landlords in twenty-seven jurisdictions.[486] While all these jurisdictions provide the tenant with a valid defense to an eviction action based on a retaliatory motive,[487] the ambit of tenant actions that are protected and the ambit of landlord actions that are restricted vary. All jurisdictions that recognize the remedy protect tenants who report code violations to state or local governmental agencies. Most states also provide protection for tenant reporting of code violations or substantial defects to the landlord.[488] Tenant organizing and joining a tenants' union are also protected activities under a majority of the cases and statutes.[489]

486. Alaska: Alaska Stat. § 34.03.310 (Supp. 1974); Arizona: Ariz. Rev. Stat. Ann. § 33-1381 (1974); California: Cal. Civ. Code § 1942.5 (West Supp. 1975); and Schweiger v. Superior Ct., 3 Cal. 3d 507, 476 P.2d 97 (1970); Connecticut: Conn. Gen. Stat. Ann. § 19-375a (Supp. 1975); Delaware: Del. Code Ann. tit. 25, § 5516 (1974); District of Columbia: D.C. Housing Regs. § 45-1624 (Supp. 1975-76); and Edwards v. Habib, 397 F.2d 687 (D.C. Cir. 1968), *cert. denied*, 393 U.S. 1016 (1969); Hawaii: Haw. Rev. Stat. tit. 28, § 521-74 (Supp. 1974); Illinois: Ill. Ann. Stat. ch. 80, § 71 (Smith-Hurd 1966); and Clore v. Fredman, 59 Ill. 2d 20, 319 N.E.2d 18 (1974); Kentucky: Ky. Rev. Stat. Ann. § 383.705 (Supp. 1974); Maine: Me. Rev. Stat. Ann. tit. 14, § 6001 (1974); Maryland: Md. Real Prop. Code Ann. § 8-208.1 (Supp. 1974); Massachusetts: Mass. Gen. Laws Ann. ch. 186, § 18 (Supp. 1975); Michigan: Mich. Comp. Laws Ann. § 600.5720 (Supp. 1975/76); Minnesota: Minn. Stat. Ann. § 566.03, .28 (Supp. 1975/76); Nebraska: Neb. Rev. Stat. § 76-1439 (1974 Cum. Supp.); New Hampshire: N.H. Rev. Stat. Ann. § 540.13 (Supp. 1973); New Jersey: N.J. Stat. Ann. § 2A:42-10.10 (Supp. 1975/76); and E.&E. Newman, Inc. v. Hallock, 116 N.J. Super. 220, 281 A.2d 544 (1971); New York: N.Y. Unconsol. Laws tit. 23, §§ 8590, 8609 (McKinney 1974); North Carolina: N.C. Gen. Stat. ch. 75, § 11 *et seq.* (enforceable by State Attorney General, Consumer Division); Ohio: Ohio Rev. Code Ann. § 5321.02 (Supp. 1974); Oregon: Or. Rev. Stat. § 91-865 (1974); 1973 Or. Laws ch. 559, § 32; Pennsylvania: Pa. Stat. Ann. tit. 35, § 1700-1 (Supp. 1975/76); Rhode Island: R.I. Gen. Laws Ann. ch. 20, § 34-20-10 (1970); Tennessee: Tenn. Code Ann. § 53-5505 (Supp. 1974); Virginia: Va. Code Ann. § 55-248.39 (Supp. 1975); Washington: Wash. Rev. Code §§ 59.18.240, 54.19.250 (Supp. 1973); Wisconsin: Dickhut v. Norton, 45 Wis. 2d 389, 173 N.W.2d 297 (1970).

487. Most statutes require tenants to be current in rent before they can raise retaliation as a defense to eviction. *See, e.g.,* Ariz. Rev. Stat. ch. 10, § 33-1381; 1973 Or. Laws ch. 559, § 32.

488. *See, e.g.,* Haw. Rev. Stat. ch. 521, § 74(a)(1)(2); Cal. Civ. Code §§ 1942, 1942.5.

489. *See, e.g.,* Edwards v. Habib, 397 F.2d at 701; Hosey v. Club Van Courtlandt, 299 F. Supp. 501, 504 (S.D.N.Y. 1969) ("There can be no doubt of the

Landlords are restricted in these states from evicting or threatening to evict tenants who engage in protected activities. Most jurisdictions also prohibit retaliatory rent increases and decreases in services.[490] In at least one state the landlord is prevented from refusing to renew a lease for a retaliatory purpose.[491] (This is not to be confused with the right of a tenant in public housing to have a lease renewed absent good cause.)[492]

All the cases declare retaliatory action invalid as against public policy.[493] Tenants, however, frequently have difficulty proving retaliatory intent or motivation on the part of the landlord. A majority of statutes attempt to resolve this problem of meeting the burden of proof by establishing a period during which specific landlord actions following a protected tenant action will be presumed to be retaliatory.[494] This presumption shifts the burden of proof to the landlord to show a nonretaliatory motive for the action taken. A small number of jurisdictions have an absolute statutory bar for enumerated retaliatory actions, subject only to specified statutory exceptions.[495] California has adopted a hybrid statute that provides protection against retaliatory action for a specified period, but it contains no presumption and the frequency of permitted use is limited.[496]

Protection against retaliatory action is a recognition by courts and legislatures of the fundamental right of tenants to fair treatment, which is equaled in its crucial value to tenants only by the prohibition against self-help eviction. This and other new laws for tenants' protection present obvious danger for abuse. A tenant with a good lawyer can usually delay a justifiable eviction for a substantial period simply through procedural maneuvering. Prior to these laws, however, the potential and actual abuses were greater still. No law

---

right of a tenant to discuss the condition of his building with his co-tenants to encourage them to use legal means to remedy improper conditions, to hold meetings, and to inform public officials of the conditions. In short, a tenant can organize the other tenants of his building to improve living conditions."). *See also* MacQueen v. Lambert, 348 F. Supp. 1334 (M.D. Fla. 1972); 1973 Or. Laws ch. 559, § 32(b).

490. *See, e.g.,* 1973 Or. Laws ch. 59, § 32(1); N.J. Stat. Ann. § 2A:48-10.10(d).

491. *Id.* at § 2A:48-10.10(1)(c).

492. *See, e.g.,* Green v. Copperstone Ltd., 346 A.2d 686 (1975).

493. *See, e.g.,* Edwards v. Habib, 397 F.2d at 701.

494. The presumption is usually for a six-month period, *see, e.g.,* 1973 Or. Laws ch. 559, § 32(2), Ariz. Rev. Stat. ch. 10, § 33-1381(B), but may vary from a low of 60 days to a high of one year.

495. *See, e.g.,* Haw. Rev. Stat. ch. 621, §§ 74 *et seq.*

496. Cal. Civ. Code § 1942.5.

could eliminate sharp practices or bad faith from landlord-tenant relationships, but the recent reforms have put landlords and tenants on a more nearly equal footing.

Distress and Distraint: Lockouts. Distress and distraint are landlord self-help measures used against tenants for nonpayment of rent. Though authorized by state landlord lien statutes,[497] they are initiated by the landlord without benefit of prior judicial hearing or court supervision. Distress is the *locking out* of the tenant from the premises by the landlord, while distraint is the taking or *locking in* of the tenant's personal property to satisfy a claim for rent. The statutes authorizing landlord use of distress and distraint have been repeatedly challenged during the last five years. These challenges have produced a string of cases holding such lien statutes to be an unconstitutional denial of due process because of their failure to provide for notice or hearing before seizure of the tenant's property.[498] Where the tenant is given the right to a hearing conditioned on deposit of a bond, this also has been held to violate due process requirements.[499] Distress and distraint have also been disallowed by statute in many states.[500]

Security Deposits. While abuse of security deposits is not a major problem facing tenants, it is a continuing source of irritation. Landlords demanding excessive security deposits can act as a bar to low-income tenants attempting to lease decent, safe, and sanitary housing. Unfair retention of security deposits is an unnecessary burden on the cost of tenancy and creates an unacceptable windfall profit for landlords. Many states have enacted legislation regulating security

---

497. *See, e.g.*, Ala. Code tit. 31, §§ 29–34; Miss. Code Ann. § 89–7–51 (Supp. 1971).

498. *See* Gross v. Fox, 319 F. Supp. 1164 (E.D. Pa. 1972); Hall v. Garson, 430 F.2d 430 (5th Cir. 1970); Barber v. Rader, 350 F. Supp. 183 (S.D. Fla. 1972); MacQueen v. Lambert, 348 F. Supp. 1334 (M.D. Fla. 1972); Dielen v. Levine, 344 F. Supp. 823 (D. Neb. 1972); Musselman v. Spies, 343 F. Supp. 528 (M.D. Pa. 1972); Collins v. Viceroy Hotel Corp., 338 F. Supp. 390 (N.D. Ill. 1972); Holt v. Brown, 36 F. Supp. 2 (W.D. Ky. 1971); Santiago v. McElroy, 319 F. Supp. 284 (E.D. Pa. 1970); Klin v. Jones, 315 F. Supp. 109. *But see* U.S.A. I. Lehndorff Vermoegensverwaltung Gmbh & Cie v. Cousins Club Inc., Ill. Sup. Ct., May 14, 1976, in which the court found no state action was involved.

499. *See* MacQueen v. Lambert, 348 F. Supp. at 1338.

500. *See, e.g.*, Ariz. Rev. Stat. ch. 10. § 33–1372; Cal. Code Civ. Proc. § 1161; Cal. Penal Code § 418; Ill. Rev. Stat. ch. 89, § 16; Mass. Gen. Laws ch. 186, § 15B, *as amended by* 1972 Mass. Acts ch. 639.

deposits.[501] The protections afforded tenants by this legislation vary significantly from state to state.

The basic protection that any security deposit legislation affords is a guarantee that deductions from the deposit must be fairly made and in reasonable amounts, and that the surplus must be returned to the tenant within a reasonable period after termination of the tenancy. This basic protection is generally afforded without the benefit of legislation in any small claims court or other court of competent jurisdiction. Additional protections that have been extended to tenants in security deposit legislation include limiting the amount deposited,[502] requiring notice of where the deposit is held,[503] barring the commingling of deposits,[504] requiring the payment of interest to the tenant on deposits,[505] requiring the written itemization of deductions,[506] and authorizing damages for landlord noncompliance.[507]

---

501. Arizona: Ariz. Rev. Stat. § 33-1321 (1974); California: Cal. Civ. Code § 1950.15 (West Supp. 1975); Colorado: Colo. Rev. Stat. Ann § 38-21-101 *et seq.* (1973); Connecticut: Conn. Gen. Stat. Ann. § 47-23a; Delaware: Del. Code Ann. tit. 25, § 5511 (Supp. 1974); District of Columbia: D.C. Housing Regs. § 103, art. 290, D.C. Law 1-7, D.C. Reg. at 291-92, § 2908 (July 17, 1975); Florida: Fla. Stat. Ann. § 83.49; Hawaii: Haw. Rev. Stat. § 521-44 (Supp. 1974); Illinois: Ill. Rev. Stat. ch. 74, §§ 91-93 (1973); Maryland: Md. Ann. Code art. 53, §§ 41-43 (1957), *as amended by* 1973 Md. Laws ch. 2, § 1.4; Massachusetts: Mass. Gen. Laws Ann. ch. 186, § 15B (Supp. 1975); Michigan: Mich. Comp. Laws Ann. §§ 554.601 to .616 (Supp. 1975/76); Minnesota: Minn. Stat. § 504.20 (Supp. 1975/76); Missouri: Mo. Ann. Stat. § 456.040; Montana: Mont. Rev. Codes Ann. §§ 42-301 to 309 (Supp. 1974); New Jersey: N.J. Stat. Ann. § 46:8-19 (Supp. 1975/76); New York: N.Y. Gen. Oblig. Law §§ 7-103, 7-105 (1964); Ohio: Ohio Rev. Code § 5321.16 (Supp. 1974); Oregon: 1973 Or. Laws ch. 559, § 12; Or. Rev. Stat. § 91.760 (1974); Pennsylvania: Pa. Stat. Ann. tit. 68, §§ 250.511a to .512 (Supp. 1975/76); Texas: Tex. Rev. Civ. Ann. art. 5236e (Supp. 1974/75); Washington: Wash. Rev. Code § 59.18.270.

502. *See, e.g.,* N.J. Stat. Ann. § 46:8-19 *et seq.* (one month's maximum deposit); Ariz. Rev. Stat. ch. 10. § 33-1321(a) (one and a half months' maximum deposit); Mass. Gen. Laws ch. 186, § 15B (two months' maximum).

503. *See, e.g.,* N.J. Stat. Ann § 46:8-19.

504. *Id.*

505. *See, e.g.,* Conn. Gen. Stat. Ann. § 47-23a; Fla. Stat. Ann. § 83.49; Ill. Rev. Stat. ch. 74, §§ 91-93 (requires 4 percent interest); Md. Ann. Code § 8-203(f); Mass. Gen. Laws Ann. ch. 15B; Minn. Stat. Ann. § 504.20; Mo. Ann. Stat. § 456.040; N.J. Stat. Ann. §§ 46:8-19 *et seq.* (requires market rate less 1 percent for cost of administration); N.Y. Gen. Oblig. Law § 7-103; Ohio Rev. Code § 5321.16(A) (5 percent interest on deposits in excess of the statutory limit); Pa. Stat. Ann. tit. 68, § 250.510 *et seq.* (requires market rate); Wash. Rev. Code § 59.18.270.

506. *See, e.g.,* Ariz. Rev. Stat. ch. 10, § 33-1321(D); Haw. Rev. Stat. ch. 521, § 44(D).

507. *See, e.g.,* N.J. Stat. Ann. § 46:8-19 *et seq.* (requires mandatory double damages); Ariz. Rev. Stat. ch. 10, § 33-1321(D) (allows discretionary double damages); Cal. Civ. Code § 1950.5(f) (actual damages plus civil penalty of up to a maximum of $200).

The URLTA: A Model Act for the Equalization of Landlord-Tenant Bargaining Positions

The Uniform Residential Landlord-Tenant Act (URLTA) is a compendium of almost all the basic reforms in both the decent housing and fair treatment areas.[508] It was drafted by the National Conference of Commissioners on Uniform State Laws and was finally approved and recommended for enactment by the Conference in August 1972. The URLTA was endorsed by the American Bar Association in February 1974. It is a product of three years work by a subcommittee of the Conference of Commissioners. They were aided in their deliberations by an advisory committee whose membership was selected to represent a wide range of viewpoints and special interests. Organizations such as the United States Savings and Loan League and the National Association of Real Estate Boards were represented, along with the National Tenants Organization and the Urban League. The reporter-draftsman of the URLTA was Professor Julian Levi of the University of Chicago Law School.

The URLTA was drafted in response to the sporadic reform of landlord and tenant law in most states, and in recognition of the value of comprehensive and uniform change. The value of uniformity was considered particularly important in view of the facts that a metropolitan housing market frequently transcends state boundaries (for instance, the Philadelphia housing market includes Pennsylvania, Delaware and New Jersey), and that housing finance is increasingly arranged in a national market.[509] The goals of the commissioners in drafting the URLTA were to equalize the bargaining position of landlords and tenants; to force landlords to meet minimum standards for providing safe and habitable housing; to spell out the responsibilities of tenants for maintaining the quality of their housing units; and to insure tenants the right to occupy a dwelling as long as they fulfill their responsibilities.[510]

In the decent housing category the URLTA includes warranty of habitability,[511] repair and deduct,[512] and rent abatement.[513] In the

508. The URLTA excludes housing codes and receivership. *See generally* Blumberg & Robbing, *The Uniform Residential Landlord and Tenant Act: The National Experience,* Hous. & Dev. Rep. 15 E-1 (Nov. 28, 1973); McCabe, *The Uniform Residential Landlord and Tenant Act: Better Law for Rental Shelter,* 6 [Special Issue] Lawyers in Housing 3 [publication of the American Bar Association's Department of State and Local Bar Services] (February 1976).

509. J. Levi, The Uniform Residential Landlord and Tenant Act: A Brief History 4 (mimeo., National Conference of Commissioners on Uniform State Laws, Chicago 1973).

510. J. McCabe, *The Uniform Residential Landlord and Tenant Act* [Article 1 of a five-part series explaining the URLTA, National Conference of Commissioners on Uniform State Laws, Chicago] (1973).

511. U.R.L.T.A. §§ 2.104, 4.101.

fair treatment category, it covers protection against retaliatory action,[514] prohibition of distress and distraint,[515] security deposit regulation,[516] and prohibition of utility shut-off.[517] The URLTA has the additional virtue of expanding the fair treatment area to include a number of other basic reform measures, which include prohibitions against abuse of access,[518] unfair landlord rules and regulations,[519] and unconscionable lease provisions.[520] Only a few non-URLTA states have adopted one or more of these additional protections.[521]

Counterbalancing the obligations of the landlord are those imposed upon the tenant. The URLTA requires the tenant to keep the premises clean and sanitary, to dispose of garbage and rubbish, to keep plumbing fixtures clean and sanitary, to use plumbing and electrical fixtures properly, to refrain from the willful or negligent destruction of property, to permit reasonable access to the lessor, not to disturb neighbors' peaceful enjoyment of the premises, and to comply with local codes.[522] Breach of any of these warranties creates an actionable violation of the tenant's obligation to his or her landlord. These obligations promote proper management of the premises.

The landlord also has specific remedies. One is the "repair and add" remedy,[523] which is the converse of the repair and deduct remedy of the tenant. If the tenant breaches any of these obligations, and the breach materially affects health and safety and can be remedied by repair, the landlord can have it done and charge the tenant. In addition, if the rental agreement requires notice of absence for an extended period, and the tenant does not give it, there are actual damages available to the landlord.[524] There are also specific remedies for a holdover tenancy[525] or for unreasonably withholding access.

---

512. *Id.* at § 4.103 (one-half periodic rent or $100, whichever is greater).
513. *Id.* at § 4.105.
514. *Id.* at § 5.101 (one-year presumption of retaliation).
515. *Id.* at § 4.107 (treble damages); *id.* at § 4.205 (abolishment of distraint).
516. *Id.* at § 2.101 (one month's rent limit on deposit).
517. *Id.* at § 4.104.
518. *Id.* at §§ 3.103, 4.302.
519. *Id.* at § 3.102.
520. *Id.* at § 3.303.
521. *See, e.g.,* on abuse of access, Ga. Code Ann. tit. 105, ch. 1401 *et seq.*; Mass. Gen. Laws ch. 186, § 15B; Jordan v. Talbot, 55 Cal. 2d 597 (1961). For unfair rules and regulations, *see, e.g.,* R.I. Gen. Laws. §§ 34-18.1, 34.20.1 *et seq.*; for unconscionable lease provisions: Mass. Gen. Laws ch. 186, § 15B.
522. U.R.L.T.A. at § 3.101.
523. *Id.* at § 4.202. See McCabe, *supra* note 510, at 7.
524. *Id.* at § 4.203.
525. *Id.* at § 4.301(c).

The obvious advantage in adopting the URLTA is that a state may in one step provide a pattern of rights and remedies consistent with residential rentals in contemporary America. This particularly desirable in states that have not yet undertaken reforms or have only achieved limited reforms. In most other states that have adopted varying degrees of piecemeal reform, the URLTA can still offer a comprehensive system of protections that are specifically geared to achieve an equitable relationship between landlords and their tenants. Only in three jurisdictions have reforms progressed to the point where the URLTA protections are not needed.[526]

Thus far the URLTA has been adopted with variations in thirteen states[527] and has been introduced into the legislatures of ten others.[528] Almost all these state adaptations substantially conform to the URLTA model, though in a minority of states considerable alterations were made.[529]

Other Reforms in Fair Treatment and Decent Housing

Retroactive Rent Abatement. Retroactive rent abatement is an affirmative damage action based in contract for past breach of the warranty of habitability by a landlord. In such an action a tenant, whether in current possession of the premises or not, files suit for damages retroactive to the date of the initial breach of the warranty of habitability. The date of the initial breach is determined as that point when the landlord, having been notified of a breach of the warranty of habitability (actual or implied notice suffices), fails or

526. New Jersey, Massachusetts, and the District of Columbia.

527. Alaska Stat. §§ 34.03.010 to .380 (1974); Ariz. Stat. Ann. §§ 33-1201 to -1381 (1974); Del. Code Ann. 25-5100 *et seq.* (1973); Fla. Stat. Ann. §§ 83-40-83.73 (Supp. 1975/76); Haw. Rev. Stat. §§ 521-1 to -76 (Supp. 1974); Kan. Stat. Ann. §§ 58-2540 to 2573 (1975); Ky. Rev. Stat. Ann. §§ 383-505, 383-715 (1974); Neb. Rev. Stat. §§ 76-1401, 76-1449 (Cum. Supp. 1974); N.M. Stat. Ann. §§ 70-7-1 *et seq.* (1975); Ohio Rev. Code Ann. §§ 5321.01, 5321.19 (1974); Or. Rev. Stat. §§ 91.700, 91.860 (1974); Va. Code Ann. §§ 55-248.2, 248.40 (Supp. 1975); Wash. Rev. Code Ann. §§ 59.18.010, 59.18.900 (Supp. 1974).

528. California: A.B. 1202 (1973/74 Reg. Sess.); Connecticut: Com. B. 1808 (1973); Idaho, S.B. 1352 (1974) (tenant proposal); and S.B. 1391 (1974) (realtor's proposal); Illinois: H.B. 1345 (78th Gen. Ass. 1974); Indiana: H.B. 1042 (1975); North Carolina: H.B. 673 (1974); Pennsylvania: S.B. 1079 (1973); Rhode Island: 73-S. 892 (1973); Vermont: S. 112 (1973); Wisconsin: A.B. 492 (1973).

529. Florida excluded protection against retaliatory actions; Hawaii's statute was enacted before the final URLTA was drafted; and the Wisconsin act was rewritten by amendment in the legislature.

refuses to make repairs within a reasonable amount of time. The retroactive damage action is limited in time only by the applicable statute of limitations for contract actions in the jurisdiction, and damages may be computed on any of the three theories of damages for breach of the warranty of habitability discussed above. At present the remedy of retroactive rent abatement is recognized only in New Jersey,[530] Massachusetts,[531] and the District of Columbia.[532]

Landlord Security Deposit Act. The Landlord Security Deposit Act (LSDA) is a statutory reform that functions as a counterpart to tenant security deposits. Tenants have traditionally been required to deposit sums of money with their landlord to insure compliance with the rental agreement. Under the LSDA, landlords are required to deposit with the city a fixed sum of money per unit to insure compliance with *their* obligations arising from the housing codes. The actual operation of the LSDA is simple. If the landlord fails to correct conditions that pose an immediate danger to the health and safety of the occupants of the unit, the city may use the landlord's security deposit funds to repair the defects that constitute the emergency. The landlord is then required to replenish the deposit fund within a set period of time, or the city will have a lien against the landlord's property.

The novel feature of the LSDA is not that it provides cities with the authority and mechanism to repair deteriorating buildings, but rather that it allows them to do so using funds placed on deposit by the offending landlord. Though many cities have broad code compliance apparatus, their use is typically limited by the potential expense of comprehensive enforcement. Thus far the LSDA has been enacted into law and is currently operating in four New Jersey cities.[533] The New Jersey courts have upheld the municipal authority to enact an LSDA pursuant to their local police powers.[534]

Security of Tenure–Just Cause Eviction. The capricious or arbitrary termination of a tenancy by a landlord is perhaps the most disturbing predicament that tenants can anticipate. Under security

---

530. Berzito v. Gambino, 63 N.J. 460, 308 A.2d 17 (1973).

531. McKenna v. Begin, 325 N.E.3d 587 (Mass. App. 1975).

532. William J. Davis, Inc. v. Slade, 271 F.2d 412 (D.C. Cir. 1970).

533. Ridgefield Ord. No. 930 (June 8, 1972); Fort Lee Ord. 73-15 (April 4, 1973); Lindenwould Ord. No. 389 (April 12, 1973); Wayne Ord. No. 55 (May 16, 1973).

534. Apartment House Council v. Mayor and Council, 123 N.J. Super. 87, 301 A.2d 484 (Law Div. 1973), *aff'd per curiam*, 128 N.J. Super. 192, 319 A.2d 507 (App. Div. 1974).

of tenure–just cause eviction, landlords no longer enjoy the right to terminate tenancies or refuse to renew a lease by simply giving statutory notice without stating a cause. (In most states, month-to-month tenancies may be terminated on 30-days notice without cause.) All tenants, no matter what the form or duration of their rental agreements, are guaranteed the right to continue in residential premises so long as they abide by all reasonable rules and obligations of the tenancy. The only exceptions to this guarantee arise when the landlord withdraws the rental unit from the public rental market for any one of a number of statutorily specified reasons.

Currently, just cause eviction protections are available only to private housing tenants in the state of New Jersey[535] and in rent-controlled units in the District of Columbia,[536] Massachusetts[537] and New York City.[538] Tenants in public housing throughout the United States are afforded just cause protections by court decisions interpreting due process requirements[539] and HUD regulations.[540] Mobile home park tenants in several states are also protected.[541]

THE REDLINING PROBLEM AND NEIGHBORHOOD CONSERVATION

In almost four decades, national housing policy has focused principally on new construction of homes and apartments for a growing population and on the removal of the substandard housing inventory. In this context, rehabilitation of the existing stock was recognized as generally desirable, but it has not constituted a major element of national policy. In recent years, however, increasing recognition has been given to the importance of meeting our housing needs by the recycling of the older housing stock. The abandonment of entire built-up neighborhoods on the one hand, and newly constructed low-density sprawl on the other hand, combine to waste important

535. N.J. Stat. Ann. § 2A:18–61.1 *et seq., amending* N.J. Stat. Ann. § § 2A-18–53 *et seq.*

536. District of Columbia Rent Control Regulations, D.C. Law 1–33, (November 1, 1975).

537. 1970 Mass. Acts ch. 842.

538. New York City Local Law No. 16–1969, § YY55–5.10(c)(9).

539. Thorpe v. Housing Authority, 393 U.S. 268 (1969); Omaha v. U.S. Housing Authority, 468 F.2d 1 (1972); Fuller v. Urstadt, 276 N.E.2d 321 (N.Y. 1971) (state public housing); Joy v. Daniels, 479 F.2d 1236 (1973); Rudder v. United States, 266 F.2d 51 (1955).

540. *See e.g.,* HUD Circulars 7465.8 and .9, February 22, 1971.

541. *See, e.g.,* 1973 N.Y. Laws ch. 1012, § 233, Real Property Law; Fla. Stat. § § 83.271, 83.281, 83.291, *upheld in* Palm Beach Mobile Homes, Inc. v. Strong, 300 So. 2d 881 (Fla. 1974). *See* discussion of landlord and tenant relations in mobile homes, *supra.*

resources. It is inefficient to finance and construct new roads and water and sewer facilities to serve low-density new construction on the urban fringe while the existing infrastructure in the midst of the central city becomes idle as neighborhoods literally crumble away.

The lack of coordination of private and public investment decisions, and the fragmentation of public decisionmaking in metropolitan areas, prevents a coherent metropolitan approach to the problem of assuring that urban growth to serve our needs will make the most efficient and equitable use of resources. All that can be said is that we are increasingly beginning to view the problems of growth in a regional context, a perspective in which the courts have begun to play a prominent role, as described in other portions of this book.

Recent federal legislation recognizes the public interest in the spatial impact of public and private investment decisionmaking in our large urban areas. The Housing and Community Development Act of 1974, for example, sets forth as a primary objective for community development assistance "the reduction of the isolation of income groups within communities and geographical areas and the promotion of an increase in the diversity and vitality of neighborhoods through the spatial deconcentration of housing opportunities for persons of lower income and the revitalization of deteriorating or deteriorated neighborhoods to attract persons of higher income."[542] In 1975 Congress enacted the Home Mortgage Disclosure Act, which requires all federally insured or regulated financial institutions in Standard Metropolitan Statistical Areas with assets of $10 million or more to disclose the location, by census tract and dollar amount, of all multiple- and single-family mortgage and home improvement loans they make.[543] In passing the act Congress found that

> some depository institutions have sometimes contributed to the decline of certain geographic areas by their failure pursuant to their chartering responsibilities to provide adequate home financing to qualified applicants on reasonable terms and conditions.

It further noted that the act was intended to enable citizens and public officials:

542. Pub. L. No. 93-383 tit. I, § 101(c)(6), 42 U.S.C. § 5301(c)(6).
543. Home Mortgage Disclosure Act of 1975, Pub. L. No. 94-200 tit. III, 12 U.S.C. §§ 2801 *et seq.* The Federal Reserve Bank, which is charged with writing the regulations under the act (although enforcement is the responsibility of the Federal Home Loan Bank Board and the National Credit Union Administration), has estimated that some 8,500 depository institutions are affected, including 4,400 commercial banks, 3,000 savings and loan associations, 470 mutual savings banks, and 600 credit unions. 4 Hous. & Dev. Rep. 72 (June 28, 1976).

. . . to determine whether depository institutions are filling [sic] their obligations to serve the housing needs of the communities and neighborboods in which they are located and to assist public officials in their determination of the distribution of public sector investments in a manner designed to improve the private investment environment.[544]

This legislation is commonly known as an anti-redlining measure. Redlining occurs when lenders designate entire inner-city neighborhoods as poor risks and refuse to finance purchases or improvements in them. While in some instances this practice reflects perceived risk and uncertainty, often it is quite arbitrary and does not examine the merits of particular cases. The practice accelerates neighborhood deterioration and makes the rehabilitation of already deteriorated neighborhoods difficult or impossible. The long-term and sometimes relatively short-term effect of this policy is disinvestment in the neighborhood.

The criteria that lead lenders to redline are characteristically the age of the homes, the racial makeup of the neighborhood, and the location within the city.[545] Disinvestment results from a variety of lending practices which tend to fall into two broad categories. The first is characterized by stricter, more onerous mortgage terms than are imposed in other neighborhoods;[546] the second by outright refusal to lend.[547] The practice is not limited to lending

544. 12 U.S.C. §§ 2801 *et seq.* (1975). For an evaluation of the law and regulations issued thereunder by the Federal Reserve Board (known as Regulation C), concluding the data required to be disclosed is of limited public utility in dealing with the redlining problem and suggesting some supplementary state initiatives, *see* Center for Community Change, The Life Blood of Housing (1976). Several state initiatives in this regard are discussed in the text accompanying notes 593–96 *infra.*

545. *See* D. Searing, *Credit Disinvestment and Redlining* 1–2 (Paper prepared for the National Committee Against Discrimination in Housing, Midwest Regional Housing Conference, January 29–30, 1974).

546. The Housing Training and Information Center of Chicago lists the following practices that fall into this category:

1. Requiring down payments of a higher amount that are usually required for financing comparable properties in other areas.
2. Fixing loan interest rates in amounts higher than those set for all or most other mortgages in other areas.
3. Fixing loan closing costs in amounts higher than those set for all or most other mortgages in other areas.
4. Fixing loan maturities below the number of years to maturity set for all or most other mortgages in other areas.
5. Charging discount "points" as a way of discouraging financing.

Governor's Commission on Mortgage Practices, Home Ownership in Illinois: The Illusive Dream 15–16 (1975).

547. This category includes:

1. Refusing to lend on properties above a prescribed maximum age.

institutions but may include insurers as well, and when these institutions redline the same areas, the problem is compounded, for the absence of insurance creates higher mortgage risks and the scarcity of improvement financing generates greater insurance risks. The symptoms of redlining are often indistinguishable from its causes. Disinvestment occurs when a neighborhood declines, and a neighborhood declines as a result of disinvestment. Thus, when a savings and loan association, for example, determines that an area is deteriorating, its prophecy is likely to be self-fulfilling.[548]

Disinvestment, however, is not the only cause of urban decay. Redlining is only one aspect of a broader, more complex, and pervasive issue.[549] The cycle usually begins when a predominantly white

---

2. Refusing to make loans in dollar amounts below a certain minimum figure, thus excluding many of the lower priced properties often found in neighborhoods where redlining is practiced.
3. Refusing to lend on the basis of presumed "economic obsolescence" no matter what the condition of an older property may be.
4. Stalling on appraisals to discourage potential borrowers.
5. Setting appraisals in amounts below what market value actually should be, thus making home purchase transactions more difficult to accomplish.
6. Applying structural appraisal standards of a much more rigid nature than those applied for comparable properties in other areas.

Id. Within this category should be included the custom of some institutions which segregate large sums to provide future financing for home buyers in multi-million-dollar subdivisions. Thus,

[A] developer is guaranteed that his customers will have access to mortgage money at attractive interest rates. In Cook County, Illinois, approximately two-thirds of available mortgage funds are committed to developers before mortgages for homes in the developers' subdivisions are actually requested, effectively placing that portion of the available mortgage money out of the reach of the individual who is seeking a mortgage on his own.

Greenberg, *Redlining—The Fight Against Discrimination in Mortgage Lending,* 6 Loyola U.L.J. 71, 73 (1975) [hereinafter cited as Greenberg].

548. Greenberg, note 547 *supra,* at 74.

549. Disinvestment is but one factor in the growing problem of inner-city decline, the ultimate end of which is abandonment. One study of the abandonment process identified six stages of deterioration which lead ultimately to abandonment:

1. Decline in neighborhood socioeconomic status as middle-class whites leave.
2. Racial or ethnic changes as urban newcomers seek space.
3. Property speculation and exploitation.
4. Weakened market conditions and the emergence of a "crisis ghetto."
5. Disinvestment, *i.e.,* lack of interest by investors.
6. Abandonment.

Center for Community Change, National Urban League, The National Survey of Housing Abandonment (1971), *cited in* Duncan, Hood, & Neet, *Redlining Practices, Racial Resegregation, and Urban Decay: Neighborhood Housing Services as a Viable Alternative,* 7 Urb. Law. 510, 511 n.4 (1975) [hereinafter cited as Duncan].

neighborhood begins to age. Appraisal values drop,[550] and conservative investors begin to impose stricter mortgage terms.[551] As the neighborhood continues to wear, typically more mobile whites begin to migrate to the suburbs where mortgages are obtainable on better terms,[552] where streets may be safer, schools better, and so on. The concentration of minorities in the neighborhood consequently becomes much greater, and new whites will increasingly decline to settle in homes vacated by white families who leave. Indeed, it is reported that lending officers not infrequently steer prospective homebuyers away from declining neighborhoods by remarking on the decline and proffering more favorable terms on suburban mortgages.[553]

Lending institutions will consider the increasing proportion of minorities as indicating decline, and redlining practices will be accelerated.[554] When conventional loans become difficult to obtain, borrowers naturally look to FHA mortgage guarantees to solve their difficulties. But FHA programs are not immune from redlining, either.[555] Moreover, when FHA guarantees are available, they may actually create an incentive for abuse. Mortgagees are not in the business of owning and managing property, and for this reason (among others) they dislike foreclosures, when forebearance with a shaky mortgagor may produce a better arrangement for all concerned.

The guaranteed or insured mortgagee is in a different position, however, and has everything to gain from speedy foreclosure. Not only is the trouble and expense of dealing with a mortgagor who is in difficulty avoided, but the mortgage money turns over faster and the mortgagee can take advantage of fluid interest rates.[556] Once this happens the last available source of funds will have been exhausted, because the FHA cannot again guarantee homes that have once been foreclosed. In addition, since mortgage funds for the purchase of homes in the area are also unavailable, resident owners cannot sell their homes. In this way, deterioration becomes an unstoppable pro-

550. Coalition to End Neighborhood Deterioration, Why Do Neighborhoods Deteriorate? Red-Lining in Indianapolis 6 (1975) [hereinafter cited as C.E.N.D.].
551. Duncan, *supra* note 549, at 516; and note 565 *infra*.
552. *Id.*
553. C.E.N.D., *supra* note 550, at 516.
554. Duncan, *supra* note 549, at 516.
555. *See* Building the American City, *supra* note 1, at 100–01; U.S. Commission on Civil Rights, Equal Opportunity in Suburbia 36–40 (1974); Chicago Sun Times, April 28, 1974, § 1-A, at 1, col. 1. *See also* F.H.A. Underwriting Manual § 937 (1938). A discussion of early FHA lending practices is in Chapter 1 *supra.*
556. *See* B. Boyer, Cities Destroyed for Cash: The F.H.A. Scandal at HUD (1973), *cited in* Duncan, *supra* note 549, at 520 n.49.

cess until residents of the area flee. The eventual abandonment of the neighborhood is thus made more likely.[557]

The subtlety of the redlining practice makes it difficult to document. There is some evidence of such discrimination in New York as early as the period of the 1920s to 1940s.[558] More recent studies suggest that the practice is widespread, occurring in neighborhoods in many of America's major cities.[559] The Civil Rights Act of 1866, in its present codification as 42 U.S.C. § 1982, mandates that:

> All citizens of the United States shall have the same right, in every State and Territory, as is enjoyed by white citizens thereof to inherit, purchase, lease, hold, and convey real and personal property.[560]

In the landmark decision of *Jones v. Alfred H. Mayer Co.*,[561] the United States Supreme Court held that Section 1982 reaches discrimination by private entities and that Congress has the power, under the Thirteenth Amendment, to prohibit such discrimination. The Court was careful to note, however, that "§ 1982 is not a comprehensive open housing law . . ." and that it "deals only with racial discrimination. . . ."[562] Thus, the utility of Section 1982 as a means of combatting redlining depends entirely on whether the discrimination complained about can be shown to be racial.

The nature and extent of racial discrimination necessary to invoke Section 1982 has been hotly contested. The conduct condemned in *Jones* was the refusal to sell a home to a black for the sole reason of his race, and the Court was careful to limit its holding when it stated, in dictum, that Section 1982 "does not refer *explicitly* to discrimination in financing arrangements. . . ."[563] Whether particular lending practices come within the *spirit* of the act depends upon the relationship between financing and the ability to purchase a home, and upon the extent to which race plays a part in the difficulty of obtaining such financing. Thus it may be hard to distinguish the refusal to finance because of race from the refusal to sell for the same reason

557. Duncan, *supra* note 549, at 521.

558. H. Swan, The Housing Market in New York City 193–94 (1944).

559. *See* C. Rapkin, The Real Estate Market in an Urban Renewal Area (1958); G. Sternlieb, The Urban Housing Dilemma (1971); Hearings on S.1281 Before the Committee on Banking, Housing and Urban Affairs, 94th Cong., 1st Sess., pt. 1, at 551–52 (1975) (Paper prepared for Senator Proxmire by G. Sternlieb, R. Burchell & D. Listokin of the Center for Urban Policy Research, Rutgers University), and sources cited therein.

560. Act of April 9, 1866, ch. 31, 14 Stat. 27.

561. 392 U.S. 409 (1968).

562. *Id.* at 413.

563. *Id.* (emphasis added).

when both effectively prohibit purchase. To proscribe the latter and not the former would contradict the power that the Court in *Jones* said Congress exercised when it enacted Section 1982: "to assure that a dollar in the hands of a Negro will purchase the same thing as a dollar in the hands of a White man."[564] Whether more subtle forms of discrimination can be reached is uncertain, as will be illustrated below.

In the 1974 decision in *Clark v. Universal Builders, Inc.,*[565] the Seventh Circuit held that a prima facie case was made under Section 1982 when: (1) dual housing markets exist by reason of racial segregation; and (2) defendant sellers took advantage of this situation by demanding prices and terms unreasonably in excess of prices and terms available to white citizens for comparable housing.[566] In terms of redlining, the opinion is particularly significant for the following language:

> Defendants can find no justification for their actions in a claim that they would have sold on the same terms to those whites who elected to enter the black market and to purchase housing in the ghetto and segregated inner-city neighborhoods at exorbitant prices, far in excess of prices for comparable homes in the white market.[567]

This is crucial to the vitality of Section 1982 in redlining situations, because one premise of the practice is that it discriminates, for whatever reason, against all, regardless of race.

Thus, under a *Clark* rationale, a redlining suit might be sustained on a showing that disparate housing markets exist as a result of racial discrimination and that lenders have exploited the existing disparity by imposing unreasonably stricter mortgage terms in redlined areas than in other comparable neighborhoods. Still, the applicability of Section 1982, even under the broad reading given it in *Clark*, must be predicated upon the showing of a close relationship between geographic and racial discrimination. (The means of showing such a relationship is discussed below.) In a suit to challenge redlining in a predominantly black neighborhood, it may therefore be necessary to locate a predominantly white but otherwise similar neighborhood where mortgage terms are substantially better.[568] Conceivably it

564. *Id.* at 433.
565. 501 F.2d 324 (7th Cir. 1974), *cert. denied*, 419 U.S. 1070 (1974).
566. *Id.* at 334.
567. *Id.* at 331.
568. In *Clark* the plaintiffs established the existence of a dual housing market by expert testimony based on statistical evidence. *Id.* at 334–35.

could even be necessary to show that redlining rarely or never occurs in such neighborhoods.

An example of the problem is presented in *Love v. DeCarlo Homes, Inc.*,[569] a case decided prior to *Clark*. There the Fifth Circuit held Section 1982 to be inapplicable when the "acts complained of do not fit within the traditional concept of racial discrimination."[570] Exploitation similar to that in *Clark* was not seen as "traditional," for even though blacks were paying more than whites for housing, the markets for each were different. In other words, since the black plaintiffs could not show that similar housing was sold to whites on more favorable terms, they were not denied "something pertaining to property that is available to whites."[571] Furthermore, a case could not be made unless it could be shown that the same lender discriminated with respect to similar housing.[572]

Congress has attacked a broader range of discriminatory housing practices in Title VIII of the 1968 Civil Rights Act. In sweeping language, discrimination in lending "because of race, color, religion, sex, or national origin" is declared unlawful.[573] Of particular importance, the act prohibits denial of loans based upon the race "of the present or prospective owners, lessees, tenants, or occupants of the dwelling or dwellings in relation to which such loan is to be made or given. . . ."[574] The first definitive interpretation of the applicability of Title VIII to redlining has been made by a federal district court in *Laufman v. Oakley Building and Loan Co.*[575] The court held that three separate provisions of Title VIII make it unlawful for a credit institution to deny home financing to a white potential borrower on the ground that the neighborhood into which the borrower wishes to move is predominantly black. In reaching this result the court gave great deference to the interpretation given Title VIII by HUD and the Federal Home Loan Bank Board (FHLBB), both of which have construed it to apply to redlining.

The court quoted approvingly the oral argument of the FHLBB's counsel in distinguishing between the denial of credit for sound

---

569. 482 F.2d 613 (5th Cir. 1973), *cert. denied*, 414 U.S. 1115 (1973).

570. *Id*. at 615.

571. *Id*. at 616.

572. In *Love* the plaintiffs failed because they could not establish that the defendant had discriminated in similar circumstances. *Id*. at 615–16. The *Clark* court noted that a traditional case could have been made had the trial court not erred and overcome "corporate formalities" to establish common ownership. 501 F.2d at 337.

573. 42 U.S.C. § 3605.

574. *Id*.

575. 408 F. Supp. 489 (S.D. Ohio 1976).

economic reasons and the denial of credit for unlawful racial reasons:

... I'd like to start by refuting or attempting to refute a couple of points made by counsel for defendants. First, counsel points out that regulations of the Federal Savings and Loan Insurance Corporation discourage savings and loans from making investments or making loans in "declining neighborhoods," and he used that term several times. I suggest that that's the gist of what Congress was attempting to make illegal in Title VIII and the gist of what the Bank Board was trying to make illegal in its regulations, was the feeling on the part of a great many lenders that a racially integrated neighborhood per se must be a declining neighborhood and per se must be a bad credit risk. There is nothing in the Board's regulations or in the Board's policies which mandates an asssociation to make a bad loan as long as the criteria they use for making the loan are legitimate business criteria, such as the credit worthiness of the borrower, the marketability, the salability of the security property, including the neighborhood in which it's located which has a bearing on its salability, the diversification of the institution's assets. All these things are legitimate criteria. But the facts have shown over the years, it's been shown time and again that a neighborhood which had changed from white to black or a neighborhood that is racially integrated, particularly an older neighborhood within city limits of an established and older city need not be a declining neighborhood, and that often a contributing factor to the decline is the refusal of lenders to provide credit for the purchase of these homes or for the rehabilitation of them. So we take issue with the defense, not on whether or not a financial institution is obligated to make loans in the declining neighborhood, but on the judgment that a declining neighborhood necessarily results when a neighborhood becomes racially integrated.

....

The Board has determined in its regulations that the racial composition of a neighborhood is not a legitimate rationale of criteria and neither is it a businesslike criteria for the making of a loan. If a neighborhood in fact is declining, if property can't be sold, for whatever reason, regardless of the racial criteria, why, that's a legitimate business judgment. A neighborhood can decline for a number of reasons. The Board is anxious that lenders not use the racial composition of the neighborhood to effect an automatic judgment that it must be declining.[576]

Given the expressed intent of Congress that it is "the policy of the United States to provide, within constitutional limitations, for fair housing throughout the United States,"[577] the court's and FHLBB's interpretation of Title VIII in *Laufman* is proper.

576. *Id.* at 501.
577. 42 U.S.C. § 3601 (1970). *See* Trafficante v. Metropolitan Life Ins. Co., 409 U.S. 205 (1972); United States v. Youritan Const. Co., 370 F. Supp. 643 (N.D. Cal. 1973), *aff'd per curiam*, 509 F.2d 623 (9th Cir. 1975).

While Title VIII is more apposite than Section 1982 in that it is aimed directly at discriminatory lending practices, it may also require a close nexus between the geographic and racial discrimination in order to bring the pattern and practice of redlining within the act.[578] Fortunately this shortcoming is to some extent alleviated, since Title VIII authorizes the Attorney General to investigate allegedly discriminatory practices on the basis of statistical data.[579] As a form of proof in cases brought either under Title VIII or under Section 1982, statistical evidence would be especially valuable, given the often subtle methods potentially employed by lenders.[580]

In the past the courts have been receptive to such proof[581] and have been willing to find prima facie discrimination, in violation of federal civil rights statutes, when only discriminatory effects have been shown.[582] The Fair Housing Act Title VIII of the Civil Rights Act of 1968, like other civil rights laws, it has been held, "prohibits conduct with discriminatory consequences as well as discriminatorily motivated practices."[583] Given the tendency of a high proportion of minorities to reside in redlined areas, Title VIII and Section 1982 will prove more effective in combating redlining practices when statistical evidence can be relied upon.

Such statistical evidence may be forthcoming if the federal govern-

578. *Compare* 42 U.S.C. § 3601 *with* 42 U.S.C. § 1982.

579. 42 U.S.C. § 3613 (1970).

580. *See* Searing, *Discrimination in Home Finance,* 48 Notre Dame Law. 1113-14 (1973).

581. "Statistical evidence can make a prima facie case of discrimination." Carter v. Gallagher, 452 F.2d 315, 323 (8th Cir. 1971), *cert. denied,* 406 U.S. 950 (1972); Clark v. Universal Builders, Inc., 501 F.2d 324; Parham v. Southwestern Bell Telephone Co., 433 F.2d 421 (8th Cir. 1970).

582. *See* Griggs v. Duke Power Co., 401 U.S. 424 (1971); United States v. West Peachtree Tenth Corp., 437 F.2d 221 (5th Cir. 1971) (brought under Title VIII). The *Griggs* case, *supra,* construed Title VII of the Civil Rights Act of 1964 to invalidate employment tests that disproportionately disadvantage the members of racial minorities (and women) unless the tests are demonstrably related to job employment. However, in Washington v. Davis, 96 S. Ct. 2040 (1976), an action challenging the verbal ability test required of applicants by the District of Columbia Police Department, the Supreme Court held that the Constitution does not incorporate the *Griggs* rule and, more broadly, that only official conduct having a "discriminatory purpose" violates that equal protection clause. The Court expressly rejected a general constitutional doctrine of "racially disproportionate impact," developed by some lower federal courts, which disapproves even colorblind decisions that disproportionately disadvantage racial minorities. *Id.* at 2050. The Davis court, however, did not question the soundness of the *Griggs* rule as statutory doctrine. Title VIII of the Civil Rights Act of 1968, prohibiting discrimination in housing, should be given the same construction. *See* discussion of *Washington v. Davis* in Chapter 2 *supra* in text accompanying notes 80-91.

583. United States v. Grooms, 348 F. Supp. 1130 (M.D. Fla. 1972) (neighbor recommendations, brought under Title VIII).

ment attacks redlining through its agencies that regulate national and state banks.[584] Most notable is the FHLBB, which regulates essentially all[585] home mortgages made by savings and loan associations.[586] The FHLBB has promulgated regulations under the authority of Title VIII[587] and Section 1982 that address the redlining problem and influenced the decision of the *Laufman* case. Its regulations prohibit member institutions from discriminating in the making of loans because of the race of "occupants of other dwellings in the vicinity of the dwelling or dwellings in relation to which such loan . . . is to be made or given."[588]

More significantly, the FHLBB has issued a regulation proscribing consideration of many factors often examined when redlining is contemplated and that have racial repercussions:

> Refusal to lend in a particular area solely because of the age of the homes or the income level in a neighborhood may be discriminatory in effect since minority group persons are more likely to purchase used housing and to live in low-income neighborhoods. The racial composition of the neighborhood where the loan is to be made is always an improper underwriting consideration.[589]

Unfortunately, these provisions have not as yet been effective.[590] The FHLBB has, however, recently amended its record-keeping regulations to require racial, ethnic, and sexual information about potential borrowers.[591] Given access to relevant data of this nature, combined with the geographic data required under the Home Mortgage Disclosure Act, could prove invaluable to litigants and public officials.

---

584. These include the Federal Home Loan Bank Board, the Comptroller of the Currency, which charters and supervises national banks, pursuant to 12 U.S.C. § 1 *et seq.* (1970); the Federal Reserve Board, which regulates state banks belonging to the Federal Reserve System, pursuant to 12 U.S.C. §§ 248(a), 325 (1970); and the Federal Deposit Insurance Corporation, which supervises state banks not belonging to the Federal Reserve System but which are nevertheless insured, pursuant to 12 U.S.C. §§ 1815-1819 (1970). All but the FHLBB have been relatively lax in their efforts to combat discrimination. *See* Searing, *supra* note 580.

585. Of all assets held in savings and loans, 97.7 percent are found in FHLBB system members. U.S. League of Savings Associations, 1974 Savings & Loan Fact Book 112 (1974).

586. 12 U.S.C. § 1437.

587. 42 U.S.C. § 3608(c).

588. 12 C.F.R. § 528.2 (Supp. 1974).

589. *Id.* at § 531.8(b) (Supp. 1974).

590. U.S. Commission on Civil Rights, Equal Opportunity in Suburbia (1974). *See* Searing, *supra* note 580.

591. 12 C.F.R. § 528.6 (1974). *See* 39 Fed. Reg. 18642 (1974); 39 Fed. Reg. 27121 (1974).

Indeed, the FHLBB's general counsel has written an opinion letter indicating that 12 C.F.R. 528.2 prohibits redlining practices when they are racially inequitable and that a showing of discriminatory effect would establish a prima facie violation of Title VIII.[592]

The states also have a significant role to play in this area; one that is now only in its seminal stages but is expanding at a rapid pace. Since June 1976, mortgage lenders have been required under the Federal Home Loan Mortgage Disclosure Act of 1975 to compile and to disseminate to the public pertinent data documenting where they make loans for the purchase and rehabilitation of housing. Four states—California, Massachusetts, Illinois, and New York—have already been exempted from the provisions of the federal law on the grounds that they have adopted state laws or regulations that "provide depositors, citizens and public officials with sufficient information to enable them to determine whether lenders are fulfilling their obligations to serve the housing needs of the communities and neighborhoods were they are located." (The exemptions vary among the states as to the type of lending institution covered and geographic area covered, enforcement, procedures, and so on.)[593]

Perhaps the most advanced step to date has been taken in New Jersey (which has also applied for an exemption from the Home Mortgage Disclosure Act), where the state legislature in January 1977 enacted a law authorizing neighborhood groups who allegedly have been subjected to geographic mortgage discrimination to bring class actions against lenders.[594] Under the law, banks are required to disclose, according to census tracts or zip codes, the dollar amounts of both loans granted and loans applied for but denied. If neighborhood mortgage discrimination is proved—when mortgage applicants can demonstrate that they were denied loans based on arbitrary geographic reasons rather than their own credit ratings—the bank or banks involved will be forced to pay damages.[595] While the law clearly permits lenders to deny mortgages after a reasonable analysis of risk, a denial can now be more objectively evaluated in light of the new lending disclosure requirements.

Finally, numerous states have statutes, substantially equivalent to federal fair housing laws, that also prohibit discrimination by mortgage lenders. Active enforcement of these laws by the states could also have a salutary effect on combating redlining.[596]

592. 2 U.S. League of Savings Associations Federal Guide 8173-3, § U-13-49.2 (1974).

593. 4 Hous. & Dev. Rep. 666 (Dec. 27, 1976).

594. *Id*. at 754–55 (Jan. 24, 1977).

595. *Id*.

596. R. Schafer, N. Betnun & A. Solomon, A Place to Live: Housing Policy in the States 24–25 (Council of State Governments 1974).

Conclusion

Neighborhood decline in large urban areas is the result of a complex of social, racial, economic, and psychological forces. At any given time some neighborhoods are widely recognized as poor, low-status, crime-ridden, and generally not desirable places to live. People with choice tend to move out of such neighborhoods. Experience also shows that in some cases such neighborhoods, because of their convenient location and basically sound housing stock, can become desired again by people with choice. Brooklyn Heights, Georgetown, Old Town, and numerous other neighborhoods have shown that neighborhood decay is not always irreversible.

No policy that attempts to cure or reverse such decline with one or two tools can succeed. This Report is addressed to housing and urban growth issues comprehensively for that reason. For example, the exclusion of low-income households from middle- and high-income areas on the urban fringe contributes to the concentration of such households in the older housing stock, and the maintenance of that stock is bound to suffer. In addition, the limited creditworthiness of such households, clustered together, can cause credit institutions to withdraw loans for sound economic reasons from individual borrowers in a large area if all those borrowers have limited incomes. Suburban land-use policy is thus inextricably connected with neighborhood decline in the older portions of our metropolitan areas.

Public funds alone, unaccompanied by the availability of private financing on reasonable terms, cannot arrest neighborhood decline. Private financing unaccompanied by imaginative public programs of rehabilitation, crime prevention, and adequate services will not succeed, either. Public officials who are concerned about the deterioration of large areas of their jurisdictions cannot ignore the impact of suburban land and housing policies.

Table of Cases

Index

About the Editor

Richard P. Fishman, an attorney and planner, has had broad ranging practical and scholarly experience in the areas of housing, land use, and planning. Prior to assuming the position of Executive Director of the A.B.A.'s Advisory Commission on Housing and Urban Growth, he was Managing Attorney of the Housing & Economic Development Unit of the Georgia Legal Services Program, where he was actively engaged in the development of federally assisted housing and in environmental and community development litigation. As Director of the A.B.A.'s National Housing Law Program he advised numerous state and local governments on a variety of housing finance, land use and community development matters. In addition to writing in various law journals and publications in the field, he has taught courses in housing, land use, and local government law in the Graduate Schools of Urban Studies and Planning of the Massachusetts Institute of Technology and Boston University. Currently, he practices law in Washington, D.C. with the law firm of Kutak Rock and Huie.